Religion and Law in the United States

Religion and Law in the United States

Second Edition

Elizabeth A. Clark
Brett G. Scharffs
Amy Lynn Andrus

This book was originally published as a monograph in the International Encyclopaedia of Laws/Religion Law.

Founding Editor: Roger Blanpain
General Editor: Frank Hendrickx
Volume Editor: Wouter Druwé

Wolters Kluwer

Published by:
Kluwer Law International B.V.
PO Box 316
2400 AH Alphen aan den Rijn
The Netherlands
E-mail: lrs-sales@wolterskluwer.com
Website: www.wolterskluwer.com/en/solutions/kluwerlawinternational

Sold and distributed by:
Wolters Kluwer Legal & Regulatory U.S.
920 Links Avenue
Landisville, PA 17538
United States of America
E-mail: customer.service@wolterskluwer.com

ISBN 978-94-035-3918-8

e-Book: ISBN 978-94-035-3928-7
web-PDF: ISBN 978-94-035-3938-6

The Authors

Elizabeth A. Clark is Associate Director of the International Center for Law and Religion Studies at the J. Reuben Clark Law School, Brigham Young University (BYU). She is also the US member of the OSCE/ODIHR Advisory Panel for Freedom of Religion or Belief (2022–2025). Professor Clark has written more than forty chapters and articles and co-written or edited several books on the topic of law and religion, including *Religion During the Russian-Ukrainian Conflict*, *Facilitating Freedom of Religion or Belief: A Deskbook*, and *Law and Religion in Post-Communist Europe*.

Professor Clark has analyzed legislation and draft legislation on religion from more than a dozen countries for the US State Department, USAID, national governments, and international NGOs. She has spoken at UN and OSCE forums and at more than one hundred academic conferences throughout the world. She has also testified before the US Congress and the US Commission on International Religious Freedom on religious freedom issues and has written amicus briefs on religious freedom issues for the US Supreme Court.

Brett G. Scharffs is the Rex E. Lee Chair and Professor of Law and the Director of the International Center for Law and Religion Studies at the J. Reuben Clark Law School, Brigham Young University (BYU). He received a BSBA in international business and an MA in philosophy at Georgetown University and, as a Rhodes Scholar, earned a BPhil in philosophy at the University of Oxford. He received his JD from Yale Law School, where he was Senior Editor of the *Yale Law Journal*.

Professor Scharffs has been a recurring visiting professor at Central European University in Budapest and at the University of Adelaide Law School. For several years, he has helped organize certificate training programs in religion and the rule of law in China and Vietnam, and he has taught and helped organize programs on sharia and human rights at several Indonesian universities. Author of more than one hundred articles and book chapters, Professor Scharffs has made more than 300 scholarly presentations in thirty countries. His casebook, *Law and Religion: National, International, and Comparative Perspectives*, published by Aspen Press / Wolters Kluwer (co-authored with his BYU Law School colleague W. Cole Durham, Jr.), has been translated into Bahasa Indonesian, Chinese, Hebrew, Spanish, Russian, Turkish, and Vietnamese, with a Portuguese translation in process.

He has served as Chair of the Law and Religion Section of the Association of American Law Schools and as Chair of the Law and Interpretation Section of the AALS. Professor Scharffs is also on the advisory board of the *Oxford Journal of Law and Religion*.

Amy Lynn Andrus is Associate Director of the International Center for Law and Religion Studies at the J. Reuben Clark Law School, Brigham Young University (BYU). She was previously an Attorney Advisor in the Attorney General's Honors Program with the US Department of Justice, Executive Office for Immigration Review. She graduated from BYU Law School in 2019, where she was a Clark Scholar and Lead Executive Editor of the *BYU Law Review*. A former writer and editor of international publications at BYU's David M. Kennedy Center Publications Office, she received an MA in International and Area Studies and graduated summa cum laude with a BA in English from BYU. Her work at the Center includes helping administer the Young Scholars Fellowship on Religion in the Rule of Law, held annually at Christ Church, Oxford.

Table of Contents

List of Abbreviations

ACA	Patient Protection and Affordable Care Act
ACHPR	African Commission on Human and Peoples' Rights
ACLU	American Civil Liberties Union
ADA	Americans with Disabilities Act
ADR	Alternative Dispute Resolution
ART	Assisted Reproductive Technologies
BFOQ	Bona Fide Occupational Qualification
CARES Act	Coronavirus Aid, Relief, and Economic Security Act
CDC	Centers for Disease Control and Prevention
CERD	International Convention on the Elimination of All Forms of Racial Discrimination
C.F.R.	Code of Federal Regulations
CLIA	Clinical Laboratory Improvement Amendments
CMS	Centers for Medicare & Medicaid Services
CPC	Country of Particular Concern
CRC	Convention on the Rights of the Child
CSS	Catholic Charitable Services
DC	District of Columbia
DOMA	Defense of Marriage Act
EEOC	Equal Employment Opportunity Commission
EPC	Entity of Particular Concern
EU	European Union
FAA	Federal Arbitration Act
FCC	Federal Communications Commission
FCPA	Foreign Corrupt Practices Act
FDA	Food and Drug Administration
FEHB	Federal Employees Health Benefits
FICA	Federal Insurance Contributions Act

List of Abbreviations

FTC	Federal Trade Commission
GDPR	General Data Protection Regulation
HIPAA	Health Insurance Portability and Accountability Act
ICCPR	International Covenant on Civil and Political Rights
ICESCR	International Covenant on Economic, Social and Cultural Rights
IDEA	Individuals with Disabilities Education Act
I.R.C.	Internal Revenue Code
IRFA	International Religious Freedom Act
IRS	Internal Revenue Service
IVF	In Vitro Fertilization
NAACP	National Association for the Advancement of Colored People
NAFTA	North American Free Trade Agreement
NGO	Non-governmental Organization
NHL	National Historic Landmark
NIH	National Institutes of Health
NLRA	National Labor Relations Act
NLRB	National Labor Relations Board
NOI	Nation of Islam
NRB	National Religious Broadcasters
NSA	National Security Agency
OAS	Organization of American States
OIRF	Office of International Religious Freedom
OSCE	Organization for Security and Co-operation in Europe
PBS	Public Broadcasting Service
PPP	Paycheck Protection Program
PRWORA	Personal Responsibility and Work Opportunity Reconciliation Act
RFMA	Respect for Marriage Act
RFRA	Religious Freedom Restoration Act
RLUIPA	Religious Land Use and Incarcerated Persons Act
RUDs	Reservations, Understandings, or Declarations (used in the context of US Senate ratification of international law)
SECA	Self-Employment Contributions Act
SWL	Special Watch List
UAA	Uniform Arbitration Act
UDHR	Universal Declaration of Human Rights
ULC	Universal Life Church

UN	United Nations
UPA	Uniform Parentage Act
US	United States of America
U.S.C.	United States Code
USCIRF	United States Commission on International Religious Freedom
USSC	United States Supreme Court

List of Abbreviations

Preface

This book is a basic introduction to law and religion in the United States. It is written primarily for comparative law scholars; we do not presume their familiarity with US law. For US lawyers, the structure will seem a little counter intuitive. While discussions of US law are usually divided between the Free Exercise Clause and the Establishment Clause, here we follow the framework of the International Encyclopaedia of Laws series.

Discussion of US law is somewhat complicated because, while the United States is a common law system, there are large areas of statutory overlay. In addition, the United States is a federal system, with large areas of law covered in this book being governed by state law, or state as well as federal law.

Due to the complexity of the US federal system, we have not been able to cover all state variations but have tried to include laws from larger jurisdictions, such as New York and California, as well as majority and minority positions. We also include illustrative examples from states where there is an important minority position or where the law is sparse and the state example helps us understand what other courts might do.

At times, the book is repetitive because some issues and cases relate to multiple parts of the *International Encyclopaedia of Law/Religion* series' standardized table of contents; therefore, issues and cases may be discussed in more than one place, with a focus on the elements of the issue or case most relevant to the topic at hand. We have tried to include cross-references to primary discussions of issues and cases, but the back matter (Table of Statutes, Table of Cases, Selected Bibliography, and Index) will be helpful to locate all discussions of a given issue, law, or case.

We would like to thank Rik Torfs, General Series Editor, for the invitation to participate in this Encyclopaedia series. We would also like to thank our colleagues and former colleagues at the International Center for Law and Religion Studies, especially its founding director, W. Cole Durham, Jr., as well as Deborah Wright, Donlu Thayer, Gary Doxey, Janet Nelson, Jeff Nelson, and Robert Smith. Cole Durham and Bob Smith are editors of the major multi-volume treatise *Religious Organizations & the Law* (Thomson Reuters), which is updated annually. We have used this as one of our primary resources and recommend it to others seeking further information on US religion law. Although credit for this work and our colleagues is evident in the footnotes of our volume, our appreciation and thanks go well beyond the value of footnotes.

We have benefited from a tremendous amount of research assistance from summer fellows at the International Center for Law and Religion Studies at Brigham

Young University. A special note of thanks is due to Tanner Bean, BYU Law Class of 2017, who served as a compiling editor and helped transform the first edition manuscript into an integrated whole. The following offered additional invaluable assistance with the first edition: Abby McKeon, Adam Forsyth, Alex Storms, Aline Longstaff, Annalee Moser, Bennett Briggs, Bryant Hinckley, Emily Page, Eva Brady, Heather Binks, Ian Collins, James Heilpern, Jarvis Yau, John Gibbons, Lauren Flores, Lauren Ravsten Robins, Leilani Maldonado, Lynn Nouri, McKenna Mills, Michael Goodrich, Roman Harper, Ryan Anderson, Ryan Jolley, Scott Ludlow, Tara Fitzgerald, Travis Hyer, and Tye Christensen.

Summer fellows who ably assisted with this second edition include Abdullah Hassan, Abigail Wadley, Andrew Birkensha, Anna Bryner, Austin Atkinson, Ayoung Tansiongco, Brooklyn Bird, Clayton Varvel, Erin Cranor, John Geilman, Jordan Phail, Kody Richardson, Liam Smith, Malea Moody, Reece Barker, Rhett Hunt, Ryan Cheney, and Tanner Hafen.

As with other volumes in this series, we hope this volume will fulfil the twin aims and objectives of the series: first, to provide a comprehensive overview of law and religion in the United States and, second, to promote comparative study through the disciplined adherence to the structure of volumes in the series.

Comments and suggestions for future editions are welcome at amy.andrus @law.byu.edu, scharffsb@law.byu.edu, and clarke@law.byu.edu.

General Introduction

§1. General Background of the Country

I. Basic Structures

1. The American Revolution, which resulted in independence from Great Britain and the founding of the United States of America, began as early as 1765 when American[1] colonists rebelled against taxes imposed by the British Parliament, claiming them to be unjust and contrary to the British Constitution.[2] These political grievances and sentiments escalated over the following decade, leading to the American Revolutionary War (1775–1783). At the outset of the War, Americans were fighting primarily for their rights as British subjects, but support for independence grew, and by the summer of 1776, the Continental Congress, America's governing body during the Revolution, convened to debate and vote on the issue.[3]

2. On July 4, 1776, thirteen American colonies declared their independence from Great Britain as "the United States of America." The Declaration of Independence, drafted by Thomas Jefferson, declared certain "self-evident truths" and enumerated a list of grievances against King George III, announcing to the world the basis and justification of the colonies' separation from their mother country:

> We hold these truths to be self-evident, that all men are created equal, that they are endowed by their Creator with certain unalienable Rights, that among these are Life, Liberty and the pursuit of Happiness.—That to secure these rights,

1. The terms "America" and "American" were used historically to distinguish the British colonies and colonists from Great Britain and British citizens who remained there. That usage continues today, although "America" and "American" can encompass all or part of North and South America and their inhabitants. In the interest of efficiency and readability, the authors continue the tradition of using America/Americans to refer to what is now "the United States of America" and its inhabitants, acknowledging that the terms have broader application. Similarly, "American" is used as an adjective throughout this volume.
2. The eighteenth-century British Constitution "was not a single written document, but rather a mixture of English laws, customs, and precedents". *The British Constitution*, Am. Revolution, https://www.ouramericanrevolution.org/index.cfm/page/view/p0006 (last visited Sep. 30, 2023); *see generally* David Ammerman, *The British Constitution and the American Revolution: A Failure of Precedent*, 17 Wm. & Mary L. Rev. 473 (1976).
3. *Parliamentary Taxation of Colonies, International Trade, and the American Revolution, 1763–1775*, U.S. Dep't State, Off. Historian, https://history.state.gov/milestones/1750-1775/parliamentary-taxation (page retired and archived) (last visited Sep. 30, 2023).

> Governments are instituted among Men, deriving their just powers from the consent of the governed.—That whenever any Form of Government becomes destructive of these ends, it is the Right of the People to alter or to abolish it, and to institute new Government, laying its foundation on such principles and organizing its powers in such form, as to them shall seem most likely to effect their Safety and Happiness.

3. The Declaration of Independence established each of the thirteen states as independent sovereigns, possessing jurisdiction and power over all property and persons within their respective territories. The Articles of Confederation, serving as America's first constitution, established the United States as a confederation of sovereign states. A Constitutional Convention, assembled in 1787 to discuss the problems of the Articles of Confederation, adopted a new constitution, which with few amendments remains the fundamental law of the United States. The Constitution of the United States (US Constitution) provided for a stronger federal government while still maintaining sovereignty among the states. *See* Subsection II (General Legal System), below. The United States is currently composed of fifty states as well as five populated and nine unpopulated territories.

4. The United States is a constitutional republic with federal powers shared between the President, Congress, and the judiciary, and with sovereignty shared between the federal government and the states, resting ultimately in "the people." *See* Subsection II (General Legal System), below. States maintain governments, as do local units within states, including counties, municipalities, and special districts. The US Congress is bicameral, consisting of the House of Representatives and the Senate. The body of the House of Representatives, comprising 435 voting representatives,[4] is determined by proportional representation. Each of the fifty states is guaranteed one seat in the House; the other 385 seats are apportioned among the states according to the most recent US census population figures.[5] These "congressional representatives" are elected for two-year terms by residents of their respective geographic "congressional districts," within their respective states. The Senate is composed of two senators from each state, for a total of one hundred, elected for six-year terms, with one-third of the Senate elected every two years. Although smaller parties exist, American politics is primarily dominated by two parties: the Democratic Party, which today is more politically liberal, and the Republican Party, which is more politically conservative.

5. The United States encompasses nearly 3.8 million square miles with a population of more than 331 million people. Due to extensive immigration from many countries, the US population is diverse in ethnicity and culture. Its composition

---

4. "In addition, there are 6 non-voting members, representing the District of Columbia, the Commonwealth of Puerto Rico, and four other territories of the United States: American Samoa, Guam, the U.S. Virgin Islands, and the Commonwealth of Northern Mariana Islands." *The Legislative Branch*, White House, https://www.whitehouse.gov/about-the-white-house/our-government/the-legislative-branch (last visited Sep. 30, 2023).
5. *About Congressional Apportionment*, U.S. Census Bureau, https://www.census.gov/topics/public-sector/congressional-apportionment/about.html (last visited Sep. 30, 2023).

includes more than 235 million Caucasians, nearly 47 million African Americans, more than 24 million Asians, more than 9.5 million American Indians and Alaska Natives, and more than 1.5 million Native Hawaiians and other Pacific Islanders. Included in these race categories are more than 62 million people of Hispanic or Latino origin. All numbers reflect individuals who identify as being of a race, either alone or in combination with another race. Nearly 34 million Americans—more than 10% of the total population—are of two or more races.[6]

II. General Legal System

6. The Constitution of the United States came into force in 1789 and was originally comprised of seven articles outlining and establishing the scope and powers of the federal government. The first ten amendments, known as the Bill of Rights (adopted in 1791), place limits on governmental powers and protect individual rights of liberty and justice. The next seventeen amendments primarily broaden individual civil rights. Additionally, the Constitution outlines the relationship between the federal government and the states, limiting the power of each.

7. The first three articles of the Constitution establish three branches of federal government—the legislative, executive, and judicial—along with the respective duties and powers of each. This "separation of powers" is designed to provide a system of "checks and balances" wherein each branch acts as a check on the others to prevent any one branch from exercising too much power. The Legislative Branch, made up of the House of Representatives and the Senate, is given the power to legislate. The Executive Branch—consisting of the President, Vice President, President's Cabinet, and executive agencies that administer federal government programs—exercises the "executive power" assigned to the President and delegated by him. The Judicial Branch, comprising the United States Supreme Court and other federal courts, is given the authority to decide questions of federal and constitutional law, as well as interstate and international law issues.

8. The Supremacy Clause of the Constitution (article VI) declares the Constitution to be the supreme law of the land, under which all other laws are subject:

> This Constitution, and the Laws of the United States which shall be made in Pursuance thereof; and all Treaties made, or which shall be made, under the Authority of the United States, shall be the supreme Law of the Land; and the Judges in every State shall be bound thereby, any Thing in the Constitution or Laws of any State to the Contrary notwithstanding.

6. *Race and Ethnicity in the United States: 2010 Census and 2020 Census*, U.S. Census Bureau (Aug. 12, 2021), https://www.census.gov/library/visualizations/interactive/race-and-ethnicity-in-the-united-state-2010-and-2020-census.html. Race and ethnicity group names are those used by the US Census.

9. Federal law is comprised of statutes passed by both houses of Congress (the House of Representatives and the Senate) and signed by the President, as supplemented by administrative regulations. The "enumerated powers" given to Congress are listed in Article I of the Constitution, including the power to tax, regulate interstate commerce, declare war, establish naturalization rules, protect intellectual property, and establish federal courts.

10. Congress delegates some of its legislative power by statute to federal agencies that have specialized expertise in certain areas. If a statute grants too much power to an agency, the courts can invalidate the statute or limit its scope. Additionally, the President may issue executive orders that are legislative in character, but this power is limited.

11. Congress holds the power to establish federal courts, and the US federal court system is comprised of three main levels: the United States Supreme Court, the courts of appeals, and the district courts. Other federal courts of limited jurisdiction also exist, including the US Court of Federal Claims, US Court of International Trade, and US Tax Court.

12. The US Supreme Court (USSC), established by the Constitution, has the authority to review all federal court decisions. The courts of appeals, comprising thirteen circuits, have the authority to review district court decisions within their jurisdiction. District courts are trial courts where both civil and criminal cases are heard, along with other matters. The Supreme Court, unlike the other federal courts, has primarily discretionary review and selects cases through the process of granting writs of certiorari.

13. Federal courts in general, but the Supreme Court in particular, have the power to declare presidential and congressional acts to be unconstitutional, as established by the landmark case *Marbury v. Madison*, under a doctrine known as "judicial review."[7] Judicial review is based on the reasoning that the Constitution is the supreme law of the land, and the judicial branch is given the power to interpret the law. Therefore, the judicial branch can declare acts of the other branches to be unconstitutional if it determines that those acts violate the Constitution. US courts may deliberate the constitutionality of a law or government act that is challenged by a party who has "standing"—that is, a party who has been or soon will be harmed by the act or law in a way that courts will likely be able to redress.[8]

14. Federalism in the United States is the division of power between the federal government and state governments. This concept reaches back to the Declaration of Independence, which declared that the United Colonies were thereafter "Free and Independent States" under a form of national government.

---

7. *Marbury v. Madison*, 5 U.S. (1 Cranch) 137 (1803).
8. *Lujan v. Defenders of Wildlife*, 504 U.S. 555, 560–561 (1992).

15. The Constitution establishes boundaries between federal and state law. Whereas the Supremacy Clause prohibits state laws from contradicting the Constitution or federal law, and whereas Congress is given the sole power to legislate in specified areas, the Tenth Amendment to the Constitution declares that the rest of the powers are reserved to the States: "The powers not delegated to the United States by the Constitution, nor prohibited by it to the States, are reserved to the States respectively, or to the people." The federal courts' ability to invalidate state laws was expanded, however, through the enactment of the Fourteenth Amendment (1868), which states, "No State shall … deprive any person of life, liberty, or property, without due process of law; nor deny to any person within its jurisdiction the equal protection of the laws."

16. Like the federal government, each state has a written constitution. State constitutions vary, but each typically establishes three branches of government and delineates various rights and powers between the government and the people. In comparison to the federal Constitution, state constitutions are often longer and contain more specific, detailed provisions. As a result, they require more frequent amendment than does the US Constitution, and states have made the amendment process less onerous than the federal amendment process.[9] State constitutions may grant more protection to individuals than that offered by the federal Constitution, but not less.

17. State law, subject to federal law and state constitutions, encompasses vast areas of substantive law including criminal, family, contract, real property, probate, and tort law. State law is of great importance, particularly in areas such as these that the US Constitution largely leaves to state control. States are divided into counties (geographic administrative and political units), which may also have legislative powers. These counties are further divided into municipalities—that is, cities, towns, townships, boroughs, and villages. Municipalities, typically governed by an elected mayor and council, also exercise a remarkable scope of legal authority over many areas of life and can enact ordinances of local interest. State and local administrative bodies may supplement state and local law in the same manner federal agencies supplement federal law. However, state constitutional provisions or statutes can pre-empt local law, just as federal constitutional provisions and statutes can pre-empt state law.

9. "[S]ince its ratification, the [US] Constitution has been amended 27 times. In order to prevent arbitrary changes, the process for making amendments is quite onerous. An amendment may be proposed by a two-thirds vote of both Houses of Congress, or, if two-thirds of the States request one, by a convention called for that purpose. The amendment must then be ratified by three-fourths of the State legislatures, or three-fourths of conventions called in each State for ratification." *The Constitution*, White House, https://www.whitehouse.gov/about-the-white-house/our-government/the-constitution (last visited Sep. 30, 2023). In contrast, states may amend their constitutions as determined by state law: through approval by the state legislature, citizen-initiated ballot proposals, state constitutional conventions, and/or proposals made by specially appointed commissions and approved by state residents. *See* John Dinan, *Constitutional Amendment Processes in the 50 States*, State Ct. Rep. (Jul. 24, 2023), https://statecourtreport.org/our-work/analysis-opinion/constitutional-amendment-processes-50-states.

18. Like the federal court system, most state judiciaries are comprised of three levels—trial courts, intermediate appellate courts, and supreme courts—though there is considerable variation from state to state.

19. Rather than cover the status of the law in all US state and territorial jurisdictions, this book will provide majority and minority positions when significant and/or a sampling of laws from more populous or illustrative states.

20. The United States is a common law system in which law is developed by judges through court decisions. Where constitutional and statutory law is silent, common law principles serve to fill the gap. Precedential weight is given to prior court decisions applying relevant principles to similar facts under a doctrine known as *stare decisis*, to facilitate consistency, fairness, and predictability. Courts are only bound, however, by decisions of higher courts within their jurisdiction; the decisions of other courts may serve as persuasive authority.

21. International law, comprised of international agreements and customary practice, is a part of US law, but it does not take precedence over domestic law. International agreements made by the United States consist of treaties and executive agreements. Treaties can be entered into by the President with a two-thirds consent of the Senate. A self-executing treaty takes effect immediately upon ratification, whereas a non-self-executing treaty takes effect upon implementation through domestic legislation. Treaties are subject to the Constitution and are equal in authority to federal statutes, with the more recent one controlling. Executive agreements with foreign nations are more numerous than treaties and have the same legal effect. These agreements can be made by the President, through powers specified in the Constitution, without the consent of Congress. For a more detailed discussion of international law, *see* Part IV (International, Transnational, and Regional Effects on Religious Communities), Chapter 1 (International Law Effects on Religious Communities).

22. Comparative law, although employed for academic purposes, is used rarely in the interpretation of US domestic law.

§2. Social Facts about Religion

I. Official Census

23. According to the latest official census in 2020, the US population is 331,449,281.[10]

10. *Quick Facts: United States*, U.S. Census Bureau, https://www.census.gov/quickfacts/fact/table/US/PST045219 (last visited Jan. 31, 2023).

II. Religious Demographics

24. Pew Research Center, a nonpartisan think tank that focuses on religion and public life, has summarized its estimates of US religious demographics as follows, based on self-reporting survey methodology:[11]

Major Religious Traditions in the US	*Percentage among All Adults (%)*
Christian	**65**
Protestant	**42**
White evangelical Protestant	17
White, not evangelical Protestant	12
Black Protestant	8
Other Protestant	6
Catholic	**21**
White Catholic	12
Hispanic Catholic	7
Other Catholic	2
Latter-day Saint ("Mormon")	2
Orthodox Christian	1
Other Faiths	**6**
Jewish	1
Muslim	1
Buddhist	1
Hindu	1
Other	2
Religiously unaffiliated (religious "nones")	**28**
Atheist	5
Agnostic	6
Nothing in particular	18

11. Pew Rsch. Ctr., *Measuring Religion in Pew Research Center's American Trends Panel* 11 (Jan. 14, 2021), https://www.pewresearch.org/religion/2021/01/14/measuring-religion-in-pew-research-centers-american-trends-panel (link to PDF) (discussing shifts in methodology and effects on 2020 surveys and estimates).

III. Religious Trends

25. Religious life in the United States is influenced by strong legal protections of religious freedom, non-establishment of religion, and an underlying culture of individualism and pluralism. Religious affiliation is largely viewed as a matter of choice rather than identity. Religious affiliation in the United States is characterized by a higher degree of fluidity than in many other countries. By some estimates, more than 40% of Americans change their religious identity at least once during the course of their life.[12]

26. Sociologists have noted the rise of the "nones", those who do not identify with a particular religion or denomination, with the percentage of nones more than tripling since the early 1990s, becoming the second largest "religious" group in America.[13] This increase of those who claim no religious affiliation has been more pronounced among younger adults, whites, and Protestants but includes individuals of different generations, religions, ethnicities, and races.[14] A 2021 Pew Research Center survey indicated that the percentage of Americans identifying as Christians had declined 15% since 2007, from 78% to 63%.[15] The implications of these trends for politics and law in the United States is an issue of considerable interest.

IV. Historical Patterns

27. Historically, Protestants have been the majority religious group in the United States. The diversity of American Protestantism makes determining the exact number of Protestant organizations difficult, with more than a dozen Protestant "denominational families" (Baptist, Episcopalian, Lutheran, Methodist, Pentecostal, etc.) comprised of numerous individual denominations.[16] The year 2012 marked the first time in US history that fewer than 50% of Americans identified as Protestant.[17] The largest single denomination of Christians in the United States is Catholic, representing approximately 21% of the population. There is a strong and dynamic Jewish community in the United States, which has the second-largest Jewish population in

12. Pew Rsch. Ctr., *America's Changing Religious Landscape* 33 (May 12, 2015), https://www.pewforum.org/2015/05/12/americas-changing-religious-landscape (link to PDF) (not counting those who revert to the religion of their youth).
13. Pew Rsch. Ctr., *Modeling the Future of Religion in America* 19 (Sep. 13, 2022), https://www.pewresearch.org/religion/2022/09/13/modeling-the-future-of-religion-in-america (link to PDF).
14. *See ibid.*, at 2; Pew Rsch. Ctr., *About Three-in-Ten U.S. Adults Are Now Religiously Unaffiliated* 5, 12 (Dec. 14, 2021), https://www.pewresearch.org/religion/2021/12/14/about-three-in-ten-u-s-adults-are-now-religiously-unaffiliated (link to PDF); Pew Rsch Ctr., *America's Changing Religious Landscape*, *supra* n. 12 at 71–72.
15. Pew Rsch. Ctr., *About Three-in-Ten U.S. Adults Are Now Religiously Unaffiliated*, *supra* n. 14 at 4.
16. Pew Rsch. Ctr., *America's Changing Religious Landscape*, *supra* n. 12 at 21–24.
17. *"Nones" on the Rise*, Pew Rsch. Ctr. (Oct. 9, 2012), https://www.pewforum.org/2012/10/09/nones-on-the-rise.

the world.[18] The relatively small Muslim, Hindu, and Buddhist populations are among the fastest-growing religions in the United States due in large measure to immigration and birth patterns.[19] A wide variety of small religious groups includes Unitarian, Deist, Humanist, and Native American religions, among others.[20] In all, there are more than 340,000 religious congregations in the United States.[21] The religious landscape is characterized by a high degree of pluralism, fluidity, and openness to a wide range of religious viewpoints.

V. Native Americans

28. Native Americans are the indigenous people of North America, historically referred to as "Indians", including in federal and state law.[22] Before European migration to the continent, between one and twelve million Native Americans, of numerous tribes, occupied land throughout what is now the United States.[23] While in many places early colonists initially achieved peace with Native Americans, disagreements about the use of land and diseases brought from Europe quickly led to fighting and decimation of the Native American population. European expansionism drove the Native American population westward in the seventeenth, eighteenth, and nineteenth centuries.[24]

29. After the United States declared independence from Great Britain, competing ideas about Native Americans struggled for pre-eminence. In the early nineteenth century, the federal government attempted several assimilation programs, including the funding of churches and other groups to build schools and teach European farming techniques, even though religious schools in the United States generally could not receive state aid.[25] During this time, churches also tried to convert the Native Americans from their own spiritual traditions to Christianity. Some Native Americans accepted the new teachings fully, while others accepted only some teachings or rejected them entirely. Those who rejected the teachings often

18. Sergio DellaPergola, *World Jewish Population, 2021, in American Jewish Year Book* 313, 315 (2021).
19. *See* Pew Rsch. Ctr., *America's Changing Religious Landscape, supra* n. 12, at 15, 54; Pew Rsch. Ctr., *The Future of World Religions: Population Growth Projections, 2010–2050* at 5, 16, 49, 54, 95–96, 106, 244 (Apr. 2, 2015), https://www.pewresearch.org/religion/2015/04/02/religious-projections-2010-2050 (link to PDF).
20. Pew Rsch. Ctr., *America's Changing Religious Landscape, supra* n. 12, at 21.
21. *The Nonprofit Sector in Brief 2019*, Urban Inst.: Nat'l Ctr. for Charitable Stat. at n.2 (Jun. 4, 2020), https://nccs.urban.org/publication/nonprofit-sector-brief-2019#the-nonprofit-sector-in-brief-2019.
22. The authors use the word "Indian" when reflecting historical or legal usage.
23. *See* John D. Daniels, *The Indian Population of North America in 1492*, 49 Wm. & Mary Q. 298, 299 (1992); Alexander Koch, Chris Brierley, Mark M. Maslin & Simon L. Lewis, *Earth System Impacts of the European Arrival and Great Dying in the Americas after 1492*, 208 Quarternary Sci. Rev. 13, 16–17 (2019). Wide divergence of estimates can exist because of varied methods for calculating pre-colonial populations and disputes about the reliability of primary sources.
24. *See* Leonard Dinnerstein, Roger L. Nichols & David M. Reimers, *Natives and Strangers: A History of Ethnic Americans* 4–7 (6th ed. 2014).
25. *See, e.g.*, Civilization Fund Act, Pub. L. No. 15-85, 3 Stat. 516 (1819).

"place[d] increasing dependence on their own cultural traditions".[26] Multiple Indian prophets emerged, including the Seneca leader Handsome Lake, who denounced alcohol and weapons.[27] Since many Americans were not satisfied with assimilation programs, Congress passed the Indian Removal Act of 1830, allowing the President to negotiate the removal of Indian tribes from east of the Mississippi to the West.[28] The Act resulted in the infamous "Trail of Tears", in which approximately 4,000 Cherokee Indians died on a forced march from the southern states to territory known now as Oklahoma.[29]

30. In the mid-nineteenth century, the US government created the reservation system, in part as attempted restitution for prior misdeeds. Under this system, the federal government holds title to land set aside as a permanent tribal homeland, or "reservation", on behalf of a tribe. Today, 574 tribes are federally recognized, and 326 reservations have been designated through treaty, federal statute, executive order, or other federal action.[30] After the reservation system was created, the United States again attempted an assimilation program, removing Native American children from reservations and placing them with white Christian families or in Indian boarding schools where they received an education, often in substandard facilities.[31] This continued until the mid-1970s when the US Congress passed legislation that recognized certain rights, freedoms, and areas of autonomy of Native American individuals and tribes, including the Indian Self-Determination and Education Assistance Act, American Indian Religious Freedom Act, and Indian Child Welfare Act.[32] Native American leaders now have the authority to create their own schools and to teach both secular and religious subjects.[33]

VI. Home-Grown Religious Movements

31. America has been fertile ground for religious innovation and creativity. In business, the United States has long been heralded as the land of opportunity, where the "American dream" can be realized. In religion, and particularly Christian religion, the United States could equally be spoken of as the land of "American visions". Men and women of faith have had a tremendous impact on the religious landscape of the states from the very beginning. Some of these early faiths ebbed

26. Dinnerstein et al., *supra* n. 24, at 29–31.
27. *Ibid.*
28. Indian Removal Act, Pub. L. No. 21-148, 4 Stat. 411 (1830).
29. Dinnerstein et al., *supra* n. 24, at 32–33.
30. *Frequently Asked Questions*, U.S. Dep't Interior: Indian Affs., https://www.bia.gov/frequently-asked-questions (last visited Sep. 30, 2023).
31. Dinnerstein et al., *supra* n. 24, at 149–153.
32. Indian Self-determination and Education Assistance Act of 1975, Pub. L. No. 93-638, 88 Stat. 2203 (codified as amended at 42 U.S.C. § 2004B and scattered ss. of 25 U.S.C. (2018)); American Indian Religious Freedom Act, Pub. L. No. 95-341, 92 Stat. 469 (1978) (codified as amended at 42 U.S.C. §§ 1996, 1996a); Indian Child Welfare Act of 1978, Pub. L. No. 95-608, 92 Stat. 3069 (codified at 25 U.S.C. §§ 1901–1903, 1911–1923, 1931–1934, 1951–1952, 1961, 1963).
33. Dinnerstein et al., *supra* n. 24, at 231.

over time, but several continue to grow today, and new faiths continue to develop. Below is an illustrative list of denominations that took root in the United States in the eighteenth and nineteenth centuries.

32. Church of Christ, Scientist (Christian Science). In 1879, Mary Baker Eddy founded the Church of Christ, Scientist. During the previous decade, Eddy experienced a rapid recovery from an accident "while reading an account of one of Jesus' healings".[34] She then wrote the book *Science and Health with Key to the Scriptures* to enable others to access similar healings in their lives.[35] Christian Science membership has been declining since 1936, when it reported more than 260,000 members worldwide, and is likely less than 100,000 today.[36] The Church owns a highly respected nonprofit news organization, *The Christian Science Monitor*, that publishes international news online and in a weekly print-edition newspaper.[37] *See also* Part XI (Religion and Culture), Chapter (Religion and Media).

33. The Church of Jesus Christ of Latter-day Saints ("Mormon"). The Church of Jesus Christ of Latter-day Saints was formally organized in 1830, ten years after the founder, Joseph Smith, experienced a vision of God the Father and Jesus Christ. Smith wrote that a heavenly messenger later showed him golden plates, or tablets, which contained an ancient history of a people living in the Americas as well as the complete gospel of Jesus Christ.[38] Smith translated the plates into the *Book of Mormon*, from which followers received the nickname "Mormons".[39] Persecution of early Latter-day Saints drove them westward, eventually leading to their settlement in territory that became the state of Utah. Today, the Church is a worldwide organization with a primarily lay ministry, more than 17 million members (6.8 million of whom live in the United States), more than 31,000 congregations, an active missionary program and educational and humanitarian programs.[40]

34. Millerites. In the early 1840s, Baptist minister William Miller gained followers, known as Millerites, by predicting that Jesus Christ's second coming would

34. *Christian Science, in Christian Science: A Sourcebook of Contemporary Materials* 5, 6 (1990).
35. *What Is Christian Science?*, Christian Sci., http://christianscience.com/what-is-christian-science#history-of-cs (last visited Sep. 30, 2023).
36. *See* Rodney Stark, *The Rise and Fall of Christian Science*, 13 J. Contemp. Religion 189, 189–191 (1998). The Church's governing manual forbids the publication of membership numbers.
37. Christian Sci. Monitor, https://www.csmonitor.com (last visited Sep. 30, 2023).
38. *Joseph Smith—History* 1:18–19, 33, *in Pearl of Great Price* (The Church of Jesus Christ of Latter-day Saints 2013).
39. In the past, the terms "Mormon Church" and "Mormons" were common nicknames for The Church of Jesus Christ of Latter-day Saints and its members. Church members now largely reject those names, in favor of the Church's full name and "Latter-day Saints" for members. *See Style Guide—The Name of the Church*, Church Jesus Christ Latter-day Saints, https://newsroom.churchofjesuschrist.org/style-guide (last visited Sep. 30, 2023).
40. *Facts and Statistics: Worldwide Church*, Church Jesus Christ Latter-day Saints, https://newsroom.churchofjesuschrist.org/facts-and-statistics (last visited Sep. 30, 2023).

take place in 1843 or 1844. A Millerite preacher, Samuel Snow, predicted the precise date would be October 22, 1844. When this did not occur, the Millerites split into various groups.[41]

35. Seventh-day Adventist Church. Joseph Bates, a Millerite preacher, and Ellen White, a young woman who experienced visions clarifying doctrines of the Bible, began preaching a return from Sunday worship to Saturday worship, the Sabbath of the Old Testament. The Seventh-day Adventists officially organized in 1863.[42] Today, the Seventh-day Adventist Church is a worldwide organization with nearly 22 million members, including 1.2 million in the United States and Canada, nearly 9,500 schools, a strong healthcare organization, and humanitarian programs.[43] Seventh-day Adventists constitute the most racially diverse religious group in the United States.[44]

36. Jehovah's Witnesses. Also emerging from the Millerite movement, the Jehovah's Witness movement is generally attributed to Charles Russell, who started a Bible study program in the late nineteenth century. Due to their interpretation of the Bible, members will not accept blood transfusions, salute the nation's flags, or participate in military service.[45] Today, Jehovah's Witnesses is a worldwide organization with a lay ministry, 8.6 million publishers (part-time missionaries) and more than 117,000 congregations.[46] The organization is known in the United States and throughout the world for its proselytizing or "witnessing" efforts, often conducted by publishers on public streets or door-to-door.

37. Shakers. The United Society of Believers in Christ's Second Appearing initially formed in England but flourished for a period in the United States. Members were known as "shaking Quakers" and eventually just "Shakers" due to their unconventional worship style that involved a convulsive style of dance. Ann Lee ("Mother Ann") and a group of believers immigrated to the colonies in August 1774.[47] Shakers formed communities intended to establish the proper "Gospel Order" through separation from the world and sin. Believers followed the three Cs: (1) celibacy, (2)

---

41. Gary Land, *Historical Dictionary of the Seventh-day Adventists* 2–8 (2d ed. 2014).
42. *Ibid.*
43. The number of schools includes primary and secondary schools, as well as worker-training and tertiary institutions. *Seventh-day Adventist World Church Statistics 2021*, Seventh-day Adventist Church, https://www.adventist.org/statistics (last visited Sep. 30, 2023); *see also Who Are Seventh-Day Adventists?*, Seventh-day Adventist Church N. Am. Div., https://www.nadadventist.org/about-our-church/who-are-adventists (last visited Sep. 30, 2023).
44. Michael Lipka, *The Most and Least Racially Diverse U.S. Religious Groups*, Pew Rsch. Ctr. (Jul. 27, 2015), https://www.pewresearch.org/short-reads/2015/07/27/the-most-and-least-racially-diverse-u-s-religious-groups.
45. *Controversial Christian Movements: History, Growth, and Outlook, in New Religious Movements and Religious Liberty in America* 1, 18–19 (Derek H. Davis & Barry Hankins eds., 2d ed. 2003).
46. *2022 Service Year Report of Jehovah's Witnesses Worldwide*, Jehovah's Witnesses, https://www.jw.org/en/library/books/2022-Service-Year-Report-of-Jehovahs-Witnesses-Worldwide/2022-Grand-Totals (last visited Sep. 30, 2023).
47. *Shaker Historical Background: An Ongoing Story*, Shaker Village: Sabbathday Lake, Me., https://www.maineshakers.com/shaker-historical-background (last visited Jan. 31, 2023).

community goods in imitation of Christ's life, and (3) confession of sin.[48] In the mid-nineteenth century, prior to the Civil War, eighteen Shaker communities reached a collective peak of about 5,000 believers. Today, one community remains, Sabbathday Lake Shaker Village, established in Maine in 1783, which claims only two full members as of March 2022.[49]

VII. Islam

38. Islam has existed intermittently in North America for half a millennium.[50] Before immigration, a notable Muslim population was brought to the United States through the institution of African slavery. When forcibly brought to the United States, between 15% and 30% of enslaved African men and less than 15% of enslaved African women were Muslim.[51] While many converted to Christianity upon arrival and over the intervening years, some did so reluctantly, under pressure or threat of force.[52]

39. Beginning in the 1930s, a religious movement called the Nation of Islam (NOI) made an appeal to African Americans with enslaved heritage. Founded in Detroit, Michigan, the Nation of Islam is considered distinct from traditional Islam.[53] The NOI believes in both the Qur'an and the Bible but believes the Bible was tampered with and must be reinterpreted. Followers seek freedom, justice, and equality for all and historically sought a state of their own. The NOI is known for its work to empower African Americans.[54]

40. The US Muslim population began to rise in the twentieth century with an increase in immigrants from India, Indonesia, Malaysia, Pakistan, and throughout the Middle East. Many Muslims who immigrated to the United States did so as refugees in pursuit of religious freedom, either coming from countries where Muslims were a minority or as members of a minority Muslim sect.[55]

41. Although the Muslim population in the United States remains small, since 2010 forty-four states have considered passing statutes or amending state constitutions to ban Islamic law or sharia. Alabama, Arizona, Arkansas, Florida, Kansas,

48. Chilton Furniture Me., *The Sabbathday Lake Shakers*, YouTube (Feb. 15, 2015), https://www.youtube.com/watch?v=8ZZbT8NVlZ8.
49. Séan Alonzo Harris, *The Last Shakers*, Deseret News (Mar. 24, 2022), https://www.deseret.com/faith/2022/3/24/22989812/the-last-shakers-sabbathday-lake-maine-shaker-village.
50. Sylviane A. Diouf, *Servants of Allah: African Muslims Enslaved in the Americas* 20–70 (15th anniversary ed. 2013).
51. Donna L. Meigs-Jaques & R. Kevin Jaques, *Islam, in Encyclopedia of Religion in the South* 394, 394–395 (Samuel S. Hill, Charles H. Lippy & Charles Reagan Wilson eds., 2d ed. 2005).
52. Diouf, *Servants of Allah, supra* n. 50, at 71–80.
53. Mother Tynnetta Muhammad, *Nation of Islam in America: A Nation of Beauty & Peace*, Nation Islam (Mar. 28, 1996), http://www.noi.org/noi-history.
54. *What the Muslims Want*, Nation Islam, http://www.noi.org/muslim-program (last visited Sep. 30, 2023) (featuring excerpts from Elijah Muhammad, *Message to the Blackman in America* (1965)).
55. Dinnerstein et al., *supra* n. 24, at 271–272.

Louisiana, Mississippi, North Carolina, Oklahoma, South Dakota, Tennessee, Texas, and Washington have enacted such laws.[56] A federal court of appeals found the Oklahoma law to be unconstitutional.[57] Such laws are widely viewed as unnecessary and a reflection of Islamophobia.[58]

VIII. Composition of US Supreme Court

42. The religious composition of the Supreme Court of the United States has been predominantly Protestant, with ninety-two of the 116 Supreme Court justices being Protestants. The remaining twenty-four justices include fifteen Catholics, eight Jews, and one with no religious affiliation. Until 2010, the bench had always included at least one Protestant. The current Supreme Court is comprised of six Catholic and two Jewish justices, one nondenominational Protestant, and one justice who has identified as both Catholic and Episcopalian[59]—a religious composition that would have been unimaginable even a generation ago. As noted in the next section, this reflects decreasing political polarization over religious denominational differences.

IX. Political Alignment over Social Issues

43. For large swaths of American history, political cleavages have largely been drawn on religious lines. Since the 1970s, however, political alignments have increasingly been along social rather than religious lines, with conservative Protestants, Catholics, and Jews increasingly identifying as Republicans, and liberal Protestants, Catholics, and Jews increasingly identifying as Democrats.[60] In the 2020 presidential election won by Joe Biden, 59% of those who reported attending church once or more per month voted for Donald Trump, the Republican candidate, while 58% of those who reported rarely or never attending church voted for Joe Biden, the Democratic candidate.[61] On the divisive issue of abortion, US adults had long

---

56. *Anti-Muslim Legislation Map*, Othering & Belonging Inst. UC Berkeley, https://belonging.berkeley.edu/islamophobia/anti-muslim-legislation-map (last visited Sep. 30, 2023); *see also Tracking Anti-Muslim Legislation Across the U.S.*, S. Poverty L. Ctr., https://www.splcenter.org/data-projects/tracking-anti-muslim-legislation-across-us (last visited Sep. 30, 2023).
57. *Awad v. Ziriax*, 670 F.3d 1111 (10th Cir. 2012).
58. *See, e.g.*, Arun Kundnani, *The Muslims Are Coming!: Islamophobia, Extremism, and the Domestic War on Terror* 233–262 (2014); Am. Bar Ass'n, Res. 113A, *Court's Use of International Law or Doctrine of Particular Religion* (Aug. 9, 2011), https://www.americanbar.org/content/dam/aba/administrative/crsj/religious-freedom.pdf (opposing "federal or state laws that impose blanket prohibitions on considerations or use by courts or arbitral tribunals of a) foreign or international law or b) the entire body of law or doctrine of a particular religion").
59. Frank Newport, *The Religion of the Supreme Court Justices*, Gallup (Apr. 8, 2022), https://news.gallup.com/opinion/polling-matters/391649/religion-supreme-court-justices.aspx.
60. Jeff Manza & Clem Brooks, *Religion, in Social Cleavages and Political Change: Voter Alignments and US Party Coalitions* 85, 85–127 (1999).
61. Justin Nortey, *Most White Americans Who Regularly Attend Worship Services Voted for Trump in 2020*, Pew Rsch. Ctr. (Aug. 30, 2021), https://www.pewresearch.org/fact-tank/2021/08/30/most-white-americans-who-regularly-attend-worship-services-voted-for-trump-in-2020.

been split almost evenly between those who describe themselves as "pro-choice", with respect to abortion, and those who describe themselves as "pro-life". The percentage of pro-choice adults nudged upward, to 55%,[62] immediately following the US Supreme Court's 2022 decision *Dobbs v. Jackson Women's Health Organization*,[63] in which the Court held that the right to abortion is not protected by the US Constitution. Views on abortion differ fairly widely by religious affiliation,[64] but Americans who attend church at least once a week are more than twice as likely to believe abortion should be illegal in all or most cases.[65] While 76% of Republicans are pro-life, 84% of Democrats are pro-choice.[66]

§3. Historical Background

I. Religion in America in the Colonial Period

44. Religion existed in the Americas for thousands of years before the arrival of Europeans. Estimates of the Native North American population in 1492 range from one to twelve million.[67] Their religious beliefs and practices were as rich and varied as their languages, cultures, and ways of living. Although many of those traditional beliefs and practices were denigrated, marginalized, and/or stripped away over the last 500 years, many live on among Native American tribes and individuals today.

45. "American religion" as we know it today was imported largely by Europeans, beginning with the arrival of Christopher Columbus in 1492. Driven by a desire to expand Christendom into Asia and shrink the borders of Muslim influence (as well as a desire for gold and personal glory), Columbus's attempt to reach the Orient by circumnavigation resulted instead in bringing the Americas to the attention of the Western world.[68] Successive explorations over the next century continued to pursue Columbus's goals with varying degrees of sincerity and aggression. Spanish voyages included mixed groups of conquistadors and missionaries. Their travels extended through the southern and western portions of the present-day United States as well as Central and South America, the result being that the majority of Latin America today still speaks the Spanish language and remains largely Catholic. French Catholics attempted to missionize in what is today Canada and northern

62. *Abortion*, Gallup, https://news.gallup.com/poll/1576/Abortion.aspx (last visited Sep. 30, 2023).
63. *Dobbs v. Jackson Women's Health Org.*, 142 S. Ct. 2228 (2022).
64. David Masci, *American Religious Groups Vary Widely in Their Views of Abortion*, Pew Rsch. Ctr. (Jan. 22, 2018), https://www.pewresearch.org/short-reads/2018/01/22/american-religious-groups-vary-widely-in-their-views-of-abortion.
65. *Religious Landscape Study: Views about Abortion*, Pew Rsch. Ctr., https://www.pewresearch.org/religion/religious-landscape-study/views-about-abortion (last visited Sep. 30, 2023).
66. *"Pro-Choice" or "Pro-Life" Demographic Table*, Gallup, https://news.gallup.com/poll/244709/pro-choice-pro-life-2018-demographic-tables.aspx (last visited Sep. 30, 2023).
67. *See supra* para. 28 and accompanying footnotes.
68. Martin E. Marty, *Pilgrims in Their Own Land: 500 Years of Religion in America* 21, 26 (1984).

New England but met with limited success, as British colonists later came to dominate the area. The methods employed by early French and Spanish Catholic missionaries to acquire baptisms have long been criticized, but while their motives may have been mixed, it can be fairly said that many came to "care greatly for the people they set out to convert and educate".[69]

46. Within a generation after the "discovery" of America, Europe's religious landscape changed with the beginning of the Reformation. Dissenters from established state churches were often persecuted, and many escaped to more tolerant countries. Several groups eventually made their way to the American colonies, seeking greater religious freedom and an opportunity to build an ideal religious community free from interference.

47. One notable group was the Separatist Pilgrims who left England in the first decade of the 1600s for Holland—Europe's most religiously diverse and tolerant country at the time—and from there obtained a charter to settle in Virginia. When their ship was blown off course and landed in present-day Massachusetts in 1620, they formed their own charter known as the "Mayflower Compact". Believing they could reform and perfect the Church of England from afar, these early settlers employed Calvinist theology to set up a "covenanted society" they hoped would be an example to the world.[70] Another group of Puritans—less inclined to cut ties entirely with the Anglican Church—settled Massachusetts Bay Colony a decade later, was far more successful in terms of population and economy, and eventually branched out into Connecticut and New Haven.

48. The irony of New England is that those who came to seek freedom quickly moved to quash dissenters. Roger Williams was a Puritan turned "seeker" who insisted that the Anglican Church was degenerate and called for a return to primitive Christianity. He also advocated for separating civil matters from religion, not because he did not support church influence in the public sphere but rather because he feared tainting the church with worldly concerns. Branded an agitator, he was cast out of Massachusetts. Williams established a new home in Rhode Island, where he sought a charter from England to set up a colonial government and put into practice his ideas of separation of church and state. Rhode Island, originally called "Rogue Island", thus became a haven for other "outsiders" and dissenters in New England.

49. Slightly to the south, a very different sort of Protestant colony was in development. The wealthy Dutch had established a port and trading post in New Amsterdam, later renamed "New York" by the English. Because Holland was more religiously diverse than other European nations, the Dutch had learned the virtue of tolerance, and that attitude carried over into the New World. Although the Dutch Reformed Church was established, the colony lacked strong clerical leadership and churches were not well supported. Attempts to preach the gospel to nearby Native

69. *Ibid.*, at 26.
70. *Ibid.*, at 60–88.

Americans were half-hearted and unsuccessful. In the 1650s, Jewish immigrants began to arrive and were allowed to stay because many European shareholders in the Dutch West India Company were Jews, much to the chagrin of New Amsterdam's leaders, who sought to hamper Jewish settlement as much as possible. New Amsterdam fell to the English in 1664 without much struggle; the settlers there were more concerned with their crops and commodities than with European politics.

50. Among other European dissenters who made their way to America, seeking their own place, were the "Quakers" or "Friends" of the Religious Society of Friends. Quakers were Christians who believed in the universal priesthood of believers, thus rejecting the need for hierarchical church authority, and who preached pacifism and equality among men. Quakers encountered serious opposition in the colonies until William Penn, a wealthy English Quaker, received the land of Pennsylvania from the King in 1681 as payment for a debt owed to Penn's father. Penn immediately sold hundreds of thousands of acres to prospective settlers and set off for America to fulfil his dream of founding a peace-loving society where religious freedom would be granted. Naming the largest city "Philadelphia" (City of Brotherly Love), Penn encouraged settlers from a variety of religious backgrounds to participate in his utopian experiment. Although successful at first, the colony soon faced political divisions and corruption among Penn's deputies. Penn had sailed back to England just before the Glorious Revolution, only to find himself imprisoned for backing the wrong side. He returned to Pennsylvania in 1699 but left again two years later when he saw that it had failed to live up to his utopian vision, and he never had anything to do with the colony again. However, Pennsylvania still set an important precedent for church-state separation and religious freedom and was held up as an example by James Madison and others at the time of the United States' founding. In the early eighteenth century, Philadelphia was larger and more economically successful than both Boston and New York, and its success has been attributed to the religious freedoms its citizens enjoyed.[71]

51. Founded in 1632 by the wealthy Calvert family, who had converted to Catholicism in Protestant England, Maryland was originally intended as a haven for English Catholics. Being few in number, however, Maryland Catholics invited Englishmen of other faiths—including Catholic-hating Puritans—to settle there and were soon outnumbered by Anglicans and other Protestants.[72] The colonial assembly passed An Act Concerning Religion in 1649 mandating religious tolerance for Trinitarian Christians.[73] The colony managed to remain tolerant until Puritans came to power in England in the Great Revolution, the Calvert charter was revoked, and the Act Concerning Religion was repealed. The Church of England became the

71. Nicholas P. Miller, *The Religious Roots of the First Amendment: Dissenting Protestants and the Separation of Church and State* 62 (2012).
72. *Ibid.*, at 83.
73. *Two Acts of Toleration: 1649 and 1826*, Md. State Archives, http://msa.maryland.gov/msa/speccol/sc2200/sc2221/000025/html/intro.html (last visited Sep. 30, 2023).

established church in 1702, and Catholic churches were closed, Catholics were forbidden to teach in public, and Catholic children were forced to take oaths of loyalty.[74] Catholics were banned from voting in 1718.[75] It was not until the Maryland State Constitution was ratified in 1776 that all Christians were given equal protection under the law, and protections were not extended to Jews until 1825 or to other religions until 1867.[76]

52. Virginia was the oldest English colony in North America, though the first few attempts at settlement failed and had to be abandoned. Jamestown, the first permanent settlement in 1607, struggled for many years due to disease, failed crops, and clashes with the local Native Americans.[77] Virginia settlers primarily came seeking economic opportunities, hoping to establish profitable plantations, rather than for the sake of religion or religious freedom. Anglicanism was the official religion, but ministers were few and generally casual in their ministry, and attendance at church was lackluster. Later in the century, however, more capable ministers arrived from England and the Church became well established.[78]

II. Revolutionary War and the Great Awakenings

53. Beginning in the 1730s, a religious revival that has come to be known as the First Great Awakening swept across the colonies. This movement was less about converting the non-religious to Christianity and more about reinvigorating Christianity by rejecting blind obedience to church authority and encouraging individuals to seek personal spiritual experiences with God. Religion came to be seen as a matter of choice and personal freedom—an important attitudinal shift that contributed to the American Revolution a generation later.[79] Calvinism, which taught predestination and the primacy of God's will, and was hitherto the dominant Protestant theology, changed as Arminianism gained influence, teaching that man had agency to reject or accept God's grace.[80] Popular preachers such as George Whitefield drew crowds in the thousands as they travelled from city to city, employing new styles of teaching that were passionate and appealed to emotions. Ministers of established churches tended to oppose "revivalism", since it threatened to encroach on their territory and undermine their authority, but a large segment of America's population was enthusiastic about this new wave of spirituality.[81]

---

74. Marty, *Pilgrims in Their Own Land*, *supra* n. 68, at 84–86.
75. Paul Finkelman, *Maryland Toleration Act (1649)*, *in* 1 *Encyclopedia of American Civil Liberties* 975, 976 (Paul Finkelman ed., 2013).
76. Md. Constitution § XXXIII (1776); *Two Acts of Toleration*, *supra* n. 73.
77. Marty, *Pilgrims in Their Own Land*, *supra* n. 68, at 54–55.
78. *Ibid.*, at 58.
79. *See ibid.*, at 108, 126; Gordon S. Wood, *The Radicalism of the American Revolution* 144–145 (1992).
80. Frank Lambert, *Religion and the American Revolution*, *in* 1 *The Cambridge History of Religions in America* 570, 583 (Stephen J. Stein ed., 2012).
81. *See generally* Marty, *Pilgrims in Their Own Land*, *supra* n. 68, at 107–128.

54. Though many political and social changes took place at the time of the American Revolution, religion played an important role in supporting the cause, and American religion itself was changed by it. Religion and politics were virtually intertwined during these years, as ministers preached sermons reinforcing the rightness of America's political position in separating from Britain and the justness of their cause. Revolutionaries tended to see America as God's chosen people—a new Israel—and themselves as crusaders in a holy war against the political and religious oppression of Europe.[82] In several instances, sermons delivered by preachers such as Jonathan Mayhew actually incited violent demonstrations against British authority.[83] Many of the Founding Fathers expressed their belief that they were guided by the hand of God in their efforts—in winning the war, in unifying the nation, and in establishing the Constitution. Such sentiments gave rise to a "civil religion" in the United States—generalized references to Deity's assistance in and approval of America's founding principles.[84] Several of the nation's early leaders were ministers, including Scottish Presbyterian John Witherspoon, a delegate to the Continental Congress and signer of the Declaration of Independence.[85] The Declaration itself cited the "Creator" as the source of human rights and expressed the signers' trust in "divine Providence".[86]

55. Up to the time of the Revolution, which began in 1775, the colonies had not received an Anglican bishop, and colonists were wary of a bishop being imposed on them. Fears about the potential for tyranny if one were sent, as well as conspiracy theories that the British monarchy was trying to control American churches, fueled Americans' desire for independence from "outside" influences.[87] Such fears also contributed to the movement for disestablishment after America's independence was won. The Bill of Rights, written a decade later, officially rejected an established church at the federal level.[88] By 1790, a majority of the states had either already disestablished or were in the process of disestablishing their state churches, although Connecticut and Massachusetts did not complete their disestablishments until 1818 and 1833, respectively.[89] During the process of state disestablishments, the concern was as much for keeping churches free from government interference as preventing abuse of government-backed ecclesiastical power.

56. From the 1820s through the 1840s, another religious revival swept the nation, this time with a different effect. Instigators of the Second Great Awakening,

---

82. Lambert, *Religion and the American Revolution*, *supra* n. 80, at 571–572.
83. *Ibid.*, at 575.
84. *Ibid.*, at 583–584.
85. *Ibid.*, at 580.
86. *The Declaration of Independence* paras. 2, 29 (U.S. 1776).
87. Lambert, *Religion and the American Revolution*, *supra* n. 80, at 572–573.
88. U.S. Const. amend. I ("Congress shall make no law respecting an establishment of religion … .").
89. Kelly Olds, *Privatizing the Church: Disestablishment in Connecticut and Massachusetts*, 102 J. Pol. Econ. 277, 278 (1994).

like those of the First, intended to rekindle the flame of faith and "reheat" lukewarm Christians, though the movement soon became very much a contest for converts.[90] Itinerant preachers set up camp meetings in the woods where people could come and hear numerous ministers contend for their respective faiths. Often, heated debates between ministers of different sects would be held. It was during this period that modern American denominationalism was born. Applying the political ideals of the Revolution to religion, churches became republicanized. Congregations came to assert greater control over their pastors, and individuals were encouraged to find truth for themselves rather than rely wholly on what others told them to believe.[91] Churches also became highly sectarian, as every doctrinal schism produced a new church.

57. One issue that divided churches was slavery, which the Founders failed to condemn or restrict in the US Constitution, largely because they believed doing so would cause southern states to reject the Constitution entirely.[92] These splits tended to separate large denominations into northern and southern branches, increasing the sectionalism that eventually led to the Civil War.[93] During this time, Methodism grew significantly, its membership increasing from less than 10,000 in 1780 to half a million in 1830.[94] A number of new faiths emerged at this time as well, including Unitarians, Universalists, Shakers, Latter-day Saints, Campbellites, Millerites, and Seventh-day Adventists, some of whom experimented with new models of societal organization and gender roles and relationships. In addition to churches, religious organizations promoting social reform also gained influence, advocating for issues such as temperance, women's rights, and abolition of slavery. These associations had a profound moral effect on politics and culture and secured the role that religious organizations would play in public affairs for the next two centuries.[95]

III. Anti-slavery and the Civil War

58. Religion played a large role in the Civil War of 1861 to 1865—both in the South (Confederacy) and in the North (Union). The Bible was used to justify both abolitionists and those who supported slavery. Consequently, both preached that God was on their side, and the campaigns of the Confederate and Union armies were highly influenced by that religious momentum and ideology.

---

90. *See* Grant Underwood, *"Awash in a Sea of Faith": America and the Second Great Awakening*, *in Lectures on Religion and the Founding of the American Republic* 97, 100–101 (John W. Welch & Stephen J. Fleming eds., 2003).
91. Wood, *The Radicalism of the American Revolution*, *supra* n. 79, at 332.
92. *See* Steven Mintz, *Historical Context: The Constitution and Slavery*, Gilder Lehrman Inst. Am. Hist., https://www.gilderlehrman.org/history-resources/teaching-resource/historical-context-constitution-and-slavery (last visited Sep. 30, 2023) (discussing how the Framers deliberately avoided the word "slave" in the Constitution but afforded slavery important, implicit protections).
93. *See generally* C.C. Goen, *Broken Churches, Broken Nation: Denominational Schisms and the Coming of the American Civil War* (1985).
94. Underwood, *"Awash in a Sea of Faith"*, *supra* n. 90, at 101.
95. *Ibid.*, at 104–105.

59. Many Christians throughout the United States, particularly in the South, believed that the Bible condoned slavery.[96] This belief encouraged the southern states to secede from the Union when they saw their lifestyle—supported, in their view, by both the Bible and the Constitution—was being challenged.[97] Therefore, as the Confederates established their new country, they believed they had been given the opportunity to establish a more religious government.[98] They attempted to do so, adding the words "invoking the favor and guidance of Almighty God" to the preamble of the Confederate Constitution and establishing the national motto of "God will avenge".[99]

60. The Union, predominantly Protestant as well, also believed that God favored their side. While not all northerners believed slavery was evil, most believed it was a wrong that would be eliminated slowly and peacefully. Abolitionism, which most northerners viewed as an extreme and destabilizing ideology, was largely a religious movement. Abolitionists like William Lloyd Garrison and the Beecher family had been calling for the immediate emancipation of black slaves since the 1830s, citing scripture as the basis for their position. They not only advocated for the end of slavery but also for full integration of African Americans into society as equals with whites. They saw churches that argued for anything less as hypocritical and un-Christian. The abolition movement arose as a grassroots effort across many denominations, and some believed it became a religion all to itself, an "uncanonical Church".[100] Although perceived as radical and potentially dangerous, abolitionism had a profound influence on shaping the religious overtones of the Civil War.[101]

61. During the Civil War's early years, after the Union suffered several devastating defeats, a popular narrative emerged in the North that God was punishing the United States for the practice of slavery.[102] More and more congregations in the North began calling for abolition of slavery in order to regain God's favor in their war efforts. This momentum encouraged and allowed President Abraham Lincoln to issue his Emancipation Proclamation, and it sustained the passage of amendments to the Constitution that allowed for the emancipation of slaves in the United States.[103]

---

96. For example, the Mosaic Law permitted the Hebrews to buy and sell "bondmen" from the "heathen", *Leviticus* 25:44–46 (King James), and Paul and Peter both encouraged "servants" to obey their masters, *Ephesians* 6:5, *1 Peter* 2:18 (King James).
97. Charles F. Irons, *Religion in the Civil War*, Encyclopedia Va., http://www.encyclopediavirginia.org/religion_during_the_civil_war (last modified Dec. 7, 2020).
98. Harry S. Stout & Christopher Grasso, *Civil War, Religion, and Communications: The Case of Richmond, in Religion and the American Civil War* 313, 321 (Randall M. Miller, Harry S. Stout & Charles Reagan Wilson eds., 1998).
99. *Ibid.*
100. 4 Wendell Phillips Garrison & Francis Jackson Garrison, *William Lloyd Garrison, 1805–1879: The Story of His Life Told by His Children* 90 (1894) (quoting Henry Ward Beecher).
101. Marty, *Pilgrims in Their Own Land, supra* n. 68, at 245–246.
102. James Howell Moorhead, *Religion in the Civil War: The Northern Perspective*, Nat'l Humans. Ctr.: TeacherServe, Divining Am., http://nationalhumanitiescenter.org/tserve/nineteen/nkeyinfo/cwnorth.htm (last modified Oct. 2000).
103. *See ibid.*

IV. Civil War Through New Deal (1865–1933)

62. After the Civil War, the United States began to focus on rebuilding and growth. Reconstruction began in the broken southern states, as the Union and adventurers throughout the country were pushing the borders of the United States further west. Throughout this period of growth and healing, the Supreme Court decided cases that shaped the law's relationship with religious freedom.

63. The increased fervor in westward expansion led to thousands of wagon trains engraving trails throughout the West as pioneers traveled and settled new territories. The Utah Territory was home to thousands of members of The Church of Jesus Christ of Latter-day Saints (sometimes called "Mormons" in the past), approximately one-quarter of whom practiced polygamy from 1840 to 1890.[104] In 1862 Congress passed the Morrill Act, criminalizing polygamy.[105] The resulting case of *Reynolds v. United States* was the US Supreme Court's first examination of the meaning of the First Amendment's Free Exercise Clause.[106] In *Reynolds*, the Supreme Court upheld the Morrill Act and drew a distinction between belief and actions, which remains a central principle of free exercise jurisprudence. The Court stated that while laws "cannot interfere with mere religious belief and opinions, they may with practices".[107]

64. Reynolds, a Latter-day Saint polygamist, argued that the Free Exercise Clause of the First Amendment protected religiously motivated acts that were *malum prohibitum* but not acts that were *malum in se*.[108] Essentially, his argument was that religion should not justify actions that are wrong by nature but can justify actions that are deemed wrong only by statute. Reynolds relied on the Bible and the majority opinion of people living in the Utah Territory to support his claim that polygamy was not wrong by nature. However, while natural law theory may have been prominent in the mid-nineteenth century, the Court's rejection of this natural law argument demonstrates a shift that was taking place by the end of the century.[109] After *Reynolds*, the US Congress passed the Edmunds-Tucker Act that unincorporated The Church of Jesus Christ of Latter-day Saints, instituted an anti-polygamy oath for voters and public officials, disenfranchised women in the Utah Territory (who up to that point had enjoyed the right to vote), and confiscated all

---

104. B. Carmon Hardy, *That "Same Old Question of Polygamy and Polygamous Living," Some Recent Findings Regarding Nineteenth and Early Twentieth-Century Mormon Polygamy*, 73 Utah Hist. Q. 212, 215 (2005) (estimating the percentage of Latter-day Saints who practiced polygamy in the latter half of the nineteenth century to be 15% to 30%); William Volf, *Mormon Polygamy in the Nineteenth Century: The Practice of "The Principle" in Reality*, 15 Neb. Anthropologist 39, 41 (1999) (citing studies estimating the same).
105. Morrill Act, Pub. L. No. 37-130, 12 Stat. 501 (1862).
106. *Reynolds v. United States*, 98 U.S. 145 (1878).
107. *Ibid.*, at 166.
108. Nathan B. Oman, *Natural Law and the Rhetoric of Empire:* Reynolds v. United States, *Polygamy, and Empire*, 88 Wash. U. L. Rev. 671, 673 (2011) (citing George Q. Cannon, *A Review of the Decision of the Supreme Court of the United States, in the Case of* Geo. Reynolds vs. The People of the United States 34 (1879)).
109. *Ibid.*, at 678–679.

church property valued over USD 50,000.[110] The Supreme Court upheld this law in *Late Corp. of The Church of Jesus Christ of Latter-day Saints v. United States*.[111] After the Church abandoned the practice of polygamy in 1890, Congress authorized the release of the Church's assets.[112]

65. An 1892 Supreme Court case, *Church of the Holy Trinity v. United States*, considered the nation's Christian heritage in evaluating the meaning of the law.[113] In *Holy Trinity*, the Church had contracted with an Anglican priest from England to come minister to them. However, an 1885 law prohibited the importation and migration of "foreigners" and "aliens" under contract or agreement to perform labor or service of any kind in the United States.[114] Justice David J. Brewer ruled that the law applied only to manual labor jobs, not professional positions such as clergy. As evidence to support his position, Justice Brewer cited numerous events from American history with religious underpinnings, as well as religious language in documents such as the Declaration of Independence and the Constitution.[115] He also appealed to traditions, customs, and practices in "American life" that demonstrated a clear Christian background, stating "These, and many other matters which might be noticed, add a volume of unofficial declarations to the mass of organic utterances that this is a Christian nation."[116] The legislature of a Christian nation, he concluded, could not possibly have intended to prohibit the employment by churches of foreign ministers, so the statute in question must be interpreted to exempt clergy.[117]

66. In the late nineteenth century, the Protestant presence in America was in the ascendant.[118] However, while numbers were growing, the Protestant church was facing increasing and unprecedented challenges. Urbanization and industrialization were accompanied by an increase in Catholic and Jewish immigrants and new sects, such as Christian Science and The Church of Jesus Christ of Latter-day Saints, which led to a more diverse religious demographic.[119] With increased diversity, the Protestant influence throughout the public sphere began to attenuate. For example, in some states religious or Bible instruction was no longer permitted—let alone

110. Edmunds-Tucker Act, Pub. L. No. 49-397, 24 Stat. 635 (1887).
111. *Late Corp. of The Church of Jesus Christ of Latter-day Saints v. United States*, 136 U.S. 1 (1890).
112. J. Res. 11, 53d Cong., 1st Sess., 28 Stat. 980 (1893).
113. *Church of the Holy Trinity v. United States*, 143 U.S. 457 (1892).
114. Alien Contract Labor Law, Pub. L. No. 48-164, 23 Stat. 332 (1885).
115. *Church of the Holy Trinity*, 143 U.S. at 465–470.
116. *Ibid.*, at 471.
117. *Ibid.*, at 471–472.
118. Robert T. Handy, *A Christian America: Protestant Hopes and Historical Realities* 69 (1971).
119. The Catholic population in the United States increased from 5% in 1850 to 17% in 1906. Julie Byrne, *Roman Catholics and Immigration in Nineteenth Century America*, Nat'l Humans. Ctr.: TeacherServe, Divining Am., http://nationalhumanitiescenter.org/tserve/nineteen/nkeyinfo/nromcath.htm (last modified Nov. 2000); *see also* Handy, *A Christian America*, *supra* n. 118, at 57–81.

required—in public schools.[120] While this period saw diversification, it also saw Protestants lamenting and resisting the weakening of their majority.[121]

67. Scholars have noted a shift from traditional Christian supernatural theology to an outlook of religious liberalism in the century between 1870 and 1970.[122] Religious liberalism focused on general application of moral principles found in the Bible rather than on individual salvation.[123] The shift contributed to what is termed the "Social Gospel" that encouraged institutional (including legislative and judicial) involvement in curbing social injustices such as wealth and class disparities and inhumane working conditions.[124] This social justice vision became influential to US policy throughout the beginning of the twentieth century.

68. This Christian morality became infused with the American concept of true democracy.[125] While the decision to support Great Britain and Allied forces in World War I was influenced by various factors, including military and economic connections, the mentality fostered by religious liberalism also inclined many Americans to feel a moral duty to support the more democratic, war-torn countries.[126] Respect for different religious practices was promoted, with a general consensus that individuals belonging to religious groups that preached pacifism should be exempt from conscription.[127]

69. Between the World Wars, the "Scopes Monkey Trial" was a significant symbol of the changing role of religion in society. Since the publication of Charles Darwin's *On the Origin of Species* in 1859, tensions grew between conservative Christians and schools over teaching evolution.[128] In 1925, Tennessee passed the Butler Act, making it illegal "to teach … that man has descended from a lower order of animals" instead of the "story of the divine creation of man as taught in the Bible".[129] The American Civil Liberties Union supported teacher John Scopes in a

---

120. *See, e.g.*, *Bd. of Educ. v. Minor*, 23 Ohio St. 211 (1872); *State ex rel. Weiss v. Dist. Bd. of Sch. Dist. No. 8 of Edgerton*, 44 N.W. 967 (Wis. 1890).
121. Steven K. Green, *Justice David Josiah Brewer and the "Christian Nation" Maxim*, 63 Alb. L. Rev. 427, 440–443 (1999). One way in which the Protestant majority attempted to resist the influence of Catholicism, in particular, was through the passage of state constitutional "Blaine Amendments", which prohibited state funding of religious schools (at the time largely Catholic). *See infra* paras. 87, 112.
122. Grant Wacker, *Religious Liberalism and the Modern Crisis of Faith*, Nat'l Humans. Ctr.: TeacherServe, Divining Am., http://nationalhumanitiescenter.org/tserve/twenty/tkeyinfo/liberal.htm (last modified Oct. 2000).
123. *Ibid.*
124. *Ibid.*
125. *See* Jonathan H. Ebel, *Religion (USA)*, 1914–1918 Online: Int'l Encyclopedia First World War, https://encyclopedia.1914-1918-online.net/article/religion_usa (last visited Sep. 30, 2023).
126. *See ibid.*
127. Selective Services Act of 1917, Pub. L. No. 65-12, § 4, 40 Stat. 76, 78.
128. Christopher Armstrong & Grant Wacker, *The Scopes Trial*, Nat'l Humans. Ctr.: TeacherServe, Divining Am., http://nationalhumanitiescenter.org/tserve/twenty/tkeyinfo/tscopes.htm (last modified Oct. 2000).
129. *Scopes v. State*, 289 S.W. 363, 363 n.1 (Tenn. 1927) (quoting Acts of 1925, ch. 27, § 1 (Butler Act or Tennessee Anti-Evolution Act)).

case challenging the constitutionality of the Butler Act.[130] While Scopes lost his case, momentum on the issue was reversed, and in *Epperson v. Arkansas* the US Supreme Court struck down an anti-evolution statute as unconstitutionally designed to protect a particular reading of the book of Genesis.[131] *See* Part IX (Education), Chapter 1 (Religious Education in Public and Private Schools).

70. With the economic crash of 1929 and subsequent Great Depression came one of the darker periods of American history, with unemployment reaching nearly 25%.[132] Hardship hit all classes, religious sects, ethnicities, and races and consequently helped break down some of the barriers separating these groups.[133] In 1933, Franklin D. Roosevelt was elected President of the United States and implemented a series of policies known collectively as "The New Deal". The New Deal increased the size and authority of the federal government to provide jobs and relief to the American public. World War II further helped break down some of the barriers between religious and ethnic groups, as soldiers from all backgrounds gave their lives for their country.[134] It is said that while people went into the Great Depression and World War II as Protestants and Jewish and Catholic immigrants, they came out as Americans.[135]

V. World War II Era Forward

71. After World War II, a newly prosperous and victorious America was looking for stability, which led newly established families to renew regular religious worship. By the 1960s, however, the United States no longer had the monolithic Protestant culture that had dominated throughout its first 150 years. New beliefs that had come to the country through immigration, intellectualism, and social movements had been forged into the culture through the trials of poverty and warfare during the Great Depression and World Wars. While religion did not fade as a fundamental part of American culture, the diversity of accepted religions practiced throughout the population had attenuated the connection between Protestantism and the government.[136]

72. The civil rights movement of the 1960s demonstrates how diversity had become an accepted and even desired part of American culture. Religion was at the

130. *See ibid.*, at 364.
131. *Epperson v. Arkansas*, 393 U.S. 97, 107–109 (1968).
132. U.S. Dep't of Com., Bureau of the Census, *Bicentennial Edition: Historical Statistics of the United States, Colonial Times to 1970* at D 85–86 (*Unemployment: 1890 to 1970*) (Sept. 1975), https://www.census.gov/library/publications/1975/compendia/hist_stats_colonial-1970.html.
133. Michael Kazin, *The American People and the New Deal*, 1 Fed. Hist. J. 1 (2009).
134. *See, e.g.*, Byrne, *Roman Catholics and the American Mainstream in the Twentieth Century*, *supra* n. 119.
135. *See, e.g.*, *ibid.*; Edward Shapiro, *World War II and American Jewish Identity*, 10 Mod. Judaism 65, 65 (1990).
136. Joanne Beckman, *Religion in Post-World War II America*, Nat'l Humans. Ctr.: TeacherServe, Divining Am., http://nationalhumanitiescenter.org/tserve/twenty/tkeyinfo/trelww2.htm (last modified Oct. 2000).

forefront of the movement's motives and rhetoric and was the impetus that brought together thousands of Americans, uniting them in the cause. Beginning with a few non-violent protests in the deep South organized by black churches and young university students, the movement grew to national proportions, garnering support from African Americans and people from all ethnic and racial backgrounds across the country. One major voice for civil rights was Reverend Martin Luther King Jr., who infused the movement with biblical language and symbols. He saw civil rights activists as a modern-day camp of Israel seeking deliverance from oppression and searching for a promised land of freedom and equality.[137] He also insisted that civil rights activists refrain from violence, citing Mahatma Gandhi—a religious and political leader who led the successful movement for India's independence—as a historical role model. King invoked early Christian theologian St. Augustine in arguing that unjust laws were not truly "laws" because they lacked the force of reason and therefore came under God's condemnation.[138]

73. While the civil rights movement is most often associated with racial equality, religious exercise rights were affected as well. The Civil Rights Act of 1964 prohibits employers from discriminating against prospective or current employees based on their religious affiliations.[139] In 1972, the Civil Rights Act was amended to further require employers to accommodate the religious practices of their employees, as far as it does not cause undue hardship.[140] Throughout the remainder of the twentieth century, there was an ongoing shift in focus from constitutional toward statutory protection of free exercise.[141] *See* Part II (Religious Freedom in General), Chapter 1 (Individual Religious Freedom).

74. In the sixty years since the Civil Rights Act was passed, many other highly charged social issues have had an important religious dimension. Issues such as abortion, poverty, women's rights, LGBTQ+ rights, and environmental issues have all seen religious arguments advanced by proponents of both sides. For instance, many pro-life advocates argue that a religious belief in the sanctity of life means that aborting fetuses amounts to murder, an act that God has explicitly forbidden.[142] Religious pro-choice advocates, in contrast, argue that God has given individuals

137. *See generally* Gary S. Selby, *Martin Luther King and the Rhetoric of Freedom: The Exodus Narrative in America's Struggle for Civil Rights* (2008).
138. Marty, *Pilgrims in Their Own Land*, *supra* n. 68, at 441–442.
139. 42 U.S.C. § 2000e-2(a) (2018).
140. Equal Employment Opportunity Act of 1972, Pub. L. No. 92-261, § 2(7), 86 Stat. 103, 103 (codified as amended at 42 U.S.C. § 2000e(j) (2018)); *see also* Andrew M. Campbell, Annotation, *What Constitutes Employer's Reasonable Accommodation of Employee's Religious Preferences under Title VII of Civil Rights Act of 1964*, 134 A.L.R. Fed. 1, § 2[a] (1996).
141. Ira C. Lupu, Hobby Lobby *and the Dubious Enterprise of Religious Exemptions*, 38 Harv. J.L. & Gender 35, 48–75 (2015).
142. *See, e.g.*, Robert M. Bowman, Jr., *Argument for the Silent: A Biblical Case Against Abortion*, Reasons to Believe (Apr. 1, 2001), http://www.reasons.org/articles/argument-for-the-silent-a-biblical-case-against-abortion.

personal stewardship over their decisions and free will to choose what is best for themselves in their circumstances.[143] *See* Part XI (Religion and Culture), Chapter 3 (Religion and Civil Society).

75. Also in the past fifty years, a view has ascended that religion should be reserved for private life, that religious symbols should be removed from the public sphere, and more importantly, that political arguments based on religious beliefs are illegitimate. *See* Part XI (Religion and Culture), Chapter 4 (Religion and Public Debate).

143. *See, e.g., The Biblical Basis for Being Pro-Choice*, Beliefnet, http://www.beliefnet.com/News/2003/01/The-Biblical-Basis-Forbeing-Pro-Choice.aspx?p=3 (last visited Sep. 30, 2023).

Part I. Legal Framework and Sources

Chapter 1. Constitutional Position of Religion

§1. Federal Constitution

76. The original text of the US Constitution only explicitly addresses religion once, in a provision prohibiting religious tests for public office.[144] Structurally, however, through the enumeration of powers (with unenumerated powers, including vis-à-vis religion, reserved to state governments and the people), the Constitution significantly disempowers the federal government in matters related to religion.[145]

---

144. Richard J. Regan, *The American Constitution and Religion* 33 (2013) ("[The No Religious Test Clause] is the only provision in the original Constitution about religion."). This does not count the casual phrase, "in the Year of our Lord", used in the written date of the Constitution's signing after article VII, neither does it count the "Sundays excepted" language in determining the time period for a presidential veto in article I, section 7—provisions that have doubtful substantive religious significance. *See* Michael I. Meyerson, *Endowed by Our Creator: The Birth of Religious Freedom in America* 141–146 (2012).

145. John Witte, Jr., and Joel A. Nichols write:

> It was commonly assumed at the convention that questions of religion and of religious liberty were for the states and the people to resolve, not the budding federal government. … Whatever was not specifically given to this new federal sovereign was to be retained by the sovereign states and the sovereign people. Federal power over religion was not considered part of this new constitutional calculus. As James Madison put it to the Virginia Ratification Convention: "There is not a shadow of right in the general government to intermeddle with religion. Its least interference with it, would be a most flagrant usurpation." ... Federal protection of religion was also considered beyond the mandate of the 1787 convention. Both the natural checks and balances inherent in the nation's religious pluralism and the new religious liberty provisions of the state constitutions were considered to be ample protection. For the emerging federal constitution to guarantee religious and civil rights was viewed to be unnecessary, if not dangerous.

John Witte, Jr. & Joel A. Nichols, *Religion and the American Constitutional Experiment* 70 (4th ed. 2016) (citation omitted).

Leo Pfeffer writes:

> Omission of reference to God in the Constitution was not the result of any oversight. Invocations of God in state constitutions were common. …
>
> The reason for the exclusion was, in Madison's words, that the Constitution was not to create "a shadow of right in the general government to meddle with religion" ... "Why," asked Alexander Hamilton in defending the absence of a Bill of Rights from the Constitution, "why declare that things shall not be done which there is no power to do?" Why forbid Congress to abridge freedom of religion when religion was completely outside its jurisdiction?

Leo Pfeffer, *Religious Freedom* 20 (1979).

77. The landmark case *Marbury v. Madison* instituted the doctrine of judicial review,[146] which recognizes the Supreme Court's power to invalidate statutes or other governmental actions that violate the Constitution. The doctrine has had significant impact on American religious exercise jurisprudence. Through judicial review, the Supreme Court has become the preeminent American institution for defining the meaning and scope of the First Amendment and other constitutional provisions. Any discussion of law and religion in the United States is in large measure an analysis of the numerous Supreme Court cases interpreting the religion clauses of the First Amendment or the meaning of other federal laws relating to religion. A number of religion cases have turned on the threshold question of whether the challenge was brought by a party with standing to sue, and in others, standing has been at least one major issue addressed by courts.[147] Generally, to have standing, plaintiffs must show that (1) they have suffered, or imminently will suffer, a

146. *Marbury v. Madison,* 5 U.S. (1 Cranch) 137 (1803); *see also* Michael Stokes Paulsen, *The Irrepressible Myth of* Marbury, 101 Mich. L. Rev. 2706 (2003) (asserting that *Marbury* "did not create the concept of judicial review" but rather "applied well-established principles").

147. *See, e.g., Little Sisters of the Poor Saints Peter & Paul Home v. Pennsylvania*, 140 S. Ct. 2367, 2379 n.6 (2020) (noting a lower court erred in its analysis of standing); *Am. Legion v. Am. Humanist Ass'n*, 139 S. Ct. 2067, 2098 (2019) (Gorsuch, J., with Thomas, J., concurring) (explaining that the "'offended observer' theory of standing has no basis in law"); *Trump v. Hawaii*, 138 S. Ct. 2392, 2416 (2018) ("We need not decide whether the claimed dignitary interest establishes an adequate ground for standing. The … plaintiffs assert another, more concrete injury: the alleged real-world effect that the Proclamation has had in keeping them separated from certain relatives who seek to enter the country [from eight Muslim-majority states]." (citations omitted)); *Ariz. Christian Sch. Tuition Org. v. Winn*, 563 U.S. 125, 138 (2011) (explaining the narrow *Flast v. Cohen* Establishment Clause exception to the general rule against taxpayer standing); *Valley Forge Christian Coll. v. Ams. United for Separation of Church & State, Inc.*, 454 U.S. 464, 472 (1982) ("[A]t an irreducible minimum, Art. III requires the party who invokes the court's authority to 'show that he personally has suffered some actual or threatened injury as a result of the putatively illegal conduct of the defendant' and that the injury 'fairly can be traced to the challenged action' and 'is likely to be redressed by a favorable decision.' In this manner does Art. III limit the federal judicial power 'to those disputes which confine federal courts to a role consistent with a system of separated powers and which are traditionally thought to be capable of resolution through the judicial process.'" (citations omitted)); *New Doe Child #1 v. Cong. of the U.S.*, 891 F.3d 578, 585–586 (6th Cir. 2018) (holding that plaintiffs had standing to challenge use of "In God we trust" motto on currency); *Ansley v. Warren*, 861 F.3d 512, 523 (4th Cir. 2017) (holding that taxpayer plaintiffs lacked standing to challenge bill that provided state funds to administer the recusals of magistrates who objected to performing marriages on religious grounds); *Barber v. Bryant*, 860 F.3d 345 (5th Cir. 2017) (holding that plaintiffs lacked "personal confrontation" and taxpayer standing to challenge law prohibiting discrimination against religious persons who disapproved of LGBT and unmarried persons); *Am. Humanist Ass'n, Inc. v. Douglas Cty. Sch. Dist. RE-1*, 859 F.3d 1243, 1253–1254 (10th Cir. 2017) (holding that only one of several plaintiffs had standing for an Establishment Clause challenge where she had "unwelcome contacts" with Christian fundraising efforts in a public school); *COPE v. Kan. State Bd. of Educ.*, 821 F.3d 1215 (10th Cir. 2016) (holding that plaintiffs lacked standing to challenge "anti-religious" science education standards); *Freedom from Religion Found., Inc. v. Lew*, 773 F.3d 815 (7th Cir. 2014) (holding that plaintiffs lacked standing to challenge constitutionality of "parsonage" tax exemption); *Awad v. Ziriax*, 670 F.3d 1111, 1120–1124 (10th Cir. 2012) (holding that plaintiff had standing to challenge state constitutional amendment that prohibited state courts from considering or using sharia); *Cath. League for Religious & C.R. v. City & County of San Francisco*, 624 F.3d 1043, 1062, 1070–1075 (9th Cir. 2010) (Graber, J., with Kozinski, C.J., and Rymer, Hawkins, and McKeown, JJ., dissenting in part, concurring in the judgment) (collecting cases involving religion and "injury in fact" standing); *U.S. Cath. Conf. (USCC) v.*

concrete, particularized injury to a legally protected interest; (2) the alleged harmful conduct caused or will cause the injury; and (3) a favorable decision by the court is likely to redress the injury.[148]

78. The First Amendment to the Constitution, ratified in 1791 as part of the Bill of Rights, directly and concisely addresses religion: "Congress shall make no law respecting an establishment of religion, or prohibiting the free exercise thereof … ."[149] These sixteen words are the bedrock of US law and religion jurisprudence. Judicial interpretation of the First Amendment has been divided into the Establishment Clause (which prohibits a state-sponsored church or religion) and the Free Exercise Clause (which protects freedom of belief and has also been interpreted to determine the scope of limitations permitted on religiously motivated actions). Until the 1940s, the First Amendment applied only to the federal government, not to state or local governments.

79. The Free Exercise Clause was incorporated, or held to apply to state governments, in *Cantwell v. Connecticut.*[150] In *Cantwell*, the US Supreme Court struck down a state law requiring religious organizations to obtain a city-issued license before soliciting donations. In a brief but direct opinion, the Court held that "[t]he First Amendment declares that Congress shall make no law respecting an establishment of religion or prohibiting the free exercise thereof. The Fourteenth Amendment has rendered the legislatures of the states as incompetent as Congress to enact such laws."[151]

80. The Establishment Clause, perhaps technically incorporated in *Cantwell*, was first explicitly applied to state governments in *Everson v. Board of Education.*[152] *Everson* tested whether the state could reimburse parents for the cost of sending children to religious private schools. While holding the reimbursement at issue constitutional, the Court emphasized the now-famous concept of a wall of separation between church and state, explaining that "[n]either a state nor the Federal Government can set up a church" under the Establishment Clause nor can government "aid one religion, aid all religions, or prefer one religion over another", compel religious attendance at any church, or support religious organizations with taxes in any form.[153]

81. Although the Free Exercise Clause and the Establishment Clause of the First Amendment are the primary constitutional provisions relating to religious freedom, a number of other constitutional provisions tangentially affect religious freedom.

Baker, 885 F.2d 1020, 1025–1026 (2d Cir. 1989) ("[B]ecause the [plaintiffs] have neither been personally denied equal treatment under the law nor in any way prosecuted … their self-perceived "stigma" does not amount to a particularized injury in fact.").

148. *Lujan v. Defenders of Wildlife*, 504 U.S. 555, 560–561 (1992).

149. U.S. Const. amend. I.

150. *Cantwell v. Connecticut*, 310 U.S. 296, 303 (1940).

151. *Ibid.*, at 303–304.

152. *Everson v. Bd. of Educ.*, 330 U.S. 1 (1946).

153. *Ibid.*, at 15–16.

These include, among others, the prohibition on religious tests for public office, in Article VI; freedoms of speech, press, and assembly, guaranteed by the First Amendment; property rights and rights to due process of law, guaranteed by the Fifth Amendment; and due process and equal protection of the laws, guaranteed by the Fourteenth Amendment.[154] These constitutional provisions, and their relation to religious freedom, will be addressed in detail throughout this work.

82. The "state action requirement" is an important limitation on the constitutional protections available for violations of individual constitutional rights. Most of the Constitution's provisions, including the First and Fourteenth Amendments, restrict only government actions. Accordingly, injured parties cannot seek relief or redress under the Constitution for private individuals' discriminatory actions. However, federal and state anti-discrimination laws do provide remedies for some violations of civil rights by private individuals.[155] Even so, the Supreme Court has held that private parties who have an indirect relationship with the government may be immune from liability under the state action doctrine, if they operate under the government's "active supervision".[156]

§2. State Constitutions

83. Each state government is subject to both the US Constitution (including, since incorporation, the Bill of Rights) and the state's own constitution. State constitutions are usually lengthier than the federal Constitution and generally address the relationship between government and the people in greater detail than does the federal Constitution. State constitutions vary considerably in their treatment of religion and religious rights; however, by the time the US Constitution went into effect in 1789, every state then in existence had some form of protection of religious freedom, with the exception of Connecticut.[157]

84. Each state constitution takes a unique tack in addressing the issue of religious freedom. For example, the Pennsylvania state constitution of 1790, Article IX, section III, provided:

154. U.S. Const. art. VI, cl. 3; amend. I, V; amend. XIV, § 1.
155. *See, e.g.*, 42 U.S.C. § 1981 (2018) (prohibiting racial discrimination in the making and enforcing of contracts); *Runyon v. McCrary*, 427 U.S. 160 (1976) (holding that § 1981 applies to both government and private actors); 42 U.S.C. § 1983 (2018) (allowing claims against a person who, acting under the color of state law, deprived a plaintiff of rights, privileges, or immunities under federal law or the US Constitution). For state laws, *see*, for example, Cal. Gov't Code § 12955 (West 2022) (prohibiting housing discrimination by any "owner of any housing accommodation"); N.Y. Lab. Law § 197 (McKinney 2022) (prescribing a civil penalty for any employers who differentiate in wages due to protected class status); and Or. Rev. Stat. § 652.220 (2022) (prohibiting types of wage discrimination against a protected class by any employer).
156. *See, e.g.*, *Patrick v. Burget*, 486 U.S. 94 (1988).
157. 1 William W. Bassett, W. Cole Durham Jr., Mark A. Goldfeder & Robert T. Smith, *Religious Organizations and the Law* § 2:10 (*The Disestablishment of Religion and the Virginia Statute for Establishing Religious Freedom*), Westlaw RELORGS (database updated Dec. 2022) [hereinafter 1 Durham et al.].

> That all men have a natural and indefeasible right to worship Almighty God according to the dictates of their own consciences; that no man can, of right, be compelled to attend, erect, or support any place of worship, or to maintain any ministry against his consent; that no human authority can, in any case whatever, controul [sic] or interfere with the rights of conscience; and that no preference shall ever be given, by law, to any religious establishments or modes of worship.[158]

In the current Pennsylvania Constitution, this list of enumerated rights has been moved from Article IX to Article I, demonstrating its importance.[159] Additionally, Article I, section 4, provides that "[n]o person who acknowledges the being of a God and a future state of reward and punishments" may be disqualified from holding public office.[160]

85. In contrast, the 1780 Massachusetts state constitution took a different approach to established religion. Massachusetts had established the Puritan Congregational Church in its original colonial charter and was the last of the original states to completely disestablish.[161] While Part I, Article II, of its new state constitution provided for individual freedom to worship "in the manner and season most agreeable to the dictates of [each person's] own conscience", Article III of that same part allowed the legislature to make church attendance, at one's chosen religion, compulsory.[162] Additionally, Article III permitted local government and religious entities to provide "support and maintenance" to religious teachers but mentioned only those of Protestant persuasion.[163] Of course, "the 1780 Massachusetts constitution was unusual in the rigor and detail of its continued endorsement of religion".[164] The current Massachusetts constitution amends Article III to allow all religious organizations to operate independently and hold property, and it declares that "all religious sects and denominations, demeaning themselves peaceably, and as good citizens[,] … shall be equally under the protection of the law; and no subordination of any one sect or denomination to another shall ever be established by law".[165]

---

158. Pa. Const. of 1790 art. IX, § III, https://www.paconstitution.org/texts-of-the-constitution/1790-2 (last visited Sep. 30, 2023).
159. Pa. Const. art. I, §§ 3–4, https://www.legis.state.pa.us/WU01/LI/LI/CT/HTM/00/00.HTM (last visited Sep. 30, 2023).
160. *Ibid.*, § 4.
161. Carl H. Esbeck, *Dissent and Disestablishment: The Church-State Settlement in the Early American Republic*, 2004 BYU L. Rev. 1385, 1457–1458.
162. Mass. Const. of 1780 pt. I, arts. II, III, http://www.nhinet.org/ccs/docs/ma-1780.htm (last visited Sep. 30, 2023).
163. *Ibid.*; *see also* Leonard W. Levy, *The Establishment Clause: Religion and the First Amendment* 29 (2d ed. 1994).
164. Witte & Nichols, *Religion and the American Constitutional Experiment*, *supra* n. 145, at 107.
165. Mass. Const. pt. 1, art. III, https://malegislature.gov/Laws/Constitution#cart046.htm (last visited Sep. 30, 2023).

86. State government involvement in religious matters was common in the early United States.[166] Of the thirteen colonies, only Rhode Island never had an established religion.[167] The Anglican (later Episcopalian) Church was the official church of the southern colonies, while Puritanism was the established religion in much of New England.[168] Even by the time the federal Constitution was ratified in 1788, seven of the thirteen states retained established churches;[169] states could do so because the Establishment Clause at the time was interpreted to apply against the federal government only. During the next forty-five years, the disestablishment movement gradually eliminated official state sponsorship of churches. Massachusetts was last to disestablish, completing the process in 1833.[170] Thus, the process of state disestablishment was complete well before the First Amendment's religion clauses were explicitly "incorporated" (that is, interpreted to apply) against the states in the 1940s.[171] For additional discussion, *see* Part XI (Religion and Culture), Chapter 3 (Religion and Civil Society).

87. Significant provisions that appear in many state constitutions are so-called Blaine Amendments, which forbid state aid to religiously affiliated schools. These amendments are named after James G. Blaine, who was a Speaker of the US House of Representatives and who proposed an amendment to the US Constitution in 1875, which was never adopted.[172] The text of his proposed amendment read:

> No State shall make any law respecting an establishment of religion or prohibiting the free exercise thereof; and no money raised by taxation in any State for the support of public schools, or derived from any public fund therefor[], nor any public lands devoted thereto, shall ever be under the control of any religious sect, nor shall any money so raised or lands so devoted be divided between religious sects or denominations.[173]

---

166. The US Constitution and the First Amendment's religion clauses were intended originally to disempower only the federal government, not states, in religious matters. *See supra* Part I, Ch. 1, s. 1; Esbeck, *Dissent and Disestablishment, supra* n. 161, at 1393; Richard Albert, *Religion in the New Republic*, 67 La. L. Rev. 1, 23 (2006) ("Most of the American colonies exhibited establishmentarian features during the revolutionary era and into the period of constitutional ratification." (citing Levy, *The Establishment Clause: Religion and the First Amendment, supra* n. 163, at 1; Jed Rubenfeld, *Antidisestablishmentarianism: Why RFRA Really Was Unconstitutional*, 95 Mich. L. Rev. 2347, 2351 (1997))).
167. Michelle J. Dye Neumann & Paul Finkelman, *Disestablishment of State Churches, in Religion and American Law: An Encyclopedia* 136, 136 (Paul Finkelman ed., 2000).
168. Esbeck, *Dissent and Disestablishment, supra* n. 161, at 1457.
169. *Ibid.*, at 1458.
170. *Ibid.*, at 1458.
171. *Everson v. Board of Education*, 330 U.S. 1 (1947) (incorporating the First Amendment's Establishment Clause, making it applicable to state and local laws); *Cantwell v. Connecticut*, 310 U.S. 296 (1940) (incorporating the First Amendment's Free Exercise Clause, making it applicable to state and local laws).
172. Mark Edward DeForrest, *An Overview and Evaluation of State Blaine Amendments: Origins, Scope, and First Amendment Concerns*, 26 Harv. J.L. & Pub. Pol'y 551, 556–573 (2003).
173. *Ibid.*, at 556 (quoting H.R.J. Res. 1, 44th Cong., 1st Sess., 4 Cong. Rec. 205 (1875)).

While Blaine's proposed federal amendment (in large part motivated by anti-Catholic sentiment) was never ratified, variations of the Blaine Amendment have been adopted in thirty-six state constitutions.[174] The purpose of Blaine Amendments is to avoid state establishment concerns, but application of the amendments can raise free exercise concerns. State constitutional jurisprudence has sometimes interpreted Blaine Amendments to restrict state aid to religion, including indirect aid, to a greater degree than is permitted under the US Constitution's Free Exercise Clause.[175] In 2020, the Supreme Court held that Montana's version of a Blaine Amendment was unconstitutional as applied. The Montana legislature created a program offering tax credits for donors to nonprofit organizations that provided scholarships for private tuition.[176] A state agency promulgated a rule that barred the scholarships from being used at religious schools, citing the state constitution's "no-aid" provision prohibiting state funding of religious organizations. The Supreme Court held that the no-aid provision, as applied to the scholarship program, discriminated based on religious status in violation of the Free Exercise Clause.[177]

88. Most state constitutions include provisions that carve out property tax exemptions for religious organizations.[178] Under eighteen state constitutions, the exemption is required and generally applies whether or not the legislature passes a statute confirming the exemption.[179] In two states, the exemptions are in force unless the legislature statutorily abrogates the exemption.[180] Under fourteen state constitutions, a religious property tax exemption is explicitly allowed if the legislature so directs.[181] "The remaining sixteen state constitutions are silent as to exemptions specifically for religious property", but their respective legislatures have all adopted statutes providing religious property tax exemptions.[182] Even so, "[n]early all state courts have adopted the position that tax exemptions are a matter of legislative grace, and therefore, statutory and constitutional tax exemption provisions must be strictly construed in favor of taxing the property".[183]

---

174. *Ibid.*, at 559–565, 573, 576–577, 602; 3 William W. Bassett, W. Cole Durham Jr., Mark A. Goldfeder & Robert T. Smith, *Religious Organizations and the Law* § 25:14 (*Blaine Amendments in State Constitutions*), Westlaw RELORGS (database updated Dec. 2022) [hereinafter 3 Durham et al.]. An amendment passed by the state of Louisiana was repealed when a new state constitution was adopted in 1974. *Compare* La. Const. of 1921 art. 4, § 8, *with* La. Const. of 1974 art. 1, § 8; art. 8, § 13(A).
175. DeForrest, *An Overview and Evaluation of State Blaine Amendments*, *supra* n. 172, at 552–555, 576–601.
176. *Espinoza v. Mont. Dep't of Revenue*, 140 S. Ct. 2246 (2020).
177. *Ibid.*, at 2260–2263.
178. 4 William W. Bassett, W. Cole Durham Jr., Mark A. Goldfeder & Robert T. Smith, *Religious Organizations and the Law* § 33:7 (*Legal Sources of Religious Property Tax Exemptions*), Westlaw RELORGS (database updated Dec. 2022) [hereinafter 4 Durham et al.]. These exemptions, however, are not necessarily derived solely from religious freedom rights. *Ibid.*, § 31:2 (*Rationale for Tax Exemptions*).
179. *Ibid.*, § 33:7 (*Legal Sources of Religious Property Tax Exemptions*).
180. *Ibid.*
181. *Ibid.*
182. *Ibid.*
183. *Ibid.*

89. The case *Locke v. Davey* altered the presumptive understanding of the relationship between federal and state constitutional protections.[184] Before *Locke v. Davey*, "an assumption ... emerged that the Free Exercise Clause required the states to allow anything not prohibited by the Establishment Clause".[185] In *Locke*, the Supreme Court stated that "there are some state actions permitted by the Establishment Clause but not required by the Free Exercise Clause"; the Court called this the "play in the joints" between establishment and free exercise/equal protection.[186] For example, in *Locke*, a university student sued to be able to use his state-funded scholarship to pursue a devotional studies degree, which was prohibited by Washington's state constitution and a state statute.[187] The Court held that "even though Washington could have included theology majors in the scholarship program without violating the Establishment Clause, neither the Free Exercise Clause nor the Equal Protection Clause prohibited their exclusion" or mandated their inclusion.[188] Therefore, state constitutions and statutes may regulate, and are considered controlling, within this "play in the joints".[189]

90. Although the exact scope of this "play in the joints" remains uncertain, a 2017 Supreme Court decision suggests that meaningful limitations remain on the ability of states to restrict religious organizations from receiving religiously neutral public benefits. In *Trinity Lutheran Church v. Comer*, the Court held that Missouri's interpretation of its Blaine Amendment violated the Free Exercise Clause; the state had interpreted it to exclude qualifying religious schools from receiving state funds through a playground-resurfacing program.[190] The Court reiterated the Free Exercise Clause requirement that a state interest be "of the highest order" to justify limiting religious groups' or individuals' access to a generally available state benefit.[191] It found that the state's asserted interest "in achieving greater separation of church and State than is already ensured under the Establishment Clause of the Federal Constitution" was insufficient to meet that requirement.[192]

184. *Locke v. Davey*, 540 U.S. 712 (2004).
185. 1 Durham et al., *supra* n. 157, § 4:45 (*State Constitutional Limitations on Religion after* Locke v. Davey—*The "Play in the Joints"*).
186. *Locke*, 540 U.S. at 718–719.
187. *Ibid.*, at 715–717.
188. 1 Durham et al., *supra* n. 157, § 4:45.
189. 1 Durham et al., *supra* n. 157, § 4:45.
190. *Trinity Lutheran Church of Columbia, Inc. v. Comer*, 582 U.S. 449 (2017).
191. *Ibid.*, at 466 (quoting *McDaniel v. Paty*, 435 U.S. 618, 628 (1978) (plurality opinion)).
192. *Ibid.* (quoting *Widmar v. Vincent*, 454 U.S. 263, 276 (1981)).

Chapter 2. Other Legislation with Regard to Religion

91. As a common law system, the United States has no organic law on religion but instead has developed a patchwork of federal and state law relating to religious exercise. In fact, comparatively little federal law on religion exists, due to the common law system, Establishment Clause limitations on federal power to regulate religions, and the fact that registration of religious organizations (which is not required) happens at the state level through nonprofit or religious corporation statutes. *See* Part III (Legal Status of Religious Communities), Chapter 1 (Formal Status of Religious Communities).

92. Generally, federal laws on religion either establish specific religious exemptions to comprehensive legislation in a given area (such as tax or healthcare) or, in a few cases, broader religious exemptions (such as the Religious Freedom Restoration Act and the Religious Land Use and Institutionalized Persons Act). *See* section 1 (Federal Laws), below. Most legislation dealing with practical regulation of religious issues happens at the state level but, again, is largely piecemeal. This chapter addresses primarily major federal legislation and areas of state legislation that affect religious exercise.

§1. Federal Laws

I. Religious Freedom Restoration Act

93. The federal Religious Freedom Restoration Act (RFRA, pronounced *rĭ-fruh*) was passed in 1993 with wide support across the political spectrum.[193] It was a reaction to the Supreme Court's decision in *Employment Division v. Smith*, which held that the Free Exercise Clause did not require religious exemptions to generally applicable laws.[194] Since 1963, the Supreme Court had applied strict scrutiny to laws that burden religious exercise, which meant that a law may substantially burden an individual's religious exercise only when the law furthers a compelling government interest and is narrowly tailored to serve that interest.[195] In *Smith,* however, the Supreme Court held that religious exemptions to generally applicable laws were the province of the legislature, not the judiciary.[196]

94. RFRA legislatively reinstated the compelling state interest test, requiring that all laws alleged to substantially burden religious exercise be examined under the strictest scrutiny, meaning courts must determine if the government adopted the

193. Religious Freedom Restoration Act, Pub. L. No. 103-141, 107 Stat. 1488 (1993) (codified as amended at 42 U.S.C. §§ 2000bb to 2000bb-4 (2018)).
194. *Emp. Div., Dep't of Hum. Res. of Or. v. Smith*, 494 U.S. 872, 890 (1990); *see also infra* paras. 138–142.
195. *Sherbert v. Verner*, 374 U.S. 398, 406 (1963).
196. *Smith*, 494 U.S. at 890.

least restrictive means of achieving a *compelling state interest*.[197] RFRA was originally designed to apply to both federal and state laws. In 1997, however, the Supreme Court held that RFRA as applied to state governments was an unconstitutional exercise of Congress's enforcement power.[198] Today, RFRA protects only against violations by the federal government.[199] Although RFRA no longer applies to state laws, many states have enacted their own state-specific Religious Freedom Restoration Acts, modelled after the federal statute. *See* Part II (Religious Freedom in General), Chapter 1 (Individual Religious Freedom).

II. Civil Rights Act of 1964

95. The Civil Rights Act of 1964 is a broad piece of legislation aimed at eliminating discrimination in commerce and in the workplace. While its primary purpose is to achieve racial equality, it also protects against discrimination based on religion and other characteristics.[200] Title II addresses religious discrimination in places of public accommodation, and Title VII deals with religious discrimination in employment.[201]

96. Title II of the Civil Rights Act states that all individuals are entitled to "the full and equal enjoyment" of the services, goods, and facilities of any place of public accommodation without segregation or discrimination on the ground of religion.[202] Under the law, a place of public accommodation encompasses any business that has a physical location, serves the public, and affects commerce, such as hotels and other places of lodging, restaurants and other places that primarily sell food, theaters and other places of entertainment, and any other business located in the same facility as another public accommodation.[203] Title II allows district courts to provide injunctive relief against actors who engage in discrimination as defined by the statute.[204]

97. Title VII is designed to provide equal employment opportunities. Its provisions apply to private-sector, state-government, and local-government employers with fifteen or more employees working twenty-plus weeks per year; to the federal

197. 42 U.S.C. § 2000bb-1 (1993); *see also City of Boerne v. Flores*, 521 U.S. 507, 535 (1997) ("[RFRA] imposes in every case a least restrictive means requirements—a requirement that was not used in the pre-*Smith* jurisprudence RFRA purported to codify … .")
198. *City of Boerne*, 521 U.S. at 532–536.
199. *Gonzales v. O Centro Espirita Beneficente Uniao do Vegetal*, 546 U.S. 418, 424 & n.1 (2006); *see also Tanzin v. Tanvir*, 141 S. Ct. 486, 493 (2020) (holding that RFRA provides for "money damages against federal officials in their individual capacities"); *Ajaj v. Fed. Bureau of Prisons*, 25 F.4th 805, 813 (10th Cir. 2022) (holding that officials sued in their individual capacities for money damages under RFRA could invoke qualified immunity as a defense).
200. Civil Rights Act of 1964, Pub. L. No. 88-352, 78 Stat. 241 (1964) (codified as amended primarily in 42 U.S.C. §§ 2000a to 2000h-6 (2018)).
201. 42 U.S.C. §§ 2000a to 2000a-6 (2018); *ibid.*, §§ 2000e to 2000e-17.
202. *Ibid.*, § 2000a(a).
203. *Ibid.*, § 2000a(b).
204. *Ibid.*, § 2000a-3(a).

government as an employer; and to employment agencies and unions.[205] Under Title VII, it is unlawful for those employers to fire, refuse to hire, or withhold any privileges of employment from individuals because of their religion, race, color, national origin, or sex (which includes sexual orientation and gender identity).[206] Employers are also prohibited from segregating or classifying their employees in a way that deprives them of employment opportunities.[207] In 1971, the US Supreme Court applied the doctrine of "disparate impact", holding that under Title VII, any test that an employer requires its employees to take that has a disparate impact on a protected group, such as an ethnic minority group, must be reasonably related to the job for which the test is required.[208] Title VII also prohibits employment agencies from discriminating against applicants in referral processes and prohibits labor organizations from excluding or segregating individuals based on their religion.[209] Notwithstanding these Title VII requirements, in general, employers may set forth discriminatory requirements for a position if the requirements are necessary to fulfilling the position or if the employers are religiously affiliated employers who are discriminating based on religion.[210] *See* discussion in Part VI (Labor Law Within Religious Communities), Chapter 3 (Other Church Employees and Labor Law).

205. *Ibid.*, § 2000e(b).
206. *Ibid.*, § 2000e-2(a)(1). *Bostock v. Clayton County*, 140 S. Ct. 1731, 1754 (2020) (interpreting Title VII's prohibition on workplace discrimination "because of ... sex" to encompass sexual orientation and gender identity). Following the *Bostock* decision, President Joe Biden issued an Executive Order on his inauguration day, stating that laws prohibiting sex discrimination also "prohibit discrimination on the basis of gender identity or orientation, so long as the laws do not contain sufficient indications to the contrary". Exec. Order No. 13988, 86 Fed. Reg. 7023 (Jan. 20, 2021). Lower courts have applied the *Bostock* interpretation of Title VII to other anti-discrimination laws, including Title IX, which prohibits discrimination under educational programs or activities receiving federal assistance. *See, e.g.*, *Grabowski v. Az. Bd. of Regents*, 69 F.4th 1110, 1116 (9th Cir. 2023) (relying on *Bostock* to hold "that discrimination on the basis of sexual orientation is a form of sex-based discrimination under Title IX"); *Grimm v. Gloucester Cty. Sch. Bd.*, 972 F.3d 586, 619 n.18 (4th Cir. 2020) ("*Bostock* forecloses that 'on the basis of sex' is ambiguous as to discrimination against transgender persons. ... So too Title IX."); *N.H. v. Anoka-Hennepin Sch. Dist. No. 11*, 950 N.W.2d 553 (Minn. Ct. App. 2020) (citing *Bostock* and other federal caselaw in determining that a Title IX-like state constitutional provision allowed for a discrimination claim by a transgender student). *But see Adams ex rel. Kasper v. Sch. Bd. of St. Johns Cnty.*, 57 F.4th 791, 808–812 (11th Cir. 2022) (en banc) (concluding that "sex" in Title IX refers to biological sex and does not necessarily encompass "gender identity" and that *Bostock* did not apply to transgender student's challenge of school's biological-sex-based bathroom policy); Memorandum from Reed Rubinstein, Principal Deputy Gen. Couns., U.S. Dep't of Educ., Off. of Gen. Couns., to Kimberly M. Richey, Acting Assistant Sec'y of Off. for C.R. (Jan. 8, 2021), https://www2.ed.gov/about/offices/list/ocr/correspondence/other/ogc-memorandum-01082021.pdf (concluding *Bostock*'s narrow holding does not construe Title IX).
207. 42 U.S.C. § 2000e-2(a)(2).
208. *Griggs v. Duke Power Co.*, 401 U.S. 424, 436 (1971).
209. 42 U.S.C. § 2000e-2(b)–(c) (2018); *Bostock*, 140 S. Ct. at 1753–1754.
210. *See* 42 U.S.C. § 2000e-1; *Griggs*, 401 U.S. at 431–432.

III. Internal Revenue Code

98. The main source of federal tax law is the Internal Revenue Code (I.R.C.).[211] Section 501(c)(3) of the I.R.C. provides tax exemptions to organizations that are "organized and operated exclusively for religious … purposes" as long as: (1) their income does not benefit private individuals, (2) a substantial part of their activities does not attempt to influence legislation, and (3) they do not participate in any political campaign by endorsing or opposing a candidate for public office in any way.[212] The exemption's benefits to religious organizations incentivize them to comply with the related regulations and guidelines; therefore, the code has a significant impact on religions throughout the United States. For more information on the effects of I.R.C. section 501(c)(3) tax exemptions, *see* Part III (Legal Status of Religious Communities), Chapter 1 (Formal Status of Religious Communities).

IV. Religious Land Use and Institutionalized Persons Act

99. The Religious Land Use and Institutionalized Persons Act (RLUIPA)[213] was enacted in response to *City of Boerne v. Flores*,[214] the Supreme Court decision that invalidated RFRA as applied to the states. In contrast to RFRA's blanket application of a strict scrutiny standard, RLUIPA applies strict scrutiny only to substantial burdens on free exercise in relation to institutionalized persons and zoning laws, two of the more common sources of free exercise claims. The US Supreme Court has upheld the Act's constitutionality as it applies to both the federal and state governments in cases involving RLUIPA's institutionalized persons provisions.[215] But while the Court has addressed a handful of claims by incarcerated individuals, it has yet to decide a land-use case under the Act. For more detailed information and case law on RLUIPA's institutionalized persons provisions, *see* Part VII (Religious Communities and Protections of the Individual), Chapter 8 (Penal Law and Religion). For more information on RLUIPA's land-use provisions, *see* Part XI (Religion and Culture), Chapter 1 (Religion and Art).

V. International Religious Freedom Act

100. The International Religious Freedom Act of 1998 (IRFA) was designed to promote religious freedom as part of US foreign policy.[216] The Act created three new entities to monitor the state of religious freedom in other countries: (1) the

---

211. Codified in Title 26 of the United States Code (U.S.C.) but commonly cited as "I.R.C."
212. I.R.C. § 501(c)(3) (2018). Federal regulations interpret "exclusively" religious to mean "primarily" religious in purpose. Treas. Reg. § 1.501(c)(3)-1(c) (2022).
213. Religious Land Use and Institutionalized Persons Act (RLUIPA), Pub. L. No. 106-274, 114 Stat. 803 (2000) (codified at 42 U.S.C. §§ 2000cc to 2000cc-5 (2018)).
214. *City of Boerne v. Flores*, 521 U.S. 507 (1997).
215. *Cutter v. Wilkinson*, 544 U.S. 709 (2005).
216. International Religious Freedom Act of 1998 (IRFA), Pub. L. No. 105-292, 112 Stat. 2787 (codified as amended at 22 U.S.C. §§ 4028, 6401–6483 (2018)).

Office of International Religious Freedom within the Department of State, with an Ambassador at Large for International Religious Freedom; (2) a bipartisan US Commission on International Religious Freedom (USCIRF); and (3) a Special Advisor to the President on International Religious Freedom within the National Security Council. The Office of International Religious Freedom compiles an annual report on international religious freedom, sets forth policies and classifications for countries based on how much religious persecution they allow, proposes actions the President should take in response to countries that violate international standards of religious freedom, encourages the involvement of international media in religious freedom issues and the giving of foreign service awards, sets forth guidelines for training immigration officials, and urges international corporations to adopt policies that promote religious freedom.[217] For more information, *see* Part IV (International, Transnational, and Regional Effects on Religious Communities), Chapter 2 (Transnational Law Effects on Religious Communities); and Part V (Religion and Politics), Chapter 3 (Interaction Between Religion and State).

VI. Laws Providing for Conscientious Objection

101. Some federal laws offer specific protections to individuals who may conscientiously object to duties associated with employment and conscription. The National Labor Relations Act (NLRA) was enacted in 1935[218] and amended in 1980, creating exemptions for union membership requirements.[219] It provides that any employee who adheres to a bona fide religion historically opposed to its members joining or supporting labor organizations may not be required to join or support an organization as a condition of employment; however, such an employee may be required to pay dues in kind to other charitable funds.

102. The "Church Amendment" (named for one of its sponsors, Senator Frank Church) was enacted as part of the Health Programs Extension Act of 1973.[220] Congress passed the amendment in part to protect both hospitals and individuals with moral objections from being required to participate in abortions, and to prohibit hospitals from conditioning individuals' employment on their willingness to perform abortions.

103. The Selective Training and Service Act was instituted in 1940 before World War II and required all men between the ages of 18 and 36 to register with the draft board in order to fill vacancies in the armed forces.[221] Although the draft was only in force between 1940 and 1973, the Selective Service System still requires men

217. *See About Us*, Off. Int'l Religious Freedom, https://www.state.gov/about-us-office-of-international-religious-freedom (last visited Sep. 30, 2023).
218. National Labor Relations Act (NLRA), Pub. L. No. 74-198, 49 Stat. 449 (1935) (codified as amended at 29 U.S.C. §§ 151–169 (2018)).
219. 29 U.S.C. § 169 (2018).
220. Health Programs Extension Act of 1973, Pub. L. No. 93-45, § 401, 87 Stat. 91, 95–96 (codified as amended at 42 U.S.C. § 300a-7 (2018)).
221. Selective Training and Service Act, Pub. L. No. 76-783, 54 Stat. 885 (1940).

aged 18 to 25 to register. Current law allows men with religious or moral objections to military service or bearing arms to conscientiously object to registration.[222] In 1965, the US Supreme Court held that conscientious objections to military service need not be based on theistic beliefs—that is, belief in a Supreme Being—as long as the beliefs are as sincere and deeply held as religious beliefs.[223] For more on conscientious objection laws, *see* Part II (Religious Freedom in General), Chapter 1 (Individual Religious Freedom) and Chapter 2 (Collective Religious Freedom); and Part VII (Religious Communities and Protections of the Individual), Chapter 2 (Freedom to Marry) and Chapter 6 (Medical Deontology).

VII. Social Security Act

104. Social Security is a federal social insurance program that provides retirement, disability, and survivor benefits, funded through payroll taxes. Under the Social Security Act of 1935, religious individuals who hold conscientious objections to receiving public benefits are exempt from paying Social Security taxes if they (1) are a member of a religious organization that the government recognizes as having tenets opposed to accepting public benefits, (2) have never received Social Security benefits, (3) waive their right to all such benefits, and (4) demonstrate that their religious organization provides in other ways for its members to retire.[224] This exemption applies mostly to the Amish and the Mennonites. Qualifying churches or church-controlled organizations who object to paying Social Security taxes for their employees for religious reasons can also apply for an exemption.[225] For more information on Social Security, *see* Part VI (Labor Law Within Religious Communities), Chapter 1 (Scope of Application of Labor Law) and Chapter 2 (Religious Ministers and Labor Law).

VIII. Patient Protection and Affordable Care Act (ACA)

105. The Patient Protection and Affordable Care Act (ACA) was passed into law in 2010.[226] It requires that nearly all Americans be enrolled in a health insurance program (the "individual mandate") but allows the possibility of exemptions for individuals who belong to certain religious groups.[227] The ACA also forbids discrimination against healthcare providers that have religious objections to participating in or supporting abortions.[228] In 2017, ACA opponents in Congress passed

222. 50 U.S.C. § 3806(j) (2018).
223. *United States v. Seeger*, 380 U.S. 163, 174, 184–188 (1965).
224. 26 U.S.C. § 1402(g) (2018).
225. *See Publication 517, Social Security and Other Information for Members of the Clergy and Religious Workers*, IRS, https://www.irs.gov/publications/p517 (last updated Dec. 29, 2022).
226. Patient Protection and Affordable Care Act, Pub. L. No. 111-148, 124 Stat. 119 (2010) (codified as amended in scattered ss. of 21, 25, 26, 29, and 42 U.S.C. (2018)).
227. 26 U.S.C. § 5000A(d)(2)(A); 42 U.S.C. § 18081(b)(5)(A) (2018) (outlining religious exemptions and their requirements). While the federal penalty for nonenrolment was reduced to USD 0 in 2018,

legislation amending the Act, which reduced the tax penalties to zero for violation of the individual mandate.[229] Previously, the Supreme Court had found the penalties to be the provision that allowed Congress to pass the ACA in the first place, under its constitutional authority to tax.[230] After elimination of the penalties, a federal district court held that the individual mandate could "no longer be fairly read as an exercise of Congress's Tax Power" and thus was unconstitutional, rendering the entire ACA invalid.[231] The US Supreme Court eventually took up the case in *California v. Texas*, holding that the individual and state plaintiffs lacked standing.[232] The Court thereby reserved the questions of whether the individual mandate, as amended, is unconstitutional and, if so, whether it is severable from the rest of the ACA.

106. The Department of Health and Human Services (HHS) and other executive agencies adopted guidelines interpreting the ACA to include a "contraceptive mandate", meaning that most employers and educational institutions must provide contraceptive coverage in their group health insurance plans covering employees and students. The mandate initially allowed narrow exemptions for organizations that served only their own religious community.[233] Agencies eventually promulgated rules allowing other qualifying nonprofit, religiously affiliated organizations to opt out of contraceptive coverage through a process of self-certification or by informing HHS of religious objections in writing.[234]

107. The reach of the contraceptive mandate was at issue in a series of Supreme Court cases beginning in 2014. In *Burwell v. Hobby Lobby*, the Court ruled that, under RFRA, "closely held" for-profit corporations may be exempt from the mandate on religious grounds because the government could achieve its interest in protecting female employees' health in a less restrictive way vis-à-vis such corporations.[235] In 2017, agencies under the President Donald Trump administration widened the exemption to include private employers opposed to providing contraception on religious or "moral" grounds.[236] The Court upheld these more

---

the ACA's individual mandate remains "on the books", and some states have implemented their own mandates and penalties. *See* Tax Cuts and Jobs Act of 2017, Pub. L. No. 115-97, tit. I, pt. VIII, 131 Stat. 2054, 2092.

228. 42 U.S.C. § 18023(a)–(b).

229. *See supra* n. 227 and accompanying text.

230. *NFIB v. Sebelius*, 567 U.S. 519 (2012).

231. *See Texas v. United States*, 340 F. Supp. 3d 579, 593 (N.D. Tex. 2018).

232. *California v. Texas*, 141 S. Ct. 2104 (2021).

233. *See* Coverage of Certain Preventive Services under the Affordable Care Act, 78 Fed. Reg. 39870–39899 (Jul. 2, 2013).

234. *See* Coverage of Certain Preventive Services under the Affordable Care Act, 80 Fed. Reg. 41318, 41337 (Jul. 14, 2015) (codified at 45 C.F.R. § 147.131 (2022)) (providing means for organizations to notify HHS directly of their eligibility for an exemption to the contraceptive mandate, responding, in part, to *Wheaton College v. Burwell*, 573 U.S. 958 (2014)).

235. *Burwell v. Hobby Lobby Stores, Inc.*, 573 U.S. 682 (2014).

236. Religious Exemptions and Accommodations for Coverage of Certain Preventive Services under the Affordable Care Act, 82 Fed. Reg. 47792, 47838 (Oct. 13, 2017) (codified at 45 C.F.R. pt. 147 (2022)).

expansive rules in *Little Sisters of the Poor v. Pennsylvania.*[237] In early 2023, President Joe Biden's administration announced a proposed rule that would retain the religious exemption for private health plans and insurers but eliminate the moral exemption.[238] For additional discussion, *see* Part VII (Religious Communities and Protections of the Individual), Chapter 6 (Medical Deontology).

IX. Other Federal Laws

108. Section 104 of the Personal Responsibility and Work Opportunity Reconciliation Act of 1996, also known as the "Charitable Choice" provision, encourages states to involve religiously affiliated organizations in providing federally funded social services.[239] For additional discussion, *see* Part VI (Labor Law Within Religious Communities), Chapter 3 (Other Church Employees and Labor Law); and Part VIII (Financing of Religious Communities), Chapter 2 (Indirect Financing).

109. In 2005, Congress passed the REAL ID Act that set forth standards state-issued ID cards and driver licenses must meet to be recognized by the federal government.[240] The REAL ID Act does not require that identification include information about religious affiliation. However, the Act does require all ID cards to include a digital photo of the cardholder, a requirement subject to challenge by religious groups and individuals who hold conscientious objections to being photographed.[241] Department of Homeland Security guidelines allow individuals to wear religious head coverings in government-issued ID cards or driver's license photos if the covering does not obscure or shadow the subject's facial features.[242] *See also* Part VII (Religious Communities and Protections of the Individual), Chapter 1 (Protection of Privacy).

237. *Little Sisters of the Poor Saints Peter & Paul Home v. Pennsylvania*, 140 S. Ct. 2367 (2020).
238. Coverage of Certain Preventive Services under the Affordable Care Act, 88 Fed. Reg. 7236, 7236 (proposed Feb. 2, 2023) (to be codified at 26 C.F.R. pt. 54; 29 C.F.R. pt. 2590; 45 C.F.R. pt. 147, 156).
239. Personal Responsibility and Work Opportunity Reconciliation Act of 1996 (PRWORA or Welfare Reform Act), Pub. L. No. 104-193, § 104, 110 Stat. 2105, 2161–2163 (codified at 42 U.S.C. § 604a (2018)).
240. REAL ID Act of 2005, Pub. L. No. 109-13, § 202, 119 Stat. 302, 312 (ID provisions contained in 49 U.S.C. § 30301, statutory note 23:401 (2018)).
241. *See* Cynthia Brougher, Cong. Rsch. Serv., R40515, Legal Analysis of Religious Exemptions for Photo Identification Requirements (Sep. 5, 2012), https://www.everycrsreport.com/reports/R40515.html (link to PDF) (discussing factors courts have used to decide questions of religious accommodation vis-à-vis government ID requirements).
242. Memorandum from Margo Schlanger, Officer for C.R. & Civ. Liberties, to U.S. Dep't Homeland Sec. Component Heads, Guidance for Accommodating Religious Beliefs in DHS Policies Requiring Fingerprinting or Photographic Identification 2 (Dec. 30, 2011), https://www.dhs.gov/publication/guidance-accommodating-religious-beliefs-dhs-policies-requiring-fingerprinting-or (link to PDF).

110. Congress passed the Equal Access Act in 1984 in an effort to end widespread discrimination against religious speech in public schools.[243] It applies to public secondary schools that already have at least one student-led extracurricular club and requires schools to treat religious clubs equal to other student clubs, allowing them to conduct meetings that are "voluntary and student-initiated". For more information, *see* Part VII (Religious Communities and Protections of the Individual), Chapter 3 (Freedom of Expression) and Chapter 7 (Non-discrimination).

§2. State Laws

I. Religious Freedom Restoration Acts

111. Since 1993, when the Supreme Court invalidated the federal Religious Freedom Restoration Act as it applied to the states, twenty-three states have enacted their own RFRAs.[244] These are mostly modelled after the federal statute but are not identical. *See* discussion in Part II (Religious Freedom in General), Chapter 1 (Individual Religious Freedom).

II. Blaine Amendments

112. The late nineteenth century was marked by strong anti-Catholic sentiments in the United States. In 1875, reacting to widespread fears of Catholic influence, Speaker of the US House of Representatives James Blaine proposed an amendment to the US Constitution that would prohibit all government funding of sectarian schools. While the amendment failed to pass the Senate, many states amended their own constitutions; thirty-six of the fifty state constitutions still include an original amendment modelled after the Blaine Amendment.[245] Although these provisions appear neutral on their face, their intent and practical effect were to disadvantage Catholic groups, especially immigrants, who created a strong system of Catholic schools largely in response to Protestant practices then prevalent in public schools. Religious rights groups in the United States have made efforts to educate the public about their discriminatory nature and call for their removal from state constitutions.[246]

113. In 2017, the Supreme Court held that an application of Missouri's Blaine Amendment violated the Free Exercise Clause of the federal constitution.[247] Missouri relied on its state amendment to disqualify a religious school—based solely

243. Equal Access Act, Pub. L. No. 98-377, 98 Stat. 1302 (1984) (codified at 20 U.S.C. §§ 4071–4074 (2018)).

244. 1 Durham et al., *supra* n. 157, § 3:26 (*State Standards of Free Exercise Review under State RFRAs and State High Court Decisions*).

245. 3 Durham et al., *supra* n. 174, § 25:14 (*Blaine Amendments in State Constitutions*).

246. *See, e.g.*, U.S. Comm'n on C.R., *School Choice: The Blaine Amendments & Anti-Catholicism* (2007), https://www.usccr.gov/files/pubs/docs/BlaineReport.pdf.

247. *Trinity Lutheran Church of Columbia, Inc. v. Comer*, 582 U.S. 449, 466–467 (2017).

on its religious character—from receiving state funds through a playground-resurfacing program. In that case, the Court found that the state's application of its amendment, resulting in greater separation of church and state than is required under the federal Establishment Clause, infringed on the free exercise rights of the qualifying religious school.[248] Three years later, the Supreme Court held that another state's application of its Blaine Amendment was unconstitutional.[249] In that case, Montana's state legislature created a program offering tax credits for donors to nonprofit organizations that provided scholarships for private tuition. A state agency promulgated a rule that barred the scholarship from being used at religious schools, citing the state constitution's Blaine Amendment, or "no-aid" provision, which prohibited state funding of religious organizations. The Supreme Court struck down the "no-aid" provision as applied to the scholarship program, holding it too discriminated based on religious status in violation of the Free Exercise Clause.[250]

III. Religious Corporation Statutes

114. Religious corporation statutes are modifications of standard not-for-profit corporation statutes designed to facilitate unique religious needs in corporate forms. Most religious organizations choose a religious nonprofit corporation structure, which is available in most states.[251] It offers religious organizations several benefits, including "the ability to own and transfer title to property, to accept contributions of property in its own name, to directly manage its resources, to prevent members from being liable for corporate debt, and to provide legal continuity".[252] In contrast, the "corporation sole" is recognized in relatively few (about a dozen) states and used by a much smaller percentage of religious organizations.[253] It allows the incorporation of a religious office, typically a Catholic official, such as a Bishop.[254] The holder of the office is the only officer of the corporation sole and "has administrative and managerial control over the affairs and property of the church".[255] Title to property passes by operation of law to the office holder's successor. Thus, major benefits of the corporation sole structure are its efficiency in providing centralized control—relatively insulated from outside pressures by members or trustees—and continuity of property ownership.[256] For further discussion, *see* Part III (Legal Status of Religious Communities), Chapter 1 (Formal Status of Religious Communities).

248. *Ibid.*
249. *Espinoza v. Mont. Dep't of Revenue*, 140 S. Ct. 2246 (2020).
250. *Ibid.*, at 2257–2263.
251. Sarah J. Hastings, *Cinderella's New Dress: A Better Organizational Option for Churches and Other Small Nonprofits*, 55 Drake L. Rev. 813, 820–821 (2007). West Virginia is the only state that does not allow religious incorporation.
252. *Ibid.*
253. *Ibid.*, at 823.
254. *Ibid.*
255. *Ibid.*
256. *Ibid.*

IV. Child Abuse Reporting and the Priest-Penitent Privilege in State Law

115. Every state imposes requirements on certain groups of professionals to report cases of suspected child abuse or neglect. These requirements sometimes come into conflict with the common law priest-penitent privilege, which protects communications between members of the clergy and their parishioners and is recognized by most states. To achieve a balance between child welfare and privacy rights, each state places limits on when church officials may refrain from reporting suspected child abuse. For a discussion of state child abuse reporting laws and their effect on religious entities, *see* Part VII (Religious Communities and Protections of the Individual), Chapter 1 (Protection of Privacy).

V. Anti-discrimination Laws

116. Civil rights laws are prevalent among the states. They typically follow the model of the federal Civil Rights Act in protecting individuals from discrimination on the basis of race, religion, sex, and national origin in places of public accommodation and employment. Most civil rights laws also protect against discrimination in housing.[257] Public accommodation and similar anti-discrimination laws are sometimes at issue in lawsuits alleging sexual orientation or gender identity discrimination by religious individuals or organizations, or when governments seek to enforce such laws against religious individuals or organizations.[258] *See* discussions in Part II (Religious Freedom in General), Chapter 1 (Individual Religious Freedom); Part V (Religion and Politics), Chapter 1 (Religious Influence in Politics); Part VI (Labor Law Within Religious Communities), Chapter 3 (Other Church

257. *See, e.g.*, Kan. Stat. Ann. § 44-1001 (2022) (Kansas Acts Against Discrimination); Minn. Stat. § 363A.09 (2022).

258. *See, e.g.*, *303 Creative LLC v. Elenis*, 600 U.S. 570, 588–590 (2023) (holding that enforcement of state public accommodation anti-discrimination statute would violate First Amendment free speech rights where enforcement would compel a wedding website to convey messages inconsistent with the owner's religious beliefs that marriage be reserved for heterosexual couples); *Fulton v. City of Philadelphia*, 141 S. Ct. 1868, 1881 (2021) (holding that a religious foster care agency was not a public accommodation subject to a city ordinance's prohibition on discrimination on the basis of sexual orientation); *New Hope Fam. Servs. v. Poole*, 966 F.3d 145, 179–180 (2d Cir. 2020) (holding that a religious adoption agency properly alleged First Amendment claims in its suit challenging threatened closure under a state anti-discrimination statute); *Telescope Media Grp. v. Lucero*, 936 F.3d 750, 758 (2d Cir. 2019) (holding that state could not apply state human rights statute to compel wedding videographers to film same-sex weddings, contrary to their religious beliefs); *Brush & Nib Studio, LC v. City of Phoenix*, 448 P.3d 890, 926 (Ariz. 2019) (holding that city's application of anti-discrimination ordinance to compel business owners to create celebratory wedding invitations for same-sex weddings violated state laws protecting free speech and free exercise); *Elane Photography, LLC v. Willock*, 309 P.3d 53, 77 (N.M. 2013), *cert. denied*, 572 U.S. 1046 (2014) (mem.) (holding that anti-discrimination law was neutral and generally applicable, did not violate the Free Exercise Clause, and did not unconstitutionally compel speech of wedding photography company that refused services to a customer based on sexual orientation); *State v. Arlene's Flowers, Inc.*, 441 P.3d 1203, 1237–1238 (Wash. 2019) (en banc) (holding state anti-discrimination law was neutral and generally applicable, did not violate florist's rights to free exercise or association, and did not violate First Amendment protections against compelled speech).

Employees and Labor Law); and Part VII (Religious Communities and Protections of the Individual), Chapter 2 (Freedom to Marry).

VI. Laws Prohibiting Foreign Law

117. Increasing immigration from Muslim countries and persistent anti-Muslim sentiment following the 9/11 attacks have led thirteen states to enact laws that ban foreign law, particularly sharia (Islamic law), from being consulted in US courts; several other states have considered or are considering similar legislation.[259] In 2012, Oklahoma's ban was held unconstitutional by the Tenth Circuit Court of Appeals.[260]

259. *See supra* para. 41.
260. *Awad v. Ziriax*, 670 F.3d 1111 (10th Cir. 2012).

Chapter 3. Typology of the System

118. In the United States, the intellectual framework for thinking about religious freedom is largely bifurcated between the Establishment Clause and the Free Exercise Clause of the US Constitution's First Amendment. Where these overlap, such as in protecting the autonomy of religious groups, commentators have struggled to determine which clause is the source of rights.[261] Courts and commentators have also noted and grappled with areas of tension between the clauses.[262] Reflecting US bifurcations, this chapter will address conceptual frameworks undergirding understandings of the Establishment Clause and Free Exercise Clause separately.

§1. Establishment Clause

119. Scholars and lawmakers have long held differing views on the purpose of the Establishment Clause. Some interpret it as entirely excluding religion from all aspects of the public sphere, while others argue for a more accommodationist approach.[263] Still others focus on neutrality as a guiding principle.[264] An extreme

261. *See* Esbeck, *Dissent and Disestablishment, supra* n. 161, at 1585 n.722; *see also Hosanna-Tabor Evangelical Lutheran Church & Sch. v. EEOC*, 565 U.S. 171, 186–189 (2012) (explaining that the autonomy of religious organizations stems from both the Establishment Clause and the Free Exercise Clause); *Our Lady of Guadalupe Sch. v. Morrissey-Berru*, 140 S. Ct. 2049, 2060 (2020) (explaining the same); *Am. Legion v. Am. Hum. Ass'n*, 139 S. Ct. 2067, 2074 (2019) ("The Religion Clauses of the Constitution aim to foster a society in which people of all beliefs can live together harmoniously … .").

262. *See, e.g., Kennedy v. Bremerton*, 142 S. Ct. 2407 (2022) (discussing establishment, free exercise, and free speech tensions in the context of private prayer at public-school events); *Good News Club v. Milford Cent. Sch.*, 533 U.S. 98, 120, 120–121 (2001) (Scalia, J., concurring) (discussing establishment, free exercise, and free speech tensions in the context of religious clubs in public schools); *Marsh v. Chambers*, 463 U.S. 783, 787 & n.5 (1983) (invoking history and tradition in holding that government funding of legislative chaplaincies is constitutional); William Clancy, *Religion as a Source of Tension, in Religion and the Free Society* 23, 28 (1958); Carl H. Esbeck, *The Establishment Clause as a Structural Restraint: Validations and Ramifications*, 18 J.L. & Pol'y 445, 469–471 (2002); Brett G. Scharffs, *The Autonomy of Church and State*, 2004 BYU L. Rev. 1217, 1231.

263. *See, e.g., Mitchell v. Helms*, 530 U.S. 793, 867, 868 (2000) (Souter, J., with Stevens and Ginsburg, JJ., dissenting) (discussing the "establishment prohibition of government religious funding"); *Witters v. Wash. Dep't of Servs. for the Blind*, 474 U.S. 481, 489 (1986) (finding no Establishment Clause violation in allowing a student to use generally available state vocational rehabilitation assistance funds at a religious college); Gerard V. Bradley, *Dogmatomachy: A "Privatization" Theory of Religion Clause Cases*, 30 St. Louis U. L.J. 275 (1986) (arguing that Supreme Court decisions "privatizing" religion keep religion "imprisoned" in a non-public sphere, contrary to Madisonian principles); Richard W. Garnett, *A Quiet Faith? Taxes, Politics, and the Privatization of Religion*, 42 B.C. L. Rev. 771 (2001) (arguing that tax-exemption limits on religious organizations' political expression privatizes religion, robbing the public square of the organizations' contributions); Howard Gillman & Erwin Chemerinsky, *The Religion Clauses: The Case for Separating Church and State* at xi (2020) ("In contrast to the accommodationist approach ..., we defend a separationist view"); Levy, *The Establishment Clause, supra* n. 163 (arguing that the Constitution's framers viewed the Establishment Clause as prohibiting any "government aid for religion, whether for all religions or one church").

no-aid separationist approach would suggest that no government funds, exemptions, or subsidies should be given to religious organizations, even to organizations that provide public services such as education, health care, and counselling. For more on the Establishment Clause, *see* Part VIII (Financing of Religious Communities), Chapter 1 (Direct Financing); Part IX (Education), Chapter 2 (Religious Schools); and Part XI (Religion and Culture), Chapter 3 (Religion and Civil Society).

120. This conflict has been reflected in the jurisprudence of the US Supreme Court. In its first few decades of Establishment Clause jurisprudence, the Court emphasized the principle of state-church separation but has softened its approach in more recent decades, moving toward a focus on accommodation and neutrality, allowing religion to engage in the public sphere so long as the government action in question is neutral.[265] In the late twentieth century, Justice Sandra Day O'Connor favored the use of an "endorsement" approach, which focuses on whether the religious activity in question appears to be endorsed by the state.[266] However, the endorsement test did not maintain much traction after her departure from the Supreme Court, and a majority of the Court eventually declared it "abandoned".[267] Occasionally, Supreme Court decisions rejected these approaches and drew on history and tradition to suggest that long-standing religious practices in public life, such as legislative prayer, comported with the Establishment Clause.[268] In 2022, the

264. *See, e.g.*, Claudia E. Haupt, *Religion-State Relations in the United States and Germany: The Quest for Neutrality* 107–108 (2011); Donald T. Kramer, Annotation, *Supreme Court Cases Involving Establishment and Freedom of Religion Clauses of Federal Constitution*, 37 L. Ed. 2d 1147, § 3[c] (LexisNexis 2012).

265. *See, e.g.*, *Everson v. Bd. of Educ.*, 330 U.S. 1, 16 (1947) (quoting Thomas Jefferson in explaining that the Establishment Clause was intended to erect "a wall of separation between church and state"); *Lynch v. Donnelly*, 465 U.S. 668, 672–673 (1984) ("It has never been thought either possible or desirable to enforce a regime of total separation ... ." (quoting *Comm. for Pub. Educ. & Religious Liberty v. Nyquist*, 413 US. 756, 760 (1973))); *Rosenberg v. Rector & Visitors of U. of Va.*, 515 U.S. 819, 839 (1995) ("[T]he guarantee of neutrality is respected, not offended, when the government, following neutral criteria and evenhanded policies, extends benefits to recipients whose ideologies and viewpoints, including religious ones, are broad and diverse.").

266. *Lynch*, 465 U.S. at 687, 688 (O'Connor, J., concurring).

267. *Kennedy v. Bremerton*, 142 S. Ct. 2407, 2427–2428 (2022).

268. *Am. Legion v. Am. Hum. Ass'n*, 139 S. Ct. 2067, 2089 (2019) (holding that use of a Latin Cross as a World War I memorial is constitutional because the symbol came to represent, through time, more than religion within the community); *Town of Greece v. Galloway*, 572 U.S. 565, 591–592 (2014) (holding that practice of opening town board meetings with prayer—even sectarian prayer—comported with US history and tradition and did not violate Establishment Clause); *Marsh v. Chambers*, 463 U.S. 783, 792–793 (1983) (holding that practice of opening state legislature with prayers in Judeo-Christian tradition did not violate Establishment Clause when "[w]eighed against the historical backdrop"); *Woodring v. Jackson County*, 986 F.3d 979 (7th Cir. 2021) (applying *American Legion*); *Kondrat'yev v. City of Pensacola*, 949 F.3d 1319 (11th Cir. 2020) (applying *American Legion*). Federal courts of appeals have applied *Town of Greece* to varying outcomes. *See, e.g.*, *Fields v. Speaker of the Pa. House of Representatives*, 936 F.3d 142, 153 (3d Cir. 2019) (holding that legislature's policy giving preference to theistic prayers did not violate Establishment Clause); *Williamson v. Brevard County*, 928 F.3d 1296, 1299, 1310 (11th Cir. 2019) (holding that process for selecting prayer-givers for board of county commissioners' meetings violated Establishment Clause when it favored monotheistic religions and categorically excluded others); *Barker v. Conroy*, 921 F.3d 1118, 1131 (D.C. Cir. 2019) (noting legislative prayer "coexisted

Court stated that such an approach—focusing on history and tradition, as well as originalism (interpreting the Establishment Clause as it was understood at the time of its adoption)—now "represent[s] the rule" in Establishment Clause jurisprudence.[269]

§2. Free Exercise Clause

121. The US Supreme Court over time has varied in approaches to the Free Exercise Clause. At times, the Court has interpreted the Clause as requiring some religious exemptions to generally applicable laws. At other times, the Court has held that the Clause bars only laws that target particular religious groups or practices because of their religious character. For more on the Free Exercise Clause, *see* Part II (Religious Freedom in General), Chapter 1 (Individual Religious Freedom) and Chapter 2 (Collective Religious Freedom); Part III (Legal Status of Religious Communities), Chapter 2 (Autonomy of Religious Communities); and Part IX (Education), Chapter 2 (Religious Schools).

122. The earliest Supreme Court free exercise case, *Reynolds v. United States*, introduced a belief/action dichotomy: while beliefs are protected absolutely, actions motivated by those beliefs are subject to important limitations, including those found in criminal law.[270] In cases such as *Minersville School District v. Gobitis*, the Court proved itself inhospitable to religious exemptions to laws, holding that religiously motivated actions can be limited if the state has a "legitimate" interest.[271] Later, in *Sherbet v. Verner*, the Court articulated a "strict scrutiny" standard, meaning that restrictions on free exercise must be narrowly tailored to meet a "compelling" state interest.[272] *Employment Division v. Smith* essentially closed a door to exemptions, holding that the Free Exercise Clause does not require the government to grant religious exemptions to generally applicable laws—that is, to laws that do not specifically target religious practices.[273] Commentators favoring this approach draw on much the same line of thought as those who favor stronger separation of

---

with the principles of disestablishment and religious freedom [f]rom colonial times through the founding of the Republic and ever since" (internal quotation marks omitted) (quoting *Marsh*, 463 U.S. at 786)); *Freedom from Religion Found., Inc. v. Chino Valley Unified Sch. Dist. Bd. of Educ.*, 896 F.3d 1132, 1150 (9th Cir. 2017) (holding that policy of beginning public portion of school board meetings with prayer violated Establishment Clause where the "policy reinforce[d] the dominance of particular religious traditions"), *reh'g en banc denied*, 910 F.3d 1297 (9th Cir. 2018); *Bormuth v. County of Jackson*, 870 F.3d 494, 497–498 (6th Cir. 2017) (en banc) (holding that practice of county commissioners opening public meetings with prayer did not violate Establishment Clause); *Lund v. Rowan County*, 863 F.3d 268, 272 (4th Cir. 2017) (en banc) (holding that county board of commissioners' exclusive, Christianity-elevating prayer practice violated Establishment Clause).

269. *Kennedy*, 142 S. Ct. at 2428 (quoting *Town of Greece*, 572 U.S. at 575).
270. *Reynolds v. United States*, 98 U.S. 145, 165 (1878).
271. *Minersville Sch. Dist. v. Gobitas*, 310 U.S. 586, 593–600 (1940) ("The religious liberty which the Constitution protects has never excluded legislation of general scope not directed against doctrinal loyalties of particular sects" where the state "end is legitimate".).
272. *Sherbert v. Verner*, 374 U.S. 398, 406–407 (1963).
273. *Emp. Div., Dep't of Hum. Res. of Or. v. Smith*, 494 U.S. 872, 877–882 (1990).

church and state under the Establishment Clause and who consider the core purpose of separation to be protection of the state from private religiosity.[274] Under this approach, the Free Exercise clause is essentially just a protection against laws targeting religious practice or a particular religious tradition.[275] Others reject this approach, favoring the *Sherbert* approach the Supreme Court used prior to *Smith*.[276] While the Court has limited *Smith*'s application in various cases, it has continued to rely on *Smith*'s standard—for example, employing *Smith* to reach its 2021 decision *Fulton v. City of Philadelphia*.[277] When government entities mandated church closures as part of their response to the COVID-19 pandemic, courts also grappled with the line between neutral, generally applicable government actions and those that unfairly target religion. *See* Part II (Religious Freedom in General), Chapter 1 (Individual Religious Freedom) and Chapter 2 (Collective Religious Freedom).

274. Frederick Mark Gedicks, *An Unfirm Foundation: The Regrettable Indefensibility of Religious Exemptions*, 20 U. Ark. Little Rock L.J. 555, 572–574 (1998); William P. Marshall, *The Case Against the Constitutionally Compelled Free Exercise Exemption*, 40 Case W. Res. L. Rev. 357, 376–378 (1989).

275. *See Church of the Lukumi Babalu Aye, Inc. v. City of Hialeah*, 508 U.S. 520, 532–534 (1993).

276. *See infra* n. 332.

277. *Fulton v. City of Philadelphia*, 141 S. Ct. 1868, 1876–1878 (2021) (declining to decide whether to overrule *Smith* because the provision at issue was not neutral and generally applicable); *see also Hosanna-Tabor Evangelical Lutheran Church & Sch. v. EEOC*, 565 U.S. 171, 190 (2012); *Church of the Lukumi Babalu Aye*, 508 U.S. at 531–532.

Part II. Religious Freedom in General

Chapter 1. Individual Religious Freedom

§1. Constitutional Frameworks

123. Protections of individual religious freedom in the US Constitution are grounded in the First Amendment and in the "religious test" clause of Article VI. The First Amendment forbids Congress from passing laws "respecting an establishment of religion, or prohibiting the free exercise thereof".[278] Article VI states that "no religious Test shall ever be required as a Qualification to any Office or public Trust under the United States".[279]

124. First Amendment protections of religious freedom have been extended to individual claims against states by incorporation under the Fourteenth Amendment.[280] "Incorporation" refers to the process of applying language from the Bill of Rights—which was traditionally understood to apply only to the federal government—to states as well, by virtue of the Fourteenth Amendment.[281] For additional discussion of incorporation, *see* Part I (Legal Framework and Sources), Chapter 1 (Constitutional Position of Religion). The Supreme Court has never resolved the question of whether the Constitution's "no religious test" requirement applies to the states. It did, however, strike down, under the First and Fourteenth Amendments, a state requirement that officeholders declare a belief in God.[282] The Supreme Court also struck down a ban on religious clergy serving in a state's legislature, holding that the ban deprived the pastor of his right to freely exercise his religion and enjoy the right to hold public office.[283] For more information on the influence of religion in American politics, *see* Part V (Religion and Politics), Chapter 1 (Religious Influence in Politics).

---

278. U.S. Const. amend. I.
279. *Ibid.*, art. VI, cl. 3.
280. Constitutional protections against establishment of religion were incorporated in *Everson v. Bd. of Educ.*, 330 U.S. 1 (1947). Free exercise protections were incorporated in *Cantwell v. Connecticut*, 310 U.S. 296 (1940).
281. The Supreme Court has adopted selective, rather than total, incorporation, choosing to incorporate "only selected portions of the Bill of Rights". James McHenry, *Fourteenth Amendment*, *in* 2 *The Encyclopedia of Civil Liberties in America* 394, 395 (David Schultz & John R. Vile eds., 2015).
282. *Torcaso v. Watkins*, 367 U.S. 488, 495–496 (1961). The decision explicitly avoided the question of whether states are bound by the "no religious test" provision of article VI. *Ibid.*, at 489 n.1.
283. *McDaniel v. Paty*, 435 U.S. 618, 626–629 (1978) (plurality opinion).

§2. THE CORE DOMAIN OF CONSCIENCE

125. While the right to manifest religious beliefs has been subject to various restrictions, the Supreme Court held in *West Virginia State Board of Education v. Barnette* that the Free Exercise Clause protects belief and prevents compelled affirmations of belief: "If there is any fixed star in our constitutional constellation, it is that no official, high or petty, can prescribe what shall be orthodox in politics, nationalism, religion, or other matters of opinion or force citizens to confess by word or act their faith therein."[284] In that case, the Supreme Court reversed its own precedent from *Minersville School District v. Gobitis*, in which the Court refused to require a state to provide religious exemptions to the requirement that students recite the Pledge of Allegiance.[285] In *Barnette,* the Court changed course and rejected a compulsory flag salute in schools, holding that "the action of the local authorities in compelling the flag salute and pledge transcends constitutional limitations on their power and invades the sphere of intellect and spirit which it is the purpose of the First Amendment to our Constitution to reserve from all official control".[286]

126. More recently, the Supreme Court extended *Barnette*'s holding against compelled speech to rule that public employees cannot be forced to subsidize a union—a decision cited in some lower court cases involving religious convictions, free speech, and non-discrimination.[287] The Court also cited *Barnette* in holding that a state anti-discrimination statute could not be enforced to compel a wedding website business owner to convey messages inconsistent with her religious beliefs that marriage be reserved to heterosexual couples.[288] The Supreme Court and lower courts have continued to hold against compelled speech in other cases as well.[289]

284. *W. Va. State Bd. of Educ. v. Barnette*, 319 U.S. 624, 642 (1943).

285. *Minersville Sch. Dist. v. Gobitis*, 310 U.S. 586, 597–600 (1940), *overruled by Barnette*, 319 U.S. at 643.

286. *Barnette*, 319 U.S. at 642. A lower court has since relied on *Barnette* to distinguish between compelled religious behavior and acquainting students with a particular religion. In *Wood v. Arnold*, 915 F.3d 308, 319 (4th Cir. 2019), the Fourth Circuit Court of Appeals employed the now-abrogated *Lemon* test to uphold the dedication of a portion of world history coursework to learning about Islam.

287. *Janus v. Am. Fed'n of State, Cnty., & Mun. Emps., Council 31*, 138 S. Ct. 2448 (2018); *see, e.g., 303 Creative LLC v. Elenis*, 6 F.4th 1160, 1190, 1194–1195 (10th Cir. 2021) (Tymkovich, C.J., dissenting) (discussing "the First Amendment's antipathy toward government-compelled speech"), *rev'd*, 600 U.S. 570 (2023); *Telescope Media Grp. v. Lucero*, 936 F.3d 740, 750–753 (8th Cir. 2019) (holding state could not apply state human rights act to compel wedding videographers to film same-sex weddings, contrary to their religious beliefs); *Brush & Nib Studio, LC v. City of Phoenix*, 448 P.3d 890, 905, 926 (Ariz. 2019) (holding city could not apply anti-discrimination ordinance to compel company owners to create celebratory wedding invitations for same-sex weddings, contrary to their religious beliefs).

288. *303 Creative LLC v. Elenis*, 600 U.S. 570, 584–586 (2023).

289. *See, e.g., Nat'l Inst. of Family & Life Advocates v. Becerra*, 138 S. Ct. 2361, 2375–2378 (2018) (holding that petitioners were likely to succeed on their claim that state law requiring pro-life centers to provide notice of state-provided abortions and other family planning services violated the First Amendment); *Otto v. City of Boca Raton*, 981 F.3d 854, 864–872 (11th Cir. 2020) (holding that ban on conversion therapy, including purely speech-based therapy, violated First Amendment prohibition on compelled speech); *Apodaca v. White*, 401 F. Supp. 3d 1040, 1053–1054, 1060 (S.D.

§3. SPEECH AND PROPAGATION

127. The landmark USSC decision rejecting limits on religious speech is *Cantwell v. Connecticut.*[290] In that case, the Supreme Court held that a statute requiring a license to engage in street proselytizing, and the subsequent conviction of three street proselytizers under the statute, violated the First Amendment.[291] Three Jehovah's Witnesses—Newton Cantwell and his two sons—were convicted for not obtaining a license before proselytizing and for inciting a public disturbance.[292] The Supreme Court held that the solicitation statute was an unlawful prior restraint on the Cantwells' free exercise and speech rights.[293] For further discussion of freedom of expression and religion, *see* Part VII (Religious Communities and Protections of the Individual), Chapter 3 (Freedom of Expression).

128. Blasphemy and hate speech fall within the First Amendment's protective scope but not necessarily within the specific scope of the amendment's religion clauses. Generally speaking, the federal and state governments cannot regulate speech, religious or otherwise, in a way that promotes or inhibits specific viewpoints. It can, however, establish *content-neutral* laws that regulate the time, place, and manner of speech.[294] The general rule regarding *content-based* government action—that is, regulation that limits speech based on its substance—is that the regulation must be "narrowly tailored to serve compelling state interests".[295] This "strict scrutiny" standard broadly protects hate speech and blasphemy from government prohibition or regulation. The US Supreme Court in *R.A.V. v. City of Saint Paul*, for example, applied strict scrutiny to a statute that prohibited the display of symbols known to "arouse[] anger, alarm or resentment in others on the basis of race, color, creed, religion or gender".[296] The Court held the law unconstitutional because a content-neutral version of the law could have served the state's interest without discriminating against particular viewpoints. For a more detailed discussion of blasphemy, defamation, and hate speech, *see* Part VII (Religious Communities and Protections of the Individual), Chapter 3 (Freedom of Expression); and Part XI (Religion and Culture), Chapter 1 (Religion and Art) and Chapter 4 (Religion and Public Debate).

Cal. 2019) (finding that university's "unbridled" discretionary process for deciding which student organizations to fund, through mandatory student fees, was not viewpoint neutral and thus violated students' First Amendment rights against compelled speech).

290. *Cantwell v. Connecticut*, 310 U.S. 296 (1940).
291. *Ibid.*, at 303.
292. *Ibid.*
293. *Ibid.*
294. *See ibid.*, at 303–305.
295. *Reed v. Town of Gilbert*, 576 U.S. 155, 163 (2015).
296. *R.A.V. v. City of St. Paul*, 505 U.S. 377, 395 (1992).

§4. Limitations on Religious Actions and Manifestations

I. Overview

129. Protections for religious actions and manifestations in US law have varied greatly over time. Initially, the Supreme Court interpreted the Free Exercise Clause to protect only belief, not manifestations of belief.[297] In the 1960s, the Court recognized the need for religious accommodations from generally applicable laws and held that the Free Exercise Clause required state accommodation for sincere religious beliefs absent a compelling state interest and a restriction narrowly tailored to serve that interest.[298] In 1990, in *Employment Division v. Smith,* the Supreme Court effectively repudiated this doctrine, holding that generally applicable laws were sufficient to meet the requirements of the Free Exercise Clause—that the clause did not require religious exemptions from such laws.[299]

130. In response, the US Congress passed the Religious Freedom Restoration Act (RFRA) in 1993, which reinstated a compelling state interest test—known as "strict scrutiny"—for claims of substantial burden to religious exercise.[300] RFRA further heightened the strict scrutiny standard, however, by requiring that state restrictions that substantially burden free exercise constitute the least restrictive means (rather than simply be narrowly tailored) to achieve a compelling state interest.[301] The Supreme Court struck down RFRA in 1997 as applied to the states, holding that the federal government lacked power under the Fourteenth Amendment to require states to analyze such claims under strict scrutiny.[302] RFRA continues to apply to federal actions.[303] The federal government has passed more specific religious freedom legislation, such as the Religious Land Use and Institutionalized Persons Act (RLUIPA), which has been upheld with regard to the states.[304] Many states have also passed statutes or upheld state constitutional standards implementing a strict scrutiny standard for free exercise claims. This section explores each of these historical developments in more detail.

---

297. *Reynolds v. United States*, 98 U.S. 145, 166 (1878).
298. *See Sherbert v. Verner*, 374 U.S. 398, 406–407 (1963).
299. *Emp. Div., Dep't of Hum. Res. of Or. v. Smith*, 494 U.S. 872, 887–882 (1990).
300. Religious Freedom Restoration Act of 1993, Pub. L. No. 103-141, 107 Stat. 1488 (codified as amended at 42 U.S.C. §§ 2000bb to 2000bb-4 (2018)).
301. *See* 42 U.S.C. § 2000bb-1 (2018); *City of Boerne v. Flores*, 521 U.S. 507, 535 (1997).
302. *City of Boerne*, 521 U.S. at 532–536.
303. *Gonzales v. O Centro Espirita Beneficente Uniao do Vegetal*, 546 U.S. 418, 424 (2006); *see also Tanzin v. Tanvir*, 141 S. Ct. 486, 493 (2020) (holding that RFRA provides for "money damages against federal officials in their individual capacities"); *Ajaj v. Fed. Bureau of Prisons*, 25 F.4th 805, 813 (10th Cir. 2022) (holding that officials sued in their individual capacities for money damages under RFRA could invoke qualified immunity as a defense).
304. *See Cutter v. Wilkinson*, 544 U.S. 709, 715–716, 719–720 (2005); *Holt v. Hobbs*, 574 U.S. 352, 357 (2015). These cases only concern the prisoner portions of RLUIPA. The land-use provisions have been upheld by federal courts of appeals, but the US Supreme Court has not decided a RLUIPA land-use case. *See St. John's United Church of Christ v. City of Chicago*, 502 F.3d 616, 640 (7th Cir. 2007); Petition for Writ of Certiorari at 16–23, *City of Salinas v. New Harvest Christian Fellowship*, 143 S. Ct. 567 (2023) (No. 22-309), 2022 WL 4781694 (discussing the split among federal courts of appeals regarding analysis of RLUIPA's "equal terms" provision).

II. Belief/Action Dichotomy: *Reynolds*

131. The earliest US Supreme Court case law addressing religious freedom distinguished between the absolute right to religious belief and the more restricted right to manifest religious belief through action. The Court's 1878 opinion in *Reynolds v. United States* specifically asked "[w]hether religious belief can be accepted as a justification of an overt act made criminal by the law of the land".[305] George Reynolds resided in Utah, then a federal territory, and worked as a secretary to Brigham Young, president of The Church of Jesus Christ of Latter-day Saints. In accordance with his religious beliefs, Reynolds married a second wife in violation of a federal statute prohibiting bigamy. After his arrest, Reynolds appealed his case to the Supreme Court, which held that religiously motivated actions did not create an exemption to laws governing general actions.[306] *Reynolds* is the foundation of the "belief-action" distinction in USSC religious liberty jurisprudence and is often considered to have placed disproportionate burdens on minority religious practices.

132. *Reynolds* continued to be good law into the twentieth century, although most free exercise claims were decided under state constitutions until incorporation of the Free Exercise Clause into the Fourteenth Amendment in *Cantwell v. Connecticut* (1940).[307] The question of free exercise arose again in 1961 in *Braunfeld v. Brown*, in which the Supreme Court refused to grant Orthodox Jews an exemption from a generally applicable law proscribing the sale of certain commodities on Sundays.[308] Because of their religious beliefs, Braunfeld and other Orthodox Jews closed their businesses on Saturdays, the Jewish Sabbath. Braunfeld and others challenged the validity of the Sunday sales ban on the grounds it imposed a unique burden by forcing them to close two days out of the week. The USSC opinion asked whether the law prohibiting Sunday commerce interfered with the free exercise of religion. Although the Court explained that "[a]bhorrence of religious persecution and intolerance is a basic part of our heritage", it held that the government is not required under the First Amendment to create exemptions to generally applicable laws like the Sunday sales ban.[309]

III. Compelling State Interest Test: *Sherbert* and *Yoder*

133. After *Braunfeld*, USSC opinions became more sympathetic to religious exemptions from generally applicable laws. The 1963 case *Sherbert v. Verner*,[310] along with the 1972 case *Wisconsin v. Yoder*,[311] marked the emergence of the compelling state interest test in religious exemption cases. This standard has also been referred to as "strict scrutiny" and is similar to the standard used by the Supreme

305. *Reynolds v. United States*, 98 U.S. 145, 162 (1878).
306. *Ibid.*, at 167.
307. *Cantwell v. Connecticut*, 310 U.S. 296, 303 (1940).
308. *Braunfeld v. Brown*, 366 U.S. 599, 601 (1961).
309. *Ibid.*, at 606.
310. *Sherbert v. Verner*, 374 U.S. 398, 403 (1963).
311. *Wisconsin v. Yoder*, 406 U.S. 205, 214 (1972).

Court in other contexts where fundamental rights are protected by the Fourteenth Amendment or where government action affects a suspect class, such as race.[312]

134. Adell Sherbert, a Seventh-day Adventist, lost her job because she would not work on Saturdays, her Sabbath day, and could not obtain other employment or unemployment benefits for the same reason.[313] The Supreme Court held that the state of South Carolina imposed an impermissible burden on Sherbert's free exercise of religion when its denial of unemployment benefits was not justified by a compelling state interest; the Court noted that had the state shown a compelling interest, it would still be required to show that no alternative means were available to achieve that interest.[314] The Supreme Court in *Yoder* imposed a similar standard to a challenge by Old Order Amish and Amish Mennonites to Wisconsin's school attendance law, which mandated attendance to age 16.[315] In contrast to *Sherbert*, the Supreme Court held that Wisconsin's interest in an educated citizenry was compelling; however, the Court invalidated the statute because the state's means of achieving that interest were not narrowly tailored, given the adequacy of the Amish informal vocational education system in meeting the Amish community's needs.[316]

135. Protections of religious manifestations under the compelling interest test were stronger than under *Reynolds* but were not always robust. Additional USSC opinions significantly limited the practical application of the compelling state interest test. In *United States v. Lee*, for example, a self-employed Amish farmer sued for a refund of taxes he paid into Social Security for his Amish employees, claiming their religious faith precluded them from paying the tax or accepting government aid through Social Security benefits.[317] The Supreme Court held that, while the tax may burden religious expression, granting a religious exemption would undermine the compelling government interest in maintaining a "sound tax system".[318]

136. In *Lyng v. Northwest Indian Cemetery Protective Association*, the Supreme Court declined to apply the compelling state interest test.[319] In that case, the Supreme Court rejected a Native American religious group's challenge to a proposed logging permit and road that would close a forest grove on federal lands used

312. *See, e.g.*, *Yick Wo v. Hopkins*, 118 U.S. 356, 373 (1886) (concluding that "no reason" existed for biased enforcement of a facially neutral law excepting "hostility" to the petitioners' race and nationality, contrary to the Fourteenth Amendment); *Skinner v. Oklahoma*, 316 U.S. 535, 541 (1942) (applying strict scrutiny in holding that sterilization law aimed at habitual criminals violated the Fourteenth Amendment); *Loving v. Virginia*, 388 U.S. 1, 11 (1967) (holding that racial classifications by the state demand the "most rigid scrutiny").

313. *Sherbert*, 374 U.S. at 401.

314. *Ibid.*, at 406–407 (finding no evidence that the government's policy furthered a state interest in eliminating unscrupulous claims by individuals "feigning religious objections to Saturday work").

315. *Yoder*, 406 U.S. at 207, 215 ("[O]nly those interests of the highest order and those not otherwise served can overbalance legitimate claims to the free exercise of religion".)

316. *Ibid.*, at 219, 221–228.

317. *United States v. Lee*, 455 U.S. 252, 254 (1982).

318. *Ibid.*, at 260.

319. *Lyng v. Nw. Indian Cemetery Protective Ass'n*, 485 U.S. 439, 447–451 (1988).

by the group for religious ceremonies. The Court did not apply strict scrutiny, arguing that it did not apply to incidental effects of government programs.[320] It noted that the government had sought to accommodate Native American beliefs but could not completely accommodate them without halting the road, which, the Court emphasized, was on government land.[321] The Court claimed that attempting to balance state and religious interests in the case would inappropriately require the Court to be the arbiter of which lands are "central" or indispensable to various religious traditions and which lands are not—a task better suited to "the legislatures and other institutions".[322] *See* additional discussion in this Part, Chapter 2 (Collective Religious Freedom), below.

137. The Supreme Court in *Goldman v. Weinberger* also declined to apply the compelling state interest test, citing a more deferential standard of review for military regulations.[323] In *Goldman,* a Jewish service member challenged an Air Force regulation prohibiting service members from wearing religious headgear.[324] The Supreme Court upheld the military requirement as "reasonably and evenhandedly regulat[ing] dress in the interest of the military's perceived need for uniformity".[325] In response, Congress enacted a military dress code allowing conservative religious headgear in the military.[326]

IV. Generally Applicable Laws: *Smith* and *Fulton*

138. In 1990, the US Supreme Court effectively abandoned the compelling state interest test in *Employment Division v. Smith.*[327] In *Smith*, similar to the underlying facts of *Sherbert*, two counselors at a private drug-rehabilitation clinic lost their jobs for using peyote in violation of state drug laws. The counselors were denied unemployment benefits under a state law that disqualified employees who are fired for "work-related 'misconduct'". Because the counselors used the controlled substance during a sacrament in a Native American Church, they claimed the right to a religious exemption to the benefits law. The Court held that the Free Exercise Clause does not require religious exemptions to generally applicable laws.[328] The opinion distinguished *Smith* from other free exercise cases such as *Cantwell v. Connecticut* and *Wisconsin v. Yoder* by labelling the latter 'hybrid cases', where an additional constitutional right applied apart from the right to free exercise of religion.[329] The Court also distinguished the facts in *Sherbert*, where the state made individualized

320. *Ibid.*
321. *Ibid.*, at 453–455.
322. *Ibid.*, at 452, 457.
323. *Goldman v. Weinberger*, 475 U.S. 503, 506–507 (1986).
324. *Ibid.*, at 504.
325. *Ibid.*, at 510.
326. Pub. L. No. 100-180, § 508(a)(2), 101 Stat. 1019, 1086 (1986) (codified at 10 U.S.C. § 774 (2018)).
327. *Emp. Div., Dep't of Hum. Res. of Or. v. Smith*, 494 U.S. 872 (1990).
328. *Ibid.*, at 878.
329. *Ibid.*, at 880–882.

assessments of conduct to determine exemptions, from the facts in *Smith*, where the state created 'an across-the-board criminal prohibition on a particular form of conduct'.[330] The Court noted that "where the State has in place a system of individual exemptions, it may not refuse to extend that system to cases of 'religious hardship' without compelling reason".[331]

139. While the Court has limited the application of *Smith* in several cases since 1990, critics have argued that lower courts continue to apply it too narrowly and have urged the Court to "return to a standard that can better balance governmental interests and fundamental rights".[332] The Court nevertheless relied on *Smith* to reach a decision more than thirty years later in *Fulton v. City of Philadelphia*.[333] The city of Philadelphia refused to renew its long-standing contract with Catholic Social Services because the agency refused to consider same-sex couples as foster parents, which the city of Philadelphia considered a violation of the contract's nondiscrimination provision. The Court found the provision neither neutral nor generally applicable because it gave the city discretionary authority to grant exceptions; therefore, strict scrutiny, rather than *Smith*, applied.[334] Even so, the Court employed *Smith* as an analytical first step to reach its holding that the city's actions unconstitutionally burdened the agency's religious exercise. *Fulton*'s three concurring opinions joined by various justices reveal the Court's divergent views on whether the Court should have overruled *Smith*.[335]

V. Federal Reaction to *Smith*: The Religious Freedom Restoration Act, *City of Boerne*, and the Religious Land Use and Institutionalized Persons Act

140. In reaction to *Employment Division v. Smith*, the US Congress enacted the Religious Freedom Restoration Act (RFRA) in 1993.[336] RFRA reinstated the compelling state interest test through legislation, requiring that "[g]overnment shall not substantially burden a person's exercise of religion even if the burden results from

330. *Ibid.*, at 884.
331. *Ibid.*
332. *See* Petition for Writ of Certiorari at 31, *Fulton v. City of Philadelphia*, 141 S. Ct. 1868 (2021) (No. 19-123), 2019 WL 3380520.
333. *Fulton*, 141 S. Ct. at 1876–1877.
334. *Ibid.*
335. *See ibid.*, at 1882, 1882–1883 (Barrett, J., with Kavanaugh, J., concurring, and with Breyer, J., joining in part) (acknowledging "serious arguments" for overruling *Smith* but agreeing the facts in *Fulton* did not trigger *Smith*); *ibid.*, at 1883, 1883–1926 (Alito, J., with Thomas and Gorsuch, JJ., concurring) (asserting *Smith* should be overruled and replaced by strict scrutiny); *ibid.*, at 1926, 1926–1931 (Gorsuch, J., with Thomas and Alito, JJ., concurring) (asserting *Smith* "committed a constitutional error" that the Court should not have "sidestep[ped]" in *Fulton*).
336. Pub. L. No. 103-141, 107 Stat. 1488 (1993) (codified as amended at 42 U.S.C. §§ 2000bb to 2000bb-4 (2018)). Congress also amended RFRA in 1994 to explicitly protect the Native American ceremonial use of peyote—the free exercise issue addressed in *Smith*. American Indian Religious Freedom Act Amendments of 1994, Pub. L. No. 103-344, 108 Stat. 3125 (codified at 42 U.S.C. § 1996a (2018)).

a rule of general applicability" unless it can demonstrate that the burden "is in furtherance of a compelling governmental interest" and "is the least restrictive means of furthering that compelling governmental interest".[337]

141. Although Congress intended to include actions by the states within the scope of RFRA, the Supreme Court opinion in *City of Boerne v. Flores* held that Congress lacked the power under the Fourteenth Amendment to address encroachments by the states on religious freedom.[338] *City of Boerne* arose when the Roman Catholic archbishop of San Antonio, Texas, applied for a zoning permit to enlarge a church in a historic preservation district. The archbishop claimed that denial of the permit amounted to an impermissible burden on religious expression. The Supreme Court considered whether the Fourteenth Amendment's enforcement power allowed Congress to apply RFRA to the states and concluded that Congress's enforcement power is solely for enforcing already-existing rights, not for declaring the substantive boundaries of rights.[339] This decision invalidated RFRA as applied to actions by states. However, as the Supreme Court recognized in *Gonzales v. O Centro Espirita Beneficente Uniao do Vegetal*, RFRA continues to be valid with respect to federal action and in federal jurisdictions.[340] In that case, the Court held that, under RFRA, the federal government failed to demonstrate a compelling interest in banning the use of a hallucinogenic tea for religious worship.[341] The Court has since held that RFRA's remedies provision allows litigants to claim "money damages against federal officials in their individual capacities".[342]

142. In response to the Supreme Court's decision in *Boerne*, Congress passed the Religious Land Use and Institutionalized Persons Act (RLUIPA), a narrower statute that imposes the compelling state interest test—also known as "strict scrutiny"—in state and federal cases involving land use and institutionalized persons.[343] The Supreme Court has upheld RLUIPA provisions with respect to incarcerated persons[344] but has yet to consider a case involving the Act's land-use provisions.[345] For discussion of RLUIPA's provisions related to incarcerated

337. 42 U.S.C. §§ 2000bb-1 (2018); *see also City of Boerne v. Flores*, 521 U.S. 507, 535 (1997) (noting that RFRA replaced the compelling state interest test's previous "narrowly tailored means" requirement with a heightened "least restrictive means" requirement).
338. *City of Boerne*, 521 U.S. at 536.
339. *Ibid.*, at 519.
340. *Gonzales v. O Centro Espirita Beneficente Uniao do Vegetal*, 546 U.S. 418, 424 (2006).
341. *Ibid.*, at 439.
342. *Tanzin v. Tanvir*, 141 S. Ct. 486, 493 (2020); *see also Ajaj v. Fed. Bureau of Prisons*, 25 F.4th 805, 813 (10th Cir. 2022) (holding that officials sued in their individual capacities for money damages under RFRA could invoke qualified immunity as a defense).
343. Pub. L. No. 106-274, 114 Stat. 803 (2000) (codified at 42 U.S.C. §§ 2000cc to 2000cc-5 (2018)) (requiring restrictions that impose a substantial burden on religious exercise to serve a compelling government interest and be the least restrictive means of furthering that interest).
344. *Cutter v. Wilkinson*, 544 U.S. 709, 714 (2005).
345. *See infra* paras. 837, 838; *Tree of Life Christian Sch. v. City of Upper Arlington*, 905 F.3d 357, 376, 378, 387 (6th Cir. 2018) (Thapar, Cir. J., dissenting) ("[T]he courts … have added requirements into RLUIPA that prevent many religious groups from seeking the shelter that Congress sought to provide. … There comes a time with every law when the Supreme Court must revisit what the [federal courts of appeals] are doing. That time has come.").

persons, *see* Part VII (Religious Communities and Protections of the Individual), Chapter 8 (Penal Law and Religion). For discussion of RLUIPA's land-use provisions, *see* Part XI (Religion and Culture), Chapter 1 (Religion and Art).

VI. State Responses to *Smith* and *Boerne*

143. Some state governments responded to *Employment Division v. Smith* and *City of Boerne v. Flores* by enacting their own RFRA laws that, like the federal RFRA law, apply strict constitutional scrutiny to substantial burdens on religious exercise. Thirty-three of the fifty states have enacted RFRA laws or have RFRA-like protections that require strict scrutiny. Twenty-three of those states have passed measures similar to RFRA as either state constitutional amendments or statutes.[346] The courts in twelve states (including Indiana and Montana, which also have state RFRAs) have interpreted their state constitutions as requiring strict scrutiny.[347]

144. Seventeen states have not enacted (legislatively) or recognized (judicially) RFRA-like protections. The courts in four of those states—Maryland, Nebraska, New Jersey, and Wyoming—have expressly rejected strict scrutiny.[348] In eight

---

346. *See generally* 1 Durham et al., *supra* n. 157, § 3:27 (*Chart: State Standards of Free Exercise Review under State RFRAs and State High Court Decisions*). *See also* (including year main provision became effective or was passed) Ala. Const. art. I, § 3.01 (1999); Ariz. Rev. Stat. Ann. §§ 41-1493 to -1493.04 (1999); Ark. Code Ann. §§ 16-123-401 to -407 (2015); Conn. Gen. Stat. § 52-571b (1993); Fla. Stat. §§ 761.01–.061 (1998); Idaho Code §§ 73-401 to -404 (2000); 775 Ill. Comp. Stat. 35/1–30, 35/99 (1997); Ind. Code §§ 34-13-9-0.7 to -9-11 (2015); Kan. Stat. Ann. §§ 60-5301 to -5322 (2013); Ky. Rev. Stat. Ann. § 446.350 (West 2013); La. Stat. Ann. §§ 13:5231–5242 (2010); Miss. Code Ann. §§ 11-61-1, -3 (2014); Mo. Rev. Stat. §§ 1.302, 1.307 (2003); Mont. Code Ann. §§ 27-33-101 to -105 (2021); N.M. Stat. Ann. §§ 28-22-1 to -5 (2000); Okla. Stat. tit. 51, §§ 251–258 (2000); 71 Pa. Cons. Stat. §§ 2401–2408 (2002); R.I. Gen. Laws § 42-80.1-1 to -4 (1998); S.C. Code Ann. §§ 1-32-10 to -60 (1999); S.D. Codified Laws § 1-1A-4 (2021); Tenn. Code Ann. § 4-1-407 (2009); Tex. Civ. Prac. & Remedies Code Ann. §§ 110.001–.012, .0031 (West 1999); Va. Code Ann. § 57-2.02 (2009).

347. *See generally* 1 Durham et al., *supra* n. 157, § 3:27 (*Chart: State Standards of Free Exercise Review under State RFRAs and State High Court Decisions*). *See also In re Tiffany O.*, 467 P.3d 1076, 1081 & n.16 (Alaska 2020); *City Chapel Evangelical Free Inc. v. City of South Bend*, 744 N.E.2d 443, 445–451 (Ind. 2001); *Fortin v. Roman Cath. Bishop of Portland*, 871 A.2d 1208, 1227–1228 (Me. 2005); *Magazu v. Dep't of Child. & Fams.*, 42 N.E.3d 1107, 1117–1118 (Mass. 2016); *McCready v. Hoffius*, 586 N.W.2d 723 (Mich. 1998), *vacated in part by* 593 N.W.2d 545 (Mich. 1999); *Odenthal v. Minn. Conf. of Seventh-day Adventists*, 649 N.W.2d 426, 442 (Minn. 2002); *St. John's Lutheran Church v. State Comp. Ins. Fund*, 830 P.2d 1271, 1276 (Mont. 1992); *State v. Mack*, 249 A.3d 423, 443 (N.H. 2020); *Humphrey v. Lane*, 728 N.E.2d 1039, 1043 (Ohio 2000); *Munns v. Martin*, 930 P.2d 318 (Wash. 1997) (en banc) (but *see State v. Arlene's Flowers, Inc.*, 441 P.3d 1203, 1229–1231 (Wash. 2019) (en banc), analyzing state anti-discrimination statute as a neutral and generally applicable law subject to rational basis review); *Matter of Kilpatrick*, 375 S.E.2d 794 (W. Va. 1988); *Coulee Cath. Sch. v. Lab. & Indus. Rev. Comm'n*, 768 N.W.2d 868, 886 n.27 (Wis. 2009).

348. *See Archdiocese of Wash. v. Moersen*, 925 A.2d 659, 661 (Md. Ct. App. 2007); *In re Interest of Anaya*, 758 N.W.2d 10, 19 (Neb. 2008); *S. Jersey Cath. Sch. Tchrs. Org. v. St. Teresa of the Infant Jesus Church Elementary Sch.*, 696 A.2d 709, 720–721 (N.J. 1997); *Trujillo v. State*, 2 P.3d 567, 575–577 (Wyo. 2000) (but *see In re Neely*, 390 P.3d 728, 736 (Wyo. 2017), applying strict scrutiny to a hybrid First Amendment claim).

states, courts have not addressed the appropriate level of scrutiny for religious exemption claims.[349] In three states, courts have explicitly noted the issue but not resolved it.[350] And courts in at least two states have employed a kind of hybrid analysis.[351]

145. The reach of state RFRA laws differs widely. Some states only bar the state from "burdening" religious exercise instead of from "substantially burdening" religious claimants,[352] while others prevent the state from "restricting" religious exercise.[353] Several states require the government to provide "clear and convincing evidence" of the compelling government interest.[354] RFRAs in Indiana and South Carolina apply to private businesses and organizations, in addition to individuals, and permit such entities to assert the law as a defense as well as a claim.[355]

146. In the wake of litigation establishing the right to same-sex marriage and the Supreme Court's determination that RFRA applies to closely held corporations in *Hobby Lobby*, state RFRAs became highly controversial. Typically, opponents of same-sex marriage have advocated for the adoption of state RFRAs while supporters have claimed such laws carve out an over-broad niche for religious expression that infringes on other rights.[356] Many LGBTQ+ advocates express fear of discrimination at places of public accommodation because they believe state RFRA protections for business owners' religious beliefs would allow owners to exclude LGBTQ+ individuals and same-sex couples. While it is unclear whether this would

---

349. *See Van Osdol v. Vogt*, 908 P.2d 1122, 1129–1131 (Colo. 1996) (en banc); *Keegan v. Univ. of Del.*, 349 A.2d 14 (Del. 1975) (applying strict scrutiny twenty-five years prior to *Smith*); *State v. Armitage*, 319 P.3d 1044, 1067–1068 (Haw. 2014) (showing an inclination to follow *Smith* but not interpreting state constitutional law); *Mitchell County v. Zimmerman*, 810 N.W.2d 1 (Iowa 2012) (showing an inclination to follow *Smith* but not interpreting state constitutional law); *State v. Carignan*, 631 S.E.2d 892 (N.C. Ct. App. 2006); *State ex rel. Heitkamp v. Family Life Servs., Inc.*, 560 N.W.2d 526, 530 (N.D. 1997) (Neumann, J. dissenting) (noting strict scrutiny standard); *Blandino v. State*, 914 P.2d 624, 626 (Nev. 1996) (holding under *Smith* that appellant had no free exercise right to self-representation but not addressing the state's free exercise provision), *cert denied*, 522 U.S. 888 (1997). Georgia's Supreme Court appears not to have considered a free exercise case since *Smith*, and several attempts by the state legislature to pass a state RFRA have failed.
350. *Cath. Charities of Sacramento, Inc. v. Superior Ct.*, 85 P.3d 67, 91 (Cal. 1996); *State v. Holm*, 2006 UT 31, ¶ 35, 137 P.3d 726, 738 (Utah 2006); *Brady v. Dean*, 790 A.2d 428, 433 (Vt. 2001).
351. *State v. Hickman*, 358 P.3d 987, 992–994 (Or. 2015); *Cath. Charities of Diocese of Albany v. Serio*, 859 N.E.2d 459, 466 (N.Y. 2006) (rejecting *Smith*'s "inflexible rule" and applying intermediate scrutiny); *Rourke v. N.Y. State Dep't of Correctional Servs.*, 603 N.Y.S.2d 647, 649–650 (N.Y. Sup. Ct. 1993) (using a balancing test offering greater protection than *Smith* but less than other states' tests); *C.F. v. N.Y. City Dep't of Health & Mental Hygiene*, 139 N.Y.S.3d 273 (N.Y. App. Div. 2020) (applying *Smith* but outlining alternate holding based on strict scrutiny analysis).
352. *See, e.g.*, Ala. Const. art. I, § 3.01; Conn. Gen. Stat. § 52-571b (2022).
353. *See, e.g.*, Mo. Rev. Stat. § 1.302 (2022); N.M. Stat. Ann. § 28-22-3 to -4 (2022); R.I. Gen. Laws § 42-80.1-3 (2022).
354. Idaho Code § 73-401 (2022); Kan. Stat. Ann. § 60-5303 (2022); Ky. Rev. Stat. Ann. § 446.350 (West 2023); Okla. Stat. tit. 51, § 252 (2022); 71 Pa. Cons. Stat. § 2405 (West 2023); Tenn. Code Ann. § 4-1-407 (2022); Va. Code Ann. § 57-2.02 (2022).
355. Ind. Code §§ 34-13-9-7, -9 (2022); S.C. Code Ann. §§ 1-32-20, -50 (2022).
356. *See* Kelsey Dallas, *Is the "DEFCON 3 Culture War" over Religious Freedom Bills Coming to an End?*, DeseretNews (May 15, 2021), https://www.deseret.com/2021/5/15/22421195/is-the-culture-war-over-state-level-religious-freedom-bills-coming-to-an-end-rfra-first-amendment.

always be the case, such objections have led to the amendment of state RFRAs and the defeat of several proposed state RFRAs.[357]

147. A disputed issue is whether RFRAs offer protections for businesses sued under a public accommodation statute that bars discrimination.[358] The RFRAs in two states expressly allow businesses to use RFRA as a defense.[359] Some federal courts of appeals have interpreted the federal RFRA to serve as a valid defense in private discrimination suits while others have not.[360] The New Mexico Supreme Court in *Elane Photography, LLC v. Willock* upheld the finding of discrimination

357. *See, e.g.*, Ark. Code Ann. §§ 16-123-401 to -407 (2022) (reflecting language of second bill passed and signed into law in 2015 after first bill was roundly criticized for being discriminatory); Ind. Code § 34-13-9-0.7 (2015) (amending state RFRA as passed by adding anti-discrimination safeguards). The amended Indiana law helped alleviate intense concerns of discrimination that had resulted in national protests, and it was the first Indiana law to include the language "sexual orientation" and "gender identity", in outlining protections. *See* Tony Cook et al., *Indiana Governor Signs Amended "Religious Freedom" Law*, USA Today (Apr. 2, 2015), http://www.usatoday.com/story/news/nation/2015/04/02/indiana-religious-freedom-law-deal-gay-discrimination/70819106; *see also* Ben Nadler, *Controversial Georgia "Religious Liberties" Bill Stalls*, AP (Mar. 4, 2019), https://apnews.com/article/b588b00d0728401d95e42bcb39749cdd.
358. Forty-five states and the District of Columbia have public accommodation statutes that prohibit discrimination based on race, sex, national origin, and religion. Alabama, Georgia, Mississippi, North Carolina, and Texas do not. Some statutes also cover marital status, sexual orientation, gender identity, age, or other status categories. State statutes vary in which businesses fall in the ambit of "public accommodations". *See generally State Public Accommodation Laws*, NCSL, http://www.ncsl.org/research/civil-and-criminal-justice/state-public-accommodation-laws.aspx (last updated Jun. 25, 2021). *See also* (codes current through Dec. 31, 2022) Alaska Stat. § 18.80.230; Ariz. Rev. Stat. Ann. § 41-1442; Ark. Code Ann. § 16-123-107; Cal. Civ. Code § 51; Colo. Rev. Stat. § 24-34-601; Conn. Gen. Stat. §§ 46a-64, -81d; Del. Code Ann. tit. 6, § 4504; Fla. Stat. §§ 413.08, 760.08; Haw. Rev. Stat. § 489-3; Idaho Code § 67-5909; 775 Ill. Comp. Stat. 5/101 to 5/103; Ind. Code § 22-9-1-2; Iowa Code § 216.7; Kan. Stat. Ann. § 44-1001; Ky. Rev. Stat. Ann. §§ 344.120, 344.145; La. Stat. Ann. § 51:2247; Me. Stat. tit. 5, §§ 4552, 4591; Md. Code Ann., State Gov't § 20-304; Mass. Gen. Laws ch. 272, § 98; Mich. Comp. Laws §§ 37.1102, 37.2302; Minn. Stat. § 363A.11; Mo. Rev. Stat. §213.065; Mont. Code Ann. § 49-2-304; Neb. Rev. Stat. § 20-134; Nev. Rev. Stat. § 651.070; N.H. Rev. Stat. Ann. § 354-A:17; N.J. Stat. Ann. § 10:5-12(f); N.M. Stat. Ann. § 28-1-7(f); N.Y. Civ. Rights Law §§ 40, 40-C, Exec. Law § 292; N.D. Cent. Code § 14-02.4-14; Ohio Rev. Code Ann. § 4112.02; Okla. Stat. tit. 25, § 1402; Or. Rev. Stat. § 659A.403; 43 Pa. Cons. Stat. § 953; R.I. Gen. Laws § 11-24-2; S.C. Code Ann. § 45-9-10; S.D. Codified Laws § 20-13-23; Tenn. Code Ann. § 4-21-501; Utah Code § 13-7-3; Vt. Stat. Ann. tit. 9, § 4502; Va. Code Ann. § 2.2-3900, -3904; Wash. Rev. Code § 49.60.215; W. Va. Code § 5-11-2, -11-9(6); Wis. Stat. § 106.52; Wyo. Stat. Ann. § 6-9-101; D.C. Code § 2-1402.31.
359. Ind. Code §§ 34-13-9-7, -9 (2022); S.C. Code Ann. §§ 1-32-20, -50 (2022).
360. *Compare, e.g., Hankins v. Lyght*, 441 F.3d 96, 103 (2d Cir. 2006) (holding RFRA provided a defense to private age discrimination action against church and bishop under federal ADEA, which permits enforcement by a federal agency or private plaintiffs), *and EEOC v. Cath. Univ. of Am.*, 83 F.3d 455, 468–469 (D.C. Cir. 2003) (holding that private plaintiff, a Catholic university, was allowed to claim a defense under RFRA, against a claim of sex discrimination under Title VII), *with Tomic v. Cath. Diocese of Peoria*, 442 F.3d 1036, 1042 (7th Cir. 2006) (holding, regarding private suit brought under federal ADEA, that "RFRA is applicable only to suits to which the government is a party"), *abrogated by Hosanna-Tabor Evangelical Lutheran Church & Sch. v. EEOC*, 565 U.S. 171, 195 & n.4 (2012). *See also Gen. Conf. Corp. of Seventh-day Adventists v. McGill*, 617 F.3d 402, 410–411 (6th Cir. 2010) (holding, in a trademark infringement action, that RFRA's statutory language and legislative history "indicate Congress did not intend the statute to apply against private parties").

under public accommodation laws where a photographer refused to photograph a same-sex commitment ceremony.[361] The photographer claimed that enforcing the public accommodation statute created a substantial burden on her religious exercise under New Mexico's RFRA, but the New Mexico Supreme Court held that the state's RFRA only applies to legal actions in which the government is a party.[362] (New Mexico, unlike some states, permits private actors to enforce public accommodations statutes without involving state entities.[363])

§5. CONSCIENTIOUS OBJECTION

148. Statutory provisions have long protected rights of conscientious objection, particularly in the military.

I. Protections for Conscientious Objection to Military Service

149. Legal recognition of conscientious objection to military service in the United States for members of religious groups that oppose military service extends back to the creation of the nation.[364] It was regulated at the state level until federal law required conscription and provided for conscientious objectors in 1864. Those wishing to exercise conscientious objection had the option to care for wounded and sick soldiers in hospitals or to pay USD 300 to their benefit.[365] During World War II, conscientious objection to armed forces service due to religious belief and training was approved through local boards that reviewed self-reporting questionnaires.[366]

150. During the twentieth century, an individual right to object to military service based on personal rather than group beliefs developed along with an individual right to object based on personal non-religious beliefs. The 1965 USSC opinion in *United States v. Seeger* interpreted the 1948 Training and Service Act's requirement that objectors sincerely believe in a Supreme Being to mean that the belief need only be personal to the believer.[367] The *Seeger* opinion holds that if a given belief is "sincere", "meaningful", and "occupies a place in the life of its possessor parallel

361. *Elane Photography, LLC v. Willock*, 309 P.3d 53, 77 (N.M. 2013), *cert. denied*, 572 U.S. 1046 (2014) (mem.).
362. *Ibid.*, at 76–77.
363. *See* Anne-Marie G. Harris, *A Survey of Federal and State Public Accommodations Statutes: Evaluating Their Effectiveness in Cases of Retail Discrimination*, 13 Va. J. Soc. Pol'y & L. 331, 342, 345 (2006) (citing twenty-four states that permit claimants to file lawsuits directly without filing a claim with a state agency, twenty-two states that require a plaintiff to file a claim with a state agency, and five states that do not permit private enforcement of public accommodations statutes).
364. Robert Paul Churchill, *Conscientious Objection*, *in An Encyclopedia of War and Ethics* 99, 100 (Donald A. Wells ed., 1996).
365. Melvin Gingerich, *Service for Peace: A History of Mennonite Civilian Public Service* 3 (1949).
366. *Ibid.*, at 76.
367. *United States v. Seeger*, 380 U.S. 163, 170 (1965).

to that filled by the orthodox belief in God", an exemption should be granted.[368] *Welsh v. United States* later held that the right to exemption extends to individuals "whose consciences, spurred by deeply held *moral, ethical, or religious beliefs*, would give them no rest or peace if they allowed themselves to become part of an instrument of war".[369] During the Vietnam War, the Supreme Court in *Gillette v. United States* made clear, however, that conscientious objection exemptions cannot be based solely on objections to specific wars.[370]

151. In the employment context, the US Supreme Court extended the rights of conscientious objectors to include exemption from arms manufacturing in *Thomas v. Review Board* in 1981.[371] Thomas was employed in a steel factory and was reassigned to a department that produced parts for tanks, which he felt violated his religious beliefs as a Jehovah's Witness. He asked to be laid off, but when the company refused, he quit his job. Much like the underlying facts of *Sherbert*, the state denied him unemployment benefits, thereby forcing Thomas to choose between his religious beliefs and a public benefit.[372] The USSC opinion found no legally significant difference between the facts in *Sherbert* and *Thomas* and subsequently upheld his right to receive unemployment benefits.[373]

II. Conscientious Objection in Provision of Medical Services

152. Medical service providers also enjoy some protection as conscientious objectors. Abortion, contraceptives, physician-assisted death, hormone therapies to treat gender dysphoria, and other debated medical treatments create religious or moral conflict for many medical professionals and service providers. For a detailed treatment of this topic, *see* Part VII (Religious Communities and Protections of the Individual), Chapter 6 (Medical Deontology).

153. In 1973, the "Church Amendment" was passed, which mandates that federal funds provided through different health programs will not require individuals or hospitals "to perform or assist in the performance of any sterilization procedure or abortion" if their doing so "would be contrary to [their] religious beliefs or moral convictions".[374] Additionally, hospitals cannot condition employment on willingness to perform or assist in these procedures, nor can they practice similar forms of discrimination.[375] Other federal amendments prohibit federal funding of local, state,

368. *Ibid.*, at 165–166.
369. *Welsh v. United States*, 398 U.S. 333, 344 (1970) (emphasis added).
370. *Gillette v. United States*, 401 U.S. 437, 447–448 (1971).
371. *Thomas v. Rev. Bd. of the Ind. Emp. Sec. Div.*, 450 U.S. 707 (1981).
372. *Ibid.*, at 713.
373. *Ibid.*, at 717–720.
374. 42 U.S.C. § 300a-7(b)(1) (2018).
375. *Ibid.*, § 300a-7(c) to (e).

or federal government entities and programs that discriminate against healthcare entities for not facilitating or providing abortions or abortion training.[376]

154. A series of federal circuit and state court cases affirm the right of private hospitals to object to treatments like abortion while still generally requiring public hospitals to perform abortions permitted under state law.[377] Forty-six states offer individual protections to medical professionals unwilling to perform abortions as well.[378]

155. Pharmacists may be granted exemptions to having to dispense certain medications, depending largely on their state of residence. Some state laws include "conscience" or "refusal" clauses that allow pharmacists to refuse to dispense contraception based on moral, ethical, or religious objections.[379] An emerging issue is the intersection of conscience clauses with non-discrimination laws, where a pharmacist might refuse to dispense hormone therapies to a transgender individual.[380]

---

376. Coats-Snowe Amendment (codified at 42 U.S.C. § 238n); Departments of Labor, Health and Human Services, and Education and Related Agencies Appropriations Act, Pub. L. No. 115-245, div. B, § 507(d), 132 Stat. 2981, 3118 (2018) (Weldon Amendment, adopted or incorporated by reference in annual Department of Health and Human Services appropriations acts).
377. *See, e.g.*, *Doe v. Bridgeton Hosp. Ass'n, Inc.*, 366 A.2d 641 (N.J. 1976) (holding quasi-public institutions—such as nonprofit, non-sectarian, private hospitals—that provide therapeutic abortions could not refuse to perform first-trimester elective abortions). *But see Poelker v. Doe*, 432 U.S. 519 (1977) (holding city's refusal to provide elective abortions in publicly funded, city-owned hospitals was constitutional). *See also* 3 Durham et al., *supra* n. 174, § 27:6 (*Abortion*).
378. *State Laws and Policies: Refusing to Provide Health Services*, Guttmacher Inst., https://www.guttmacher.org/state-policy/explore/refusing-provide-health-services (last updated Aug. 31, 2023); 3 Durham et al., *supra* n. 174, § 27:5 (*Conscience Clauses Generally*); *see, e.g.*, (codes current through Mar. 20, 2023) Ala. Code §§ 22-21B-3, -4; Alaska Stat. § 18.16.010(b); Ariz. Rev. Stat. Ann. § 36-2154; Cal. Health & Safety Code § 123420; Del. Code Ann. tit. 24, § 1791; Haw. Rev. Stat. § 453-16(e); Idaho Code §§ 18-611, -612; 745 Ill. Comp. Stat. 70/4; Ind. Code §§ 16-34-1-4 to -6; Iowa Code § 146.1; Kan. Stat. Ann. § 65-443; Ky. Rev. Stat. Ann. § 311.800(4); La. Stat. Ann. § 40:1061.2; Mich. Comp. Laws §§ 333.20181–20183; Minn. Stat. §§ 145.42, 145.414; Mo. Rev. Stat. § 197.032; Mont. Code Ann. § 50-20-111; Neb. Rev. Stat. § 28-338; Nev. Rev. Stat. § 632-475; N.Y. Civ. Rights Law § 79-i; N.C. Gen. Stat. § 14-45.1(e); N.D. Cent. Code § 23-16-14; Ohio Rev. Code Ann. § 4731.91; Okla. Stat. tit. 63, § 1-741; 18 Pa. Stat. and Cons. Stat. Ann. § 3213(d); S.C. Code Ann. § 44-41-50; S.D. Codified Laws § 34-23a-12; Tex. Occ. Code Ann. § 103.001; Utah Code § 76-7-306; Va. Code Ann. § 18.2-75.
379. A 2022 study found that "[e]leven states have conscience clauses present in their pharmacy administrative code", nearly double the number found in 2006: Delaware, Georgia, Kansas, New York, North Carolina, Oregon, Pennsylvania, Rhode Island, South Carolina, South Dakota, and Texas. Thomas S. Achey & Ashley T. Robertson, *Conscientious Objection: A Review of State Pharmacy Laws and Regulations*, 57 Hosp. Pharmacy 268, 270 (2022). Approximately ten other states have statutory conscientious objection provisions that cover pharmacists specifically or that cover healthcare providers broadly and may include pharmacists. *See State Laws and Policies: Refusing to Provide Health Services*, *supra* n. 378.
380. For example, Georgia's State Board of Pharmacy regulations establish that "[i]t shall not be considered unprofessional conduct for any pharmacist to refuse to fill any prescription based on his/her professional judgment or ethical or moral beliefs". Ga. Comp. R. & Regs § 480-5-.03(n) (2022). This broad protection would allow pharmacists to refuse to dispense hormone-related medications prescribed to treat gender dysphoria. *See* Movement Advancement Project & Nat'l Ctr. for Transgender Equality, *Religious Refusals in Health Care: A Prescription for Disaster* 2–3 (Mar. 2018), https://www.lgbtmap.org/file/Healthcare-Religious-Exemptions.pdf.

156. The COVID-19 pandemic brought to the forefront conscientious objection exemptions to both administering and receiving vaccines. Another developing area related to conscientious objections is the provision of medical transitioning or other treatment to transgender children and adults.[381] Objections to administering vaccines or providing transitioning treatment may be accommodated under federal or state anti-discrimination or conscientious objection laws and regulations; federal or state RFRAs; or Title VII of the Civil Rights Act, which requires that employee objections be based on sincerely held religious beliefs that can be reasonably accommodated without imposing undue hardship to the employer.[382] For a more detailed discussion of vaccine mandates and exemptions, *see* Part VII (Religious Communities and Protections of the Individual), Chapter 6 (Medical Deontology).

381. *See, e.g.*, *Franciscan Alliance, Inc. v. Becerra*, 47 F.4th 368 (5th Cir. 2022) (holding that private religious healthcare providers had standing and claim under RFRA to seek permanent injunction against federal regulations requiring healthcare providers to provide abortions and gender-transitioning treatments).

382. *See ibid.*; 42 U.S.C. § 2000e(j) (2018); *United States v. Seeger*, 380 U.S. 163, 185 (1965) (explaining that "the threshold question of sincerity … must be resolved in every [conscientious objection] case").

Chapter 2. Collective Religious Freedom

§1. Freedom of Association

157. Freedom of association is an important dimension of the collective expression of religious freedom and is an integral part of the fundamental right of religious freedom. As the Supreme Court explained in *Roberts v. U.S. Jaycees*, "we have long understood as implicit in the right to engage in activities protected by the First Amendment a corresponding right to associate with others in pursuit of a wide variety of political, social, economic, educational, *religious*, and cultural ends".[383] The *Jaycees* case, however, illustrates the limits of the rights of freedom of association. The US Jaycees restricted regular membership in its nonprofit national membership corporation to men between the ages of 18 and 35. Men outside of this age group and women could be associate members, but their participation was limited: they could not vote or hold national or local office. In the mid-1970s, two Minnesota chapters began admitting women as regular members. In 1978, the president of the national organization informed the chapters that their charters were in jeopardy of being revoked, and the local chapters filed discrimination charges with Minnesota's Department of Human Rights. In turn, the US Jaycees filed suit against the acting commissioner of the Department of Human Rights. Because the local chapters were "neither small nor selective", the Supreme Court found them to be "places of public accommodation" subject to the Minnesota Human Rights Act.[384] The Court reasoned that, although application of the Act requiring the Jaycees to admit women as regular members was "an intrusion into the internal structure or affairs of an association", the Jaycees' right to associate was not absolute.[385] The Court ruled that regulations infringing on the right to association may be justified to serve compelling state interests, such as eliminating discrimination and ensuring equal access to public goods and services.[386]

158. While it may be limited, freedom of association has fundamental liberty, privacy, and autonomy dimensions. As the Court explained in *U.S. Jaycees*, individual choices to "enter into and maintain certain intimate human relationships must be secured against undue intrusion by the State because of the role of such relationships in safeguarding the individual freedom that is central to our constitutional scheme".[387] Therefore, "freedom of association receives protection as

383. *Roberts v. U.S. Jaycees*, 468 U.S. 609, 622 (1984) (emphasis added).
384. *Ibid.*, at 615 (defining a place of accommodation as "a business, accommodation, refreshment, entertainment, recreation, or transportation facility of any kind, whether licensed or not, whose goods, services, facilities, privileges, advantages or accommodations are extended, offered, sold, or otherwise made available to the public").
385. *Ibid.*, at 623.
386. *Ibid.*
387. *Ibid.*, at 617–618; *see also Hartwell v. Houghton Lake Cmty. Sch.*, 755 Fed. App'x 474, 476–478 (6th Cir. 2018) (asserting that freedom of intimate association is protected by the Fourteenth Amendment as a fundamental liberty, not by the First Amendment's express protection of freedom to associate).

a fundamental element of personal liberty".[388] The Court also noted that there are two sides to this coin: the freedom of association not only protects an individual's freedom to associate but also "presupposes a freedom not to associate" with any group or organization contrary to a person's beliefs.[389] In other words, the freedom to associate implies the freedom to disassociate.

§2. Freedom of Worship and the Collective Dimension

159. The Supreme Court has recognized that an important part of protecting individuals is protecting the groups with which they associate. Thus, the Court has noted that while freedom of association exists in part to protect individuals, groups must also be protected because "[a]n individual's freedom to speak, to worship, and to petition the government for the redress of grievances could not be vigorously protected from interference by the State unless a correlative freedom to engage in group effort toward those ends were not also guaranteed".[390] Accordingly, "[t]he right to freedom of association is a right enjoyed by religious and secular groups alike".[391] Religious groups, however, receive special consideration based on the text of the First Amendment.[392]

160. In 2020, pleas for injunctive relief reached the Supreme Court when states imposed COVID-19 pandemic-related restrictions on freedom to associate for religious worship. In early pandemic cases, the Court showed great deference to the political branches of government, acknowledging the broad latitude owed lawmakers in "areas fraught with medical and scientific uncertainties".[393] As the pandemic continued, however, the Court demonstrated decreasing deference, asserting "we should respect the judgment of those with special expertise and responsibility in [public health]. But even in a pandemic, the Constitution cannot be put away and forgotten".[394] In *Roman Catholic Diocese of Brooklyn v. Cuomo*, the Court enjoined

388. *U.S. Jaycees*, 468 U.S. at 618.
389. *Ibid.*, at 623.
390. *Ibid.*, at 622.
391. *Hosanna-Tabor Evangelical Lutheran Church & Sch. v. EEOC*, 565 U.S. 171, 189 (2012).
392. *Ibid.*
393. *S. Bay United Pentecostal Church v. Newsom*, 140 S. Ct. 1613, 1613 (2020) (mem.) (Roberts, C.J., concurring) (internal quotation marks omitted) (quoting *Marshall v. United States*, 414 U.S. 417, 427 (1974)); *see also Calvary Chapel Dayton Valley v. Sisolak*, 140 S. Ct. 2603, 2605 (2020) (mem.) (Alito, J., with Thomas and Kavanaugh, JJ., dissenting from denial of application for injunctive relief).
394. *Roman Cath. Diocese of Brooklyn v. Cuomo*, 141 S. Ct. 63, 68 (2020) (per curiam); *see also S. Bay United Pentecostal Church v. Newsom (II)*, 141 S. Ct. 716 (2021) (mem.) (statement of Gorsuch, J., with Thomas and Alito, JJ., joining) ("Government actors have been moving the goalposts on pandemic-related sacrifices for months, adopting new benchmarks that always seem to put restoration of liberty just around the corner. As this crisis enters its second year—and hovers over a second Lent, a second Passover, and a second Ramadan—it is too late for the State to defend extreme measures with claims of temporary exigency, if it ever could. Drafting narrowly tailored regulations can be difficult. But if Hollywood may host a studio audience or film a singing competition while not a single soul may enter California's churches, synagogues, and mosques, something has gone seriously awry.")

state regulations that strictly limited attendance at religious services in zones with high COVID-19 rates.[395] The Court reasoned that because restrictions limited religious facilities more than comparable "essential" secular facilities—such as campgrounds, stores, laundromats, and acupuncture clinics—the restrictions were not neutral and generally applicable; therefore, strict scrutiny would apply.[396] The Court concluded that the state's restrictions were not narrowly tailored, since the state could adopt less restrictive rules to safeguard public health, such as correlating maximum-attendance restrictions to the size of a synagogue or church.[397]

161. The Supreme Court, in support of the freedom of association, has also cited the value of diversity: "According protection to collective effort on behalf of shared goals is especially important in preserving political and cultural diversity and in shielding dissident expression from suppression by the majority".[398] Thus, the Court has recognized that giving both large and small groups the freedom to gather, worship, learn, teach, serve, and govern is vital to their success and to maintaining a democratic, pluralistic society.

§3. Conscientious Objection

162. The right to be exempted from military service on grounds of conscience began as a collective religious freedom right. Individuals who belonged to churches that had an institutional objection to military service (for example, Quakers, Mennonites, the Brethren) were generally exempt under state laws from serving in the military during the Revolution, on provision of "alternative service or assessments".[399] It was not until the Federal Conscription Act of 1864 that the US Congress made a specific exception for members of religious denominations that prohibited bearing arms, so long as they "pay a substitute assessment or accept non-combatant service".[400] Over time, the right was extended to individuals who based their conscientious objections on religious training and beliefs as defined in section 6(j) of the Universal Military Training and Service Act.[401] Eventually, the principle

395. *Roman Cath. Diocese of Brooklyn*, 141 S. Ct. at 65.
396. *Ibid.*, at 66–67; *see also ibid.*, at 69, 69 (Gorsuch, J., concurring).
397. *Ibid.*, at 67.
398. *Roberts v. U.S. Jaycees*, 468 U.S. 609, 622 (1984).
399. 1 Durham et al., *supra* n. 157, § 3:47 (*Conscientious Objection to War*).
400. *Ibid.*
401. *United States v. Seeger*, 380 U.S. 163, 164–165 (1965). The Court quoted the 1958 edition of the Universal Military Training and Service Act, which defined "religious training and belief … as an individual's belief in a relation to a Supreme Being involving duties superior to those arising from any human relation, but (not including) essentially political, sociological, or philosophical views or a merely personal moral code". *Ibid.* The Court also established an objective test to determine whether an individual's refusal to serve in combatant military roles is based on "religious training and belief" that falls under the Act's definition. *Ibid.*, at 165–166, 184. The test asks, "does the claimed belief occupy the same place in the life of the objector as an orthodox belief in God holds in the life of one clearly qualified for exemption?" *Ibid.*, at 184.

was extended to individuals who objected based on "deeply held moral, ethical, or religious beliefs".[402] Thus, the protection of religious institutions paved the way for expanding protections to individuals.

§4. Separation of Church and State

163. The concept of separation of church and state, although not explicit in the First Amendment, has been used to forge an institutional independence of religion and the state. An important case in the development of this idea was *Engel v. Vitale*, which addressed whether daily classroom prayer in public schools violated the Establishment Clause.[403] In 1955, the New York Board of Regents composed a prayer they recommended for the school districts within their jurisdiction, which became known as the Regents' prayer. At the beginning of every school day, each class would state, "Almighty God, we acknowledge our dependence upon Thee, and we beg Thy blessings upon us, our parents, our teachers and our Country."[404] The parents of ten students sued the school district for its adoption of the prayer, arguing that it "was contrary to the beliefs, religions, or religious practices of both themselves and their children" and amounted to an establishment of religion.[405] The Supreme Court agreed, affirming that "by using its public school system to encourage recitation of the Regents' prayer, the State of New York has adopted a practice wholly inconsistent with the Establishment Clause".[406] The separation of religion and the state, of course, can protect the autonomy of both the state and religious institutions.[407] For further discussion concerning religion in public schools, *see* Part IX (Education), Chapter 1 (Religious Education in Public and Private Schools).

§5. Free Exercise and the Compelling State Interest Test

164. The saga of the "compelling state interest" in law and religion jurisprudence is discussed elsewhere. *See* this part, Chapter 1 (Individual Religious Freedom), above. The test has been an important mechanism for protecting not only individual but also collective religious freedom. The US Supreme Court articulated

402. *Welsh v. United States*, 398 U.S. 333, 343–344 (1970). The Court allowed Welsh to claim protection under the Universal Military Training and Service Act because he believed that the taking of life was morally wrong. *Ibid.* Although he did not base his objection on religious beliefs, the Court exempted him because he held his beliefs "with the strength of more traditional religious convictions". *Ibid.*, at 343 (quoting the earlier opinion of the Ninth Circuit Court of Appeals in the case).
403. *Engel v. Vitale*, 370 U.S. 421, 422 (1962); U.S. Const. amend. I ("Congress shall make no law respecting an establishment of religion … .").
404. *Engel*, 370 U.S. at 422.
405. *Ibid.*, at 423.
406. *Ibid.*, at 424; *see also Freedom from Religion Found., Inc. v. Chino Valley Unified Sch. Dist. Bd. of Educ.*, 896 F.3d 1132, 1150 (9th Cir. 2017) (holding that policy of beginning public portion of school board meetings with prayer violated Establishment Clause where the "policy reinforce[d] the dominance of particular religious traditions"), *reh'g en banc denied*, 910 F.3d 1297 (9th Cir. 2018).
407. *See* Scharffs, *The Autonomy of Church and State*, *supra* n. 262, at 1248–1251.

the compelling state interest test in *Sherbert v. Verner*, which involved Adele Sherbert, a Seventh-day Adventist who was denied unemployment benefits because she refused to work on Saturdays, the Sabbath day of her church.[408] The Court observed that, in denying benefits, the state was essentially forcing Sherbert "to choose between following the precepts of her religion and forfeiting benefits, on the one hand, and abandoning one of the precepts of her religion in order to accept work, on the other hand".[409] It found that eliminating fraud did not constitute a compelling state interest warranting "substantial infringement of religious liberties", since no evidence existed of a pattern of "fraudulent claims by unscrupulous claimants feigning religious objections to Saturday work".[410] The Court noted that, even if evidence of fraudulent claims existed, the state would still be required "to demonstrate that no alternative forms of regulation would combat such abuses without infringing First Amendment rights".[411] This reasoning became known as the compelling state interest test or "strict scrutiny" analysis. Under that test, government must demonstrate that a regulation shown to burden religious exercise is (1) related to a compelling state interest and (2) narrowly tailored—meaning that no less restrictive alternative exists to achieve that interest. The compelling state interest test has not provided a "free pass" to conscientious objectors. Where government has met its burden of proof under the test, courts have found that laws and policies that burden religious exercise do not violate the Constitution.[412]

165. Even after the US Supreme Court rejected the compelling state interest in *Smith*, it hasrecognized the protection that the Free Exercise Clause affords religious entities to be free of official discrimination.[413] *See* this part, Chapter 1 (Individual Religious Freedom), above.

§6. Church Autonomy

166. Another constitutional idea important to collective religious freedom is church autonomy. In *Gonzalez v. Roman Catholic Archbishop of Manila*, the Supreme Court stated, "In the absence of *fraud*, *collusion*, or *arbitrariness*, the decisions of the proper church tribunals on matters purely ecclesiastical, although affecting civil rights, are accepted in litigation before the secular courts as conclusive,

408. *Sherbert v. Verner*, 374 U.S. 398 (1963).
409. *Ibid.*, at 404.
410. *Ibid.*, at 406–407.
411. *Ibid.*, at 407.
412. *See, e.g.*, *Silva v. Bacon*, No. C19-619-RAJ-MLP, 2020 WL 4754950, at *8 (W.D. Wash. May 12, 2020) (concluding that a "compelling government interest in order and security" justified burden on the religious exercise of inmate whose self-styled religious diet required eating meat on the bone, where the bones could be used to fashion weapons).
413. *See, e.g.*, *Church of the Lukumi Babalu Aye, Inc. v. City of Hialeah*, 508 U.S. 520, 546–547 (1993) (holding that city ordinances targeting a church's Santeria practices were unjustified and unconstitutional where government interests were not shown to be compelling and ordinances restricting practices were overbroad).

because the parties in interest made them so by contract or otherwise".[414] This standard was eventually modified in *Serbian Eastern Orthodox Diocese for the United States of America and Canada v. Milivojevich*; in that case, the Court ruled that allowing courts to determine the arbitrariness of ecclesiastical decisions violated the right of churches to function without judicial intervention.[415]

167. In the 1871 case *Watson v. Jones*, the Supreme Court was asked to determine which members had authority over church property after a Presbyterian congregation became divided. The Court ruled that because the particular congregation at issue was part of a church that had an internal system of government, the civil courts had to defer to the rulings of church authorities.[416] The Court reasoned that "[t]he right to organize voluntary religious associations … and to create tribunals … for the ecclesiastical government of all the individual members, congregations, and officers within the general association, is unquestioned."[417] The various approaches the Supreme Court has taken to church property disputes are discussed in greater detail in Part III (Legal Status of Religious Communities), Chapter 2 (Autonomy of Religious Communities).

168. In 1952, in *Kedroff v. St. Nicholas Cathedral of Russian Orthodox Church in North America*, the Court ruled that because the Russian Orthodox Church in Moscow still had administrative control over the North American Diocese, the civil courts had to defer to the authority of the Russian Orthodox Church concerning the "disposition or use of property".[418]

§7. Church Employment

169. The right of religious groups to choose whom to employ or dismiss is another important dimension of collective religious freedom. In *Corporation of the Presiding Bishop of The Church of Jesus Christ of Latter-day Saints v. Amos*, former employees of church-owned corporations claimed their dismissals were due to religious discrimination in violation of Title VII of the Civil Rights Act of 1964.[419] The Church claimed immunity under section 702 of the Act, which had been amended to exempt both secular and religious nonprofit activities of religious organizations from Title VII's prohibition on religious discrimination in employment. In turn, the plaintiffs claimed that section 702—if interpreted to permit religious discrimination in "nonreligious" jobs—violated the Establishment Clause. The Court upheld section 702 of the Act, as amended, explaining that the exemption helps religious organizations avoid significant government interference in carrying out their respective

414. *Gonzalez v. Roman Cath. Archbishop*, 280 U.S. 1, 7–8 (1929) (emphasis added).
415. *Serbian E. Orthodox Diocese for the U.S. & Can. v. Milivojevich*, 426 U.S. 696, 713–715 (1976).
416. *See Watson v. Jones*, 80 U.S. (13 Wall.) 679, 727–730 (1871).
417. *Ibid.*, at 728–729.
418. *Kedroff v. St. Nicholas Cathedral of Russian Orthodox Church in N. Am.*, 344 U.S. 94, 120 (1952).
419. *Corp. of the Presiding Bishop of The Church of Jesus Christ of Latter-day Saints v. Amos*, 483 U.S. 327 (1987).

religious missions.[420] Church employment issues are discussed in detail in Part VI (Labor Law Within Religious Communities), Chapter 1 (Scope of Application of Labor Law), Chapter 2 (Religious Ministers and Labor Law), and Chapter 3 (Other Church Employees and Labor Law).

170. The constitutional basis of church autonomy was settled in the 2012 case *Hosanna-Tabor Evangelical Lutheran Church and School v. EEOC.*[421] The Supreme Court held that the First Amendment barred an employment discrimination claim by a teacher who held the title Minister of Religion at a religious elementary school.[422] In doing so, the Court applied *Kedroff* (relevant to church self-governance) and referenced federal courts of appeals decisions that "uniformly recognized the existence of a 'ministerial exception'".[423] The Court ruled that, under the ministerial exception, the teacher could not bring her discrimination claim because "[b]y imposing an unwanted minister, the state infringes the Free Exercise Clause, which protects a religious group's right to shape its own faith and mission through its appointments".[424]

171. Eight years later, the Supreme Court clarified that there is no "rigid formula" for determining if an employee falls within the ministerial exception, but the Court agreed with most federal courts of appeals that an employee's "ministerial function should be the key focus" of the analysis.[425] In that case, *Our Lady of Guadalupe School v. Morrissey-Berru*, the Court consolidated claims brought by two teachers at Catholic schools who instructed students in religious tenets, in addition to their other teaching duties.[426] The Court held that the employees were sufficiently entrusted "with the responsibility of educating and forming students in the faith" that "judicial intervention into disputes between the school and the teacher threaten[ed] the school's independence in a way that the First Amendment does not allow".[427] These cases and the ministerial exception are discussed in detail in Part III (Legal Status of Religious Communities), Chapter 2 (Autonomy of Religious Communities).

---

420. *Ibid.*, at 335–339.
421. *Hosanna-Tabor Evangelical Lutheran Church & Sch. v. EEOC*, 565 U.S. 171 (2012).
422. *Ibid.*, at 177 ("The Synod classifies teachers into two categories: 'called' and 'lay.' 'Called' teachers are regarded as having been called to their vocation by God through a congregation. ... Once called, a teacher receives the formal title "Minister of Religion, Commissioned.'").
423. *Ibid.*, at 186, 188 & n.2, 195.
424. *Ibid.*, at 188; *see also EEOC v. Cath. Univ. of Am.*, 83 F.3d 455, 461 (D.C. Cir. 1996) (explaining the ministerial exception as follows: "[T]he Free Exercise Clause exempts the selection of clergy from Title VII and similar statutes and, as a consequence, precludes civil courts from adjudicating employment discrimination suits by ministers against the church or religious institution employing them.").
425. *Our Lady of Guadalupe Sch. v. Morrissey-Berru*, 140 S. Ct. 2049, 2055, 2060 (2020) (internal quotation marks omitted) (quoting *Biel v. St. James Sch.*, 926 F.3d 1238, 1239, 1239 (9th Cir. 2019) (mem.) (Nelson, J., dissenting)).
426. *Ibid.*, at 2059–2060.
427. *Ibid.*, at 2069.

172. Although the ministerial exception does bar some Title VII and other employment discrimination claims from being brought against churches, the applicability of the ministerial exception to certain claims remains unclear. The Ninth Circuit has stated that the ministerial exception does not bar Title VII claims that do not require the court to "evaluate religious doctrine or the 'reasonableness' of the religious practices".[428] That court allowed a former novice to pursue a sexual harassment claim against his former Jesuit order because it did not require the court to become entangled in religious doctrine.[429] In contrast, the Seventh Circuit has held that "the ministerial exception protects a religious organization's employment relationship with its ministers, from hiring to firing and the supervising in between", and therefore precludes "hostile work environment claims based on minister-on-minister harassment".[430] Other circuits have followed similar reasoning.[431] In 2020, the Supreme Court ruled in *Bostock v. Clayton County* that Title VII's prohibition on employment discrimination based on "sex" encompasses sexual orientation and gender identity. The Court acknowledged that its opinion did not explicitly address how *Bostock* intersects with free exercise protections for religious organizations as employers; however, the Court noted that existing constitutional and statutory protections could continue to apply to religious organizations in employment, including the ministerial exception, section 702 of Title VII, and the Religious Freedom Restoration Act.[432] Federal courts of appeals have split regarding application of the ministerial exception to employment-related suits brought as tort claims.[433]

§8. Indigenous Peoples

173. Indigenous people in the United States have repeatedly had to fight for recognition of their individual and collective religious rights. Two Supreme Court cases illustrate this struggle: *Employment Division v. Smith* and *Lyng v. Northwest.*

428. *Bollard v. Cal. Province of the Soc'y of Jesus*, 196 F.3d 940, 950 (9th Cir. 1999); *see also Puri v. Khalsa*, 844 F.3d 1152, 1167–1168 (9th Cir. 2017) (applying the "neutral-principles" approach in a management dispute where the ministerial exception did not apply, explaining the approach similarly avoided unconstitutional inquiry into doctrine or religious practices).

429. *Bollard*, 196 F.3d at 950; *see also Elvig v. Calvin Presbyterian Church*, 375 F.3d 951, 953 (9th Cir. 2004) (holding that a minister's Title VII suit regarding claims of a hostile work environment—involving sexual harassment and retaliation—could proceed but that the ministerial exception foreclosed her claim of wrongful termination).

430. *Demkovich v. St. Andrew the Apostle Par.*, 3 F.4th 968, 973, 984–985 (7th Cir. 2021) (noting a circuit split in application of the ministerial exception to hostile environment claims).

431. *Skrzypczak v. Roman Cath. Diocese of Tulsa*, 611 F.3d 1238, 1245–1246 (10th Cir. 2010) ("[The Seventh Circuit's] approach provides greater clarity in the exception's application and avoids the kind of arbitrary and confusing application the Ninth Circuit's approach has created."); *Gellington v. Christian Methodist Episcopal Church, Inc.*, 203 F.3d 1299, 1304 (11th Cir. 2000); *Combs v. Cent. Tex. Annual Conf. of United Methodist Church*, 173 F.3d 343, 350 (5th Cir. 1999).

432. *Bostock v. Clayton County*, 140 S. Ct. 1731, 1753–1754 (2020).

433. *Compare McRaney v. N. Am. Mission Bd. of the S. Baptist Convention, Inc.*, 966 F.3d 346, 347 (5th Cir. 2020) (holding that the district court's dismissal of a tort case for lack of jurisdiction, citing the ministerial exception, was premature), *cert. denied* 141 S. Ct. 2852 (2021) (mem.), *with Bell v. Presbyterian Church (U.S.A.)*, 126 F.3d 328, 329 (4th Cir. 1997) (holding the court lacked subject matter jurisdiction over tort claim related to a minister's termination, due to the ministerial exception).

174. In *Employment Division v. Smith*, two members of the Native American Church were fired from their jobs for ingesting peyote, a hallucinogenic drug, as part of a religious ceremony. They were also denied unemployment compensation because their dismissal was based on "misconduct" under Oregon law.[434] The Court reasoned that denying unemployment benefits based on violation of a law specifically directed at restricting religiously motivated behavior would violate the Free Exercise Clause.[435] But because the employees' peyote use was prohibited by a "neutral law of general applicability", the Court held that the denial of unemployment benefits was constitutional.[436] The Court concluded its opinion by noting that some states had taken legislative measures to exempt sacramental peyote use from their drug laws and thus prevent the constitutional conflict presented by *Smith*. The Oregon state legislature responded by creating an affirmative defense for religious peyote use.[437] The US Congress responded to *Smith* by enacting the Religious Freedom Restoration Act, which requires strict scrutiny of federal laws that impose a substantial burden on religious exercise—including exercise of Native American religions—even if the laws are generally applicable.[438] The *Smith* case, as well as legislative and judicial reactions to it, are discussed in more detail in this part, Chapter 1 (Individual Religious Freedom), above.

175. In a case predating *Smith*, several individuals, organizations, and the state of California brought suit when the federal government planned to construct a road through land used by American Indian tribes for religious rituals. The primary question in *Lyng v. Northwest Indian Cemetery Protective Association* was whether the Free Exercise Clause prohibited the US government from constructing a road through, or permitting timber harvesting in, a portion of sacred land now designated as national forest.[439] The Supreme Court acknowledged the tribes' religious interests, reaffirming that "[t]he Constitution does not permit government to discriminate against religions that treat particular physical sites as sacred", but ultimately found that, "[w]hatever rights the Indians may have to the use of the area … do not divest the Government of its right to use what is, after all, *its* land".[440] Citing precedent, the Court reiterated that the "Free Exercise Clause affords an individual protection from certain forms of governmental compulsion," but "it does not afford an individual a right to dictate the conduct of the Government's internal procedures."[441] In short, the Court found that the significant religious interests of Indians

434. *Emp. Div., Dep't of Hum. Res. of Or. v. Smith*, 494 U.S. 872, 872 (1990).
435. *Ibid.*, at 877–879.
436. *Ibid.*, at 881–882.
437. *See* Or. Rev. Stat. § 475.752(4)–(5) (2022).
438. Religious Freedom Restoration Act of 1993, Pub. L. No. 103-141, 107 Stat. 1488 (codified as amended at 42 U.S.C. §§ 2000bb to 2000bb-4 (2018)).
439. *Lyng v. Nw. Indian Cemetery Protective Ass'n*, 485 U.S. 439, 441–442 (1988).
440. *Ibid.*, at 453.
441. *Ibid.*, at 448 (quoting *Bowen v. Roy*, 476 U.S. 693, 699–700 (1986)). *But see* Stephanie Hall Barclay & Michalyn Steele, *Rethinking Protections for Indigenous Sacred Sites*, 134 Harv. L.R. 1294, 1340–1343 (2020) (arguing that the Court in *Lyng* employed a double standard, since the government has been required to accommodate free exercise rights in other spheres involving its "internal affairs"—such as in prisons or the military—and the government has treated the sacred sites of other groups very differently).

in regard to sacred lands did not trump federal government rights to that same land. In response to the litigation, Congress designated the area in question "wilderness" under the Wilderness Act (in 1984) and added it to the Siskiyou Wilderness Area (in 1990), thus preventing both the road from being built and the timber from being harvested.[442] It is interesting to note that once again it was Congress, an institution that ostensibly vindicates majority interests, that was more protective of minority rights than the Supreme Court.

§9. Collective Dimension of Individual Freedoms

176. As the previous sections illustrate, while the First Amendment is generally understood to comprise an enumeration of individual rights, nothing in the Amendment's text limits these protections strictly to individuals. On the contrary, three of the five rights specifically mentioned—press, assembly, and petition—are impossible to exercise outside a collective context. The collective dimension of the remaining two—speech and religion—has also been specifically and repeatedly protected by the Supreme Court.

177. For example, in 2010 in *Citizens United v. FEC*, the Court held that "political speech does not lose First Amendment protection simply because its source is a corporation", since "[c]orporations and other associations, like individuals, contribute to the discussion, debate, and the dissemination of information and ideas that the First Amendment seeks to foster."[443] This decision has been controversial, since it clears the way for big-money donors to have a louder voice in the US political system, but it also stands for the idea that free speech rights are collective as well as individual interests.[444]

178. The Religious Freedom Restoration Act (RFRA), introduced in Part I, Chapter 2, also protects the religious exercise of organizations. RFRA prohibits the government from "substantially burden[ing] a person's exercise of religion" unless it is "in furtherance of a compelling governmental interest" and "is the least restrictive means of furthering that compelling governmental interest".[445] RFRA was Congress's effort to restore this strict scrutiny standard—also known as the compelling

---

442. Amy Bowers & Kristen Carpenter, *Challenging the Narrative of Conquest: The Story of* Lyng v. Northwest Indian Cemetery Protective Association, *in Indian Law Stories* 489, 491, 527 (Carole Goldberg, Kevin K. Washburn & Philip P. Frickey eds., 2011).

443. *Citizens United v. FEC*, 558 U.S. 310, 342–343 (2010) (internal quotation marks omitted) (quoting *First Nat'l Bank of Bos. v. Bellotti*, 435 U.S. 765, 784 (1978); *Pac. Gas & Elec. Co. v. Pub. Utils. Comm'n of Cal.*, 475 U.S. 1, 8 (1986)).

444. *See* Richard A. Epstein, Citizens United v. FEC: *The Constitutional Right That Big Corporations Should Have but Do Not Want*, 34 Harv. J.L. & Pub. Pol'y 639 (2011) (asserting that "hysterical predictions" of post-*Citizens United* political activism by corporations is "overblown"); Zephyr Teachout, *The Historical Roots of* Citizens United v. FEC: *How Anarchists and Academics Accidentally Created Corporate Speech Rights*, 5 Harv. L. & Pol'y Rev. 163 (2011) (theorizing why Supreme Court jurisprudence has shifted to focus largely on "First Amendment concerns at the expense of a greater focus on corruption").

445. 42 U.S.C. § 2000bb-1 (2018).

state interest test—in religious freedom cases. Enacted in direct response to *Employment Division v. Smith*, it established that strict scrutiny should be applied to government actions even if the burden on religion "results from a rule of general applicability".[446] The Supreme Court has subsequently held that the federal RFRA applies only to federal law.[447]

179. The term "person" was not specifically defined in RFRA, so in *Burwell v. Hobby Lobby*, the Supreme Court looked to the Dictionary Act for a definition.[448] That Act defines "person" to include "corporations, companies, associations, firms, partnerships, societies, and joint stock companies, as well as individuals".[449] The Court concluded that the term should be construed broadly to include both non-profit and for-profit corporations, or at least for-profit corporations that are "closely held".[450] In doing so, however, the Court emphasized that "[w]hen rights, whether constitutional or statutory, are extended to corporations, the purpose is to protect the rights of [individuals]".[451] As the Court explained, "Corporations, separate and apart from the human beings who own, run, and are employed by them, cannot do anything at all."[452] The Court did not decide whether RFRA applied to publicly traded corporations but observed that intrinsic institutional factors would make it unlikely that such a corporation would assert a claim under RFRA.[453]

180. The collective exercise of religion is not limited to the freedom to believe or profess faith but includes "the performance of (or abstention from) physical acts that are engaged in for religious reasons".[454] Nevertheless, a plaintiff corporation or association must prove that its asserted beliefs are, in fact, sincerely held and not simply a pretext for obtaining an exemption to a generally applicable law for the purpose of gaining a financial advantage or windfall.[455]

---

446. *Ibid.*; *Emp. Div., Dep't of Hum. Res. of Or. v. Smith*, 494 U.S. 872 (1993).
447. *City of Boerne v. Flores*, 521 U.S. 507, 532–536 (1997) (holding that the federal RFRA exceeded Congress's enforcement powers insofar as it applied to the states); *Gonzales v. O Centro Espirita Beneficente Uniao do Vegetal*, 546 U.S. 418, 424 & n.1 (2006) (explaining that RFRA still applies to federal government action).
448. *Burwell v. Hobby Lobby Stores, Inc.*, 573 U.S. 682, 707–708 (2014).
449. 1 U.S.C. § 1 (2018).
450. *Hobby Lobby Stores, Inc.*, 573 U.S. at 707–708.
451. *Ibid.*, at 706–707.
452. *Ibid.*, at 707 (internal quotation marks deleted).
453. *Ibid.*, at 717 (noting that "numerous practical restraints would likely prevent" publicly traded corporations from making frequent RFRA claims, such as the improbability "that unrelated shareholders—including institutional investors with their own set of stake holders—would agree to run a corporation under the same religious beliefs").
454. *Ibid.*, at 710 (internal quotation marks omitted) (quoting *Emp. Div., Dep't of Hum. Res. of Or. v. Smith*, 494 U.S. 872, 877 (1993)).
455. *Ibid.*, at 717 n.28.

Chapter 3. Organizational Religious Freedom

§1. Right to Religious Schools

181. One of the early cases where the Court recognized an institutional dimension to religious freedom involved the right of parents to send their children to religiously affiliated schools. In *Pierce v. Society of the Sisters of the Holy Names of Jesus and Mary*, two private organizations filed suit against the governor of Oregon, as well as others, to enjoin enforcement of the Compulsory Education Act of 1922.[456] The Act required that all children between the ages of eight and sixteen attend public schools during the school year. One of the plaintiff organizations ran private primary, high school, and junior college schools, which taught Roman Catholic doctrine as part of the curriculum. Public officers threatened to enforce the Act. The organization alleged that enforcement would damage both their business and property. In its decision, the Supreme Court recognized that parents have a constitutional right "to direct the upbringing and education" of their children without unreasonable inference from the government.[457] This includes the right to send their children to private, religious schools.[458] For further discussion of religious schools, *see* Part IX (Education), Chapter 2 (Religious Schools).

§2. Finances of Religious Communities

182. Religious organizations in the United States rely almost entirely on member donations for their financing. Such organizations can solicit donations without any direct government supervision or oversight. But rules governing nonprofit organizations' use and solicitation of funds create an oversight mechanism for abusive practices such as fraud and theft.[459] Because of the special constitutional position of religion, the IRS grants most religious organizations greater latitude in the management of their finances than other nonprofit organizations. In addition, the usual IRS disclosure rules do not apply.[460] For further discussion of the financing of religious communities, *see* Part VIII (Financing of Religious Communities), Chapter 1 (Direct Financing) and Chapter 2 (Indirect Financing).

183. Congress has imposed special limitations, found in section 7611 of the Internal Revenue Code, on how and when the IRS may conduct civil tax inquiries and examinations of "churches" (a generic term the IRS uses for places of worship that meet requirements for specific tax rules).[461] The IRS may only conduct a church

456. *Pierce v. Soc'y of the Sisters of the Holy Names of Jesus & Mary*, 268 U.S. 510 (1925).
457. *Ibid.*, at 534–535 (citing *Meyer v. Nebraska*, 262 U.S. 390 (1923)).
458. *Ibid.*
459. *See Charitable Solicitation—State Requirements*, IRS, https://www.irs.gov/charities-non-profits/charitable-organizations/charitable-solicitation-state-requirements (last visited Sep. 30, 2023).
460. *See* Internal Revenue Serv., Pub. No. 1828, *Tax Guide for Churches & Religious Organizations* 30–31, https://www.irs.gov/pub/irs-pdf/p1828.pdf (last visited Sep. 30, 2023) [hereinafter *Tax Guide for Churches & Religious Organizations*].
461. *Ibid.*, at 1, 31, 33.

tax inquiry if "an appropriate high-level Treasury official reasonably believes" there is a violation.[462] The reasonable belief must be based on "facts and circumstances recorded in writing" that an organization either does not qualify for an exemption generally or is engaged in an unrelated activity that should be subject to appropriate taxation.[463] To date, section 7611 has not been interpreted, discussed, or reviewed in any case by the Supreme Court. The only other oversight of churches related to the IRS is via the US House of Representatives Ways and Means Oversight Subcommittee, which over the past several decades has held hearings to address concerns about certain churches' tax-exempt status and exempt activities.[464]

184. The State Attorney General (or similar state authority) in the state where a nonprofit organization is incorporated or organized also has authority to bring a suit on behalf of the public if those who control a nonprofit's finances and activities conduct abusive practices. For a more detailed discussion of nonprofit organizations, *see* Part III (Legal Status of Religious Communities), Chapter 1 (Formal Status of Religious Communities).

§3. Church Autonomy

185. An essential component of the religion clauses of the First Amendment is the right of religious communities to govern themselves without state interference. This right includes the freedom to "independently determine their own doctrines and teachings, their missions, their organizational and communal structures …, and in general, their own authentic natures and aspirations".[465] Of particular note are the Supreme Court decisions in *Hosanna-Tabor Evangelical Lutheran Church and School v. EEOC* and *Our Lady of Guadalupe School v. Morrissey-Berru.*[466] In *Hosanna-Tabor*, a teacher hired by the member congregation was fired after threatening to file a lawsuit under the Americans with Disabilities Act (ADA). The teacher and the Equal Employment Opportunity Commission then brought suit alleging retaliation and unlawful dismissal in violation of the ADA. Hosanna-Tabor maintained that, under the First Amendment's religion clauses, a "ministerial exception" exempted the school from the ADA's employment requirements with respect to employees who were also ministers. The Supreme Court held that both the Free

462. I.R.C. § 7611 (2018); *see also Special Rules Limiting IRS Authority to Audit a Church*, IRS, https://www.irs.gov/charities-non-profits/churches-religious-organizations/special-rules-limiting-irs-authority-to-audit-a-church (last updated Apr. 25, 2023).

463. I.R.C. § 7611.

464. *See, e.g.*, Staff of the J. Comm. on Tax'n, JCX-29-05, Historical Development and Present Law of the Federal Tax Exemption for Charities and Other Tax-Exempt Organizations (Apr. 19, 2005), https://www.jct.gov/CMSPages/GetFile.aspx?guid=91d1c71d-866b-4423-84a7-0f1ec352edf8 (summarizing the development of federal tax exemptions for charitable and other organizations, in preparation for a House Ways and Means Committee public hearing).

465. W. Cole Durham, Jr. & Brett G. Scharffs, *Law and Religion: National, International, and Comparative Perspectives* 433 (2d ed. 2019).

466. *Hosanna-Tabor Evangelical Lutheran Church & Sch. v. EEOC*, 565 U.S. 171 (2012); *Our Lady of Guadalupe Sch. v. Morrissey-Berru*, 140 S. Ct. 2049 (2020).

Exercise and Establishment Clauses mandated the inclusion of a ministerial exception to generally applicable labor laws. Writing for a unanimous Court, Chief Justice John Roberts explained, "The Establishment Clause prevents the Government from appointing ministers, and the Free Exercise Clause prevents it from interfering with the freedom of religious groups to select their own".[467] In other words, religious communities are free to select their own leaders and terminate their employment in accordance with the methods and qualifications they deem appropriate.

186. Hosanna-Tabor did not resolve disagreement among federal courts of appeals as to who qualifies as a minister for purposes of the ministerial exception. In 2020, the Supreme Court addressed the issue in *Our Lady of Guadalupe School v. Morrissey-Berru.*[468] Two elementary school teachers filed separate discrimination claims against their Catholic schools after their teaching contracts were not renewed. A central question was whether the teachers qualified as ministers for purposes of the ministerial exception. Reflecting on the factors relevant to identifying a "minister" in *Hosanna-Tabor*, the Court reasoned that relevant factors will not be the same in every case, nor will occupation title and formal religious training always determine whether an individual is a minister. Instead, the Court explained, "What matters, at bottom, is what an employee *does*."[469] The Court found that the teachers' core responsibilities qualified them as ministers, including responsibilities to guide their students "toward the goal of living their lives in accordance with their faith" and "playing a vital part in carrying out the mission of the church".[470] The applicability of the ministerial exception to hostile work environment claims and tort claims remains unclear.[471] For more information about the ministerial exception, *see* Part III (Formal Status of Religious Communities), Chapter 2 (Autonomy of Religious Communities).

187. Churches are explicitly exempted from the prohibition on discrimination based on religion in many non-discrimination laws, including some Title VII prohibitions on discrimination in employment. Such exemptions allow religious organizations to give preference to members of their faith in hiring decisions. For a detailed discussion of religious exemptions and employment, *see* Part III (Legal Status of Religious Communities), Chapter 2 (Autonomy of Religious Communities).

---

467. *Hosanna-Tabor*, 565 U.S. at 184.
468. *Morrissey-Berru*, 140 S. Ct. at 2049.
469. *Ibid.*, at 2063–2066 (emphasis added).
470. *Ibid.*, at 2066.
471. *See supra* para. 172.

Part III. Legal Status of Religious Communities

Chapter 1. Formal Status of Religious Communities

§1. Registration and Incorporation

I. No Formal Registration Required

188. The federal government has no department of religious affairs. A religious group's ability to register any legal entity does not depend on government officials' administrative discretion. In fact, to begin operating in the United States, religious organizations are not required to register with the government at all. Legal recognition is advantageous, however, in that it facilitates many dimensions of ordinary operations—including opening bank accounts, renting or buying real property, entering into contracts, and clarifying succession rights in church property.

189. Most religious organizations in the United States qualify as "churches"[472] under federal law; as such, they are automatically considered by the federal Internal Revenue Service (IRS) to have legal status as tax-exempt nonprofit "501(c)(3)" organizations.[473] Churches are not required to obtain an IRS declaration of 501(c)(3) status before claiming tax exemptions, but many seek such official recognition so they can guarantee income tax exemptions to donors.[474] For more information, *see* this chapter, section 2 (Definition of Religion), below; and Part VIII (Financing of Religious Communities), Chapter 2 (Indirect Financing).

190. Legal registration as a 501(c)(3) organization or other entity is typically a matter of filling out a few forms and paying a small fee.[475] State law governs the

472. The IRS uses "church" and "churches" as generic terms of art. *See Tax Guide for Churches & Religious Organizations*, *supra* n. 460, at 1.

473. Tax-exempt status for religious organizations is derived from I.R.C. section 501(c)(3) (2018). *See also Tax Guide for Churches & Religious Organizations*, *supra* n. 460, at 2, 33.

474. *Tax Guide for Churches & Religious Organizations*, *supra* n. 460, at 2–3.

475. *See* 1 Durham et al., *supra* n. 157, § 10:2 (*Forming Corporations Used for Religious Purposes*) (citing Patty Gerstenblith, *Associational Structures of Religious Organizations*, *in Religious Organizations in the United States: A Study of Identity, Liberty, and the Law* 223, 226 (James A. Serritella et al. eds., 2006) (originally published in 1995 BYU L. Rev. 439)).

recognition of legal structures such as corporations, associations, and trusts.[476] Thus, the legal mechanisms available for religious organizations to register as these types of entities vary somewhat from state to state.[477]

II. Forms of Religious Organizations

191. While religious organizations in the United States most frequently form nonprofit corporations, a wide variety of other legal structures are available, including informal associations, trusts, for-profit corporations, and partnerships (a form of business association limited to for-profit businesses).[478] Each legal form has characteristic advantages and limitations.

192. In the 1990s, the DePaul Center for Church/State Studies found that religious organizations adopted organizational structures in the following percentages:

Religious not-for-profit corporation	87%
Unincorporated association	8%
Not-for-profit corporation	3%
Charitable/religious trust	1%
Corporation sole	1%
For-profit corporation	1%
Other	1%[479]

476. *Ibid.*

477. *Ibid.*, § 10:2 (*Forming Corporations Used for Religious Purposes*), § 10:50 (*Chart: State Incorporation Resources for Nonprofit Organizations*).

478. Compare to the United Kingdom, where religious organizations typically are trusts. *Ibid.*, § 9:2 (*History of Legal Organizations for Religious Organizations*), § 9:4 (*Chart: Advantages and Disadvantages of Different Legal Organization Structures*); James J. Fishman, *The Development of Nonprofit Corporation Law and an Agenda for Reform*, 34 Emory L.J. 617, 620–621 (1985). For information on partnerships, *see* Robert R. Keatinge & Ann E. Conaway, *Keatinge and Conaway on Choice of Business Entity: Selecting Form and Structure for a Closely Held Business* § 2:5 (*Organic Statutes-Partnership Statutes*), Westlaw CHOICEBE (database updated Oct. 2023) (citing Unif. Partnership Act § 6(a) (1914); *ibid.*, § 202(a) (1997); *ibid.*, § 102(11) (2013)) ("Statutes governing general partnerships provide the basis upon which most of the organic statutes regulating all unincorporated business organizations are based. The principal organic statutes governing general partnerships are: (1) UPA [Uniform Partnership Act] (1914), which at one point had been adopted in all states except Louisiana, and (2) UPA (1997), sometimes referred to as "RUPA," [Revised Uniform Partnership Act] which has been adopted in the majority of the states. … General partnerships have several characteristics that differ significantly from corporation statutes. Unlike corporation, limited partnership, and limited liability company organic statutes, the organic statutes governing general partnerships define the rules that apply when two or more persons associate as co-owners *to conduct a business for profit*." (emphasis added) (footnotes omitted)).

479. Patty Gerstenblith, *Associational Structures of Religious Organizations*, *supra* n. 475, at 225 (citing Center for Church/State Studies, DePaul University College of Law, 1994 Report on the Survey of Religious Organizations at the National Level, Q4 (unpublished survey on file with the Center for Church/State Studies, DePaul University College of Law)).

193. The religious not-for-profit corporation structure used by most religious organizations offers several advantages over the usual nonprofit corporation, such as not being subject to certain IRS auditing procedures.[480]

194. Occasionally, a religious organization will choose to form as a for-profit corporation to avoid restrictions placed on nonprofit corporations. For example, a for-profit corporation enjoys a much broader scope of protection for political speech, and the rules barring private inurement of the corporation's directors are not applicable. The disadvantage of the for-profit structure is that it is not exempt from taxes.[481] More frequently, religious organizations set up separate for-profit corporations, which are subject to ordinary taxes and other regulations, to carry out their business activities.

195. Religious groups sometimes have religious reasons for favoring a particular form of legal organization.[482] Considerations such as legal liability, organizational efficiency, disposition of property in the event of dissolution, and tax advantages also affect decisions about legal structure.[483] A religious organization may choose to create several legal entities, which may take a variety of legal forms, to carry out various aspects of its mission.[484]

196. The legal forms available to religious organizations vary from state to state. Some states have unique legal regimes, most notably New York and California. Some legal structures, such as a corporation sole, are not available in every state.[485] Even two states that offer the same choice of entities may have different requirements for formation and different legal regimes under which the rules are administered. To address these differences, the American Bar Association developed the Model Nonprofit Corporation Act (MNCA), a model set of statutes states can adapt

480. I.R.C. § 7611 (2018).

481. Of course, a religious organization, even if generally exempt from taxes as a 501(c)(3) organization, may have to pay taxes on business income "unrelated to their tax-exempt purposes", such as gift shops, coffee shops, raffle sales, or other for-profit enterprises run by the church. *See Tax Guide for Churches & Religious Organizations*, *supra* n. 460, at 19–21; *see also Jimmy Swaggart Ministries v. Bd. of Equalization of Cal.*, 493 U.S. 378, 392 (1990).

482. *See generally* 1 Durham et al., *supra* n. 157, ch. 8 (*Legal Entities and Religious Polity*), ch. 9 (*Legal Organization Choices of Religious Organizations*).

483. *Ibid.*, §§ 8:19–8:26 (*Initial Considerations When Choosing a Legal Structure*), § 9:1 (*Overview of Legal Organization Choices*).

484. At English Common Law each congregation of the Church of England was a separate legal entity. This model has been continued by some, but certainly not all, American religious organizations. In The Church of Jesus Christ of Latter-day Saints, for example, each congregation is not a separate legal entity but rather an internal division of the Church. Religious organizations may also choose to create legal entities that are affiliated with, but not technically part of, the official "church" function; for example, Brigham Young University is an independent educational entity affiliated with The Church of Jesus Christ of Latter-day Saints. *See ibid.*, § 8:1 (*Introduction to Legal Entities*); *see also generally ibid.*, ch. 8 (*Legal Entities and Religious Polity*).

485. *Ibid.*, § 9:26 (*Corporation Sole*) (citing, *inter alia*, James B. O'Hara, *The Modern Corporation Sole*, 93 Dick. L. Rev. 23, 30–31 (1988)).

or adopt, in whole or in part, to govern nonprofit corporations.[486] Most states have enacted some version of the MNCA, providing a measure of consistency in rules governing nonprofit formation. *See also* Part I (Legal Framework and Sources), Chapter 2 (Other Legislation with Regard to Religion).

III. Mechanics of Registration

197. The requirements for creating a nonprofit corporation are similar in each state.[487] In Texas, for example, the process consists of (1) choosing a name that is available, distinguishable, and legal; (2) filing a certificate of formation with the Texas Secretary of State; (3) preparing bylaws; and (4) holding an organizational meeting with the board of directors.[488] The required state forms are generally simple to complete, inexpensive to file, and fast to process: Texas charges a USD 25 filing fee to process and issue a certificate of formation, which is completed generally within five to seven business days of submission.[489] After the initial formation procedure, a Texas nonprofit corporation may apply for and be granted federal and state tax exemptions.[490] Similarly simple mechanisms are available for organizing under alternative legal structures.

IV. Role of State Attorneys General in Oversight

198. Unlike for-profit corporations, nonprofit corporations do not have shareholders who may sue the corporation's officers. Therefore, the state attorney general is typically assigned as the authority to sue any trustees, officers, or directors who allegedly violate the law or their fiduciary duties to the nonprofit. This authority has been extended to other legal structures used by religious organizations.[491] An attorney general's authority is discretionary, and the attorney general cannot be compelled to bring an action against a religious organization. It is rare for the attorney general to sue religious leaders for their exercise of trust in the operation of a church. More common are legal actions against religious groups or their leaders to

486. The Model Nonprofit Corporation Act (MNCA) has undergone several revisions since its original drafting in 1952, with the fourth edition published in 2021. *See* ABA Nonprofit Orgs. Comm., Model Nonprofit Corporation Act (4th ed. 2021).

487. "Although each state has its own unique statutory provisions regarding the incorporation of a nonprofit or other corporations used for religious purposes, the provisions generally contain common elements, including 'a purpose clause, a procedure to incorporate, an enumeration of general powers, a method for merger and dissolution, and a provision for distribution of assets upon dissolution'". Patty Gerstenblith, *Associational Structures of Religious Organizations*, *supra* n. 475, at 226–227.

488. Texas CBAR, *Forming a Nonprofit Tax-Exempt Corporation in Texas* 5–12 (2018), https://www.sos.state.tx.us/corp/nonprofit_org.shtml (link to PDF) (last visited Sep. 30, 2023).

489. *Filing & Other General FAQs*, Tex. Sec'y State, http://www.sos.state.tx.us/corp/filingandothergeneralfaqs.shtml (last visited Sep. 30, 2023); *Business Filings & Trademarks Fee Schedule*, Tex. Sec'y State, https://direct.sos.state.tx.us/help/help-corp.asp?pg=fee (last visited Sep. 30, 2023).

490. Texas CBAR, *Forming a Nonprofit Tax-Exempt Corporation in Texas*, *supra* n. 488, at 10–14.

491. *See* 1 Durham et al., *supra* n. 157, § 11:56 (*Attorneys General*).

enforce ordinary provisions of civil and criminal law involving, for example, financial mismanagement or improper personal emolument of those who control a church's finances.[492]

§2. Definition of Religion

199. The question of what qualifies as a religion occasionally arises in certain contexts, such as in tax law (where a group may be seeking tax-exempt status as a religious organization) or in laws dealing with employment discrimination. Under US law, religion is defined pragmatically, rather than by an ontological or metaphysical approach, and depends on the particular legal issue in question. For tax law purposes, a "religion" is an organization that is exclusively religious in purpose and meets several listed criteria.[493] Yet for purposes of conscientious objection, the definition of "religion" depends on how fundamental a particular belief is to the individual's subjective belief system.[494] In determining whether something is a "religion" or "religious", US courts have utilized a variety of general approaches introduced by social scientists.[495]

I. Categories of Definitions

A. *Essentialist*

200. An essentialist definition of religion looks for an essential characteristic that is common to all religions. For example, this approach may focus on belief in a Supreme Being and an afterlife. Essentialists acknowledge the existence of features that most religions share but accept that all are not necessary for a movement or belief system to be defined as a religion. Early US Supreme Court decisions often

492. *See, e.g.*, *Att'y Gen. v. First United Baptist Church of Lee*, 601 A.2d 96 (Me. 1992) (upholding lower court's decision ordering church to give accounting of trust assets); *Att'y Gen. v. Clark*, 167 Mass. 201 (1896); 1 Durham et al., *supra* n. 157, § 10:11 (*Articles of Incorporation-Protecting Religious Polity*) (citing *People ex rel. Deukmejian v. Worldwide Church of God, Inc.*, 178 Cal. Rptr. 913 (Cal. Ct. App. 1981); *Worldwide Church of God, Inc. v. California*, 623 F.2d 613 (9th Cir. 1980)), § 11:47 (*Misappropriation of Funds*), § 11:56 (*Attorneys General*); 9 B.E. Witkin et al., Witkin Summary of California Law, at ch. XIII.X.D, § 404 (*Examination by Attorney General*), Westlaw WITSUM (database updated May 2023) ("The [California] Attorney General has broad authority to supervise public benefit corporations. ... The Attorney General's supervision of religious corporations is limited."); Barry W. Taylor, *Diversion of Church Funds to Personal Use: State, Federal and Private Sanctions*, 73 J. Crim. L. & Criminology 1204 (1982).

493. *See infra* para. 210. Federal regulations interpret exclusively" religious to mean "primarily" religious in purpose. Treas. Reg. § 1.501(c)(3)-1(c) (2022).

494. *See supra* para. 150.

495. *See generally* W. Cole Durham, Jr. & Elizabeth A. Clark (Sewell), *Definition of Religion*, *in Religious Organizations in the United States: A Study of Identity, Liberty, and the Law* 3 (James A. Serritella et al. eds., 2006); Durham & Scharffs, *Law and Religion*, *supra* n. 465, 39–58.

utilized essentialist approaches. In an 1890 case, for example, the Court defined religion in terms of one's belief in, reverence for, and obedience to a Creator.[496]

201. Critics charge that the essentialist approach relies excessively on definitions that assume the metaphysical reality of the thing they define and, therefore, cannot provide an objective view.[497]

B. Functionalist

202. From a functionalist's perspective, popular among social scientists of the twentieth century, religion should be defined by its effects. Functionalists look at the behaviors that religion produces in its adherents and the role that it plays in an individual's life and in society. "In this view, anything that plays the role of a religion is, by definition, a religion."[498] For example, *United States v. Seeger* involved would-be conscientious objectors who wished to be exempt from a military draft; they had moral objections to military service even though those objections were not based on belonging to any traditional religious sect.[499] The right to conscientious objection, the Court held, must extend to individuals whose opposition to war is as central to their belief system as a Supreme Being is to followers of more traditional religions.[500] In other words, the Court examined the role belief played in the objectors' lives. In recent decades, functional definitions have often comprised simple lists of intrinsic factors in religions. Such definitions have been criticized as either over- or under-inclusive.[501]

C. Limited Deference

203. The limited deference approach seeks to allow religious communities to be defined on their own terms, while maintaining the authority of the state to ultimately decide whether to recognize or protect particular "religious" groups and

---

496. *Davis v. Beason*, 133 U.S. 333, 342 (1890); *see also United States v. MacIntosh*, 283 U.S. 605, 627, 633–634 (1931) (Hughes, C.J., dissenting) ("The essence of religion is belief in a relation to God involving duties superior to those arising from any human relation.")

497. Durham & Clark, *Definition of Religion, supra* n. 495, at 9.

498. Durham & Scharffs, *Law and Religion, supra* n. 465, at 48.

499. *United States v. Seeger*, 380 U.S. 163 (1965).

500. *Ibid.*, at 165–166, 185 ("[W]e hasten to emphasize that while the 'truth' of a belief is not open to question, there remains the significant question whether it is 'truly held.' This is the threshold question of sincerity [and]a prime consideration to the validity of every claim for exemption as a conscientious objector."). *Seeger* has been applied by lower courts considering the definition of religion. *See, e.g., Fallon v. Mercy Cath. Med. Ctr. of Se. Pa.*, 877 F.3d 487, 490–491 (3d Cir. 2017); *see also St. Augustine Sch. v. Evers*, 906 F.3d 591, 605 n.15 (7th Cir. 2018) (Ripple, J., dissenting), *vacated*, 141 S. Ct. 186 (2020) (mem.); *Real Alternatives, Inc. v. Sec'y Dep't of HHS*, 867 F.3d 338, 349 (3d Cir. 2017) (echoing lower court's finding that a nonprofit anti-abortion organization was "an employer, a company, and not a belief system … and its single mission statement cannot guide believers comprehensively throughout life as a religion can" (internal quotation marks omitted)).

501. Durham & Clark, *Definition of Religion, supra* n. 495, at 9–11.

activities.[502] The deference given to would-be religious communities helps guard against intentional and unintentional discriminatory state behavior.

II. Church of Scientology Cases

204. The Church of Scientology's fight for religious classification illustrates the limited deference approach. Author L. Ron Hubbard organized and incorporated the first Church of Scientology in 1953, based on his writings.[503] The Church's umbrella organization, Church of Scientology International (often called the "Mother Church"), was organized the following year in California.[504] Although the Mother Church of Scientology was granted 501(c)(3) tax-exempt status in 1957, a "battle between Scientology and the Internal Revenue Service began in 1967" when the IRS revoked that status.[505] The Mother Church challenged the revocation, which was upheld by both the Tax Court and the Ninth Circuit Court of Appeals. In response, "[t]he Church of Scientology began a two-pronged plan to win back tax-exempt status. It began a campaign of constant litigation against the IRS, coupled with organized harassment, and began reshaping its "creed" into a form more consistent with traditional religion."[506] In October 1993, the IRS once again granted the Mother Church tax exemption under section 501(c)(3) of the Internal Revenue Code (I.R.C.).[507]

205. During this same time period, the US Supreme Court heard *Hernandez v. Commissioner*, examining the tax deductibility of Scientologists' payments to the Church of Scientology in exchange for counselling meetings (known as "auditing") with Scientologist officials.[508] The Supreme Court affirmed the rulings of both the Tax Court and the appellate courts and ruled that payments for these services were not "charitable contributions" under I.R.C. section 170 because they involved a

502. *Ibid.*, at 33–55.

503. *How Did Scientology Start*, Scientology Newsroom, https://www.scientologynews.org/faq/how-did-scientology-start.html (last visited Sep. 30, 2023).

504. *Scientology Religion*, Scientology Newsroom, https://www.scientologynews.org/quick-facts/scientology.html; *Church of Scientology International*, Scientology Newsroom, https://www.scientologynews.org/quick-facts/church-of-scientology-international.html (last visited Sep. 30, 2023).

505. James Walsh, *Tax Treatment of the Church of Scientology in the United States and the United Kingdom*, 19 Suffolk Transnat'l L. Rev. 331, 337–338 & n.39 (1995) ("An extensive audit of the Church's records revealed that church income was inuring to the benefit of L. Ron Hubbard and Scientology practitioners. *Church of Scientology v. Comm'r*, 83 T.C. 381, 404 (1984), *aff'd*, 823 F.2d 1310 (9th Cir. 1987).").

506. *Ibid.*, at 338.

507. *Ibid.*, at 339 ("While commentators have suggested that the IRS in fact succumbed to intimidation by granting tax exempt status to the Scientologists in … 1993, the IRS explained that a two year examination revealed that Scientology was a religious organization within the scope of … section 501(c)(3).").

508. *Hernandez v. Comm'r*, 490 U.S. 680, 683–689 (1989). The Church of Scientology provides religious services, known as "auditing" to its members in exchange for a "fixed donation"—at the time of the lawsuit, between USD 625 and 4,250. *Ibid.*, at 684–685. The Church of Scientology teaches that such payments are necessary under the "doctrine of exchange". *Ibid.*, at 685.

quid pro quo for payment.[509] The Court rejected the Church's arguments (1) that the payments should not be considered a *quid pro quo* arrangement because the benefits were entirely religious and (2) that denying the tax deduction violated the First Amendment's religion clauses.[510] The Court also found I.R.C. section 170 to be "neutral both in design and purpose" and not born of animus toward religions like Scientology, which earn funds from fixed costs imposed for "participation in certain religious practices".[511] The limited deference approach allowed the government to grant a degree of autonomy to the Church of Scientology in defining itself as a religion (within certain limits, as shown by the Mother Church's struggle to regain tax-exempt status) while drawing lines at activities (e.g., paying for "auditing") that were, for tax purposes, more transactional in nature.

III. Tax-Exempt Status

206. Tax-exempt status is granted to religious organizations under section 501(c)(3) of the Internal Revenue Code, and tax-exempt organizations are often referred to colloquially as "501(c)(3)s". The exemption covers organizations that are "organized and operated" for exclusively religious purposes, as well as foundations whose purpose is exclusively charitable, scientific, literary, safety, educational, humane, or athletic. The tax exemption does not apply to organizations whose income benefits private individuals, whose net earnings are used to endorse or oppose a candidate for public office in any way, or whose activities substantially consist of distributing propaganda, lobbying, or otherwise attempting to influence legislation.

207. A religious organization's ability to qualify as tax-exempt depends on whether it meets the organizational and operational requirements of I.R.C. section 501(c)(3). To pass the organizational test, the organization's purpose must be expressly religious. This purpose can be verified either in the written document creating the legal entity or in the bylaws, one of which must state that the entity is organized exclusively for one of the tax-exempt purposes set forth in section 501(c)(3).[512] The operational test examines whether an organization operates as an exempt organization, focusing on its ongoing activities.[513] As mentioned above, the operational test also denies tax-exempt status to organizations that are substantially involved in politics or for-profit activities.[514] For additional discussion, *see* Part V (Religion and Politics), Chapter 1 (Religious Influence in Politics); Part VIII (Financing of Religious Communities), Chapter 2 (Indirect Financing); and Part XI (Religion and Culture), Chapter 4 (Religion and Public Debate).

---

509. *Ibid.*, at 689–694.
510. *Ibid.*, at 694–702.
511. *Ibid.*, at 695–698.
512. 26 C.F.R. § 1.501(c)(3)-1(b) (2022). Federal regulations interpret "exclusively" religious to mean "primarily" religious in purpose. Treas. Reg. § 1.501(c)(3)-1(c) (2022).
513. *Ibid.*, § 1.501(c)(3)-1(c).
514. *Ibid.*, § 1.501(c)(3)-1; Rev. Rul. 2007-41, 2007-25 I.R.B. 1421.

208. The legal structure of a religious organization does not affect its ability to qualify as tax-exempt. Indeed, "a church may simply hold itself out as tax exempt and receive the benefit of that status without applying for" and obtaining official IRS recognition of tax-exempt status under I.R.C. section 501(c)(3).[515] Individuals who donate to churches that qualify for tax-exempt status under 501(c)(3) but have not sought or received IRS recognition of that status may still claim their donations as "charitable deductions" for federal income tax purposes.[516] However, many organizations seek official "IRS recognition of tax-exempt status because that recognition provides reliance to church leaders, members, and contributors that a church … is eligible to receive tax-deductible contributions".[517]

209. Religious organizations, referred to collectively as "churches" in regulations, are not required to file an annual tax return.[518] However, religious organizations that qualify for income tax exemptions under section 501(c)(3) may still need to pay other taxes. These may include unrelated business taxes, as well as state and local government taxes and assessments.[519] State laws may be more or less restrictive than section 501(c)(3) in granting tax exemptions to religious organizations. For further discussion, *see* Part VIII (Financing of Religious Communities), Chapter 2 (Indirect Financing).

IV. "Church"

210. No commonly accepted definition of "church" exists in US law. The IRS distinguishes, however, between "churches" and "religious organizations" in its application of certain tax rules. For example, organizations that qualify as "churches" and meet section 501(c)(3) requirements "are automatically considered tax exempt and are not required to apply for and obtain recognition of tax-exempt status from the IRS".[520] Moreover, "churches" qualify for the application of special auditing rules.[521] To determine which organizations qualify as churches, the IRS considers fourteen characteristics:[522]

(1) distinct legal existence,
(2) recognized creed and form of worship,
(3) definite and distinct ecclesiastical government,
(4) formal code of doctrine and discipline,
(5) distinct religious history,

515. 4 Durham et al., *supra* n. 178, § 32:3 (*Federal Income Tax Privileges Accorded to Religious Organizations*) (citing I.R.C. § 508(c)(1)(A)).
516. I.R.C. § 170 (2018).
517. *Churches, Integrated Auxiliaries, and Conventions or Associations of Churches*, IRS, https://www.irs.gov/charities-non-profits/churches-integrated-auxiliaries-and-conventions-or-associations-of-churches (last updated Apr. 26, 2023).
518. I.R.C. § 508(c)(1)(A).
519. *Ibid.*, § 512.
520. *Tax Guide for Churches & Religious Organizations*, *supra* n. 460, at 3.
521. *Ibid.*, at 1, 31–32.
522. *Ibid.*, at 33.

(6) membership not associated with any other church or denomination,
(7) organization of ordained ministers,
(8) ordained ministers selected after completing prescribed courses of study,
(9) literature of its own,
(10) established places of worship,
(11) regular congregations,
(12) regular religious services,
(13) Sunday schools for religious instruction of the young, and
(14) schools for the preparation of its ministers.

Not one of these factors is considered required; rather, "[t]he IRS generally uses a combination of these characteristics, together with other facts and circumstances, to determine whether an organization is considered a church for tax exemption purposes".[523] Additionally, the IRS is careful to note that it "makes no attempt to evaluate the content of whatever doctrine a particular organization claims is religious" but only requires that "the particular beliefs of the organization are truly and sincerely held by those professing them and the practices and rites associated with the organization's belief or creed are not illegal or contrary to clearly defined public policy".[524] The IRS has gained media attention when it has recognized as 'churches' organizations considered by some to be anti-religious or otherwise controversial.[525]

523. *Ibid.*, at 33.
524. *Ibid.*
525. *See, e.g.*, Sarah Pulliam Bailey, *Major Evangelical Nonprofits Are Trying a New Strategy with the IRS That Allows Them to Hide Their Salaries*, Wash. Post (Jan. 17, 2020), https://www.washingtonpost.com/religion/2020/01/17/major-evangelical-nonprofits-are-trying-new-strategy-with-irs-that-allows-them-hide-their-salaries; Roberta Medford, Opinion, *In Theory: The IRS Gave Nonprofit Status to a Satanic Church. Will All Hell Break Loose?*, L.A. Times (Jul. 2, 2019), https://www.latimes.com/socal/burbank-leader/opinion/tn-blr-me-intheory-20190702-story.html.

Chapter 2. Autonomy of Religious Communities

§1. General Principles

211. Religious communities in the United States enjoy a high degree of freedom in how they structure and govern their religious organization. This autonomy is rooted in the basic concept of non-establishment and expressed in ideas including separation of church and state, non-entanglement, and church autonomy.

I. Separation of Religion and the State

212. The phrase "separation of church and state" is not found in any of the United States' founding documents. However, Thomas Jefferson used a similar phrase in a letter written to the Danbury Baptist Association of Danbury, Connecticut, in response to their complaint about infringement on their religious liberties by the Connecticut state legislature.[526] The US Supreme Court quoted Jefferson's metaphor of "a wall of separation between church and State" in an important nineteenth-century case, calling it an "authoritative declaration of the scope and effect" of the Establishment Clause.[527]

213. Jefferson's figure of speech has been invoked frequently by the Supreme Court.[528] However, many scholars and some Supreme Court justices do not believe the metaphor is helpful in determining the meaning and scope of non-establishment.[529] Even proponents of the metaphor's use have recognized challenges in its application.[530] Perhaps unsurprisingly, then, the history of the Supreme Court's use of the concept has proven arbitrary to some extent, rather than reflecting fixed legal principles.[531] Whatever its limitations, the concept of separation does both illuminate and reflect the idea of institutional autonomy of both religion and the state.

---

526. Letter from Thomas Jefferson to Danbury, Connecticut, Baptist Association (Jan. 1, 1802) (The Thomas Jefferson Papers at the Library of Congress: Series 1, General Correspondence, 1651 to 1827, Manuscript Division), https://www.loc.gov/item/mtjbib010955 (last visited Sep. 30, 2023).
527. *Reynolds v. United States*, 98 U.S. 145, 164 (1878).
528. *See, e.g.*, *Everson v. Bd. of Educ.*, 330 U.S. 1, 16 (1947).
529. *See, e.g.*, Ronald F. Thiemann, *Religion in American Public Life: A Dilemma for Democracy* 164–168 (1996) (asserting that introducing the concept of separation into the Court's jurisprudence led to confusion because "[t]he only sense in which religious communities and the modern welfare state are to remain 'separate' is that neither should exercise final authority over the values, beliefs and practices of the other"); *Wallace v. Jaffree*, 472 U.S. 38, 84, 107 (1985) (Rehnquist, J., dissenting) ("The 'wall of separation between church and State' is a metaphor based on bad history, a metaphor which has proved useless as a guide to judging. It should be frankly and explicitly abandoned.").
530. *See, e.g.*, *Illinois ex rel. McCollum v. Bd. of Educ.*, 333 U.S. 203, 232, 237–238 (1948) (Jackson, J., concurring) ("The task of separating the secular from the religious in education is one of magnitude, intricacy and delicacy.").
531. *Cf.* Marci A. Hamilton, *The Endorsement Factor*, 43 Ariz. St. L.J. 349, 351–352 (2011) (describing the conflicting perspectives of Supreme Court justices on the *Lemon* test).

II. Historical Significance of Non-entanglement

214. Another important concept in Establishment Clause jurisprudence has been the idea of non-entanglement. In 1971, the Supreme Court articulated a three-pronged test for Establishment Clause cases in *Lemon v. Kurtzman.*[532] The first and second prongs focused on the purpose and effect of a law and whether it advanced or favored religion. The third prong focused on whether the law or practice would create "undue entanglement" of church and state. Although many courts—and even Supreme Court justices—were critical of it, the *Lemon* test was the dominant test in Establishment Clause jurisprudence for fifty years.[533] In 2022, however, the Supreme Court abrogated the *Lemon* test in *Kennedy v. Bremerton School District*, concluding the Court had clearly abandoned the test in previous cases.[534] It is unclear how or if the principle of non-entanglement will survive outside of the *Lemon* test. But because Establishment Clause jurisprudence has often referenced or relied on the concept of non-entanglement, even prior to *Lemon*, it is important to understand where and how the Supreme Court has employed it.

215. Non-entanglement has arisen in cases involving internal church disputes, for example.[535] In this context, the non-entanglement principle meant that courts would not only defer to decisions made by "properly authorized leaders" of religious organizations but would also give "legal protection and implementation" to those decisions.[536] This deferential approach has contrasted with the other primary method of addressing internal church disputes, which employs religiously neutral principles of law and secular legal tools. How far the non-entanglement principle reaches has been a matter of some disagreement. However, courts have consistently

---

532. *Lemon v. Kurtzman*, 403 U.S. 602, 612–613 (1971), *abrogated by Kennedy v. Bremerton Sch. Dist.*, 142 S. Ct. 2407, 2427–2428 (2022).
533. For a discussion of the *Lemon* test among Supreme Court justices, *see* the majority, plurality, concurring, and dissenting opinions in *Am. Legion v. Am. Humanist Ass'n*, 139 S. Ct. 2067 (2019). For examples of courts applying the *Lemon* analysis, *see Agostini v. Felton*, 521 U.S. 203 (1997); *Bd. of Educ. v. Grumet*, 512 U.S. 687, 717 (1994); *Gaylor v. Mnuchin*, 919 F.3d 420 (7th Cir. 2019); *Wood v. Arnold*, 915 F.3d 308 (4th Cir. 2019); *Buxton v. Kurtinitis*, 862 F.3d 423 (4th Cir. 2017); *Access Fund v. U.S. Dep't of Agric.*, 499 F.3d 1036 (9th Cir. 2007); *Roark v. S. Iron R-1 Sch. Dist.*, 540 F. Supp. 2d 1047 (E.D. Mo. 2008) (discussing first prong of the *Lemon* test), *aff'd in part, rev'd in part on other grounds*, 573 F.3d 556 (8th Cir. 2009). *But see Lynch v. Donnelly*, 465 U.S. 668, 679 (1984) ("[W]e have repeatedly emphasized our unwillingness to be confined to any single test or criterion in [Establishment Clause cases]."); *Brown v. Collier*, 929 F.3d 218, 247 (5th Cir. 2019) (collecting USSC cases saying *Lemon* was not a go-to test); *Doe v. United States*, 901 F.3d 1015, 1019 (8th Cir. 2019) (asserting the USSC had not committed to any one test).
534. *Kennedy*, 142 S. Ct. at 2426–2428 (citing *Am. Legion*, 139 S. Ct. at 2079–2081); *Town of Greece v. Galloway*, 572 U.S. 565, 575–577 (2014)); *see also Groff v. DeJoy*, 600 U.S. 447, 460 & n.7 (2023) (acknowledging *Kennedy*'s abrogation of the *Lemon* test).
535. *See* 2 William W. Bassett, W. Cole Durham Jr., Mark A. Goldfeder & Robert T. Smith, *Religion Organizations and the Law* § 19:5 (*Church Autonomy*), § 19:6 (*The Rule of Deference*), Westlaw RELORGS (database updated Dec. 2022) [hereinafter 2 Durham et al.].
536. *Ibid.*, § 19:6 (*The Rule of Deference*).

employed the principle in two areas: (1) disputes over "the meaning or significance of religious concepts or doctrines" and (2) disputes over who has legitimate authority within the church.[537]

216. The significance of the non-entanglement doctrine is that it resulted not only in the autonomy of religious organizations to make important decisions regarding doctrine and personnel but also in state recognition and enforcement of those decisions. The Supreme Court first articulated this idea in 1871 in *Watson v. Jones*.[538] According to the Court in *Watson*, when a church decides issues such as discipline, faith, or "ecclesiastical rule, custom, or law", then civil courts must recognize such decisions as binding.[539] The Court in *Watson* explained that deferring to religious organizations' decisions about these matters maintains proper jurisdictional separation between church and state.[540]

217. However, not all decisions made by religious organizations are exempt from the oversight and decision-making of civil courts. Specifically, the Supreme Court has allowed courts to use "neutral principles" to address issues that are not strictly religious, for example, property or contract disputes.[541] In addition, in some circumstances, courts can directly address issues regarding religious organizations that involve "fraud, collusion, or arbitrariness".[542] For more on the neutral principles approach in Establishment Clause jurisprudence, *see* this same chapter, below; and Part VIII (Financing of Religious Communities), Chapter 1 (Direct Financing).

III. Belief/Action Distinction

218. One important distinction in US Free Exercise jurisprudence is between belief and action, which is analogous to the distinction between belief and manifestation in human rights jurisprudence. In general, the freedom to believe, sometimes described as freedom of conscience, is absolute, whereas the freedom to act on one's

537. *Ibid.*

538. *Watson v. Jones*, 80 U.S. (13 Wall.) 679 (1871).

539. *Ibid.*, at 727; *see also* Peter Shannon, *Deference or Neutral Principles: The Dual Approach by Civil Courts to Ecclesiastical Disputes*, 49 Canon L. Soc'y Am. Proc. 105 (1987).

540. *Watson*, 80 U.S. at 727–729, 732–734.

541. *See, e.g.*, *Presbyterian Church in the U.S. v. Mary Elizabeth Blue Hull Mem'l Presbyterian Church*, 393 U.S. 440, 449 (1969) ("[T]he First Amendment severely circumscribes the role that civil courts may play in resolving church property disputes. It is obvious, however, that not every civil court decision as to property claimed by a religious organization jeopardizes values protected by the First Amendment. Civil courts do not inhibit free exercise of religion merely by opening their doors to disputes involving church property. And there are neutral principles of law, developed for use in all property disputes, which can be applied without 'establishing' churches to which property is awarded."); *Presbyterian Church in the U.S. v. E. Heights Presbyterian Church*, 167 S.E.2d 658 (Ga. 1969) (applying on remand the USSC's announced rule).

542. *Gonzalez v. Roman Cath. Archbishop of Manila*, 280 U.S. 1, 16 (1929), *abrogated by Serbian E. Orthodox Diocese for the U.S. & Can. v. Milivojevich*, 426 U.S. 696 (1976).

beliefs, or the freedom to act according to one's conscience, is not.[543] In *Cantwell v. Connecticut* (1940), the first case applying the Free Exercise Clause to the states, the Supreme Court reiterated that the First Amendment "embraces two concepts,—freedom to believe and freedom to act. The first is absolute but, in the nature of things, the second cannot be".[544]

219. As discussed earlier, this belief/action dichotomy was first articulated in 1878 in *Reynolds v. United States*, an early Supreme Court case about limitations on the freedom to act based on religious principles.[545] *Reynolds* addressed the religiously motivated practice of polygamy, then engaged in by a minority of members of The Church of Jesus Christ of Latter-day Saints.[546] The Court discussed the general historical prohibition on polygamy, the public policy concerns underlying that prohibition, and the "legitimate scope of the power of every civil government to determine whether polygamy or monogamy shall be the law of social life under its dominion".[547] The Court reasoned that, allowing individuals to act on their beliefs in defiance of the enacted "law of social life" would "allow every citizen to become a law unto himself" and, thus, delegitimize government.[548] This reasoning was echoed in 1990 by Justice Antonin Scalia in *Employment Division v. Smith*, which returned to a *Reynolds*-like standard in scaling back exemptions to generally applicable laws for religiously motivated acts.[549]

IV. Autonomy Grounded in Establishment or Free Exercise Clause

220. Consensus does not exist within the legal community regarding whether the church autonomy doctrine is rooted in the Establishment Clause, the Free Exercise Clause, or both. Oftentimes, the Supreme Court has avoided distinguishing between the two clauses by basing their rulings on the First Amendment as a whole.[550] While

543. *Cantwell v. Connecticut*, 310 U.S. 296, 303–304 (1940).
544. *Ibid.*
545. *Reynolds v. United States*, 98 U.S. 145, 166–168 (1878).
546. *Ibid.*; *see also* Hardy, *That "Same Old Question of Polygamy and Polygamous Living"*, *supra* n. 104, at 215; Volf, *Mormon Polygamy in the Nineteenth Century*, *supra* n. 104, at 41; 1 Durham et al., *supra* n. 157, § 3:2 (*The Polygamy Cases and the Belief vs. Action Distinction*).
547. *Reynolds*, 98 U.S. at 164–166.
548. *Ibid.*, at 166–167.
549. *Emp. Div., Dep't of Hum. Res. of Or. v. Smith*, 494 U.S. 872, 879 (1990) (quoting *Reynolds*, 98 U.S. at 166–167); *see also Fulton v. City of Philadelphia*, 141 S. Ct. 1868 (2021) (invoking the *Smith* standard to determine the provisions in question were not neutral and generally applicable and, therefore, strict scrutiny was required). *But see ibid.*, at 1882–1931 (concurring opinions, joining by various justices, acknowledging or indicating dissatisfaction with the *Smith* standard); 1 Durham et al., *supra* n. 157, ch. 3.IV (*Congressional Responses to* Smith: *Reestablishment of Free Exercise Protections*) (explaining developments surrounding the Religious Freedom Restoration Act, which legislatively restored the compelling state interest test for federal claims).
550. *See, e.g., Smith*, 494 U.S. at 872, 877.

some legal scholars believe distinguishing between the two is unnecessary, many others believe church autonomy is based on either the Establishment Clause or the Free Exercise Clause.[551]

221. The view that autonomy is based on the Free Exercise Clause has been supported by arguments that the Establishment Clause focuses on government not supporting religious organizations, whereas the Free Exercise Clause aims to prevent government from interfering with a religious organization.[552] After the Supreme Court decided *Employment Division v. Smith* in 1990,[553] however, plaintiffs increasingly invoked the Establishment Clause to address church autonomy issues.

222. Other scholars have argued that the Establishment Clause underpins church autonomy because the structural nature of the Clause assumes that both government and religion have equal "competence".[554] The idea here is that religious organizations must alone address anything "respecting an establishment of religion".[555] This view coincides with the approach of courts that say religious matters are outside the court's jurisdiction, thus emphasizing the structural nature of the separation of church and state.[556]

223. Instead of choosing one clause over the other or generically referring to the First Amendment in determining religious issues, some scholars believe that the underpinnings of the church autonomy doctrine are found in both the Free Exercise and Establishment Clauses.[557] The Supreme Court supported this approach in *Hosanna-Tabor Evangelical Lutheran Church and School v. EEOC* and again in *Our Lady of Guadalupe School v. Morrissey-Berru*.[558] The Court specifically

551. *See* Kathleen A. Brady, *Religious Organizations and Free Exercise: The Surprising Lessons of* Smith, 2004 BYU L. Rev. 1633, 1664–1672; Lael Weinberger, *The Limits of Church Autonomy*, 98 Notre Dame L. Rev. 1254, 1259 (2023). On religious autonomy as fundamentally a matter of free exercise, *see* for example Douglas Laycock, *Towards a General Theory of the Religion Clauses: The Case of Church Labor Relations and the Right to Church Autonomy*, 81 Colum. L. Rev. 1373, 1373, 1416–1417 (1981). For views on church autonomy as an Establishment Clause matter, *see* for example Carl H. Esbeck, *The Establishment Clause as a Structural Restraint on Government Power*, 84 Iowa L. Rev. 1, 42–51 (1998); Laurence Tribe, *American Constitutional Law*, at ch. 14, §§ 1–9, at 812–846 (1st ed. 1978).

552. *See* Laycock, *Towards a General Theory of the Religion Clauses*, *supra* n. 551, at 1416–1417.

553. *Smith*, 494 U.S. at 890.

554. *See, e.g.*, Esbeck, *The Establishment Clause as a Structural Restraint on Government Power*, *supra* n. 551, at 10 & nn.34–35.

555. *Ibid.*, at 104–109.

556. *Ibid.*, at 51–54.

557. *See, e.g.*, Carl H. Esbeck, *An Extended Essay on Church Autonomy*, 22 Federalist Soc'y Rev. 244, 246 (2021); Arlin M. Adams & William R. Hanlon, Jones v. Wolf*: Church Autonomy and the Religion Clauses of the First Amendment*, 128 U. Pa. L. Rev. 1291, 1297 (1980); Perry Dane, *"Omalous" Autonomy*, 2004 BYU L. Rev. 1715, 1718–1720.

558. *Hosanna-Tabor Evangelical Lutheran Church & Sch. v. EEOC*, 565 U.S. 171, 181 (2012); *Our Lady of Guadalupe Sch. v. Morrissey-Berru*, 140 S. Ct. 2049, 2060 (2020).

addressed how the two clauses work with each other in *Hosanna-Tabor*,[559] explaining that "[t]he Establishment Clause prevents the Government from appointing ministers, and the Free Exercise Clause prevents it from interfering with the freedom of religious groups to select their own [ministers]."[560] *Hosanna-Tabor*, it should be noted, was specifically about a religious organization's ability to appoint or fire its ministers.[561] Thus, the combined application of both clauses may not be appropriate in all cases involving aspects of the church autonomy doctrine.[562]

§2. Intra-church Disputes

I. Church Property Disputes

224. Resolving church property-related disputes between its members often comes down to determining who has been properly designated as the legal owner or trustee of the property.[563] The Supreme Court and lower courts have taken two main approaches to such disputes. In *Watson v. Jones*, the Supreme Court articulated a "deference to polity" doctrine, which courts have applied to property disputes.[564] Under this doctrine, in issues involving hierarchical churches, courts accept as binding the decision of the highest church judicatory on "questions of discipline, or of faith, or ecclesiastical rule, custom, or law".[565] In contrast, under that doctrine, courts resolve such questions involving independent, self-governing churches through "ordinary principles which govern voluntary associations".[566] More than one hundred years after *Watson*, the Supreme Court approved an alternate "neutral principles of law" approach to resolving disputes involving intra-church property.[567] In *Jones v. Wolf*, the Court found that if key documents contained clear language regarding property ownership, then courts could rely on those documents to help determine legal ownership of the disputed property.[568] Specifically, the Court

559. *Hosanna-Tabor*, 565 U.S. at 181–191; *see also Morrissey-Berru*, 140 S. Ct. at 2061–2066 (applying the reasoning of *Hosanna-Tabor*).

560. *Hosanna-Tabor*, 565 U.S. at 184.

561. 1 Durham et al., *supra* n. 157, § 5:3 (*Free Exercise and Establishment Clause Roots of Church Autonomy*); *see also Trinity Lutheran Church of Columbia, Inc. v. Comer*, 582 U.S. 449, 461 n.2 (2017) ("Recently, in *Hosanna-Tabor* … this Court held that the Religion Clauses required a ministerial exception to the neutral prohibition on employment retaliation … . Distinguishing *Smith*, we explained that while that case concerned government regulation of physical acts, '[t]he present case, in contrast concerns government interference with an internal church decision that affects the faith and mission of the church itself.'" (quoting *Hosanna-Tabor*, 565 U.S. at 190)).

562. 1 Durham et al., *supra* n. 157, § 5:3 (*Free Exercise and Establishment Clause Roots of Church Autonomy*).

563. *See, e.g., In re Graham's Est.*, 218 P. 84 (Cal. Ct. App. 1923).

564. *Watson v. Jones*, 80 U.S. (13 Wall.) 679 (1871).

565. *Ibid.*, at 727; 1 Durham et al., *supra* n. 157, § 5:18 (*Church Property Disputes*), § 8:6 (*Congregational, Hierarchical, Connectional*).

566. *Watson*, 80 U.S. at 725; 1 Durham et al., *supra* n. 157, § 5:18 (*Church Property Disputes*), § 8:6 (*Congregational, Hierarchical, Connectional*).

567. *Jones v. Wolf*, 443 U.S. 595 (1979).

568. *Ibid.*, at 602–605.

noted the relevance of deeds, local church charters, and general church constitutions, all of which are to be considered in "purely secular terms" and in light of state statutes governing equivalent, non-sectarian organizational documents.[569] The Court cautioned, however, that if the interpretation of documents "would require the civil court to resolve a religious controversy", then the civil court must invoke the deference to polity doctrine.[570] State courts have divided in their approaches to church property disputes, with some using a deference to polity approach, some using a neutral principles approach, and others using a hybrid of the two.[571]

II. Disputes over Leadership

225. The phrase "church polity" or "church order" is used to describe the internal framework of a religious organization—its "patterns of association, cooperation, and governance", as well as the processes and structures it uses to implement its doctrine.[572] Church polity determines the relationship between a general church and its local units. It also determines the relationship between religious organizations and the broader national and international religious community. An organization's exercise of polity is not only a reflection of its theological belief system; it is an exercise of faith that may also shape aspects of the organization's doctrine and belief system.[573] Because the polity of a religious organization is so inextricably related to its beliefs, polity itself is not within the jurisdiction of civil courts.[574]

226. Kedroff v. St. Nicholas Cathedral is a significant case involving leadership disputes within a religious organization.[575] In *Kedroff*, the Supreme Court invalidated a New York State statute[576] that worked to transfer control of a cathedral from the Patriarch of Moscow to the Russian Orthodox Church in America, which had essentially seceded from the larger church body in Russia.[577] Relying on the deference to polity doctrine,[578] the Court explained that the right to use the cathedral depended on whether the valid ruling hierarch of the Church in America was selected by the Patriarch of Moscow or elected by a convention of the American churches.[579] The Court found that the Russian Orthodox Church maintained administrative control of the Church in America, including control over the appointment

569. *Jones*, 443 U.S. at 602–605; 1 Durham et al., *supra* n. 157, § 5:18 (*Church Property Disputes*).
570. *Jones*, 443 U.S. at 604.
571. 1 Durham et al., *supra* n. 157, § 5:18 (*Church Property Disputes*).
572. *Ibid.*, § 8:5 (*Religious Polity*).
573. *Ibid.*
574. "The government may not compel affirmation of religious belief, punish the expression of religious doctrines it believes to be false, impose special disabilities on the basis of religious views or religious status, or lend its power to one or the other side in controversies over religious authority or dogma." *Emp. Div., Dep't of Hum. Res. of Or. v. Smith,* 494 U.S. 872, 877 (citations omitted).
575. *Kedroff v. St. Nicholas Cathedral of Russian Orthodox Church in N. Am.*, 344 U.S. 94 (1952); *see* 1 Durham et al., *supra* n. 157, § 5:9 (Watson*'s Progeny:* Kedroff *and* Milivojevich).
576. *Kedroff*, 344 U.S. at 107.
577. *Ibid.*, at 100–105.
578. *Ibid.*, at 115–116; *see also supra* para. 224.
579. *Ibid.*, at 96–97.

of a ruling hierarch. As a result, the Court held the New York statute invalid because it "directly prohibit[ed] the free exercise of an ecclesiastical right, the Church's choice of its hierarchy".[580]

227. Another important case regarding internal leadership disputes is *Serbian Eastern Orthodox Diocese v. Milivojevich.*[581] The US Supreme Court overruled an attempt by the Illinois State Supreme Court to overturn a church's decision to remove a bishop from power.[582] The US Supreme Court reasoned that civil courts must "accept the decisions of the highest judicatories of a religious organization of hierarchical polity on matters of discipline, faith, internal organization, or ecclesiastical rule, custom, or law".[583] Ultimately, the Court concluded that the Illinois court ruling allowed the state to become improperly entangled with the church's internal polity.[584]

228. In *Milivojevich*, the US Supreme Court did not address how deference to the church might apply to other "quintessentially religious" issues or other issues "at the core of ecclesiastical affairs".[585] Moreover, *Milivojevich* involved a hierarchical structure with tribunals in place, and thus the Court did not discuss the level of deference required were a congregational religious organization with a different organizational structure to face the same issue.[586]

III. Ministerial Exception

229. After decades of recognition by lower courts, the Supreme Court acknowledged the existence of the ministerial exception for the first time in 2012.[587] Lower courts developed the ministerial exception to reconcile two principles that at times conflict in US law: (1) the principle that religious organizations have the constitutional freedom to choose their leaders without state interference and (2) the principle that employers cannot discriminate based on certain protected classes, including religion.[588] The ministerial exception creates an exception to employment non-discrimination law for religious organizations making employment decisions that involve individuals who act as ministers.[589] Every federal court of appeals had

580. *Ibid.*, at 119–121.
581. *Serbian E. Orthodox Diocese for the U.S. & Can. v. Milivojevich*, 426 U.S. 696 (1976); *see* 1 Durham et al., *supra* n. 157, § 5:9 (Watson*'s Progeny:* Kedroff *and* Milivojevich).
582. *Milivojevich*, 426 U.S. at 698.
583. *Ibid.*, at 713.
584. *Ibid.*, at 698, 708–709, 720–725.
585. *Ibid.*, at 720–721.
586. 1 Durham et al., *supra* n. 157, § 5:9 (Watson*'s Progeny:* Kedroff *and* Milivojevich).
587. *Hosanna-Tabor Evangelical Lutheran Church & Sch. v. EEOC*, 565 U.S. 171, 188 (2012); *see* 2 Durham et al., *supra* n. 535, § 15:9 (*The Ministerial Exception Upheld:* Hosanna-Tabor Lutheran Church and School v. Equal Employment Opportunity Commission).
588. 2 Durham et al., *supra* n. 535, § 15:6 (*The Ministerial Exception to Employment Discrimination Law*).
589. *Ibid.*

previously recognized the existence of the ministerial exception.[590] The Supreme Court did not recognize it, however, until *Hosanna-Tabor Evangelical Lutheran Church and School v. EEOC*. As noted above,[591] the Court found in *Hosanna-Tabor* that the ministerial exception is rooted in both the Free Exercise Clause and the Establishment Clause. Conceptually, the ministerial exception is part of the broader concept of church autonomy, where religious organizations have the right to determine their own internal governance issues.[592] Even though the Court acknowledged the existence of the exception, it did not explain how to determine who qualifies as a minister.[593]

230. In 2020, in *Our Lady of Guadalupe School v. Morrissey-Berru*,[594] the Supreme Court offered additional guidance on who qualifies for the ministerial exception. In that case, two elementary school teachers filed separate discrimination claims against their Catholic schools after their teaching contracts were not renewed. Reflecting on significant factors in *Hosanna-Tabor*, the Court reasoned that occupation title and formal religious training will not always determine whether an individual is a minister. Instead, the Court explained, "What matters, at bottom, is what an employee does."[595] The Court found that the two teachers' "core responsibilities as teachers of religion were essentially the same" as the teacher in *Hosanna-Tabor*, allowing Our Lady of Guadalupe School to exercise the ministerial exception.[596]

231. The Ninth Circuit Court of Appeals has stated that claims alleging a Title VII (federal unlawful employment discrimination) violation are not barred by the ministerial exception if they do not require the court to "evaluate religious doctrine or the 'reasonableness' of the religious practices".[597] That court allowed a sexual harassment suit to be brought because it did not require the court to rule on issues involving religious doctrine. The Seventh Circuit and others, however, have held that in the employment context, "[t]he 'ministerial exception' applies without regard to the type of claims being brought."[598] In 2020, the Supreme Court ruled that Title

---

590. *Ibid.*, § 15:9 (*The Ministerial Exception Upheld:* Hosanna-Tabor Lutheran Church and School v. Equal Employment Opportunity Commission).
591. *See supra* para. 185.
592. 2 Durham et al., *supra* n. 535, § 15:9 (*The Ministerial Exception Upheld:* Hosanna-Tabor Lutheran Church and School v. Equal Employment Opportunity Commission).
593. *Hosanna-Tabor Evangelical Lutheran Church & Sch. v. EEOC*, 565 U.S. 171, 190 (2012) ("We are reluctant … to adopt a rigid formula for deciding when an employee qualifies as a minister. It is enough for us to conclude, in this our first case involving the ministerial exception, that the exception covers [respondent] Perich, given all the circumstances of her employment.").
594. *Our Lady of Guadalupe Sch. v. Morrissey-Berru*, 140 S. Ct. 2049 (2020).
595. *Ibid.*, at 2064.
596. *Ibid.*, at 2066.
597. *Bollard v. Cal. Province of the Soc'y of Jesus*, 196 F.3d 940, 950 (9th Cir. 1999); *see also Puri v. Khalsa*, 844 F.3d 1152, 1167–1168 (9th Cir. 2017) (applying the "neutral-principles" approach in a management dispute where the ministerial exception did not apply, explaining the approach similarly avoided unconstitutional inquiry into doctrine or religious practices).
598. *Alicea-Hernandez v. Cath. Bishop of Chi.*, 320 F.3d 698, 703 (7th Cir. 2003); *see also Demkovich v. St. Andrew the Apostle Par.*, 3 F.4th 968, 973, 984–985 (7th Cir. 2021) (clarifying that the ministerial exception covers hostile work environment claims while noting a circuit split on the issue);

VII's prohibition on employment discrimination based on "sex" encompasses sexual orientation and gender identity. While the Court failed to explicitly address the holding's implications for religious organizations as employers, it suggested that existing free exercise protections for religious organizations would apply, including the ministerial exception and statutory exemptions.[599] For more about the ministerial exception, *see* Part VI (Labor Law Within Religious Communities), Chapter 2 (Religious Ministers and Labor Law).

IV. Exemptions from Employment Non-discrimination Laws

232. Generally, religious employers are exempt from federal employment law prohibitions on discriminating based on religion.[600] In 1972, Congress added an exemption to section 702 of the Civil Rights Act, which further insulated the activities of religious organizations from the Act's prohibition on employment discrimination based on religion.[601] In 1987, the Supreme Court addressed whether the exemption extended to church employment in secular activities in *Corporation of the Presiding Bishop of The Church of Jesus Christ of Latter-day Saints v. Amos*.[602] The corporation fired a building engineer, who worked in one of its nonprofit entities, on religious grounds.[603] Specifically, the building engineer failed to uphold behavioral standards to qualify for a "temple recommend"—a requirement for church employment.[604] The engineer and other similarly situated individuals sued, claiming that the exemption from civil rights law violated the Establishment Clause because the exemption helped to "directly and immediately advance religious tenets and practices".[605] The Supreme Court upheld the amended section 702 exemption, reasoning that it merely permits religious organizations to "advance religion, which is their very purpose",[606] and accommodates religious organizations rather than unconstitutionally advancing them.[607] In *Amos*, a concurring opinion cautioned that the exemption should apply categorically to a religious organization's nonprofit activities but not to for-profit operations.[608] The concurrence noted a danger of

---

Skrzypczak v. Roman Cath. Diocese of Tulsa, 611 F.3d 1238, 1245–46 (10th Cir. 2010); *Gellington v. Christian Methodist Episcopal Church, Inc.*, 203 F.3d 1299, 1304 (11th Cir. 2000); *Combs v. Cent. Tex. Annual Conf. of United Methodist Church,* 173 F.3d 343, 350 (5th Cir. 1999).

599. *Bostock v. Clayton County*, 140 S. Ct. 1731, 1753–1754 (2020).

600. *See* 2 Durham et al., *supra* n. 535, § 15:1 (*Employment Discrimination Protections for Religious Employers: Introduction*).

601. Equal Employment Opportunity Act of 1972, Pub. L. No. 92-261, § 3, 86 Stat. 103, 103–104 (codified as amended at 42 U.S.C. § 2000e-1 (2018)).

602. *Corp. of the Presiding Bishop of The Church of Jesus Christ of Latter-day Saints v. Amos*, 483 U.S. 327 (1987).

603. *Ibid.*, at 330.

604. *Ibid.*

605. *Ibid.*, at 333.

606. *Ibid.*, at 337.

607. *See ibid.*, at 338; 2 Durham et al., *supra* n. 535, § 15:15 (*Upholding Statutory Religious Exemptions:* Corporation of Presiding Bishop of Church of Jesus Christ of Latter-day Saints v. Amos).

608. *Corp. of the Presiding Bishop of The Church of Jesus Christ of Latter-day Saints v. Amos*, 483 U.S. 327, 340, 345 (Brennan., J., with Marshall, J., concurring).

excessive entanglement in allowing the government to determine whether activities are secular or religious on a case-by-case basis.[609]

233. While cases like *Amos* and *Bostock* focused on federal anti-discrimination laws, each state has its own set of anti-discrimination laws.[610] Some states try to limit the level of protection given to religious organizations under *Amos*, some states give the same level of protection, and some states go so far as to exempt religious organizations from all state anti-discrimination laws.[611] For further discussion of exemptions for religious organizations from non-discrimination statutes, *see* Part VI (Labor Law Within Religious Communities), Chapter 3 (Other Church Employees and Labor Law).

V. Church Names

234. To protect their names, some religious organizations have turned to trademark law.[612] Nothing in the Free Exercise Clause or the Establishment Clause prevents a religious organization from using a trademark to protect its name.[613] Additionally, court enforcement of one religious organization's trademark against another religious organization does not infringe on the religious rights of the organization against which the trademark is enforced.[614] Part of the justification for religious organizations' use of trademarks is that the name of a religious organization is inextricably linked to the organization's identity.[615] Moreover, two religious organizations using the same name can lead to confusion.[616] When ruling on cases of this nature, courts have weighed whether a name was descriptive or generic, whether the plaintiff organization will be damaged if not granted control over a trademark's use, and what the historical relationship is between original organizations and splinter groups.[617]

609. *Ibid.*, at 340–346.
610. 2 Durham et al., *supra* n. 535, § 15:22 (*State Statutory Protections: Exceptions for Religious Employers*).
611. For a compilation of the anti-discrimination laws and religious exemptions of all fifty states, see *ibid.*.
612. 4 Durham et al., *supra* n. 178, § 30:43 (*Overview and Applicability of Trademark Law to Religious Organizations*), § 30:44 (*Consumer Perception and the Purpose of Protecting Trademarks*).
613. *Nat'l Bd. of Young Women's Christian Ass'n of the U.S. v. Young Women's Christian Ass'n of Charleston*, 335 F. Supp. 615, 624–625 (D.S.C. 1971).
614. *Ibid.*
615. 4 Durham et al., *supra* n. 178, § 30:60 (*Judicial Tests for Determining Likelihood of Confusion*).
616. *Ibid.*
617. *Ibid.*, § 30:62 (*Exemplary Trademark Infringement Cases Involving Religious Organizations*); *see, e.g.*, *TE-TA-MA Truth Foundation-Family of Uri, Inc. v. The World Church of the Creator*, 297 F.3d 662, 666–667 (7th Cir. 2002) (holding that a trademarked name used by two religious groups, which had "diametrically opposed" views, was descriptive, rather than generic, and thus could not be used by the infringing group); *Purcell v. Summers*, 145 F.2d 979, 983 (4th Cir. 1944) ("[F]or dissident members to use the name of the [united] church will enable them to appear in the eyes of the community as the continuation of that church and to make the united church, which is in reality the continuation of the old church, appear as an intruder. … [I]t is not fair to it that such name be used by persons over whose professions of faith and practices it can exercise no control.")

VI. Rights of Membership

235. Generally speaking, religious organization's membership decisions are considered to be ecclesiastical decisions not subject to review by secular courts. Religious organizations are able to determine membership based on both religious belief and conduct.[618] Deciding who is a member of a religious organization and deciding if a member is able to fully participate in the organization's functions is a protected function of the organization.[619] In fact, *only* the religious organization has the authority to make these decisions.[620] As long as the decision on membership is "fundamentally religious", civil courts must defer to the religious organization's choice, even if the organization did not follow its own internal guidelines or rules.[621] This principle holds true even if the religious organization has no established internal rules on the disputed aspect of membership.[622]

236. Courts do not necessarily treat hierarchical and congregational religious organizations the same way, however.[623] While membership decisions of religious hierarchical organizations are beyond civil courts' adjudication,[624] courts do not

618. *See* 1 Durham et al., *supra* n. 157, § 10:43 (*Determining Membership*); Revised Model Nonprofit Corp. Act §§ 1.80, 6.01, 6.21(a) (Am. Bar Ass'n 4th ed. 2022); *Marks v. Est. of Hartgerink*, 528 N.W.2d 539 (Iowa 1995) (affirming holding that excommunication was "purely ecclesiastical" decision with which the court could not interfere and affirming summary judgment for church in suit alleging intentional infliction of emotional distress and defamation in the excommunication process), *abrogated by Barreca v. Nickolas*, 683 N.W.2d 111 (Iowa 2004) (abrogating *Marks* on the "actual malice" test relevant to qualified privilege).

619. 1 Durham et al., *supra* n. 157, § 5:24 (*The Rule of Deference and the Selection of Members*), § 10:43 (*Determining Membership*).

620. *Ibid.*, § 10:43 (*Determining Membership*).

621. *See ibid.* The exception mentioned by the Supreme Court in 1929 that a court may override a church decision that is "arbitrary" and contrary to canon law, *Gonzalez v. Roman Catholic Archbishop of Manila*, 280 U.S. 1, 7–8 (1929), has not been followed in religious membership selection or removal decisions. In fact, the "arbitrariness" exception to deference was rejected by the Court in *Serbian Eastern Orthodox Diocese for the United States of America and Canada v. Milivojevich*, 426 U.S. 696, 712–717 (1976). *See also Schofield v. Superior Ct.*, 118 Cal. Rptr. 3d 160, 165–167 (Cal. Ct. App. 2010) (explaining that the lower court should have deferred to the internal decision-making processes of the Church in determining the "ecclesiastical fact" of who was properly appointed bishop); *Smith v. Emmanuel Temple Pentecostal Churches of the Apostolic Faith, Inc.*, 946 N.E.2d 608, 615 (Ind. Ct. App. 2011) ("[C]ivil courts are precluded from resolving disputes involving church affairs if resolution of the disputes cannot be made without extensive inquiry into religious law and polity." (internal quotation marks omitted) (quoting *Cole v. Holt*, 725 N.E.2d 145, 148 (Ind. Ct. App. 2000))); *Evans v. Shiloh Baptist Church, Inc.*, 77 A.2d 160, 163 (Md. 1950) (reiterating that the court does not decide questions of church discipline "where no property interest is involved"); *Temple-Ashram v. Satyanandji*, 923 N.Y.S.2d 664, 667 (N.Y. App. Div. 2011) (holding that determining the spiritual leader of temple necessarily implicates ecclesiastical issues and cannot be resolved by applying neutral principles of law); *Hutterville Hutterian Brethren, Inc. v. Waldner*, 791 N.W.2d 169 (S.D. 2010) (holding that state courts lacked subject matter jurisdiction in disputes between two factions because of the disputes' doctrinal nature, relating to church leadership and excommunications).

622. *See* 1 Durham et al., *supra* n. 157, § 10:43 (*Determining Membership*).

623. *Ibid.*

624. *See Milivojevich*, 426 U.S. at 708–709; *Kedroff v. St. Nicholas Cathedral of Russian Orthodox Church in N. Am.*, 344 U.S. 94, 114–115 & n.20 (1952); *Bouldin v. Alexander*, 82 U.S. (15 Wall.)

always afford congregational religious organizations the same deference.[625] Civil courts have a small window of review of congregational organizations' membership decisions when "civil, property or contract rights depend" on the parties following the organization's internal policies and procedures.[626]

VII. Failure to Follow Internal Procedures

237. Even though precedent allows civil courts to review claims that a religious organization has not followed its own internal procedures, the scope of review is very limited.[627] The US Supreme Court opinion in *Gonzalez v. Roman Catholic Archbishop of Manila* seemingly opened the door for courts to examine failures in following internal procedures when "fraud, collusion, or arbitrariness" was involved (though the Court later characterized these categories as "dicta").[628]

238. While *Gonzalez* cracked open the door for civil court review, courts must still defer to internal decisions of religious organizations that are "essentially related to church order, appointments to ministry, church discipline, and the interpretation of fundamental beliefs and church law".[629] In a Kentucky State Supreme Court case, *Music v. United Methodist Church*, a minister claimed violation of an employment

---

131, 139–140 (1872); *Watson v. Jones*, 80 U.S. (13 Wall.) 679, 732–734 (1871); *Grunwald v. Bornfreund*, 696 F. Supp. 838, 840–841 (E.D.N.Y. 1988); *Nunn v. Black*, 506 F. Supp. 444, 448 (W.D. Va. 1981), *aff'd*, 661 F.2d 925 (4th Cir. 1981); *St. John's Greek Cath. Hungarian Russian Orthodox Church of Rahway v. Fedak*, 233 A.2d 663, 673–674 (N.J. Sup. Ct. App. Div. 1967); *Congregation Yetev Lev D'Satmar, Inc. v. Kahana*, 879 N.E.2d 1282, 1286 (N.Y. 2007).

625. 1 Durham et al., *supra* n. 157, § 10:43 (*Determining Membership*).

626. *Ibid.*; *see Soc'y of the Holy Transfiguration Monastery, Inc. v. Archbishop Gregory of Denver*, 685 F. Supp. 2d 217, 225 & n.12 (D. Mass. 2010) (considering a copyright infringement claim and explaining that property disputes are justiciable in both congregational and hierarchical contexts); *Sapp v. Callaway*, 69 S.E.2d 734, 737–738 (Ga. 1952) (explaining that church membership is not a property right and courts lack jurisdiction to review congregational decisions, absent violation of civil or property rights); *Stewart v. Jarriel*, 59 S.E.2d 368, 370 (Ga. 1950) (finding membership does not constitute a property interest and that a member dissatisfied with congregational decisions lacks a justiciable claim, absent a violation of civil rights); *Cooper v. Bell*, 106 S.W.2d 124, 126–127 (Ct. App. Ky. 1937) (holding "the courts will not intervene" where a congregational decision was made by the majority, absent a showing that a civil right "secured by contract" has been violated); *Baugh v. Thomas*, 265 A.2d 675, 677–678 (N.J. 1970) (finding church membership is a civil right and that civil courts have jurisdiction to determine if a religious organization has followed its established procedures in expelling members); *Randolph v. First Baptist Church of Lockland*, 120 N.E.2d 485, 488–489 (Ohio Ct. Com. Pl. 1954) (finding church membership is a property right). *But see Alexander v. Shiloh Baptist Church*, 592 N.E.2d 918, 922–923 (Ohio Ct. Com. Pl. 1991) (declining to follow *Randolph*, noting that *Randolph* had not been followed by any other court and finding that the concept of church membership as a property right is outweighed by First Amendment interests).

627. 2 Durham et al., *supra* n. 535, § 19:6 (*The Rule of Deference*).

628. *Gonzalez v. Roman Cath. Archbishop of Manila*, 280 U.S. 1, 16 (1929), *abrogated by Serbian E. Orthodox Diocese for the U.S. & Can. v. Milivojevich*, 426 U.S. 696, 712 (1976) (characterizing *Gonzalez*'s "fraud, collusion, or arbitrariness" exception as "dictum only"); *see also* 2 Durham et al., *supra* n. 535, § 19:6 (*The Rule of Deference*); Shannon, *Deference or Neutral Principles*, *supra* n. 539, at 105–107.

629. 2 Durham et al., *supra* n. 535, § 19:6 (*The Rule of Deference*).

contract.[630] The court found that the claim required examination of "internal church discipline, faith, and organization" and interpretation of church law, which would create excessive government entanglement.[631] Relying on US Supreme Court precedent, the state court explained that the "neutral principles" doctrine is reserved for church-related property disputes and did not apply to the minister's employment claim, which was a matter of "church government or order and discipline".[632] The Supreme Court of Kentucky later clarified that the "ecclesiastical abstention" doctrine does not preclude it from hearing "*types* of cases, only *specific* cases pervaded by religious issues".[633]

630. *Music v. United Methodist Church*, 864 S.W.2d 286 (Ky. 1993), *abrogated by St. Joseph Cath. Orphan Soc'y v. Edwards*, 449 S.W.3d 727, 736–737 (Ky. 2014).
631. *Ibid.*, at 288–289.
632. *Ibid.*, at 287–288 (citing *Jones v. Wolf*, 443 U.S. 595, 599 (1979)).
633. *St. Joseph Cath. Orphan Soc'y v. Edwards*, 449 S.W.3d 727, 736–737 (Ky. 2014).

Chapter 3. Fundamental Rights and Religious Communities

239. Much of the information that could be included in this chapter is set forth in other sections of this book. Part II, Chapter 2, discusses the collective freedoms of religious communities; Part II, Chapter 3, covers organizational religious freedom; and Part VII, Chapter 1, discusses the individual right to privacy in religious practice. This chapter focuses specifically on the right of religious communities to exercise their beliefs, operate religious schools, and exercise choice in education.

240. Religious communities enjoy a broad array of legal protections under US law. In the Constitution, these protections are derived from the individual rights of free exercise of religion, freedom of association, freedom of speech, due process, and equal protection.[634] In addition, the federal and state governments enforce laws to promote religious freedom and prevent undue burdens on religious exercise.[635]

§1. "Compelling State Interest" Test Versus "General and Neutral Laws"

241. For many years, the US Supreme Court interpreted the Free Exercise Clause to protect religious groups and believers under the compelling interest test.[636] By this standard—also known as "strict scrutiny"—the federal or state government had to show that any substantial burden imposed on religious exercise was justified by a compelling state interest and that the government had employed the least restrictive means of achieving that interest.[637]

242. In the 1990 case *Employment Division v. Smith*, however, the Supreme Court held that the compelling interest test should not be applied to require religious exemptions from a generally applicable criminal law—that the religious beliefs of individuals cannot excuse them from complying with a law that applies neutrally to all and proscribes conduct that the state is free to regulate.[638] The Court more recently invoked the *Smith* standard in *Fulton v. City of Philadelphia*[639] but ultimately found *Smith* did not apply, because the provision in question was not neutral and generally applicable. The justices authored and joined various concurring opinions, however, to acknowledge and express dissatisfaction with *Smith* and even urge the Court to overrule it.[640]

---

634. U.S. Const. amend. I, XIV.
635. *See, e.g.*, I.R.C. § 501(c)(3) (2018); Religious Freedom Restoration Act (RFRA), 42 U.S.C. §§ 2000bb to 2000bb-4 (2018); Religious Land Use and Institutionalized Persons Act (RLUIPA), 42 U.S.C. §§ 2000cc to 2000cc-5 (2018).
636. *Sherbert v. Verner*, 374 U.S. 398, 403, 406–408 (1963).
637. *Ibid.*
638. *Emp. Div., Dep't of Hum. Res. of Or. v. Smith*, 494 U.S. 872, 884–885 (1990).
639. *Fulton v. City of Philadelphia*, 141 S. Ct. 1868, 1876–1877 (2021).
640. *See ibid.*, at 1882, 1882–1883 (Barrett, J., with Kavanaugh, J., concurring, and with Breyer, J., joining in part) (acknowledging "serious arguments" for overruling *Smith* but agreeing the facts in *Fulton* did not trigger *Smith*); *ibid.*, at 1883, 1883–1926 (Alito, J., with Thomas and Gorsuch, JJ.,

243. Three years after *Employment Division v. Smith*, the US Congress passed the Religious Freedom Restoration Act (RFRA), which reinstated the compelling interest test for claims of government violations of individual religious freedom.[641] The Supreme Court later ruled that RFRA was constitutional only as applied to federal laws, invalidating RFRA's application to state laws.[642] In response, twenty-three states have passed their own Religious Freedom Restoration Acts as state statutes or constitutional amendments.[643] Additionally, the highest state courts of at least ten states have interpreted the free exercise clause in their state constitutions to require strict scrutiny.[644] For a detailed discussion of RFRA and its aftermath, *see* Part I (Legal Framework and Sources), Chapter 2 (Other Legislation with Regard to Religion).

§2. Religious Schools

244. A fundamental freedom of religious communities is the right to operate religiously affiliated schools and send children to them. State compulsory education laws are prevalent and are generally deemed constitutional exercises of state power.[645] Typical mandatory school attendance laws require children, generally between the ages of six to eighteen years old, to enroll in and attend school, whether public or private.[646] Educational programs outside of public or private schools, including religiously oriented programs, can be acceptable alternatives but may require approval and some supervision by the state board of education.[647] Additionally, children may be exempted from compulsory attendance, through written consent of a parent or by court order, when they have reached sixteen or seventeen years of age, depending on the state.[648]

---

concurring) (asserting *Smith* should be overruled and replaced by strict scrutiny); *ibid.*, at 1926, 1926–1931 (Gorsuch, J., with Thomas and Alito, JJ., concurring) (asserting *Smith* "committed a constitutional error" that the Court should not have "sidestep[ped]" in *Fulton*).

641. Religious Freedom Restoration Act (RFRA), Pub. L. No. 103-141, 107 Stat. 1488 (1993) (codified as amended at 42 U.S.C. §§ 2000bb to 2000bb-4 (2018)).

642. *City of Boerne v. Flores*, 521 U.S 507, 532–536 (1997) (holding that RFRA, at least as applied to state action, exceeded Congress's authority under the Constitution's Enforcement Clause); *Gonzales v. O Centro Espirita Beneficente Uniao do Vegetal*, 546 U.S. 418, 424 & n.1 (2006) (affirming that RFRA still applied to federal action).

643. *See supra* para. 143 and accompanying footnotes (listing state statutes and constitutional provisions); *see also* 1 Durham et al., *supra* n. 157, § 3:27 (*Chart: State Standards of Free Exercise Review under State RFRAs and State High Court Decisions*).

644. S*ee supra* para. 143 and accompanying footnotes (listing state cases); *see also* 1 Durham et al., *supra* n. 157, § 3:27 (*Chart: State Standards of Free Exercise Review under State RFRAs and State High Court Decisions*).

645. *See, e.g.*, *Farrington v. Tokushige*, 273 U.S. 284 (1927); *Pierce v. Soc'y of Sisters of the Holy Names of Jesus & Mary*, 268 U.S. 510 (1925).

646. *50-State Comparison: Free and Compulsory School Age Requirements*, Educ. Comm'n States (Aug. 2020), https://reports.ecs.org/comparisons/free-and-compulsory-school-age-requirements-all.

647. *See, e.g.*, Iowa Code § 299.24 (2022) (outlining exemptions for religious groups from compulsory education but requiring department of education approval and testing of children's comprehension of basic subjects).

648. *See, e.g.*, Minn. Stat. § 120A.22, subdiv. 8 (2022).

245. Rights in education necessarily involve the rights of parents and legal guardians to direct how their children are educated. In 1923, the Supreme Court held that a state law prohibiting foreign language education interfered unconstitutionally with the right of parents to supervise the education of their children.[649] Two years later, the Court ruled that the Fourteenth Amendment prevented the state from requiring students to attend public schools and that children therefore had a right to attend private schools if their guardians so desired.[650] A parent's decision for a child to attend a religious school is a permissible exercise of parental discretion and is upheld as long as the school meets basic state requirements for educational quality. *See* Part IX (Education), Chapter 2 (Religious Schools).

246. The Supreme Court has also upheld religiously motivated exemptions from mandatory school attendance laws. For example, *Wisconsin v. Yoder* limited the applicability of state compulsory education laws to the Amish.[651] To reach its holding, the Court balanced Wisconsin's compelling interest in universal formal education against the free exercise rights of Amish parents to remove their children from schools for religious and vocational training, after the eighth grade.[652] The Court effectively concluded that the state's compulsory education law was not narrowly tailored, given that the Amish community's alternative to formal education enabled its children "to function effectively in their day-to-day life" and prepared them for future community obligations.[653] Thus, the Court held that the law burdened Amish parents' rights in violation of the Free Exercise Clause.[654]

247. State funding of religious schools is subject to complex constitutional limits, based on varying, and sometimes inconsistent, Supreme Court interpretations of the Establishment Clause. For a detailed description of the law governing state funding of religious schools, including indirect funding, *see* Part IX (Education), Chapter 2 (Religious Schools).

248. A small but growing alternative to public schools is homeschooling. In 1999, only 1.7% of children in the United States were homeschooled; by 2016, 3.3% were homeschooled.[655] That percentage increased dramatically by 2021—with estimates ranging from 7 to 11%—due in large part to circumstances surrounding the COVID-19 pandemic.[656] The percentage of homeschooled children

649. *Meyer v. Nebraska*, 262 U.S. 390, 400–403 (1923).
650. *Pierce*, 268 U.S. at 510, 354–535.
651. *Wisconsin v. Yoder*, 406 U.S. 205 (1972).
652. *Ibid.*, at 215.
653. *Ibid.*, at 219, 225, 233–234.
654. *Ibid.*, at 234.
655. *Chapter 2.206 Homeschooling and School Choice*, Digest of Educ. Stat., Nat'l Ctr. for Educ. Stat., https://nces.ed.gov/programs/digest/2021menu_tables.asp (last visited Sep. 30, 2023).
656. *See* Brian D. Ray, *Research Facts on Homeschooling: General Facts, Statistics, and Trends*, Nat'l Home Educ. Rsch. Inst. (revised Jul. 20, 2023), https://www.nheri.org/research-facts-on-home schooling; Casey Eggleston & Jason Fields, *Census Bureau's Household Pulse Survey Shows Significant Increase in Homeschooling Rates in Fall 2020*, U.S. Census Bureau (Mar. 22, 2021), https://www.census.gov/library/stories/2021/03/homeschooling-on-the-rise-during-covid-19-pande mic.html.

decreased in 2022 but was still above pre-pandemic levels, at approximately 6%.[657] While parents often cite health and safety concerns as a reason for homeschooling, many parents homeschool to provide their children religious or moral instruction.[658] Every state allows parents to homeschool their children: twenty-two states simply require parents to notify local school officials of their intent to homeschool; twelve states require parents to send initial notification as well as periodic evaluations of the child's academic progress; five states impose further requirements, such as home visits by state officials, state approval of curriculum, or "teacher qualification of parents"; the remaining eleven states impose few or no requirements on homeschooling parents.[659]

249. Although the right to attend a religious private school or homeschool is generally recognized, religious groups may not receive special treatment from the state. *Board of Education v. Grumet* dealt with a New York statute that had been passed specifically to create a separate school district for Kiryas Joel, a village within the town of Monroe, comprised entirely of highly religious Satmar Hasidic Jews.[660] Most children in the village attended private religious schools, but those with special educational needs were forced to attend outside public schools—a jarring experience for children raised in a highly religious, insular group.[661] The New York state legislature decided to solve the problem by creating an independent school district for Kiryas Joel, thereby allowing the formation of public special education and remedial programs within the village that would benefit the Jewish children exclusively.[662] The Supreme Court ruled that the special treatment rendered to Kiryas Joel, as essentially a religious community, violated the Establishment Clause. The Court reiterated that any government accommodation of religions or special religious needs must reflect neutrality between religions and between religion and non-religion.[663]

---

657. Brian D. Ray, *How Many Homeschool Students Are There in the United States During the 2021–2022 School Year?*, Nat'l Home Educ. Rsch. Inst. (Sep. 9, 2021), https://www.nheri.org/how-many-homeschool-students-are-there-in-the-united-states-during-the-2021-2022-school-year.
658. Nat'l Ctr. for Educ. Stat., *Homeschooled Children and Reasons for Homeschooling* 4 (May 2022), https://nces.ed.gov/programs/coe/indicator/tgk/homeschooled-children#suggested-citation (link to PDF).
659. *Homeschool Laws by State*, Home Sch. Legal Def. Ass'n (HSLDA), https://hslda.org/legal (last visited Sep. 30, 2023).
660. *Bd. of Educ. v. Grumet*, 512 U.S. 687, 690–694 (1994).
661. *Ibid.*, at 691–92.
662. *Ibid.*, at 693.
663. *Ibid.*, at 696–697, 705–707, 709.

Chapter 4. Contractual Religious Freedom

250. Contractual religious freedom in the United States relates to the rights of religious groups to contract or avoid contracts. This chapter will discuss contractual religious freedom in the contexts of (1) employment non-discrimination laws that forbid religious discrimination and the exemptions that exist for religious institutions and religious business owners, (2) religious objections to unions by individuals and religious groups, and (3) arbitration clauses incorporating religious law. For more information on church autonomy, *see* this part, Chapter 2 (Autonomy of Religious Communities), above.

§1. Employment Non-discrimination Laws and Exemptions

251. The Constitution provides protections against religious discrimination by the federal and state governments to individuals, private employers, and institutions. The First Amendment prohibits Congress from making any "law respecting an establishment of religion, or prohibiting the free exercise thereof".[664] The First Amendment's Free Speech Clause protects religious speech from government interference.[665] And the Fourteenth Amendment has been interpreted to require that states provide these First Amendment guarantees as well.[666] While private employers are not required to provide these same constitutional protections to their employees, several statutes have been enacted since the 1960s that protect individuals from private discrimination, which will be discussed in this section below.

252. Religious autonomy, or church autonomy, is the doctrine that religious organizations should be free to "select their own leaders, define their own doctrines, resolve their own disputes, and run their own institutions".[667] The first church autonomy case brought to the Supreme Court held that the courts defer to a religious institution's governing body, if one exists, when internal "ecclesiastical" disputes arise.[668] If there is no governing body, then the courts defer to the majority of the congregation.[669] When ecclesiastical matters are non-determinative, courts may resolve disputes using "neutral principles of law".[670]

253. In *Hosanna-Tabor Evangelical Lutheran Church and School v. EEOC*, the Supreme Court affirmed that religious groups are exempt from certain non-discrimination laws in relation to employment of ministers.[671] The "ministerial

664. U.S. Const. amend. I.
665. *Ibid.* ("Congress shall make no law … abridging the freedom of speech … .").
666. U.S. Const. amend. XIV; *Cantwell v. Connecticut*, 310 U.S. 296, 303 (1940).
667. *Corp. of the Presiding Bishop of The Church of Jesus Christ of Latter-day Saints v. Amos*, 483 U.S. 327, 340, 341 (1987) (Brennan, J., with Marshall, J., concurring) (quoting Laycock, *Towards a General Theory of the Religion Clauses*, *supra* n. 551, at 1389).
668. *Watson v. Jones*, 80 U.S. (13 Wall.) 679, 733 (1871).
669. *Ibid.*
670. *Jones v. Wolf*, 443 U.S. 595, 602–603 (1979).
671. *Hosanna-Tabor Evangelical Lutheran Church & Sch. v. EEOC*, 565 U.S. 171, 188–189 (2012).

exception" relieves religious groups from providing due process in hiring ministers or terminating their employment. Requiring due process otherwise might "impos[e] an unwanted minister" on a congregation, violating both the Establishment Clause and Free Exercise Clause of the First Amendment.[672] *Hosanna-Tabor* did not resolve disagreement among federal courts of appeals as to who qualifies as a minister for purposes of the exception. In a later opinion, *Our Lady of Guadalupe School v. Morrissey-Berru*, the Court reasoned that occupation title and formal religious training will not always determine whether an individual is a minister.[673] Instead, the Court concluded, "What matters, at bottom, is what an employee *does*."[674] For additional discussion, *see* this part, Chapter 2 (Autonomy of Religious Communities), above.

I. Title VII of the Civil Rights Act of 1964

254. Beyond constitutional protections, a number of federal and state laws prohibit employment discrimination based on protected characteristics, including religion. The most notable federal law is Title VII of the Civil Rights Act of 1964.[675]

255. Title VII applies to the federal government as an employer and to most state, local, and private employers. To prevent burdens on small business owners, Title VII defines an employer as "a person engaged in ... commerce who has fifteen or more employees" working at least twenty weeks per year.[676] It prohibits employment decisions from being based on "race, color, religion, sex, or national origin".[677] In 2020, the Supreme Court held in *Bostock v. Clayton County* that Title VII's prohibition on "sex" discrimination encompasses sexual orientation and gender identity.[678] Sections 702 and 703 of Title VII contain exemptions for religious institutions. A religious corporation, association, educational institution, or society may discriminate based on religion but not based on race, color, sex, or national origin, except as provided by the ministerial exception—the legal recognition of religious organizations' autonomy in employment decisions.[679]

II. Title VII Protections for Individuals

256. Individuals are protected from disparate treatment because of their religion. Title VII states that it is unlawful for an employer:

672. *Ibid.*
673. *Our Lady of Guadalupe Sch. v. Morrissey-Berru*, 140 S. Ct. 2049, 2063–2064 (2020).
674. *Ibid.*, at 2064 (emphasis added).
675. 42 U.S.C. §§ 2000e to 2000e-17 (2018).
676. 42 U.S.C. § 2000e(b).
677. *Ibid.*, § 2000e-2.
678. *Bostock v. Clayton County*, 140 S. Ct. 1731, 1737 (2020).
679. *Ibid.*, § 2000e-1(a) (also known as § 702), § 2000e-2(e)(2) (also known as § 703); *see also Bostock*, 140 S. Ct. at 1753–1754 (explaining constitutional and statutory exemptions from Title VII requirements, available to religious organizations).

(1) to fail or refuse to hire or to discharge any individual, or otherwise to discriminate against any individual with respect to his compensation, terms, conditions, or privileges of employment, because of such individual's … religion … or

(2) to limit, segregate, or classify his employees or applicants for employment in any way which would deprive or tend to deprive any individual of employment opportunities or otherwise adversely affect his status as an employee, because of such individual's … religion.[680]

257. Additionally, since an amendment to the definition of religion passed in 1972, Title VII has required employers to "reasonably accommodate" the religious observance and practices of employees as long as doing so does not cause "undue hardship" to their business.[681] In 1977, in *Trans World Airlines, Inc. v. Hardison*, the Supreme Court appeared to define "undue hardship" as anything constituting more than *de minimis* cost,[682] a vague standard that made it difficult for employees to seek relief under this provision. In 2023, in *Groff v. DeJoy*, a unanimous Court explained that *Hardison* had been misinterpreted and that the *de minimus* test was incorrect.[683] Instead, it held, "an employer must show that the burden of granting an accommodation would result in *substantial* increased costs in relation to the conduct of its particular business".[684] The Court further explained that Title VII requires employers to actually reasonably accommodate an employee's religious practice and not just assess the reasonableness of one or more accommodations. For example, if an employee requests scheduling accommodation for religious worship, "it would not be enough for an employer to conclude that forcing other employees to work overtime would constitute an undue hardship. Consideration of other options, such as voluntary shift swapping, would also be necessary."[685] Moreover, the Court clarified that only impacts on coworkers that "affec[t] the conduct of the business" are relevant to the undue hardship inquiry; in contrast, a coworker's animus toward religion generally, a particular religion, or religious accommodation in the workplace would not be relevant in determining undue hardship.[686] Even given the Court's clarification and guidance in *Groff*, questions remain regarding the type of coworker impacts that would constitute undue hardship in "the conduct of business".[687]

680. 42 U.S.C. § 2000e-2(a).
681. *Ibid.*, § 2000e(j).
682. *Trans World Airlines, Inc. v. Hardison*, 432 U.S. 63, 84 (1977).
683. *Groff v. DeJoy*, 600 U.S. 447, 469–471 (2023).
684. *Ibid.* (emphasis added).
685. *Ibid.*, at 473.
686. *Ibid.*, at 2296 (internal quotation marks omitted).
687. *See ibid.*, at 2297, 2298 (Sotomayor, J., with Jackson, J., concurring); 3 Lex K. Larson, *Labor and Employment Law*, at ch. 76, § 76.10[3] (*Reasonable Accommodation-General*), Lexis/Matthew Bender (database updated May 2023).

258. In 1986, the Supreme Court held that in cases where a religious accommodation is required, an employer need not choose the exact accommodation proposed by the employee; rather, the employer can create its own accommodation, as long as it is reasonable.[688]

259. In 2015, in *EEOC v. Abercrombie & Fitch Stores, Inc.*, the Supreme Court held that Abercrombie & Fitch unlawfully discriminated against a job applicant when it did not hire her because the Muslim headscarf she wore violated the store's dress policy prohibiting 'caps', even though she was otherwise qualified for the job. The Court deemed this a scenario in which an employer is required to accommodate a religious practice.[689]

III. Exemptions from Title VII for Religious Institutions

260. It is often challenging to determine if an institution should qualify for Title VII's religious exemptions. An institution with a religious name that does not conduct any religious activities does not qualify.[690] However, an institution that does engage in religious activities may also engage in non-religious activities and still qualify.[691] Thus, nonprofit, secularly focused organizations that are operated by churches qualify for the exemption.

261. An educational institution must have "extremely close ties to organized religion" to qualify for the religious exemption.[692] Institutions that are at least substantially "owned, supported, controlled, or managed by a particular religion" qualify and may base employment on affiliation with a specific religion.[693]

262. The Equal Employment Opportunity Commission (EEOC), charged with enforcing Title VII, has interpreted the religious exemption to apply only to decisions regarding hiring and firing employees.[694] The Supreme Court has not decided

688. *Ansonia Bd. of Educ. v. Philbrook*, 479 U.S. 60, 69 (1986).

689. *EEOC v. Abercrombie & Fitch Stores, Inc.*, 575 U.S. 768, 773–775 (2015).

690. *Fike v. United Methodist Children's Home*, 547 F. Supp. 286, 290 (E.D. Va. 1982), *aff'd*, 709 F.2d 284 (4th Cir. 1983).

691. *Corp. of the Presiding Bishop of The Church of Jesus Christ of Latter-day Saints v. Amos*, 483 U.S. 327, 340 (1987).

692. *EEOC v. Kamehameha Sch./Bishop Est.*, 990 F.2d 458, 460 (9th Cir. 1993) (as amended on denial of rehearing); *see also Garcia v. Salvation Army*, 918 F.3d 997, 1003 (9th Cir. 2019) ("The entity seeking the benefit of [Title VII's exemption for religious entities] bears the burden of proving it is exempt." (citing *Kamehameha Sch.*)); *LeBoon v. Lancaster Jewish Cmty. Ctr. Ass'n*, 503 F.3d 217, 226–227 (3d Cir. 2007) (discussing factors relevant to determining whether an entity's "purpose and character are primarily religious").

693. *Kamehameha Sch.*, 990 F.2d at 460 n.4.

694. EEOC Comp. Man. § 2.B.I (*Threshold Issues: Partial Exemptions/Exemptions for Discrimination Based on Religion*) (May 12, 2000), https://www.eeoc.gov/laws/guidance/section-2-threshold-issues (explaining that Title VII requirements do "not apply to discrimination by a religious organization on the basis of religion in *hiring and discharge*" (emphasis added)). *But cf. ibid.*, § 12.C.1 (*Religious Discrimination: Exceptions/Religious Organizations*) (Jan. 15, 2021), https://www.eeoc.gov/laws/guidance/section-12-religious-discrimination (explaining the exemption to Title VII

this issue, but federal appellate courts have rejected the EEOC's interpretation because Congress did not specifically apply the exemption only to hiring and firing but could have, had it intended to.[695]

IV. Bona Fide Occupational Qualification Exception

263. Employers must give Title VII non-discrimination protections to religious individuals except in specific circumstances, such as when the employer is a religious institution (*see* above) or when the nature of the job requires a member of a specific faith. A subsection of Title VII known as the "bona fide occupational qualification" (BFOQ) exception states, "It shall not be an unlawful employment practice for an employer to hire and employ employees … on the basis of … religion … in those certain instances where religion … is a bona fide occupational qualification reasonably necessary to the normal operation of that particular business or enterprise … ."[696]

264. Two cases illustrate how courts determine which discriminatory practices qualify for a Title VII BFOQ exception. In *Kern v. Dynalectron Corp.*, a US firm doing business in Saudi Arabia hired only Muslim pilots for flights into Mecca because Saudi Arabian law prohibited entry of non-Muslims to that area, under penalty of death. A federal district court held that the company's discriminatory hiring of only Muslim pilots, as well as its offer to reassign an employee who declined to convert to Islam, were based on a BFOQ because non-Muslims were unable to perform the job safely.[697] Because the BFOQ was reasonably necessary to the business's operation, the court concluded that the company's religious discrimination qualified for the Title VII exception. In contrast, in *Abrams v. Baylor College of Medicine*, a federal district court held that a medical school's exclusion of Jewish doctors from a rotation program in a Saudi Arabian hospital was not based on a BFOQ. The court found that school officials had failed to inquire about the "actual policy of the Kingdom of Saudi Arabia toward Jews participating in the program"; moreover, the court noted that similarly situated US schools had stipulated that their agreements with Saudi officials include non-discrimination clauses.[698] The court

applies to religious organizations "with respect to *the employment* of individuals of a particular religion to perform work connected with the carrying on … of its activities" (emphasis added) (quoting § 702(a)).

695. *Kennedy v. St. Joseph's Ministries, Inc.*, 657 F.3d 189, 193 (4th Cir. 2011); *Garcia*, 918 F.3d at 1004–1005 (following *Kennedy*).

696. 42 U.S.C. § 2000e-2(e)(1) (2018); *see also ibid.*, § 2000e-1(a) (also known as § 702), § 2000e-2(e)(2) (also known as § 703).

697. *Kern v. Dynalectron Corp.*, 577 F. Supp. 1196, 1201 (N.D. Tex. 1983), *aff'd*, 746 F.2d 810 (5th Cir. 1984).

698. *Abrams v. Baylor Coll. of Med.*, 581 F. Supp. 1570, 1576 (S.D. Tex. 1984), *aff'd in relevant part*, 805 F.2d 528 (5th Cir. 1986).

concluded that the medical school's policy was not a business necessity and did not qualify for a BFOQ exception and, thus, unlawfully discriminated under Title VII.[699]

V. Federal Protections under RFRA

265. Business owners, or employers, do have some protections from being compelled to support activities that violate their faith. The Religious Freedom Restoration Act prohibits the federal government from "substantially burden[ing] a person's exercise of religion" unless it uses "the least restrictive means" of furthering a "compelling governmental interest".[700] In *Burwell v. Hobby Lobby Stores, Inc.*, the Supreme Court held that "closely held corporations" could be exempt from an otherwise generally applicable law that required employers, through their group insurance plans, to: (1) pay for certain forms of birth control for their employees, including the "morning-after pill", or (2) pay a substantial fine.[701] The business owners claimed the law substantially burdened their free exercise of religion because compliance would facilitate abortions and noncompliance would result in significant financial loss.[702] The Supreme Court agreed with the business owners and found that the contraception mandate was not the least restrictive means of furthering a compelling government interest in ensuring access to birth control; therefore, it was unlawful under RFRA.[703] For additional discussion of *Hobby Lobby*, *see* Part VII (Religious Communities and Protections of the Individual), Chapter 6 (Medical Deontology).

VI. State Laws

266. Most states have enacted or recognized RFRA-like protections. *See* Part II (Religious Freedom in General), Chapter 1 (Individual Religious Freedom). Most states have also enacted laws similar to Title VII, using similar language regarding reasonable accommodation. California requires an employer to explore "any available reasonable alternative means of accommodating … religious belief or observance" before refusing to hire or before terminating an individual.[704] The law

699. *Abrams*, 581 F. Supp. at 1579. *But see Buxton v. Kurtinitis*, 862 F.3d 423, 431–433 (4th Cir. 2017) (concluding denial of college admission was lawful, where denial was due in part to applicant's repeated self-initiated references to religion in admissions interview, evidencing applicant's lack of interpersonal skills and awareness of social norms).

700. 42 U.S.C. § 2000bb-1.

701. *Burwell v. Hobby Lobby Stores, Inc.*, 573 U.S. 682, 689–691 (2014). "Generally, a closely held corporation is a corporation that: Has more than 50% of the value of its outstanding stock owned (directly or indirectly) by 5 or fewer individuals at any time during the last half of the tax year, and isn't a personal service corporation." *Frequently Asked Questions*, IRS, https://www.irs.gov/faqs/small-business-self-employed-other-business/entities/entities-5 (last updated Jun. 15, 2023).

702. *Hobby Lobby Stores, Inc.*, 573 U.S. at 720.

703. *Ibid.*, at 728–730, 736.

704. Cal. Gov't Code § 12940(l)(1) (West 2022).

specifically mentions accommodating Sabbath or other holy days, as well as religious dress and grooming standards, unless doing so would cause "undue hardship". New York similarly requires employers to reasonably accommodate an employee's Sabbath or holy day and "the wearing of [religious] attire, clothing, or facial hair", unless it would result in undue hardship.[705]

267. Some states and municipalities have enacted anti-discrimination laws that prohibit discrimination on the basis of sexual orientation and/or gender identity.[706] The Supreme Court's 2020 decision in *Bostock v. Clayton County* indicates that exemptions to such laws for religious employers may be granted under the First Amendment, RFRA, Title VII, and state laws offering similar protections.[707] Anti-discrimination laws have been challenged in cases where small businesses were sued for refusing to provide services in connection with same-sex weddings because owners believed doing so would violate their religious beliefs. For more information on these cases, *see* Part VII (Religious Communities and Protections of the Individual), Chapter 2 (Freedom to Marry).

§2. Religious Objections to Unions

268. Some religious organizations and individuals oppose the unionization of church employees or the participation in labor unions by individual members. For example, the Catholic Church has objected to unionization in church-owned entities.[708] Historically, the Seventh-day Adventist Church prohibited the organization of or participation in labor unions. However, in a 2003 statement, the Church acknowledged that circumstances may be "considerably different today" and appears to encourage members to base decisions on careful, individual study of the Church's teachings.[709]

I. Church Objections

269. In the 1970s the National Labor Relations Board (NLRB) ordered a number of schools owned by the Catholic Church to engage in negotiations with labor

---

705. N.Y. Exec. Law § 296(10)(a) (McKinney 2022).
706. For information on states that have enacted anti-discrimination laws prohibiting discrimination on the basis of sexual orientation and/or gender identity, *see Equality Maps: Nondiscrimination Laws*, MAP: Movement Advancement Project, https://www.lgbtmap.org/equality-maps/non_discrimination_laws (last visited Sep. 30, 2023).
707. *Bostock v. Clayton County*, 140 S. Ct. 1731, 1753–1754 (2020).
708. *See NLRB v. Cath. Bishop of Chi.*, 440 U.S. 490, 494 (1979).
709. *Employer and Employee Relationships*, Seventh-day Adventist Church, https://www.adventist.org/guidelines/employer-and-employee-relationships (noting that founder Ellen G. White "gave stern warnings about the trade union practices of her day. … [But s]ome would assert that the situation is considerably different today") (last visited Sep. 30, 2023).

unions over the employment of lay teachers because the schools taught both religious and secular subjects, or were not "completely religious".[710] To avoid difficult constitutional questions, the Supreme Court pointed to "the absence of a clear expression of Congress' [sic] intent to bring teachers in church-operated schools within the jurisdiction of the Board"[711] and concluded that the Board lacked authority to require such schools to engage in negotiations.[712]

II. Individual Objections

270. Individual members of a religious group may also object to union membership on religious grounds. In 1980, Congress amended the National Labor Relations Act (NLRA), exempting members of religious groups from being compelled into union membership:

> Any employee who is a member of and adheres to established and traditional tenets or teachings of a bona fide religion, body, or sect which has historically held conscientious objections to joining or financially supporting labor organizations shall not be required to join or financially support any labor organization as a condition of employment; [however] such employee may be required … to pay sums equal to such dues and initiation fees to a nonreligious, nonlabor organization charitable fund … .[713]

271. Essentially, the amendment allows members of a religious group historically opposed to union membership to substitute union dues with a contribution to charity. Based on Title VII's reasonable accommodation provision, this protection is also routinely extended to individuals who may not be members of a religious group but can prove that union membership is contrary to their own sincerely held personal religious beliefs.[714] For example, in *International Association of Machinists & Aerospace Workers, Lodge 751 v. Boeing Co.*, a woman was allowed to pay the equivalent of union dues to a charitable organization instead of the union because her personal study of the Bible led her to believe she should not join a union, even though the church she attended permitted union membership.[715] The EEOC's interpretation of Title VII also suggests this is the correct outcome.[716]

710. *Cath. Bishop*, 440 U.S. at 493–495.
711. *Ibid.*, at 507.
712. *Ibid.*
713. Pub. L. 96-593, 94 Stat. 3452, 3452 (1980) (codified at 29 U.S.C. § 169 (2018)).
714. *See, e.g., Int'l Ass'n of Machinists & Aerospace Workers, Lodge 751 v. Boeing Co.*, 833 F.2d 165, 169–170 (9th Cir. 1987).
715. *Ibid.*, at 168.
716. 29 C.F.R. § 1605.2(d)(2) (2022).

§3. ARBITRATION CLAUSES INCORPORATING RELIGIOUS LAW

272. Although not in widespread use, religious arbitration has had a long history in the United States, predating American independence.[717] Today, the Federal Arbitration Act (FAA) and the Uniform Arbitration Act (UAA) are the governing instruments for arbitration.[718] Due to the authority of the FAA and UAA, there are only minor differences among the states in religious arbitration enforcement.[719] Some Christians, Jews, and Muslims use religious-based arbitration aligned with the teachings and values of their faith traditions.[720] Religious arbitration awards are generally upheld by courts.[721] However, an arbitration award may be overturned on public policy grounds if it violates a state statute or regulation.[722] Arbitration agreements may also be nullified on public policy or even constitutional grounds. A California state court held that an arbitration agreement between a church and its members—which stipulated internal resolution of disputes using church rules of procedure—was not binding after the petitioners left the church. The court noted that neutral tort principles, rather than internal religious matters, were at issue and that the church's alleged tortious conduct occurred after the petitioners had terminated their membership. The court reasoned that the "petitioners' First Amendment rights to leave a faith" outweighed the church's "right to resolve disputes with its members without court intervention".[723]

273. The Tenth Circuit struck down an Oklahoma state constitutional amendment that proscribed state courts from "considering or using Sharia" (Islamic law), including in arbitration agreements.[724] The Tenth Circuit held that the Muslim plaintiff had standing under the Establishment Clause because he alleged direct injury

717. William E. Nelson, *Dispute and Conflict Resolution in Plymouth County, Massachusetts, 1725–1825*, at 43–44 (1981).
718. Federal Arbitration Act, Pub. L. No. 68-401, 43 Stat 883 (1925) (codified as amended at 9 U.S.C. §§ 1–16 (2018)). The UAA was promulgated by the National Conference of Commissioners on Uniform State Laws in 1955 and revised in 2000. Versions of the UAA have been adopted by thirty-five states. *See* Unif. Arbitration Act (Nat'l Conference of Comm'rs of Unif. State Laws 2010), https://www.uniformlaws.org/committees/community-home?CommunityKey=a0ad71d6-085f-4648-857a-e9e893ae2736 (last visited Sep. 30, 2023); Timothy J. Heinsz, *The Revised Uniform Arbitration Act: Modernizing, Revising, and Clarifying Arbitration Law*, 2001 J. Disp. Resol. 1, 1–2.
719. Nicholas Walter, *Religious Arbitration in the United States and Canada*, 52 Santa Clara L. Rev. 501, 516 (2012).
720. R. Seth Shippee, *"Blessed Are the Peacemakers": Faith-Based Approaches to Dispute Resolution*, 9 ILSA J. Int'l & Compar. L. 237 (2002).
721. *See, e.g.*, *Prescott v. Northlake Christian Sch.*, 141 F. App'x 263, 265, 275 (5th Cir. 2005).
722. *See, e.g.*, *Berg v. Berg*, 873 N.Y.S.2d 231 (N.Y. Sup. Ct. 2008), *aff'd as modified*, 926 N.Y.S.2d 568 (N.Y. App. Div. 2011) (vacating child support award and remanding the issue to Beth Din (Jewish) arbitration, on grounds that the award failed to comply with child support statute).
723. *Bixler v. Superior Ct.*, 2022 WL 167792, at *9 (Cal. Ct. App. Jan. 19, 2022). *But see* Daniel Kroll, *Faith-Based Arbitration: First Amendment Freedom or Major Concern?*, Colum. Undergraduate L. Rev. (Jan. 8, 2023), https://www.culawreview.org/journal/faith-based-arbitration-first-amendment-freedom-or-major-concern ("[I]t can be argued that an agreement to engage in religious arbitration … is the same as a secular arbitration contract; it merely compels parties to resolve claims according to a specific set of religious rules. Therefore, unless the agreement explicitly binds both parties to a religion, religious arbitration agreements can be enforced even if a party has left the faith.").
724. *Awad v. Ziriax*, 670 F.3d 1111, 1118, 1130–1133 (10th Cir. 2012).

from the amendment—that it exposed him to disfavored treatment, since Oklahoma law did not prohibit people of other faiths from relying on their religions' legal precepts in state court.[725] The Tenth Circuit further held that the amendment violated the Establishment Clause, on grounds that it was not narrowly tailored to serve a compelling state interest.[726] For more on religion-based alternative dispute resolution, *see* Part X (Matrimonial and Family Law), Chapter 2 (Legal Position of Religious Family Law).

725. *Ibid.*, at 1123.

726. *Ibid.*, at 1131 (declining to reach the appellee's free exercise claim since the "Establishment Clause claim provide[d] sufficient grounds to uphold the preliminary injunction").

Part IV. International, Transnational, and Regional Effects on Religious Communities

Chapter 1. International Law Effects on Religious Communities

§1. Basic Principles of International Law in the United States

274. Relative to international law and relations, the Constitution grants the executive branch the power, upon approval of the Senate, to make treaties with foreign nations and to appoint ambassadors.[727] The Constitution also authorizes the President to "receive Ambassadors and other public Ministers".[728] The legislative branch is expressly given the power to declare war and, in connection with that power, can "raise and support Armies".[729]

275. International law is implicated in the US system either through international agreements or through customary international law. US law distinguishes among three types of international agreements: (1) treaties, (2) congressional-executive agreements, and (3) sole executive agreements.[730] As a technical matter, congressional-executive agreements and sole executive agreements are not considered treaties under US domestic law, although there is no generally understood agreement as to the difference in effect between treaties and non-treaty agreements.[731] The Supreme Court held in *Dames & Moore v. Regan* that the President is able to make, with foreign states, unilateral executive agreements that have the force of the supreme law of the land.[732] The Court emphasized the narrowness of its decision, explaining that it did not mean that the President "possesses plenary power to settle claims, even as against foreign governmental entities"; however, the

727. U.S. Const. art. II, § 2, cl. 2 (Treaty Clause).
728. *Ibid.*, art. II, § 3.
729. *Ibid.*, art. I, § 8, cls. 11, 12.
730. In *United States v. Pink*, 315 U.S. 203, 229–231 (1942), the Supreme Court held that international executive agreements, while having the same legal status as treaties, did not require Senate approval; *see also About Treaties*, U.S. Senate, https://www.senate.gov/about/powers-procedures/treaties.htm (last visited Sep. 30, 2023).
731. Bradford R. Clark, *Domesticating Sole Executive Agreements,* 93 Va. L. Rev. 1573, 1579–1580 (2007).
732. *Dames & Moore v. Regan*, 453 U.S. 654, 688 (1981).

Court was "not prepared to say that the President lacks the power to settle such claims" if settlement was integral to resolving major disputes with foreign sovereignties.[733]

276. Under US law, the domestic effectiveness of a treaty, covenant, or agreement is not whether the agreement is styled as a treaty or covenant but rather how the agreement is ratified or implemented.[734]

I. Declarations

277. Declarations by their nature require no ratification. They provide guidelines to the participating states as to the development and implementation of laws. Declarations are not legally binding in the United States.

II. Treaties

278. Legal obligations of a treaty accrue upon ratification, which, under the US Constitution, requires a two-thirds vote of approval in the Senate.[735] In considering a treaty, the Senate may make its consent conditional on reservations, understandings, declarations (collectively known as RUDs), or provisos regarding the treaty application. Any of these conditions may modify or limit the United States' obligations under the treaty.[736]

III. Congressional-Executive Agreements

279. If the President gains approval of any international agreement by a joint House and Senate majority vote instead of by a two-thirds vote of the Senate alone, the resulting document is referred to as a congressional-executive agreement. Congress may authorize the agreement before negotiation and signing, or it may be retroactively authorized. US trade agreements such as the North American Free Trade Agreement (NAFTA), the World Trade Organization agreements, and bilateral free

733. *Ibid.*

734. *See* Cong. Rsch. Serv., S. Prt. 106-71, Treaties and Other International Agreements: The Role of the United States Senate 52–53 (Jan. 2001), https://www.congress.gov/106/cprt/SPRT66922/CPRT-106SPRT66922.pdf; *see also generally* Stephen P. Mulligan, Cong. Rsch. Serv., RL32528, International Law and Agreements: Their Effect upon U.S. Law (update Jul. 13, 2023), https://crsreports.congress.gov/product/pdf/RL/RL32528.

735. U.S. Const. art. II, § 2, cl. 2 (Treaty Clause). Note that international law suggests signing an unratified treaty creates a good faith obligation to "refrain from the acts which would defeat the object and purpose of [the] treaty". *See* Vienna Convention on the Law of Treaties, May 23, 1969, 1155 U.N.T.S. 331, arts. 10, 18.

736. Mulligan, International Law and Agreements, *supra* n. 734, at 4 & nn.28–31 (explaining the difference between the four types of conditions).

trade agreements (FTAs) are all examples of congressional-executive agreements.[737] These can be legally binding without additional action by Congress, unless the original congressional authorization requires such action.

IV. Sole Executive Agreement

280. The President may also choose to leverage the areas in which he has inherent authority to make a sole executive agreement, without the involvement of Congress. A large percentage of US international agreements are executed this way. Congress is typically notified of these agreements within sixty days of entry.[738] More than 18,500 executive agreements have been executed by the United States since 1789, the majority of which (17,300) have been executed after World War II.[739] These are effective and binding without action by Congress.

281. These agreements must be made pursuant to the inherent powers provided to the President under Article II of the Constitution. The authorities that Presidents may leverage in making such agreements include (1) their general executive authority under Article II, section 1; (2) their role as Commander in Chief of the Army and Navy under Article II, section 2, clause 1; and (3) their duty to "take Care that the Laws be faithfully executed" in Article II, section 3.[740] Courts have indicated that these agreements can supersede state law.[741]

V. Customary International Law

282. The Supreme Court has determined that "where there is no treaty and no controlling executive or legislative act or judicial decision, resort must be had to the customs and usages of civilized nations".[742] Customary international law is composed of two elements: state practice and *opinio juris*. State practice exists when all or nearly all nation states, including those that are specially affected, follow a custom or practice out of a sense of legal obligation. If they do so with a sense of legal obligation, often referred to as *opinio juris*, the practice becomes binding.

283. The United States often avoids being subject to customary international law either (1) through the international law doctrine of being a persistent objector, meaning it repeatedly explicitly renounces or rejects the custom and thereby distinguishes itself from the other nation states that practice the custom under a sense of

737. Mulligan, International Law and Agreements, *supra* n. 734, at 7.

738. 1 U.S.C. § 112b(a) (2018).

739. Michael J. Garcia, Cong. Rsch. Serv., RL32528, International Law and Agreements: Their Effect upon U.S. Law 4–5 (Sep. 24, 2015), https://www.everycrsreport.com/files/20150924_RL32528_2ce3cbc59891da783bdb9fa34756754810d4d301.pdf.

740. Cong. Rsch. Serv., Treaties and Other International Agreements, *supra* n. 734, at 5.

741. *See United States v. Pink*, 315 U.S. 203, 230–231 (1942); *United States v. Belmont*, 301 U.S. 324, 330–331 (1937).

742. *The Paquete Habana*, 175 U.S. 677, 700 (1900).

obligation; or (2) by passing a contradictory statute. Under the domestic "later-in-time" rule, the more recent statute will be controlling.[743]

§2. Effects of International Agreements

284. Article VI, clause 2, of the US Constitution indicates that the Constitution, federal laws, and all treaties made under federal authority shall be the "supreme Law of the Land" and shall bind the judicial system. This is known as the "Supremacy Clause". While a textual interpretation of the clause could suggest that the Constitution, federal laws, and treaties share equal weight or power, courts have considered international law to be equal in force with statutes enacted by Congress but subordinate to the US Constitution.[744] Although statutes may be equal in force with international law, courts generally employ the canon that statutes be interpreted in a way that avoids conflicts with treaties. In 1804, in *Murray v. Schooner Charming Betsy*, Supreme Court Chief Justice John Marshall stated that "an act of Congress ought never to be construed to violate the law of nations if any other possible construction remains".[745] If it is not possible to interpret a statute in a way that avoids conflict with a treaty, then the "last in time" prevails.[746]

285. In conflicts between international agreements and federal or state laws, the controlling authority of international agreements depends in part on whether they are deemed self-executing or non-self-executing.

I. Self-Executing Agreements

286. Self-executing agreements are international agreements with provisions that have the force of law without necessitating subsequent action by Congress.[747] In contrast, a non-self-executing treaty requires subsequent legislation by governmental bodies to implement the agreement's obligations or for the agreement to

743. Mulligan, International Law and Agreements, *supra* n. 734, at 28.

744. *See, e.g., Cunard S.S. Co. v. Mellon*, 262 U.S. 100, 128–131 (1923) (upholding legislation that both domestic and foreign ships in US territory could be subject to seizure of liquor during the Prohibition era); *United States ex. rel. Pfefer v. Bell*, 248 F. 992, 995 (E.D.N.Y. 1918) (holding that "the rules of international law, like those of existing treaties or conventions, are subject to the express acts of Congress").

745. *Murray v. Schooner Charming Betsy*, 6 U.S. (2 Cranch) 64, 118 (1804); *see also* Curtis A. Bradley, *The* Charming Betsy *Canon and Separation of Powers: Rethinking the Interpretive Role of International Law*, 86 Geo. L.J. 479, 485–488 (1998).

746. *See Reid v. Covert*, 354 U.S. 1, 18 (1957) ("[W]hen a statute which is subsequent in time is inconsistent with a treaty, the statute to the extent of conflict renders the treaty null."); Alina Kaczorowska-Ireland, *Public International Law* 158 (5th ed. 2015) ("Where there is a conflict between a federal statute and a treaty, the last in time prevails."). *But see generally* Vasan Kesavan, *The Three Tiers of Federal Law*, 100 Nw. U. L. Rev. 1479 (2006) (proposing a superiority-of-statutes approach to replace the "weak" last-in-time approach to resolving statute-treaty conflicts).

747. *Cook v. United States*, 288 U.S. 102, 119 (1933) ("For in a strict sense the Treaty was self-executing, in that no legislation was necessary to authorize executive action pursuant to its provisions.").

apply to private parties.[748] A ratified self-executing treaty is placed "on the same footing" as federal law and "no superior efficacy is given to either over the other".[749] If there is a conflict between a self-executing treaty and a statute, the Supreme Court has ruled that the one enacted later in time controls.[750] A self-executing executive agreement is likely to be found "superior to [US] state law, but inferior to the Constitution".[751]

II. Non-self-executing Agreements

287. Treaties and executive agreements, or provisions therein, that cannot be enforced judicially unless Congress has enacted "implementing legislation" are deemed non-self-executing.[752] Treaties have been found non-self-executing for the following reasons: (1) the agreement demonstrates an intent not to take effect in the absence of legislation; (2) in the approval process, the appropriate legislative body (either the Senate in ratification of a treaty or Congress through resolution) required implementing legislation; or (3) the Constitution requires it.[753] Traditionally, the Constitution requires implementing legislation to accompany a non-self-executing agreement when the subject of the agreement lies within the legislative power granted to Congress in the Constitution.[754]

§3. International Instruments Addressing Religious Issues to Which the United States Is a Party

I. Declarations

288. While the United States is a party to the following declarations, they are not legally binding and have no force of law in the United States.

---

748. Mulligan, International Law and Agreements, *supra* n. 734, at 15.
749. *Whitney v. Robertson*, 124 U.S. 190, 194 (1888).
750. Ralph G. Steinhardt, Paul L. Hoffman & Christopher N. Camponovo, *International Human Rights Lawyering: Cases and Materials* 148 (1st ed. 2008).
751. Mulligan, International Law and Agreements, *supra* n. 734, at 20 (citing *Ware v. Hylton*, 3 U.S. (3 Dall.) 199, 237 (1796) ("[L]aws of any of the States, contrary to a treaty, shall be disregarded.")).
752. *See Foster v. Neilson*, 27 U.S. (2 Pet.) 253, 314 (1829), *overruled by United States v. Percheman*, 32 U.S. 51 (1833) ("Our constitution declares a treaty to be the law of the land. It is, consequently, to be regarded in courts of justice as equivalent to an act of the legislature, whenever it operates of itself without the aid of any legislative provision. But when the terms of the stipulation import a contract, when either of the parties engages to perform a particular act, the treaty addresses itself to the political, not the judicial department; and the legislature must execute the contract before it can become a rule for the Court.").
753. Restatement (Third) of the Foreign Rels. L. of the U.S. § 111(4) (Am. L. Inst. 1987), Westlaw REST 3d FOREL (database updated 2023).
754. *Ibid.*, cmt. i.

289. The Universal Declaration of Human Rights (UDHR) was adopted in the third session of the United Nations General Assembly on December 10, 1948.[755] It was the first global document to set forth standards for human rights. Article 18 of the Declaration declares, "Everyone has the right to freedom of thought, conscience and religion". A subsequent international treaty, the International Covenant on Civil and Political Rights (ICCPR), was adopted in the twenty-first session of the United Nations General Assembly on December 16, 1966.[756] Unlike the UHDR, the ICCPR is legally binding on nations that have ratified it, including the United States. Article 18 of the ICCPR is similar to Article 18 of the UDHR, stating that all have the right to "freedom of thought, conscience and religion", including the "freedom to have or to adopt a religion or belief"[757] and to manifest their "religion or belief in worship, observance, practice and teaching".

290. The American Declaration of the Rights and Duties of Man was adopted by the Ninth International Conference of American States in Bogota, Columbia, in May 1948.[758] While not legally binding like a treaty, the Inter-American Court of Human Rights and the Inter-American Commission on Human Rights consider its provisions obligatory for participating member states.[759] It outlines a set of civil, political, economic, social, and cultural rights due to the citizens of signatory nations. Chapter One, Article III, protects the right to profess, practice, and manifest religious faith, both in private and public. For additional discussion, *see* this part, Chapter 3 (Regional Law Effects on Religious Communities), below.

291. The Declaration on the Elimination of All Forms of Intolerance and of Discrimination Based on Religion or Belief (also known as the "1981 Declaration") was approved in the thirty-sixth session of the United Nations General Assembly on November 25, 1981.[760] Article 1 states that individuals should not be subject to coercion that would impair their freedom to have religious or personal beliefs. Article 6 outlines specific protected manifestations of individuals' right to freedom of thought, conscience, and belief. And Article 5 gives parents and legal guardians the authority to organize and raise their families according to their beliefs or religion, provided doing so does not injure a child's physical or mental health and development.

292. The Declaration on the Human Rights of Individuals Who Are Not Nationals of the Country in Which They Live was adopted without a vote in the fortieth

---

755. G.A. Res. 217 A (III), Universal Declaration of Human Rights (Dec. 10, 1948).
756. G.A. Res. 2200A (XXI), International Covenant on Civil and Political Rights (Dec. 16, 1966).
757. Article 18 of the UDHR, in contrast, states that "[e]veryone has the … freedom to change his religion or belief".
758. OAS Res. XXX, American Declaration of the Rights and Duties of Man, May 2, 1948, 1 *Annals of the O.A.S.* 130 (1949).
759. *See* Christina M. Cerna, *Reflections on the Normative Status of the American Declaration of the Rights and Duties of Man*, Inter-Am. Ct. H.R. (Feb. 2, 2009), https://www.corteidh.or.cr/tablas/r31598.pdf (explaining the Commission's and Court's reasoning in finding the American Declaration obligatory but arguing that such a finding "is a useful mechanism, but a legal fiction").
760. G.A. Res. 36/55, Declaration on the Elimination of All Forms of Intolerance and of Discrimination Based on Religion or Belief (Nov. 25, 1981).

session of the United Nations General Assembly on December 13, 1985.[761] Article I of this declaration sets forth the definition and human rights of resident "aliens". Referencing the UDHR and the ICCPR and other covenants, Article 5(e) affirms that the freedoms of "thought, opinion, conscience and religion" should be afforded not only to a country's citizens but also to its non-citizens.

293. The Declaration on the Rights of Persons Belonging to National or Ethnic, Religious and Linguistic Minorities was adopted by the UN General Assembly on December 18, 1992.[762] Inspired by Article 27 of the ICCPR, this declaration explains that states have an obligation to acknowledge and promote the rights of minority cultures, identities, languages, and religions.

II. Relevant International Instruments That Have Been Signed and Ratified by the United States

294. The Convention Relating to the Status of Refugees, adopted in 1950, identifies refugees as those who either experienced past persecution or have a well-founded fear of future persecution on account of religion or other protected ground.[763] It also identifies the fundamental human rights of those who qualify as refugees that should be recognized and protected. The Convention is based on the principle of "non-refoulement", which prohibits the expulsion or return of refugees to a territory where their life or freedom would be threatened because of religion or other protected ground.[764] The United States has ratified the Protocol Relating to the Status of Refugees, which incorporates Articles 2 through 34 of the Convention Relating to the Status of Refugees.[765]

295. The International Convention on the Elimination of All Forms of Racial Discrimination (CERD) was signed by the United States on September 28, 1966 but not ratified until October 21, 1994.[766] It entered into force on November 20, 1994. Article 5 of the Convention states that civil rights include "[t]he right to freedom of thought, conscience and religion". The United States filed three reservations, one understanding, and one declaration concerning the document that effectually exempted the United States from any obligations not found in US law.[767] First, the

761. G.A. Res. 40/144, Declaration on the Human Rights of Individuals Who Are Not Nationals of the Country in Which They Live (Dec. 13, 1985).
762. G.A. Res. 47/135, Declaration on the Rights of Persons Belonging to National or Ethnic, Religious and Linguistic Minorities (Dec. 18, 1992).
763. Convention Relating to the Status of Refugees, *approved* Jul. 28, 1951, 19 U.S.T. 6259, 189 U.N.T.S. 150 (recognizing the protected characteristics of race, religion, nationality, membership of a particular social group, and political opinion).
764. *Ibid.*, art. 33(1).
765. U.S. Dep't of State, *Treaties in Force: A List of Treaties and Other International Agreements of the United States in Force on January 1, 2020*, at 30, https://www.state.gov/treaties-in-force (link to PDF) (last visited Sep. 30, 2023).
766. International Convention on the Elimination of All Forms of Racial Discrimination, *opened for signature* Dec. 21, 1965, 660 U.N.T.S. 195.
767. *See* 140 Cong. Rec. 14,326 (1994).

United States indicated that the US Constitution contains enough provisions for the protection of individual freedoms and that nothing in the Convention should be deemed to require or authorize legislation or other action. Second, the United States did not accept obligations under Article 4, which criminalizes hate speech, or Article 7, which prohibits racism in education, because they conflict with constitutional rights of expression, speech, and association. Third, the United States distinguished between areas of "public life", which government can regulate, and private conduct, which the US government does not customarily regulate, and did not accept any obligation to enact legislation to regulate private conduct outside the scope of the Constitution. Fourth, the United States stipulated that its consent was required before any dispute (to which the United States is a party) could be submitted to the jurisdiction of the International Court of Justice.

296. The International Covenant on Civil and Political Rights (ICCPR) is a multilateral treaty that commits parties to uphold civil and political rights and to promote "universal respect for, and observance of, human rights and freedoms", including the right to freedom of religion or belief.[768] The US Senate ratified the Convention in 1992, but with five reservations, five understandings, and four declarations. The first understanding clarified that "[t]he United States understands distinctions based upon race, color, sex, language, religion, political or other opinion, national or social origin, property, birth or any other status … to be permitted when such distinctions are, at minimum, rationally related to a legitimate governmental objective."[769] This understanding points to "rational basis review" that US courts apply to cases under the Fourteenth Amendment's Equal Protection Clause.

III. Relevant International Instruments That the United States Has Signed but Not Ratified

297. The International Covenant on Economic, Social and Cultural Rights (ICESCR) was adopted by the United Nations General Assembly on December 16, 1966.[770] President Jimmy Carter signed the treaty on October 5, 1977. Part II, Article 2, section 2, of the Covenant states, "[t]he State Parties … undertake to guarantee that the rights enunciated in the … Covenant will be exercised without discrimination of any kind as to race, colour, sex, language, religion, political or other opinion, national or social origin, property, birth or other status." The reasons for lack of political will to ratify the ICESCR have varied through US presidential administrations.[771]

---

768. International Covenant on Civil and Political Rights, *adopted* Dec. 19, 1966, 999 U.N.T.S. 171, pmbl., art. 18.
769. 138 Cong. Rec. 8071 (1992).
770. International Covenant on Economic, Social and Cultural Rights, *adopted* Dec. 16, 1966, 993 U.N.T.S. 3.
771. *See* Amnesty Int'l USA, *Economic, Social and Cultural Rights: Questions and Answers* 6 (Jun. 26, 2008), https://web.archive.org/web/20080626051117/http://www.amnestyusa.org/escr/files/escr_qa.pdf.

298. All UN member countries except the United States and Somalia have ratified the Convention on the Rights of the Child (CRC), which President Bill Clinton signed in 1995.[772] Resistance to the treaty in the United States comes largely from conservatives who are "concerned that CRC could interfere in the private lives of families, particularly the rights of parents to educate or discipline their children".[773]

299. The American Convention on Human Rights was adopted in San Jose, Costa Rica, on November 22, 1969.[774] The United States signed it in 1977 but has never ratified it. The American Convention contains numerous references to freedom of religion.[775] Article 12 is largely modelled on Article 18 of the Universal Declaration of Human Rights and states, "Everyone has the right to freedom of conscience and of religion. This right includes freedom to maintain or to change one's religion or beliefs, and freedom to profess or disseminate one's religion or beliefs, either individually or together with others, in public or in private." Article 12, paragraph 3, dictates that limitations on these rights must be prescribed by law and necessary to protect "public safety, order, health, or morals, or the rights or freedoms of others".[776] The United States' failure to ratify is due partly to the "right to life" provisions in Article 4.1, which indicate that life should be protected from "the moment of conception". This concept has, in more recent history, contradicted US abortion laws.

§4. References to International Law in US Cases

300. The Supremacy Clause states that "all treaties made, or which shall be made, under the authority of the United States, shall be the supreme law of the land; and the judges in every state shall be bound thereby, anything in the Constitution or laws of any State to the contrary notwithstanding".[777] Customary international law may be applied directly by US courts, but international law generally appears in cases in the form of "codification by Congress; implementation through executive branch orders or regulations; indirect application through statutory interpretation; or a fusion of international and domestic legal principles in judicially developed common law".[778]

301. While international law is not typically considered in US courts, a number of US cases have dealt with religious groups and international laws. In *Gonzales v.*

772. Convention on the Rights of the Child, *adopted* Nov. 20, 1989, 1577 U.N.T.S. 3.
773. Cong. Rsch. Serv., R40484, The United Nations Convention on the Rights of the Child, at i (Summary), 9 (updated Jul. 27, 2015), https://crsreports.congress.gov/product/pdf/R/R40484/25.
774. Org. of Am. States, American Convention on Human Rights, *adopted* Nov. 22, 1969, S. Treaty Doc. No. 95-21, 1144 U.N.T.S. 123, O.A.S.T.S. No. 36 [hereinafter American Convention on Human Rights].
775. *See ibid.*, art. 1, para. 1; art. 12, paras. 1–4; art. 13, para. 5; art. 16, para. 1; art. 22, para. 8; art. 27, paras. 1–2.
776. *Ibid.*, art. 12, para. 3.
777. U.S. Const. art. VI, cl. 2.
778. Curtis A. Bradley, *International Law in the U.S. Legal System* 345 (3d ed. 2020).

O Centro Espirita Beneficente Uniao do Vegetal, the US Supreme Court rejected the idea that enforcement of the United Nations Convention on Psychotropic Substances necessarily creates a compelling state interest that would justify a substantial burden on a claimant's religious freedom.[779]

302. In another case, the Presbyterian Church of Sudan, several individuals, and an American nonprofit corporation brought a class action suit in the United States alleging that a Canadian oil company conspired with the Sudanese government to violate international law. Along with claims of human rights violations, the plaintiffs alleged that at least seventeen churches were deliberately destroyed due to their proximity to the company's oil fields.[780] The federal district court explained that it was an "inferior court" and unlike international courts, which are not governed by *stare decisis*, it was obligated to rely not only on sources of international law but also interpretations of that law by the US Supreme Court and Second Circuit Court of Appeals.[781] Relying on both international and US precedent, the district court held that the oil company was potentially liable for international human rights violations and that the plaintiffs, including the church, had standing to sue.[782] The Second Circuit later applied international law standards, however, to find that the plaintiffs failed to show the Canadian oil company acted purposely to advance human rights abuses by the Sudanese government.[783]

303. In *American Baptist Churches in the U.S.A. v. Meese*, religious and refugee organizations alleged discriminatory application of immigration laws and challenged government prosecution of members for "harboring illegal aliens".[784] The religious organizations asserted that their "determin[ation] to offer sanctuary to persons from El Salvador and Guatemala" was "a matter of religious faith and practice".[785] The organizations also pointed to international treaties and customary international law that conferred on refugees the right to temporary relief in the United States. The US district court held that the religious organizations lacked standing relative to their free exercise claim because they sought an injunction against prosecution under a prior version of a statute and, therefore, did not show a substantial likelihood that their requested relief would prevent future prosecutions under the revised law. The court also held that the Geneva Convention Relative to the Protection of Civilian Persons in Time of War did not provide a right of temporary refuge to the Salvadorans or Guatemalans within the United States.[786]

---

779. *Gonzales v. O Centro Espirita Beneficente Uniao do Vegetal*, 546 U.S. 418, 437–438 (2006).
780. *Presbyterian Church of Sudan v. Talisman Energy, Inc.*, 244 F. Supp. 2d 289, 301 (S.D.N.Y. 2003).
781. *Ibid.*, at 305.
782. *Ibid.*, at 296.
783. *Presbyterian Church of Sudan v. Talisman Energy, Inc.*, 582 F.3d 244, 247–248 (2d Cir. 2009); *see also Kiobel v. Royal Dutch Petroleum Co.*, 621 F.3d 111, 138 (2d Cir. 2010) (noting that the district court in *Presbyterian Church* had "erroneously overvalued the importance of a number of international treaties in finding that corporate liability has attained the status of customary international law").
784. *Am. Baptist Churches in the U.S.A. v. Meese*, 712 F. Supp. 756, 764 (N.D. Cal. 1989).
785. *Ibid.*, at 759.
786. *Ibid.*, at 769–770.

Eventually, however, the Guatemalan and Salvadoran nationals involved in the case reached a class action settlement agreement with the US government relative to their claims of discriminatory application of immigration laws.[787]

787. *See Am. Baptist Churches v. Thornburgh*, 760 F. Supp. 796 (N.D. Cal. 1991) (approving and outlining "ABC" class action agreement).

Chapter 2. Transnational Law Effects on Religious Communities

§1. US Law with International Effects

I. International Religious Freedom Act

304. The International Religious Freedom Act of 1998 (IRFA) was adopted by the United States to promote freedom of religion throughout the world.[788] The Act creates an Office of International Religious Freedom within the Department of State. The duties of this office include (1) releasing an annual report on the status of religious liberty in all countries of the world, (2) contributing religious freedom-related information to the State Department's individual Country Reports on Human Rights Practices, and (3) helping identify governments or entities that either engage in or tolerate violations of religious freedom.[789] The latter are designated by the President as Countries of Particular Concern (CPCs), Special Watch List (SWL) Countries, or Entities of Particular Concern (EPCs).[790] The Ambassador at Large, who leads the office, acts as a policy advisor to the President and the Secretary of State and as a diplomatic representative abroad in matters concerning religious freedom abroad.[791]

305. The Ambassador at Large also serves as a non-voting member on the United States Commission on International Religious Freedom (USCIRF). The rest of the Commission is composed of members appointed by the President, the President pro tempore of the Senate, and the Speaker of the House of Representatives.[792] USCIRF was designed to monitor the State Department's Office of Religious Freedom, evaluate policy, and make policy recommendations in response to circumstances—either progression or deterioration—of religious freedom throughout the world.[793]

306. IRFA provides a list of fifteen potential responses the President is required to choose from in responding to violations, ranging from a private demarche to heavy sanctions on the governments that are either participating in or tolerating violations of religious liberties.[794] When violations are considered severe under IRFA, the President must choose from the more serious responses on the list.[795] This process allows the United States to help focus attention on the condition of religious

788. International Religious Freedom Act of 1998 (IRFA), Pub. L. No. 105-292, 112 Stat. 2787 (codified as amended at 22 U.S.C. §§ 4028, 6401–6483 (2018)).
789. 22 U.S.C. § 6412 (2018).
790. *Ibid.*; *Countries of Particular Concern, Special Watch List Countries, Entities of Particular Concern*, U.S. Dep't State [hereinafter *Countries of Particular Concern*], https://www.state.gov/countries-of-particular-concern-special-watch-list-countries-entities-of-particular-concern (last visited Sep. 30, 2023).
791. 22 U.S.C § 6411.
792. *Ibid.*, § 6431.
793. *Ibid.*, § 6432.
794. *Ibid.*, §§ 6441, 6445.
795. *Ibid.*, § 6442.

freedom throughout the world as well as provide incentives to governments to protect and promote freedom of religion or belief. Many outside the United States criticize US "name and shame" policies. However, US policy promoting religious freedom focuses largely on positive reinforcement and persuasive methods, such as providing human rights education and training in foreign countries and supporting international human rights organizations, rather than coercive methods, such as imposing sanctions.[796]

307. IRFA creates an avenue for the United States to influence religious freedom policy abroad by mandating an annual Report to Congress on International Religious Freedom. The annual report facilitates awareness of current conditions worldwide, and the findings allow the United States to condemn violations and encourage improved laws, policies, and practices relative to freedom of religion or belief. Past and current reports can be found at https://www.state.gov/international-religious-freedom-reports. For additional discussion, *see* Part I (Legal Framework and Sources), Chapter 2 (Other Legislation with Regard to Religion); and Part V (Religion and Politics), Chapter 3 (Interaction Between Religion and State).

II. Foreign Corrupt Practices Act

308. The Foreign Corrupt Practices Act (FCPA) was passed in 1977 after a study revealed that more than 400 US businesses were participating in suspicious business practices.[797] The FCPA is intended to prevent US parties from giving anything of value to foreign officials or third parties to gain their assistance in obtaining or retaining business.

309. While not directly concerned with religion or religious organizations, the FCPA is significant for its extraterritorial reach and valuable for its efforts to promote transparency. Religious organizations, like other groups, face demands internationally for bribes in efforts to obtain routine government approvals, and the FCPA reflects a major attempt to address this issue internationally through US law.

§2. Foreign Laws with Effects in the United States

310. Various laws of other countries may affect the functioning of individuals and religious organizations in the United States, particularly religious organizations with international scope. These organizations are affected by national laws on immigration, taxation, currency exchange, import and export duties, privacy, land ownership, and more.

---

796. *See About Us*, Off. Int'l Religious Freedom, *supra* n. 217; *Frequently Asked Questions: IRF Report and Countries of Particular Concern*, U.S. Dep't State, https://www.state.gov/frequently-asked-questions-irf-report-and-countries-of-particular-concern (last visited Sep. 30, 2023).

797. Foreign Corrupt Practices Act of 1977, Pub. L. No. 95-213, 91 Stat. 1494 (codified as amended at 15 U.S.C. §§ 78m, 78o, 78dd-1 to -3, 78ff (2018)).

I. EU Data Privacy Protections

311. One significant set of laws that affect transnational US religious organizations is data privacy laws, particularly those in the European Union. In 1995, the European Union adopted the Common Position on the Protection of Individuals with Regard to the Processing of Personal Data and on the Free Movement of Such Data (EU directive), which had considerably more stringent requirements than US law. The directive was superseded by the more expansive, modern General Data Protection Regulation (GDPR), which was enacted by the European Union in 2016 and went into effect in 2018.[798] The regulation is directly binding on member states[799] but also affects any organization outside the European Union that offers services to individuals within the European Union or collects, stores, or uses their personal data.

312. To continue their information storing and transmitting activities within the European Union (EU), US religious and other organizations that have a presence there must conform to very specific information-handling requirements under the GDPR, such as seeking permission from organization members to keep or transmit their personal information.[800] In contrast, in the United States, religious organizations operate under the self-governance framework created by the US government.

313. In an effort to close the gap between the EU and US data protection frameworks, the US Department of Commerce and the European Commission developed the EU-US Safe Harbor (2000–2015) and EU-US Privacy Shield (2016–2020) Frameworks, through which US organizations could agree to meet EU data protection standards. Both frameworks, however, were declared invalid by the European Court of Justice.[801] A new Trans-Atlantic Data Privacy Framework was approved by US and EU authorities in 2022 and 2023 and went into effect in 2023. In the

798. Regulation (EU) 2016/679 of the European Parliament and of the Council of April 27, 2016 on the Protection of Natural Persons with Regard to the Processing of Personal Data and on the Free Movement of Such Data, and Repealing Directive 95/46/EC (General Data Protection Regulation), 2016 OJ (L 119/1).

799. The UK incorporated GDPR provisions into UK law through its 2018 Data Protection Act (DPA) and (post-Brexit) 2021 amendments, resulting in the "UK GDPR".

800. For example, article 9.1 of the GDPR states that "Processing of personal data revealing … religious or philosophical beliefs … shall be prohibited." 2016 OJ (L 119/1) art. 9.1. Nonprofit religious organizations are exempt from this general rule if the processing relates "solely to the members or to former members of the body or to persons who have regular contact with it in connection with its purposes and that the personal data are not disclosed outside that body without the consent of the data subjects". *Ibid.*, art. 9.2(d).

801. *See* Case C-362/14, *Schrems v. Data Prot. Comm'r (Schrems I)*, ECLI:EU:C:2015:650 (finding the Safe Harbor Framework provided inadequate protections against US government access to data); Case C-311/18, *Data Prot. Comm'r v. Facebook Ireland Ltd. (Schrems II)*, ECLI:EU:C:2020:559 (invalidating the Privacy Shield Network for similar reasons).

interim, before the new framework went into effect, organizations generally relied on private contracts to facilitate data transfers.[802]

II. Religious Asylum Law

314. International treaties, US law, and foreign law (and its enforcement or lack thereof) all help define and determine who qualifies for religious asylum in the United States. The United States follows the 1951 Hague Convention Relating to the Status of Refugees in recognizing and granting religious refugee status based on the international human rights principle of non-refoulement.[803] The Immigration and Nationality Act of 1952 (INA) governs immigration to the United States and US citizenship.[804] The Act both reflects and codifies broad deference historically granted to the President and the executive branch in immigration matters, due to immigration's implications for national security.[805] President Donald Trump, for example, relied on executive authority under the INA to implement sweeping measures to severely restrict refugee and other migrant inflows into the United States, both before and during the COVID-19 pandemic.[806] In *Trump v. Hawaii*, the Supreme Court held that a 2017 Presidential Proclamation restricting travel to the United States from eight countries—six with Muslim-majority populations—was within the President's broad authority under the INA.[807] Applying "rational basis" review, the Court also held that the Proclamation did not violate the Establishment Clause, given that the list of restricted countries was limited to countries previously deemed security risks, included non-Muslim-majority countries, and applied to "just 8% of the world's Muslim population".[808]

315. The INA empowers the Attorney General to grant asylum to non-US citizens who have experienced or fear persecution in their home countries on account

802. Although the court in *Schrems II* did not find contracts such as standard contractual clauses (SCCs) invalid per se, it did indicate that SCCs must include monitoring safeguards to ensure US law did not undermine their guaranteed adequate level of data protection. *See* Case C-311/18, ¶¶ 94–96, 105, 108, 121.

803. Convention Relating to the Status of Refugees, *supra* n. 763.

804. Immigration and Nationality Act, Pub. L. No. 82-414, 66 Stat. 163 (1952) (codified as amended in scattered ss. of 8 U.S.C. § 1101–1778 (2018)).

805. *See Trump v. Hawaii*, 138 S. Ct. 2392, 2421–2422 (2018) ("[W]e cannot substitute our own assessment for the Executive's predictive judgments on [national security] matters, all of which are delicate, complex, and involve large elements of prophecy. While we of course do not defer to the Government's reading of the First Amendment, the Executive's evaluation of the underlying facts is entitled to appropriate weight, particularly in the context of litigation involving sensitive and weighty interests of national security and foreign affairs." (citations and internal quotation marks omitted)).

806. *See generally* Sarah Pierce & Jessica Bolter, Migration Pol'y Inst., *Dismantling and Reconstructing the U.S. Immigration System: A Catalog of Changes under the Trump Presidency* (July 2020), https://www.migrationpolicy.org/sites/default/files/publications/MPI_US-Immigration-Trump-Presidency-Final.pdf (noting, for example, that "the administration … largely dismantled the U.S. asylum system" and "set the lowest annual refugee admission ceilings of any administrations").

807. *Trump*, 138 S. Ct. at 2420–2423 (2018).

808. *Ibid.*, at 2421, 2423.

of a protected ground: religion, race, nationality, political opinion, or membership in a particular social group.[809] Bars to asylum include convictions for certain types of crimes, participation in the persecution of others, "firm resettlement" in another country prior to arrival in the United States, and a determination that the applicant poses a national security risk.[810] To receive asylum, applicants must file an application within one year of their arrival in the United States. Applicants seeking asylum on religious grounds must demonstrate that they either have suffered past persecution or have a "well-founded fear" of future persecution on account of their religion.[811] In addition, applicants must show that the persecution was or would be committed by their home government or by actors their home government is unable or unwilling to control.[812] In *INS v. Cardoza-Fonseca*, the Supreme Court held that the "well-founded fear" standard has both objective and subjective components and can be satisfied even if there is a "less than 50% chance of the [persecution] taking place".[813]

316. To avoid abuse of the asylum system, the US government requires applicants to provide credible testimony and, in addition, generally requires corroborating evidence.[814] Therefore, applicants with religion-based claims may be questioned about their religious practices, or applicants may ask clergy members to testify on their behalf as evidence of involvement in their respective churches. In such cases, church authorities may have to evaluate their members' asylum applications and verify their truthfulness before they testify for applicants. Failure to do so can subject an organization and/or its representatives to claims of fraud or conspiracy to commit fraud.[815]

809. 8 U.S.C. § 1158(b) (2018).
810. *See ibid.*, § 1158(b)(2).
811. *Ibid.*, §§ 1101(a)(42), 1158(b).
812. *Villegas Sanchez v. Garland*, 990 F.3d 1173, 1179 (9th Cir. 2021).
813. *INS v. Cardoza-Fonseca*, 480 U.S. 421, 431, 440 (1987). Though not as an explicit holding, the Court further stated, "There is simply no room in the United Nations' definition for concluding that because an applicant only has a 10% chance of being … persecuted, that he or she has no 'well-founded fear' of the event happening." *Ibid.*, at 440. Courts interpret this to mean that "even a ten percent chance of persecution may establish a well-founded fear". *See, e.g.*, *Al-Harbi v. INS*, 242 F.3d 882, 888 (9th Cir. 2001) (citing *Cardoza-Fonseca*, 480 U.S. at 440); *Sanchez Jimenez v. U.S. Att'y Gen.*, 492 F.3d 1223, 1234 (11th Cir. 2007) (citing the same).
814. 8 U.S.C. § 1158(b)(1)(B)(ii).
815. 18 U.S.C. §§ 371, 1546(a) (2018); *see, e.g.*, Press Release, FBI, Liying Lin Found Guilty of Immigration Fraud Offenses Following One-Week Jury Trail in Manhattan Federal Court (Feb. 26, 2014), https://archives.fbi.gov/archives/newyork/press-releases/2014/liying-lin-found-guilty-of-immigration-fraud-offenses-following-one-week-jury-trial-in-manhattan-federal-court.

Chapter 3. Regional Law Effects on Religious Communities

§1. Organization of American States

317. A significant regional community of which the United States is a member is the Organization of American States (OAS), which was formed by a charter signed in 1948 by twenty-one nations of the American continents. In large part, the OAS was born of an urgency to create a system that would protect against the ravages of continental warfare experienced in the World Wars. The Organization now includes all thirty-five independent states of the Americas.

318. The OAS Charter implicitly addressed religious freedom and a concern for the religions of the Americas by seeking "consolidation on this continent, within the framework of democratic institutions, of a system of individual liberty and social justice based on respect for the essential rights of man".[816] Nonetheless, the primary focus of the OAS was to provide solidarity, not to "intervene in matters that are within the internal jurisdiction of the Member States".[817] Even so, the Organization has been foundational to the creation of other regional institutions that affect religious communities in member states. These institutions include the autonomous Inter-American Commission on Human Rights and Inter-American Court of Human Rights, which are responsible for overseeing compliance with the American Convention on Human Rights.[818]

319. The OAS Charter created the Inter-American Commission on Human Rights, which is charged with promoting and protecting human rights within the OAS.[819] The Commission reviews the status of human rights protections in member states, makes policy in significant human rights areas, and maintains a petition system that allows individuals and NGOs to present allegations of human rights violations under the American Convention on Human Rights. Few petitions to the Commission have involved the United States. Judicial remedies within member countries, including the United States, must be exhausted before the submission of a petition.[820] The Commission's responses to petitions contain politically binding recommendations, which can be rejected by the United States.

320. The Inter-American Commission on Human Rights has created a series of special rapporteurs, although none addresses religion issues specifically. The Special Rapporteur for Freedom of Expression has touched on religious issues. That rapporteur issued a 2008 joint declaration concerning the defamation of religions,

816. Charter of the Org. of Am. States pmbl., para. 4, 2 U.S.T. 2394, 119 U.N.T.S. 3 (Apr. 30, 1948) [hereinafter OAS Charter].
817. *Ibid.*, art. 1, para. 2.
818. *See* American Convention on Human Rights, *supra* n. 774, art. 33.
819. OAS Charter, *supra* n. 816, art. 106.
820. Org. of Am. States & Inter-Am. Comm'n on Hum. Rts., *Informational Booklet: Petition and Case System* 14 (2022), https://www.oas.org/en/IACHR/jsForm/?File=/en/iachr/mandate/petitions.asp (link to PDF).

in conjunction with authorities from other international and regional bodies,[821] and has publicly condemned government acts that repress religious expression.[822]

321. The American Convention on Human Rights was held in 1969 and resulted in the Pact of San José, Costa Rica. Article 12 of the Pact protects "the right to freedom of conscience and of religion".[823] Although the United States has signed the Pact, it has never ratified it. As a result, the Inter-American Court of Human Rights, created in 1979 as an independent judicial institution with authority to review the Pact's application and interpretation, has no jurisdiction over the United States. Individuals have no ability to petition the Court directly; it receives referrals from the Commission and member states. For a discussion of the significance of ratification in the US system, *see* this part, Chapter 1 (International Law Effects on Religious Communities), above.

821. Catalina Botero (OAS/IACHR Special Rapporteur on Freedom of Expression) et al., *Joint Declaration on Defamation of Religions, and Anti-Terrorism and Anti-Extremism Legislation* (Dec. 9, 2008), https://www.osce.org/files/f/documents/4/b/35639.pdf.

822. E.g., Press Release, IACHR, IACHR and Its Special Rapporteurship for Freedom of Expression Urge the State of Nicaragua to End Persecution of the Church and to Enable a Plurality of Voices (May 27, 2022), https://www.oas.org/en/iachr/jsForm/?File=/en/iachr/media_center/preleases/2022/119.asp.

823. American Convention on Human Rights, *supra* n. 774, art. 12.

Part V. Religion and Politics

Chapter 1. Religious Influence in Politics

§1. Constitutional Principles

322. Individuals have a constitutional right to participate in the political process. Throughout US history, a decreasing number of states excluded clergymen from holding political office. But in 1978, in *McDaniel v. Paty*, the US Supreme Court considered a still-valid exclusionary state law challenged by a Baptist minister who sought to serve as a delegate to a state constitutional convention. Tennessee's constitution forbade ministers from being members of the state legislature, and in 1977 this prohibition was statutorily integrated into requirements for delegates to Tennessee's constitutional convention.[824] The US Supreme Court held that the statute's exclusionary provision was unconstitutional because it forced the minister to choose between his free exercise rights and his right to seek public office.[825]

---

824. In *McDaniel*, the Court explains the historical background of similar exclusions:

> The disqualification of ministers from legislative office was a practice carried from England by seven of the original States; later six new States similarly excluded clergymen from some political offices. …
>
> As the value of the disestablishment experiment was perceived, 11 of the 13 States disqualifying the clergy from some types of public office gradually abandoned that limitation. … Only Maryland and Tennessee continued their clergy-disqualification provisions into this century and, in 1974, a District Court held Maryland's provision violative of the First and Fourteenth Amendments' guarantees of the free exercise of religion. Today Tennessee remains the only state excluding minsters from certain public offices.
>
> The essence of this aspect of our national history is that in all but a few States the selection or rejection of clergymen for public office soon came to be viewed as something safely left to the good sense and desires of the people.

McDaniel v. Paty, 435 U.S. 618, 622, 625 (1978) (plurality opinion) (citations omitted); *see also* Tenn. Const. art. 9, § 1 (disqualifying "Minister[s] of the Gospel" or "priest[s] of any denomination" from service in the legislature); 1976 Tenn. Pub. Acts ch. 848 § 4 (limiting convention delegates to state citizens who qualify for service in the legislature).

825. *McDaniel*, 435 U.S. at 626 ("Yet under the clergy-disqualification provision, McDaniel cannot exercise both [the right to free exercise of religion and the right to run for public office] simultaneously because the State has conditioned the exercise of one on the surrender of the other. Or, in James Madison's words, the State is 'punishing a religious profession with the privation of a civil right.'")

323. Religious groups sometimes themselves restrict their leaders or clergy from holding public office. For example, the Reverend Robert Drinan, S.J., a Catholic Jesuit Priest, represented a district in Massachusetts for a number of years, before having "to leave the Congress because of world-wide edict from [Pope] John Paul II that members of the priesthood could not hold public office".[826] Father Drinan resigned from Congress and had a lengthy second career as a law professor at Georgetown University.[827] In contrast, Ezra Taft Benson, one of twelve apostles of The Church of Jesus Christ of Latter-day Saints, accepted President Dwight D. Eisenhower's nomination to serve as Secretary of Agriculture in 1952.[828] With the approval of Church President David O. McKay, he served in that capacity for eight years, the entire time actively continuing as part of the senior leadership of the Church.[829]

324. The US Supreme Court has held that corporations have significant free speech rights, including in the political arena, which could have implications for religious corporations—but likely only in theory. In *Citizens United v. Federal Election Commission*, the nonprofit corporation Citizens United sought a declaratory judgment that its politically charged documentary about Hillary Clinton (at the time, a candidate for the 2008 Democratic Party presidential nomination) did not violate federal election law. The law prohibited "corporations and unions from using general treasury funds to make … independent expenditures that expressly advocate the election or defeat of a candidate, through any form of media".[830] The federal district court initially ruled against Citizens United. The appeal reached the Supreme Court, which held that, although Citizens United's movie had clearly violated the statutory prohibition, the provision was unconstitutional under the First Amendment.[831] The Court reiterated that "First Amendment protection extends to corporations" and held that "the Government may not suppress political speech on the basis of the speaker's corporate identity".[832] The Court stressed that "[n]o sufficient governmental interest justifies limits on the political speech of nonprofit or for-profit corporations."[833] On its face, the *Citizens United* holding would appear to apply to the free speech rights of religious organizations. However, the Supreme Court has yet to decide how the holding would interplay with restrictions on the political speech of tax-exempt nonprofit religious corporations under section 501(c)(3) of the Internal Revenue Code (I.R.C.).[834]

---

826. Robert Pitofsky, *Father Robert F. Drinan*, 95 Geo. L.J. 1721, 1721 (2007).
827. *Ibid.*
828. Reed A. Benson & Sheri Dew, *Benson, Ezra Taft, in Encyclopedia of Mormonism* 100, 102 (Daniel H. Ludlow ed., 1992).
829. *Ibid.*
830. *Citizens United v. FEC*, 558 U.S. 310, 320 (2010).
831. *Ibid.*, at 322–336.
832. *Ibid.*, at 342 (citing twenty-two cases to illustrate the Court's recognition of First Amendment protections for corporations), 365.
833. *Ibid.*, at 365.
834. *See* Brandon S. Boulter, Note, *Expensive Speech:* Citizens United v. FEC *and the Free Speech Rights of Tax-Exempt Religious Organizations*, 2010 BYU L. Rev. 2243.

325. Indeed, the scope of free speech rights of religious organizations in political matters is largely unknown and untested, due to IRS restrictions on the political campaigning and lobbying activities of religious organizations that wish to qualify for tax-exempt status, under I.R.C. section 501(c)(3).[835] The principal benefits of 501(c)(3) status include, for the qualifying organization, being exempt from paying income tax and, for those who donate to the organization, qualifying for tax-deductions for their own charitable contributions.[836] Since the benefits of tax-exempt status are considerable, churches, for the most part, are quite cautious about their involvement in politics.[837] The IRS is not particularly strict about enforcing the political activity prohibition; in the entire history of section 501(c)(3)'s prohibition

---

835. Internal Revenue Code (I.R.C.) section 501(c)(3) provides that "[c]orporations … organized and operated exclusively for religious … purposes" will be tax-exempt under I.R.C. s. 501(a) only if:

> no part of the net earnings of [the corporation] inures to the benefit of any private shareholder or individual, no substantial part of the activities of [the corporation] is carrying on propaganda, or otherwise attempting, to influence legislation …, and [the corporation] does not participate in, or intervene in (including the publishing or distributing of statements), any political campaign on behalf of (or in opposition to) any candidate for public office.

Under section 501(h), a narrow exemption allows 501(c)(3) organizations to spend money to influence legislation, but churches are explicitly disqualified from claiming this exemption. I.R.C. § 501(h)(5) (2018).

836. According to the Internal Revenue Service:

> The benefits of having 501(c)(3) status include exemption from federal income tax and eligibility to receive tax-deductible charitable contributions. … Another benefit is that some organizations may be exempt from certain employment taxes.
>
> Individual … donors are more likely to support organizations with 501(c)(3) status because their donations can be tax deductible. …
>
> An IRS determination of 501(c)(3) status is recognized and accepted for other purposes. For example, state and local officials may grant exemption from income, sales or property taxes. In addition, the U.S. Postal Service offers reduced postal rates to certain organizations.

Internal Revenue Serv., Pub. No. 4220, *Applying for 501(c)(3) Tax-Exempt Status* 3, https://www.irs.gov/pub/irs-pdf/p4220.pdf (last accessed Sep. 30, 2023).

837. Keith S. Blair describes such a situation:

> A real-life example of this occurred in the controversy over the remarks made by Reverend Jeremiah Wright and then-Senator Obama's subsequent speech in response to the furor. Then-Senator Obama's speech occurred just days before Easter Sunday, and some ministers thought that would be an appropriate time to address the issues of race raised by then-Senator Obama. *Some ministers, however, were afraid to speak on the subject for fear of triggering an investigation by the Internal Revenue Service.*

Keith S. Blair, *Praying for a Tax Break: Churches, Political Speech, and the Loss of Section 501(c)(3) Tax Exempt Status*, 86 Denv. U. L. Rev. 405, 423 n.126 (2009) (emphasis added) (citing Laurie Goodstein & Neela Banerjee, *Obama's Talk Fuels Easter Sermons*, N.Y. Times, Mar. 23, 2008, at A1); *see also* David Shipler, *The Faustian Bargain Between Church and State*, Atlantic (May 7, 2015), http://www.theatlantic.com/politics/archive/2015/05/the-faustian-bargain-between-church-and-state/392630 (quoting a pastor who decided not to endorse a candidate from the pulpit: "I don't want to be a test case, no sir. … Let's let somebody else—yes, I'm that much of a coward.").

on political activity, "[t]here has been only one court case where a church has lost tax-exempt status for violating the ban on political activity."[838]

§2. IRS Rules Regarding Political Activities of Tax-Exempt Organizations

326. The tax-exempt status of nonprofit organizations, including religious organizations, is governed by section 501(c)(3) of the Internal Revenue Code (I.R.C.).[839] The Internal Revenue Service (IRS) has adopted regulations to interpret and implement this section.[840] Two provisions in I.R.C. section 501(c)(3) significantly affect the ability of churches to engage in politics. The first is a bright-line rule prohibiting endorsing (or opposing) candidates, and the second is a less-definite standard prohibiting churches from substantially engaging in political activities such as lobbying or endorsing legislation. These limits were first incorporated into the 1954 tax code through the "Johnson Amendment", which had wide, bipartisan support and went into effect without debate.[841] Conservative critics since then, however, have argued that the 501(c)(3) prohibitions unconstitutionally stifle religious exercise and speech. Claims by President Donald Trump to have "got[ten] rid of the Johnson Amendment" through an executive order were unfounded.[842] It

---

838. Blair, *Praying for a Tax Break*, *supra* n. 837, at 428. *See Branch Ministries v. Rossotti*, 211 F.3d 137 (D.C. Cir. 2000). Blair further explains:

> An additional problem is that the law has historically not been stringently enforced. …
>
> The IRS's minimal enforcement of Section 501(c)(3) undoubtedly leads to enforcement that is at best inequitable for similarly situated churches [based on how public the church's actions are]. … While there were very few examinations of churches during the 2004 election cycle and fewer determinations of noncompliance, it is likely that noncompliance with Section 501(c)(3) was more widespread.

Blair, *Praying for a Tax Break*, *supra* n. 837, at 428–429. *See also* Cong. Rsch. Serv., RL34447, Churches and Campaign Activity: Analysis under Tax and Campaign Finance Laws 1 (Oct. 9, 2012), https://www.everycrsreport.com/files/20121009_RL34447_22d86a9c9b98adab4e9846c34dccff3dc741b652.pdf (indicating a second church lost "501(c)(3) status due to campaign intervention", though its identity "is not clear").

839. I.R.C. § 501(c)(3) (2018); *see supra* n. 835 for relevant statutory text. Additionally, donations to a 501(c)(3) tax-exempt church may be deducted from the donor's income tax under I.R.C. ss. 170(a)(1) and 170(c)(2).

840. *See* 26 C.F.R. § 1.501(c)(3)-1 (2022).

841. Johnson Amendment, Pub. L. No. 83-591 § 501(c)(3) (1954).

842. *See* Jeremy Schwartz & Jessica Priest, *Churches Are Breaking the Law and Endorsing Elections, Experts Say. The IRS Looks the Other Way*, Tex. Trib. (Oct. 30, 2022), https://www.texastribune.org/2022/10/30/johnson-amendment-elections-irs (noting that "[e]liminating the Johnson Amendment would require congressional or judicial action"); Exec. Order No. 13798, 82 Fed. Reg. 21675 (May 9, 2017) (ordering that the Department of Treasury essentially maintain the status quo in "not tak[ing] any adverse action against any individual, house of worship, or other religious organization on the basis that such individual or organization speaks or has spoken about moral or political issues from a religious perspective").

should be noted that these rules do not restrict 501(c)(3) nonprofit religious organizations from encouraging their members to be politically informed, be politically active, and vote for the candidates and issues of the members' choice.

I. No Candidate Endorsement: A Bright-Line Rule

327. A bright-line rule forbids nonprofit organizations claiming tax-exempt status, including religious organizations, from endorsing candidates for political office. Section 501(c)(3) of the I.R.C. provides, in relevant part, that a tax-exempt organization under that section may "not participate in, or intervene in (including the publishing or distributing of statements), any political campaign on behalf of (or in opposition to) any candidate for public office".[843] Ministers and other religious leaders may still personally endorse candidates.[844]

328. To work around the institutional endorsement prohibition, churches sometimes distribute informational voter checklists (or "voter guides") comparing the positions of candidates for public office on issues important to the church. For example, in 2020 the Christian Coalition of America website offered such voter guides as a free download, for the presidential election and Senate elections in

843. I.R.C. § 501(c)(3). IRS regulations with regard to I.R.C. s. 501(c)(3) somewhat further explain what this means for tax-exempt organizations:

> An organization is an action organization [i.e., not eligible for tax-exempt status under I.R.C. section 501(c)(3)] if it participates or intervenes, directly or indirectly, in any political campaign on behalf of or in opposition to any candidate for public office.
>
> The term candidate for public office means an individual who offers himself, or is proposed by others, as a contestant for an elective public office, whether such office be national, State, or local. Activities which constitute participation or intervention in a political campaign on behalf of or in opposition to a candidate include, but are not limited to, the publication or distribution of written or printed statements or the making of oral statements on behalf of or in opposition to such a candidate.

26 C.F.R. § 1.501(c)(3)-1(c)(3)(iii) (2022).

844. The IRS has stated:

> The political campaign intervention prohibition [in I.R.C. s. 501(c)(3)] is not intended to restrict free expression on political matters by leaders of organizations speaking for themselves, as individuals. Nor are leaders prohibited from speaking about important issues of public policy. However, for their organizations to remain tax-exempt under section 501(c)(3), leaders cannot make partisan comments in official organization publications or at official functions of the organization.

Rev. Rul. 2007-41, 2007-25 I.R.B. 1421, 1422; *see also* 4 Durham et al., *supra* n. 178, § 32:15 (*Political Activities Test—Right of Clergy and Congregational Members to Participate in Political Activities*), § 32:16 (*Political Activities Test—Permissible Participation by Religious Organizations in Political Activity*).

thirty-three different states.[845] These voter guides were specifically designed for distribution to church congregations to "help[] educate tens of millions of citizens across [the United States] as to where candidates for public office stand on key faith and family issues".[846] The IRS has stated that "[s]ection 501(c)(3) organizations are permitted to conduct certain voter education activities (including … the publication of voter education guides) if they are carried out in a non-partisan manner".[847]

II. No Substantial Political Activities: A Less-Clear Rule

329. The limits on other political activities are less defined. A religious organization can participate in political lobbying and issue advocacy, including taking positions on specific legislation and referenda, as long as the activity does not constitute a "substantial part" of the organization's activities.[848] IRS regulations explain only that "[a]n organization will not be … regarded [as tax-exempt] *if more than an insubstantial part of its activities*" involve political lobbying and advocacy.[849] Furthermore:

> An organization is [not tax-exempt] if a substantial part of its activities is attempting to influence legislation by propaganda or otherwise. For this purpose, an organization will be regarded as attempting to influence legislation if the organization:
>
> (a) Contacts, or urges the public to contact, members of a legislative body for the purpose of proposing, supporting, or opposing legislation; or
> (b) Advocates the adoption or rejection of legislation.
>
> The term legislation, as used in this subdivision, includes action by the Congress, by any state legislature, by any local council or similar governing body, or by the public in a referendum, initiative, constitutional amendment, or similar procedure. An organization will not fail to meet the operational test merely because it advocates, as an insubstantial part of its activities, the adoption or rejection of legislation.[850]

The meaning of "substantial part" (never defined, except circularly, in either the I.R.C. or the relevant regulations) is unclear, and significant ambiguity exists as to

845. *Download 2020 Voter Guides*, Christian Coal. of Am., https://cc.org/download-2020-voter-guides (last visited Mar. 31, 2023).
846. *2020 Christian Coalition Voter Guide: Presidential Election*, Christian Coal. of Am., https://cc.org/wp-content/uploads/2020/10/2020-Voter-Guide-President-1-sided_N.pdf (last visited Sep. 30, 2023) (highlighting, with questionable accuracy, fifteen issues, four of which Republican candidate Donald Trump "oppos[ed]" and ten of which Democratic candidate Joe Biden "oppos[ed]").
847. Rev. Rul. 2007-41, 2007-25 I.R.B. 1421, 1422.
848. I.R.C. § 501(c)(3) (2018); 26 C.F.R. § 1.501(c)(3)-1(c)(1) (2022); Rev. Rul. 2007-41 2007-25 I.R.B. 1421, 1421; 4 Durham et al., *supra* n. 178, § 32:16 (*Political Activities Test—Permissible Participation by Religious Organizations in Political Activity*).
849. 26 C.F.R. § 1.501(c)(3)-1(c)(1) (emphasis added).
850. *Ibid.*, § 1.501(c)(3)-1(c)(3)(ii).

what constitutes an attempt to "participate in, or intervene in … any political campaign".[851] In fact, the IRS published Revenue Ruling 2007-41 ("Exemption From Tax on Corporations, Certain Trusts, etc.")[852] to "clarify the situations for tax-exempt organizations because the I.R.C. and the regulations are so vague. The revenue ruling describes twenty-one situations and, in each hypothetical situation, attempts to answer the question of whether the entity has intervened in a political campaign."[853] For additional discussion, *see* Part III (Legal Status of Religious Communities), Chapter 1 (Formal Status of Religious Communities); Part VIII (Financing of Religious Communities), Chapter 2 (Indirect Financing); and Part XI (Religion and Culture), Chapter 4 (Religion and Public Debate).

III. Challenges to IRS Rules and Non-enforcement

330. Despite the restrictions on church political involvement, the IRS rarely attempts to enforce these restrictions by actually revoking a church's tax-exempt status.[854] One noteworthy exception is *Branch Ministries v. Rossotti*, which involved the "first time in its history" that the IRS "revoked a bona fide church's tax-exempt status because of its involvement in politics".[855] The Branch Ministries Church placed full-page advertisements in the *Washington Times* and *USA Today* four days prior to the 1992 presidential election. "Each bore the headline 'Christians Beware' and asserted that then-Governor Bill Clinton's positions concerning abortion, homosexuality, and the distribution of condoms to teenagers in schools violated Biblical precepts."[856] After investigation, the IRS revoked Branch Ministries' tax-exempt status; Branch Ministries sued, claiming that the political activity restrictions in I.R.C. section 501(c)(3) were unconstitutional limitations on the Church's free exercise rights under the First Amendment.[857] The federal district court granted summary judgment against Branch Ministries, and the DC Circuit

851. *See ibid.*, § 1.501(c)(3)-1(b)(3)(ii); Blair, *Praying for a Tax Break*, *supra* n. 837, at 415–418; *see also* Cong. Rsch. Serv., Churches and Campaign Activity, *supra* n. 838, at 2 & n.12 ("Some case law suggests that 'no substantial part' is between 5% and 20% of an organization's expenditures, although courts generally examine the lobbying in the broad context of the group's purposes and activities" (citing cases)); Meghan J. Ryan, *Can the IRS Silence Religious Organizations?*, 40 Ind. L. Rev. 73, 77, 80 (2007) ("The lack of meaningful legislative history as to what constitutes impermissible intervention in a political campaign makes the § 501(c)(3) limitation difficult to apply. … Despite the IRS's attempt to clarify the scope of the § 501(c)(3) limitation on intervening in a political campaign, organizations remain unclear as to which activities may constitute impermissible intervention in a political campaign. This is especially true with respect to religious organizations.").

852. Rev. Rul. 2007-41, 2007-25 I.R.B. 1421.

853. Blair, *Praying for a Tax Break*, *supra* n. 837, at 415–416.

854. Schwartz & Priest, *Churches Are Breaking the Law*, *supra* n. 842; Shipler, *The Faustian Bargain*, *supra* n. 837 ("IRS enforcement has been erratic and unpredictable. Secular nonprofits have been watched a little more closely than religious organizations, but only egregious violations trigger action.").

855. *Branch Ministries v. Rossotti*, 211 F.3d 137, 139 (D.C. Cir. 2000).

856. *Ibid.*, at 140.

857. *Ibid.*, at 140–141.

Court of Appeals upheld summary judgment on appeal.[858] The DC Circuit's unanimous decision dismissed Branch Ministries' constitutional claim, finding that section 501(c)(3) restrictions on political speech did not impose a substantial burden on the Church's free exercise rights because the Church could pursue its political advocacy through another avenue—by forming a separate, non-501(c)(3) nonprofit organization—and the Church did not "maintain that a withdrawal from electoral politics would violate its beliefs".[859] Therefore, the DC Circuit concluded, the government could constitutionally restrict religious organizations' political speech under I.R.C. section 501(c)(3), and the revocation of the Church's 501(c)(3) status was upheld.[860] It should be noted that, while *Branch Ministries* predates the Supreme Court's *Citizens United* decision (discussed in this chapter, above), the case would likely be decided in the same way today, given the significant policy concerns undergirding 501(c)(3) restrictions.

331. In the past, the IRS has declined to revoke a church's tax-exempt status even where investigation showed that the church had, in fact, violated section 501(c)(3) campaigning prohibitions.[861] In a regularly occurring protest known as "Pulpit Freedom Sunday", as many as 1,500 religious leaders nationwide have publicly endorsed candidates from the pulpit in an attempt to attract IRS attention.[862]

---

858. *Ibid.*, at 141.
859. *Ibid.*, at 142–144.
860. *Ibid.*, at 144–145.
861. While audits involving churches increased in the early 2000s, and the IRS "has issued dozens of warning letters aimed at halting advocacy for political candidates, it has only twice revoked a church's tax-exempt status since the tax law was amended in 1954". Suzanne Sataline, *Obama Pastors' Sermons May Violate Tax Laws*, Wall St. J. (Mar. 10, 2008), http://www.wsj.com/articles/SB120511457633523621. For example:

> Two days before the 2004 [presidential] election, the Reverend George Regas preached a sermon entitled, "If Jesus Debated President [George W.] Bush and Senator [John] Kerry." …
>
> It is clear that the Reverend—in all likelihood because he was aware of the prohibition against campaigning in church—attempted to make his sermon as neutral as possible. But, it is also clear that the sermon, despite best efforts, was more critical of President Bush than Senator Kerry.

Blair, *Praying for a Tax Break*, *supra* n. 837, at 429–430. The IRS conducted an investigation into the All Saints Church (with which the Church did not cooperate), where that sermon was delivered. In September 2007, "the IRS informed the Church that it had concluded its investigation. The IRS's letter to All Saints stated that All Saints had, indeed, intervened in the 2004 presidential campaign, but that the intervention appeared to be a one-time occurrence and All Saints still qualified for tax-exempt status." *Ibid.*, at 430–431. Similarly, Reverend Jeremiah Wright famously said during the 2008 Democratic presidential primaries, "Barack [Obama] knows what it means to be a black man living in a country and a culture that is controlled by rich white people. Hillary can never know that." *Ibid.*, at 405. However, "[t]he IRS never investigated or punished Reverend Wright for his statements made from the pulpit, even though his statements in support of Barack Obama's presidential campaign were widely reported and posted on the Internet for public review." Erik W. Stanley, *LBJ, the IRS, and Churches: The Unconstitutionality of the Johnson Amendment in Light of Recent Supreme Court Precedent*, 24 Regent U. L. Rev. 237, 257 (2012).
862. *See* Shipler, *The Faustian Bargain*, *supra* n. 837 ("They [the participating ministers] are trying to provoke the Internal Revenue Service into an adverse ruling so they can challenge the constitutionality of the law, which they believe violates the First Amendment."). Some pastors who participate

The IRS typically ignores such provocations.[863] Supporters of 501(c)(3) prohibitions who might wish to compel the IRS to enforce the law lack standing to sue, under Supreme Court precedent.[864] Non-enforcement has also produced protests from religious organizations that desire to challenge the constitutionality of the prohibitions under the Free Speech and Free Exercise provisions of the First Amendment, but they too lack standing to sue if the IRS has not taken action against them.[865] Ultimately:

> The IRS's minimal enforcement of Section 501(c)(3) undoubtedly leads to enforcement that is at best inequitable for similarly situated churches. While a high-profile church might be investigated for an alleged violation of Section 501(c)(3), a church with a lower profile might engage in the same conduct and not draw the attention and scrutiny of the IRS. Because of the confidentiality rules of Section 501(c)(3), neither church might be aware of the disparate treatment.[866]

Critics of minimal and disparate enforcement argue that it potentially undermines public faith in both the IRS and religious organizations, discouraging "the public from respecting and complying with [IRS] administrative actions" and discouraging charitable giving.[867]

---

in "Pulpit Freedom Sunday" even record and mail their sermons to the IRS to prove their violations. Meredith Bennett-Smith, *Pastors to Challenge IRS Ban on Political Speech with "Pulpit Freedom Sunday"*, Huffington Post (Sep. 20, 2012), https://www.huffpost.com/entry/pastors-conservative-groups-challenge-irs-pulpit-free-sunday_n_1901080.

863. Shipler, *The Faustian Bargain*, *supra* n. 837 ("For many years, the IRS has refrained from taking the bait, and citizen complaints about churches's [sic] electioneering have disappeared into the agency's bureaucratic abyss."). "In 2008, 33 pastors took part in the first Pulpit Freedom Sunday … . [E]ven though all the pastors involved recorded their sermons and sent them to the IRS, only one church was investigated by the IRS, and the audit was dropped after several months." Kevin Dolak, *"Pulpit Freedom Sunday" to Defy IRS*, ABC News (Sep. 25, 2010), http://abcnews.go.com/US/defiant-pastors-irs-pulpit-freedom-sunday/story?id=11726610. In 2011, counsel from the nonprofit legal defense group that sponsors "Pulpit Freedom Sunday" expressed frustration with the lack of IRS enforcement, explaining it leaves "churches in limbo". Stephanie Strom, *The Political Pulpit*, N.Y. Times, Sep. 30, 2011, at B1. Counsel further noted, "None of the churches involved in previous pulpit Sunday events have received anything beyond a form letter from the I.R.S. thanking them for the tapes … . They [the I.R.S.] haven't done anything to clarify what the law is and what pastors can and can't say … ." *Ibid.* (internal quotation marks omitted).

864. *See* Samuel Brunson, *Dear I.R.S., It Is Time to Enforce the Campaigning Prohibition. Even Against Churches*, 87 U. Colo. L. Rev. 143, 161–167 (2016) (citing, e.g., *Lujan v. Defs. of Wildlife*, 504 U.S. 555, 560 (1992) (rejecting generalized taxpayer standing); *Ariz. Christian Sch. Tuition Org. v. Winn*, 563 U.S. 125, 138–145 (2011) (rejecting Establishment Clause standing where the government merely declines to impose a tax)). A 2011 *New York Times* article noted that supporters of the campaign activity prohibitions are "vexed by the tax agency's perceived inaction". Strom, *The Political Pulpit*, *supra* n. 863, at B1. A July 2011 letter from thirteen Ohio ministers to then—Treasury Secretary Timothy F. Geithner expressed their "grave concerns over the current inability of the I.R.S. to enforce the federal tax laws applicable to churches." *Ibid.*

865. *See* Brunson, *Dear I.R.S.*, *supra* n. 864, at 143, 145–146, 179–182.

866. Blair, *Praying for a Tax Break*, *supra* n. 837, at 429.

867. Brunson, *Dear I.R.S.*, *supra* n. 864, at 175–176.

§3. Role of Religion in Political and Social Movements

332. Despite legal limitations on religious involvement in political matters, both historically and today, religion has played an important role in many of the most significant social and political movements in United States history.

I. Independence

333. The Declaration of Independence proclaims, "We hold these truths to be self-evident, that all men are created equal, that they are endowed by their Creator with certain unalienable Rights, that among these are Life, Liberty and the pursuit of Happiness."[868] Religious leaders and church institutions were at the forefront of the pro-independence movement in the latter half of the eighteenth century. To an extent not appreciated by many Americans today, the American Revolution was based on advocacy of independence by religious leaders and groups. "Preachers in congregations supporting the revolution would praise revolutionary efforts in their sermons, when previously their sermons would have praised the king. … Preachers thus reassured the revolutionaries and their families that what they were doing was right in God's eyes."[869] In general, American churches "became increasingly identified with the Patriot tide of opinion and contributed powerfully to its rise."[870] One famous minister who openly advocated the patriot cause was Baptist Isaac Backus, who "denounced many Parliamentary laws … as acts of tyranny", "urged others to support the patriot cause" in his sermons, and visited and "encouraged soldiers to continue fighting for a righteous cause".[871]

334. Loyalist (pro-British) religious influences existed in the colonies during the American Revolution as well. "[T]he chief strength of Loyalism lay in the Anglican clergy everywhere and in the Anglican laity of the middle and northern colonies. There was also considerable Tory [Loyalist] sentiment among the wealthier Quakers, the older Lutheran clergy, and the leaders of the pacifistic German sects."[872]

II. Abolition of Slavery

335. The abolitionist movement in opposition to slavery was also in large measure a religious movement.[873] Members of the Religious Society of Friends, known

868. *The Declaration of Independence* para. 2 (U.S. 1776).
869. 1 Scott A. Merriman, *Religion in Times of War, in Religion and the Law in America: An Encyclopedia of Personal Belief and Public Policy* 72, 72 (2007).
870. Sydney E. Ahlstrom, *A Religious History of the American People* 361 (1972).
871. Milton V. Backman Jr., *Religion at War in Support of the American Revolution, in Lectures on Religion and the Founding of the American Republic* 77, 82 (John W. Welch & Stephen J. Fleming eds., 2003).
872. Ahlstrom, *A Religious History*, *supra* n. 870, at 361.
873. "There is no direct command in the Bible to oppose slavery, so abolitionists had to look to interpretations of the Bible for religious support. Specific passages used by abolitionists included words

as Quakers, were early opponents of slavery.[874] In the first half of the nineteenth century, in the years leading to the Civil War, many of the most forceful and eloquent northern abolitionist voices, who were often considered to be dangerous radicals, were religious leaders who opposed slavery for religious reasons. Religious voices were not incidental to the anti-slavery movement; in fact, to a large extent the anti-slavery movement was a religious movement.[875] Harriet Beecher Stowe, who wrote the famous anti-slavery novel *Uncle Tom's Cabin*, was "the wife of a Congregational professor of Old Testament—and an able lay theologian herself".[876] Julia Ward Howe's famous abolitionist "Battle Hymn of the Republic" contained the line "As He [Jesus Christ] died to make men holy, Let us die to make men free".[877]

336. Many of the most vocal and forceful defenders of slavery were also religious leaders who justified their views based on scripture and religious tradition. In fact, "[t]hose defending slavery had an easier time finding textual support for the[ir] position. The Bible states, in Ephesians 6:5, that slaves should obey their masters, and many pro-slavery advocates used this to justify the practice. … Similar biblical passages also occur in the New Testament books of 1 Timothy, Colossians, Titus, and 1 Peter."[878] Pro-slavery advocates also used the Bible to promulgate the "curse of Ham" narrative, which portrayed African slaves as descendants of Ham, whose Biblical indiscretions led the prophet Noah to declare that Ham's descendants would be servants to Shem's descendants.[879]

---

encouraging empathy with those who suffered. The Bible was also used in petitions to end slavery." 2 Scott A. Merriman, *Religion and the Defense of Slavery, in Religion and the Law in America: An Encyclopedia of Personal Belief and Public Policy* 413, 414 (2007).

874. *See Welcome*, Quakers & Slavery Conf., https://web.tricolib.brynmawr.edu/speccoll/quakersandslavery (last visited Sep. 30, 2023); 1 Durham et al., *supra* n. 157, § 2:18 (*Impacts of Religion in Modern History*). For a selection of primary documents related to Quaker opposition to slavery in the United States, *see Quaker Opposition to the Constitution's Provisions Concerning Slavery*, Univ. Wis.—Madison: Ctr. for Study Am. Const., http://csac.history.wisc.edu/quaker_opposition.htm (last visited Sep. 30, 2023).

875. "In New England, New York, and the Northwest antislavery and evangelicalism had struck a close and powerful alliance … ." Ahlstrom, *A Religious History*, *supra* n. 870, at 653. Ahlstrom writes that, between 1840 and 1860:

> [t]he many voluntary associations for evangelism and moral reform became inseparable from the humanitarian crusades, including the most powerful of these, the crusade against slavery. … The churches were slow in joining the antislavery cause, but they did most of the pioneering; and as the movement gained momentum the countless auxiliary organizations of mainstream Protestantism became radiating centers of concern and agitation. The national antislavery societies, now moribund and faction-ridden, were superseded by ecclesiastical organizations in which an antislavery "social gospel" was forging ahead, winning new leaders, trampling on compromisers, and bringing schism or conflict when the occasion demanded.

Ahlstrom, *A Religious History*, *supra* n. 870, at 657.

876. *Ibid.*, at 657.

877. *See ibid.*, at 658.

878. 2 Merriman, *Religion and the Defense of Slavery*, *supra* n. 873, at 414.

879. *Ibid.*; *Genesis* 9:20–27 (King James).

337. Many religious denominations suffered denominational splits on the basis of their support or opposition to slavery. John Calhoun observed on the US Senate floor in 1850 that "'three great evangelical churches have been torn asunder' by the slavery issue", referring to the Presbyterian, Methodist, and Baptist churches.[880] Southern Baptists separated from Northern Baptist institutions and formed the Southern Baptist Convention to avoid northern influence on the issue of slavery.[881]

III. Women's Right to Vote

338. Women's suffrage was supported by some religious organizations and opposed by others who cited biblical scripture to support their idea that women were never meant to have political influence.[882] Anti-suffragists quoted the epistles of Paul, arguing that because women should be silent in the churches, they should be silent in politics as well. Additionally, they believed that because Eve caused the fall of man in the book of Genesis, women were cursed to be subordinate to men.[883] Suffragists had several viewpoints on the matter: some believed Paul was speaking from a cultural perspective rather than a divine, some turned to passages of scripture supporting women, while others rejected the Bible as a source of enlightenment on the subject altogether.[884]

339. In 1870, the Utah territory, demographically dominated by members of The Church of Jesus Christ of Latter-day Saints (then often called "Mormons"), became the second political jurisdiction in the United States to allow women to vote, largely to preserve the influence of Church members. Although the federal government later removed this right from Utah women in 1887, it was restored in 1895 when Utah became a state. The first territory to give women the right to vote was Wyoming, in 1869, but a desire to preserve culture, rather than religion, was the major impetus for passage of that territory's suffrage bill.[885]

IV. Temperance Movement

340. The temperance movement emphasized the immoral influences of alcohol, particularly on the family. Similar to other major social movements in the United States, the moral framework for the movement was religious, and many leaders of temperance movements were explicitly religious in their motivations and messages.

> One of the leading [early] temperance groups … was the Washington Society, made up of reformed drunkards. A continuing theme was that these former

880. Ahlstrom, *A Religious History*, *supra* n. 870, at 660.
881. *Ibid.*, at 664–665.
882. 1 Durham et al., *supra* n. 157, § 2:18 (*Impacts of Religion in Modern History*).
883. *See, e.g.*, Matilda Joslyn Gage, *Woman, Church, and State* 482–483, 509 (Google Books 1893).
884. Marty, *Pilgrims in Their Own Land*, *supra* n. 68, at 247–248.
885. Marty, *Pilgrims in Their Own Land*, *supra* n. 68, at 247–248.

> inebriates had found God … . Some …, however, did not like the Washington Society, finding it too secular. Thus, there was debate even among religious reformers who promoted temperance as to how much God was enough.[886]

The beginnings of the Temperance Movement included "pray-ins" led by women. In 1873, "Eliza Trimble Thompson of Hillsboro, Ohio, led more than seventy determined women from a prayer meeting to one of the town's liquor vendors. … [T]hey prayed, sang, pleaded, and in other ways besought the proprietor to close and desist. During succeeding days they dealt similarly with the twelve other saloons in town … ."[887] Later, in 1893, "the Anti-Saloon League was organized … as a church-oriented direct action political pressure association".[888] "Methodism … gave the league its unanimous institutional support and supplied most of its most militant leadership. The Baptists and Presbyterians … were not far behind."[889] Indeed, in the words of one scholar, "the temperance movement united Protestant Americans as nothing else ever had or would".[890]

V. Civil Rights

341. To an extent more broadly appreciated among contemporary Americans, the civil rights movement was a religious movement as well. "The civil rights movement was fueled by a number of religious individuals and groups, and [the way] that movement changed the law … demonstrates how religion and the law interacted in this area. … [R]eligious rhetoric infused the movement, drawing on the language of Christian love to insist upon legal change."[891] Two leaders of the movement were Martin Luther King Jr. and Fred Shuttlesworth, both of whom were Baptist preachers and founders of the Southern Christian Leadership Conference.[892] In King's most well-known speech, titled *I Have a Dream*, he famously declared, with religious overtones:

> Now is the time to make justice a reality for all of God's children. …
>
> [W]e are not satisfied, and we will not be satisfied until justice rolls down like waters and righteousness like a mighty stream. …
>
> I have a dream that one day every valley shall be exalted, every hill and mountain shall be made low. The rough places will be made plain, and the crooked places will be made straight. And the glory of the Lord shall be

886. 2 Scott A. Merriman, *Religion and Nineteenth-Century Reform, in Religion and the Law in America: An Encyclopedia of Personal Belief and Public Policy* 416, 417 (2007).
887. Ahlstrom, *A Religious History*, *supra* n. 870, at 867.
888. *Ibid.*, at 870.
889. *Ibid.*, at 871.
890. *Ibid.*, at 872.
891. 2 Scott A. Merriman, *Religious Elements of the Civil Rights Movement, in Religion and the Law in America: An Encyclopedia of Personal Belief and Public Policy* 428, 428 (2007); *see also* 1 Durham et al., *supra* n. 157, § 2:18 (*Impacts of Religion in Modern History*).
892. 2 Merriman, *Religious Elements of the Civil Rights Movement*, *supra* n. 891, at 428.

> revealed, and all flesh shall see it together. This is our hope. … With this faith we will be able to work together, to pray together, to struggle together, to go to jail together, to stand up for freedom together, knowing that we will be free one day.
>
> [W]e will be able to speed up that day when all of God's children … will be able to join hands and sing in the words of the old Negro spiritual, "Free at last, Free at last, Great God a-mighty, We are free at last."[893]

Even in the twenty-first century, some of the most visible American civil rights advocates continue to be ordained Protestant ministers.[894]

VI. The Anti-abortion Movement

342. Abortion is one of the most divisive issues in US politics.[895] Although religious views differ on exactly when human life begins during pregnancy, much of the opposition to abortion is religiously based.[896] Gallup polls have consistently

---

893. Martin Luther King, Jr., *"I Have a Dream … ", Speech by the Rev. Martin Luther King at the "March on Washington"* 2, 4, 5–6 (1963), https://teachtnhistory.org/file/I%20Have%20A%20Dream%20Speech.pdf (last visited Sep. 30, 2023).

894. For more information on modern civil rights advocates Reverend Jesse Jackson and Reverend Al Sharpton, *see Jesse Jackson*, Britannica, https://www.britannica.com/biography/Jesse-Jackson (last updated Oct. 4, 2023); *Al Sharpton*, Britannica, https://www.britannica.com/biography/Al-Sharpton (last updated Sep. 29, 2023).

895. *See* 3 Durham et al., *supra* n. 174, § 23:49 (*Abortion*).

896. "The whole topic of religion is inextricably tied up with the issue of abortion. Most of those who favor banning abortion do so, at least in large part, because they believe that life begins at conception. This idea comes, for many, from their religion." 2 Scott A. Merriman, Roe v. Wade, *in Religion and the Law in America: An Encyclopedia of Personal Belief and Public Policy* 439, 439 (2007). The general positions of various religions practiced in the United States vary:

> Christians reflect a range of positions on abortion, with some liberal and mainline denominations permitting abortion in some cases and others, such as the Roman Catholic Church along with other conservative and evangelical denominations, maintaining a stricter stance against all elective abortions. Most schools of Islamic law and scholarship believe that the fetus becomes a living soul at 120 days and thus permit abortion for the first four months of pregnancy, but other Islamic schools take a stricter view permitting abortion during this period only in cases of rape or where pregnancy poses a threat to the life of the mother. Hindu teachings generally condemn abortion as a violation of the principle of nonviolence, but it is permissible where a woman's life is at risk[.] Buddhist teachings say that taking the life of any living thing is wrong and that through reincarnation, life begins at the moment of conception; however, the Dalai Lama has said that there are exceptions such as when the woman's life is in danger.

3 Durham et al., *supra* n. 174, § 23:49 (*Abortion*); *see also* Masci, *American Religious Groups Vary Widely in Their Views of Abortion*, *supra* n. 64; David Masci, *Where Major Religious Groups Stand on Abortion*, Pew Rsch. Ctr. (Jun. 21, 2016), https://www.pewresearch.org/fact-tank/2016/06/21/where-major-religious-groups-stand-on-abortion. One early post-*Roe v. Wade* study showed that "religious conservatism was indeed positively related to opposition to abortion. Education, church attendance, and religious liberalism/conservatism were found to be the most important predictors of abortion attitudes." Larry R. Peterson & Armand L. Mauss, *Religion and the "Right to Life": Correlates of Opposition to Abortion*, 37 Socio. Analysis 243, 243 (1976). A survey of more

shown that "Christians have stronger anti-abortion views than non-Christians, and those who frequently attend church have stronger anti-abortion views than those who attend less frequently"; these views hold true within Republican, Democratic, and politically independent groups.[897] Most litigation of abortion rights has not directly invoked questions under the First Amendment's religion clauses. An exception is the 1980 Supreme Court decision in *Harris v. McRae*. In that case, the Court held that a law limiting the use of federal funds to reimburse abortion costs under Medicaid (a government insurance program) did not violate the Establishment Clause simply because the limits coincided with the tenets of some religions.[898]

343. Many states have conscientious objector laws that protect doctors and other medical professionals (such as nurses and pharmacists) who refuse to participate in abortions for religious reasons. For example, "[forty-six] states allow some health care providers to refuse to provide abortion services. ... [Forty-four] states allow health care institutions to refuse to provide abortion services; [thirteen] limit the exemption to private health care institutions, and [one] state allows only religious health care entities to refuse to provide such care."[899] Additionally, the Church Amendment, passed by the US Congress in 1973, protects both individuals and hospitals from being required to participate in abortions when they have moral or religious objections and prohibits hospitals from conditioning employment on an individual's willingness to perform abortions.[900] For more on abortion and related issues, *see* Part VII (Religious Communities and the Protections of the Individual), Chapter 1 (Protection of Privacy) and Chapter 6 (Medical Deontology).

VII. LGBTQ+ Rights

344. In the recent past, US Supreme Court opinions have acknowledged the rights of both LGBTQ+ individuals and religious individuals and institutions who do not sanction same-sex marriage or other LGBTQ+ rights. In 2015, in *Obergefell v. Hodges*, the Supreme Court held that "[T]he right to marry is a fundamental right inherent in the liberty of the person, and under the Due Process and Equal Protection Clauses of the Fourteenth Amendment couples of the same-sex [sic] may not

---

recent research on predictors of abortion attitudes noted the continued significance of those predictors but echoed the 1976 study's call for more nuanced research. Amy Adamczyk, Chunrye Kim & Leevia Dillon, *Examining Public Opinion about Abortion: A Mixed-Methods Systematic Review of Research over the Last 15 Years*, 90 Socio. Inquiry 920, 925–929 (2020).

897. Frank Newport & Lydia Saad, *Religion, Politics Inform Americans' Views on Abortion*, Gallup (Apr. 3, 2006), http://www.gallup.com/poll/22222/religion-politics-inform-americans-views-abortion.aspx; Frank Newport, *Personal Religiosity and Attitudes Toward Abortion*, Gallup (May 13, 2022), https://news.gallup.com/opinion/polling-matters/392648/personal-religiosity-attitudes-toward-abortion.aspx; *see also "Pro-Choice" or "Pro-Life" Demographic Table*, *supra* n. 66.

898. *Harris v. McRae,* 448 U.S. 297, 318–320 (1980).

899. *State Laws and Policies: Refusing to Provide Health Services*, *supra* n. 378.

900. Health Programs Extension Act of 1973, Pub. L. No. 93-45, § 401, 87 Stat. 91, 95–96 (codified as amended at 42 U.S.C. § 300a-7 (2018)).

be deprived of that right and that liberty."[901] At the same time, the Court emphasized that the First Amendment still protects religious groups and others who oppose same-sex marriage.[902] In 2017, the Court reiterated this principle when it reversed sanctions imposed on a wedding cake baker by a state human rights commission, on grounds that the commission exhibited "hostility toward the sincere religious beliefs" of the baker.[903] In 2020, the Supreme Court ruled that the statutory prohibition on employment discrimination based on "sex", in Title VII of the Civil Rights Act, encompasses discrimination based on sexual orientation or gender identity; the Court's opinion indicated that existing free exercise protections, in statutes and common law, could exempt religious organizations from abiding by the prohibition in employment decisions.[904] The Supreme Court's 2022 decision in *Dobbs v. Jackson Women's Health Organization*, overruling *Roe v. Wade*, created concern that *Obergefell* and other decisions similarly grounded in the concept of substantive due process might also be overturned.[905] In response, Congress passed the Respect for Marriage Act, providing statutory protections for same-sex and interracial civil marriages while also protecting religious liberty interests.[906] The Act ensures, for example, that nonprofit religious organizations and their employees "shall not be required to provide services … for the solemnization or celebration of a marriage".[907]

345. US public opinion is split with regard to "claims of religious liberty or traditional morality against non-discrimination policies".[908] As with previous movements in the United States, the issue of LGBTQ+ rights has divided religious organizations and members. Many religious organizations have opposed the expansion of LGBTQ+ rights in the United States. Some of this opposition arises out of a concern that anti-discrimination laws may negatively impact the rights of religious organizations and members to practice their beliefs without government interference. These concerns have been both augmented and assuaged by contradictory holdings in court cases weighing anti-discrimination and religious interests, such as cases involving religious owners of wedding-related "public accommodation" businesses who object to providing services to same-sex couples.[909] At least one state,

901. *Obergefell v. Hodges*, 576 U.S. 644, 675 (2015).
902. *Ibid.*, at 679–680.
903. *Masterpiece Cakeshop, Ltd. v. Colo. C.R. Comm'n*, 138 S. Ct. 1719, 1727–1729 (2018) (quoting *Obergefell*, 576 U.S. at 679–680).
904. *Bostock v. Clayton County*, 140 S. Ct. 1731, 1753–1754 (2020).
905. *See Dobbs v. Jackson Women's Health Org.*, 142 S. Ct. 2228, 2300–2304 (2022) (Thomas, J., concurring) (asserting that the Court should "reconsider all of [its] substantive due process precedents, including *Griswold*, *Lawrence*, and *Obergefell*. Because any substantive due process decision is demonstrably erroneous". (internal quotation marks omitted)).
906. Respect for Marriage Act, Pub. L. No. 117-228, 136 Stat. 2305 (2022).
907. Pub. L. No. 117-228, § 6, 136 Stat. 2305, 2306.
908. *16 Striking Findings from 2016*, Pew Rsch. Ctr. (Dec. 21, 2016), https://www.pewresearch.org/fact-tank/2016/12/21/16-striking-findings-from-2016.
909. *See supra* paras. 516–517. *Compare, e.g., Masterpiece Cakeshop, Ltd. v. Colo. C.R. Comm'n*, 138 S. Ct. 1719, 1727–1732 (2018) (holding that a state commission's actions in a case brought against a cakeshop owner violated the Free Exercise Clause requirement of neutrality toward religion but explaining that, "while … religious … objections are protected, it is a general rule that such objections do not allow business owners and other actors in the economy and in society to deny

Mississippi, expressly provides broad religious exemptions from public accommodation laws with regard to LGBTQ+ individuals.[910] For additional discussion, *see* Part VII (Religious Communities and Protections of the Individual), Chapter 3 (Same-Sex Marriage).

346. Other religious organizations have accepted and even advocate for LGBTQ+ rights, including same-sex marriage. Some of these organizations compare the campaign for LGBTQ+ rights with other important social movements, like the mid-twentieth-century civil rights movement, in which religion played an important role.[911] Still other religious organizations have recognized the need for civil protection for LGBTQ+ individuals while trying to preserve legal protections afforded to religious organizations.[912] Some scholars have noted legal similarities in

---

protected persons equal access to goods and services under a neutral and generally applicable public accommodations law"), *and State v. Arlene's Flowers, Inc.*, 441 P.3d 1203, 1237 (Wash. 2019) (en banc) (holding that refusal to provide flowers for a same-sex wedding violated "a neutral, generally applicable law that serves our state government's compelling interest in eradicating discrimination in public accommodations"), *and Elane Photography, LLC v. Willock,* 309 P.3d 53, 58–60 (N.M. 2013), *cert. denied*, 572 U.S. 1046 (2014) (mem.) (holding that state anti-discrimination public accommodations law was neutral, generally applicable, and required wedding photography business to serve same-sex couples on the same basis it serves opposite-sex couples), *with 303 Creative LLC v. Elenis*, 600 U.S. 570, 588–589 (2023) (holding state could not apply anti-discrimination law to compel "expression" of wedding website owner—that is, to create content for same-sex couples—contrary to her religious beliefs), *and Telescope Media Grp. v. Lucero*, 936 F.3d 740, 752 (8th Cir. 2019) (holding state could not apply human rights act to compel wedding videographers to film same-sex weddings, contrary to their religious beliefs), *and Brush & Nib Studio, LC v. City of Phoenix*, 448 P.3d 890, 896, 926 (Ariz. 2019) (holding city could not apply anti-discrimination ordinance to compel company owners to create celebratory wedding invitations for same-sex weddings, contrary to their "sincere conviction that, by divine precepts, same-sex marriage should not be condoned") (quoting *Obergefell*, 576 U.S. 644, 679)), *and Chelsey Nelson Photography LLC v. Louisville/Jefferson Cnty. Metro Gov't*, 479 F. Supp. 3d 543, 558 & n.122 (W.D. Ky. 2020) (declining to follow *Elane Photography*'s "more narrow[]" reading of the First Amendment and expressing approval of interpretations in *Telescope Media Group* and *Brush & Nib Studio, LC*, based partly on the amendment's protections against compelled speech).

910. Miss. Code Ann. § 11-62-5 (2022).

911. *See, e.g.*, Kelsey Dallas, *How Should Black Churches Respond to the Fight for LGBTQ Rights?*, Deseret News (Apr. 30, 2022), https://www.deseret.com/faith/2022/4/30/23045434/how-should-the-black-church-respond-to-the-fight-for-lgbtq-rights-gay-transgender; *Black Churches and Gay Marriage*, PBS: Religion & Ethics News Weekly (Jul. 16, 2004), https://www.pbs.org/wnet/religionandethics/2004/07/16/july-16-2004-black-churches-and-gay-marriage/13200 (discussing differing views among African American clergy of the relationship between the civil rights and gay rights movements).

912. The 2015 "Utah Compromise", for example, involved the collaborative efforts of LGBTQ+ community leaders, majority-conservative state lawmakers, and leaders of the state's predominant faith (The Church of Jesus-Christ of Latter-day Saints) and other faiths to draft and pass legislation securing non-discrimination protections for LGBTQ+ individuals while ensuring religious freedoms for individuals and organizations. *See* Antidiscrimination and Religious Freedom Amendments, S.B. 296, 2015 Gen. Sess. (Utah 2015) (codified in scattered sections of Utah Code §§ 34A, 57 (2022)) (protecting "LGBT" individuals from employment and housing discrimination and guaranteeing employees' freedom of expression both in and outside of the workplace); Protections for Religious Expression and Beliefs about Marriage, Family, or Sexuality, S.B. 297, 2015 Gen. Sess. (Utah 2015) (codified in scattered sections of Utah Code §§ 17, 30, 63G (2022)) (giving religious organizations discretion in performing marriages and conducting counselling, ensuring access to state-authorized celebrants for all lawful marriages, and guaranteeing professionals freedom of

LGBTQ+ rights and religious freedom claims and have called for protection of both under the same recognition of civil liberty as to one's identity.[913]

VIII. Public Reason and the Marginalization of Religion

347. There is a perception that the influence of religion in public life is waning.[914] A 2014 Pew Research poll found that many Americans believe religious organizations should make more of an effort to make their voices heard in the public square.[915] This may be seen as a reaction to a perceived decline of religious involvement in public debate and politics over the past several decades.

348. The idea of public reason, as articulated by the philosopher John Rawls, has considerable influence in the United States, which has resulted in many calling for religious groups to stand down in political debates and for religious reasons to be rejected as a basis for public policy. As religious diversity has increased in the United States, so has religious polarization, which has intensified the call to remove religion from the political sphere.[916] For a more detailed discussion of public reason, *see* Part XI (Religion and Culture), Chapter 4 (Religion and Public Debate).

§4. Role of Religion in Political Campaigns

349. The US Constitution prohibits any religious tests for holding political office.[917] Nevertheless, the religious bona fides of candidates for office has often

---

expression in non-work settings); *see also* Jonathan Rauch, *Meeting in the Middle on Religious and LGBTQ Rights*, Deseret News (May 4, 2021), https://www.deseret.com/2021/5/4/22417652/meeting-in-the-middle-religious-freedom-lgbtq-rights-fairness-for-all-equality-act; Jonathan Rauch & Peter Wehner, Opinion, *We Can Find Common Ground on Gay Rights and Religious Liberty: It Does Not Have to Be All or Nothing*, N.Y. Times (Jun. 22, 2020), https://www.nytimes.com/2020/06/22/opinion/gay-rights-religious-liberty.html.

913. *See, e.g.*, Thomas C. Berg, *What Same-Sex Marriage and Religious-Liberty Claimants Have in Common*, 5 Nw. J.L. & Soc. Pol'y 206, 202–226 (2010); W. Cole Durham, Jr., et al., *Response to the UN's Call for Input to a Thematic Report: Freedom of Religion or Belief (FoRB) and Sexual Orientation and Gender Identity*, Talk About: L. & Religion (Feb. 16, 2023), https://talkabout.iclrs.org/2023/02/16/response-to-the-uns-call-for-input; Douglas Laycock, *The Wedding-Vendor Cases*, 41 Harv. J.L. & Pub. Pol'y 49, 61 (2018); William N. Eskridge, Jr., *A Jurisprudence of "Coming Out": Religion, Homosexuality, and Collisions of Liberty and Equality in America*, 106 Yale L.J. 2411, 2416–2430 (1997); *Religious Freedom, LGBT Rights, and the Prospects for Common Ground* (William N. Eskridge, Jr. & Robin Fretwell Wilson eds., 2018).

914. *Public Sees Religion's Influence Waning*, Pew Rsch. Ctr. (Sep. 22, 2014), http://www.pewforum.org/2014/09/22/public-sees-religions-influence-waning-2; *see also* Michael Lipka, *Republicans and Democrats Agree Religion's Influence Is Waning, but Differ in Their Reactions*, Pew Rsch. Ctr. (Nov. 15, 2019), https://www.pewresearch.org/fact-tank/2019/11/15/republicans-and-democrats-agree-religions-influence-is-waning-but-differ-in-their-reactions.

915. *Public Sees Religion's Influence Waning*, *supra* n. 914.

916. *See* Natalie Sherman & David Gergen, *Religion & Politics: Seeking a Reconciliation*, *in Religion & Public Policy* 307, 308–311 (Sumner B. Twiss, Marian Gh. Simion & Rodney L. Petersen eds., 2015).

917. U.S. Const. art. VI, cl. 3 ("[N]o religious Test shall ever be required as a Qualification to any Office or public Trust under the United States.").

been an issue. John F. Kennedy's status as a Catholic was a major campaign issue in the 1960 presidential campaign, and he gave an important speech to Protestant clergy proclaiming his political independence from the Catholic Church.[918] More than a half-century later, 2012 Republican Party presidential nominee Mitt Romney's membership in The Church of Jesus Christ of Latter-day Saints was an issue in both the Republican primary and the general election. Even so, Congress reflects the religious diversity of America today more than ever. While the majority of its members are still Protestant Christians, Congress also includes Catholic, Latter-day Saint, Orthodox Christian, Jewish, Muslim, Hindu, Buddhist, and unaffiliated members, many of whom represent districts where they are a religious minority.[919]

I. Perceived Necessity of Some Religious Affiliation/Belief

350. Historically, conventional wisdom has held that a candidate, at least on a national level, must have some religious affiliation or belief to be successful. A 2016 Pew Research poll reported that voters are more likely to vote for a candidate who has had a past extramarital affair than an atheist.[920] However, the two major political parties perceive very differently the importance of candidates being religious, with it being more important for Republicans and less important for Democrats.[921] President Donald Trump, who was popular among conservative Republicans despite not being widely viewed as religious "even by those in his own party", was something of an outlier.[922]

351. While a candidate's religiosity remains important for many voters, there is evidence that religious affiliation is less important today than it has been in the past.[923] Compared to the role religion played in John F. Kennedy's 1960 presidential campaign, candidate Joe Biden's Catholicism was rarely discussed in the 2020 presidential campaign. The 2020 election also saw the southern "Bible Belt" state of Georgia elect as US senators an African American Baptist pastor and a white Jewish journalist. In 2023, the Supreme Court had only one justice who was Protestant

918. *Transcript: JFK's Speech on His Religion*, NPR, http://www.npr.org/templates/story/story.php?storyId=16920600 (last visited Sep. 30, 2023) ("I believe in an America that is officially neither Catholic, Protestant nor Jewish; where no public official either requests or accepts instructions on public policy from the Pope, the National Council of Churches or any other ecclesiastical source; where no religious body seeks to impose its will directly or indirectly upon the general populace or the public acts of its officials; and where religious liberty is so indivisible that an act against one church is treated as an act against all.").
919. Jeff Diamant, *Faith on the Hill*, Pew Rsch. Ctr. (Jan. 3, 2023), https://www.pewresearch.org/religion/2023/01/03/faith-on-the-hill-2023.
920. Pew Rsch. Ctr., *Faith and the 2016 Campaign* 3 (Jan. 27, 2016), https://www.pewforum.org/2016/01/27/faith-and-the-2016-campaign (link to PDF).
921. While negativity toward atheist candidates is decreasing overall, a 2016 survey showed that 65% of Republicans would still "be less likely to support an atheist candidate", while 41% of Democrats would be less likely to support an atheist. *Ibid.*, at 23.
922. *Ibid.*, at 2.
923. *Ibid.*, at 4.

and one who "was raised Catholic" but now attends Episcopal services.[924] The remainder of the Court was composed of six Catholic justices and one Jewish justice—a religious composition that would have been unimaginable fifty years ago.

II. Civil Religion

352. American civil religion is the idea of a non-sectarian religious belief surrounding the American Revolution and the United States' role in the world. Robert Bellah wrote: "Until the Civil War, the American civil religion focused above all on the event of the Revolution, which was seen as the final act of the Exodus from the old lands across the waters. The Declaration of Independence and the Constitution were the sacred scriptures and Washington the divinely appointed Moses who led his people out of the hands of tyranny."[925] Civil religion embraces Christian as well as patriotic symbolism. Traditionally, popular belief has held that politicians must embrace and evoke this civil religion to be politically successful. Though weakening, this belief still holds true, particularly for those who seek to appeal to more conservative voters. America's unique conception of civil religion is discussed more fully in Part XI (Religion and Culture), Chapter 3 (Religion and Civil Society).

---

924. Daniel Burke, *What Is Neil Gorsuch's Religion? It's Complicated*, CNN (Mar. 22, 2017), https://www.cnn.com/2017/03/18/politics/neil-gorsuch-religion.

925. Robert N. Bellah, *Civil Religion in America*, 96 Dædalus 1, 9 (1967).

Chapter 2. Political Influence on Religion

§1. Introduction

353. Political influence on religion in the United States exists to a relatively low degree. This is largely based on deep constitutional structural provisions, most importantly the constitutional principles of non-establishment, which prohibits direct government funding or other involvement in religious affairs, and free exercise, which broadly protects religious freedom. Also important is the separation of powers among the branches of the federal government and the reservation of unenumerated powers to the states.

354. Issues relating to the political influence on religion are addressed in various chapters in this book. For example, issues of collective religious freedom are addressed in Part II (Religious Freedom in General), Chapter 2 (Collective Religious Freedom); autonomy of religious communities is addressed in Part III (Legal Status of Religious Communities), Chapter 2 (Autonomy of Religious Communities); and state funding of religion is addressed in Part VIII (Financing of Religious Communities), Chapter 1 (Direct Financing) and Chapter 2 (Indirect Financing).

355. Below is a discussion of the constitutional framework, the ways in which political pressures are brought to bear on religious groups, what happens when religious groups run afoul of fundamental public policies, and the extent to which religious groups can participate in government funding programs that address social needs and issues.

§2. Constitutional Framework

356. The First Amendment of the US Constitution prevents the government from establishing a religion and protects individuals' right to exercise religion within certain limits. For the most part, non-establishment and free exercise of religion have been understood to enjoin state involvement in religion, thus creating religious and ecclesiastical autonomy. *See* Part I (Legal Framework and Sources), Chapter 1 (Constitutional Position of Religion).

§3. Political Pressure on Religious Groups

357. At times political pressure has been brought to bear on religious groups to change fundamental religious beliefs. One of the most salient examples is the legal and political pressure exerted on The Church of Jesus Christ of Latter-day Saints in the nineteenth century with respect to the issue of polygamy.

358. Beginning in the mid-1850s and running until the early 1890s, federal officials targeted the Church and its members in a number of ways but focused most specifically on polygamy, which was a doctrine of the Church then practiced by a minority of its members.[926] This issue was taken to the Supreme Court in 1878 in *Reynolds v. United States*.[927] Defendant George Reynolds had been convicted under a federal anti-bigamy statute. The Court examined whether the statute was unconstitutional under the Free Exercise Clause if plural marriage was an integral part of the defendant's religious belief. The Supreme Court upheld the statute and differentiated between belief and action in the free exercise of religion, reasoning that laws cannot interfere with religious beliefs but can interfere with religious practices. Twelve years later, in *Davis v. Beason*, the Supreme Court held that mere membership in a religious organization that believed in plural marriage was sufficient grounds for denying voting rights.[928] The US Congress had earlier enacted legislation that prohibited past or present polygamists from serving on juries and voting.[929]

359. Congress targeted plural marriage in a number of other ways: It passed legislation in 1887 that denied women in the Utah Territory the right to vote—a right granted by Utah's territorial legislature in 1870.[930] It abolished the common law protection of spousal immunity in the Utah Territory.[931] And it excluded members of The Church of Jesus Christ of Latter-day Saints from holding public office and prohibited wives and children of polygamous marriages from inheriting property.[932] The Church's Perpetual Emigration Fund, created to help foster migration of less well-to-do converts from abroad, was dissolved and its assets seized.[933] And finally, congressional legislation dissolved the Church and confiscated its property.[934] The Supreme Court upheld this confiscation as constitutional in *Late Corp. of The Church of Jesus Christ of Latter-day Saints v. United States*.[935]

360. Under these and other laws and court rulings, many church members and leaders who practiced polygamy were imprisoned. Church members were faced with dissonance between these legal mandates and a central tenet of the Church expressing belief in "being subject to … magistrates[and] in obeying, honoring,

926. Hardy, *That "Same Old Question of Polygamy and Polygamous Living"*, *supra* n. 104, at 215; Volf, *Mormon Polygamy in the Nineteenth Century*, *supra* n. 104, at 41.
927. *Reynolds v. United States*, 98 U.S. 145 (1878).
928. *Davis v. Beason*, 133 U.S. 333 (1890), *abrogated by Romer v. Evans*, 517 U.S. 620, 634 (1996) ("To the extent *Davis* held that persons advocating a certain practice may be denied the right to vote, it is no longer good law. To the extent it held that the groups designated in the statute may be deprived of the right to vote because of their status, its ruling could not stand without surviving strict scrutiny, a most doubtful outcome." (citations omitted)).
929. Edmunds Act, Pub. L. No. 47-47, §§ 5, 8, 22 Stat. 30, 31–32 (1882) (repealed 1983); Edmunds-Tucker Act, Pub. L. No. 49-397, § 24, 24 Stat. 635, 639–640 (1887) (repealed 1978).
930. Edmunds-Tucker Act, Pub. L. No. 49-397, § 20.
931. *Ibid.*, § 1.
932. *Ibid.*, §§ 11, 18, 24; *see also* Edwin Brown Firmage & R. Collin Mangrum, *Zion in the Courts: A Legal History of The Church of Jesus Christ of Latter-day Saints, 1830–1900*, at xv, 199, 240, 336 (1988).
933. Edmunds-Tucker Act, Pub. L. No. 49-397, § 15.
934. *Ibid.*, § 13.
935. *Late Corp. of The Church of Jesus Christ of Latter-day Saints v. United States,* 136 U.S. 1, 65 (1890).

and sustaining the law".[936] In 1890, Church President Wilfred Woodruff issued a "manifesto" that led to the termination of the practice of plural marriage within the Church.[937] Since that time, the official policy of The Church of Jesus Christ of Latter-day Saints has prohibited polygamy. The memberships of individuals who practice polygamy are withdrawn from the Church. Some independent fundamentalist groups unassociated with the Church still continue the practice, however, mostly in rural areas.

361. More than a decade after The Church of Jesus Christ of Latter-day Saints had abandoned polygamy, a Church leader who had never been a polygamist, Reed Smoot, was elected to the US Senate. In hearings that lasted nearly four years, the US Senate grappled with the terms of admission—legally, politically, and socially—of Latter-day Saints into US society. The Smoot hearings demonstrated how the political process can pressure religious organizations to modify their policies and conform to majority points of view to obtain political acceptance. Although the essential facts relevant to the hearings are unique to Latter-day Saint history, general principles and lessons can be understood to apply to other religious minorities in the United States.

362. Reed Smoot won the Utah legislature's election for US senator in January 1903, but resistance to Smoot's seating in the Senate quickly arose. The basic justifications for resisting Smoot's appointment were his church's history of polygamy and doubts about Smoot's independence from the opinions of his church's leadership.

363. Congressional hearings began in 1903 and continued until 1907. The Senate eventually approved Smoot's seating, but the process undoubtedly affected the institutional church as well as Latter-day Saint society. Although the Church had already renounced polygamy in 1890, during the hearings it reaffirmed and clarified its position, apparently to address concerns that had been raised during the evolving political situation. The hearings illustrated that much of the concern actually centered on Smoot's capacity to function independently from church leadership, something not formally compelled by the US Constitution or law.

364. For Smoot to be seated, The Church of Jesus Christ of Latter-day Saints had to conform to the religious environment of the United States in three ways.[938] The first requirement was absolute abandonment of polygamy in both word and deed. The second was a demonstration by both benevolent actions and military enlistment that the Church created loyal citizens who could contribute to the

936. Joseph Smith, *The Articles of Faith of the Church of Jesus Christ of Latter-Day Saints*, at art. 12, Church of Jesus Christ of Latter-day Saints, https://www.churchofjesuschrist.org/comeuntochrist/article/articles-of-faith (last visited Sep. 30, 2023).

937. Wilford Woodruff, *Official Declaration—1*, *in Doctrine and Covenants* 291 (The Church of Jesus Christ of Latter-day Saints 2013).

938. Kathleen Flake, *The Politics of American Religious Identity: The Seating of Senator Reed Smoot, Mormon Apostle* 8 (2004).

nation's common good. The third requirement was a more clearly democratic process in Utah government, which prompted an announcement by the Church that it was not a political institution with political objectives.

365. A more modern example of political influence on a minority religion and pressures for political acceptance involved proposals for an Islamic worship center near the World Trade Center site. Branded the "ground zero mosque" by opponents, Park51, or the Cordoba House, was proposed as an Islamic community center and mosque with space dedicated to promoting interfaith relations and memorializing the lives lost on September 11, 2001. Muslims historically have faced difficulties obtaining acceptance in US society, which were only heightened by the backlash against Muslims after the 9/11 attacks by extremists. The Park51 development proposal represented a kind of olive branch sent from a religious minority to engage with "mainstream" society. Political pressure eventually prevailed, however, and the development proceeded as a condominium complex, under a different name, without the mosque, and with plans for a scaled-back Islamic cultural space.[939]

366. Land use and zoning issues are handled at the local level in the United States. There is evidence to suggest that minority and new religious groups face more obstacles in land use and zoning issues than do larger, well-known religious groups.[940] One study analyzed 196 cases where zoning decisions were challenged by religious organizations, on free exercise grounds.[941] The study concluded that minority groups face "a substantially greater level of problems in the zoning area than mainline churches".[942] For discussion of federal statutory provisions prohibiting religious discrimination in land use, *see* Part XI (Religion and Culture), Chapter 1 (Religion and Art).

§4. Religious Organizations That Violate Fundamental Public Policy

367. The 1983 Supreme Court case *Bob Jones University v. United States* is a significant example of the use of legal leverage against religious organizations that depart from social norms.[943] In that case, the IRS revoked the tax-exempt status of a private university because it prohibited interracial dating and marriage on its campus. This policy was based on the university's genuinely held religious belief that the Bible prohibits interracial marriage and dating. All students admitted to Bob Jones were screened for religious beliefs, and their private and public conduct was strictly regulated by university standards. The IRS determined that because of this

939. Ronda Kaysen, *Condo Tower to Rise Where Muslim Community Center Was Proposed*, N.Y. Times (May 12, 2017), https://www.nytimes.com/2017/05/12/realestate/muslim-museum-world-trade-center.html.

940. Brief of The Church of Jesus Christ of Latter-day Saints as Amicus Curiae in Support of Respondents 29–30, app.1A, *City of Boerne v. Flores*, 521 U.S. 507 (1997) (No. 95-2074).

941. *Ibid.*

942. *Ibid.*, at 8a.

943. *Bob Jones Univ. v. United States*, 461 U.S. 574 (1983).

policy the university was not a charitable organization within common law concepts of the tax code. Common law interpretation requires that, to be considered "charitable", an institution's purposes must be in harmony with the law and established public policy. The Supreme Court majority upheld this interpretation, stating that withdrawal of tax-exempt status from the university was justified—even though it was based on sincere, genuinely held religious beliefs—because racial discrimination in education is contrary to fundamental public policy. A concurring opinion took issue with the Court's analysis of what qualifies as a charitable organization because it allows the government to dictate which social and political views are acceptable and "ignores the important role played by tax exemptions in encouraging diverse, indeed often sharply conflicting, activities and viewpoints".[944] Bob Jones University eventually lifted its ban on interracial dating seventeen years later, in 2000; issued a public apology for its "racially hurtful" institutional policies in 2008; and regained its tax-exempt status in 2017.[945]

368. As communities and federal, state, and local policymakers increasingly regard LGBTQ+ anti-discrimination law as central to a healthy society, religious beliefs in heterosexual marriage are sometimes analogized to the religious beliefs opposing interracial dating and marriage that were at issue in *Bob Jones University*. In *Obergefell v. Hodges* and *Masterpiece Cakeshop, Ltd. v. Colorado Civil Rights Commission*, the Supreme Court effectively rejected this analogy, noting constitutional protections for religious opposition to same-sex marriage and calling for "open and searching debate" and pluralistic solutions.[946] The Respect for Marriage Act of 2022 also distinguishes views on same-sex marriage from those on interracial marriage; it affirms that people with diverse religious "beliefs about the role of gender in marriage" and the beliefs themselves "are due proper respect" but does not affirm the same for beliefs opposing interracial marriage.[947] Some scholars have noted legal similarities in LGBTQ+ rights and religious freedom claims and have called for protection of both under the same recognition of civil liberty as to one's identity.[948] For additional discussion, *see* Part VII (Religious Communities and Protections of the Individual), Chapter 2 (Freedom to Marry).

---

944. *Ibid.*, at 606, 609 (Powell, J., concurring in part and concurring in the judgment); *see also ibid.*, at 612, 622 (Rehnquist, J., dissenting) (agreeing Congress has power to further anti-discrimination policy by denying tax-exempt status "to organizations that practice racial discrimination" but asserting Congress "failed to do so" in the statute).
945. Nathaniel Cary, *Bob Jones University Regains Nonprofit Status 17 Years after It Dropped Discriminatory Policy*, Greenville News (Feb. 16, 2017), https://www.greenvilleonline.com/story/news/education/2017/02/16/bju-regains-nonprofit-status-17-years-after-dropped-discriminatory-policy/98009170; *Statement about Race at BJU*, Bob Jones Univ. (Nov. 20, 2008), https://www.bju.edu/about/what-we-believe/race-statement.php.
946. *Masterpiece Cakeshop, Ltd. v. Colo. C.R. Comm'n*, 138 S. Ct. 1719, 1729–1731 (2018); *Obergefell v. Hodges*, 576 U.S. 644, 679–680 (2015).
947. Respect for Marriage Act, Pub. L. No. 117-228, § 2, 136 Stat. 2305, 2305 (2022).
948. *See* sources cited *supra* n. 913.

§5. Participation in Government Funding Programs

369. The Personal Responsibility and Work Opportunity Reconciliation Act of 1996 adopted during the Bill Clinton administration implemented the idea of "Charitable Choice", which expanded the eligibility of religiously affiliated groups in the United States to provide social services through government-funded programs.[949] Charitable Choice was expanded further by the George W. Bush administration. President Bush's first executive order in office established the White House Office of Faith-Based and Community Initiatives to inform faith-based and community organizations of federal support available to them and connect them with federal agencies "to lower the legal and institutional barriers that prevented government and faith-based groups from working as partners".[950] Under the Office and its later iterations, participant religious groups are not allowed to discriminate based on religion in the provision of services, but they are allowed to have a religious character. They can also make employment decisions based on religion. President Barack Obama's administration changed the name of the Office to the White House Office of Faith-Based and Neighborhood Partnerships. The administration also created an advisory board that included secular leaders who sought to protect the rights of minorities. President Donald Trump issued an executive order effectually replacing the Office with a "Faith and Opportunity Initiative" that focused primarily on helping faith-based organizations gain equal access to government funding.[951] President Joe Biden re-established the White House Office of Faith-Based and Neighborhood Partnerships with a charge to collaborate with religious and community organizations to "address the COVID-19 pandemic and boost economic recovery; combat systemic racism; increase opportunity and mobility for historically disadvantaged communities; … strengthen pluralism" and advance US diplomatic, development, and humanitarian work worldwide.[952] *See also* Part XI (Religion and Culture), Chapter 3 (Religion and Civil Society).

949. Personal Responsibility and Work Opportunity Reconciliation Act of 1996 (PRWORA or Welfare Reform Act), Pub. L. No. 104-193, § 104, 110 Stat. 2105, 2161–2163 (codified at 42 U.S.C. § 604a (2018)).

950. Press Release, White House Off. of the Press Sec'y, President Bush Attends Office of Faith-Based and Community Initiatives' National Conference (Jun. 26, 2008) [hereinafter White House Press Release (Jun. 26, 2008)], http://georgewbush-whitehouse.archives.gov/news/releases/2008/06/20080626-20.html; *see also* President George W. Bush, *Rallying the Armies of Compassion* (Jan. 2001), http://archives.hud.gov/reports/rally.pdf.

951. Exec. Order No. 13831, 83 Fed. Reg. 20715 (May 3, 2018).

952. Press Release, White House Briefing Room, Fact Sheet: President Biden Reestablishes the White House Office of Faith-Based and Neighborhood Partnerships (Feb. 14, 2021) [hereinafter White House Press Release (Feb. 14, 2021)], https://www.whitehouse.gov/briefing-room/statements-releases/2021/02/14/fact-sheet-president-biden-reestablishes-the-white-house-office-of-faith-based-and-neighborhood-partnerships; Exec. Order No. 14015, 86 Fed. Reg. 10007 (Feb. 18, 2021).

Chapter 3. Interaction Between Religion and State on a Political and Legal Level

§1. Overview

370. Although the First Amendment's Establishment Clause has been said to erect "a wall of separation between Church and State",[953] the wall metaphor has always been an incomplete and perhaps misleading image of the relationship between religion and the state in the United States.[954] For example, in 2014, the Supreme Court reconfirmed the acceptability of holding prayer before public legislative and governmental deliberations (*see* section 2 below). Similarly, with a few exceptions, the Supreme Court has generally found that government displays of religious objects and symbols do not per se violate the Establishment Clause (*see* section 3 below). A robust civil religion is evident in the United States (*see* section 4 below), and there are numerous other ways that religious leaders and organizations informally influence government (*see* section 5 below).

§2. Legislative Prayer

371. In *Marsh v. Chambers*, the Supreme Court considered an Establishment Clause challenge to the Nebraska state legislature's practice of retaining a chaplain, paid with public funds, to offer a prayer to begin each legislative day. The same chaplain, a Presbyterian clergyman, had served in the position for roughly sixteen years. In a 6-3 decision, the Court held that legislative prayer, as practiced by the Nebraska legislature, did not violate the Establishment Clause, stating that "[t]he opening of sessions of legislative and other deliberative public bodies with prayer is deeply embedded in the history and tradition of this country."[955] The Court noted that "the First Congress, as one of its early items of business, adopted the policy of selecting a chaplain to open each session with prayer".[956] Both the first Senate and the first House of Representatives selected chaplains in April and May of 1789 and, shortly thereafter, provided for these chaplains to be paid with public funds.[957] Not long thereafter, "final agreement was reached on the language of the Bill of Rights", including the First Amendment.[958] The Court emphasized that the concurrence of these events clearly showed that "the men who wrote the First Amendment Religion Clauses did not view paid legislative chaplains and opening prayers as a violation of that Amendment"; moreover, "the practice of opening sessions with prayer has continued without interruption ever since that early session of Congress".[959]

953. Letter from Thomas Jefferson to Danbury, Connecticut, Baptist Association, *supra* n. 526.
954. The Establishment Clause has been made applicable to the states through the Fourteenth Amendment. *Everson v. Bd. of Educ.*, 330 U.S. 1, 15–16 (1947).
955. *Marsh v. Chambers*, 463 U.S. 783, 786 (1983).
956. *Ibid.*, at 787–788.
957. *Ibid.*, at 788.
958. *Ibid.* (citing S. Journal, 1st Cong., 1st Sess., 88 (1789); H.R. Journal, 1st Cong., 1st Sess., 121 (1789)).
959. *Ibid.*, at 788 & n.10.

This historical perspective was viewed by the Court as being particularly important because "[a]n act 'passed by the first Congress assembled under the Constitution, many of whose members had taken part in framing that instrument, … is contemporaneous and weighty evidence of its true meaning.'"[960] The Court stated that legislative prayer was "simply a tolerable acknowledgment of beliefs widely held among the people of this country".[961] The Court held that Nebraska's particular implementation of legislative prayer was constitutional, even though a single Christian (Presbyterian) minister had held the chaplaincy for sixteen years, because there was no proof that the state legislature hired that particular minister out of "impermissible motive", and "there [was] no indication that the prayer opportunity ha[d] been exploited to proselytize or advance any one, or to disparage any other, faith or belief".[962] Some courts have more recently upheld policies of theist-only or religious-only legislative prayer on "history and tradition" grounds.[963]

372. It should be noted that, until the Supreme Court's 2022 decision *Kennedy v. Bremerton School District*,[964] the Court did not exclusively endorse or widely utilize the "historical significance" or "history and tradition" test as an interpretive methodology in other establishment or free exercise cases.[965] Prior to that decision,

---

960. *Ibid.*, at 790 (citing *Wisconsin v. Pelican Ins. Co.*, 127 U.S. 265, 297 (1888)).
961. *Ibid.*, at 792.
962. *Ibid.*, at 793, 794–795.
963. *See, e.g., Fields v. Speaker of the Pa. House of Representatives*, 936 F.3d 142, 149 (3d Cir. 2019) ("Because the House's policy preferring theistic over nontheistic prayers fits squarely within the historical tradition of legislative prayer, we … uphold the prayer policy."); *Barker v. Conroy*, 921 F.3d 1118, 1131 (D.C. Cir. 2019) ("[T]he House's decision to limit the opening prayer to religious prayer fit[s] 'within the tradition long followed in Congress and the state legislatures[.]'") (quoting *Town of Greece v. Galloway*, 572 U.S. 565, 577 (2014))); *Bormuth v. County of Jackson*, 870 F.3d 494, 497–498 (6th Cir. 2017) (en banc) (finding county board's tradition of opening public meetings with prayer was "consonant with … historical practice" and constitutional, applying *Marsh* and *Town of Greece*). *But see Williamson v. Brevard County*, 928 F.3d 1296, 1299, 1310 (11th Cir. 2019) (holding that process for selecting prayer-givers for board of county commissioners' meetings violated Establishment Clause when it favored monotheistic religions and categorically excluded others).
964. *Kennedy v. Bremerton Sch. Dist.*, 142 S. Ct. 2407, 2427–2428 (2022) (finding that the *Lemon* and endorsement tests had been "abandoned", in light of more recent Supreme Court precedent instructing that the Establishment Clause "be interpreted by 'reference to historical practices and understandings'" (quoting *Town of Greece v. Galloway*, 572 U.S. 565, 576 (2014), and citing *Am. Legion v. Am. Humanist Assoc.*, 139 S. Ct. 2067, 2087 (2019) (plurality section))).
965. *See Edwards v. Aguillard*, 482 U.S. 578, 583 n.4 (1987) (noting *Marsh v. Chambers* as the only relevant decision not to apply the *Lemon* test since its adoption and up to that point, and explaining that *Marsh*'s historical approach was "not useful in determining the proper roles of church and state in public schools, since free public education was virtually nonexistent at the time the Constitution was adopted"). Citing *Aguillard*, federal courts of appeals more recently rejected the historical significance test for Establishment Clause questions involving public-school settings. *See, e.g., Freedom from Religion Found., Inc. v. Chino Valley Unified Sch. Dist. Bd. of Educ.*, 896 F.3d 1132, 1149 (9th Cir. 2018), *reh'g en banc denied*, 910 F.3d 1297 (9th Cir. 2018); *Doe v. Indian River Sch. Dist.*, 653 F.3d 256, 280–281 (3d Cir. 2011); *see also Am. Humanist Ass'n v. McCarty*, 851 F.3d 521, 528 (5th Cir. 2017) (applying *Marsh* to hold that school board's prayer practice was constitutional but noting that the school board in question did not include students, unlike other cases that had rejected *Marsh* in public-school board settings). *But see Am. Legion v. Am. Humanist Ass'n*, 139 S. Ct. 2067, 2080, 2090–2103 (2019) (applying historical test in a religious symbol case

Marsh and subsequent legislative prayer cases were outliers, inasmuch as the Court did not employ the three-part "*Lemon* test"[966] or other tests focusing on neutrality or endorsement that it had utilized in other Establishment Clause contexts.

373. Town of Greece v. Galloway gave the Court a chance to re-examine legislative prayer thirty-one years after *Marsh*.[967] The town of Greece, New York, began in 1999 to open its board meetings with a prayer offered by local clergy. In contrast to *Marsh*, the opportunity to offer the invocation was rotated among various willing clergy in the Town of Greece, who were not compensated. Town leaders did not exclude anyone or deny opportunities to those willing to pray: "[A] minister or layperson of any persuasion, including an atheist, could give the invocation. But nearly all of the congregations in the town were Christian; and from 1999 to 2007, all of the participating ministers were too."[968] Two residents who attended a board meeting objected to the practice of invocation and brought an Establishment Clause claim against the town. In a 5-4 decision, the Court again upheld the practice of legislative prayer. Relying heavily on *Marsh*, the Court reiterated the long history of legislative prayer in the United States and held that the Town of Greece's particular implementation did not violate the Establishment Clause. Although the prayers at issue in *Town of Greece* were more explicitly Christian than those in *Marsh*, the Court nevertheless held that this fact alone did not constitute an Establishment Clause violation, pointing out that:

> [t]he town made reasonable efforts to identify all of the congregations located within its borders and represented that it would welcome a prayer by any minister or layman who wished to give one. ... So long as the town maintains a policy of nondiscrimination, the Constitution does not require it to search beyond its borders for non-Christian prayer givers in an effort to achieve religious balancing.[969]

Importantly, a plurality[970] of the Court rejected the idea that the board's practice created a coercive situation in which residents in attendance felt forced to participate in a religious ceremony with which they did not agree.[971]

---

in a plurality section of the opinion and, in multiple concurrences, discussing decline of the *Lemon* test and/or asserting it should be overruled); *Woodring v. Jackson County*, 986 F.3d 979 (7th Cir. 2021) (applying *American Legion*); *Kondrat'Yev v. City of Pensacola*, 949 F.3d 1319 (11th Cir. 2020) (applying *American Legion*); *Gaylor v. Mnuchin*, 919 F.3d 420, 435 (7th Cir. 2019) (citing *Van Orden v. Perry*, 545 U.S. 677 (2005), as the first case in the development of what the circuit court calls the "historical significance test").

966. *Lemon v. Kurtzman*, 403 U.S. 602, 612–613 (1971), *abrogated by Kennedy*, 142 S. Ct. at 2427–2428.

967. *Town of Greece v. Galloway*, 572 U.S. 565 (2014).

968. *Ibid.*, at 571.

969. *Ibid.*, at 579, 585–586. "*Marsh* nowhere suggested that the constitutionality of legislative prayer turns on the neutrality of its content. ... To the contrary, the Court instructed that 'the content of the prayer is not of concern to judges,' provided 'there is no indication that the prayer opportunity has been exploited to proselytize or advance any one, or to disparage any other, faith or belief.'" *Ibid.*, at 580–581 (quoting *Marsh v. Chambers*, 463 U.S. 783, 794–795); *see also supra* para. 371 and accompanying footnotes.

970. A plurality opinion means that while five or more of the nine Supreme Court justices agree on the end result of the ruling, only four or fewer agree on the legal rationale detailed in the opinion.

374. In a significant dissenting opinion, Justice Stephen Breyer provided useful principles to guide a public prayer practice that strives to be inclusive and pluralistic. He cited, as an example, guidelines given by the US House of Representatives to clergy who are invited to open sessions of that body with prayer. Those guidelines recommend, but do not require, that clergy be sensitive to the fact that their audience includes "[m]embers of many different faith traditions", that the prayer be no longer than 150 words, and that the prayer-giver refrain from expressing their "personal political views" or their views on "sectarian controversies".[972] Justice Breyer also suggested he might have approved of the Town of Greece's legislative prayer practices had the town made a greater effort to extend invitations to religious minorities within the community and the wider county and had it better advertised its inclusive policy through its website and announcements at board meetings.[973]

§3. Religious Symbols on Public Property

375. In *Lynch v. Donnelly*, the Court held that including a crèche (Christian nativity scene) in a city holiday display that included other secular elements—such as a Christmas tree, a Santa Claus house, and a "Seasons Greetings" banner—did not violate the Establishment Clause. In contrast, the Court held in *County of Allegheny v. ACLU* that a crèche erected by a local religious group in a prominent area of a local government building was unconstitutional under the Establishment Clause. The main factor distinguishing the two crèche displays was the overall context: the constitutional *Lynch* crèche was part of a larger display with a secular purpose, while the unconstitutional *County of Allegheny* display was part of an overwhelmingly religious exhibit, which included angels and Bible excerpts but no Santa Claus or other secular elements.[974]

Because a majority of the justices do not agree on the reasoning found in the plurality opinion, that reasoning constitutes persuasive, not binding, authority. *See Glossary*—U.S. v. Avarez, U.S. Cts., https://www.uscourts.gov/educational-resources/educational-activities/glossary-us-v-alvarez (last visited Aug. 30, 2023); *see also* Kimura, *Legitimacy Model for the Interpretation of Plurality Decisions*, *infra* n. 1459, at 1595–1596.

971. *Town of Greece*, 572 U.S. at 586–592.

972. *Ibid.*, at 610, 614 (Breyer, J., dissenting). Distinctions raised in Justice Breyer's dissent parallel primary differences between federal courts of appeals cases that have applied *Town of Greece* to different outcomes. *Compare, e.g.*, *Bormuth v. County of Jackson*, 870 F.3d 494, 497–498, 512 (6th Cir. 2017) (en banc) (holding county board's commissioner-led prayer tradition was constitutional where pattern of prayers was overwhelmingly Christian, due to the board's composition, but did not "denigrate, proselytize, or betray an impermissible government purpose" (quoting *Town of Greece*, 572 U.S. at 567)), *with Lund v. Rowan County*, 863 F.3d 268, 272 (4th Cir. 2017) (en banc) (holding county board of commissioners' prayer tradition was unconstitutional where it "referenced one and only one faith and veered from time to time into overt proselytization" (citing *Town of Greece*, 572 U.S. at 565)).

973. *Town of Greece*, 572 U.S. at 610, 613 (Breyer, J., dissenting).

974. *Lynch v. Donnelly*, 465 U.S. 668, 679–686 (1984); *County of Allegheny v. ACLU*, 492 U.S. 573, 580, 598–603 (1989), *abrogation acknowledged by Kennedy v. Bremerton*, 142 S. Ct. 2407, 2427–2428 (2022) ("Here, unlike in *Lynch*, nothing in the context of the display detracts from the crèche's religious message. The *Lynch* display composed a series of figures and objects, each group of which had its own focal point. Santa's house and his reindeer were objects of attention separate

376. Public display of the Ten Commandments has been another controversial question in Establishment Clause jurisprudence, where the Court has made subtle distinctions, with the display's purpose and context being determinative factors in the constitutionality analysis. Like the tradition of legislative prayer, displaying the Ten Commandments is an established and common governmental practice.[975] However, in *McCreary County v. ACLU*, the Court held that the Ten Commandments displays in two Kentucky county courthouses were unconstitutional because evidence showed that the displays were religiously motivated.[976] On the same day, it decided *McCreary County*, the Court also released a plurality opinion[977] upholding the constitutionality of a different Ten Commandments display included among the "17 monuments and 21 historical markers" that surround the Texas State Capitol.[978] As in the crèche cases, the Court focused on whether there was a permissible secular purpose in the religious display and reached similar conclusions in each context—that the government is allowed to publicly display religious symbols and messages if a non-pretextual secular purpose exists.

377. In certain public forum situations, where the government has broadly invited the public to participate in expression, the government may allow overtly religious displays and messages without violating the Establishment Clause.[979] However, when governments are themselves speaking or acting in a "curatorial"

---

from the crèche, and had their specific visual story to tell. Similarly, whatever a "talking" wishing well may be, it obviously was a center of attention separate from the crèche. Here, in contrast, the crèche stands alone: it is the single element of the display on the Grand Staircase.").

975. For example, representations of the Ten Commandments, or Moses with the Ten Commandments, appear on the walls of the Supreme Court's chambers, on the Supreme Court building's exterior, on the Supreme Court's gates and doors, in the Library of Congress, on the floor of the National Archives, in the Department of Justice building, in front of the Ronald Reagan Building, and in the House of Representatives' legislative chambers. *McCreary County v. ACLU*, 545 U.S. 844, 874 (2005); *ibid.*, at 885, 906 (Scalia, J., with Roberts, C.J., and Thomas, J., dissenting, and Kennedy, J., joining in part); *Van Orden v. Perry*, 545 U.S. 677, 688–689 (2005) (plurality opinion).

976. *McCreary County*, 545 U.S. at 859–874 ("The reasonable observer could only think that the Counties meant to emphasize and celebrate the Commandments' religious message.")

977. For an explanation of a plurality opinion, *see supra* n. 970; *see also* Kimura, *Legitimacy Model for the Interpretation of Plurality Decisions*, *infra* n. 1459, at 1595–1596.

978. *Van Orden*, 545 U.S. at 681, 691–692 ("Texas has treated its Capitol grounds monuments as representing the several strands in the State's political and legal history. The inclusion of the Ten Commandments monument in this group has a dual significance, partaking of both religion and government."); *ibid.*, at 698, 701–703 (Breyer, J., concurring) ("Here the tablets have been used as part of a display that communicates not simply a religious message, but a secular message as well. The circumstances surrounding the display's placement on the capitol grounds and its physical setting suggest that the State itself intended the latter, nonreligious aspects of the tablets' message to predominate. And the monument's 40-year history on the Texas state grounds indicates that that has been its effect.").

979. *Shurtleff v. City of Boston*, 596 U.S. 243, 247–248 (2022) (concluding that a city's exclusion of a religious flag from a public forum displaying flags with various viewpoints unconstitutionally discriminated based on viewpoint); *Capitol Square Rev. & Advisory Bd. v. Pinette*, 515 U.S. 753, 770 (1995) (requiring the state to allow the Ku Klux Klan to erect a temporary cross in a public area where other religious groups have been allowed to construct temporary religious displays); *see also Am. Legion v. Am. Humanist Ass'n*, 139 S. Ct. 2067 (2019) (holding that the display of a Latin Cross as a World War I memorial on public land does not violate the Establishment Clause because, within the community, the symbol has come to represent more than its original religious meaning).

manner and not creating a public forum where the public is invited to speak, they may be selective in the monuments displayed in publicly owned parks.[980] Additionally, in situations where a religious monument has existed long enough for the community to form a sense of "familiarity and historical significance", government action to remove the monument may no longer be viewed as content neutral.[981] For additional discussion about public displays of religious symbols, *see* Part VII (Religious Communities and Protections of the Individual), Chapter 3 (Freedom of Expression) and Chapter 7 (Non-discrimination); and Part XI (Religion and Culture), Chapter 1 (Religion and Art).

§4. Civil Religion

378. A kind of civil religion permeates US history, society, and culture. Although it draws on Christian tenets and symbols, it is "neither sectarian nor in any specific sense Christian" but includes a belief in a God who "is actively interested and involved in history, with a special concern for America".[982] For example, in 1956 Congress officially adopted "In God we trust" as the United States' motto.[983] This national motto is required to appear on all coins and bills minted by the US Treasury.[984] US Presidents almost always conclude state of the union, inaugural, or other significant public addresses with the phrase, "God bless America" or

---

980. In *Pleasant Grove City v. Summum*, the Court held that Pleasant Grove City could permissibly refuse the request of Summum, a small religious organization, to place a Summum-funded monument in a public park that featured other displays, including a Ten Commandments monument, because the city's "practice was to limit monuments in the park to those that 'either (1) directly relate to the history of Pleasant Grove, or (2) were donated by groups with long-standing ties to the Pleasant Grove community'". 555 U.S. 460, 465 (2009). Summum challenged the refusal under the public forum free speech doctrine. The Court held the analysis did not apply because, unlike free speech requirements to reasonably and temporarily accommodate speakers or leaflet distributors in the park, the city could not be expected to accommodate every permanent monument donated to the park. *Ibid.*, at 478–480. The Court also distinguished *Capitol Square Review*, which involved a request for a temporary display rather than a permanent monument. *Ibid.*, at 480. The Court did not directly address the Establishment Clause issue because it was not raised on appeal. *See also infra* para. 637 and accompanying footnotes.
981. *Am. Legion v. Am. Humanist Ass'n*, 139 S. Ct. 2067, 2084 (2019). In *American Legion*, a Latin Cross was erected as a World War I memorial, after the fashion of the era, to honor forty-nine local men who died and were buried overseas. *Ibid.*, at 2047. The Court held that the cross did not violate the Establishment Clause, noting that in the eighty-nine years prior to the suit being filed, the memorial had become a gathering place for patriotic events and had become viewed by the community less as a religious symbol and more as a historical monument. *Ibid.*, at 2077, 2089; *see also Woodring v. Jackson County*, 986 F.3d 979 (7th Cir. 2021) (applying *American Legion* in finding county's nativity display constitutional); *Kondrat'yev v. City of Pensacola*, 949 F.3d 1319 (11th Cir. 2020) (applying *American Legion* in finding cross maintained on city property did not violate Establishment Clause).
982. Bellah, *Civil Religion in America*, *supra* n. 925, at 7–8; *see also supra* para. 352.
983. H.R.J. 396, 84th Cong., Pub. L. No. 84-851, 70 Stat. 732 (1956) (codified at 36 U.S.C. § 302 (2018)) ("'In God we trust' is the national motto.").
984. H.R. 619, 84th Cong., Pub. L. 84-140, 69 Stat. 290 (1955) (codified at 31 U.S.C. §§ 5112(d)(1), 5114(b) (2018)).

some variant thereof.[985] And the Supreme Court begins oral arguments each day only after the clerk proclaims "God save the United States and this Honorable Court!"[986] For more on civil religion, *see* Part XI (Religion and Culture), Chapter 3 (Religion and Civil Society).

379. In *Elk Grove Unified School District v. Newdow*, the atheist father of an elementary school student claimed that a school district policy, requiring each elementary school class to recite daily the Pledge of Allegiance, violated the Establishment Clause by repeatedly exposing his daughter to a religious affirmation—specifically the words "one Nation under God".[987] (The words "under God" were added to the Pledge during the Cold War as a mechanism for distinguishing American democracy from Soviet communism.) The right of a student to opt out of participating in the recitation of the Pledge had been recognized by the Court a half-century earlier.[988] Newdow's objection was not based on a claim of coerced participation in recitation of the pledge; rather, he objected to his daughter being continually exposed to what he believed was an unconstitutional establishment of religion. Although the majority opinion briefly discussed the Pledge of Allegiance as a "patriotic exercise" (rather than a religious one), the Court ultimately dismissed Newdow's case based on his lack of standing to bring the lawsuit on behalf of his daughter.[989] The child's father and mother were not married, the mother had legal custody of the child, and the mother did not object to the Pledge.[990] Thus, the court declined to rule on the substantive Establishment Clause issue, and that question remains unresolved by the Supreme Court. The trend in lower courts, however, has been to follow the Supreme Court's suggestion that the Pledge is primarily a patriotic exercise.[991]

---

985. *McCreary County v. ACLU*, 545 U.S. 844, 885, 885 (2005) (Scalia, J., with Roberts, C.J., and Thomas, J., dissenting, and Kennedy, J., joining in part); *see, e.g.*, 167 Cong. Rec. S77–78 (daily ed. Jan. 21, 2021) (inaugural address of President Joseph R. Biden, Jr.); 163 Cong. Rec. S364–365 (daily ed. Jan. 20, 2017) (inaugural address of President Donald J. Trump); 155 Cong. Rec. S668–669 (daily ed. Jan. 20, 2009) (first inaugural address of President Barack Obama); 147 Cong. Rec. S422–423 (daily ed. Jan. 22, 2001) (first inaugural address of President George W. Bush); 139 Cong. Rec. S384–385 (daily ed. Jan. 20, 1993) (first inaugural address of President Bill Clinton).

986. *McCreary County*, 545 U.S. at 885, 886, 888 (Scalia, J., with Roberts, C.J., and Thomas, J., dissenting, and Kennedy, J., joining in part); *The Court and Its Procedures*, Sup. Ct. U.S., http://www.supremecourt.gov/about/procedures.aspx (last visited Sep. 30, 2023).

987. The Pledge of Allegiance states, in full: "I pledge allegiance to the Flag of the United States of America, and to the Republic for which it stands, *one Nation under God*, indivisible, with liberty and justice for all." 4 U.S.C. § 4 (2018) (emphasis added); *Elk Grove Unified Sch. Dist. v. Newdow*, 542 U.S. 1, 4–7 (2004).

988. *W. Va. State Bd. of Educ. v. Barnette*, 319 U.S. 624, 642 (1943) ("We think the action of the local authorities in compelling the flag salute and pledge transcends constitutional limitations on their power and invades the sphere of intellect and spirit which it is the purpose of the First Amendment to our Constitution to reserve from all official control."). *Barnette* officially overruled *Minersville Sch. Dist. v. Gobitis*, 310 U.S. 586 (1940), which had reached the opposite result only a few years earlier.

989. *Elk Grove*, 542 U.S. at 15–18.

990. *Ibid.*, at 9–10, 13–14.

991. Concurrently with the *Elk Grove* suit, Newdow joined a US district court suit along with several other atheist parents to question the constitutionality of the Pledge and the practice of four California public-school districts in leading students to recite it. *Newdow v. Cong. of the U.S.*, 383 F.

§5. Religion and Politics

380. The Constitution provides that "[t]he Senators and Representatives … and all executive and judicial Officers, both of the United States and of the several States, *shall be bound by Oath or Affirmation*, to support this Constitution; *but no religious Test shall ever be required* as a Qualification to any Office or public Trust under the United States."[992] The option that public officers "be bound by Oath *or* Affirmation" finds its origins in laws passed by the English Parliament, which allowed Quakers (members of the Society of Friends, who believed that swearing oaths was a sin) to make an affirmation, rather than swear an oath, to testify in court.[993] The final clause, known as the No Religious Test Clause, prohibits oaths of office from containing sectarian religious material that would present conflicts of conscience for people of certain faiths; this arose as a response to the English practice of forcing public officers to swear allegiance to the authority of the king, presumably so as not to be influenced by the Catholic pope.[994] The No Religious Test Clause does not prevent people from considering religion when deciding for whom to vote, and as noted earlier, the religious affiliation and bona fides of candidates for office are sometimes an issue in contests for public office. *See* this part, Chapter 1 (Religious Influence in Politics), above.

381. Although the United States Congress is more religiously diverse today than it was in the 1960s, Christianity is still the religion of most of its members. In

---

Supp. 2d 1229 (E.D. Cal. 2005). The district court judge concluded that, while the US Supreme Court reversed *Elk Grove* on the basis of Newdow's prudential standing, the opinion of the Ninth Circuit Court regarding his Establishment Clause claims (that is, that the school's policy was unconstitutional) remained binding. *Ibid.*, at 1240–1242. On appeal, the Ninth Circuit reversed, pointing out that, since Newdow did not have standing in *Elk Grove*, the court erred in reaching the merits of the case, so its opinion was not binding on any lower court. *Newdow v. Rio Linda Union Sch. Dist.*, 597 F.3d 1007, 1041 (9th Cir. 2010). Furthermore, the Ninth Circuit Court rejected Newdow's claim, holding that the Pledge does not violate the Establishment Clause because Congress's ostensible and predominant purpose was to inspire patriotism and that the context of the Pledge—its wording as a whole, the preamble to the statute, and this nation's history—demonstrate that it is a predominantly patriotic exercise. For these reasons, the Ninth Circuit reasoned, the phrase "one Nation under God" does not turn the patriotic exercise into a religious activity. *Ibid.*, at 1014. The Supreme Court later upheld the presence of a Latin cross on public land, using similar reasoning, in *American Legion v. American Humanist Association*, 139 S. Ct. 2067 (2019). The Court reasoned that "the Bladensburg Cross carries special significance in commemorating World War I" and had "acquired additional layers of historical meaning" over the 89 years it had stood as a community monument. *Am. Legion*, 139 S. Ct. at 2089. The Court acknowledged it is "undoubtedly a Christian symbol, but that fact should not blind us to everything else that the Bladensburg Cross has come to represent. … For many …, destroying or defacing the Cross … would not be neutral and would not further the ideas of respect and tolerance embodied in the First Amendment." *Ibid.*, at 2089–2090.

992. U.S. Const. art. VI, cl. 3 (emphasis added).

993. Frederick B. Jonassen, *"So Help Me?": Religious Expression and Artifacts in the Oath of Office and the Courtroom Oath*, 12 Cardozo Pub. L. Pol'y & Ethics J. 303, 319–320 (2014).

994. *Ibid.*, at 322–323 ("Many British oaths included explicit religious statements, which made it difficult, if not impossible, for Catholics, Jews, and minority Protestant sects to take the oaths for public office. These were religious tests.").

January 2023, 88% (469 out of 534 members) identified as Christian.[995] Fifty-seven percent were Protestant, and 28% were Catholic.[996] These figures differ in degree from the makeup of the total US adult population, which in 2023 was 63% Christian, 40% Protestant, and 21% Catholic.[997] About 6% of congressional representatives were Jewish, compared to 2% of American adults, and members of The Church of Jesus Christ of Latter-day Saints made up about 2%, similar to their percentage among American adults.[998] Muslims, Buddhists, and Hindus, who have only been elected to Congress in this century and only to the House of Representatives, comprised less than 1.5% of members, though they made up 3% of the US population.[999] Three representatives were Unitarian Universalists.[1000] The one group that remained underrepresented was the religious "nones", or unaffiliated. In 2023, an increasing number of American adults—29%—identified themselves as "unaffiliated", but only one member of Congress did so.[1001] One explanation for this is that, while "unaffiliated" does not necessarily mean atheist, politicians may be cautious about the designation because "fully half of American adults say they would be less likely to vote for a hypothetical presidential candidate who does not believe in God, while just 6% say they would be more likely to vote for a nonbeliever".[1002]

382. Pursuant to the Establishment Clause, the United States has no official church, no federal or state departments of religious affairs, and no federal or state religious bureaucracies of any sort. Recognizing the powerful influence that religion has on civil society, however, the federal government has created formal offices and initiatives charged with establishing connections to religious organizations to facilitate collaborations in promoting community development and providing social services. Under different administrations, the name, purposes, and objectives of the executive office responsible for fostering these connections are subject to change. Under the Biden and Obama administrations, the office has been called the White House Office of Faith-Based and Neighborhood Partnerships.[1003] For more information on the history and purposes of this office, *see* this part, Chapter 2 (Political Influence in Religion), above; and Part XI (Religion and Culture), Chapter 3 (Religion and Society).

383. Although the United States has no established religion or church, religious groups and people can and do influence both politics and government in myriad informal ways. For example, the Reverend Billy Graham famously met with each

995. Diamant, *Faith on the Hill*, *supra* n. 919 (noting that one seat remained unfilled at the beginning of the 118th Congress).
996. Diamant, *Faith on the Hill*, *supra* n. 919.
997. *Ibid.*
998. *Ibid.*
999. *Ibid.*
1000. *Ibid.*
1001. *Ibid.*
1002. *Faith and the 2016 Campaign*, *supra* n. 920, at 2.
1003. Exec. Order No. 14015, 86 Fed. Reg. 10007 (Feb. 18, 2021).

president, from Harry Truman in 1950 to Barack Obama in 2010.[1004] He offered political advice in support of Richard Nixon during the 1960 election and was Lyndon B. Johnson's "chief spiritual counselor".[1005] Of course, religious leaders are free to run for public office, which can bring religious influence into the political process in various ways. Pat Robertson, a famous televangelist and founder of the Christian Coalition and Christian Broadcasting Network, ran unsuccessfully for the Republican presidential nomination in 1987; his platform focused on returning to and maintaining America's "Christian roots" and traditional "family values".[1006] Reverend Jesse Jackson, a Baptist minister and former protégé of Martin Luther King Jr., surprised many by placing second and third, respectively, for the 1987 and 1983 Democratic presidential nominations; Jackson proposed creating a "Rainbow Coalition" of minority groups and emphasized the financing of social welfare programs.[1007] Joseph Smith, the nineteenth-century founder of The Church of Jesus Christ of Latter-day Saints, launched a campaign for US President a few months before his assassination in 1844; his platform included abolition of slavery, radical reform of the prison system, and westward expansion contingent on Indian tribes' consent.[1008]

384. Political candidates who are not professional clergy sometimes express religious views to attract voters. For example, Mike Huckabee (who had once been a Baptist minister) won the 2008 Iowa Republican caucus by casting himself as "the Christian candidate",[1009] and Donald Trump gained wide appeal among conservative Christian voters in his 2016 campaign by casting himself as a champion of their values, despite admittedly not living them.[1010] Conversely, religious leaders and organizations may seek to influence governmental leaders and processes through less public ways, such as meeting privately with public officials and submitting amicus curiae briefs in court cases.[1011]

1004. Stephen J. Whitfield, The Preacher and the Presidents: Billy Graham in the White House *by Nancy Gibbs and Michael Duffy*, 123 Pol. Sci. Q. 523, 523–524 (2008) (book review); *Billy Graham: Pastor to the Presidents*, Billy Graham Evangelistic Ass'n (Feb. 17, 2023), https://billygraham.org/gallery/billy-graham-pastor-to-the-presidents.

1005. Richard V. Pierard, *Billy Graham and the U.S. Presidency*, 22 J. Church & St. 107, 119–122 (1980).

1006. Stephen D. Johnson, Joseph B. Tamney & Ronald Burton, *Pat Robertson: Who Supported His Candidacy for President?*, 28 J. Sci. Study Religion 387, 387–399 (1989).

1007. Howell Raines, *A Provocative Candidate*, N.Y. Times, Nov. 4, 1983, at A1.

1008. Richard Lyman Bushman, *Joseph Smith: Rough Stone Rolling* 514–517, 544–550 (2007); Spencer W. McBride, *Joseph Smith for President: The Prophet, the Assassins, and the Fight for American Religious Freedom* 89–106, 181–198 (2021).

1009. Stephen M. Feldman, *Divided We Fall: Religion, Politics, and the* Lemon *Entanglements Prong*, 7 First Amend. L. Rev. 253, 255–256 (2009).

1010. *See* Jessica Taylor, *True Believer? Why Donald Trump Is the Choice of the Religious Right*, NPR (Sep. 13, 2015), https://www.npr.org/sections/itsallpolitics/2015/09/13/439833719/true-believer-why-donald-trump-is-the-choice-of-the-religious-right.

1011. *See, e.g.*, Ruby Mellen, *The History of Meetings Between U.S. Presidents and Pontiffs*, Wash. Post (Oct. 29, 2021), https://www.washingtonpost.com/world/interactive/2021/biden-francis-popes-presidents; News Release, The Church of Jesus Christ of Latter-day Saints, President Uchtdorf, Other Faith Leaders Meet with President Obama on Immigration (Apr. 15, 2014),

385. As early as the election contest between John Adams and Thomas Jefferson, religion has been an issue in political campaigns, with Adams's supporters attacking Jefferson for his unorthodox religious views. Federalists frequently decried Jefferson as a "howling atheist" and an anti-Christian "infidel".[1012] If elected, they feared, Jefferson would turn the country into an immoral and godless nation; Bibles would be burned and traditional religious establishments destroyed. One newspaper said the election would force voters to choose between "GOD—AND A RELIGIOUS PRESIDENT or impiously declare for JEFFERSON—AND NO GOD".[1013] Notwithstanding these attacks, Jefferson won the election. The Federalists' strategy may have backfired, giving the impression that the Federalists had little to offer politically, other than criticism of their opponent.[1014] When his first term as President "did not bear out the dire predictions of his detractors, the question of his faith received much less attention" in the next election.[1015] Perhaps the Federalists had learned a lesson about the ineffectiveness of such tactics; the majority of the American people seemed to care more about Jefferson's policies and his ability to lead the country than his private beliefs.[1016] Even so, the issue remained a significant obstacle for Jefferson to overcome; he spent a great deal of time after the election redefining himself as a Christian and trying to prove his spirituality by attending church and continuing to advocate for religious liberty.[1017]

386. At the time of the United States' founding, widespread anti-Catholic sentiment existed among both voters and government officials.[1018] Based on stereotypes and misinformation, these anti-Catholic feelings can also be seen as born in

---

https://newsroom.churchofjesuschrist.org/article/church-apostle-joins-other-faith-leaders-in-meeting-with-president-obama-on-immigration; *Franklin Roosevelt Administration: Report on Meeting of Jewish Leaders with Roosevelt (December 8, 1942)*, Jewish Virtual Libr., https://www.jewishvirtuallibrary.org/report-on-meeting-of-jewish-leaders-with-roosevelt-december-1942 (last visited Sep. 30, 2023); Letter from Stephen Wise, President, Am. Jewish Cong., to President Franklin D. Roosevelt (Dec. 2, 1942) (on file with National Archives), https://www.docsteach.org/documents/document/american-jewish-congress-fdr; Brief Amicus Curiae of United States Conference of Catholic Bishops in Support of Respondents and Supporting Affirmance, *Obergefell v. Hodges*, 574 U.S. 1118 (2015) (mem.) (Nos. 14-556, 14-562, 14-574); Brief of National Ass'n of Evangelicals as Amicus Curiae Supporting Hobby Lobby and Conestoga, et al., *Burwell v. Hobby Lobby Stores, Inc.*, 573 U.S. 682 (2015) (Nos. 13-354, 13-356).

1012. John E. Ferling, *Adams vs. Jefferson: The Tumultuous Election of 1800*, at 154 (2004).

1013. *Ibid.*; Robert M. S. McDonald, *Was There a Religious Revolution of 1800?*, *in The Revolution of 1800: Democracy, Race, and the New Republic* 173, 182 (James Horn, Jan Ellen Lewis & Peter S. Onuf eds., 2002).

1014. McDonald, *Was There a Religious Revolution of 1800?*, *supra* n. 1013, at 180–181.

1015. *Ibid.*, at 190, 187.

1016. *Ibid.*, at 184–189.

1017. *See ibid.*, at 194.

1018. *See* Michael W. McConnell, Essay, *Is There Still a "Catholic Question" in America? Reflections on John F. Kennedy's Speech to the Houston Ministerial Association*, 86 Notre Dame L. Rev. 1635, 1638–1642 (2011) ("Let us consider what some historians have called the oldest prejudice in America, the history of anti-Catholicism in the United States."); Daniel J. Morrissey, *The Separation of Church and State: An American-Catholic Perspective*, 47 Cath. U. L. Rev. 1, 5–7 (1997); Douglas Laycock, *Continuity and Change in the Threat to Religious Liberty: The Reformation Era and the Late Twentieth Century*, 80 Minn. L. Rev. 1047, 1060–1069 (1996).

part from an impulse to protect the state apparatus from the improper influence of a religious group that many believed sought to demolish the "wall of separation" between church and state.[1019] Running as the Democratic candidate in the 1960 presidential campaign, John F. Kennedy famously assured the country that he would not be a papal puppet if elected President of the United States.[1020] Kennedy's victory marked an inflection point in anti-Catholic sentiment in the United States.[1021] In recent years, nearly one-third of US Congress members have been Catholic.[1022] In 2023, seven of the nine US Supreme Court justices identified or once identified as Catholic.[1023] Joe Biden, who openly discussed and observed his faith throughout his long political career, became the second Catholic President in US history in 2021. It is safe to say that Catholicism is no longer a barrier to being elected or appointed, even to national office.

387. Religious affiliation does tend to mark divides in Americans' voting behavior. In 2017, Pew Research Center conducted polling that found white, non-Hispanic evangelical Protestants (77%) and members of The Church of Jesus Christ of Latter-day Saints (72%) are the religious groups most likely to identify as or "lean" Republican, though the latter has leaned increasingly independent and Democratic in more recent elections.[1024] Meanwhile, 87% of black Protestants and 67% of Jews identify with or lean toward the Democratic Party, compared to just 7% and 31%, respectively, who identify with or lean toward the Republican Party.[1025] Catholic voters split fairly evenly between the two major parties, though

---

1019. *See, e.g.*, Thomas C. Berg, *Anti-Catholicism and Modern Church-State Relations*, 33 Loy. U. Chi. L.J. 121, 138–147 (2002); McConnell, *Is There Still a "Catholic Question" in America?*, *supra* n. 1018, at 1638–1640 ("Philosopher George Santayana … declared that '[i]f … the Catholic church ever became dominant in America, it would without doubt … transform American life and institutions. … [I]t would abolish religious liberty, the freedom of the press, divorce, and lay education.' … In 1948, critics of the Church formed a new organization, called Protestants and Other Americans United for the Separation of Church and State (POAU) with the objective of 'resist[ing] the declared purposes of the Roman Catholic Church further to breach the wall of separation between church and state.'"); *see also Lynch v. Donnelly*, 465 U.S. 668, 673 (1984) (discussing "wall of separation" metaphor).

1020. John F. Kennedy, Address to the Greater Houston Ministerial Association (Sep. 12, 1960), https://www.jfklibrary.org/learn/about-jfk/historic-speeches/address-to-the-greater-houston-ministerial-association (link to transcript) (last visited Sep. 30, 2023) ("I believe in an America where the separation of church and state is absolute … ."); *see also* McConnell, *Is There Still a "Catholic Question" in America?*, *supra* n. 1018, at 1643–1644.

1021. McConnell, *Is There Still a "Catholic Question" in America?*, *supra* n. 1018, at 1635–1636, 1653.

1022. Diamant, *Faith on the Hill*, *supra* n. 919.

1023. Newport, *The Religion of the Supreme Court Justices*, *supra* n. 59.

1024. Pew Rsch. Ctr., *Wide Gender Gap, Growing Educational Divide in Voters' Party Identification* 18, 20 (Mar. 20, 2018) [hereinafter *Voters' Party Identification*], https://www.pewresearch.org/politics/2018/03/20/wide-gender-gap-growing-educational-divide-in-voters-party-identification (link to PDF); *see also* Christian Sagers, Opinion, *Are Latter-day Saint Voters Turning Blue?*, Deseret News (May 12, 2021), https://www.deseret.com/opinion/2021/5/12/22432312/latter-day-saint-voters-turning-blue-mormon-trump-republican-democrat.

1025. *Voters' Party Identification*, *supra* n. 1024, at 18, 20.

Hispanic Catholics, who make up an increasing share of the US Catholic population, identify or lean much more Democratic (64%).[1026] In recent decades, the percentage of religiously unaffiliated voters has more than quadrupled (from 5% in 1997 to 24% in 2017) and leans increasingly Democratic (from 52% in 1997 to 68% in 2017).[1027] Other social scientists have found that "[i]dentifying a candidate as an evangelical … increases Republican support for, and Democratic opposition to, the candidate, while identifying the candidate as a Catholic … has no bearing on partisan voting".[1028] Interestingly, "affiliation with an evangelical tradition works in opposite directions for African Americans and whites. African American evangelicals, perhaps because of the messages on economics and civil rights that are preached in the traditional black church, are more likely than other African Americans to vote Democratic".[1029]

§6. Religious Freedom and International Affairs

388. In 1998, the International Religious Freedom Act (IRFA) was passed by Congress and signed by President Bill Clinton. The Act created two government institutions to monitor, advise, and report on international religious freedom: the United States Commission on International Religious Freedom (USCIRF) and the US State Department Office of International Religious Freedom.[1030] The Act also created the position of Ambassador at Large for International Religious Freedom, responsible for coordinating international religious freedom policies and activities across the federal government.[1031]

389. USCIRF is a bipartisan, independent federal agency that monitors the right to freedom of religion or belief abroad based on international standards; "makes policy recommendations to the President, Secretary of State, and Congress"; and tracks implementation of those recommendations.[1032] The Commission is comprised of nine voting commissioners, including a chair and vice-chair, who are supported by a professional staff. Commissioners are appointed by the President and leaders of Congress from both political parties.[1033] The Ambassador at Large serves as a non-voting member of USCIRF.[1034] The Ambassador also heads the Office of

1026. *Ibid.*, at 19.
1027. *Ibid.*, at 21, 28.
1028. David E. Campbell, John C. Green & Geoffrey C. Layman, *The Party Faithful: Partisan Images, Candidate Religion, and the Electoral Impact of Party Identification*, 55 Am. J. Pol. Sci. 42, 42 (2011).
1029. Brad Lockerbie, *Race and Religion: Voting Behavior and Political Attitudes*, 94 Soc. Sci. Q. 1145, 1145 (2013).
1030. International Religious Freedom Act of 1998 (IRFA), Pub. L. No. 105-292, 112 Stat. 2787 (codified as amended at 22 U.S.C. §§ 4028, 6401–6483 (2018)).
1031. 22 U.S.C. § 6411 (2018).
1032. *Ibid.*, § 6432; *About Us*, U.S. Comm'n on Int'l Religious Freedom, https://www.uscirf.gov/about-uscirf/about-us (last visited Sep. 30, 2023).
1033. *See* 22 U.S.C. § 6431; *Commissioners*, U.S. Comm'n on Int'l Religious Freedom, https://www.uscirf.gov/commissioners (last visited Sep. 30, 2023).
1034. 22 U.S.C. § 6431.

International Religious Freedom (OIRF), part of the Bureau of Democracy, Human Rights, and Labor in the US State Department.[1035] Pursuant to IRFA, the State Department is required to submit annual reports on human rights and religious freedom in every country other than the United States. In addition to contributing to these individual reports, OIRF helps produce an annual Report to Congress on International Religious Freedom worldwide.[1036] The Office also advises the Secretary of State in designating Countries of Particular Concern (CPCs—nations that engage in or tolerate "particularly severe" religious freedom violations), Special Watch List countries (SWL countries—nations that engage in or tolerate "severe violations"), and Entities of Particular Concern (EPCs—"non-state actors that have engaged in particularly severe violations").[1037] Nations so designated may be subject to economic sanctions or other federal action. In addition to its advisory role, OIRF seeks to support non-governmental organizations (NGOs) that promote reconciliation in religious disputes in foreign countries.[1038] For additional discussion, *see* Part I (Legal Framework and Sources), Chapter 2 (Other Legislation with Regard to Religion); and Part IV (International, Transnational, and Regional Effects on Religious Communities), Chapter 2 (Transnational Law Effects on Religious Communities).

1035. *Ibid.*, § 6411; *Office of International Religious Freedom*, U.S. Dep't State, https://www.state.gov/bureaus-offices/under-secretary-for-civilian-security-democracy-and-human-rights/office-of-international-religious-freedom (last visited Sep. 30, 2023).
1036. 22 U.S.C. § 6412; *International Religious Freedom Reports*, U.S. Dep't State, https://www.state.gov/international-religious-freedom-reports (last visited Sep. 30, 2023).
1037. 22 U.S.C. § 6442; *Countries of Particular Concern*, *supra* n. 790.
1038. *About Us*, Off. Int'l Religious Freedom, *supra* n. 217.

Part VI. Labor Law Within Religious Communities

Chapter 1. Scope of Application of Labor Law

§1. General Background

390. US labor law involves numerous issues that affect religious and religiously affiliated organizations, such as non-discrimination in employment, labor relations and collective bargaining, Social Security (federal retirement benefits system), and tax withholding. This chapter will give a brief overview of each of these areas of law and relevant exemptions for religious communities.

391. Exemptions to labor law for religious and religiously affiliated organizations stem from either explicit statutory protections or constitutional requirements. In determining whether the Constitution requires exemptions, courts will look at the demands of religious autonomy, the requirements of the Free Exercise Clause, and requirements of the Establishment Clause. *See* Part II (Religious Freedom in General) generally; Part III (Legal Status of Religious Communities), Chapter 2 (Autonomy of Religious Communities); and Part VIII (Financing of Religious Communities), Chapter 2 (Indirect Financing). In keeping with the canon of constitutional avoidance, courts will also seek to interpret labor laws in ways that avoid constitutional conflict.[1039]

392. The Supreme Court has upheld labor laws providing exemptions for religious communities from Establishment Clause challenges. In *Corporation of the Presiding Bishop of The Church of Jesus Christ of Latter-day Saints v. Amos*, for example, the Supreme Court upheld religious exemptions to Title VII, a federal law prohibiting discrimination in employment, concluding the exemptions did not violate the Establishment Clause.[1040] For a more detailed discussion of *Amos*, *see* Part III (Legal Status of Religious Communities), Chapter 2 (Autonomy of Religious Communities); and this Part, Chapter 3 (Other Employees and Labor Law), below.

1039. *See, e.g.*, *Church of the Holy Trinity v. United States*, 143 U.S. 457, 458–460 (1892).
1040. *Corp. of the Presiding Bishop of The Church of Jesus Christ of Latter-day Saints v. Amos*, 483 U.S. 327, 339 (1987).

§2. NON-DISCRIMINATION IN EMPLOYMENT DECISIONS

I. Non-discrimination Law

393. State and federal laws prevent discrimination in employment. State laws vary from state to state in breadth of protection and enforcement.[1041] Currently, however, all states prohibit some employment discrimination based on religion or "creed".[1042] The federal law, located in Title VII of the Civil Rights Act of 1964, prohibits employment discrimination based on "race, color, religion, sex, or national origin".[1043] Under the Act, unlawful employer practices include the following when done on any of those bases: (1) failing or refusing to hire or discharge an individual, or otherwise discriminating, with respect to "compensation, terms, conditions, or privileges of employment"; and (2) limiting, segregating, or classifying employees or applicants "in any way which would deprive or tend to deprive any individual of employment opportunities or otherwise adversely affect his status as an employee".[1044]

II. Religious Exemptions

394. Section 702 of Title VII of the Civil Rights Act provides an exception to federal anti-discrimination laws for "a religious corporation, association, educational institution, or society with respect to the employment of individuals of a particular religion to perform work connected with the carrying on by such corporation, association, educational institution, or society of its activities".[1045] Many states have adopted similar statutes, providing exemptions where religious organizations or

1041. *See Employment: Private Employment, Unlawful Discrimination*, 50 State Statutory Surveys, Westlaw 0060 Surveys 25 (database updated Nov. 2022) [hereinafter *Unlawful Discrimination*, 50 State Statutory Surveys]; *Discrimination and Harassment in the Workplace*, NCSL, https://www.ncsl.org/labor-and-employment/discrimination-and-harassment-in-the-workplace (last updated Aug. 12, 2021) (summarizing federal and individual state laws related to non-discrimination and harassment in the workplace, as well as employer exemptions and affirmative defenses).

1042. *Unlawful Discrimination*, 50 State Statutory Surveys, *supra* n. 1041. Regulations, rather than statutes, prohibit employment discrimination based on religion in Alabama and Georgia. *Ibid.*; Ala. Admin. Code § 670-X-4-.01 (2022); Ga. Comp. R. & Regs. §§ 186-1-.02 to -.03 (2022) (applying to state but not private employees). Mississippi does not have statutes or regulations prohibiting employment discrimination based on religion; however, "certain private employers are covered by applicable federal law governing equal employment opportunity". *Discrimination and Harassment in the Workplace*, NCSL, *supra* n. 1041.

1043. 42 U.S.C. § 2000e-2 (2018); *see also Bostock v. Clayton County*, 140 S. Ct. 1731, 1737 (2020) (holding that Title VII's prohibition against sex discrimination includes discrimination "for being homosexual or transgender").

1044. 42 U.S.C. § 2000e-2(a).

1045. *Ibid.*, § 2000e.

foundations are employers or where religion is a bona fide occupational qualification.[1046] *See* Part VI (Labor Law Within Religious Communities), Chapter 3 (Other Church Employees and Labor Law).

395. Protections of religious autonomy in the US Constitution have led courts to create the "ministerial exemption", which also exempts religious organizations from the mandates of labor law with respect to religious leaders or teachers. *See* Part VI (Labor Law Within Religious Communities), Chapter 2 (Religious Ministers and Labor Law).

§3. Unions and Labor Organizations

I. Law on Collective Bargaining and Labor Organizations

396. The National Labor Relations Board (NLRB) was created to strengthen ties between employers and labor unions and to facilitate bargaining discussions between the two. Congress passed the National Labor Relations Act (NLRA) in 1935, allowing the Board to oversee this process and help resolve any disputes that may arise.[1047] The Board participates in this process by placing agents to supervise bargaining meetings. An employer's refusal to participate in the bargaining process is considered an unfair labor practice.[1048]

397. States are split on the issue of collective bargaining: twenty-seven states have adopted "right-to-work" provisions while twenty-three have not.[1049] "Right-to-work" states bar union security agreements between labor unions and employers that compel employee support for the union. In these states, employees generally cannot be forced as a condition of employment to join or pay fees or dues to a union, but they are still covered by any collective bargaining agreement the union negotiates.[1050] In contrast, companies in states that are not "right-to-work" may be either a *closed shop*, in which employees must be a member of a union to be employed; a *union shop*, where non-union employees may be hired if they join the union within a certain period; an *agency shop*, in which employees must pay the equivalent of

1046. *See Unlawful Discrimination*, 50 State Statutory Surveys, *supra* n. 1041; *Discrimination and Harassment in the Workplace*, NCSL, *supra* n. 1041.

1047. National Labor Relations Act (Wagner-Connery Labor Relations Act), Pub. L. No. 74-198, 49 Stat. 449 (1935) (codified as amended at 29 U.S.C. § 151–169 (2018)).

1048. 29 U.S.C. § 159 (2018).

1049. *See Right to Work States Timeline*, Nat'l Right to Work Comm., https://nrtwc.org/facts/state-right-to-work-timeline-2016 (last Sep. 30, 2023) (noting that repeal of the Michigan Right to Work law will be effective December 2023).

1050. *About NLRB: Employer/Union Rights and Obligations*, Nat'l Lab. Rels. Bd., https://www.nlrb.gov/about-nlrb/rights-we-protect/your-rights/employer-union-rights-and-obligations (last visited Sep. 30, 2023); *FAQ—What's a Right to Work Law?*, Nat'l Right to Work Comm. (Oct. 1, 2019), https://nrtwc.org/faqs-right-to-work-laws.

union dues but need not formally join the union; or an *open shop*, in which employees cannot be compelled to join a union or fired for joining a union.[1051]

II. Religious Exemptions

398. Under federal law, employees who adhere to a bona fide religious tradition that has "historically held conscientious objections to joining or financially supporting labor organizations [are not] required to join or financially support [such an] organization as a condition of employment".[1052] The Supreme Court has ruled that employees cannot be forced to subsidize a union, on grounds that speech may not be compelled under the First Amendment—a ruling that has since been cited in some lower court cases involving the First Amendment's religion clauses.[1053]

399. Authority granted to the NLRB includes "statutory jurisdiction over private sector employers whose activity in interstate commerce exceeds a minimal level".[1054] By definition, religious organizations and non-commercial religiously affiliated organizations should therefore be exempt from NLRB jurisdiction. In *NLRB v. Catholic Bishop of Chicago*, the Supreme Court held that the Board's jurisdiction, under the terms of the NLRA, does not include teachers in church-operated elementary or secondary schools.[1055] The Board continued to assert jurisdiction over religiously affiliated institutions of higher education, however, claiming such institutions lacked "substantial religious character" (because their primary purpose is to provide secular education—unlike elementary or secondary schools, whose primary

1051. *See* 29 U.S.C. §§ 151–169. The Taft-Hartley Act of 1947 amended the NLRA by outlawing *closed shops* and allowing states to outlaw *union shops* through "right-to-work" provisions. Labor-Management Relations Act (Taft-Hartley Act), ch. 120, tit. 1, §§ 8(a)(3), (b)(3), 61 Stat. 136, 140–141 (1947) (codified at 29 U.S.C. §§ 158(a)(3), (b)(3)). The result is that *closed-shop* agreements are still used today in certain states and contexts but generally are not included in contracts and not enforceable. *See About NLRB: Collective Bargaining (Section 8(d) & 8(b)(3))*, Natl'l Lab. Rels. Bd., https://www.nlrb.gov/about-nlrb/rights-we-protect/the-law/collective-bargaining-section-8d-8b3 (last visited Sep. 30, 2023) ("Section 8(b)(3) of the Act makes it unlawful for a labor organization or its agents to … [i]insist to impasse on an illegal subject of bargaining, or include an illegal clause in a collective-bargaining agreement. Illegal subjects include, for example, closed-shop provisions … ."); *see also About NLRB: 1947 Taft-Hartley Substantive Provisions*, Nat'l Lab. Rels. Bd., https://www.nlrb.gov/about-nlrb/who-we-are/our-history/1947-taft-hartley-substantive-provisions (last visited Sep. 30, 2023).

1052. 29 U.S.C. § 169.

1053. *Janus v. Am. Fed'n of State, Cnty., & Mun. Emps., Council 31*, 138 S. Ct. 2448 (2018); *see also supra* para. 126 and accompanying footnotes.

1054. *About NLRB: Jurisdictional Standards*, Nat'l Lab. Rels. Bd., https://www.nlrb.gov/about-nlrb/rights-we-protect/the-law/jurisdictional-standards (last visited Sep. 30, 2023).

1055. *NLRB v. Cath. Bishop of Chi.*, 440 U.S. 490, 504 (1979).

purpose is to inculcate religious values) or the faculty lacked "religious function".[1056] These and similar jurisdictional standards were rejected by some federal courts of appeals as inconsistent with *Catholic Bishop*.[1057]

400. The NLRS has since adopted a DC Circuit Court of Appeals three-pronged test to determine whether it has jurisdiction over faculty at a religious institution of higher education.[1058] Under this test, the Board lacks jurisdiction where an institution of higher education "(a) holds itself out to the public as a religious institution, (b) is nonprofit, and (c) is religiously affiliated".[1059] It remains to be seen if the test will apply to jurisdictional questions involving non-faculty employees of colleges or universities, or to employees of other, similar organizations.

401. The Board has exercised jurisdiction over church employees involved in commercial operations and employees involved in operating religiously affiliated organizations that do not have a religious character, such as healthcare institutions. The Ninth Circuit Court of Appeals has upheld this approach, approving NLRB jurisdiction over commercial aspects of an evangelical organization and over a hospital owned and operated by an order of the Catholic Church where employees were not required to be members of the order or the Catholic Church.[1060]

§4. Social Security and Tax Laws

I. Overview of Social Security and Tax Laws for Religious Organizations

402. In general, religious organizations are considered tax-exempt organizations under Internal Revenue Code (I.R.C.) section 501(c)(3).[1061] But even though they

1056. *See, e.g.*, *Universidad Central de Bayamon*, 273 N.L.R.B. 1110 (1984) (claiming jurisdiction because the primary purpose of a religiously affiliated university was to provide secular education); *Univ. of Great Falls*, 331 N.L.R.B. 1663 (2000) (applying a "substantial religious character" test); *Pac. Lutheran Univ.*, 361 NLRB 1404 (2014) (outlining a "religious function" of faculty test).

1057. *See, e.g.*, *Universidad Central de Bayamon v. NLRB*, 793 F.2d 383, 402–403 (1st Cir. 1985) (evenly divided en banc) (Breyer, J., with Campbell, C.J., and Torruella, J., joining) (rejecting the Board's "primary purpose" distinction because the inquiry would involve entanglement in religious affairs prohibited under *Catholic Bishop*); *Univ. of Great Falls v. NLRB*, 278 F.3d 1335 (D.C. Cir. 2002) (rejecting the Board's "substantial religious character" inquiry for similar reasons); *Duquesne Univ. of the Holy Spirit v. NLRB*, 947 F.3d 824 (D.C. Cir. 2020) (rejecting the Board's inquiry as to the "religious function" of faculty for similar reasons).

1058. *Bethany Coll.*, 369 N.L.R.B. No. 98, slip op. at 1, 6 (2020) (adopting the DC Circuit's three-pronged standard from *University of Great Falls*, as a "faithful application of the constitutional principles set forth in *Catholic Bishop*").

1059. *Ibid.*

1060. *St. Elizabeth Cmty. Hosp. v. NLRB*, 708 F.2d 1436, 1440–1441 (9th Cir. 1983) (distinguishing private religious schools and the predominantly secular environment of the hospital); *NLRB v. World Evangelism, Inc.*, 656 F.2d 1349, 1352 (9th Cir. 1981) (requiring an evangelical organization to recognize a labor union, sign a pre-existing contract, and pay employees for lost wages relative to its ownership of a commercial center, a convention center, motels, and a swimming pool).

1061. I.R.C. § 501(c)(3) (2018).

themselves are tax exempt, religious organizations are generally required to withhold income, Social Security, and Medicaid taxes for their employees, unless specific exemptions apply.[1062] For more detailed information about the tax-exempt status of religious organizations, *see* Part VIII (Financing of Religious Communities), Chapter 2 (Indirect Financing).

403. The Social Security (federal retirement benefits) program is financed by two tax systems, the Federal Insurance Contributions Act (FICA) and the Self-Employment Contributions Act (SECA).[1063] FICA collects a tax based on a percentage of an employee's wages, both from employers and employees, while SECA is specifically for self-employed persons and collects based on the net earnings of self-employed persons. Employers, including churches and other religious organizations, are required to withhold FICA and other taxes from employees' paychecks.[1064]

II. Religious Exemptions

404. Individuals may waive payment of Social Security taxes and receipt of Social Security benefits if they are members of a religious organization that conscientiously objects to receiving public benefits.[1065] In *United States v. Lee,* the Supreme Court held that this statutory exemption is extended only to self-employed individuals and not to employers and employees.[1066]

405. However, ministers and religious organizations may obtain exemptions from Social Security and Medicare taxes in other ways. For more details about ministerial payment of Social Security taxes, *see* Part VI (Labor Law Within Religious Communities), Chapter 2 (Religious Ministers and Labor Law).

1062. *See* Internal Revenue Serv., Publication 15-A, *Employer's Supplemental Tax Guide* 9–10 (Dec. 19, 2022) [hereinafter *Employer's Supplemental Tax Guide*], https://www.irs.gov/pub/irs-pdf/p15a.pdf.

1063. *See* I.R.C. §§ 3101–3128 (FICA); *ibid.*, §§ 1401–1403 (SECA).

1064. *But see Publication 517*, *supra* n. 225 (explaining that churches and church organizations "opposed for religious reasons for the payment of social security and Medicare taxes may elect to exclude their employees from FICA coverage" but that employees' wages are then subject to SECA).

1065. I.R.C. §§ 1402(g)(1), 3127.

1066. *United States v. Lee*, 455 U.S. 252, 256 (1982).

Chapter 2. Religious Ministers and Labor Law

§1. Historical Background

I. Deferential Interpretation of Labor Laws

406. Historically, US courts have interpreted labor laws in ways that protect the autonomy of religious organizations in defining and carrying out their religious missions, including in selecting and hiring religious personnel.[1067] *See* Part III (Legal Status of Religious Communities), Chapter 2 (Autonomy of Religious Communities).

407. An early example of such deference is the US Supreme Court decision *Church of the Holy Trinity v. United States.*[1068] The Alien Contract Labor Act of 1885 prohibited US entities from contracting with and assisting aliens in immigrating to "labor or [provide] service of any kind" in the United States. The Court interpreted the Act to permit a church to contract with an English clergyman to migrate to New York and be the local pastor. In its opinion, the Court reviewed evidence that the United States "is a religious nation", concluding that the right to religious autonomy is so ingrained in American life that Congress could not have intended to infringe that right.[1069]

§2. Ministerial Exception

408. The ministerial exception is a court-made doctrine that protects the autonomy of religious employers in employment decisions involving religious ministers and teachers, grounded in both the Establishment Clause and the Free Exercise Clause. As the Supreme Court explained in *Hosanna-Tabor Evangelical Lutheran Church and School v. EEOC*, "The Establishment Clause prevents the Government from appointing ministers, and the Free Exercise Clause prevents it from interfering with the freedom of religious groups to select their own".[1070] In that case, the Court recognized the right of a religiously affiliated school to fire a "called" teacher who provided both secular and religious instruction and was designated a "commissioned minister", even though she claimed her termination violated the Americans with Disabilities Act.

409. The ministerial exception, naturally, only applies to ministers, but who qualifies as a "minister" has been disputed. In *Hosanna-Tabor*, the Supreme Court was "reluctant ... to adopt a rigid formula for deciding when an employee qualifies as a minister", but relied on factors such as the employee's title, relationship to

1067. 1 Durham et al., *supra* n. 157, § 5:23 (*The Rule of Deference and the Selection of Employees*).
1068. *Church of the Holy Trinity v. United States*, 143 U.S. 457 (1892).
1069. *Ibid.*, at 472.
1070. *Hosanna-Tabor Evangelical Lutheran Church & Sch. v. EEOC*, 565 U.S. 171, 184 (2012).

other members, and training, duties, and activities in the church.[1071] The Court also indicated that courts should give deference to a church's interpretation of who is classified as a minister.[1072] This explanation by the Supreme Court did not resolve disagreement among federal courts of appeals as to *who qualifies* as a minister for purposes of the exception, and the Supreme Court re-examined the question in *Our Lady of Guadalupe School v. Morrissey-Berru.*[1073] In that case, two elementary school teachers filed separate discrimination claims against their Catholic schools after their teaching contracts were not renewed. Reflecting on factors considered in *Hosanna-Tabor*, the Court reasoned that occupation and formal religious training will not always determine whether an individual qualifies as a minister. Instead, the Court reasoned, "What matters, at bottom, is what an employee does."[1074] The Court found that the two teachers' "core responsibilities as teachers of religion were essentially the same" as the teacher in *Hosanna-Tabor*, allowing their schools to exercise the ministerial exception.[1075]

410. Since *Hosanna-Tabor,* certain federal courts of appeals have concluded that, because the "ministerial exception is a structural limitation imposed on the government by the Religion Clauses", it applies to state law as well as federal law and cannot be waived.[1076] At least one court of appeals has relied on language in *Hosanna-Tabor* to conclude that the ministerial exception constitutes an affirmative defense rather than a guarantee against litigation or a jurisdictional bar on courts' authority to hear certain types of claims[1077] (though courts often refer to the ministerial exception both as an "affirmative defense" and a "bar" to claims[1078]). Indeed, courts must have jurisdiction to conduct the factual inquiry of determining whether an employee qualifies as a minister, for purposes of the exception.[1079]

411. The exact *breadth* of applicability of the ministerial exception remains unclear. The Ninth Circuit Court of Appeals has held that Title VII (federal unlawful employment discrimination) claims that do not require the court to "evaluate religious doctrine or the 'reasonableness' of the religious practices" are not barred by the ministerial exception.[1080] That court allowed a suit to be brought concerning

1071. *Ibid.*, at 190–192.
1072. *Ibid.*, at 196.
1073. *Our Lady of Guadalupe Sch. v. Morrissey-Berru*, 140 S. Ct. 2049 (2020).
1074. *Ibid.*, at 2064.
1075. *Ibid.*, at 2066.
1076. *Tucker v. Faith Bible Chapel Int'l*, 36 F.4th 1021, 1027 n.2 (10th Cir. 2022); *Lee v. Sixth Mount Zion Baptist Church*, 903 F.3d 113, 118 n.4 (3d Cir. 2018); *Puri v. Khalso*, 844 F.3d 1152, 1158 (9th Cir. 2017); *Conlon v. InterVarsity Christian Fellowship/USA*, 777 F.3d 829, 836 (6th Cir. 2015).
1077. *Tucker*, 36 F.4th at 1030, 1036–1037.
1078. *See, e.g., Demkovich v. St. Andrew the Apostle Par.*, 3 F.4th 968, 977, 984 (7th Cir. 2021).
1079. *Tucker*, 36 F.4th at 1029–1030.
1080. *Bollard v. Cal. Province of the Soc'y of Jesus*, 196 F.3d 940, 950 (9th Cir. 1999); *see also Puri*, 844 F.3d at 1154, 1167–1168 (applying the "neutral-principles" approach in a management dispute where the ministerial exception did not apply, explaining the approach similarly avoided unconstitutional inquiry into doctrine or religious practices).

sexual harassment because it did not require the court to become entangled in religious doctrine. The Seventh Circuit and others have concluded that the ministerial exception is much broader, protecting "a religious organization's employment relationship with its ministers, from hiring to firing and the supervising in between".[1081] In 2020, the Supreme Court ruled in *Bostock v. Clayton County* that Title VII's prohibition on employment discrimination based on "sex" encompasses sexual orientation and identity; while the opinion did not explicitly address the holding's implications for religious organizations as employers, it indicated that the ministerial exception and existing statutory exemptions for religious organizations could apply.[1082] Federal courts of appeals have split on whether the ministerial exception applies to employment-related tort claims.[1083] For further discussion on the autonomy of religious communities, *see* Part III (Legal Status of Religious Communities), Chapter 2 (Autonomy of Religious Communities).

§3. Personal Income Tax

I. General Provisions

412. Ministers are required to file personal income tax returns and report earnings from their ministerial service.[1084] Under the common law, clergy are considered employees if the church or organization they perform services for has the legal right to control what they do and how they do it, even if the clergy members enjoy considerable discretion and freedom of action.[1085] If congregations employ clergy for a salary, the clergy members are generally considered common law employees, and their salary is considered wages for income tax purposes.

1081. *Demkovich*, 3 F.4th at 973, 984–985 (noting a circuit split in application of the ministerial exception to hostile environment claims); *see also Alicea-Hernandez v. Cath. Bishop of Chi.*, 320 F.3d 698, 703 (7th Cir. 2003); *Skrzypczak v. Roman Cath. Diocese of Tulsa*, 611 F.3d 1238, 1245–46 (10th Cir. 2010) (reasoning that the Seventh Circuit's "approach provides greater clarity in the exception's application and avoids the kind of arbitrary and confusing application the Ninth Circuit's approach has created"); *Gellington v. Christian Methodist Episcopal Church, Inc.*, 203 F.3d 1299, 1304 (11th Cir. 2000); *Combs v. Cent. Tex. Annual Conf. of the United Methodist Church*, 173 F.3d 343, 350 (5th Cir. 1999).

1082. *Bostock v. Clayton County*, 140 S. Ct. 1741, 1753–1754 (2020).

1083. *Compare McRaney v. N. Am. Mission Bd. of the S. Baptist Convention, Inc.*, 966 F.3d 346, 347 (5th Cir. 2020) (holding that the district court's dismissal of a tort case for lack of jurisdiction, citing the ministerial exception, was premature), *cert. denied* 141 S. Ct. 2852 (2021) (mem.), *with Bell v. Presbyterian Church (U.S.A.)*, 126 F.3d 328, 329 (4th Cir. 1997) (holding the court lacked subject matter jurisdiction over tort claim related to a minister's termination, due to the ministerial exception).

1084. *See Employer's Supplemental Tax Guide*, *supra* n. 1062, at 10.

1085. *Employer's Supplemental Tax Guide*, *supra* n. 1062, at 10; *Topic No. 417, Earnings for Clergy*, IRS (last updated Aug. 24, 2023), https://www.irs.gov/taxtopics/tc417.

413. Income received by clergy directly from members of the congregation, such as fees for performing marriages, baptisms, or other personal services, are generally treated by the IRS as earnings from self-employment for income tax purposes.[1086]

414. Regardless of whether clergy income is received from a religious organization or as self-employment earnings, federal income tax must be withheld from clergy wages. However, special tax rules allow religious organizations an exemption from requirements to withhold Social Security and Medicare taxes. Organizations seeking this exemption must file paperwork with the IRS detailing their opposition to these programs due to religious beliefs.[1087] The purpose of this law is to avoid forced participation of churches in programs contrary to their religious tenets.

II. Parsonage Exemption

415. Ministers in the United States can receive a tax benefit under the IRS provision known as the parsonage exemption.[1088] The provision exempts ministers from the requirement to include either their parsonage or their parsonage allowance as gross income.

416. For ministers to claim the exemption for a parsonage, the church must provide the parsonage to the minister as compensation for services rendered.[1089] A "parsonage" is defined as "the rental value of a home furnished" to the minister.[1090]

417. In the alternative, ministers may exempt their parsonage allowance—a rental allowance paid to them as compensation. To qualify for the parsonage exemption under this provision, the rental allowance must be used "to rent or provide a home" and must "not exceed fair rental value of the home, including furnishings and appurtenances such as a garage, plus the cost of utilities".[1091] Ministers must verify that they are "minister[s] of the gospel", that the payment is designated as an allowance, that the designator is a religious organization, that the amount does not exceed fair market rental value, and that any excess amount is included in the ministers' income.[1092] Consequently, proper record keeping is vital to secure the tax exemption for a parsonage allowance.[1093]

418. In 2013, the parsonage exemption was challenged by two atheists who argued that it violated the Establishment Clause due to its preferential treatment of

1086. *Topic No. 417, Earnings for Clergy*, *supra* n. 1085.
1087. *Publication 517*, *supra* n. 225.
1088. *See* I.R.C. § 107 (2018).
1089. *Ibid.*, § 107(1), (2).
1090. *Ibid.*, § 107(1).
1091. *Ibid.*, § 107(2).
1092. 4 Durham et al., *supra* n. 178, § 34:16 (*Overview of Parsonage Benefits*).
1093. *Ibid.*

ministers.[1094] Although a federal district court initially held that the exemption violated the Establishment Clause, the Seventh Circuit Court of Appeals reversed the ruling and remanded the case on standing grounds, since the plaintiffs could identify no individual harm.[1095] Challengers to the exemption in a subsequent case brought before the Seventh Circuit succeeded in demonstrating standing, and the court upheld the exemption as constitutional.[1096]

§4. Social Security (Public Pensions)

419. Before 1967, ministers were exempt from paying into Social Security, to prevent religious leaders from being forced to comply with a government-financed public insurance program.[1097] After 1967, the IRS changed the process, instead requiring ministers to opt out of Social Security or else automatically be placed in the program. Under this process, ministers may pay into Social Security and receive benefits, but an exemption is available for those whose beliefs conflict with participating in government-run insurance programs.[1098]

420. Ministers are considered self-employed under Social Security law, regardless of whether they report as common law employees for income tax purposes, allowing them more independence when filing for Social Security.[1099] To opt out of Social Security, ministers must declare they are "conscientiously opposed" to accepting public insurance for services performed as a minister. This objection must be based on either the minister's own values or the church's religious principles. The minister applying for the exemption must be "ordained, commissioned, or licensed" by a tax-exempt religious organization.[1100] Because the exemption from Social Security tax requires ministers to conscientiously object to public insurance—and "is generally irrevocable"—the exemption is not pursued by many ministers.[1101]

1094. *Freedom from Religion Found., Inc. v. Lew*, 983 F. Supp. 2d 1051 (W.D. Wis. 2013).

1095. *Ibid.*, at 1073; *Freedom from Religion Found., Inc. v. Lew (II)*, 773 F.3d 815, 818 (7th Cir. 2014).

1096. *Gaylor v. Mnuchin*, 919 F.3d 420, 426, 437 (7th Cir. 2019).

1097. *See Online Social Security Handbook* § 1130.5, Soc. Security Admin., https://www.ssa.gov/OP_Home/handbook/handbook.11/handbook-1130.html (last visited Sep. 30, 2023); 4 Durham et al., *supra* n. 178, § 34:14 (*Requirements for Ministers Claiming an Exemption from Self-Employment Taxes*).

1098. *See Online Social Security Handbook* § 1130.3, *supra* n. 1097; 4 Durham et al., *supra* n. 178, § 34:15 (*Social Security Payments*).

1099. 26 C.F.R. § 1.1402(e)-2A (2022); 4 Durham et al., *supra* n. 178, § 34:13 (*Ministers Treated as Self-Employed for Social Security Tax Purposes*).

1100. 26 C.F.R. § 1.1402(e)-2A(a); 4 Durham et al., *supra* n. 178, § 34:14 (*Requirements for Ministers Claiming an Exemption from Self-Employment Taxes*).

1101. *See* 4 Durham et al, *supra* n. 178, § 34:13 (*Ministers Treated as Self-Employed for Social Security Tax Purposes*).

Chapter 3. Other Church Employees and Labor Law

§1. Exemptions from General Non-discrimination Laws

I. Federal Non-discrimination Laws

A. Prohibition on Discrimination Based on Religion

421. Title VII of the Civil Rights Act of 1964 prohibits employment discrimination based on race, color, religion, sex, and national origin.[1102] Under the statute, the term *religion* "includes all aspects of religious observance and practice, as well as belief", which employers must accommodate unless they can demonstrate that they are unable to do so "reasonably … without undue hardship on the conduct of [their] business".[1103]

422. Unlawful employer practices under Title VII include the following, when done on the basis of religion or another protected characteristic: (1) failing or refusing to hire or discharge an individual or to otherwise discriminate in respect to "compensation, terms, conditions, or privileges of employment"; and (2) limiting, segregating, or classifying employees or applicants "in any way which would deprive or tend to deprive any individual of employment opportunities or otherwise adversely affect his status as an employee".[1104]

B. Scope of Entities Required to Comply

423. The entities required to comply with Title VII non-discrimination provisions fall into three categories: employers, employment agencies, and labor organizations. As defined by the statute, an *employer* is "a person engaged in an industry affecting commerce who has fifteen or more employees" working twenty or more weeks per year.[1105] The definition encompasses private employers, state and local government employers, and the federal government as an employer; it does not include Indian tribes or private clubs exempt from taxation. Courts generally have interpreted "affecting commerce" provisions broadly, in a way that has included the activities of religiously affiliated nonprofit entities and can potentially include the activities of religious organizations themselves.[1106]

1102. 42 U.S.C. § 2000e-2 (2018); *see also Bostock v. Clayton County*, 140 S. Ct. 1731, 1737 (2020) (holding that Title VII's prohibition against sex discrimination includes discrimination "for being homosexual or transgender").
1103. 42 U.S.C. § 2000e(j).
1104. *Ibid.*, § 2000e-2(a).
1105. *Ibid.*, § 2000e(b).
1106. *See, e.g.*, *Camps Newfound/Owatonna, Inc. v. Town of Harrison*, 520 U.S. 564, 572–573 (1997) (concluding that church camp's services provided to out-of-state campers substantially affected commerce, for taxation purposes); *EEOC v. St. Francis Xavier Parochial Sch.*, 928 F. Supp. 29, 32 (D.D.C. 1996) (finding religiously affiliated school was an industry "affecting commerce", for

424. Employment agencies are also prohibited from failing or refusing to refer an individual for employment on a discriminatory basis.[1107] An *employment agency* is "any person regularly undertaking with or without compensation to procure employees for an employer or to procure for employees opportunities to work for an employer and includes an agent of such a person".[1108]

425. Likewise, labor organizations cannot exclude or refuse membership, or classify, segregate, or limit members, in a way that deprives or tends to deprive "any individual of employment opportunities" because of a protected characteristic; nor can such organizations "cause or attempt to cause an employer to discriminate against an individual" in violation of the Act.[1109] *Labor organization* is defined as an organization "engaged in an industry affecting commerce … in which employees participate and which exists for the purpose … of dealing with employers concerning grievances, labor disputes, wages, rates of pay, hours, or other terms or conditions of employment".[1110] A labor organization affects commerce if it (1) maintains a hiring office that "procures employees for an employer" or vice versa, or (2) has fifteen or more members and meets additional criteria.[1111]

426. Similar prohibitions apply to employee training programs conducted by "any employer, labor organization, or joint labor-management committee controlling apprenticeship or other training".[1112] Finally, it is illegal for any "employer, labor organization, employment agency, or joint labor-management committee controlling … training" to indicate preferences "based on race, color, religion, sex, or national origin" in printing or publication of notices or advertisements unless "religion, sex, or national origin is a bona fide occupational qualification for employment".[1113]

C. Bona Fide Occupational Qualification

427. Businesses or enterprises may be allowed to qualify or classify individuals based on "religion, sex, or national origin" in cases where these classifications are a "bona fide occupational qualification reasonably necessary to the normal operation of that particular business or enterprise",[1114] often abbreviated as a BFOQ. The United States also reserves the right of employers, employment agencies, or labor

employment law purposes, where it purchased out-of-state books and supplies, made out-of-state calls, and mailed out-of-state correspondence), *reversed on other grounds*, 117 F.3d 621 (D.C. Cir. 1997).

1107. *Ibid.*, § 2000e-2(b).
1108. *Ibid.*, § 2000e(c).
1109. *Ibid.*, § 2000e-2(c).
1110. *Ibid.*, § 2000e(d).
1111. *Ibid.*, § 2000e(e).
1112. *Ibid.*, § 2000e-2(d).
1113. *Ibid.*, § 2000e-3(b).
1114. *Ibid.*, § 2000e-2(e).

organizations to perform such classifications in the interest of national security.[1115] For more on BFOQ exemptions, *see* Part III (Legal Status of Religious Communities), Chapter 4 (Contractual Religious Freedom).

II. State Non-discrimination Laws

428. State non-discrimination laws in many instances overlap with Title VII principles, standards, and protected classifications. However, state laws may offer more expansive protections than Title VII and may have different procedural requirements.[1116] Title VII technically requires that aggrieved parties first file a complaint under state law if state law provides relief, but it also encourages cooperation between federal, state, and local agencies.[1117] Interagency "worksharing agreements" allow individuals to file a claim with either the relevant federal agency (Equal Employment Opportunity Commission—EEOC) or state/local agency (Fair Employment Practices Agency—FEPA), which then ensure the claim is filed in the proper jurisdiction.[1118]

429. State laws differ in the protection they offer to churches and religious organizations. Some states completely exempt religious associations from non-discrimination laws, while others have narrower exemptions permitting discrimination only where there is a bona fide occupational qualification.[1119] For example, Connecticut, Georgia, Iowa, New Jersey, and Ohio (among others) require a bona fide occupational qualification for religious discrimination, whereas Colorado, Indiana, and Wyoming (among others) exempt religious organizations broadly from non-discrimination laws. Some states, such as North Carolina, appear never to allow religious organizations to discriminate in employment decisions.[1120] Some states have carved out very narrow exemptions in certain contexts; for example, California allows religiously affiliated healthcare organizations to discriminate based on religion but only for those employees who perform "religious duties".[1121]

1115. *Ibid.*, § 2000e-2(g).

1116. Wisconsin non-discrimination statutes, for example, prohibit employment discrimination based on additional classifications, including marital status, military service, and pregnancy. *See* Wis. Stat. §§ 111.321, .322, .345, .355, .36 (2022). Where Title VII applies to employers with more than fifteen employees, Wisconsin's law applies to employers of "at least one individual". *Ibid.*, § 111.32(6)(a). The statute of limitations for filing a complaint under Title VII is 180 days; under Wisconsin law, it is 300 days. *Ibid.*, § 111.39.

1117. 42 U.S.C. § 2000e-8 (2018).

1118. *See Fair Employment Practices Agencies (FEPAs) and Dual Filing*, U.S. Equal Emp. Opportunity Comm'n, https://www.eeoc.gov/fair-employment-practices-agencies-fepas-and-dual-filing (last visited Sep. 30, 2023).

1119. *See* 2 Durham et al., *supra* n. 535, § 15:22 (*Exceptions for Religious Employers*).

1120. *Ibid.*, § 15:23 (*Chart: State Anti-Discrimination Laws and Applicable Religious Exemptions*).

1121. *Ibid.*; Cal. Gov't Code § 12926.2 (West 2022).

III. Exemptions from Labor Law for Religious Communities

430. Broad exemptions from federal labor laws exist for religious communities in the United States. Section 702 of Title VII of the Civil Rights Act states that there is an exception for "[a] religious corporation, association, educational institution, or society, with respect to the employment of individuals of a particular religion to perform work connected with the carrying on by such [entity] of its activities".[1122] This exemption permits religious organizations to discriminate based on religion in employment decisions concerning all employees, not just religious leaders or teachers.[1123]

431. The Supreme Court upheld the section 702 exemption against an Establishment Clause challenge in *Corporation of the Presiding Bishop of The Church of Jesus Christ of Latter-day Saints v. Amos.*[1124] In *Amos*, church employees engaged in non-religious jobs had been terminated for failing to adhere to church standards and brought an action claiming religious discrimination. When the Church claimed an exemption under section 702, the former employees counterargued that application of the exemption would violate the Establishment Clause.[1125] Analyzing section 702 under the *Lemon* test, the Court found the exemption constitutional, concluding that it had a permissible secular purpose, did not advance religion, and did not create excessive state entanglement with religion. In reaching its decision, the Court distinguished advancement of religion by the government and by religious organizations themselves. In doing so, it noted that the Founders wrote the Establishment Clause to prevent government from advancing religion by providing "sponsorship, financial support, and active involvement … in religious activity".[1126] The Court explained that a law does not violate the Establishment Clause just because it allows religious organizations to "advance religion, which is their very purpose".[1127]

432. The concurrences to *Amos* suggest that the question of whether section 702 applies to for-profit activities of religious organizations remains open.[1128]

433. Title VII, section 702, also provides a specific exemption for schools, colleges, universities, and other educational institutions to select employees of a particular religion if the institution is, "in whole or in substantial part, owned,

1122. 42 U.S.C. § 2000e (2018) (as amended).

1123. *Corp. of the Presiding Bishop of The Church of Jesus Christ of Latter-day Saints v. Amos*, 483 U.S. 327, 329–331, 339 (1987).

1124. *Ibid.*

1125. *Ibid.*, at 335–339.

1126. *Ibid.*, at 337 (internal quotation marks omitted) (quoting *Walz v. Tax Comm'n of N.Y.*, 397 U.S. 664, 668 (1970)); *see also Gaylor v. Mnuchin*, 919 F.3d 420, 433–434 (7th Cir. 2019) (concluding *Amos* and *Walz* had not been superseded).

1127. *Amos*, 483 U.S. at 337.

1128. *Ibid.*, at 340, 340, 345–346 (Brennan, J., with Marshall, J., concurring); *ibid.*, at 346, 346 (Blackmun, J., concurring); *ibid.*, at 346, 346–349 (O'Connor, J., concurring).

supported, controlled, or managed by a particular religion or by a particular religious corporation, association, or society", or if the curriculum of the institution propagates a particular religion.[1129]

§2. Non-discrimination in Federal Government Contracting

434. Federal contractors are prohibited from discriminating in employment based on "race, color, religion, sex, or national origin".[1130] An executive order signed by President Barack Obama in 2014 also prevents federal contractors from discriminating in employment based on sexual orientation or gender identity.[1131]

435. An executive order signed by President George W. Bush in 2002 permits religious organizations to discriminate in employment decisions based on religion, even if the organization receives federal funds for social service programs.[1132] A subsequent executive order signed by President Barack Obama amended the 2002 order, in part to clarify that any organization receiving federal assistance to provide social services—including religious organizations—may not discriminate against applicants or recipients of services based on religious belief, non-belief, or non-practice.[1133]

§3. Non-discrimination and Provision of Government-Funded Social Services

I. Overview

436. The federal government and many states provide funding for provision of social services—such as through hospitals, family service agencies, and drug and alcohol rehabilitation services—and for provision of international aid. Religiously

1129. 42 U.S.C. § 2000e-2(e) (2018). Regarding whether an educational institution qualifies as "primarily religious" for purposes of an exemption under s. 702, *see Garcia v. Salvation Army*, 918 F.3d 997, 1003 (9th Cir. 2019) ("The entity seeking the benefit of [a Title VII exemption for religious entities] bears the burden of proving it is exempt."); *LeBoon v. Lancaster Jewish Cmty. Ctr. Ass'n*, 503 F.3d 217, 226–227 (3d Cir. 2007) (discussing factors used to determine whether an entity's "purpose and character are primarily religious"); *EEOC v. Kamehameha Sch./Bishop Est.*, 990 F.2d 458, 460–464 (9th Cir. 1993) (as amended on denial of rehearing) (discussing the same).

1130. Exec. Order No. 11478, 34 Fed. Reg. 12985 (Aug. 13, 1969); Exec. Order No. 11246, 30 Fed. Reg. 12319, 12935 (Sep. 29, 1965).

1131. Exec. Order No. 13672, 79 Fed. Reg. 42971 (Jul. 21, 2014).

1132. Exec. Order No. 13279, 67 Fed. Reg. 77139 (Dec. 12, 2002).

1133. Exec. Order No. 13559, 75 Fed. Reg. 71317 (Nov. 17, 2010); *see also* Federal Agency Final Regulations Implementing Executive Order 13,559: Fundamental Principles and Policymaking Criteria for Partnerships with Faith-Based and Other Neighborhood Organizations, 81 Fed. Reg. 19353 (Apr. 4, 2016) (noting a change in the final rule implementing the order from "should not discriminate" to "may not discriminate"); *Faith-Based and Other Neighborhood Organizations*, U.S. Dep't Housing & Urb. Dev., https://www.hud.gov/program_offices/faith_based/execorders (last visited Sep. 30, 2023).

affiliated organizations have been able to receive this funding, but the funds generally may not be used for religious worship, instruction, or proselytizing, and the organizations receiving funds may not discriminate in the provision of services on the basis of race, color, national origin, sex, disability, or age.[1134] No federal statute generally bars federally funded service providers from discriminating against applicants or beneficiaries based on religious belief, non-belief, or non-practice; however, executive orders as well as legislation governing some individual programs contain such prohibitions.[1135]

II. "Charitable Choice"

437. In the 1990s and early 2000s, the "Charitable Choice" movement sought to include organizations openly teaching or engaging in religious instruction within the ambit of laws providing funds for provision of social services.

438. Most significantly, Charitable Choice provisions were enacted in section 104 of the Personal Responsibility and Work Opportunity Reconciliation Act (PRWORA or Welfare Reform Act) of 1996.[1136] Section 104 protects a religious organization's "independence from Federal, State, and local governments, including [its] control over the definition, development, practice, and expression of its religious beliefs".[1137] This includes affording participating religious organizations the continued freedom to make employment decisions based on religion.[1138] For more on PRWORA, *see* Part VIII (Financing of Religious Communities), Chapter 2 (Indirect Financing). For more on the institutionalization of Charitable Choice through

1134. *See* (all citations from the 2018 official code) Personal Responsibility and Work Opportunity Reconciliation Act of 1996 (PRWORA or Welfare Reform Act), 42 U.S.C. § 609a(j) (prohibiting the use of federal funds "for sectarian worship, instruction, or proselytization"); Title IX of the Educational Amendments of 1972, 20 U.S.C. §§ 1681–1688 (prohibiting sex-based discrimination in federally funded education programs or activities); Title V of Civil Rights Act of 1964, 42 U.S.C. §§ 2000d to 2000d-7 (prohibiting discrimination on the basis of race, color, or national origin in federally funded programs or activities); 29 U.S.C. § 794 (prohibiting discrimination against individuals with disabilities in federally funded programs or activities); Age Discrimination Act of 1975, 42 U.S.C. §§ 6101–6107 (prohibiting age discrimination in federally funded programs or activities). *See generally* Carl H. Esbeck, *Regulation of Religious Organizations via Governmental Financial Assistance, in Religious Organizations in the United States: A Study of Identity, Liberty, and the Law* 349, 349–390 (James A. Seritella ed. 2006).

1135. *See* Exec. Order No. 13559, 75 Fed. Reg. 71317 (Nov. 17, 2010); Exec. Order No. 13279, 67 Fed. Reg. 77139 (Dec. 12, 2002); Cynthia Brougher, Cong. Rsch. Serv., R41099, Faith-Based Funding: Legal Issues Associated with Religious Organizations That Receive Federal Public Funds 10 (Feb. 9, 2011), https://www.everycrsreport.com/reports/R41099.html (link to PDF).

1136. Personal Responsibility and Work Opportunity Reconciliation Act of 1996 (PRWORA or Welfare Reform Act), Pub. L. No. 104-193, § 104, 110 Stat. 2105, 2163 (codified at 42 U.S.C. § 604a(d)(1) (2018)).

1137. 42 U.S.C. § 604a(d)(1) (2018).

1138. *Ibid.*, § 604a(f); *see also Bostock v. Clayton County*, 140 S. Ct. 1731, 1753–1754 (2020) (holding that Title VII of the Civil Rights Act of 1964 prohibits employers from taking adverse employment actions against individuals due to their sexual orientation or gender identity but emphasizing the existence of both statutory exemptions for religious organizations and the constitutional guarantee of church autonomy).

the establishment of a dedicated White House Office, *see* Part V (Religion and Politics), Chapter 2 (Political Influence in Religion); and Part XI (Religion and Culture), Chapter 3 (Religion and Civil Society).

III. State Restrictions on Discrimination for State-Funded Social Service Organizations

439. States have adopted different approaches to the treatment of faith-based social service organizations that receive public funds. Arizona and Wisconsin exemplify a trend among states, allowing faith-based social services to accept public funds and continue in their religious nature if the organizations do not discriminate against beneficiaries because of their religion, though they may discriminate in employment because of religion.[1139] Laws in other states, such as Arkansas and Florida, simply require that contracts with faith-based organizations comply with federal non-discrimination requirements.[1140] Some states have more specific provisions, allowing religious discrimination to a greater or lesser extent. On its face, section 104 of PRWORA fails to indicate whether the US Congress intended federal Charitable Choice provisions generally to pre-empt state non-discrimination statutes; lack of litigation in the area leaves the question open.[1141]

440. Some courts have held that receipt of state funds turns religious social service providers into state actors who further "state action"; accordingly, these providers must comply with constitutional demands on the state, such as neutrality in religious matters.[1142] This has led to state bars on adoption and foster care agencies favoring their own religious traditions in child placement and bars on religious organizations prohibiting foster children's use of contraceptives.[1143] If applied more broadly, this concept of state action would also bar religious organizations receiving state funding from engaging in religious persuasion[1144] or discriminating based on religion in employment.

1139. Ariz. Rev. Stat. Ann. § 41-3751(E)–(F) (2022); Wis. Stat. § 46.027(5)–(6) (2022).

1140. Ark. Code Ann. § 20-76-109(4)(B) (2022); Fla. Stat. § 445.024(5)(d) (2022).

1141. *See* Brougher, Faith-Based Funding, *supra* n. 1135; Melissa McClellan, Note, *Faith and Federalism: Do Charitable Choice Provisions Preempt State Nondiscrimination Employment Law?*, 61 Wash. & Lee L. Rev. 1437 (2004).

1142. *See, e.g.*, *Arneth v. Gross*, 699 F. Supp. 450, 452–453 (S.D.N.Y. 1988); *Scott v. Fam. Ministries*, 135 Cal. Rptr. 430, 438–439 (Cal. Ct. App. 1976).

1143. *See* Carl H. Esbeck, *Government Regulation of Religiously Based Social Services: The First Amendment Considerations*, 19 Hastings Const. L.Q. 343, 402–405 (1992).

1144. *See Teen Ranch, Inc. v. Udow*, 479 F.3d 403, 409–410 (6th Cir. 2007), *cert. denied*, 552 U.S. 1039 (2007) (concluding state's moratorium on funding of faith-based residential treatment program for troubled youth was constitutional where the program incorporated religious teachings in activities and treatment). *But see Whalen v. Allers*, 302 F. Supp. 2d 194, 202–203 (S.D.N.Y. 2003) (concluding religious organization was a "state actor" but did not act unconstitutionally when a teenager in its residential facility was baptized voluntarily into a different Christian faith where the teen's mother did not make it known she wished her child to be raised in the Jewish faith).

441. In a narrow, case-specific 2021 ruling, *Fulton v. City of Philadelphia*, the Supreme Court upheld a religiously affiliated foster care agency's right to free exercise in selecting only heterosexual couples for foster placements.[1145] The city refused to renew its long-standing contract with Catholic Social Services (CSS) because it deemed the agency's refusal to consider same-sex couples as foster parents a violation of the contract's non-discrimination provision. Although the city allowed exceptions to the contract's non-discrimination requirement, it refused to grant CSS an exception. The Court noted that the equal treatment of same-sex couples is a weighty government interest but that the city "offer[ed] no compelling reason why it ha[d] a particular interest in denying an exception to CSS while making them available to others".[1146]

1145. *Fulton v. City of Philadelphia*, 141 S. Ct. 1868, 1882 (2021); *see also New Hope Fam. Servs. v. Poole*, 966 F.3d 145 (2d Cir. 2020) (finding a religious adoption agency properly alleged First Amendment claims in its suit challenging threatened closure under a state anti-discrimination statute).

1146. *Fulton*, 141 S. Ct. at 1882.

Part VII. Religious Communities and Protections of the Individual

Chapter 1. Protection of Privacy

§1. Introduction

442. In the United States, the legal concept of privacy has undergone significant doctrinal development. Early common law protections of privacy recognized only the physical aspects of interference with the life or property of another. Over time, however, the concept of a right to privacy expanded to proscribe interference with every form of possession—whether physical or intellectual, tangible or intangible—and to protect the "right to be let alone" by the government.[1147] Eventually, it became the doctrinal basis for finding a right to abortion (a finding later overturned)[1148] and to adult sexual relationships once proscribed by law.[1149] This chapter addresses US privacy laws as they affect the religious freedoms of individuals.

§2. The Common Law Tort of Invasion of Privacy

443. Before individual privacy rights became a matter of federal constitutional and statutory law, remedies were available in the common law tort of invasion of privacy. Today, the tort can be invoked for intrusion of solitude, appropriation of name or likeness, publicity that places another in a false light, and public disclosure of private facts.[1150]

I. Public Figures

444. The law has always recognized a diminished right to privacy for "public figures", such as celebrities, politicians, prominent business leaders, leaders of

1147. Samuel D. Warren & Louis D. Brandeis, *The Right to Privacy*, 4 Harv. L. Rev. 193, 193 (1890).
1148. *Roe v. Wade*, 410 U.S. 113 (1973), *overruled by Dobbs v. Jackson Women's Health Org.*, 142 S. Ct. 2228 (2022).
1149. *Lawrence v. Texas*, 539 U.S. 558 (2003).
1150. *See* Danielle Keats Citron & Daniel J. Solove, *Privacy Harms*, 102 B.U. L. Rev. 793, 809 (2022); William L. Prosser, *Privacy*, 48 Cal. L. Rev. 383, 388–389 (1960).

movements, and individuals caught up in events of public interest. Their privacy rights frequently come into conflict with the free speech rights of the press. While public figures may, like private individuals, sue for defamation, their diminished privacy rights mean they must reach a higher burden of proof to win a defamation claim.[1151] Although courts rarely address defamation claims involving ministers, they have required clergy to meet the higher burden of proving actual malice in a libel or slander claim.[1152]

§3. Protection of Privacy under the US Constitution

I. The Constitution and State Action

445. In the United States, privacy and other rights under the Constitution are not enforceable against private third parties, including religious groups. Under what is known as the "state action doctrine", the protections established by the Bill of Rights apply only to actions taken by government.[1153] Thus, for example, in 1985 the Supreme Court held that private companies have the right to fire an employee who refuses to work on his Sabbath day, since the First Amendment restricts only state actions.[1154] Such private discrimination, however, is often addressed through state and federal non-discrimination laws. In contrast to European Court of Human Rights jurisprudence,[1155] the US Supreme Court's understanding of state action would bar claims by individuals against religious organizations for violation of privacy rights (unless, of course, such rights were created statutorily).

1151. *See Time, Inc. v. Hill*, 385 U.S. 374, 386–387 (1967) (explaining the relationship between libel and the right to privacy, and requiring a showing of "actual malice"—that is, "knowledge that the statements are false or in reckless disregard of the truth"—for damages to be awarded in libel action brought by a public official).

1152. *See, e.g., Washington v. N.Y. News Inc.*, 322 N.Y.S.2d 896, 896–897 (N.Y. Sup. Ct. 1971) (finding that a gossip column item reporting a clergyman "had attended a performance at a nightclub at which a choir singer of his church was featured" was "of general interest" and that "absence of a showing of malice require[d] dismissal of the [libel] complaint"); Richard R. Hammar, *Pastor, Church & Law* § 4.02.02 (*Pastors Who Are Victims of Defamation*) (5th ed. 2019) (explaining that it "should be assumed that ministers will be deemed to be public figures" for defamation purposes).

1153. *Cantwell v. Connecticut*, 310 U.S. 296, 303 (1940); Wilson R. Huhn, *The State Action Doctrine and the Principle of Democratic Choice*, 34 Hofstra L. Rev. 1379, 1382 (2006) ("The state action doctrine does not protect the rights of individuals to be free of governmental control, but rather the right of people to democratically determine, for themselves, what kind of society they wish to live in."); Erwin Chemerinsky, *Rethinking State Action*, 80 Nw. U. L. Rev 503 (1985) (arguing that the state action doctrine should not be interpreted to allow infringements of the basic values of free speech, privacy, and equality by private actors).

1154. *Est. of Thornton v. Caldor, Inc.*, 472 U.S. 703 (1985) (holding that a state statute unconstitutionally imposed on private employers a duty to accommodate employees' preferred Sabbath-leave days).

1155. *See, e.g., Schüth v. Germany*, App. No. 1620/03 (Eur. Ct. H.R. 2010) (ruling that the state violated article 8 of the European Convention on Human Rights by failing to uphold a former church employee's right to privacy when his dismissal was based on choices in his private and family life).

II. No Direct Constitutional Right to Privacy

446. The original Constitution contains no express right to privacy. However, the Supreme Court has held that the freedoms granted in the Bill of Rights express the intent of the framers to protect various aspects of privacy. For example, the First Amendment protects freedom of religion, speech, and assembly—guarantees that imply a promise that the government will not intrude into an individual's private beliefs and belief-based conduct.[1156] Other aspects of privacy implied in the Bill of Rights include the privacy of the home against the military (the Third Amendment), of one's person and property against unreasonable searches and seizures (the Fourth Amendment), and of oneself against self-incrimination (the Fifth Amendment). In 1965, the Supreme Court held that the First Amendment, as well as the Third, Fourth, and Fifth, create "penumbra[s] where privacy is protected from government intrusion".[1157] The guarantees of the Fourteenth Amendment to due process in matters of life, liberty, and property have also been interpreted to protect significant privacy rights.[1158] Furthermore, the Ninth Amendment seeks to protect all rights not enumerated elsewhere in the Constitution and has been cited by at least one Supreme Court justice as constitutional support for a right to privacy.[1159]

447. From the 1920s to the early 2000s, the Supreme Court found constitutionally based justifications for the protection of privacy in matters of child-rearing,[1160] procreation,[1161] personal relationships,[1162] family living arrangements,[1163] and medical decisions.[1164] Citing a line of cases, the Court concluded in its 1973 decision *Roe v. Wade* that the constitutional right to privacy extends only to personal rights that can be deemed fundamental to the "concept of ordered liberty".[1165] In 2022, the Court overturned *Roe*, rejecting *Roe*'s reasoning that the right to have an

---

1156. *Griswold v. Connecticut*, 381 U.S. 479, 483–484 (1965) (holding that a state law forbidding the use of contraceptives unconstitutionally intruded on a protected "zone of privacy"—the right of marital privacy).

1157. *Ibid. But see Dobbs v. Jackson Women's Health Org.*, 142 S. Ct. 2228, 2300, 2301 & n.* (2022) (Thomas, J., concurring) (discussing "the facial absurdity of *Griswold*'s penumbral argument" and asserting that the Court has since reframed *Griswold* as rooted in "substantive due process").

1158. *Griswold*, 381 U.S. at 499, 499–500 (Harlan, J., concurring); *see also Eisenstadt v. Baird*, 405 U.S. 438, 443 (1972) (recognizing unmarried individuals' right of privacy to purchase contraceptives); *Roe v. Wade*, 410 U.S. 113, 153 (1972) ("This right of privacy … founded in the Fourteenth Amendment's concept of personal liberty … is broad enough to encompass a woman's decision whether or not to terminate her pregnancy."); *Lawrence v. Texas*, 539 U.S. 558, 564, 578 (2003) (noting petitioners were "entitled to respect for their private lives" in holding that a state prohibition on same-sex intimate relations violated their right to liberty under the due process clause). *But see Dobbs*, 142 S. Ct. at 2237, 2245, 2267–2271 (2022) (overturning *Roe v. Wade* and finding that *Roe*'s holding based in a "constitutional 'right of personal privacy'" was an improper, "remarkably loose" interpretation of the Constitution).

1159. *Griswold*, 381 U.S. at 486, 486–499 (Goldberg, J., with Warren, C.J., and Brennan, J., concurring).

1160. *Pierce v. Soc'y of the Sisters of the Holy Names of Jesus & Mary*, 268 U.S. 510, 534–535 (1925).

1161. *Roe*, 410 U.S. at 153.

1162. *Lawrence*, 539 U.S. at 564, 578.

1163. *Moore v. City of E. Cleveland*, 431 U.S. 494, 498–499 (1977).

1164. *Cruzan v. Dir., Mo. Dep't of Health*, 497 U.S. 261, 278 (1990).

1165. *Roe*, 410 U.S. at 152.

abortion was one of those constitutionally protected fundamental rights to privacy. It remains unclear whether Supreme Court decisions that relied on reasoning similar to *Roe*'s, decided both before and after *Roe*, might be similarly overturned.[1166] For further discussion of *Roe v. Wade*, *see* this section, subsection V (Access to Contraceptives and Abortion), below; and this part, Chapter 6 (Medical Deontology), below.

III. Searches and Seizures

448. The possibility of citizens' property being seized or searched by the government without good cause was one of the earliest privacy concerns in the United States, finding expression in the Declaration of Independence as well as other writings and debates.[1167] The Constitution's Fourth Amendment, ratified in 1791 as part of the Bill of Rights, protects the "right of the people to be secure in their persons, houses, papers, and effects, against unreasonable searches and seizures". In general terms, searches of a person or property may be conducted only if there is a reasonable suspicion of illegal conduct, and seizures or arrests must be supported by probable cause. To invoke the protections of the Fourth Amendment, criminal defendants must demonstrate that they had a "legitimate expectation of privacy", both by subjective and objective standards.[1168]

449. Courts have considered whether the Fourth Amendment's protection applies to church property, worship services, and religious leaders. In a case before a Florida state court of appeals, a pastor moved to exclude evidence that had been gathered from his church office and computer in a warrantless search. The court granted the motion, explaining that a pastor has a legitimate expectation of privacy in his office and on his workplace computer.[1169] Local Arizona churches and their national parent organizations brought claims of First and Fourth Amendment violations against the federal Immigration and Naturalization Service (INS) when the INS hired undercover informants to infiltrate and record church services without a warrant; the INS suspected the churches of unlawfully aiding and harboring unauthorized immigrants.[1170] A federal district court held that the state had a compelling

1166. *Compare Dobbs v. Jackson Women's Health Org.*, 142 S. Ct. 2228, 2277–2278 (majority opinion) ("Nothing in this opinion should be understood to cast doubt on precedents that do not concern abortion."), *with ibid.*, at 2300, 2301–2302 (Thomas, J., concurring) (urging the Court to "correct the error" of reliance on *Roe*-like reasoning in *Griswold*, *Lawrence*, and *Obergefell*), *and ibid.*, at 2317, 2319–2320 (Breyer, Sotomayor, and Kagan, JJ., dissenting) (warning that precedents such as *Griswold*, *Lawrence*, and *Obergefell* are at risk of being overruled under *Dobbs*-like reasoning).

1167. Fred H. Cate, *The Changing Face of Privacy Protection in the European Union and the United States*, 33 Ind. L. Rev. 173, 198–199 (1999).

1168. *Smith v. Maryland*, 442 U.S. 735, 740–741 (1979) (internal quotation marks omitted) (quoting *Rakas v. Illinois*, 439 U.S. 128, 143–144 (1978)).

1169. *State v. Young*, 974 So. 2d 601, 608–610 (Fla. Dist. Ct. App. 2008).

1170. *Presbyterian Church (U.S.A.) v. United States*, 752 F. Supp. 1505, 1507–1508 (D. Ariz. 1990).

interest in national security to justify conducting an investigation and that the informants' actions did not constitute a "search" under the Fourth Amendment. However, the court also held that the government's authority and scope are limited in conducting investigations of groups engaged in First Amendment activities, explaining that "[t]he government is constitutionally precluded from unbridled and inappropriate covert activity which has as its purpose or objective the abridgement of the first amendment freedoms of those involved."[1171]

IV. Family Life

450. The Due Process Clause of the Fourteenth Amendment has been interpreted by the Supreme Court to broadly protect private and family life, including living arrangements, marriage, procreation, and child-rearing. In an early case, *Meyer v. Nebraska,* the Court overturned a statewide ban on teaching the German language in public schools, finding it an unconstitutional interference with the right of parents to educate their children as they see fit.[1172] Of its decision in *Meyer*, the Supreme Court has said it "respected the private realm of family life which the state cannot enter".[1173] In *Moore v. City of East Cleveland*, the Court rejected "intrusive regulation of the family" in the form of an ordinance that limited the occupancy of a dwelling to a single nuclear family (a couple and their dependent children).[1174] The Court held that the ordinance violated due process by "forcing all to live in certain narrowly defined family patterns" and failing to encompass the national tradition of extended family households.[1175]

V. Access to Contraceptives and Abortion

451. The right of privacy related to contraception was addressed in a series of cases involving married and unmarried couples and individuals. In *Griswold v. Connecticut*, the US Supreme Court held that a state cannot interfere with a couple's access to contraceptives. The *Griswold* Court asserted the importance of protecting privacy within the home and considered the use of contraceptives by a married couple within the meaning of the "right of privacy".[1176] The Supreme Court extended this protection to unmarried couples in 1972.[1177]

452. Later, in the landmark case *Roe v. Wade*, the Supreme Court held that the right to privacy rooted in the Fourteenth Amendment also extended to a woman's

1171. *Ibid.*, at 1513, 1516.
1172. *Meyer v. Nebraska*, 262 U.S. 390 (1923).
1173. *Prince v. Massachusetts*, 321 U.S. 158, 166 (1944).
1174. *Moore v. City of E. Cleveland*, 431 U.S. 494, 499 (1977).
1175. *Ibid.*, at 504–506.
1176. *Griswold v. Connecticut*, 381 U.S. 479, 484–485 (1965).
1177. *Eisenstadt v. Baird*, 405 U.S. 438, 443 (1972).

decision to obtain an abortion, balanced against the state's interest in protecting prenatal life and the woman's health.[1178] In a subsequent case, *Planned Parenthood of Southeastern Pennsylvania v. Casey*, the Court affirmed that the right to abortion was absolute until the stage of fetal viability and held that state laws may not impose an undue burden on a woman's decision to terminate a pregnancy before that stage.[1179] In 2022, the Supreme Court—comprising six conservative and three liberal justices—considered the constitutionality of a state law that banned abortions before viability, at 15 weeks, in *Dobbs v. Jackson Women's Health Organization*.[1180] The majority opinion upheld the state law and overturned *Roe* and *Casey*, criticizing their reasoning and holding that the right to an abortion was not a privacy right or substantive due process right guaranteed by the US Constitution.[1181] The opinion emphasized that "the authority to regulate abortion must be returned to the people and their elected representatives", effectually making abortion rights a state issue.[1182]

453. Upon the overturning of *Roe*, "trigger bans" (state laws banning abortion that were "on the books" but unenforceable under *Roe* and *Casey*) went into immediate effect in some states; legislatures in other states have since passed near-total bans on abortion.[1183] These restrictive state laws vary in imposing civil or criminal penalties, or both. In the wake of *Dobbs*, abortion laws in nearly every state have been challenged in the courts, resulting in an uncertain legal landscape regarding abortion rights.[1184] Courts in some states have interpreted their state constitutions to protect the right to abortion as a privacy right or fundamental right.[1185] For a more detailed discussion, *see* this part, Chapter 6 (Medical Deontology), below.

1178. *Roe v. Wade,* 410 U.S. 113, 153–154 (1972).
1179. *Planned Parenthood of Se. Pa. v. Casey*, 505 U.S. 833, 846, 876–879 (1992).
1180. *Dobbs v. Jackson Women's Health Org.*, 142 S. Ct. 2228 (2022).
1181. *Ibid.*, at 2266–2271, 2279.
1182. *Ibid.*, at 2279.
1183. *See After* Roe *Fell: Abortion Laws by State*, Ctr. for Reproductive Rts., https://reproductiverights.org/maps/abortion-laws-by-state (last visited Sep. 30, 2023).
1184. *See ibid.*
1185. *See ibid.*; *see also, e.g.*, *Planned Parenthood of The Great Nw. v. State*, 375 P.3d 1122, 1129 (Alaska 2016) (reiterating that "a woman's fundamental privacy right to reproductive choice is more broadly protected by the Alaska Constitution than the United States Constitution" (citing *Valley Hosp. Ass'n, Inc. v. Mat-Su Coal. for Choice*, 948 P.2d 966, 969 (Alaska 1997))); *Gainesville Woman Care, LLC v. State*, 210 So. 3d 1243, 1254 (Fla. 2017) ("Florida's constitutional right of privacy encompasses a woman's right to choose to end her pregnancy."); *Women of State of Minn. by Doe v. Gomez*, 542 N.W.2d 17, 27 (Minn. 1995) ("We therefore conclude that the right of privacy under the Minnesota constitution encompasses a woman's right to decide to terminate her pregnancy."); *Armstrong v. State*, 1999 MT 261, 296 Mont. 361, 989 P.2d 364, 373–374 (Mont. 1999) (upholding abortion rights, noting that "Montana adheres to one of the most stringent protections of its citizens' right to privacy in the United States—exceeding even that provided by the federal constitution"); *Planned Parenthood S. Atl. v. State*, 882 S.E.2d 770, 774 (S.C. 2023) ("We hold that the decision to terminate a pregnancy rests upon the utmost personal and private considerations imaginable, and implicates a woman's right to privacy.").

VI. LGBTQ+ Rights

454. In the mid-twentieth century, every state had laws criminalizing homosexual conduct. A 1986 constitutional challenge to Georgia's statute resulted in a Supreme Court ruling that long-standing societal objections to sodomy were sufficient reason to uphold the law.[1186] In 2003, however, the Court took up a similar case and struck down state laws criminalizing homosexual conduct as unconstitutional invasions of privacy, extending the liberties protected by due process to all sexual relations between consenting adults.[1187] For subsequent developments relating to LGBTQ+ rights, including same-sex marriage, *see* Part VII (Religious Communities and Protection of the Individual), Chapter 2 (Freedom to Marry).

§4. State Law Protections of Privacy

455. While a few Supreme Court cases have established the legal recognition of privacy rights, federal legislation on the topic is patchwork and sparse. Federal privacy protection includes regulations on the use of children's information online,[1188] identity information,[1189] medical records,[1190] and a few other subjects, mostly data related (*see* section 5 below).[1191] In the absence of comprehensive congressional legislation on privacy-related issues, each state has developed its own set of privacy laws. While these differ greatly from state to state, many afford broader protections of privacy than those provided by federal law. For example, California has more than twenty general privacy statutes that regulate health information dissemination, unsolicited commercial communication, voter privacy, electronic surveillance, and more; general California statutes also protect the information of witnesses and victims, and they criminalize identity theft and misuse of another person's data. In

---

1186. *Bowers v. Hardwick*, 478 U.S. 186, 196 (1986), *overruled by Lawrence v. Texas*, 539 U.S. 558 (2003).

1187. *Lawrence,* 539 U.S. at 558, 577–579.

1188. *See* Children's Online Privacy Protection Act of 1998 (COPPA), Pub. L. No. 105-277, 112 Stat. 2681 (codified at 15 U.S.C §§ 6501–6506 (2018)) (requiring regulations to protect children's online privacy, now codified at 16 C.F.R. pt. 312 (2022)).

1189. 18 U.S.C. § 1028A (2018).

1190. *See* Health Insurance Portability and Accountability Act of 1996 (HIPAA), Pub. L. 104-191, 110 Stat. 1936 (codified as amended in scattered sections of 18, 26, 29, and 42 U.S.C. (2018)) (requiring privacy regulations to protect individuals' identifiable health information, now codified at 45 C.F.R. parts 160 and 164 (2022)).

1191. *See* (all citations from the 2018 official code) 15 U.S.C. §§ 7701–7713 (unsolicited marketing); 47 U.S.C. § 227 (telemarketing); 18 U.S.C. § 1030 (computer fraud); 5 U.S.C. § 552a (government records); 18 U.S.C. §§ 2721–2725 (motor vehicle records); 18 U.S.C. §§ 1367, 2521, 2701–2711, 3117, 3121–3127 (electronic communications); 20 U.S.C. § 1232g (educational records); 15 U.S.C. §§ 1681–1681x (credit reporting); 15 U.S.C. §§ 1692–1692p (debt collection); 15 U.S.C. §§ 6801–6809 (financial information); 18 U.S.C. § 2710 (video consumer privacy).

addition to these general privacy laws, California has enacted various specific statutes relating to these subjects and others, such as computer spyware and cyberbullying.[1192] The California Privacy Rights Act (CPRA) of 2020 was enacted through a ballot initiative; the Act expanded consumer privacy protections in the state and is the most comprehensive data privacy statute among the states.[1193]

§5. Federal Laws Concerning Privacy

456. While no comprehensive privacy law exists at the federal level, several statutes protect various aspects of privacy. In addition, the information and communications of church organizations are protected to a certain extent by Supreme Court decisions and federal rules of discovery.

I. Data Privacy Laws

457. Compared with laws in Europe, US laws on data privacy are less developed. Historically, sector-specific legislation and self-regulation by private companies in various industries have been the primary mechanism for dealing with data privacy.[1194] A federal Privacy Act was passed in 1974 but regulates only the use of data maintained by federal agencies.[1195] Data privacy has been viewed in the United States more as an economic issue rather than a fundamental right.[1196] For example, the Fair Credit Reporting Act prohibits the disclosing of identity and other credit information unless the disclosure is based on one of several "permissible purposes", such as the need to investigate a specific transaction.[1197]

458. That approach worked well for international business until the European Union adopted comprehensive privacy legislation in 1995, necessitating changes for US companies engaged in international business.[1198] *See* Part IV (International, Transnational, and Regional Effects on Religious Communities), Chapter 2 (Transnational Law Effects on Religious Communities). Although the United States still lacks an overarching data privacy law, federal protections for privacy exist through legislation covering distinct sectors, such as the Health Insurance Portability and Accountability Act of 1996 (HIPAA),[1199] the Drivers Privacy Protection Act of

1192. *See generally Privacy*, State Cal. Dep't Just., https://oag.ca.gov/privacy (last visited Sep. 30, 2023).
1193. California Privacy Rights Act of 2020, Cal. Civ. Code §§ 1798.100 to 1798.199.100 (West 2023).
1194. Morey Elizabeth Barnes, Comment, *Falling Short of the Mark: The United States Response to the European Union's Data Privacy Directive*, 27 Nw. J. Int'l L. & Bus. 171, 175–177 (2006).
1195. Privacy Act of 1974, 5 U.S.C. § 552a (2018).
1196. Barnes, *Falling Short of the Mark*, *supra* n. 1194, at 175.
1197. 15 U.S.C. § 1681b (2018).
1198. Barnes, *Falling Short of the Mark*, *supra* n. 1194, at 191–192.
1199. Health Insurance Portability and Accountability Act of 1996 (HIPAA), Pub. L. 104-191, 110 Stat. 1936 (codified as amended in scattered sections of 18, 26, 29, and 42 U.S.C. (2018)) (requiring privacy regulations to protect individuals' identifiable health information, which are now codified at 45 C.F.R. parts 160 and 164 (2022)).

1994,[1200] the Electronic Communications Privacy Act of 1986,[1201] the Family Education and Privacy Rights Act of 1974,[1202] and an act that protects personal financial information.[1203] HIPAA regulates the use and disclosure of protected health information, such as an individual's identification and health condition. In most cases, this rule does not affect a church's ability to disclose health-related information in the context of prayer lists, which many churches traditionally publish to encourage prayers for hospitalized parishioners.[1204]

459. Privacy-related concerns have grown significantly in the United States in recent decades. Shortly after the September 11, 2011 terrorist attacks, which killed nearly 3,000 people in New York City, Washington, DC, and Pennsylvania, Congress passed the PATRIOT Act. The Act facilitated and greatly expanded the government's ability to gather intelligence on US citizens to detect terrorist activity.[1205] Controversy erupted in 2013 when it became known that the National Security Agency (NSA), drawing on powers implied in section 215 of the Act, had been conducting a secret mass surveillance program with the cooperation of various governments and entities.[1206] In 2015, Congress amended section 215 to expressly bar the NSA from continuing its mass data collection.[1207]

460. In 2022, the Supreme Court considered a case involving Muslim community members who claimed the FBI had "illegally surveilled them because of their religion".[1208] An undercover FBI informant had collected "hundreds of phone numbers", "thousands of email addresses", "hundreds of hours of video recordings", and "thousands of hours of audio recordings of conversations … public discussion groups, classes, and lectures" from private homes and mosques in California.[1209] The petitioners claimed the FBI's actions violated the religion clauses of the First Amendment, the Fourth Amendment, the due process clause of the Fifth Amendment, the Religious Freedom Restoration Act, and other federal and state laws. A lower court dismissed those claims pursuant to the "state secrets privilege", which

1200. Drivers Privacy Protection Act of 1994, 18 U.S.C. §§ 2721–2725 (2018).

1201. Electronic Communications Privacy Act of 1986, 18 U.S.C. §§ 1367, 2521, 2701–2711, 3117, 3121–3127.

1202. Family Education and Privacy Rights Act of 1974, 20 U.S.C. § 1232g (2018).

1203. Gramm-Leach-Bliley Act of 1999 (Financial Services Modernization Act), tit. V, §§ 501–509 (codified at 15 U.S.C. §§ 6801–6809 (2018)).

1204. David O. Middlebrook, *Pastoral Confidentiality: An Ethical and Legal Responsibility*, Assemblies God (Feb. 2, 2010), https://news.ag.org/en/Features/Pastoral-Confidentiality-An-Ethical-and-Legal-Responsibility.

1205. PATRIOT Act (United and Strengthening America by Providing Appropriate Tools Required to Intercept and Obstruct Terrorism Act of 2001), Pub. L. No. 107-56, 115 Stat. 262 (2001) (codified as amended in scattered sections of 8, 15, 18, 22, 31, 34, 42, 49, and 50 U.S.C. (2018)).

1206. *See NSA Spying*, Electronic Frontier Found., https://www.eff.org/nsa-spying (last visited Sep. 30, 2023).

1207. *See* 50 U.S.C. §§ 1861–1862 (2018) (amended in part by USA FREEDOM Act of 2015, Pub. L. No. 114-23 tit. 1, §§ 101–107, § 705(a), (c), 129 Stat. 269, 300).

1208. *FBI v. Fazaga*, 142 S. Ct. 1051 (2022).

1209. *Ibid.*, at 1058.

prevents court-ordered disclosure of information that would threaten national security.[1210] The US Supreme Court addressed the very narrow question of whether the state secrets privilege displaced a provision of the Foreign Intelligence Surveillance Act (FISA), which established procedures for courts to review and determine the admissibility and legality of electronic surveillance. The Court held that the state secrets privilege trumped FISA's procedural requirements; however, the opinion left questions open for lower courts to (re)consider, such as whether the government's evidence qualified as privileged and whether the petitioner's claims under other statutory and constitutional provisions were properly dismissed.[1211]

461. The US Congress has passed some consumer privacy laws to protect individuals from the loss of privacy arising from failures of corporate data collectors. The Gramm-Leach-Bliley Act of 1999, for example, requires companies that offer any financial products to explain their data-sharing practices to customers and to safeguard sensitive information.[1212] However, with the explosion of online data collection, many believe that government protections of consumer data are insufficient and that government, corporations, and other actors have far too much power to access, collect, disseminate, share, and otherwise misuse personal data.[1213] The Federal Trade Commission, US Government Accountability Office, and other public and private entities have issued reports urging Congress to pass more powerful consumer data protection laws.[1214]

II. Non-disclosure of Church Finances

462. Most nonprofit organizations that have tax-exempt status under section 501(c) of the Internal Revenue Code are required to file Form 990, which makes the organization's tax return available to the public. However, churches, associations of churches, and other religious organizations receive a special exemption and generally are not required to disclose financial information to the public, to the IRS, or even to their donors.[1215]

1210. *Ibid.*, at 1058–1059.
1211. *Ibid.*, at 1062–1063.
1212. 15 U.S.C. §§ 6801–6809 (2018).
1213. *See* Thorin Klosowski, *The State of Consumer Data Privacy Laws in the US (and Why It Matters)*, N.Y. Times: Wirecutter (Sep. 6, 2021), https://www.nytimes.com/wirecutter/blog/state-of-privacy-laws-in-us.
1214. *See, e.g.*, U.S. Gov't Accountability Off., GAO-22-106096, Consumer Data: Increasing Use Poses Risks to Privacy (Sept. 2022), https://www.gao.gov/products/gao-22-106096 (link to PDF); Fed. Trade Comm'n, FTC Report to Congress on Privacy and Security 10 (Sep. 13, 2021), https://www.ftc.gov/reports/ftc-report-congress-privacy-security (link to PDF).
1215. I.R.C. § 6033(3) (2018).

463. Section 7611 of the Internal Revenue Code imposes special limitations on the extent to which the IRS may conduct financial inquiries of religious organizations. Such an inquiry may only be initiated if a high-level IRS official has a factual basis for believing that an organization claiming to be a church is engaged in taxable activities.[1216]

464. Although the government exempts religious organizations from disclosing financial information to the IRS, the common law has placed limits on this privilege. The current broad scope of trial discovery allows opposing parties in civil litigation to force the production of a church's financial reports when the judge deems it likely to help in general discovery.[1217] Moreover, churches that issue securities are generally required to register those securities with federal and state securities commissions.[1218] Religious organizations that maintain equity investments or other securities over a certain amount are required to regularly report their holdings to the US Securities and Exchange Commission and may have to meet state reporting requirements as well.[1219]

§6. The Priest-Penitent Privilege

465. In the United States, confessional privilege protects many of the confidential communications made between clergy and penitents.[1220] Since at least 1813, common law has held that information obtained by a pastor under the seal of confession is privileged, meaning that it is allowed to remain confidential.[1221] A pastor who violates his trust may be sued for defamation or invasion of privacy.[1222]

466. Most states have laws that protect communications between clergy and parishioners; each sets its own standard for which communications are privileged and to which parties the privilege extends. Many states extend only a limited privilege, requiring the communication to be a formal confession made to a clergyman

1216. *Ibid.*, §7611(a)(2).

1217. *See generally* Fed. R. Civ. P. 26. Courts have held that churches are not inherently immune from the power of subpoena and have frequently ordered churches to disclose personnel and financial records to ensure a complete remedy to victims in a civil matter. *See* Richard R. Hammar, *Essential Guide to Liabilities and Duties for Church Boards*, at pt. 2, https://store.churchlawandtax.com/essential-guide-to-liabilities-and-duties-for-church-boards; *see also* 2 Durham et al., *supra* n. 535, § 20:17 (*Punitive Damage Awards and Compelled Disclosure of Financial Records*).

1218. *See* Hammar, *supra* n. 1152, § 9.04 (*Federal and State Securities Law*).

1219. *See ibid.*; *Form 13F—Reports Filed by Institutional Investment Managers*, U.S. Sec. & Exch. Comm'n: Investor.gov, https://www.investor.gov/introduction-investing/investing-basics/glossary/form-13f-reports-filed-institutional-investment (last visited Sep. 30, 2023).

1220. *See* 2 Durham et al., *supra* n. 535, § 20:10 (*Application of the Clergy-Penitent Privilege*).

1221. *People v. Phillips*, 1 W. L. J. 109 (N.Y. Ct. Gen. Sess. 1813).

1222. Middlebrook, *Pastoral Confidentiality*, *supra* n. 1204; *see also* Hammar, *supra* n. 1152, § 04.02.01 (*Pastors Who Are Sued for Making Defamatory Statements*).

"in his professional character in the course of discipline enjoined by the denomination's rules of practice".[1223] The wording of such statutes severely restricts the ability of non-Catholic priests to invoke the privilege, although some courts have interpreted these laws liberally to further the public policy of encouraging communications in relationships of confidentiality.[1224] Most other states have more recent statutes that broaden the privilege to cover more than confessions, and many of them do away with the course of discipline requirement.[1225]

467. Regardless of how liberally or narrowly a state protects the confessional privilege, each places certain limits on what information clergy can withhold from discovery. In states with mandatory reporting laws for child abuse and neglect, for example, clergy are only exempt from an obligation to report abuse/neglect when state law provides a specific exemption, either in the mandatory reporting statute itself or through more general priest-penitent privilege provisions.[1226] In twenty-eight states, clergy are specifically required by law to report known or suspected incidents of child abuse or neglect: in their reporting laws, twenty-four of those states grant the priest-penitent privilege for pastoral communications, two deny the privilege where child abuse or neglect is suspected, and two do not address the privilege.[1227] Fifteen other states require "any person" who suspects child abuse or neglect to report it: in their reporting laws, seven of those states grant the privilege for pastoral communications, four deny the privilege where child abuse or neglect is suspected, and five do not address the privilege.[1228] The laws of eight states do not list mandated reporters, but two of those states grant the priest-penitent privilege in their reporting laws, relative to pastoral communications.[1229]

468. A church's right to privacy is limited even further in cases of sexual misconduct by members of the clergy. Scandal erupted on an international scale in the late twentieth century, when thousands of adults began to reveal that they had been sexually abused in their childhood by Catholic priests.[1230] In the United States,

1223. Fred L. Kuhlmann, *Communications to Clergymen—When Are They Privileged?*, 2 Val. U. L. Rev. 265, 267 (1968) (internal quotation marks omitted) (quoting N.Y. Rev. Stat. tit. 3, § 72 (1820)); 2 Durham et al., *supra* n. 535, § 20:11 (*Summary of State Clergy-Penitent Privilege Laws*).

1224. Kuhlmann, *Communications to Clergymen*, *supra* n. 1223, at 267–273; 2 Durham et al., *supra* n. 535, § 20:11 (*Summary of State Clergy-Penitent Privilege Laws*).

1225. Kuhlmann, *supra* n. 1223, at 277; 2 Durham et al., *supra* n. 535, § 20:11 (*Summary of State Clergy-Penitent Privilege Laws*); *see People v. Carmona*, 82 N.Y.2d 603, 608–609 (N.Y. 1993) (discussing the history of the priest-penitent privilege in New York state).

1226. Child Welfare Info. Gateway, Children's Bureau, U.S. Dep't of Health & Hum. Servs., *Clergy as Mandatory Reporters of Child Abuse and Neglect* 2–3 (Apr. 2019), https://www.childwelfare.gov/topics/systemwide/laws-policies/statutes/clergymandated (link to PDF) (summarizing which states deny or limit the priest-penitent privilege as to child abuse and neglect, and the scope of limitations).

1227. *Ibid.*

1228. *Ibid.*

1229. *Ibid.*

1230. *See Timeline of a Crisis*, Nat'l Cath. Rep. (Jul. 6, 2015), https://www.ncronline.org/blogs/ncr-today/timeline-crisis; *Roman Catholic Church Sex Abuse Cases*, N.Y. Times, https://www.nytimes.com/topic/organization/roman-catholic-church-sex-abuse-cases (collecting articles

lawsuits by victims against the Catholic Church raised the question of whether the Church could legally be forced to disclose internal records.[1231] On the one hand, the Church's policy toward priestly misconduct had been to encourage full disclosure to spiritual authorities to facilitate interventions and treatment for troubled priests, and allowing private records to be made public could undermine trust in the Church's confidentiality and deter disclosure.[1232] On the other hand, allowing discovery of internal communications revealed information relevant to cases, particularly whether Church authorities were aware of sexual misconduct.

469. A California court of appeals weighed these and other considerations in a 2005 case, holding that disclosure of documents subpoenaed in a grand jury investigation of sexual abuse by priests was not prohibited by clergy-penitent privilege, as the priests were aware their communications would be shared with others.[1233] Addressing claims that disclosure violated the First Amendment, the court reasoned that the Free Exercise Clause did not relieve the priests or church of their obligations to comply with neutral laws of general applicability; in addition, the ministerial exception did not apply since the matter was criminal rather than employment related.[1234] Further, the Court held that ordering disclosure did not constitute excessive government entanglement with religion, in violation of the Establishment Clause, as the government was investigating sexual abuse rather than the Church's doctrine or "internal workings".[1235] The court emphasized that the Church could only be relieved of its duty to disclose by statute, not by the court.[1236]

§7. Church Autonomy Doctrine

470. The legal principle of church autonomy effectuates Establishment Clause safeguards against governmental interference with a church's doctrine and administration, preventing courts from adjudicating disputes that are ecclesiastical in nature. The legal scope of church autonomy has been well developed by various court decisions and extends to religious leadership appointments, church administration, and interpretation of doctrine. In 1952 and 1960, the US Supreme Court held that the government does not have the power to pass control of purely ecclesiastical

related to sexual abuse within the Catholic Church in the United States and other countries) (last visited Sep. 30, 2023).

1231. *See, e.g.*, Randal C. Archibold, *Archdiocese Loses Case to Keep Former Priests' Records Secret*, N.Y. Times (Apr. 18, 2006), http://www.nytimes.com/2006/04/18/washington/18church.html.

1232. William Bassett, *Church Records and the Courts: Recent Court Rulings Undermine the Churchs* [sic] *Promise of Confidentiality*, Am.: Jesuit Rev. (Oct. 29, 2007), http://americamagazine.org/issue/631/article/church-records-and-courts.

1233. *Roman Cath. Archbishop of L.A. v. Superior Court*, 32 Cal. Rptr. 3d 209, 226–227 (2005), *as modified on denial of reh'g* (Aug. 16, 2005), *cert denied*, 547 U.S. 1071 (2006) (mem.).

1234. *Ibid.*, at 220–221.

1235. *Ibid.*, at 221–222.

1236. *Ibid.*, at 227.

matters from one church to another.[1237] Subsequent Supreme Court decisions established that the resolution of doctrinal disputes is also protected from governmental intrusion and that it is unconstitutional for a court to inquire into the "decisions of the highest authorities of a hierarchical church" in matters of ecclesiastical "polity".[1238] The court's only role is to determine whether an issue is purely ecclesiastical; if so, the court lacks jurisdiction.[1239] For additional discussion on church autonomy, *see* Part I (Religious Freedom in General), Chapter 2 (Collective Religious Freedom) and Chapter 3 (Organizational Religious Freedom).

§8. Disclosure of Religious Affiliation

471. Under federal law, employers generally may not ask candidates for employment about their religious identification.[1240] This prohibition applies to most employers, except small businesses and small local and state government agencies with fewer than fifteen employees.[1241]

472. Neither the federal nor state governments require religious affiliation to be published on government identification cards. However, other privacy-related issues have arisen related to religion and identification cards. The federal REAL ID Act of 2005 establishes requirements for state-issued identification cards to be used for "official" purposes (such as boarding an airplane or entering a federal building).[1242] The Act sparked controversy across the political and religious spectrum, and only half of all the states have met its minimum standards.[1243] A common objection was that it created unconstitutional invasions of privacy by effectively implementing a

1237. *Kedroff v. St. Nicholas Cathedral of Russian Orthodox Church in N. Am.*, 344 U.S. 94, 106–108 (1952) (holding unconstitutional a state statute that effectively transferred control of a church's cathedral to a religious body ungoverned by the church's ecclesiastical hierarchy, finding the statute effectively wrested "control of matters strictly ecclesiastical" from the church by displacing its chosen leader with another); *Kreshik v. St. Nicholas Cathedral*, 363 U.S. 190, 191 (1960) (applying *Kedroff* in holding that the state judiciary could not do the same through common law).

1238. *Presbyterian Church in the U.S. v. Mary Elizabeth Blue Hull Mem'l Presbyterian Church*, 393 U.S. 440, 450–452 (1969) (holding the First Amendment precluded court's resolution of a property dispute between churches that centered on doctrinal disputes); *Serbian E. Orthodox Diocese for the U.S. & Can. v. Milivojevich*, 426 U.S. 696, 708–709 (1976) (reiterating that civil courts may not extensively inquire into "religious law and polity" but must accept the decisions of the "highest ecclesiastical tribunal within a church").

1239. *See Watson v. Jones*, 80 U.S. (13 Wall.) 679, 727 (1872) (explaining that civil courts must accept as final the decisions of "the highest" church adjudicating body in questions of church governance, discipline, faith, custom, and law); *Bouldin v. Alexander*, 82 U.S. (15 Wall.) 131, 139–140 (1872) (reaffirming that the courts may not inquire into whether an excommunication is warranted).

1240. *Pre-employment Inquiries and Religious Affiliation or Beliefs*, U.S. Equal Emp. Opportunity Comm'n, https://www.eeoc.gov/pre-employment-inquiries-and-religious-affiliation-or-beliefs (last visited Sep. 30, 2023).

1241. 42 U.S.C. §§ 2000e(b), 2000e-2 (2018).

1242. REAL ID Act of 2005, Pub. L. No. 109-13, § 202, 119 Stat. 302, 312 (ID provisions contained in 49 U.S.C. § 30301, statutory note 23:401 (2018)).

1243. *See About REAL ID*, U.S. Dep't Homeland Sec., https://www.dhs.gov/real-id/about-real-id (last updated Nov. 16, 2022).

national ID system that recorded personal images and information. Denominations that object to having their personal images recorded, including some Amish, oppose the Act's mandate that identification cards include a photograph of the card-holder.[1244] These objections have been taken to court; in such lawsuits, the courts consistently base their decisions on whether the plaintiff's beliefs that forbid them from complying with photo requirements are sincerely held, whether the requirement imposes a substantial burden on religious exercise, whether the government's security interests are compelling, and whether those interests could still be achieved by allowing a religious exemption.[1245] The Supreme Court has never adjudicated the issue of religious exemptions to photo ID requirements, but in a case that predated the REAL ID Act, the Eighth Circuit Court of Appeals required state authorities to allow driver's licenses without photos.[1246] *See also* Part I (Legal Framework and Sources), Chapter 2 (Other Legislation with Regard to Religion).

1244. Brougher, Legal Analysis of Religious Exemptions for Photo Identification Requirements, *supra* n. 241, at 3.

1245. *Ibid.*

1246. *Quaring v. Peterson*, 728 F.2d 1121, 1127–1128 (8th Cir. 1984), *aff'd*, 472 U.S. 478 (1985) (per curiam decision of an equally divided court).

Chapter 2. Freedom to Marry

§1. Introduction

473. The United States, like other countries, has long treated marriage as a legal contract between two people that also implicates important societal interests.[1247] Thus, an extensive regulatory framework has been created relative to family law matters. As is true in many other countries, in recent decades the United States has experienced a dramatic change in the legal status and social attitudes toward marriage as a social institution, particularly same-sex marriage.

474. The most significant transformation may be the percentage of children born to single mothers. In 1940, less than 4% of children in the United States were born to single mothers.[1248] That percentage rose to roughly 18% in 1980.[1249] In 2021, 40% of all children born were born to unmarried mothers: 70% of children born to African American mothers, 53% of children born to Hispanic mothers, and 28% of children born to white mothers were born to unmarried mothers.[1250]

475. These figures are significant because social science research indicates that economic and social outcomes for children raised in single-parent homes are, on average, below those raised by two biological parents.[1251] The United States exhibits other stark demographic variations with respect to marriage. College-educated individuals are more likely to marry before having children than individuals without a college education, though the number of college-educated women who are unmarried when they give birth to their first child is rising.[1252]

1247. *See generally* Sanford N. Katz, *Marriage*, *in Family Law in America* 43, 43–116 (3d ed. 2021); Lynn Dennis Wardle, William C. Duncan & Laurence C. Nolan, *Family and Succession Law in the USA*, at pt. II, ch. 1, § 1 (4th ed. 2019).

1248. Stephanie J. Ventura & Christine A. Bachrach, Ctrs. for Disease Control & Prevention, *Nonmarital Childbearing in the United States, 1940–99*, Nat'l Vital Stat. Rep., Oct. 18, 2000, at 1–2, https://pubmed.ncbi.nlm.nih.gov/11060989 (link to PDF).

1249. *Ibid.*, at 1.

1250. Michelle J.K. Osterman, Brady E. Hamilton, Joyce A. Martin, Anne K. Driscoll & Claudia P. Valenzuela, Ctrs. for Disease Control & Prevention, *Births: Final Data for 2021*, Nat'l Vital Stat. Rep., Jan. 31, 2023, at 9, https://www.cdc.gov/nchs/data/nvsr/nvsr72/nvsr72-01-tables.pdf.

1251. *See, e.g.*, Timothy J. Biblarz & Greg Gottainer, *Family Structure and Children's Success: A Comparison of Widowed and Divorced Single-Mother Families*, 62 J. Marriage & Fam. 533, 534 (2000); Gretchen Livingston, Pew Research Ctr., *The Changing Profile of Unmarried Parents* 9 (Apr. 25, 2018), https://www.pewresearch.org/social-trends/wp-content/uploads/sites/3/2018/04/Unmarried-Parents-Full-Report-PDF.pdf; W. Bradford Wilcox, Wendy Wang & Ian Rowe, *Less Poverty, Less Prison, More College: What Two Parents Mean for Black and White Children*, Inst. for Fam. Stud. (Jun. 17, 2021), https://ifstudies.org/blog/less-poverty-less-prison-more-college-what-two-parents-mean-for-black-and-white-children. *But see* Christina Cross, Opinion, *The Myth of the Two-Parent Home*, N.Y. Times (Dec. 9, 2019), https://www.nytimes.com/2019/12/09/opinion/two-parent-family.html (discussing research indicating that "access to resources, more than family structure, matters for black kids' success").

1252. Andrew J. Cherlin, *Rising Nonmarital First Childbearing Among College-Educated Women: Evidence from Three National Studies*, Proc. Nat'l Acad. Scis., Jun. 25, 2021, at 2, https://www.pnas.org/doi/full/10.1073/pnas.2109016118.

476. In 1980, approximately 50% of first marriages were likely to end in divorce.[1253] In more recent years, however, the national trend reflects a decrease in both marriage and divorce rates.[1254]

I. Constitutional Right to Marry

477. Although the Constitution is silent with respect to marriage, the US Supreme Court has long considered the right to marry a fundamental constitutional right. In 1888, in *Maynard v. Hill*, the Court stated, "[Marriage] is an institution, in the maintenance of which in its purity the public is deeply interested, for it is the foundation of the family and of society, without which there would be neither civilization nor progress."[1255]

478. Although marriage is typically under state jurisdiction, the Supreme Court can impose constitutional limitations on state requirements, which the Court traces back to the creation of the Constitution.[1256] As described in detail below, the federal constitutional framework is directed primarily at questions involving the fundamental right to marry, including restrictions based on capacity, race, and more recently, sexual orientation.

479. The Supreme Court has affirmed marriage as a fundamental right of other classes of persons as well. In 1978, the Court overturned a Wisconsin law that required individuals obliged to provide child support to submit evidence of compliance and obtain a court order before they could acquire a marriage license; the Supreme Court held that such a law violates the Equal Protection and Due Process Clauses of the Fourteenth Amendment.[1257] The Court has also held that prisoners may not be denied the right to marry.[1258] Section 3 of this chapter contains a separate discussion concerning same-sex marriage.

1253. W. Bradford Wilcox, *The Evolution of Divorce*, 1 Nat'l Aff. 81, 88 (2009).

1254. *Ibid.*; *Marriage and Divorce*, Ctrs. for Disease Control & Prevention, https://www.cdc.gov/nchs/fastats/marriage-divorce.htm (last updated Apr. 24, 2023); *see also* Virginia Pelley, *What Is the Divorce Rate in America?*, Fatherly (last updated Jul. 4, 2022), https://www.fatherly.com/life/what-is-divorce-rate-america (discussing the difficulty of determining the divorce rate in the US but citing current projections that 45 percent of marriages will end in divorce).

1255. *Maynard v. Hill*, 125 U.S. 190, 211 (1888).

1256. *See United States v. Windsor*, 570 U.S. 744, 766 (2013); *see also Sosna v. Iowa*, 419 U.S. 393, 404 (1975); *Loving v. Virginia*, 388 U.S. 1, 11–12 (1967); *Ohio ex rel. Popovici v. Agler*, 280 U.S. 379, 383–384 (1930).

1257. *See Zablocki v. Redhail*, 434 U.S. 374, 375–376 (1978); U.S. Const. amend. XIV, § 1 ("No State shall … deprive any person of life, liberty, or property, without due process of law; nor deny to any person within its jurisdiction the equal protection of the laws.").

1258. *See Turner v. Safley*, 482 U.S. 78, 97–100 (1987) (ruling that prison restrictions constituting a near complete ban on marriages were constitutionally infirm and did not reasonably relate to security or rehabilitation concerns).

II. State Law

480. Largely, marriage is a matter of state rather than federal law. Each state determines eligibility for marriage in the form of regulations concerning mental and physical capacity, age, civil status, and consanguinity or affinity. Many states view marriage as a civil contract and require both parties entering into a marriage to exhibit the proper capacity, which includes satisfying age requirements or providing evidence they have the mental capacity to enter into the contract.[1259]

481. Typically, each state determines the requirements for and limitations on marriage, primarily related to the following:

(1) licensing (form),
(2) voiding a marriage (annulment),
(3) entering marriage (age),
(4) marrying while in confinement (prisoner's marriage),
(5) marrying while suffering some kind of mental or emotional disorder (mental competency),
(6) marrying with a family member (incestuous marriage), and
(7) marrying while being married to someone else (bigamous marriage).[1260]

482. Marriage must be entered into voluntarily. Fraud, misrepresentation, duress, or incapacity typically invalidate a marriage contract. Similar to the standard for voiding other contracts on grounds of duress, for a marriage to be invalidated, a threat must be so substantial "as to overcome the will and bring about a marriage to which consent would not otherwise have been given".[1261]

483. After two people are married, the law expects them to pool their resources and provide mutual support for one another. Even if one partner provides most or all of the income, both partners are typically expected to share financial responsibility concerning debts and credit.[1262] Some of the financial benefits that accrue through sharing economic responsibility in a marriage relate to Social Security benefits; taxes; worker's compensation; life, health, and car insurance; bank loans;

1259. *See* 52 Am. Jur. 2d *Marriage* § 17 (*Minimum Age for Capacity to Marry*), § 21 (*Criteria for Determination of Mental Capacity to Marry*), Westlaw AMJUR MARRIAGE §§ 17, 21 (database updated May 2023); *see also Mahan v. Mahan*, 88 So. 2d 545, 548 (Fla. 1956) (ruling that the level of intoxication of both parties prevented them from entering into a binding marital contract); *In re Guardianship of O'Brien*, 847 N.W.2d 710, 715 (Minn. Ct. App. 2014) ("The mental capacity requisite to a valid marriage is a capacity to understand the nature of the contract and the duties and responsibilities it creates." (quoting *Martin v. Martin*, 157 Fla. 835, 836, 836 (1946) (Chapman, C.J., concurring))).

1260. Katz, *Marriage*, *supra* n. 1247, at 49.

1261. M.L. Cross, Annotation, *What Constitutes Duress Sufficient to Warrant Divorce or Annulment of Marriage*, 16 A.L.R.2d 1430, § 1 (1951); *see, e.g.*, *Worthington v. Worthington*, 352 S.W.2d 80, 84 (Ark. 1961) (finding insufficient evidence that the husband had entered into the marriage based solely on the father-in-law's threats to kill the husband and his family).

1262. *See, e.g.*, *Sharpe Furniture, Inc. v. Buckstaff*, 299 N.W.2d 219, 224 (Wis. 1980) (holding that a husband was responsible for his wife's credit purchase of a "legally necessary" sofa, under the "common law doctrine of necessaries").

retirement accounts; and death and survivorship.[1263] Among non-economic marital benefits are the ability to obtain durable power of attorney and status as next-of-kin.[1264]

484. State law also regulates divorce and the dissolution of marriages. Historically, divorces were only granted if evidence proved one of the parties was at fault, for example, through cruelty, desertion, or adultery. However, reforms in the 1960s and 1970s moved divorce statutes toward a no-fault system. Today, thirty-three states still have aspects of the fault-based divorce system, but all fifty states have adopted no-fault provisions in their divorce laws.[1265] There are two types of no-fault statutes: the pure no-fault model does not require a spouse to prove any fault, while the contest model requires that a spouse present factors that could have established fault.

485. After a marriage is terminated, the court may be responsible for equitable division of the property.[1266] In addition to equitably dividing the property, the court may also be responsible for determining alimony awards, child support amounts, and child custody.[1267]

III. Civil Effect of Religious Marriages

486. Religious marriages have civil effect in the United States, and couples are not required to have a civil marriage in addition to a religious marriage. The state, however, issues marriage licenses and regulates the eligibility of parties to get married. Civil, rather than religious, law also regulates marriage and family law after marriage. *See* Part X (Matrimonial and Family Law), Chapter 1 (Legal Position of Religious Marriage).

1263. Wardle, Duncan & Nolan, *Family and Succession Law*, *supra* n. 1247, paras. 189, 869; *see, e.g.*, I.R.C. § 2056 (2018) (allowing tax-free transfer to a surviving spouse of up to half of a decedent's estate); Katz, *Marriage*, *supra* n. 1247, at 101 (stating the general rule that most wives today are given priority in a deceased husband's estate, depending on the number of children, and can acquire one-third, one-half, or the entire estate).

1264. *See* Sara M. Moorman & Megumi Inoue, *Persistent Problems in End-of-Life Planning among Young- and Middle-Aged American Couples*, 68 J. Gerontology Series B Psych. Scis. & Soc. Scis. 97, 97 (2013) (explaining that "most states designate the spouse as the surrogate decision maker if the patient has not appointed a [durable power of attorney for health care]", which is a person who can make medical decisions on behalf of an incapacitated patient).

1265. Katz, *Marriage*, *supra* n. 1247, at 2–3, 124–127.

1266. *See* Unif. Marriage & Divorce Act § 307(a) (Unif. Law Comm'n 1973) ("In making apportionment the court shall consider the duration of the marriage, and prior marriage of either party, antenuptial agreement of the parties, the age, health, station, occupation, amount and sources of income, vocational skills, employability, estate, liabilities, and needs of each of the parties, custodial provisions, whether the apportionment is in lieu of or in addition to maintenance, and the opportunity of each for future acquisition of capital assets and income.").

1267. *See* Katz, *Marriage*, *supra* n. 1247, at 140 ("[T]he conventional view [is] that alimony is based on reaching an equitable balance between the needs of the dependent spouse and the ability of the supporting spouse to pay".).

487. Currently, all jurisdictions in the United States allow religious leaders to perform civilly binding marriages.[1268] The government grants power to religious organizations to ordain or authorize their leaders to perform religious marriages for both their members and non-members. Most states do not require religious leaders to be licensed or approved by the state directly, although thirteen states do require some form of state licensing or registration.[1269] The officiator of the religious marriage signs the marriage license provided by the state, and then the state recognizes the marriage as legally binding.[1270]

488. In 1962, an organization known as the Universal Life Church (ULC) began ordaining laypeople as ministers through mailed certificates without any training and regardless of religion or personal ideology. ULC now offers ordination online and claims that more than 20 million ministers have become ordained through this process.[1271] In the years following the creation of ULC, some states considered marriages performed by ULC ministers invalid.[1272] However, in more recent years, states have generally recognized marriages solemnized by "mail-order clergy" as valid unions.[1273] The exigencies of the COVID-19 pandemic precipitated the development of virtual wedding licensing and even virtual wedding ceremonies in some states. At least one US jurisdiction now issues marriage licenses online and performs virtual marriages for local and US couples and for non-US couples abroad,

1268. *See, e.g.*, Unif. Marriage & Divorce Act § 206(a) (Unif. Law Comm'n 1973).

1269. *See* (all codes current through 2022) Ark. Code Ann. § 9-11-213; Del. Code Ann. tit. 13 § 106; Haw. Rev. Stat § 572-12; La. Stat. Ann. § 9:202; Mass. Gen. Laws ch. 207 § 38; Minn. Stat. § 517.04; Nev. Rev. Stat. § 122.062; N.H. Rev. Stat. Ann. § 457:31; Ohio Rev. Code Ann. § 3101.08; Vt. Stat. Ann. tit. 18 § 5144; Va. Code Ann. § 20-23; W. Va. Code § 48-2-401. New York state law requires that individuals who perform marriages in New York City register with the city clerk. One-day marriage officiant licenses area available. *See Marriage Officiant Registration*, Off. City Clerk, City N.Y., https://www.cityclerk.nyc.gov/content/marriage-officiant-registration (last visited Sep. 30, 2023).

1270. *See* 3 Durham et al., *supra* n. 174, § 23:5 (*Performing Marriages*).

1271. *Universal Life Church—Free Online Ordination*, Universal Life Church Monastery, http://www.themonastery.org/ordination (last visited Sep. 30, 2023).

1272. *See, e.g.*, *Ravenal v. Ravenal*, 338 N.Y.S.2d 324, 328 (N.Y. App. Div. 1972) (ruling that a ULC minister who obtained ministerial credentials by filling out a form did not fall under the statutory definition of "clergyman or minister"); *State v. Lynch*, 272 S.E.2d 349, 354–355 (N.C. 1980) (invalidating a marriage solemnized by a layman who purchased ULC ministerial credentials through a mail order certificate); Tenn. Code Ann. § 36-3-301(a)(2) (2022) ("Persons receiving online ordinations may not solemnize the rite of matrimony"); *Cramer v. Commonwealth*, 202 S.E.2d 911, 917 (Va. 1974) (limiting ministers with the power to solemnize marriages to those who are leaders of religious faiths, as opposed to the general population).

1273. *See, e.g.*, *In re Last Will & Testament of Blackwell v. Magee*, 531 So. 2d 1193, 1194 (La. 1988); N.C. Gen. Stat. § 51-1.1 (2021) (validating marriages performed by ULC ministers prior to Jul. 3, 1981 but leaving open the question of whether marriages performed after that date are valid); *Universal Life Church v. Utah*, 189 F. Supp. 2d 1302, 1317– 1318 (D. Utah 2002) (ruling that a state statute violated the Equal Protection Clause because there was no rational basis for differential treatment between officiates ordained after submitting applications by phone, fax, or in person and officiates ordained after submitting applications over the internet or by mail); 01-057 Op. Va. Att'y Gen. (2001), https://www.oag.state.va.us/files/Opinions/2001/01-057.pdf (Virginia State Attorney General opinion giving court clerks discretionary authority to authorize a ULC-ordained officiant to perform a marriage).

which have been recognized in their home countries.[1274] *See* Part X (Matrimonial and Family Law), Chapter 1 (Legal Position of Religious Marriage) for additional discussion.

IV. No Religious Freedom Right to Practice Polygamy

489. As discussed in Part II (Religious Freedom in General), Chapter 1 (Individual Religious Freedom), the Supreme Court held in 1878 that the Free Exercise Clause of the US Constitution's First Amendment does not protect the right to practice polygamy.[1275]

§2. Marriage and Race

490. Today, there are no race-based restrictions on marriage. However, this was not always the case in the United States.

I. Anti-miscegenation Statutes

491. Even before the United States was established as an independent nation, prohibitions on interracial marriage were common.[1276] Many early laws focused on interracial sexual behavior and, more particularly, on the sexual and reproductive behavior of white women in an attempt to prevent "bastardy".[1277] Following independence, explicit anti-miscegenation statutes were enacted in most states.[1278] For example, Virginia's 1792 miscegenation legislation "[banned] marriages between free whites and Negroes or mulattoes, and set the penalty for the white partner to

1274. *See, e.g.*, Lois M. Collins, *Israel Must Recognize Marriages Performed Online Through Utah County Portal*, Deseret News (Mar. 17, 2023), https://www.deseret.com/u-s-world/2023/3/17/23644985/israel-must-recognize-marriages-performed-online-by-utah-county; N.Y. Exec. Order No. 202.20 (Apr. 18, 2020) (permitting marriage licenses to be issued virtually during New York State's COVID-19 state of emergency).

1275. *Reynolds v. United States*, 98 U.S. 145 (1878).

1276. *See* Peggy Pascoe, *Race, Gender, and Intercultural Relations: The Case of Interracial Marriage*, 12 Frontiers J. Women Stud. 5, 6 (1991) (summarizing the history of anti-miscegenation laws). Anti-miscegenation laws targeted at preventing interracial sex and marriage, which were passed as early as the colonial period, were repealed in some states after the Civil War but remained in much of the South and West until 1967. *Ibid.* These laws and prohibitions on marriages between whites and non-whites—including blacks, Chinese, Japanese, Filipinos, Hawaiians, Hindus, and Native Americans—reflected the race hierarchy of the United States and the desire to maintain a white majority. *Ibid.*

1277. Peggy Pascoe, *What Comes Naturally: Miscegenation Law and the Making of Race in America* 20 (2009).

1278. *Ibid.*, at 21 ("Between the formation of the American republic and the outbreak of the Civil War, twenty-eight American states relied on [laws prohibiting interracial marriage].").

such a union at six months in jail and a fine of thirty dollars".[1279] After the Civil War, anti-miscegenation laws spread throughout the western states.

492. Determining the legality of interracial marriage fell under state jurisdiction. National anti-miscegenation laws were proposed to Congress from time to time but were never passed. In the wake of the high-profile marriage between a black professional boxer and a white woman in 1912, Georgia Congressman Seaborn Roddenbery introduced a constitutional amendment to make interracial marriages illegal across the United States and its territories. While Roddenbery's amendment proposal awaited further action, the House of Representatives in 1913 passed Congress's proposal for an anti-miscegenation law covering Washington, DC (but the proposal later died in Senate subcommittees).

493. Although the National Association for the Advancement of Colored People (NAACP) was only a few years old, Congress's actions in 1912 and 1913 motivated the NAACP to begin fighting the spread of anti-miscegenation laws throughout individual states.[1280] Over the next few decades, various civil rights organizations led efforts to repeal state anti-miscegenation laws and gain recognition of a fundamental right to marriage.[1281]

494. In the landmark 1967 case *Loving v. Virginia*, the Supreme Court held that laws prohibiting interracial marriage were unconstitutional.[1282] In 1958, a black woman and a white man violated section 20-58 of the Virginia Code when they left their home state of Virginia to be married in Washington, DC.[1283] At the time of the *Loving* case, sixteen states still had prohibitions on interracial marriage, and the Supreme Court was faced with deciding whether anti-miscegenation laws violated the Fourteenth Amendment of the US Constitution.[1284] Relying on the principles that marriage is a fundamental right to be afforded to every person and that racial discrimination is contrary to the values of the United States, the Court determined that laws prohibiting interracial marriage violated the Fourteenth Amendment.[1285]

495. In the aftermath of *Loving v. Virginia*, all state laws prohibiting access to marriage based on race were invalid, although it took time for state and local authorities and laws to conform to the ruling. Even after *Loving*, many interracial couples in the South were forced to appeal to federal courts because they could not

---

1279. Walter Wadlington, *The* Loving *Case: Virginia's Anti-miscegenation Statute in Historical Perspective*, 52 Va. L. Rev. 1189, 1194 (1966).

1280. *See* Pascoe, *What Comes Naturally*, *supra* n. 1277, at 163–173.

1281. *See ibid.*, at 246–283 (tracing the dismantling of miscegenation laws through Supreme Court decisions and other efforts).

1282. *Loving v. Virginia*, 388 U.S. 1, 12 (1967).

1283. *Ibid.*, at 4 ("If any white person and colored person shall go out of this State, for the purpose of being married, and with the intention of returning, and be married out of it, and afterwards return to and reside in it, cohabitating as man and wife, they shall be punished … ." (quoting Va. Code § 20-58 (1958))).

1284. *Ibid.*, at 2, 6.

1285. *Ibid.*, at 11–12.

obtain marriage licenses. Some local officials tried to delay repealing state miscegenation laws, waiting for a copy of the Supreme Court ruling or "until state attorney generals [sic] or federal district courts issued definitive rulings".[1286] The 2022 Respect for Marriage Act codifies federal protections for interracial marriage, prohibiting persons "acting under the color of State law" from denying, on the basis of race or other protected characteristics, full faith and credit to a marriage performed and recognized in any state.[1287]

§3. Same-Sex Marriage

I. Constitutional Status of Same-Sex Marriage

496. The legal and social status of same-sex marriage has undergone significant transformation in the United States in the twenty-first century. The text of the Constitution does not address the issue. As recently as 2002, same-sex marriage was not legal in any state. In 1972, the US Supreme Court summarily dismissed a case claiming a right to same-sex marriage on the grounds that the case did not raise a substantial federal question.[1288]

497. In 1996, Congress passed, and President Bill Clinton signed, the Defense of Marriage Act (DOMA), which defined marriage as between one man and one woman only.[1289] DOMA expressed deference to state laws banning same-sex marriage and provided that the federal government did not recognize same-sex marriages or issue federal benefits for such marriages, regardless of the legality of such marriages in their respective states. After DOMA, forty-two states followed the federal example and, through constitutional amendment and/or state statute, defined marriage as exclusively between one man and one woman.[1290] Some states also refused to recognize same-sex marriages granted by other states and considered same-sex marriage a violation of the state's public policy.

498. In 2003, Massachusetts became the first state to recognize a right to same-sex marriages, in the state supreme court decision *Goodridge v. Department of Public Health*.[1291] The court noted that civil marriage was a civil right with enormous benefits and ruled that denying anyone the right to choose to marry violated the state

1286. Pascoe, *What Comes Naturally*, *supra* n. 1277, at 289–290.

1287. Respect for Marriage Act, Pub. L. No. 117-228, § 4, 136 Stat. 2305, 2305 (2022).

1288. *Baker v. Nelson*, 409 U.S. 810 (1972) (mem.).

1289. Defense of Marriage Act, Pub. L. No. 104-199, 110 Stat. 2419 (1996) (codified at 1 U.S.C. § 7; 28 U.S.C. § 1738C (2000)) ("[T]he word 'marriage' means only a legal union between one man and one woman as husband and wife, and the word 'spouse' refers only to a person of the opposite sex who is a husband or a wife".), *invalidated by United States v. Windsor*, 570 U.S. 744, 769–770 (2013). *But see Obergefell v. Hodges*, 576 U.S. 644 (2015) (holding that states are required to license and recognize same-sex marriage, under the Fourteenth Amendment).

1290. James G. Pawelski et al., *The Effects of Marriage, Civil Union, and Domestic Partnership Laws on the Health and Well-Being of Children*, 118(1) Pediatrics 349, 352–355 (2006).

1291. *Goodridge v. Dep't of Pub. Health*, 798 N.E.2d 941, 959 (Mass. 2003).

constitution, which protected "both 'freedom from' unwarranted government intrusion into protected spheres of life and 'freedom to' partake in benefits created by the State for the common good".[1292]

499. After *Goodridge*, many East Coast states followed Massachusetts's lead. For example, the Connecticut Supreme Court ruled that prohibiting same-sex marriage violated the state constitution in 2008, and Maine voters approved a same-sex marriage referendum in 2012.[1293] In 2009, Iowa became one of the first Midwestern states to legalize same-sex marriage; the Iowa Supreme Court in *Varnum v. Brien* ruled that the state statute limiting civil marriage to heterosexual couples violated the Iowa Constitution.[1294] Farther west, courts in Oregon and Washington rejected same-sex marriage claims.[1295]

500. In response to the changing status of same-sex marriage, a number of states enacted additional provisions to ensure marriage was limited to heterosexual unions. Between 2004 and 2008, twenty-seven states passed constitutional amendments banning same-sex marriage.[1296] For example, just before the Oregon Supreme Court ruled on the same-sex marriage issue, a state constitutional amendment referendum banning same-sex marriage in Oregon passed in 2004 with 57% support.[1297]

501. California's Proposition 8 was the most publicized and controversial referendum designed to define marriage as between one man and one woman. In 2008, the California Supreme Court held that a previous state law banning same-sex marriage was unconstitutional.[1298] Proposition 8 proposed an amendment to California's state constitution that was designed to re-implement the ban on same-sex marriage.[1299] It passed by a margin of 54% to 48% in 2008. Religious groups were involved on both sides of Proposition 8, with vocal support for traditional marriage coming from a number of religious organizations.[1300] Same-sex couples sued,

1292. *Ibid.*
1293. Jason Pierceson, *Same-Sex Marriage in the United States: The Road to the Supreme Court* 158, 160 (2013); *see also Kerrigan v. Comm'r of Pub. Health*, 957 A.2d 407 (Conn. 2008).
1294. *Varnum v. Brien*, 763 N.W.2d 862, 872 (Iowa 2009).
1295. *See Li v. State*, 110 P.3d 91, 98 (Or. 2004) (en banc) (ruling that the constitutional amendment banning same-sex marriage prohibited the court from granting this right), *abrogated by Obergefell v. Hodges*, 576 U.S. 644 (2015); *Andersen v. King County*, 138 P.3d 963, 980, 990 (Wash. 2006) (en banc) (ruling that plaintiffs failed to establish sexual orientation as a classification that requires strict scrutiny and upholding the constitutionality of Washington's Defense of Marriage Act), *abrogated by Obergefell*, 576 U.S. at 644.
1296. *See* Pierceson, *Same-Sex Marriage in the United States*, *supra* n. 1293, at 153 tbl.6.2.
1297. *Ibid.*, at 181.
1298. *In re Marriage Cases*, 183 P.3d 384, 400 (Cal. 2008) (relying on the principle that in California the right to enter into a long-term committed relationship and the right to raise children are fundamental constitutional rights guaranteed to all Californians, regardless of sexual orientation), *superseded by constitutional amendment (Proposition 8) as stated in Hollingsworth v. Perry*, 570 U.S. 693, 701 (2013).
1299. *Strauss v. Horton*, 207 P.3d 48, 59 (Cal. 2009).
1300. *See* Pierceson, *Same-Sex Marriage in the United States*, *supra* n. 1293, at 191.

claiming that Proposition 8 was "*a constitutional revision* rather than ... *a constitutional amendment*" and, therefore, "could not lawfully be adopted through the initiative process".[1301] The California Supreme Court determined that Proposition 8 was a valid constitutional amendment and declined to invalidate it based on the Attorney General's alternative theory that Proposition 8 infringed on inalienable rights set out in California's constitution.[1302] On the federal level, opponents to Proposition 8 prevailed in lower courts, and the case was appealed to the US Supreme Court.[1303] Because the state of California declined to defend the law, a group of citizens stepped in, but in the 2013 case *Hollingsworth v. Perry*, the US Supreme Court held that the group of citizens defending the law did not have legal standing.[1304] As a result, the lower court decisions stood, meaning same-sex marriage was once again legal in California.

502. Also in 2013, in *United States v. Windsor*, the US Supreme Court held that the definition of marriage in the Defense of Marriage Act was unconstitutional.[1305] The plaintiff, a widow who had married her female spouse in New York after the state legalized same-sex marriage, challenged DOMA because it prevented her from qualifying for the federal estate tax exemption. She could not qualify for the exemption when her wife died because her marriage, though recognized in her home state of New York, was not recognized by the federal government. In a 5-4 decision, the Supreme Court held that DOMA violated the Due Process Clause of the Fifth Amendment and the Equal Protection Clause of the Fourteenth Amendment. According to Justice Anthony Kennedy, who wrote the 5-4 majority opinion, DOMA had been motivated by unconstitutional animus against gay individuals.[1306]

503. The 2013 *Windsor* opinion did not address whether a constitutional right to same-sex marriage exists. But in the two years following that decision, a number of federal courts in rapid succession, and with few exceptions,[1307] held that laws limiting marriage to unions between a man and a woman were unconstitutional.[1308]

1301. *Strauss*, 207 P.3d at 60.

1302. *Ibid.*, at 116–119.

1303. *See Perry v. Schwarzenegger*, 704 F. Supp. 2d 921, 1004 (N.D. Cal. 2010) (holding that Proposition 8 violated the Due Process and Equal Protection Clauses); *Perry v. Brown*, 671 F.3d 1052, 1095 (9th Cir. 2012) (ruling that Proposition 8 was evidence of the majority imposing its disapproval of gay and lesbian relationships and violated the Equal Protection Clause), *vacated and remanded by Hollingsworth*, 570 U.S. at 715.

1304. *Hollingsworth*, 570 U.S. at 715.

1305. *United States v. Windsor*, 570 U.S. 744, 769–770, 775 (2013).

1306. *Ibid.*, at 770 ("DOMA's unusual deviation from the usual tradition of recognizing and accepting state definitions of marriage here operates to deprive same-sex couples of the benefits and responsibilities that come with the federal recognition of their marriages. ... The avowed purpose and practical effect of the law here in question are to impose a disadvantage, a separate status, and so a stigma upon all who enter into same-sex marriages made lawful by the unquestioned authority of the States.").

1307. *See DeBoer v. Snyder*, 772 F.3d 388 (6th Cir. 2014) (constituting an exception by upholding a ban on same-sex marriage—the first federal court of appeals to do so); *see also* Stephen Macedo, *Just Married: Same-Sex Couples, Monogamy, & the Future of Marriage* 4 (2015).

1308. *See, e.g.*, *Bostic v. Schaefer*, 760 F.3d 352, 384 (4th Cir. 2014); *Kitchen v. Herbert*, 755 F.3d 1193, 1229–1230 (10th Cir. 2014).

504. At the beginning of 2015, same-sex marriage was legal in thirty-five states, including eleven states that had legalized same-sex marriages through legislation or referenda[1309] and twenty-four states where courts had found a constitutional right to same-sex marriage.[1310]

505. In June 2015, in *Obergefell v. Hodges*, the US Supreme Court held 5-4 that same-sex couples may not be deprived of the right to marry, under the Due Process and Equal Protection Clauses of the Constitution's Fourteenth Amendment. The majority found that denying same-sex marriage violated four fundamental principles: (1) "the right to personal choice regarding marriage is inherent in the concept of individual autonomy"; (2) "the right to marry is fundamental because it supports a two-person union unlike any other in its importance to the committed individuals"; (3) "the right to marry … safeguards children and families and thus draws meaning from related rights of childrearing, procreation, and education"; and (4) "marriage is a keystone of the Nation's social order".[1311] Although not expressly mentioned, the majority opinion was based at least partly on the concept of "substantive due process", which the Court had used to establish other fundamental unenumerated constitutional rights. While the Court ruled that banning same-sex marriage was unconstitutional, Justice Kennedy stated for the majority that the First Amendment protects religious organizations and individuals that wish to "continue to advocate with utmost, sincere conviction that, by divine precepts, same-sex marriage should not be condoned".[1312]

506. Chief Justice John Roberts's dissenting opinion warned against the Court's "aggressive application of substantive due process" and relied on the principle of federalism, expressing concern that the Court's decision bypassed the democratic process, thus removing the question from the realm of public debate and flexible legislative decision-making.[1313] He noted, for example, that while the majority opinion relied on the Constitution to protect same-sex marriage and acknowledge the rights of religious believers to advocate other views of marriage, states that adopted same-sex marriage through legislation were able to include specific, nuanced accommodations for religious practice.[1314] Chief Justice Roberts also expressed concern about religious exercise questions unaddressed by the majority opinion, such as religious colleges that do not offer housing to same-sex couples, religious

---

1309. Md. Off. of the Att'y Gen., *The State of Marriage Equality in America* 3 (Apr. 2015), https://www.marylandattorneygeneral.gov/Reports/The%20State%20of%20Marriage%20Equality%20in%20America%202015.pdf; *see also* Jeremiah A. Ho, *Once We're Done Honeymooning:* Obergefell v. Hodges, *Incrementalism, and Advances for Sexual Orientation and Anti-Discrimination*, 104 Ky. L.J. 207, 212 (2016) (citing the number of states permitting same-sex marriage in early 2015 as thirty-seven).
1310. Md. Off. of the Att'y Gen., *supra* n. 1309.
1311. *Obergefell v. Hodges*, 576 U.S. 644, 665–669 (2015).
1312. *Ibid.*, at 679.
1313. *Ibid.*, at 686, 699, 710–711 (Roberts, C.J., with Scalia and Thomas, JJ., dissenting).
1314. *Ibid.*, at 711–712.

adoption agencies that refuse to place children with same-sex couples, and religious institutions that wish to retain tax exemptions and oppose same-sex marriage.[1315]

507. The 2022 Supreme Court decision *Dobbs v. Jackson Women's Health Organization*, which overturned *Roe v. Wade*, raised concerns that the now-more-conservative Court might also overturn *Obergefell* and other decisions similarly grounded in the concept of substantive due process.[1316] In response, Congress passed the Respect for Marriage Act (RFMA), which repealed the Defense of Marriage Act and requires that marriages recognized in one state—including same-sex and interracial marriages—be recognized in all states.[1317] RFMA also acknowledges that "reasonable and sincere people based on decent and honorable religious or philosophical premises" may hold "diverse beliefs about the role of gender in marriage" and that those "beliefs are due proper respect".[1318] Accordingly, it guarantees that nonprofit religious organizations and their employees cannot be required to "provide services … for the solemnization or celebration of a marriage".[1319]

II. Conscientious Objection to Performing Same-Sex Marriages and Providing Wedding-Related Services

508. With the recognition of same-sex marriage, issues arose involving those who objected on conscientious or religious grounds to performing same-sex marriages or providing wedding-related services. At least one state, Mississippi, has carved out broad exemptions for religious organizations and individuals from providing wedding-related and other services to LGBTQ+ individuals.[1320] The law in this area has evolved rapidly, and some conscience exemptions have been controversial, especially for owners of wedding-related for-profit businesses, such as photographers, bakers, and florists. Public opinion has been fairly evenly split with regard to "claims of religious liberty or traditional morality against non-discrimination policies" and laws.[1321]

509. Some scholars have noted legal similarities in LGBTQ+ rights and religious freedom claims and have called for protection of both under the mutual recognition of human dignity and civil liberty as to one's identity.[1322] Utah,

1315. *Ibid.*; *see also ibid.*, at 720, 733–734 (Thomas, J., with Scalia, J., dissenting) (similarly warning against the "danger of substantive due process" and asserting that leaving the legality of same-sex marriages to the political process would have allowed the people to consider religious liberty implications before amending the traditional definition of marriage).

1316. *See Dobbs v. Jackson Women's Health Org.*, 142 S. Ct. 2228, 2300, 2300–2304 (2022) (Thomas, J., concurring) (asserting that the Court should "reconsider all of [its] substantive due process precedents, including *Griswold*, *Lawrence*, and *Obergefell*. Because any substantive due process decision is demonstrably erroneous". (internal quotation marks omitted)).

1317. Respect for Marriage Act, Pub. L. No. 117-228, §§ 3–5, 136 Stat. 2305, 2305–2306 (2022).

1318. Pub. L. No. 117-228, § 2, 136 Stat. 2305, 2305.

1319. Pub. L. No. 117-228, § 6, 136 Stat. 2305, 2306.

1320. Miss. Code Ann. § 11-62-5 (2022).

1321. *16 Striking Findings from 2016*, *supra* n. 908.

1322. *See* sources cited *supra* n. 913.

traditionally a religiously and politically conservative state, is distinct as the first and only state to pass comprehensive non-discrimination legislation that protects rights related to marriage, employment, housing, and free speech of both LGBTQ+ and religious individuals.[1323] In 2022, the US Congress passed the Respect for Marriage Act, which contains some dual protections: it ensures the legal recognition of interracial and opposite-sex unions while simultaneously acknowledging the existence of diverse religious and philosophical beliefs about the role of gender in marriage and exempting religious organizations and their employees from requirements to solemnize or celebrate same-sex marriages.[1324]

A. *State Officials*

510. All jurisdictions that adopted same-sex marriage legislation before the Supreme Court's decision in *Obergefell* built in protections for religious organizations and individuals who do not support same-sex marriage.[1325] However, these protections did not always extend to government officials with similar beliefs. For example, following the ruling on same-sex marriage in Massachusetts, justices of the peace were required to perform same-sex marriages or "face possible legal action for discrimination".[1326] In 2015, Utah passed Senate Bills 296 and 297—known collectively as the Utah Compromise—to protect the rights of LGBTQ+ community members as well as religious organizations and individuals, including government employees. That legislation guarantees same-sex marriage and ensures access to state-authorized celebrants for all lawful marriages while permitting religious organizations and officiants to decline involvement in same-sex marriages; a county clerk may decline to perform a same-sex marriage if the clerk's office can appoint another employee to perform the marriage.[1327] Many states that enacted same-sex legislation before *Obergefell v. Hodges* included similar protections for religious organizations and individuals, but Mississippi and North Caroline are the only other states to expressly exempt officials from the duty to

---

1323. *See supra* para. 346, *infra* para. 510, and accompanying footnotes.

1324. *See supra* para. 507.

1325. Robin Fretwell Wilson, *When Governments Insulate Dissenters from Social Change: What* Hobby Lobby *and Abortion Conscience Clauses Teach about Specific Exemptions*, 48 UC Davis L. Rev. 703, 771, 788–790 & app. (2014) (explaining that, in order to get legislation passed, all jurisdictions that "voluntarily embraced same-sex marriage built in important, if imperfect, protections for religious organizations and individuals who adhere to a heterosexual view of marriage").

1326. Allison L. Collins, *"I Will Not Pronounce You Husband and Husband": Justice and the Justice of the Peace*, 61 Ala. L. Rev. 847, 849–850 (2010).

1327. The Utah Compromise also bans housing and employment discrimination, protects employee expression inside and outside the workplace, allows employers to create workplace regulations aligned with their values, allows religious organizations to provide faith-based counselling, and protects personal expressions of belief by licensed individuals in non-professional settings. *See supra* para. 346 and accompanying footnotes; Robin Fretwell Wilson, *Summary of the Utah Compromise* (Mar. 24, 2015), https://papers.ssrn.com/sol3/papers.cfm?abstract_id=2584543; J. Stuart Adams & Robin Fretwell Wilson, *Protecting Religious Liberty Requires Protections for All*, Religious Freedom Inst. (Jul. 12, 2016), https://religiousfreedominstitute.org/2016-7-12-protecting-religious-liberty-requires-protections-for-all.

solemnize same-sex marriages.[1328] Challenges to the Mississippi and North Carolina recusal statutes have failed for lack of standing.[1329] In most states, to avoid discrimination and maintain a uniform marriage system, state officials are expected to license and perform same-sex marriages when licensing and performing lawful marriages is within their ordinary duties.[1330]

B. Churches and Religious Officials

511. Nonprofit religious organizations and their employees cannot be forced to perform same-sex marriages in the United States. Religious officials, whether paid or unpaid, have traditionally been protected by the First Amendment, and their positions and actions within those positions are within the control of their churches. *See* Part II (Religious Freedom in General), Chapter 2 (Collective Religious Freedom) and Chapter 3 (Organizational Religious Freedom). Churches have long been allowed to stipulate religious qualifications for those who are married in a church or by church officials. Some states have enacted statutes expressly exempting clergy from officiating marriages in violation of their religious beliefs.[1331] The 2022 Respect for Marriage Act (RFMA) established a federal exemption for nonprofit religious organizations and their employees from any legal requirement to "provide services, accommodations, advantages, facilities, goods, or privileges for the solemnization or celebration of a marriage".[1332]

1328. *See* Miss. Code Ann. § 11-62-5(8) (2022) ("Any person employed or acting on behalf of the state government who has authority to authorize or license marriages … may seek recusal … based upon … a sincerely held religious belief or moral conviction … ."); N.C. Gen. Stat. § 51-5.5 (2022) (granting certain public officials the right to recuse from performing marriages or issuing marriage licenses "based upon any sincerely held religious objection"); *see also* Del. Code Ann. tit. 13, § 106(f) (2022) (allowing any person authorized to solemnize marriages to refuse "for any reason to solemnize a marriage" but requiring "a Clerk of the Peace who issues a marriage license, or a deputy thereof … to perform a solemnization of such marriage if requested by the applicants for such license"). *See also generally Religious Exemption Laws: Marriage Solemnization*, Movement Advancement Project, https://www.lgbtmap.org/equality-maps/religious_exemption_laws/religious_exemption_solemnization (updated Oct. 27, 2023).

1329. *Ansley v. Warren*, 861 F.3d 512, 522–523 (4th Cir. 2017); *Barber v. Bryant*, 860 F.3d 345, 358 (5th Cir. 2017).

1330. *See, e.g.*, *Inquiry Concerning a Judge (Day)*, 413 P.3d 907, 921–922 (Or. 2018) (ordering suspension of judge for screening same-sex marriages off calendar and other misconduct); *Neely v. Wyo. Comm'n on Judicial Conduct & Ethics*, 390 P.3d 728 (Wyo. 2017) (holding that judicial discipline was proper for judge who refused to perform same-sex marriages), *cert. denied*, 138 S. Ct. 639 (2018) (mem.); *see also Miller v. Caudill*, 936 F.3d 442, 445–447 (6th Cir. 2019) (reviewing procedural history of action against clerk who refused to issue marriage licenses on grounds of religious beliefs against same-sex marriages).

1331. *See, e.g.*, Colo. Rev. Stat. § 24-34-601(1) (2022) (exempting churches, synagogues, and mosques from public accommodation law); Haw. Rev. Stat. §§ 572B-4(c), 572B-9.5 (2022) (exempting clergy and religious organizations from solemnizing unions contrary to their beliefs); N.H. Rev. Stat. Ann. § 457:37(I), (II) (2022) (exempting clergy from officiating at—and religious organizations from participating in—any marriage contrary to their beliefs).

1332. Respect for Marriage Act, Pub. L. No. 117-228, § 6, 136 Stat. 2305, 2306 (2022).

C. Church-Affiliated Nonprofits

512. RFMA also provides a federal exemption for "nonprofit entities whose principal purpose is the study, practice, or advancement of religion" from legal requirements to provide marriage celebration or solemnization services.[1333] What remains unclear is whether nonprofits affiliated with churches will be granted exemptions from discriminating against those in same-sex marriages. In Chief Justice John Roberts's dissenting *Obergefell v. Hodges* opinion, he anticipated that the Court would have to resolve conflicts that arise concerning the same-sex marriage decision and its impact on university housing, religiously affiliated adoption programs, and the tax-exempt status of some religious organizations.[1334]

513. The most common example of a church-affiliated nonprofit that intersects with same-sex marriage is an adoption agency. Some church-affiliated nonprofit organizations that facilitate adoption placements have closed because of state non-discrimination requirements that such adoption organizations place children in the homes of same-sex couples. For example, in 2006, Catholic Charities of Massachusetts chose to stop its adoption program after bishops learned that thirteen children had been placed with gay and lesbian parents; and in 2010, the Catholic Archdiocese of Washington decided to end a foster care placement program to avoid violating non-discrimination laws after the District of Columbia passed a new same-sex marriage law.[1335] In a 2021 narrow ruling in *Fulton v. City of Pennsylvania*, the Supreme Court held that the city acted unconstitutionally when it forced a foster care agency affiliated with the Catholic Church to choose between certifying same-sex couples or curtailing operations.[1336] The Court found that a non-discrimination requirement in the city's foster care contract was not generally applicable because it allowed for exemptions, even though the city refused to exempt the agency based on religious beliefs.[1337] Because the non-discrimination requirement was not generally applicable, the Court applied strict scrutiny and held that the city failed to demonstrate a compelling interest to justify burdening the agency's free exercise by not granting an exception.[1338]

514. As telegraphed in Chief Justice Roberts's *Obergefell* dissent, a significant unsettled issue is whether religiously affiliated universities that discriminate against

1333. *Ibid.*

1334. *Obergefell v. Hodges*, 576 U.S. 644, 686, 711–712 (2015) (Roberts, C.J., with Scalia and Thomas, JJ., dissenting).

1335. *See* Robin Fretwell Wilson, *The Calculus of Accommodation: Contraception, Abortion, Same-Sex Marriage, and Other Clashes Between Religion and the State*, 53 B.C. L. Rev. 1417, 1446–1447 (2012).

1336. *Fulton v. City of Philadelphia*, 141 S. Ct. 1868, 1876–1882 (2021).

1337. *Ibid.*, at 1876–1878.

1338. *Ibid.*, at 1881–1882.

same-sex couples or conduct will lose their tax-exempt status.[1339] In 1983, Bob Jones University lost a case in which it argued it had a free exercise right to racially discriminate in its university policies regarding dating and marriage. The Supreme Court upheld the IRS withdrawal of the university's tax-exempt status because the university policies violated "fundamental public policy" against racial discrimination.[1340] Similar tax policies remain in place today.[1341] In 2013, the IRS withdrew tax-exempt status from a church and a religiously affiliated nonprofit organization that promoted polygamy because they were engaged in activity that was illegal and contrary to public policy, even though they claimed a religious basis for the activity.[1342]

515. As communities and their federal, state, and local policymakers increasingly regard LGBTQ+ anti-discrimination law as fundamental to a free and fair society, religious beliefs in marriage as a covenant between a man and a woman are sometimes analogized to the religious belief opposing interracial dating and marriage at issue in *Bob Jones University*.[1343] In *Masterpiece Cakeshop, Ltd. v. Colorado Civil Rights Commission* and *Obergefell v. Hodges*, the Supreme Court implicitly rejected the race analogy, distinguished and protected religious opposition to same-sex marriage, and called for pluralistic solutions where LGBTQ+ and religious rights seemingly conflict.[1344] Additionally, in *Bostock v. Clayton County*, the Supreme Court noted the existence of constitutional and statutory protections for employers' free exercise rights vis-à-vis employment non-discrimination laws.[1345] The 2022 Respect for Marriage Act also distinguishes religious views on same-sex marriage and race; it affirms that people with diverse religious "beliefs about the role of gender in marriage" and the beliefs themselves "are due proper respect" but does not affirm the same for beliefs opposing interracial marriage.[1346]

1339. *See* David R. Wheeler, *Gay Marriage and the Future of Evangelical Colleges*, Atlantic (Jul. 14, 2015), http://www.theatlantic.com/education/archive/2015/07/evangelical-colleges-struggle-gay-marriage-ruling/398306 (discussing the decisions of Christian-affiliated colleges to retain traditional policies banning "homosexual practice" or revise them to reflect changing social mores and public policy, the impact of *Obergefell* on those decisions, and the possible implications for funding).

1340. *Bob Jones Univ. v. United States*, 461 U.S. 574, 595 (1983) ("Whatever may be the rationale for such private schools' policies, and however sincere the rationale may be, racial discrimination in education is contrary to public policy.").

1341. *See, e.g.*, I.R.C. §§ 170, 501(c)(3); *see also Bob Jones Univ.*, 461 U.S. at 597–598 ("[T]he IRS has the responsibility, in the first instance, to determine whether a particular entity is "charitable" for purposes of [I.R.C.] § 170 and § 501(c)(3). This may in turn necessitate later determinations of whether given activities so violate public policy that the entities involved cannot be deemed to provide a public benefit worthy of "charitable" status. We emphasize, however, that these sensitive determinations should be made only where there is no doubt that the organization's activities violate fundamental public policy.")

1342. I.R.S. Priv. Ltr. Rul. 201325015 (Jun. 21, 2013); I.R.S. Priv. Ltr. Rul. 201323025 (Jun. 7, 2013); I.R.S. Priv. Ltr. Rul. 201310047 (Mar. 8, 2013).

1343. *Cf. Masterpiece Cakeshop, Ltd. v. Colo. C.R. Comm'n*, 138 S. Ct. 1719, 1729 (2018).

1344. *See ibid.*; *Obergefell v. Hodges*, 576 U.S. 644, 679–680 (2015).

1345. *Bostock v. Clayton County*, 140 S. Ct. 1731, 1754 (2020).

1346. Respect for Marriage Act, Pub. L. No. 117-228, § 2, 136 Stat. 2305, 2305 (2022).

D. For-Profit Businesses

516. State and municipal anti-discrimination laws that prohibit discrimination on the basis of sexual orientation and/or gender identity[1347] have been challenged in cases where small businesses refused to provide services for same-sex weddings based on the owners' religious beliefs. Some of these businesses—bakeries, photography studios, florist shops, and others—have been fined or otherwise sanctioned and have challenged such sanctions on free exercise and/or free speech grounds. In 2018, in *Masterpiece Cakeshop, Ltd. v. Colorado Civil Rights Commission*, the US Supreme Court reached a narrow holding, avoiding free speech questions in the case of a baker who refused to design a custom wedding cake for a same-sex couple.[1348] The Court reversed state sanctions against the baker on grounds that the state civil rights commission failed to practice religious neutrality, as required by the Free Exercise Clause, and instead exhibited "hostility toward the sincere religious beliefs" of the baker.[1349]

517. In similar cases, however, courts have considered the issue in terms of competing free speech and non-discrimination interests. In a well-known early case, *Elane Photography, LLC v. Willock*, the New Mexico Supreme Court held that the state's anti-discrimination law was neutral, generally applicable, and prohibited "public accommodations", like a wedding photography company, from discriminating on the basis of sexual orientation.[1350] Addressing the photography company's free speech claim, the court reasoned that the law did not impermissibly compel the company "to either speak a government-mandated message or to publish the speech of another"; moreover, the court reasoned, because the state was not a party to the case, the state's RFRA did not apply.[1351] Other courts have ruled in favor of similar businesses on grounds that requiring a business to render services in support of same-sex marriage ceremonies constitutes compelled speech, in violation of the First Amendment's Free Speech Clause.[1352] In 2023, in *303 Creative LLC v. Elenis*,[1353] the Supreme Court—which had denied certiorari to review *Elane*

1347. For information on states that have enacted anti-discrimination laws prohibiting discrimination on the basis of sexual orientation and/or gender identity, *see Equality Maps: Nondiscrimination Laws*, MAP, *supra* n. 706.

1348. *Masterpiece Cakeshop, Ltd. v. Colo. C.R. Comm'n*, 138 S. Ct. 1719 (2018); *see ibid* at 1723–1724 (avoiding the free speech question).

1349. *Ibid.*, at 1729–1731.

1350. *Elane Photography, LLC v. Willock*, 309 P.3d 53, 59 (N.M. 2013), *cert. denied*, 572 U.S. 1046 (2014) (mem.).

1351. *Ibid.*, at 63–77. Unlike some states, New Mexico permits private actors to enforce public accommodations statutes without necessarily involving state entities. *See also State v. Arlene's Flowers, Inc.*, 441 P.3d 1203, 1237–1238 (Wash. 2019) (en banc) (holding state anti-discrimination law was neutral and generally applicable, did not violate florist's free exercise, and did not violate First Amendment protections against compelled speech).

1352. *See, e.g., Telescope Media Grp. v. Lucero*, 936 F.3d 740, 750–753 (8th Cir. 2019) (holding state could not apply state human rights act to compel wedding videographers to film same-sex weddings, contrary to their religious beliefs); *Brush & Nib Studio, LC v. City of Phoenix*, 448 P.3d 890, 926 (Ariz. 2019) (holding city's application of anti-discrimination ordinance to compel business owners to create celebratory wedding invitations for same-sex weddings violated state laws protecting free speech and free exercise); *Chelsey Nelson Photography LLC v. Louisville/*

Photography—considered a wedding website designer's pre-enforcement challenge to the same state anti-discrimination statute at issue in *Masterpiece Cakeshop*. In a 6-3 decision, the Court acknowledged the state's "compelling interest in eliminating discrimination in places of public accommodation".[1354] The Court held, however, that enforcement would violate the Free Speech Clause if it compelled the website designer to "convey messages inconsistent with her religious belief that marriage … be reserved to [opposite-sex] unions".[1355] The Court distinguished speech expressed through creation of an "expressive", customized wedding website from "the sale of an ordinary commercial product".[1356] In doing so, it noted that the First Amendment does not allow the government to "compel anyone who speaks for pay on a given topic to accept all commissions on that same topic—no matter the underlying message"; for example, the Free Speech Clause would not allow the government to "force a male website designer married to another man to design websites for an organization that advocates against same-sex marriage".[1357] The majority opinion was based solely on finding that the statute impermissibly compelled speech; the Court did not address free exercise nor did it perform a formal strict scrutiny analysis. It remains to be seen how courts will interpret and apply *303 Creative*'s holding, including how courts will determine what constitutes "expressive" commercial services that qualify for free speech protections.

E. State Religious Freedom Restoration Acts

518. Following the Supreme Court's invalidation in 1997 of the federal Religious Freedom Restoration Act (RFRA) as applied to states, most states adopted their own state RFRAs, through statute or amendment of their state constitutions. *See* discussion in Part II (Religious Freedom in General), Chapter 1 (Individual Religious Freedom). However, claims arising under state RFRAs are uncommon, and plaintiffs who do bring state RFRA claims often have difficulty winning.[1358] Some courts have held that RFRA does not protect small business owners, either because RFRA does not cover for-profit businesses or because small-business cases do not involve limitations on religious freedom directly imposed by government.[1359]

Jefferson Cnty. Metro Gov't, 479 F. Supp. 3d 543, 558 & n.122 (W.D. Ky. 2020) (declining to follow *Elane Photography*'s "more narrow[]" reading of the First Amendment and expressing approval of interpretations in *Telescope Media Group* and *Brush & Nib Studio, LC*, based partly on the amendment's protections against compelled speech).

1353. *303 Creative LLC v. Elenis*, 600 U.S. 570 (2023).

1354. *Ibid.*, at 590 (internal quotation marks omitted).

1355. *Ibid.*, at 588–589.

1356. *Ibid.*, at 593.

1357. *Ibid.*, at 589–590.

1358. Christopher C. Lund, *Religious Liberty after* Gonzales: *A Look at State RFRAs*, 55 S.D. L. Rev. 466, 467 (2010).

1359. *See Elane Photography, LLC*, 309 P.3d at 76–77 ("[T]he New Mexico Religious Freedom Restoration Act is inapplicable to disputes in which a government agency is not a party".); *First Vagabonds Church of God v. City of Orlando*, 578 F. Supp. 2d 1353, 1361 (M.D. Fla. 2008) (declining to apply Florida's RFRA in a church's challenge to a municipal "Large Group Feeding Ordinance" because it did not substantially burden free exercise according to the RFRA definition),

Chapter 3. Freedom of Expression

§1. Right to Profess

519. The right to profess personal religious beliefs is one of the few near-absolute rights Americans enjoy. The first US Supreme Court opinion discussing religious expression, *Reynolds v. United States*, stated that while the government may restrict actions motivated by religious belief, it may not restrict belief itself.[1360] A later decision in *West Virginia State Board of Education v. Barnette* affirmed the absolute right to freedom of belief, overruling *Minersville School District v. Gobitis* in holding that compulsory recitation of the Pledge of Allegiance for students was unconstitutional.[1361] But *Barnette* also signified a move away from the belief/action distinction in *Reynolds*, providing religious observers greater ability to express their beliefs through action or, in that case, inaction.[1362] More recently, in *Trinity Lutheran Church v. Comer*, the Court reaffirmed that a law "may not discriminate against some or all religious beliefs. Nor may a law regulate or outlaw conduct *because* it is religiously motivated. And … [t]he Free Exercise Clause protects against laws that impose[] special disabilities on the basis of … religious status."[1363] For a more complete discussion of Pledge of Allegiance cases, *see* Part II (Religious Freedom in General), Chapter 1 (Individual Religious Freedom). For a more complete discussion of *Trinity Lutheran, see* Part VIII (Financing of Religious Communities), Chapter 1 (Direct Financing).

---

aff'd in part, vacated in part, rev'd in part, 638 F.3d 756 (11th Cir. 2011). *But see Brush & Nib Studio, LC*, 448 P.3d at 926–927 (holding anti-discrimination ordinance as applied to wedding-invitation business owner substantially burdened her free exercise of religion under Arizona's RFRA (known as FERA)).

1360. *Reynolds v. United States*, 98 U.S. 145, 166 (1878) ("Laws are made for the government of actions, and while they cannot interfere with mere religious belief and opinions, they may with practices. Suppose one believes that human sacrifices were a necessary part of religious worship, would it be seriously contended that the civil government under which he lived could not interfere to prevent a sacrifice?"). *But see Church of the Lukumi Babalu Aye, Inc. v. City of Hialeah*, 508 U.S. 520, 538 (1993) (explaining "[i]t is not unreasonable to infer … that a law which visits 'gratuitous restrictions' on religious conduct" is unconstitutional (citation omitted)).

1361. *W. Va. State Bd. of Educ. v. Barnette*, 319 U.S. 624, 642 (1943); *see also ibid.*, at 644, 646 (Murphy, J., concurring) ("Any spark of love for country which may be generated in a child or his associates by forcing him to make what is to him an empty gesture and recite words wrung from him contrary to his religious beliefs is overshadowed by the desirability of preserving freedom of conscience to the full."); *Minersville Sch. Dist. v. Gobitis*, 310 U.S. 586 (1940), *overruled by Barnette*, 319 U.S. at 624.

1362. *Barnette*, 319 U.S. at 642 ("[T]he action of the local authorities in compelling the flag salute and pledge transcends constitutional limitations on their power and invades the sphere of intellect and spirit which it is the purpose of the First Amendment of our Constitution to reserve from all official control".)

1363. *Trinity Lutheran Church of Columbia, Inc. v. Comer*, 582 U.S. 449, 461 (2017) (quoting *Church of the Lukumi Babalu Aye*, 508 U.S. at 532–533) (citations and internal quotation marks omitted) (emphasis added).

§2. RIGHT TO PROPAGATE

520. The right to propagate religion, or any viewpoint, was first examined in *Cantwell v. Connecticut.*[1364] Newton Cantwell and his two sons were Jehovah's Witnesses who proselytized in a predominantly Roman Catholic neighborhood, spreading a message that denounced "organized religious systems" and specifically condemned Catholicism.[1365] Two residents of the neighborhood took offense to their message and, after discovering Cantwell and his sons did not have a soliciting license, brought an action against them for violating the licensing statute. Cantwell claimed that the licensing statute itself violated his constitutional right to free exercise of religion. The Supreme Court agreed, holding that the Connecticut licensing statute, as applied to Cantwell, deprived him of his right to free exercise under the First Amendment and denied him due process under the Fourteenth Amendment. The Court explained:

> The state is … free to regulate the time and manner of solicitation generally, in the interest of public safety, peace, comfort, or convenience. But to condition the solicitation of aid for the perpetuation of religious views or systems upon a license, the grant of which rests in the exercise of a determination by state authority as to what is a religious cause, is to lay a forbidden burden upon the exercise of liberty protected by the Constitution.[1366]

In other words, the Court explained, the statute unconstitutionally authorized religious censorship in granting licensing officers "too wide a discretion" to determine the religiosity of a cause and grant or withhold soliciting licenses accordingly.[1367] Although the facts surrounding *Cantwell* arose in a religious context, the Supreme Court broadly characterized free exercise to encompass both religious and nonreligious expression. It emphasized that the "state may not unduly supress free communication of views, religious or other, under the guise of conserving desirable conditions".[1368] For additional discussion of *Cantwell, see* Part II (Religious Freedom in General), Chapter 1 (Individual Religious Freedom).

521. Government restraints on religious propagation are scrutinized under principles articulated in *Cantwell*, even if the propagation resembles commercial activity. The Supreme Court's thinking on this topic underwent a remarkable transformation in the early 1940s. In 1942, in the combined cases of *Jones v. City of Opelika*, *Bowden v. City of Fort Smith*, and *Jobin v. Arizona*, the Supreme Court upheld local ordinances taxing door-to-door sales and requiring fee-based business licenses in cases where Jehovah's Witnesses requested contributions in exchange for

---

1364. *Cantwell v. Connecticut*, 310 U.S. 296 (1940).
1365. *Ibid.*, at 301, 309.
1366. *Ibid.*, at 306–307.
1367. *Ibid.*, at 305, 308.
1368. *Ibid.*, at 308.

religious literature. The Court found that because such laws did not target religious adherents, but rather treated them as other social actors, no First Amendment obstacle existed to applying the laws.[1369]

522. Just a year later, in 1943, the Supreme Court abandoned this position. In *Murdock v. Pennsylvania* the Court articulated what has become the current legal approach to government regulations indirectly affecting religious propagation.[1370] As in *Jones v. City of Opelika*, Jehovah's Witnesses failed to conform to a local ordinance requiring outdoor solicitors, religious or otherwise, to purchase a solicitor's license. Although the petitioners behaved like commercial actors in exchanging money for religious tracts, the Supreme Court concluded that a tax on religious speech, even though indirect, is prohibited by the First Amendment. Therefore, requiring a religious distributor to pay for a license constituted an unconstitutional tax on the free exercise of religion. The Court explained that distributing religious materials is a time-honored form of spreading religious messages. Allowing government to tax this activity would either promote or prohibit religious views.[1371] *Murdock* also established the "preferred position" doctrine, which granted expressive rights—the rights to freedom of press, speech, and religion—a preferred position and special protection under the Constitution.[1372] Because the *Murdock* opinion conflicted so fundamentally with *Jones*, the Court explicitly vacated its judgment in *Jones*, making *Murdock* the controlling precedent in similar cases.[1373]

523. The Supreme Court reinforced its stance in *Murdock* when it reviewed a similar fact pattern in the 1944 case *Follett v. Town of McCormick*. Again, in that case, a Jehovah's Witness refused to buy a local book vendor's license before propagating his religious views. The Court, invoking *Murdock*, reiterated that "[f]reedom of religion is not merely reserved for those with a long purse" but rather occupies a special protected status along with other expressive freedoms protected under the First Amendment.[1374]

524. In 2002, the Supreme Court upheld this position in *Watchtower Bible and Tract Society of New York, Inc. v. Village of Stratton*.[1375] *Stratton* involved a small community that passed an ordinance requiring a city-issued permit for anyone soliciting on private property.[1376] The ordinance offended a Jehovah's Witness congregation nearby, which believed the language of the ordinance was intended, at least

1369. *Jones v. City of Opelika*, 316 U.S. 584, 611 (1942), *vacated*, 319 U.S. 103 (1943) (mem.).
1370. *Murdock v. Pennsylvania*, 319 U.S. 105, 111 (1943).
1371. *See ibid.*, at 111–114.
1372. *Ibid.*, at 115.
1373. *Ibid.*, at 117.
1374. *Follett v. Town of McCormick*, 321 U.S. 573, 575–576 (1944).
1375. *Watchtower Bible & Tract Soc'y of N.Y., Inc. v. Village of Stratton*, 536 U.S. 150 (2002).
1376. The city ordinance required individuals seeking a permit to provide (1) their name and home addresses for the previous five years, (2) a description of their cause, (3) the name and address of affiliated organization and credentials from such organization, (4) the length of time desired for soliciting, and (5) the addresses of every private residence an applicant intended to visit. *Ibid.*, at 156 n.2.

in part, to block its door-to-door proselytizing efforts.[1377] In court, the Village of Stratton argued that the ability of local government to protect homeowners from fraud and invasion of privacy was critical.[1378] While the Supreme Court weighed this argument, it focused more on the ordinance's effect on the right to "anonymous political speech"—that is, the right to support causes anonymously. Because the permit application process required both time and substantial disclosure of identifying information, the Court concluded it invalidly interfered with the right to anonymity and burdened spontaneous speech on religious, political, and other subjects.[1379] Although the Court framed its holding in the context of the First Amendment generally and the Free Speech Clause specifically, it nonetheless affirmed the free exercise rights of religious groups to propagate their beliefs through door-to-door proselytizing.

§3. Government-Compelled Speech

525. Government-compelled speech, be it religious or not, violates the First Amendment. Religious oaths are expressly prohibited in the Constitution itself.[1380] The Supreme Court initially allowed, but later prohibited, schools to compel students to participate in the Pledge of Allegiance. The Court's opinions in *Minersville School District v. Gobitis* and *West Virginia State Board of Education v. Barnette* highlight the tension between the government'smotivating interests in some forms of compelled speech, like national unity, and the individual right of free expression.[1381] Ultimately, the Court sided in *Barnette* with individual freedom of expression in cases where such expression is "peaceable and orderly".[1382] The *Barnette* Court stated, "If there is any fixed star in our constitutional constellation, it is that no official, high or petty, can prescribe what shall be orthodox in politics, nationalism, religion, or other matters of opinion or force citizens to confess by word or act their faith therein."[1383] More recently, the Supreme Court held that a state could not enforce an anti-discrimination statute to compel a business owner to create speech, in the form of wedding websites celebrating same-sex marriages, contrary

---

1377. Kathryn Lusty, Note, *Proselytizers, Pamphleteers, Pests, and Other First Amendment Champions:* Watchtower Bible and Tract Society of New York, Inc. v. Village of Stratton, 18 BYU J. Pub. L. 229, 233 (2003).
1378. *See Watchtower Bible & Tract Soc'y*, 563 U.S. at 164–165.
1379. *Ibid.*, at 164–169.
1380. U.S. Const. art. VI, cl. 3; *see Torcaso v. Watkins*, 367 U.S. 488, 496 (1961) (invalidating the Maryland Declaration of Rights religious test oath required to assume public office); *see also McDaniel v. Paty*, 435 U.S. 618, 628–629 (1978) (plurality opinion) (invalidating a Tennessee constitutional provision barring ministers or priests of any denomination from participating as delegates in a constitutional convention).
1381. *Minersville Sch. Dist. v. Gobitis*, 310 U.S. 586 (1940) (holding local school board's requirement that students salute the flag and recite the Pledge of Allegiance was constitutional as applied to students with religious objections); *W. Va. State Bd. of Educ. v. Barnette*, 319 U.S. 624 (1943) (holding state school board's requirement that students daily salute the flag and recite the Pledge of Allegiance violated the First Amendment's Free Speech and Free Exercise Clauses).
1382. *Barnette*, 319 U.S. at 630.
1383. *Ibid.*, at 642.

to her religious beliefs.[1384] For a more complete discussion of *Gobitis*, *Barnette*, and government-compelled speech, *see* Part II (Religious Freedom in General), Chapter 1 (Individual Religious Freedom). For discussion of more recent tensions between free (non-compelled) speech and non-discrimination rights, *see* Part VII (Religious Communities and Protections of the Individual), Chapter 2 (Freedom to Marry).

§4. Viewpoint Discrimination

526. In public fora, the government is prohibited from discriminating against or among speakers based on viewpoint, whether religious or not. Due to the specific protection of free exercise and the prohibition of an establishment of religion, religious speech in particular cannot be hindered or helped by the government.[1385] In *Shurtleff v. City of Boston*, the city refused to grant a citizen's request to fly a Christian flag in a public space outside city hall.[1386] For years, the city had consistently, and without review, granted citizens' requests to fly flags expressing other viewpoints. But city officials believed that flying a Christian flag in the space would violate the Establishment Clause. The question before the US Supreme Court was whether the flying of flags constituted private expression or government speech. In cases of private expression, the First Amendment's Free Speech Clause prohibits viewpoint discrimination by the government; in cases of government speech, discrimination is permissible, as "the First Amendment does not demand airtime for all views".[1387] The Court concluded that the flags did not constitute government speech, since the city did not actively review the flags or control their content. Because the flags constituted private expression and because the city refused to fly the Christian flag based on its viewpoint, the Court unanimously held that the city had discriminated in violation of the Free Speech Clause.[1388] A concurring opinion noted the city's Establishment Clause concerns but emphasized that "a government does not violate the Establishment Clause merely because it treats religious … speech equally with secular … speech" in public fora. "On the contrary, a government *violates* the Constitution when (as here) it *excludes* religious … speech because of religion … ."[1389]

1384. *303 Creative LLC v. Elenis*, 600 U.S. 570 (2023).
1385. U.S. Const. amend. I ("Congress shall make no law respecting an establishment of religion, or prohibiting the free exercise thereof … .").
1386. *Shurtleff v. City of Boston*, 596 U.S. 243 (2022).
1387. *Ibid.*, at 247–248.
1388. *Ibid.*, at 258–259.
1389. *Ibid.*, at 261, 261 (Kavanaugh, J., concurring) (citing *Espinoza v. Mont. Dep't of Rev.*, 140 S. Ct. 2246 (2020); *Good News Club v. Milford Cent. Sch.*, 533 U.S. 98 (2001); *McDaniel v. Paty*, 435 U.S. 618 (1978) (plurality opinion)).

§5. Protecting Religious Sensitivities

I. Blasphemy

527. Government protection of religious sensitivities is impermissible if it patently promotes a particular religion. During the eighteenth and nineteenth centuries, several states enacted blasphemy laws to protect Christianity from public ridicule.[1390] When challenged, several laws of this kind were upheld on the grounds that they were "designed to prevent the incitement of violence and therefore serve the needs of society rather than the needs of the Christian religion".[1391] In 1970, a Maryland blasphemy statute was invalidated in *State v. West* precisely because "the statute was intended to protect and preserve the Christian religion" rather than preserve order in society, enable "unmolested" worship, or prevent violence or breaches of the peace.[1392] The few blasphemy statutes that exist today are generally linked with obscenity and profanity statues, which aim to curtail the use of offensive language. But even these statutes, unassociated with religion, have been invalidated. In *Kalman v. Cortes*, Pennsylvania's blasphemy statute prohibited companies from using names that incorporated words constituting "blasphemy, profane cursing or swearing", or profaning "the Lord's name".[1393] A filmmaker applied to register his company as "I Choose Hell Productions LLC", but his application was rejected because "Hell" appeared on the statute's list of "suspect words".[1394] After the filmmaker challenged the law, a state employee eliminated religious terms from the list of suspect words; nonetheless, the court determined that the statute required enforcers "to make standardless determinations as to what constitutes blasphemy, profane cursing or swearing, or what profanes the Lord's name".[1395] The trend toward favoring "access to discussion, debate, and the dissemination of information and ideas"[1396]—even if doing so facilitates outrageous, inflammatory, or offensive speech—was confirmed by the Supreme Court in 2017.[1397] For additional discussion of blasphemy and offensive speech, *see* Part XI (Religion and Culture), Chapter 1 (Religion and Art).

1390. *See* Robert A. Brazener, Annotation, *Validity of Blasphemy Statutes or Ordinances*, 41 A.L.R.3d 519 (1972).

1391. 12 Am. Jur. 2d *Blasphemy and Profanity* § 5 (*Validity of Blasphemy Laws*), Westlaw AMJUR BLASPHEMY § 5 (database updated Oct. 2023) (citations omitted); *see, e.g.*, *Oney v. Oklahoma City*, 120 F.2d 861 (10th Cir. 1941); *Lynch v. City of Muskogee*, 47 F. Supp. 589 (E.D. Okla. 1942); *State v. Mockus*, 120 Me. 84 (1921); *State v. Chandler*, 2 Del. (2 Harr.) 553 (1837).

1392. *State v. West*, 263 A.2d 602, 604–605 (Md. Ct. Spec. App. 1970); *see also* Brazener, *Validity of Blasphemy Statutes or Ordinances*, *supra* n. 1390.

1393. *Kalman v. Cortes*, 723 F. Supp. 2d 766, 776 (E.D. Pa. 2010) (internal quotation marks omitted) (quoting Pa. Cons. Stat. § 1303(c)(2)(ii) (1989)); *see also* Samuel G. Freedman, *A Man's Existentialism, Construed as Blasphemy*, N.Y. Times (Mar. 20, 2009), https://www.nytimes.com/2009/03/21/us/21religion.html.

1394. *Kalman*, 723 F. Supp. 2d at 780.

1395. *Ibid.*, at 781–782, 791.

1396. *First Nat'l Bank v. Bellotti*, 435 U.S. 765, 783 (1978).

1397. *Matal v. Tam*, 582 U.S. 218 (2017) (holding that a federal law prohibiting trademark registration of names that might disparage, bring contempt, or bring disrepute to persons, living or dead, violated the Free Speech Clause).

II. Defamation

528. Defamation is the "[m]alicious or groundless harm to the reputation or good name of another by the making of a false statement to a third person".[1398] Defamation law is largely a creature of common law and state law, which means variation exists across US jurisdictions. But common principles in most state defamation laws apply to religious organizations. Indeed, defamation laws can apply to speech targeting religious groups. However, a defendant may only be subject to liability if the targeted group is small enough that the defamation is reasonably understood to refer to a particular member of the group.[1399] For a religious organization to succeed in making a defamation claim, it must demonstrate that the defendant harbored "actual malice" in making a defamatory communication.[1400] This high standard exists for religious groups because other interests exist in tension with a group's interest in its own reputation and right to compensation for suffering defamatory harm; those other interests include the First Amendment's presumption in favor of free expression, respect for a religious group's internal decision-making process, and a group's ability to rebut defamation through its own efforts.[1401]

529. Courts have held that the heightened "actual malice" standard applies to defamation claims not only by religious organizations but against them as well. In a California court of appeals case, a former church member sued the church and individual leaders after the leaders made statements critical of her, orally and in a church publication, related to her divorce and her leaving the church. The California court held that the Free Exercise Clause did not bar the defamation action, finding that "protection of a person's good name is a sufficiently important state interest" to allow limitations on the leaders' actions.[1402] Acknowledging the significant free exercise interests at stake, however, the court held that the plaintiff must prove actual malice, requiring her to show by clear and convincing evidence that church leaders' statements were made with knowledge of their falsity or reckless disregard of whether they were true or false.[1403]

III. Hate Speech

530. In a seminal free speech case, *Brandenburg v. Ohio*, the US Supreme Court held that hate speech is prohibited only when such speech constitutes incitement to imminent unlawful action.[1404] A Ku Klux Klan leader was convicted of advocating

1398. *Defamation*, Black's Law Dictionary (11th ed. 2019), Westlaw.
1399. Restatement (Second) of Torts § 564A (Am. L. Inst. 1977) (noting that "cases in which recovery has been allowed usually have involved numbers of 25 or fewer").
1400. *N.Y. Times Co. v. Sullivan*, 376 U.S. 254, 279–280 (1964).
1401. *See* 3 Durham et al., *supra* n. 174, § 22:13 (*Defamation*).
1402. *McNair v. Worldwide Church of God*, 242 Cal. Rptr. 823, 830 (Cal. Ct. App. 1987).
1403. *Ibid.*, at 833.
1404. *Brandenburg v. Ohio*, 395 U.S. 444, 447–448 (1969).

violence to accomplish political reform after he gave a speech at a Klan rally, threatening the possibility of "some revengeance [sic]" if the government continued to suppress the white race.[1405] The leader challenged the constitutionality of the statute of conviction, alleging it violated the Free Speech Clause. The Supreme Court agreed, holding that the statute failed to distinguish between "advocacy", which is a constitutionally protected form of speech, and "incitement to imminent lawless action", which is not.[1406] For a more detailed discussion of *Brandenburg*, *see* Part XI (Religion and Culture), Chapter 3 (Religion and Civil Society).

531. In another significant hate speech case, the Supreme Court reiterated that, under the First Amendment's Free Speech Clause, regulation of speech must either be content neutral or meet "strict scrutiny" requirements. In *R.A.V. v. City of St. Paul*, the Supreme Court considered a bias-motivated crime ordinance enacted by the city of St. Paul, Minnesota. The ordinance prohibited a particular form of expression: the placing of symbols on private or public property, including "a burning cross or Nazi swastika, which one knows or has reasonable grounds to know arouses anger, alarm or resentment in others on the basis of race, color, creed, religion or gender".[1407] After several youths burned a crudely built cross on an African American family's property, the city of St. Paul charged them with a misdemeanor under the ordinance. Because the ordinance was not content neutral, prohibiting speech "solely on the basis of the subjects [it] addresse[d]", the Court found it facially invalid under the First Amendment.[1408] The Court noted that a content-neutral ordinance could encompass the targeted behavior, but targeting specific content requires a law "narrowly tailored to serve compelling state interests" to withstand strict scrutiny.[1409] The Court acknowledged the city's compelling interest in ensuring the rights of groups historically subject to discrimination; however, because the ordinance targeted specific content when a content-neutral ordinance would have sufficed, it was not sufficiently tailored to meet that compelling interest.[1410]

532. A prevalent justification for employing the First Amendment to protect antisocial speech is the concept of a free "marketplace of ideas". A key component of the free marketplace of ideas is the expectation that socially beneficial ideas will persist in the face of competing views.[1411] The prominent American jurist Oliver Wendell Holmes's dissenting opinion in *Abrams v. United States* conceptualized the principle that "'truth' should emerge from the free and competitive exchange of ideas".[1412] Other Supreme Court justices have used this idea when discussing the bounds of First Amendment protection as well. Justice William Douglas, for

1405. *Ibid.*, at 446.
1406. *Ibid.*, at 448–449.
1407. *R.A.V. v. City of St. Paul*, 505 U.S. 377, 380 (1992). Cross burning evokes the violence the Ku Klux Klan has inflicted on African American communities since the nineteenth century.
1408. *Ibid.*, at 381, 391.
1409. *Ibid.*, at 395–396.
1410. *Ibid.*
1411. Joseph Blocher, *Institutions in the Marketplace of Ideas*, 57 Duke L.J. 821, 823–824 (2008).
1412. *Ibid.*, at 830; *Abrams v. United States*, 250 U.S. 616, 624, 630 (1919) (Holmes, J., dissenting).

example, expressed the idea that any form of censorship, even if directed against antisocial ideas, harmed the "market place [sic] of ideas" the First Amendment protects.[1413] For additional discussion, *see* Part XI (Religion and Culture), Chapter 4 (Religion and Public Debate).

§6. Free Speech at Public Universities

533. Universities, both public and private, sometimes implement speech codes to limit expression they deem undesirable. The rationale for such limitation is usually the protection of students from threatening, harassing speech and the fostering of a positive and safe learning environment. The trend in recent years has been for universities to be more restrictive of speech than in the past, to maintain what has been termed a "politically correct" environment—an environment some lament and others praise.[1414]

534. Public universities have less legal room to restrict student speech, including religious speech. According to the Department of Education's Office for Civil Rights, speech is only considered harassment when it is "sufficiently serious to deny or limit a student's ability to participate in or benefit from the educational program".[1415] Public universities, which are generally designated public forums, have a limited ability to enact speech codes that restrict individual speech and expression beyond reasonable time, place, and manner regulations. In *Roberts v. Haragan*, a law student filed a complaint against a public university's speech code that required students to obtain permission at least two days in advance before they could make a speech on campus, other than in designated "public forum areas".[1416] The student wanted to distribute literature and make a speech in an area of campus not designated as a public forum, to express his political and religious views that homosexuality was "a sinful, immoral, and unhealthy lifestyle".[1417] A federal district court acknowledged the need for order on a university campus and the university's legitimate interest in controlling some expressive activities, stating, "First Amendment protections should apply with less force on college campuses than in the community at large."[1418] However, the court held that the speech code was too broad,

1413. *United States v. Rumely*, 345 U.S. 41, 48, 56–57 (1953) (Douglas, J., with Black, J., concurring).

1414. *Compare* Bret Stephens, Opinion, *Diversity, Inclusion and Anti-Excellence*, N.Y. Times (Aug. 2, 2019), https://www.nytimes.com/2019/08/02/opinion/university-campus-diveristy-inclusion-free-speech.html (asserting that an emphasis on political correctness on US college campuses had eroded academia), *with* Opinion Letters, *College Campuses: Are They Too P.C.?*, N.Y. Times (Aug. 14, 2019), https://www.nytimes.com/2019/08/14/opinion/letters/college-diversity.html (featuring reader letters responding to Stephens's editorial), *and* Sally Kohn, *When Minorities Demand Equal Respect*, Atlantic (Nov. 13, 2015), https://www.theatlantic.com/politics/archive/2015/11/the-revealing-roots-of-political-correctness/415812 (asserting that "[p]olitical correctness is a good thing").

1415. Letter from Gerald Reynolds, Assistant Sec'y, Off. for C.R., Dep't of Educ., to "Colleague" (Jul. 28, 2003), https://www2.ed.gov/about/offices/list/ocr/firstamend.html.

1416. *Roberts v. Haragan*, 346 F. Supp. 2d 853, 866 (N.D. Tex. 2004).

1417. *Ibid.*, at 856.

1418. *Ibid.*, at 858, 870.

imposing "a burden on a substantial amount of expression".[1419] The court reasoned that "[t]he legitimacy of the University's concerns is not an absolute value, but rather it must be weighed relative to the student's rights it would suppress and the need to avoid a chilling effect on freedom of expression."[1420]

§7. Free Speech at Private Universities

535. Because private universities are not state actors, the First Amendment does not bar them from creating more restrictive speech codes.[1421] Private religiously affiliated schools in particular implement speech codes aligned with their "beliefs and mission", and most courts have upheld their restrictions.[1422] In disputes about private university speech codes, most courts have validated the codes because students agree to them on admission. Courts assume "[t]he basic legal relation between a student and a private university or college is contractual in nature."[1423] This prevailing understanding essentially holds that students "know what they are getting into" when they attend an institution with speech restrictions. Thus, because student agreement and attendance are voluntary, the codes do not violate free speech rights.[1424] Even California's "Leonard Law", which regulates private universities' ability to restrict personal expression, acknowledges the need for religious universities to implement religiously motivated speech codes, granting them an exemption.[1425] For further discussion on university speech codes, *see* this part, Chapter 7 (Non-discrimination), below.

§8. Religious Newspapers and Broadcast Companies

536. Religious groups are generally free to own and operate newspapers, radio stations, and television networks. As in other areas of the law related to the First Amendment, the government may not regulate speech based on what the speaker

1419. *Ibid.*, at 870; *see also DeJohn v. Temple Univ.*, 537 F.3d 301, 320 (3d Cir. 2008) (finding university sexual harassment policy, which prohibited certain expressive conduct "of a sexual or gender-motivated nature", was overbroad in violation of the Free Speech Clause); *Bair v. Shippensburg Univ.*, 280 F. Supp. 2d 357, 370 (M.D. Pa. 2003) (finding portion of university speech code that prohibited certain "acts of intolerance" was overbroad in violation of the Free Speech Clause).

1420. *Roberts*, 346 F. Supp. 2d at 872.

1421. Kelly Sarabyn, *Free Speech at Private Universities*, 39 J.L. & Educ. 145, 145 (2010).

1422. 3 Durham et al., *supra* n. 174, § 25:52 (*Speech Code Restrictions*).

1423. *Zumbrun v. Univ. of S. Cal.*, 101 Cal. Rptr. 499, 504 (Cal. Ct. App. 1972); *see also Ross v. Creighton Univ.*, 957 F.2d 410, 416 (7th Cir. 1992) (quoting *Zumbrun*); *Corso v. Creighton Univ.*, 731 F.2d 529, 531 (8th Cir. 1984) ("The relationship between a university and a student is contractual in nature.").

1424. *State of the Law: Speech Codes*, Found. for Individual Rts. in Educ., https://www.thefire.org/in-court/state-of-the-law-speech-codes (last visited Sep. 30, 2023).

1425. Cal. Educ. Code § 94367(c) (West 2022); *see* 3 Durham et al., *supra* n. 174, § 25:52 (*Speech Code Restrictions*).

has said or will likely say without using narrowly tailored means to meet a compelling state interest. Government action can rarely meet this burden. Content-neutral regulations, however, face a lower standard of legal scrutiny.

537. As discussed in section 2 of this chapter, above, the right of religious groups to publish their views through print has historic protection under the First Amendment, as affirmed in *Murdock v. Pennsylvania*, *Jones v. City of Opelika*, and *Cantwell v. Connecticut*.[1426] Radio and television, however, require broadcast licenses. Beginning with the Radio Act of 1927, Congress delegated the ability to grant broadcast licenses to a federal commission that eventually became the Federal Communications Commission (FCC).[1427] The criteria under which the FCC grants licenses is a primary area of legal controversy. The DC Circuit Court of Appeals held in *King's Garden v. FCC* that the FCC could require licensees to observe non-discriminatory hiring practices unless an exemption applied for "persons hired to espouse a particular religious philosophy over the air".[1428]

538. However, the FCC changed its non-discrimination policy in 1998, in accord with *Corporation of the Presiding Bishop of The Church of Jesus Christ of Latter-day Saints v. Amos*, which allowed religious discrimination by nonprofit religious organizations in hiring for nonreligious jobs.[1429] The FCC expanded regulations to "permit religious broadcasters to establish religious belief or affiliation as a job qualification for all station employees", not just those who would "espouse religious views over the air".[1430] The FCC emphasized that the policy change in no way permitted religious broadcasters to conduct employment discrimination on other bases, including race, color, national origin, or gender. In *Lutheran Church-Missouri Synod v. FCC*, also decided in 1998, the DC Circuit held that the FCC could not require a Lutheran radio station to observe diversity-based hiring practices.[1431] As a result, the FCC adopted new rules eschewing hiring quotas related to the composition of a broadcasting licensee's workforce; religious broadcasters filling a position with a religious qualification are still required, however, to make good faith efforts to recruit applicants without regard to race, color, national origin, or gender.[1432] For further discussion of religious print and broadcast media, *see* Part XI (Religion and Culture), Chapter 2 (Religion and Media).

1426. *See supra* paras. 520–524.
1427. 1 Durham et al., *supra* n. 157, § 4:40 (*Religious Broadcasting*).
1428. *See King's Garden, Inc. v. FCC*, 498 F.2d 51, 52–53 & n.1, 60–61 (D.C. Cir. 1974).
1429. *Corp. of the Presiding Bishop of The Church of Jesus Christ of Latter-day Saints v. Amos*, 483 U.S. 327 (1987).
1430. *In re Streamlining Broad. EEO Rule & Policies, Vacating the EEO Forfeiture Pol'y Statement & Amending Section 1.80 of the Comm'n's Rules to Include EEO Forfeiture Guidelines*, 13 FCC Rcd. 6322 at 2–3 (1998); 47 C.F.R. § 73.2080(a) (2022).
1431. *Lutheran Church-Mo. Synod v. FCC*, 154 F.3d 487 (D.C. Cir. 1998).
1432. *See In re Rev. of the Comm'n's Broad. & Cable Equal Emp. Opportunity Rules & Policies & Termination of the EEO Streamlining Proc.*, 2000 WL 45531 (FCC Jan. 20, 2000); 47 C.R.F. § 73.2080(c)(1).

§9. Content-Neutral Regulation of Speech

539. When regulating speech based on content, local, state, or federal government must narrowly tailor laws to serve a compelling state interest in order to survive "strict" constitutional scrutiny. In contrast, content-neutral regulations trigger a lower standard of constitutional scrutiny, allowing governments to regulate speech based on the time, place, and manner of expression.[1433] In the case of *Heffron v. International Society for Krishna Consciousness*, the Supreme Court held that content-neutral restrictions governing pavilions at the Minnesota State Fair did not violate the Krishna Society's right to express its religious beliefs.[1434] The regulation in question required that "any exhibitor conduct its sales, distribution, and fund solicitation operations" from a rented booth.[1435] The local Krishna Society argued that the regulation unconstitutionally burdened its free exercise by not permitting the Society to employ its preferred method of proselytization—handing out fliers and small gifts and soliciting donations while mingling with crowds. The Court noted that the rule did not prevent Society members from using alternative fora and means to express their beliefs, such as renting a booth, proselytizing outside of the fairgrounds, or wandering the fairgrounds and discussing their beliefs with attendees.[1436] Because the content-neutral regulation was the least restrictive means to serve the "substantial state interest" of managing crowd control, and because alternative fora for expression existed at the site, the regulation did not infringe on the Society's First Amendment rights.[1437]

§10. Limited Public Fora and Equal Access

540. A limited public forum exists where the government reserves a public facility or area and limits expressive activity to certain groups or types of speakers or to "the discussion of certain subjects".[1438] The government may not restrict speech in

1433. This lower standard is known as "intermediate scrutiny". While the US Supreme Court has not used or defined it as consistently as it has strict scrutiny, intermediate scrutiny generally requires the government to use *substantially* or *reasonably* tailored means to serve an *important* state interest. *See United States v. Virginia*, 518 U.S. 515, 566, 570–571 (1975) (Scalia, J., dissenting).

1434. *Heffron v. Int'l Soc'y for Krishna Consciousness*, 452 U.S. 640, 654–655 (1981); *see also* 1 Durham et al., *supra* n. 157, § 3:35 (*Neutral Time, Place, and Manner Restrictions*).

1435. *Heffron*, 452 U.S. at 643–644.

1436. *Ibid.*, at 654–655.

1437. *Ibid.*

1438. 16 Am. Jur. 2d *Constitutional Law* § 542 (*Limited Public Forums for Purposes of Free Speech and Press Protections*) n.2, Westlaw AMJUR CONSTLAW § 542 (database updated May 2023); *see also Walker v. Tex. Div., Sons of Confederate Veterans, Inc.*, 576 U.S. 200, 215–220 (2015) (holding state's vehicle license plates were not a limited public forum and state could refuse to issue plates with proposed designs); *Good News Club v. Milford Cent. Sch.*, 533 U.S. 98, 120 (2001) (holding public school violated Free Speech Clause by denying religious club access to school's limited public forum, based on its religious nature).

a limited public forum based on a speaker's viewpoint; it may restrict the discussion to certain topics, however, if such restrictions are "reasonable in light of the purpose served by the forum".[1439]

541. Constitutional doctrine concerning limited public fora is often implicated in cases involving religious student groups or extracurricular activities at public universities. For example, in *Widmar v. Vincent* the Supreme Court held that a public university can only exclude a group from a forum open generally to all student groups if it has a compelling interest achieved through a narrowly drawn regulation.[1440] *Widmar* arose when the University of Missouri at Kansas City, a public university, made its campus a limited public forum available to its student groups. The university also enacted a regulation prohibiting the use of university buildings for religious purposes, which effectively excluded use by religious student groups. A religious student group that had previously been permitted to meet on campus sued the university. The Supreme Court examined whether a state university can create an open forum and subsequently exclude student groups that intended to use the forum for religious worship or discussion. The Court struck down the university's regulation, holding that a content-neutral, open-forum policy that permitted religious student groups to use public university facilities would not constitute "excessive government entanglement with religion" or have the primary effect of advancing religion, in violation of the Establishment Clause.[1441] Because such a policy provided adequate protections under the Establishment Clause, the university's content-based regulation lacked a state interest compelling enough to override students' free exercise and free speech rights.[1442]

1439. *Good News Club*, 533 U.S. at 107 (quoting *Cornelius v. NAACP Legal Def. & Educ. Fund, Inc.*, 473 U.S. 788, 806 (1985)); 16 Am. Jur. 2d *Constitutional Law* § 542, *supra* n. 1438. Lower courts have split regarding the application of this doctrine to religious or anti-religious advertising in public transportation. *Compare Archdiocese of Wash. v. Wash. Metro. Area Transit Auth.*, 897 F.3d 314, 324, 331 (D.C. Cir. 2018) (finding transit policy that prohibited religious and anti-religious advertising "was consonant with recognition by the Supreme Court that the government has wide latitude to restrict subject matters … in a nonpublic forum as long as it maintains viewpoint neutrality and acts reasonably"), *with Ne. Pa. Freethought Soc'y v. Lackawanna Transit Sys.*, 938 F.3d 424, 435–437, 442 (3d 2019) (disagreeing with the DC Circuit's analysis in *Archdiocese of Washington* and holding government ban of religious and atheistic messages on public transportation constituted unreasonable viewpoint discrimination where content-based restriction did not restrict speech based on subject but instead distinguished between religious and secular views "on the same subjects"). *See also Iancu v. Brunetti*, 139 S. Ct. 2294, 2304, 2305–2306 (2019) (Breyer, J., concurring in part and dissenting in part) ("As for the concepts of 'viewpoint discrimination' and 'content discrimination,' I agree … that the boundaries between them may be difficult to discern.").

1440. *Widmar v. Vincent*, 454 U.S. 263, 269–270 (1981).

1441. *Ibid.*, at 270–275 (quoting *Lemon v. Kurtzman*, 403 U.S. 602, 612–613 (1971), *abrogated by Kennedy v. Bremerton Sch. Dist.*, 142 S. Ct. 2407, 2427–2428 (2022)), 272 n.11.

1442. *Ibid.*, at 275–277 (also noting the narrow basis for the Court's decision and emphasizing the university's ability to "establish reasonable time, place, and manner restrictions").

542. Board of Education v. Mergens addressed a similar issue in the context of a public secondary school. *Mergens* arose when a group of students tried to establish an after-school Christian club at a Nebraska high school.[1443] The school's policy on student clubs and organizations required after-school groups to have a faculty sponsor and prohibited sponsorship by religious or political groups. The school posited that student clubs were a component of the overall educational experience but that allowing a Christian club would violate the Establishment Clause. Because the high school received federal government funding, it was subject to Equal Access Act requirements. The Act requires that public secondary schools receiving federal funds not restrict access to limited public fora based on the "religious, political, philosophical, or other content" of student speech.[1444] Following the Court's reasoning in *Widmar*, a majority of the Court held that the Equal Access Act prohibited the school from denying students access to the school's limited public fora based on the content of their speech; a plurality opinion[1445] concluded that the Act did not violate the Establishment Clause.[1446] For additional discussion of *Mergens*, *see* Part IX (Education), Chapter 1 (Religious Education in Public and Private Schools).

543. Limited public fora may also exist in a non-physical space. *Rosenberger v. Rector and Visitors of the University of Virginia* involved the university's refusal to reimburse a student group's religiously oriented publication through student activity funds.[1447] The university had a policy that allowed recognized student groups to request and receive funds from their Student Activities Fund (SAF) for a wide range of purposes.[1448] Wide Awake Productions (WAP) was a qualified student group whose stated mission was to publish a Christian magazine that explored religious expression and experience on the university's campus.[1449] When WAP requested funds from the SAF to cover the cost of printing their publication, the university denied their request, stating that the publication was a "religious activity" and did not qualify for reimbursement under university guidelines.[1450] The Supreme Court concluded that SAF constituted a "metaphysical" public forum[1451] and, therefore, its restriction on religious speech was tantamount to viewpoint discrimination.[1452] It explained that "[t]he government must abstain from regulating speech when the specific motivating ideology or the opinion or perspective of the speaker is the rationale for the restriction."[1453] Furthermore, the Court emphasized that classifying and monitoring individual thought, speech, and expression is particularly dangerous "in the University setting, where the State acts against a background and tradition of

1443. *Bd. of Educ. v. Mergens*, 496 U.S. 226 (1990).
1444. *Ibid.*, at 235 (internal quotation marks omitted) (quoting 20 U.S.C. § 4071(a)).
1445. For an explanation of a plurality opinion, *see supra* n. 970; *see also* Kimura, *Legitimacy Model for the Interpretation of Plurality Decisions*, *infra* n. 1459, at 1595–1596.
1446. *Mergens*, 496 U.S. at 246–247. *But see ibid.*, at 258–291 (concurring and dissenting opinions discussing the adequacy of, or necessity for, the plurality opinion's Establishment Clause analysis).
1447. *Rosenberger v. Rector & Visitors of the Univ. of Va.*, 515 U.S. 819 (1995).
1448. *Ibid.*, at 824–825.
1449. *Ibid.*, at 825–826.
1450. *Ibid.*, at 825, 827.
1451. *Ibid.*, at 830.
1452. *Ibid.*, at 831, 845.
1453. *Ibid.*, at 829.

thought and experiment that is at the center of our intellectual and philosophic tradition".[1454] Similar to holdings in *Widmar* and *Mergens*, the Supreme Court held that the university could not exclude viewpoints without a compelling interest and that funding the publication did not implicate the Establishment Clause.[1455] For additional discussion of *Rosenberger* and the Establishment Clause, *see* this part, Chapter 7 (Non-discrimination), below.

544. The Court followed this line of reasoning again in *Good News Club v. Milford Central School.* In *Good News Club*, a public school district in New York State had a "community use policy adopting seven … purposes for which [a school] building could be used after school".[1456] None of those purposes included religious activities. The Good News Club applied to use school facilities after school to hold children's Bible classes, but its application was denied. The school district believed that, due to the school's receipt of government funds, allowing religious groups to meet in the building would violate the Establishment Clause.[1457] As in other cases involving limited public fora, the Supreme Court found that the school district wrongfully excluded the club based on viewpoint and that Establishment Clause concerns did not justify violation of the club's free speech rights.[1458] For additional discussion of *Good News Club*, *see* this part, Chapter 7 (Non-discrimination), below; and Part IX (Education), Chapter 1 (Religious Education in Public and Private Schools).

545. Although the Supreme Court has repeatedly found in favor of granting religious groups access to limited public fora, many of its opinions, including some discussed here, were not simple majority decisions. The prevailing opinion in some limited public fora cases garners the support of only a plurality[1459] of the justices. The Court's opinion in *Christian Legal Society v. Martinez* demonstrates the Court's unsure stance on the access public entities should grant religious groups to limited public fora. Hastings Law School established a registry of student organizations.

1454. *Ibid.*, at 835.

1455. *Ibid.*, at 831–846; *see also* cases cited *supra* n. 1439 (showing the circuit split on *Rosenberger*'s application to religious and atheist advertising on public transportation).

1456. *Good News Club v. Milford Cent. Sch.*, 533 U.S. 98, 102 (2001).

1457. *See ibid.*, at 112.

1458. *Ibid.*, at 111–113; *see also Matal v. Tam*, 137 S. Ct. 1744, 1763 (2017) (citing *Good News Club*, 533 U.S. at 106–107; *Rosenberger v. Rector & Visitors of the Univ. of Va.*, 515 U.S. 819, 830–831 (1995)). Lower courts have split regarding the application of *Rosenberger* and *Good News Club* to religious or anti-religious advertising in public transportation. *See* cases cited *supra* n. 1439.

1459. Ken Kimura explains that:

> [p]lurality decisions are unique because of a conceptual gap between the legal rule and the outcome. In 'simple majority' decisions, a numerical majority of Justices agree on both a single legal rule and a single outcome. On the other hand, in plurality decisions, no single legal rule carries the support of all of the concurring Justices. Instead, at least two coalitions of concurring Justices articulate different legal rules in an attempt to justify the same outcome. … The absence of a simple majority creates precedential uncertainty in plurality decisions.

Ken Kimura, Note, *Legitimacy Model for the Interpretation of Plurality Decisions*, 77 Cornell L. Rev. 1593, 1595–1596 (1992); *see also supra* n. 970.

Student organizations that met certain requirements, including compliance with a non-discrimination policy, received recognition, financial assistance paid out of mandatory student activity fees, and the ability to use school facilities for group functions.[1460] The law school denied the local chapter of the Christian Legal Society official recognition because the Society's religiously motivated bylaws opposed homosexuality. The Court's opinion addressed whether the Society's free exercise and free speech rights were violated when the law school denied it recognition. Although the school's registry of recognized organizations constituted a limited public forum, the Court found the non-discrimination policy was viewpoint neutral and thus, as applied to the Christian Legal Society, constitutional.[1461]

§11. PUBLIC FORA AND UNPOPULAR VIEWPOINTS

546. While expression in limited public fora can be restricted as to topic, expression in public fora cannot be limited. This opens the door to the expression of potentially offensive content by antisocial or socially unpopular groups. The case *Capitol Square Review and Advisory Board v. Pinette* arose when the Ku Klux Klan applied for a permit to display a cross on grounds near the Ohio state capitol building.[1462] While the display carried with it divisive political and social implications about race relations in the United States and the state of Ohio, the Supreme Court addressed only whether a permit to display a cross near the capitol building would violate the Establishment Cause.[1463] The Court's opinion noted that the state had permitted the display of Christmas trees and menorahs in the public space in the past. The Court also noted that the state could institute content-neutral time, place, and manner regulations to avoid misperceptions of official endorsement of religion. Ultimately, the Court concluded that because the religious expression in question was "purely private" and occurred in a designated public forum "open to all on equal terms", the cross display did not violate the Establishment Clause.[1464] For another discussion of *Capitol Square Review and Advisory Board v. Pinette, see* this part, Chapter 7 (Non-discrimination), below.

1460. *Christian Legal Soc'y Chapter of the Univ. of Cal. v. Martinez*, 561 U.S. 661, 669–671 (2010).

1461. *Ibid.*, at 697. *But see Fellowship of Christian Athletes v. San Jose Unified Sch. Dist. Bd. of Educ.*, 82 F.4th 664, 694–696 (9th Cir. 2023) (en banc) (distinguishing *Martinez* in finding that a district's all-comers policy, which prohibited discriminatory criteria for members and leaders of official student clubs, was "replete with exemptions that treat[ed] comparable secular groups more favourably" than a Christian club, failed strict scrutiny, and likely would not withstand Christian club's free exercise claim).

1462. *Capitol Square Rev. & Advisory Bd. v. Pinette*, 515 U.S. 753 (1995).

1463. *Ibid.*, at 759–760.

1464. *Ibid.*, at 770.

Chapter 4. Due Process Norms and Religious Groups

§1. Due Process under the Fifth and Fourteenth Amendments

547. The Fifth and Fourteenth Amendments to the US Constitution prohibit the federal and state governments, respectively, from depriving any person "of life, liberty, or property, without due process of law".[1465] Claiming roots back to the Magna Carta, the Due Process Clauses protect not only citizens but also foreign nationals residing in the United States, corporations, labor unions, and some business partnerships.[1466]

548. Due process is divided into two categories: procedural and substantive. Procedural due process is the government's responsibility to implement adequate procedures before a person's rights can be restricted. This includes providing notice that a right is in jeopardy and allowing an opportunity to be heard by an impartial judge.[1467] Substantive due process prohibits the government from infringing on certain fundamental rights, "no matter what process is provided, unless the infringement is narrowly tailored to serve a compelling state interest".[1468] These rights include those enumerated in the Constitution as well as others recognized by common law, such as the right to marry and to autonomously parent one's children.[1469]

1465. U.S. Const. amend. V; *ibid.*, amend. XIV, § 1.

1466. *Magna Carta*, cls. 29, 30 (1215), https://www.bl.uk/magna-carta/articles/magna-carta-english-translation (last visited Sep. 30, 2023) ("No free man shall be seized or imprisoned, or stripped of his rights or possessions, or outlawed or exiled, or deprived of his standing in any way, nor will we proceed with force against him, or send others to do so, except by the lawful judgment of his equals or by the law of the land. To no one will we sell, to no one deny or delay right or justice."); Rhonda Wasserman, *Procedural Due Process: A Reference Guide to the United States Constitution* 24–25 (2004). Enemy combatants inside or outside the United States are not granted due process but may submit a petition for writ of habeas corpus. *See Hamdi v. Rumsfeld*, 542 U.S. 507 (2004).

1467. *Goldberg v. Kelly*, 397 U.S. 254, 267, 270–271 (1970).

1468. *Reno v. Flores*, 507 U.S. 292, 301–302 (1993); *see also* Wasserman, *Procedural Due Process*, *supra* n. 1466, at 1.

1469. *See Troxel v. Granville*, 530 U.S. 57, 65–66 (2000) ("[T]he interests of parents in the care, custody, and control of their children … is perhaps the oldest of the fundamental liberty interests recognized by this Court."); *Zablocki v. Redhail*, 434 U.S. 374, 383–386 (1978) (collecting USSC cases recognizing the right to marry as fundamental). Courts have not responded favorably, however, to assertions of fundamental parenting and privacy rights when parents and students have raised challenges—including challenges based on religious belief—to policies that allow transgender students access to school bathrooms and locker rooms aligned with their gender identity. E.g., *Parents for Privacy v. Barr*, 949 F.3d 1210 (9th Cir. 2019); *Doe v. Boyertown Area Sch. Dist.*, 897 F.3d 518 (3d Cir. 2018).

§2. Application of Due Process to Religious Groups and Other Private Actors

549. Religious groups are not subject to the due process constraints that apply to state action or the activities of the federal government, state or local governments, or other instrumentalities of the state. They may condition membership on the acceptance of beliefs and practices (both prescribed and proscribed) and create their own procedures for the hiring of clergy, the admittance and excommunication of members, and other internal affairs. The government may only infringe on the practices, but not the beliefs, of religious groups when doing so is "not the object … but merely the incidental effect of a *generally applicable* and otherwise valid" statute and due process is adequately provided.[1470] For further discussion of church autonomy, *see* Part II (Religious Freedom in General), Chapter 2 (Collective Religious Freedom) and Chapter 3 (Organizational Religious Freedom); and this Part, Chapter 1 (Protection of Privacy), above.

550. The Constitution does not require due process of the private sector or religious groups, but employees who are represented by unions receive some protection by means of a "just cause" requirement coupled with an arbitration system; such systems represent only about 10% of the private sector.[1471] This form of due process, known as "industrial due process," differs from constitutional due process in that it is a collective right. This means that the union ultimately gets to decide whether a grievance will go through an arbitration process.[1472]

551. While the private sector is typically not required to provide due process, the actions of private actors may be entwined with the state in such a way that due process is required.[1473] In *Brentwood Academy v. Tennessee Secondary School Athletic Association*, the Supreme Court held that a statewide interscholastic association, which regulated athletic competitions between both public and private schools, was a state actor subject to Fourteenth Amendment scrutiny because state school officials were "pervasive[ly] entwine[d]" in the association's structure.[1474] The association's various committees were composed of principals, assistant principals, and superintendents representing member schools. No school, public or private, was forced to join the association, but as the state's sole interscholastic athletic coordinator, it "enjoy[ed] the memberships of almost all the State's public high schools …, far outnumbering the 55 private schools that belong[ed]", including religious private schools.[1475] Ultimately, the court held that the "close nexus" between the

---

1470. *Emp. Div., Dep't of Hum. Res. of Or. v. Smith*, 494 U.S. 872, 878 (1990) (emphasis added).

1471. Cynthia L. Estlund, *Free Speech and Due Process in the Workplace*, 71 Ind. L.J. 101, 136 (1995).

1472. *Ibid.*, at 138.

1473. *See Brentwood Acad. v. Tenn. Secondary Sch. Athletic Ass'n*, 531 U.S. 288, 295–298 (2001) (listing factors and examples of private entities qualifying as state actors); *see also Manhattan Cmty. Access Corp. v. Halleck*, 139 S. Ct. 1921, 1928 (2019) (listing the same).

1474. *Brentwood Acad.*, 531 U.S. at 291.

1475. *Ibid.*

state and the association meant that the association's "seemingly private behavior may be fairly treated as that of the State itself".[1476]

§3. Due Process under Statutory Law

552. Questions of due process may arise in the context of employment and enrolment in religiously affiliated schools. Unlike public schools, private schools enjoy certain exemptions under federal and state employment and anti-discrimination laws.[1477] A private school's liability is based on both contract and common law torts rather than federal and state law, and private school employees have a contract-based relationship with their employer.[1478] In accordance with the principles of contract law, a school may be required to complete payment of a contract if it is breached.[1479] But unless stated otherwise in a contract, a private school teacher is not entitled to contract renewal after a term ends or due process in the form of a hearing or proof of good cause.[1480]

553. Title 42, section 1983, of the US Code provides for a cause of action for any person who has been deprived of constitutional rights through state action. To file suit under section 1983 for deprivation of civil rights, the defendant must have acted "under color" of state law. Although some private schools receive federal funds to support scholarships and other academic programs, this funding alone does make school action "state action" for purposes of section 1983.[1481] In *Rendell-Baker v. Kohn*, the Supreme Court held that although a private school received almost 90% of its budget from the government, "the school's fiscal relationship with the State [was] not different from that of many contractors performing services for the government" and did not constitute the "symbiotic relationship" required to invoke the state action doctrine.[1482] Similarly, the fact that the school performed a "public function" in providing services for the public's benefit was not enough to make its actions "state action".[1483]

554. In a public education setting, a student who is expelled has a right to a formal hearing under the Due Process Clause of the federal or relevant state constitution.[1484] A student who is expelled or dismissed from a private learning institution

1476. *Ibid.*, at 295 (internal quotation marks omitted) (quoting *Jackson v. Metro. Edison Co.*, 419 U.S. 345, 351 (1974)).
1477. *See, e.g.*, *Petruska v. Gannon Univ.*, 462 F.3d 294, 303, 306–309 (3d Cir. 2006) (holding that the ministerial exception barred some employment-related claims made by a former chaplain against her former employer, a private Catholic university).
1478. *See* 3 Durham et al., *supra*, n. 174, § 25:57 (*Establishing a Religious Identity*).
1479. *See, e.g.*, *Dunn v. Bessie F. Hiern Sch., Inc.*, 209 So. 2d 538, 542 (La. Ct. App. 1968).
1480. *See, e.g.*, *Tichener v. Avery Coonley Sch.*, 350 N.E.2d 502, 508 (Ill. App. Ct. 1976).
1481. *Spark v. Cath. Univ. of Am.*, 510 F.2d 1277, 1282 (D.C. Cir. 1975).
1482. *Rendell-Baker v. Kohn*, 457 U.S. 830, 842–843 (1982).
1483. *Ibid.*, at 842.
1484. E.H. Schopler, Annotation, *Right of Student to Hearing on Charges Before Suspension or Expulsion from Educational Institution,* 58 A.L.R.2d 903 (1958).

has no constitutional basis for a claim of violation of due process, unless such a procedure was mentioned in an enrolment contract or student handbook.[1485] Because a private school is not a state actor, courts tend to inquire as to basic fairness, rather than standard due process, regarding the enforcement of their rules and regulations.[1486] Dismissed students bear the burden of proving that a private institution acted arbitrarily in their removal, but they may face the challenge of not having access to the source of the charge, the evidence that supports it, and the overall nature of the charge.[1487]

1485. *See Babcock v. New Orleans Baptist Theological Seminary*, 554 So. 2d 90, 95–98 (La. Ct. App. 1989). Many courts, but not all, "define[] the relationship between a private university and its students as contractual". *Oiyra v. Brigham Young Univ.*, No. 2:16-cv-01121-BSJ, 2020 WL 110280 (D. Utah Jan. 9, 2020) (citing courts with contrary holdings).

1486. *See Doe v. Brandeis Univ.*, 177 F. Supp. 3d 561, 602 (D. Mass. 2016); *Mu Chapter of Delta Kappa Epsilon v. Colgate Univ.*, 578 N.Y.S.2d 713, 715 (N.Y. App. Div. 1992); *Gorman v. St. Raphael Acad.*, 853 A.2d 28, 37–38 (R.I. 2004).

1487. *See* Warren A. Seavey, Comment, *Dismissal of Students: "Due Process"*, 70 Harv. L. Rev. 1406, 1409 (1957).

Chapter 5. Professional Secrecy

§1. Introduction

555. In general, communications between clergy and the members of a religious organization are privileged when made in confidence by the penitent. Privileged information is confidential information protected by the law. The priest- or clergy-penitent privilege governs reporting obligations, the disclosure of confidential information, and testimony of those involved in legal proceedings. Each state determines the scope of the privilege, and variations among states can have a profound impact on the exercise of the privilege. These variations include regulations and interpretations about who has or is protected by the privilege and, thus, who can waive it, and what types of communications are protected under what conditions.[1488]

556. The protection of the priest-penitent privilege is an extension of the Free Exercise Clause.[1489] It stems from the concept of confessional privilege—the idea that, for individuals to be able to freely confess sinful behaviors and thoughts, and to receive guidance to correct them, individuals must trust that their confessions to a spiritual counselor will remain confidential.[1490] It is also considered vital to spiritual leaders' ability to freely "exercise [their] religion in a priestly function".[1491] Privileged communication between a religious leader and a follower is treated similarly in the law to privileged communication between an attorney and a client.

557. In the exercise of privilege, it is the content of the communication that is deemed privileged. For a communication to be privileged, the giver must intend the communication to be confidential, the intent of the giver must be reasonable, and the giver must maintain the confidentiality of that communication.[1492]

558. The communication continues to be privileged unless the privilege is waived. Waiving the privilege can occur by express waiver or by certain actions that imply grant of a waiver. For example, if the giver shares the privileged information with a third party who is neither the receiver nor the receiver's agent, the information is no longer privileged.[1493]

1488. *See* 2 Durham et al., *supra* n. 535, § 20:5 (*Chart: State-by-State Summary of Reporting Laws and Clergy Privilege*), § 20:11 (*Summary of State Clergy-Penitent Privilege Laws*). *See generally* Child Welfare Info. Gateway, *Clergy as Mandatory Reporters of Child Abuse and Neglect*, *supra* n. 1226.
1489. U.S. Const. amend. I.
1490. *See* 2 Durham et al., *supra* n. 535, § 20:9 (*The Clergy-Penitent Privilege*) (citing *Mockaitis v. Harcleroad*, 104 F.3d 1522, 1530–1531 (9th Cir 1997), *overruled on other grounds by City of Boerne v. Flores*, 521 U.S. 507 (1997)); *People v. Phillips*, 1 W. L. J. 109 (N.Y. Ct. Gen. Sess. 1813) (holding in an early, seminal case that the Free Exercise Clause did not allow the state to compel a priest to disclose information obtained in a confession).
1491. *Mockaitis*, 104 F.3d at 1530.
1492. 2 Durham et al., *supra* n. 535, § 20:8 (*History of Privileges*).
1493. *Ibid.*

559. Normally, the public would have a right to all evidence obtained by rational means. But courts and legislatures have noted that there is a "public good" in protecting communications between penitents and spiritual advisors because penitents are seeking to reform themselves. Because that public good derogates public interest in obtaining the truth, however, the privilege is often construed strictly.[1494] The clergy-penitent privilege is explained further in Sections 2 through 4, below; for additional discussion, *see also* Part I (Legal Framework and Sources), Chapter 2 (Other Legislation with Regard to Religion); and this Part, Chapter 1 (Protection of Privacy), above.

§2. Basic Protections and State Variances

560. Clergy-penitent privilege is codified in all fifty states.[1495] Nuances in state law may affect which types of communications are deemed privileged. Some states require that the communication be of a confessional nature. In other words, if the communication is sufficiently casual, or does not pertain to some profession of guilt or a request for forgiveness, the communication may not be protected.[1496]

561. While laws differ by state, generally communications are privileged if a member of a congregation or religious society communicates personally to a spiritual leader (acting in a professional capacity as one who advises on spiritual matters) in confidence in a religious context. Communications with a minister that do not relate to seeking spiritual advice or with a minister who was not acting as an advisor in a professional capacity will generally not be privileged.

562. A religious organization cannot invoke the privilege to protect institutional communication, as only natural persons can exercise this privilege.[1497]

563. Each state defines who is entitled to the priest-penitent privilege. When there is a question as to whether a particular position within a religious organization qualifies as clergy for purposes of the privilege, courts look to the language of the statute.[1498] When the issue is whether an individual who is not considered a religious functionary may claim the privilege, courts look to the denomination's doctrine and the individual's role.[1499] This means that, in general, courts will defer to the religious organization's definition of who is a spiritual leader.

1494. *Ibid.*, § 20:9 (*The Clergy-Penitent Privilege*) (quoting *People v. Edwards*, 248 Cal. Rptr. 53, 55–56 (Cal. Ct. App. 1988)).

1495. *Ibid.*, § 20:11 (*Summary of State Clergy-Penitent Privilege Laws*).

1496. *Ibid.*

1497. *Ibid.*, § 20:9 (*The Clergy-Penitent Privilege*) (citing *United States v. Luther*, 481 F.2d 429, 432 (9th Cir. 1973)).

1498. 2 David M. Greenwald, Michele L. Slachetka & Caroline L. Meneau, Testimonial Privileges § 6:5 (3d ed.), Westlaw PRIVILEGES (database updated Feb. 2023).

1499. *Ibid.*; *see, e.g., Corp. of the President of The Church of Jesus Christ of Latter-day Saints v. Cardinal*, No. 2 CA-SA 2022-0047, 2022 WL 17727582, at *3–4 (Ariz. Ct. App. Dec. 15, 2022), *review denied* (Ariz. Apr. 7, 2023) (unpublished).

564. For example, in one case, the Texas Court of Appeals looked to legislative definitions to determine whether a police officer who served as a church youth director and teacher was considered clergy while carrying out police duties. In Texas, "[a] member of the clergy may be a religious functionary similar to a minister, priest, rabbi, or an accredited Christian Science practitioner, or a person that the consulting individual believes is a 'religious functionary.'"[1500] In this case, the accused had known the police officer as a church youth leader and had attended weekly religious classes taught by the officer prior to being escorted by the officer and another officer to the police station, where he confessed to committing a crime. The court ruled that, because the accused did not "reasonably believe[the police officer] was acting as a religious functionary" at the station, the communication was not privileged.[1501] The court found that the parties' discussion did not concern church business and that their discussion of God or religion did "not automatically elevate the conversation to privileged communication".[1502]

§3. Assertion of Privilege

565. The manner in which privilege is claimed also varies among states. In some states, both the penitent and the clergy member may invoke the privilege. That is, the penitent and clergy member may refuse to disclose privileged information independent of the other claiming the privilege. For example, California's statute "provides the penitent with a privilege to refuse to disclose, and to prevent another from disclosing, a penitential communication".[1503] But it also "provides the clergyman with a privilege in his own right. Moreover, he may claim this privilege even if the penitent has waived the privilege granted him by [statute]."[1504]

566. In many states, the penitent can assert the privilege to prevent the minister from disclosing any content of the communication, and the clergy member may only claim the privilege on behalf of the penitent. If the privilege is not claimed, it will likely be unavailable on appeal, and if the penitent has waived the privilege, then the minister can no longer claim it.[1505]

567. In New Jersey, the privilege belongs to both the clergy member and the penitent. When the communication relates to a "future criminal act", the clergy member "may, but is not required to, waive the privilege", without the penitent's consent.[1506]

568. Usually, the presence of a third party during the communication will negate the claim of privilege, but each state determines which third parties do not void the

1500. *Snyder v. State*, 68 S.W.3d 671, 674 (Tex. Ct. App. 2000).
1501. *Ibid.*, at 676.
1502. *Ibid.*, at 675.
1503. Cal. Evid. Code § 1033 Law Rev. Comm'n Comments (West 2023).
1504. *Ibid.*, § 1034 Law Rev. Comm'n Comments.
1505. *See, e.g.*, Fla. Stat. § 90.505 (2022).
1506. N.J. Stat. Ann. § 2A:84A-23(2) (West 2022).

privilege. If the penitent were a minor, for example, and a parent were present for the communication, the parent would not be considered a third party sufficient to nullify the privilege. Also, essential administrative assistants present for the confidential communications would not eliminate the privilege. But if the penitent were to repeat the confessional communication to a third party, that would void the privilege on the penitent's behalf.[1507]

§4. Child Abuse Reporting Statutes

569. In general, clergy must report when they have reasonable cause to believe or have observed that a child has been neglected or abused. But while most states mandate that clergy report suspected or known abuse, these reporting obligations usually do not apply to privileged information received by clergy in confidence in their official capacity as a religious adviser.[1508]

570. Six states do require clergy to report reasonable belief of child abuse, despite the otherwise privileged nature of the communication.[1509] If clergy fail to report the abuse according to the applicable state requirements, they may face criminal liability. In some states, the victim in an abuse case may have a civil cause of action against a clergy member who had a duty to report and failed to do so.[1510]

571. In some states, the priest-penitent exemption from child abuse reporting only applies to clergy and does not exempt other members of the religious organization in other types of leadership roles from the duty to report known or suspected child abuse: for example, child care providers, teachers and other school staff, doctors, mental health professionals, or others who care for or manage the care of children.[1511] For more on laws mandating reporting of child abuse and their intersection with the priest-penitent privilege, *see* this part, Chapter 1 (Protection of Privacy), above.

1507. 2 Durham et al., *supra* n. 535, § 20:8 (*History of Privileges*).

1508. *Ibid.*, § 20:5 (*Chart: State-by-State Summary of Reporting Laws and Clergy Privilege*), § 20:11 (*Summary of State Clergy-Penitent Privilege Laws*). *See generally* Child Welfare Info. Gateway, *Clergy as Mandatory Reporters of Child Abuse and Neglect*, *supra* n. 1226. *See also, e.g.*, *Corp. of the President of The Church of Jesus Christ of Latter-day Saints v. Cardinal*, No. 2 CA-SA 2022-0047, 2022 WL 17727582 (Ariz. Ct. App. Dec. 15, 2022), *review denied* (Ariz. Apr. 7, 2023) (unpublished).

1509. New Hampshire, North Carolina, Oklahoma, Rhode Island, Texas, and West Virginia. 2 Durham et al., *supra* n. 535, § 20:11 (*Summary of State Clergy-Penitent Privilege Laws*); Child Welfare Info. Gateway, *Clergy as Mandatory Reporters of Child Abuse and Neglect*, *supra* n. 1226, at 3.

1510. 2 Durham et al., *supra* n. 535, § 20:4 (*Duty to Report*).

1511. *See* Child Welfare Info. Gateway, *Mandatory Reporters of Child Abuse and Neglect*, *supra* n. 1226, at 2.

Chapter 6. Medical Deontology

§1. Abortion

I. Constitutional Abortion Rights

572. In 1973, in *Roe v. Wade*, the US Supreme Court upheld the right to abortion as part of a constitutional right to privacy implicit in the First, Fourth, Fifth, Ninth, and Fourteenth Amendments.[1512] The Court held that a woman's right to an abortion could only be limited on the basis of a compelling state interest, including protecting maternal health and the life of the unborn child. It determined that these rights were not compelling enough during the first trimester, thus barring state intervention in a woman's decision to have an abortion during that period. The Court reasoned, however, that during the second trimester a state could "regulate abortion to the extent that the regulation reasonably relate[d] to the preservation and protection of maternal health".[1513] The Court held that during the third trimester, which the Court determined was the measuring stick for fetal viability, the state interest in protecting the fetus became compelling and the state could prohibit abortions except when abortion was necessary to protect maternal life or health.[1514]

573. *Roe*'s analytical, trimester-based regime was altered by the Supreme Court nearly two decades later in *Planned Parenthood of Southeastern Pennsylvania v. Casey.*[1515] Whereas the Court in *Roe* focused on the right to abortion as a privacy right, the Court in *Casey* found the right to abortion to be a substantive due process right under the Fourteenth Amendment.[1516] *Casey* maintained *Roe*'s essential proposition that the state may not interfere with a woman's ultimate decision to terminate her pregnancy prior to viability because "the State's interests are not strong enough to support prohibition of abortion or imposition of a substantial obstacle to a woman's right to elect the procedure".[1517] However, the Court determined that the "undue burden" test, rather than *Roe*'s trimester framework, should be used to evaluate abortion restrictions before viability.[1518] The Court explained that, under this test, "[a]n undue burden exists, and therefore a provision of law is invalid, if its purpose or effect is to place substantial obstacles in the path of a woman seeking an abortion before the fetus attains viability."[1519]

574. In 2022, in *Dobbs v. Jackson Women's Health Organization*, a conservative-majority Supreme Court considered the constitutionality of a Mississippi law that banned abortions before fetal viability, at 15 weeks, with exceptions

1512. *Roe v. Wade*, 410 U.S. 113, 151–154 (1973).
1513. *Ibid.*, at 163.
1514. *Ibid.*, at 160, 163–164.
1515. *Planned Parenthood of Se. Pa. v. Casey*, 505 U.S. 833 (1992).
1516. *Ibid.*, at 846.
1517. *Ibid.*
1518. *Ibid.*, at 876.
1519. *Ibid.*, at 837.

for medical emergencies and "severe fetal abnormality".[1520] In a controversial opinion, the Court overruled *Roe* and *Casey*, concluding that both decisions erred in finding a basis for the right to abortion in the US Constitution.[1521] Finding no constitutional foundation for abortion rights, the Court held that "the authority to regulate abortion must be returned to the people and their elected representatives", thus making abortion a state issue.

575. The immediate aftermath of the *Dobbs* decision has been a chaotic legal landscape. In at least ten states, restrictive "trigger laws" enacted prior to *Dobbs* went into near-immediate effect with the overturning of *Roe* and *Casey*;[1522] such laws, deemed unconstitutional under *Roe*, were kept "on the books" by state lawmakers in anticipation of *Roe* being overruled. In general, these trigger laws ban abortion with few or no exceptions; some impose civil penalties or criminal penalties or both.[1523] Many states have enacted new laws post-*Dobbs*, some guaranteeing the right to abortion and expanding access to abortion care, and others severely restricting abortion or banning it outright.[1524] Courts in some states have interpreted their state constitutions to protect abortion as a fundamental or privacy right.[1525] In some states, trigger bans coexist with earlier or later laws, leading to confusion over conflicting terminology or provisions.[1526]

576. For example, Texas has numerous laws on its books restricting abortion, some of which pre-date *Roe* while others are more recent. In 2021, Texas passed SB 8, which prohibits physicians from performing or inducing an abortion "if the physician detected a fetal heartbeat" (at or after about six weeks), with an exception for undefined "medical emergencies".[1527] SB 8 directs enforcement through suits brought by private citizens, rather than through criminal prosecutions or civil

---

1520. *Dobbs v. Jackson Women's Health Org.*, 142 S. Ct. 2228 (2022).

1521. *Ibid.*, at 2242–2243. *Dobbs* also abrogated several decisions, including decisions where the Supreme Court had found that state laws unconstitutionally burdened a woman's right to choose an abortion where laws required abortion providers to maintain admitting privileges at local hospitals and required abortion facilities to meet ambulatory surgical center standards. *Ibid.*; *see Whole Woman's Health v. Hellerstedt*, 579 U.S. 582 (2016); *June Med. Servs. LLC v. Russo*, 140 S. Ct. 2103 (2020) (plurality opinion).

1522. *See After* Roe *Fell: Abortion Laws by State*, *supra* n. 1183; *see, e.g.*, Idaho Code § 18-622 (setting forth law criminalizing abortion, "to become effective thirty (30) days following ... [t]he issuance of the judgment in any decision of the United States supreme court that restores to the states their authority to prohibit abortion").

1523. *After* Roe *Fell: Abortion Laws by State*, *supra* n. 1183.

1524. *Ibid. Compare* H.F. 1, 93d Gen. Assem., Reg. Sess. (Minn. 2023) (enacting post-*Dobbs* statutory right of "reproductive freedom" in Minnesota), *with* S.B. 1, 122d Leg., 1st Spec. Sess. (Ind. 2022) (enacting in Indiana a post-*Dobbs* statutory ban on abortions, excepting where the life or health of the mother is in danger, where rape or incest caused the pregnancy (up to ten weeks), or where a lethal fetal anomaly exists (up to 20 weeks)).

1525. *See supra* para. 453 and accompanying footnotes.

1526. *See, e.g.*, *Texas Abortion Ban Emergency Exceptions Case*: Zuraski v. State of Texas, Ctr. for Reproductive Rts. (Mar. 6, 2023), https://reproductiverights.org/case/zurawski-v-texas-abortion-emergency-exceptions/zurawski-v-texas (discussing suit requesting that Texas "clarify the scope" of the term "medical emergency" in its abortion laws).

1527. Tex. Health & Safety Code Ann. §§ 171.204 to .205 (West 2023); *Whole Woman's Health v. Jackson*, 142 S. Ct. 522, 530 (2021).

actions by state officials. Parties who bring a suit, alleging violation of the law by patients or providers, earn USD 10,000 if their suit is successful.[1528] This novel enforcement system has been criticized as state-sanctioned vigilantism.[1529] Texas also passed a trigger law in 2021 that bans abortion outright, with an exception for the life and health of the mother, and allows for criminal and civil penalties.[1530] Other, more targeted statutes—aimed at restricting abortion facilities and providers, for example—contribute to the complexity of Texas abortion laws.[1531]

577. In the post-*Dobbs* era, trigger laws, new laws, and state constitutional provisions are being challenged in and interpreted by the courts.[1532] Thus, significant uncertainty exists regarding the exact contours of state laws and how state laws will interact to affect access to abortion services and abortifacients (medications that induce abortion) across the United States. In the meantime, public discussions of abortion remain politically and religiously charged. For additional discussion of the role of religion in public debates on abortion, *see* Part V (Religion and Politics), Chapter 1 (Religious Influence in Politics); and Part XI (Religion and Culture), Chapter 4 (Religion and Public Debate).

II. Conscientious Objection to Abortion

A. *Federal Protections for Conscientious Objection to Abortion*

578. Since the *Roe* decision in 1973, the US Congress has passed several pieces of legislation protecting those who have religious or other conscientious objections to performing or facilitating abortion. These laws focus primarily on controversial areas of reproductive health and non-discrimination laws meant to protect those who object to participation in abortion on any grounds.

579. The Church Amendment of 1973 (named after its sponsor, Senator Frank Church) safeguards private facilities receiving healthcare-related federal funding from being required to (1) participate in abortion and sterilization procedures or (2) make facilities or personnel available where entities or personnel have moral or religious objections to those procedures.[1533] It also prohibits hospitals from engaging in employment discrimination against doctors or other medical personnel who object to participating in those procedures.[1534]

1528. *See* Tex. Health & Safety Code Ann. § 171.208 (West 2023).
1529. E.g., R. Alta Charo, *Vigilante Injustice—Deputizing and Weaponizing the Public to Stop Abortions*, N. Eng. J. Med. (Oct. 14, 2021), https://www.nejm.org/doi/full/10.1056/NEJMp2114886.
1530. Tex. Health & Safety Code Ann. §§ 170A.001 to .007 (West 2023).
1531. *See After* Roe *Fell: Abortion Laws by State*, *supra* n. 1183.
1532. *See ibid.*
1533. Enacted as part of the Health Programs Extension Act of 1973. Pub. L. No. 93-45, § 401, 87 Stat. 91, 95 (codified as amended at 42 U.S.C. § 300a-7 (2018)).
1534. 42 U.S.C. § 3001-7(c) (2018).

580. The Hyde Amendment, first passed in 1976, affords additional protection by denying funding to government grant recipients that discriminate against institutions or individuals exercising conscientious objection to their own participation in abortion.[1535]

581. The Danforth Amendment, adopted by Congress in 1996, further protects entities that refuse to provide training for abortions. Federal, state, and local governments may not discriminate against healthcare entities that refuse to provide or undergo abortion training, perform abortions, or provide referrals for training or abortions.[1536]

582. In 1997, Congress extended conscientious objection protections to companies that pay for medical care. These "managed care plans" may not restrict the ability of healthcare professionals to discuss the full range of treatment options with their patients (including contraception or abortion). But a managed care plan may refuse to provide, reimburse, or provide coverage of counselling or referral services if it objects to the service on moral or religious grounds.[1537]

583. The Weldon Amendment, first passed in 2005, prevents the federal Departments of Labor, Health and Human Services, and Education from subjecting "any institutional or individual health care entity to discrimination on the basis that the health care entity [including physicians, hospitals, health insurance plans, etc.] does not provide, pay for, provide coverage of, or refer for abortions".[1538]

584. Similarly, the 2010 Patient Protection and Affordable Care Act (ACA) prevents health plans that participate in the Act's health insurance exchange program from discriminating against healthcare providers or facilities that do not "provide, pay for, provide coverage of, or refer for abortions".[1539]

585. In 2013, the National Defense Authorization Act endorsed the protection of religious freedom and conscience rights of chaplains and other military personnel.[1540] Unless doing so would adversely affect "military readiness, unit cohesion, and good order and discipline", the armed forces are charged with accommodating

1535. Pub. L. No. 94-439, § 209, 90 Stat. 1418, 1434 (1976). Since 1976, the Hyde Amendment has been re-enacted each year as part of an annual appropriations bill, but its language has varied. *See* Edward C. Liu & Wen W. Shen, Cong. Rsch. Serv., IF 12167, The Hyde Amendment: An Overview (Jul. 20, 2022), https://crsreports.congress.gov/product/pdf/IF/IF12167.

1536. Omnibus Consolidated Recissions and Appropriations Act of 1996, Pub. L. No. 104-134, § 515, 110 Stat. 1321, 1321-245 (codified as amended at 42 U.S.C. § 238n).

1537. Balanced Budget Act of 1997, Pub. L. No. 105-33, §§ 1852(j)(3)(B), 4704(b)(3)(B), 11 Stat. 251, 295, 496 (codified as amended at 42 U.S.C. §§ 1395w-22(j)(3)(B), 1396u-2(b)(3)(B)).

1538. *See, e.g.*, Consolidated Appropriations Act of 2005, Pub. L. No. 108-447, div. F, § 508(d), 118 Stat. 2809, 3163; *see also* 45 C.F.R. § 88.3(c) (2022). Since 2005, the Weldon Amendment has been incorporated by reference or readopted into the departments' annual appropriations act.

1539. Patient Protection and Affordable Care Act, Pub. L. No. 111-148, § 1303, 124 Stat. 119, 168–171 (2010) (codified at 42 U.S.C. § 18023).

1540. *See* National Defense Authorization Act for Fiscal Year 2013, Pub. L. No. 112-239, § 533, 126 Stat. 1632, 1727.

members' expression of "sincerely held conscience, moral principles, or religious beliefs" and may not base adverse personnel actions or assignments on such expression.[1541] In addition, the armed forces may not require chaplains to perform rites, rituals, or ceremonies contrary to their beliefs, nor may the armed forces discriminate against chaplains for refusing to perform such functions based on belief.[1542] These rights for military personnel and chaplains are broad in scope and extend to objections to providing abortion-related services.

B. State Protections for Conscientious Objection to Abortion Services

586. Forty-six states have statutes providing some form of protection for healthcare providers who refuse to participate in abortion services.[1543] In each of these states, *individual* healthcare providers may refuse to provide abortion services. Only two of these states do not provide the same option to *institutional* healthcare providers. A conscientious objection exemption is limited to private institutions in thirteen states. California is the only state that limits the exemption to religious healthcare institutions.[1544]

§2. CONTRACEPTION

I. Constitutional Contraception Rights

587. In 1965, the US Supreme Court held in *Griswold v. Connecticut* that laws prohibiting married couples from using birth control violated a "zone of [marital] privacy created by several fundamental constitutional guarantees".[1545] Two years later, in *Eisenstadt v. Baird*, the Supreme Court held that a state law prohibiting single individuals from obtaining contraceptives, while permitting married couples to obtain them, violated the Equal Protection Clause of the Fourteenth Amendment.[1546] The Court's 2022 decision in *Dobbs v. Jackson Women's Health Organization* held that *Roe v. Wade* and *Casey v. Planned Parenthood* erred in finding a constitutional basis for abortion, as a privacy right and a substantive due process right, respectively.[1547] The majority opinion asserted that nothing in *Dobbs* "should be understood to cast doubt on precedents that do not concern abortion", including

1541. Dep't of Def., DoD Instruction 1300.17, Religious Liberty in the Military Services 4–5 (Sep. 1, 2020), https://www.esd.whs.mil/Portals/54/Documents/DD/issuances/dodi/130017p.pdf.
1542. Dep't of Def., DoD Instruction 1304.28, The Appointment and Service of Chaplains 4 (May 12, 2021), https://www.esd.whs.mil/Portals/54/Documents/DD/issuances/dodi/130428p.pdf.
1543. *See supra* para. 154 and accompanying footnotes.
1544. *State Laws and Policies: Refusing to Provide Health Services*, *supra* n. 378.
1545. *Griswold v. Connecticut*, 381 U.S. 479, 485–486 (1965).
1546. *Eisenstadt v. Baird*, 405 U.S. 438, 443 (1972).
1547. *Dobbs v. Jackson Women's Health Org.*, 142 S. Ct. 2228 (2022).

Griswold and *Eisenstadt*.[1548] It distinguished the abortion cases as uniquely involving the destruction of "potential life".[1549] Nevertheless, the dissenting opinion warned that *Dobbs could*—and the concurring opinion encouraged that *Dobbs should*—lead to the overruling of *Griswold*, *Eisenstadt*, and other opinions with similar reasoning.[1550]

II. Conscientious Objection to Provision of Contraceptives

A. *General Background: Contraceptives and Abortifacients*

588. Conscientious objection to provision of contraceptives has become a larger issue since the development of emergency contraceptives. Some consider emergency contraception (which is taken post-intercourse to prevent pregnancy) to be equivalent to abortion or abortifacients (which terminate an established pregnancy). Medically and legally, however, they are distinguished.

589. In 1997, the Food and Drug Administration (FDA), the federal agency responsible for approving pharmaceuticals, approved a prescription emergency contraception pill (the "morning-after pill"). The morning-after pill became available over the counter (without a prescription required) in 2006. The Supreme Court's 2022 decision in *Dobbs v. Jackson Women's Health Organization* gave states the power to determine access to or restrictions on abortion.[1551] After *Dobbs*, the FDA clarified that forms of emergency contraception, such as the morning-after pill, are not abortifacients.[1552] Accordingly, emergency contraception has remained legal in all fifty states.

590. In 2000, the FDA approved the use of the abortifacients mifepristone and misoprostol, taken together to medically induce early abortion (up to ten weeks). Post-*Dobbs*, in 2023, the FDA lifted some restrictions on access to abortifacients, allowing individuals to obtain them from retail pharmacies, not just from physicians. However, access to abortifacients post-*Dobbs* has been more challenged and restricted by states than access to emergency contraceptives.[1553] States that now ban

1548. *Ibid.*, at 2277–2278, 2280.
1549. *Ibid.*, at 2256–2258.
1550. *See ibid.*, at 2317, 2319 (Breyer, J., with Sotomayor and Kagan, JJ., dissenting) (warning that the majority's reasoning in overruling *Roe* and *Casey* logically leads to the overruling of *Griswold*, *Eisenstadt* and similar cases); *ibid.*, at 2300, 2301–2302 (Thomas, J., concurring) (asserting that *Griswold* and other cases should be reconsidered because their foundation in substantive due process is "demonstrably erroneous").
1551. *Ibid.*, at 2283–2284.
1552. *Plan B One-Step (1.5 Levonorgestrel) Information*, U.S. Food & Drug Admin. (Dec. 23, 2022), https://www.fda.gov/drugs/postmarket-drug-safety-information-patients-and-providers/plan-b-one-step-15-mg-levonorgestrel-information.
1553. *See, e.g.*, *Danco Labs., LLC v. All. for Hippocratic Med.*, 143 S. Ct. 1075 (2023) (mem.) (putting a hold on a lower court order, which would have suspended FDA approval of mifepristone and made the drug unavailable, until federal courts could reach a final decision in a case questioning the drug's safety).

abortion procedures also ban residents' access to abortifacients; some other states have restricted access to abortifacients prior to ten weeks, require that a patient obtain them directly from a physician, and/or require that they be administered in-person by a physician.[1554]

591. Because the United States does not maintain a universal, public health care system, health insurance costs are borne largely by employers and educational institutions, which work with private insurance companies to offer various insurance plans to employees and students. This system naturally results in gaps in health care coverage. In 2010, the United States adopted the Patient Protection and Affordable Care Act (ACA), which requires all US citizens to obtain health insurance, while providing some subsidies. To facilitate access to insurance, the ACA requires states to establish health insurance exchanges, also known as "marketplaces", where residents and small businesses can purchase private health insurance (or obtain public insurance coverage when applicable).[1555] One of the ACA's provisions requires health insurance plans to provide contraceptives without cost to employees.[1556]

B. The Affordable Care Act's Contraceptive Mandate

592. Final rules issued under the Affordable Care Act clarified that the Act's "contraceptive mandate" exempted group health plans of "religious employers" from having to provide coverage for contraceptive services.[1557] The definition of "religious employer" for purposes of the exemption is an organization that is organized and operates as a nonprofit entity including "churches, their integrated auxiliaries, and conventions or associations of churches".[1558] A house of worship is exempt even if it provides charitable social services to, or employs, persons of different religious faiths.[1559]

593. The final rules of the Act also provided an accommodation for other qualifying nonprofit religious organizations that object on religious grounds to providing contraceptive services coverage.[1560] Such organizations must opt out of coverage through a process of self-certification or by informing the Department of Health and Human Services of their religious objections in writing.[1561]

1554. *See State Laws and Policies: Medication Abortion*, Guttmacher Inst., https://www.guttmacher.org/state-policy/explore/medication-abortion (last updated Aug. 31, 2023).
1555. Patient Protection and Affordable Care Act, Pub. L. No. 111-148, 124 Stat. 119 (2010) (codified as amended in scattered sections of 21, 25, 26, 29, and 42 U.S.C. (2018)); *see also* 26 U.S.C. § 5000A (2018); Vanessa C. Forsberg, Cong. Rsch. Serv., R44065, Overview of Health Insurance Exchanges (Mar. 17, 2023), https://sgp.fas.org/crs/misc/R44065.pdf.
1556. 42 U.S.C. § 300gg-13(a)(4) (2018); 45 C.F.R. § 147.130(a)(1)(iv); 29 C.F.R. § 2590.715-2713(a)(1)(iv); 26 C.F.R. § 54.9815-2713(a)(1)(iv) (2022).
1557. 45 C.F.R. §§ 147.130(a)(1)(iv), 147.131(c)(1), 147.132(a)(1).
1558. 26 U.S.C. § 6033(a)(3)(A)(i).
1559. *See* 45 C.F.R. § 147.132(a)(1), (a)(2).
1560. *Ibid.*, §§ 147.131(c)(1), 147.132(a)(1).
1561. *Ibid.*, § 147.131(c), (d); *see also* Coverage of Certain Preventive Services under the Affordable Care Act, 80 Fed. Reg. 41318, 41337 (Jul. 14, 2015) (providing means for organizations to notify

594. In the 2014 case *Burwell v. Hobby Lobby Stores, Inc.*, the US Supreme Court held that, under the Religious Freedom Restoration Act (RFRA), the government must exempt for-profit, closely held companies from providing health insurance coverage for methods of contraception that violate the sincerely held religious beliefs of the companies' owners.[1562] For additional discussion of this case, *see* Part I (Legal Framework and Sources), Chapter 2 (Other Legislation with Regard to Religion); Part II (Religious Freedom in General), Chapter 2 (Collective Religious Freedom); and Part III (Legal Status of Religious Communities), Chapter 4 (Contractual Religious Freedom).

595. In 2017, federal agencies promulgated rules widening exemptions to the contraceptive mandate to include private employers opposed to providing contraception on either religious or "moral" grounds.[1563] These more expansive exemptions were upheld in 2020 by the Supreme Court in *Little Sisters of the Poor v. Pennsylvania*.[1564] In early 2023, however, President Joe Biden's administration announced a proposed rule that would retain the religious exemption but eliminate the moral exemption for private health plans and insurers.[1565]

596. Since the ACA's passage, amendments and regulatory changes to the Act's contraceptive and individual mandates have given rise to numerous court challenges. For additional discussion of the ACA, *see* Part I (Legal Framework and Sources), Chapter 2 (Other Legislation with Regard to Religion).

C. Conscientious Objection Protections: Contraceptives to Federal Employees

597. The Financial Services and General Government Appropriations Act, passed annually, includes a provision exempting religious health plans from a Federal Employees Health Benefits (FEHB) program mandate that requires participating health plans to provide contraceptive coverage. A provision also protects individuals who object to prescribing or providing contraceptives on moral or religious grounds from discrimination by any FEHB health plans.[1566]

HHS directly of their eligibility for an exemption to the contraceptive mandate, responding, in part, to *Wheaton College v. Burwell*, 573 U.S. 958 (2014)).

1562. *Burwell v. Hobby Lobby Stores, Inc.*, 134 S. Ct. 2751 (2014).

1563. Religious Exemptions and Accommodations for Coverage of Certain Preventive Services under the Affordable Care Act, 82 Fed. Reg. 47792, 47838 (Oct. 13, 2017) (codified at 45 C.F.R. pt. 147 (2022)).

1564. *Little Sisters of the Poor Saints Peter & Paul Home v. Pennsylvania*, 140 S. Ct. 2367 (2020).

1565. Coverage of Certain Preventive Services under the Affordable Care Act, 88 Fed. Reg. 7236, 7236 (proposed Feb. 2, 2023) (to be codified at 26 C.F.R. pt. 54; 29 C.F.R. pt. 2590; 45 C.F.R. pt. 147, 156).

1566. *See, e.g.*, Consolidated and Further Continuing Appropriations Act, 2015, Pub. L. No. 113-235, div. E, tit. VII, § 726, 128 Stat. 2130, 2385.

598. A separate provision affirms Congress's intent that a "conscience clause" protecting religious beliefs and moral convictions be part of any contraceptive mandate in the District of Columbia.[1567] Other than this specific provision regarding Washington, DC, Congress has largely left protection of religious objections to contraceptives in the hands of the states.

D. State Protections for Conscientious Objection to Contraceptives

599. Most states do not have laws explicitly providing exemptions for pharmacists or pharmacies who conscientiously object to dispensing contraceptives. In fact, some states maintain "duty to dispense" laws; New Jersey, for example, requires pharmacies to fill any legal prescriptions "without undue delay, despite any conflicts … due to sincerely held moral, philosophical or religious beliefs".[1568] A small but growing number of states, however, have codified conscience clauses protecting pharmacists who object to providing contraceptives or other medications on religious, moral, or ethical grounds.[1569] In 2022, the pharmacy administrative codes of eleven states contained conscience clauses, up from five states in 2006.[1570] Conscience clauses also appear in the broader health- or pharmacy-related statutory or regulatory schemes of several other states.[1571] These clauses vary widely: some apply explicitly to emergency contraception and abortion,[1572] some urge or require pharmacists to notify their employers of their objections in advance,[1573] and some contain "language intended to protect patients' rights to access healthcare" where accommodation is made for a pharmacist's beliefs.[1574]

§3. Assisted Reproductive Technologies

600. Assisted reproductive technologies (ART) refers to fertility treatments where sperm and/or ova (gametes) are handled outside of the body, including in vitro fertilization, intrauterine insemination, cryopreserved embryos, and surrogacy.

1567. *See, e.g.*, Pub. L. No. 113-235, div. E, tit. VIII, § 808, 128 Stat. 2394. The US Constitution mandates that the US Congress maintains jurisdiction over the District of Columbia (Washington, DC). U.S. Const. art. I, § 3, cl. 17.
1568. N.J. Stat. Ann. § 45:14-67.1 (West 2022).
1569. Achey & Robertson, *Conscientious Object: A Review of State Pharmacy Laws and Regulations*, *supra* n. 379, at 268.
1570. *Ibid.*
1571. *Ibid.*; *State Laws and Policies: Refusing to Provide Health Services*, *supra* n. 378.
1572. E.g., Kan. Stat. Ann § 65-443 (2022) (allowing pharmacists in Kansas to refuse to participate in "the prescription or administration of any device or drug which result in the termination of a pregnancy or an effect of which the person reasonably believes may result in the termination of a pregnancy").
1573. E.g., 216 R.I. Admin. Code § 40-15-1.16 (West 2022) (requiring licensed pharmacists in Rhode Island to notify pharmacy owners in writing of the drugs or devices they object to dispensing).
1574. E.g., 24 Del. Admin. Code § 2500-3.0 (3.1.2.4) (2022) (requiring supervising pharmacists in Delaware to "establish procedures … that maintain standard of practice" if another pharmacist conscientiously objects to dispensing a pharmaceutical); Achey & Robertson, *Conscientious Object: A Review of State Pharmacy Laws and Regulations*, *supra* n. 379, at 269.

ART is highly regulated at the state and federal levels and by a number of self-regulating professional societies.[1575] The ethics and morals associated with ART and related practices remain topics of public debate in the United States. Because ART involves the creation of life, which many view as divinely appointed, religious views are part of the public discussion. *See also* Part V (Religion and Politics), Chapter 1 (Religious Influence in Politics); and Part XI (Religion and Culture), Chapter 4 (Religion and Public Debate).

I. Federal Law

601. Three federal agencies regulate ART. The Centers for Disease Control and Prevention (CDC) is charged with collecting and publishing data on ART procedures. The Food and Drug Administration (FDA) "controls approval and use of drugs, biological products, and medical devices", in addition to having "jurisdiction over the screening and testing of reproductive tissues".[1576] And the Centers for Medicare and Medicaid Services (CMS) is responsible for ensuring laboratory testing standards are met.

602. The Clinical Laboratory Improvement Amendments of 1988 (CLIA) established standards for clinical laboratory testing performed on human specimens, as regulated by the CMS.[1577] In 1992, Congress enacted the Fertility Clinic Success Rate and Certification Act, which established standard definitions and mandated that all ART clinics provide the CDC with data for all procedures performed.[1578]

II. State Law

603. State laws vary widely on the enforceability of gestational carrier or surrogacy agreements, but many have adopted all or parts of the Uniform Parentage Act (UPA)[1579] as state law governing the use of ART. The Model Act Governing Assisted Reproductive Technology attempts to foster national consensus on ART legal issues unresolved by the UPA; while the Model Act does not have the force of law, it provides states with an additional framework for regulating legal rights and

---

1575. *See generally* Am. Soc'y for Reprod. Med., *Oversight of Assisted Reproductive Technology* (2021), https://www.asrm.org/about-us/media-and-public-affairs/public-affairs/oversight-of-assisted-reproductive-technology (link to PDF).

1576. *Ibid.*, at 3.

1577. Clinical Laboratory Improvement Amendments of 1988 (CLIA), Pub. L. No. 100-578, 102 Stat. 2903 (1988) (codified as amended at 42 U.S.C. § 263a (2018)).

1578. Fertility Clinic Success Rate and Certification Act of 1992, Pub. L. No. 102-493, § 2, 106 Stat. 3146, 3146 (codified at 42 U.S.C. § 263a-1 (2018)).

1579. Unif. Parentage Act (Nat'l Conf. of Comm'rs on Unif. State L. 2017); *see also Parentage Act*, Unif. L. Comm'n, https://www.uniformlaws.org/committees/community-home?CommunityKey=c4f37d2d-4d20-4be0-8256-22dd73af068f (last visited Sep. 30, 2023) (showing map of states that have enacted or introduced versions of the UPA).

obligations.[1580] The majority of issues arising from ART involve determining the legal parentage of children resulting from assisted insemination[1581] or surrogacy.[1582]

A. *Artificial Insemination*

604. Assisted insemination is the transfer of sperm to a woman's uterus or cervix using a device such as a syringe. To protect sperm donors, many states have enacted statutes providing that "if the sperm is given to a licensed physician for use in a woman other than the man's wife, then the sperm donor is not [legally] the father of the resulting child".[1583] However, because the procedure does not necessarily require a medical professional, paternity and other legal issues can arise when the sperm is provided directly to the woman.[1584]

B. *Surrogacy*

605. Under the UPA, parties to a state-recognized surrogacy agreement must follow a process much like adoption.[1585] This includes meeting age requirements, completing medical evaluations, participating in mental health consultations, and having independent legal representation throughout the agreement.[1586] Some states have adopted modified versions of the UPA, customizing certain requirements for persons pursuing surrogacy.[1587] UPA provisions extended only to heterosexual couples prior to *Obergefell v. Hodges*, the 2015 US Supreme Court decision finding a constitutional right to same-sex marriage.[1588] For surrogacy agreements, this meant that

1580. Model Act Governing Assisted Reproductive Tech. (Am. Bar Ass'n 2019); *see Assisted Reproductive Technologies*, 20 Geo. J. Gender & L. 313, 318 (Jenna Casolo et al. eds., 2019).
1581. *See, e.g.*, *Jhordan C. v. Mary K.*, 224 Cal. Rptr. 530 (Cal. Ct. App. 1986); *E.E. v. O.M.G.R.*, 20 A.3d 1171 (N.J. Super. Ct. Ch. Div. 2011).
1582. *See, e.g.*, *In re Baby M*, 537 A.2d 1227 (N.J. 1988); *see also, e.g.*, (all codes current through 2022) Colo. Rev. Stat. § 15-11-121; Fla. Stat. § 742.16; N.D. Cent. Code § 30.1-04-20; N.H. Rev. Stat. Ann. § 168-B:16; Tex. Fam. Code Ann. § 160.755; Utah Code § 78B-15-803; Va. Code Ann. § 20-160.
1583. Kristine S. Knaplund, *Assisted Reproductive Technology: The Legal Issues*, Prob. & Prop., Mar./Apr. 2014, 48, 49.
1584. *See Jhordan C.*, 224 Cal. Rptr. at 531 (holding that a donor who donates semen directly to a woman for artificial insemination, rather than through a licensed physician, may be declared the resulting child's father in a paternity action); *E.E.*, 20 A.3d at 1177 (holding the same).
1585. *See* Unif. Parentage Act § 803 cmt. (2017).
1586. *Ibid.*, § 802 & cmt.
1587. *Compare, e.g.*, Tex. Fam. Code Ann. § 160.755 (West 2022) (requiring judicial approval of the surrogacy agreement), *and* Utah Code § 78B-15-803 (2022) (requiring the same), *with* Fla. Stat. § 742.16 (2022) (requiring commissioning couple to seek judicial affirmation of parental status within three days after the child's birth); *see also* Utah Code § 78B-15-801 (requiring one intended parent to be a genetic parent for agreement to be enforceable against the gestational carrier).
1588. *See, e.g.*, Unif. Parentage Act § 801(b) (2002) ("The man and woman who are the intended parents must both be parties to the gestational agreement."); *see also Obergefell v. Hodges*, 576 U.S. 644 (2015).

a court in a UPA-adopted state would not validate the agreement of same-sex couples and the gestational carrier would legally be the child's mother.[1589] In response to *Obergefell* and a related Supreme Court case ensuring the recognition of same-sex couples as parents on their children's birth certificates,[1590] UPA provisions were revised in 2017 to apply equally to same-sex couples and their children.[1591] In light of these US Supreme Court decisions, at least one state supreme court has struck down a pre-2017 UPA discriminatory surrogacy provision as unconstitutional, while retaining the remainder of the old UPA statute.[1592]

606. Notwithstanding the UPA and Model Act, actual state statutes and common law vary widely, from statutory unenforceability of surrogacy at one extreme, to legalization of compensated surrogacy at the other, with some states still silent on the matter in both statute and case law.[1593]

C. In Vitro Fertilization

607. In vitro fertilization (IVF) requires extracting sperm from a man and ova from a woman and combining them in a laboratory. This embryo is then implanted into the woman's uterus by a medical professional. Because the procedure requires the assistance of licensed medical professionals and written agreements are required, legal issues are less common; however, issues regarding parentage may arise in cases where donated sperm or ova are used.[1594] Legal issues also arise when a relationship dissolves and "custody" of embryos is contested.[1595]

1589. *See* Unif. Parentage Act § 809.

1590. *Pavan v. Smith*, 137 S. Ct. 2075, 2078–2079 (2017).

1591. Unif. Parentage Act Prefatory Note (2017). In addition, some UPA provisions now differentiate between gestational and genetic surrogacy agreements. *Ibid.*, art. 8 cmt.

1592. *In re Gestational Agreement*, 2019 UT 40, ¶¶ 50–55, 449 P.3d 69 (Utah 2019).

1593. *See, e.g.*, N.Y. Dom. Rel. § 122 (McKinney 2022) ("Genetic surrogate parenting agreements are hereby declared contrary to the public policy of this state, and are void and unenforceable."); *ibid.*, § 123 (establishing penalties for arranging a genetic surrogacy for compensation: maximum USD 10,000 fine and forfeiture of the compensation for the first offense and criminal felony charge for the second offense); N.H. Rev. Stat. Ann. § 168.B-11 (2022) (allowing for "reasonable compensation" to gestational carriers); Wash. Rev. Code §§ 26.26A.700 to 26.26A.730 (2022) (reflecting 2019 repeal of § 26.26.230, which allowed "altruistic" surrogacy only, thereby implicitly providing for and regulating compensated surrogacy); Wyo. Stat. Ann. § 14-2-4-403(d) ("This act does not authorize or prohibit [a surrogacy agreement] … ."). *See generally Surrogacy Laws by State*, Legal Pro. Grp.: Am. Soc'y Reproductive Med., https://connect.asrm.org/lpg/resources/surrogacy-by-state?ssopc=1 (last visited Sep. 30, 2023).

1594. Knaplund, *Assisted Reproductive Technology*, *supra* n. 1583, at 49.

1595. *See* Jenny Gross & Maria Cramer, *The Latest Issue in Divorces: Who Gets the Embryos?*, N.Y. Times (Apr. 3, 2021), https://www.nytimes.com/2021/04/03/health/IVF-frozen-embryo-disputes.html.

D. Exemptions for Religious Organizations and Other Limits to Access

608. Nineteen states require a form of insurance coverage for some infertility treatments; eight of those states permit exemptions for religious institutions whose religious or moral beliefs conflict with assisted reproductive technologies.[1596] Religious exemptions apply either to issuers of health insurance plans or to employers to whom plans are issued—or, in some states, to both.[1597] Other states, such as Minnesota and Oklahoma, have limited access to infertility services for people who receive public medical assistance by explicitly excluding fertility drugs from their public medical assistance programs.[1598] Some states more generally limit access to infertility-related services to all recipients of Medicaid, the state children's health insurance program, or other state medical assistance programs.[1599]

§4. Stem Cell Research

609. While no federal laws ban stem cell research outright, federal laws do limit its funding and use. In 1996, President Bill Clinton accepted the general recommendation from the National Institutes of Health (NIH) Human Embryo Research Panel to fund embryo research, but shortly thereafter, the newly elected Congress passed the Dickey-Wicker Amendment. The Amendment forbade the funding of "the creation of a human embryo or embryos for research purposes; or [for] research in which a human embryo or embryos are destroyed, discarded, or knowingly subjected to risk of injury or death greater than that allowed for research on fetuses in utero [under the relevant human subjects protection regulations]".[1600]

610. In 1998, debates surrounding this issue intensified when US researchers derived stem cells from human embryos for the first time.

1596. California, Colorado, Connecticut, Delaware, Illinois, Maryland, New Jersey, and Texas allow for religious exemptions. *See* (all codes current through 2022) Cal. Health & Safety Code § 1374.55; Colo. Rev. Stat. § 10-16-104; Conn. Gen. Stat. §§ 38a-509, 38a-536; Del. Code Ann. tit. 18, § 3556; 215 Ill. Comp. Stat. 5/356m; Md. Code Ann., Ins. § 15-810; N.J. Stat. Ann. §§ 17:48-6x, 17:48A-7w, 17:48E-35.22, 17B:27-46.1x, 26:2J-4.23; Tex. Ins. Code Ann. § 1366.006. *See generally Insurance Coverage by State*, Resolve: Nat'l Infertility Ass'n, https://resolve.org/learn/financial-resources-for-family-building/insurance-coverage/insurance-coverage-by-state (last visited Sep. 30, 2023); *State and Territory Infertility Insurance Laws*, Am. Soc'y for Reproductive Med.: ReproductiveFacts.org, https://www.reproductivefacts.org/patient-advocacy/state-and-territory-infertility-insurance-laws (last visited Sep. 30, 2023).

1597. *See, e.g.*, Cal. Health & Safety Code § 1374.55(e)–(f) (West 2022) (providing religious exemptions for both issuers of plans and employers). Connecticut allows individuals to request a policy or rider that excludes such services due to their religious or moral beliefs. Conn. Gen. Stat. §§ 38a-509(c)(2), 38a-536(c)(2) (2022).

1598. Minn. Stat. § 256B.0625, subdiv. 13 (2022); Okla. Stat. tit. 56, § 204 (2022).

1599. *See, e.g.*, (all provisions current through 2022) Mont. Admin. R. 37.85.207; N.J. Stat. Ann. §§ 17:48-6x, 17:48A-7w, 17:48E-35.22, 17B:27-46.1x, 26:2J-4.23; Ohio Admin. Code § 5160-2-03; 62 Pa. Cons. Stat. § 443.6; R.I. Gen. Laws §23-13-21.

1600. Balanced Budget Downpayment Act, Pub. L. No. 104-99, § 128, 110 Stat. 26, 34 (1996).

611. Before the issue could be addressed by President Clinton or Congress, President George W. Bush became president. In 2001, President Bush issued a statement announcing new guidelines that federal funds were not to be used to create incentives to destroy, clone, or create living embryos for purposes of research.[1601] The statement limited federal funding of stem cell research to non-embryonic stem cell research and funding of embryonic stem cell research to stem cell lines in existence before August 9, 2001. The statement was implemented by executive order in 2007.[1602]

612. In 2009, President Barack Obama issued an executive order revoking President Bush's statement and executive order, thereby removing the previous administration's restrictions on funding and developing stem cell research.[1603] During the administration of President Donald Trump, federal agencies began eliminating funding and changing policies, moving toward prohibition of research dependent on the acquisition of human fetal tissue from elective abortions, citing a priority to "promot[e] the dignity of human life from conception to natural death".[1604] Under the administration of President Joe Biden, the NIH reversed course, effectually restoring Obama-era policies and guidelines.[1605]

613. In 2011, two scientists challenged the NIH's funding of embryonic stem cell research, made legal under President Obama's 2009 executive order, citing the Dickey-Wicker Amendment as valid authority restricting these actions. A federal court of appeals held that the Amendment was ambiguous and the NIH had reasonably interpreted the Amendment to prohibit federal funding of the destruction of embryos but permit federal funding of embryonic stem cell research.[1606]

§5. Right to Object to Medical Procedures and Vaccines for Self and Minors

614. The right of an adult to object to medical treatment has both constitutional and common law foundations and is generally accepted. However, the right for parents or individuals acting *in loco parentis* to object on behalf of minors, or for minors to object on their own, is less clear. This issue is particularly acute when

1601. *See* Press Release, White House Off. of the Press Sec'y, Fact Sheet: Embryonic Stem Cell Research (Aug. 9, 2001), https://georgewbush-whitehouse.archives.gov/news/releases/2001/08/20010809-1.html.
1602. Exec. Order No. 13435, 72 Fed. Reg. 34591 (Jun. 20, 2007).
1603. Exec. Order No. 13505, 74 Fed. Reg. 10667 (Mar. 9, 2009).
1604. Establishment of Safeguards and Program Integrity Requirements for Health and Human Services-Funded Extramural Research Involving Human Fetal Tissue, 86 Fed. Reg. 2615, 2615 (proposed Jan. 13, 2021).
1605. *See* Off. of the Dir., Nat'l Insts. of Pub. Health, Notice No. NOT-OD-21-111, Update on Changes to NIH Requirements Regarding Proposed Human Fetal Tissue Research (Apr. 16, 2021), https://grants.nih.gov/grants/guide/notice-files/NOT-OD-21-111.html.
1606. *Sherley v. Sebelius*, 644 F.3d 388, 394–397 (D.C. Cir. 2011).

minors are unable to make decisions for themselves. In general, states and the courts take a more active role in determining when adults *must* obtain medical care for children.[1607]

615. More specific issues arise when parents refuse medical help on behalf of their children due to religious beliefs. At the federal level, the Child Abuse Prevention and Treatment Act (CAPTA) was amended to clarify that no federal requirement exists for parents or legal guardians to provide medical services or treatments for a child contrary to their religious beliefs.[1608] Moreover, thirty-one states and the District of Columbia have laws protecting from criminal liability parents who fail to provide medical care to a child because of their religious beliefs.[1609] However, these protections are not always absolute. Indeed, some state laws establish that religious belief alone cannot be a basis for criminal liability but also allow courts to compel medical treatment "when the health of the child so requires".[1610] Wide discrepancies exist in court decisions regarding the validity of religious exemptions in such cases. Most decisions focus on the ailment of the child, the type of procedure in question, and/or the risk to the child with or without preventive or remedial measures.[1611]

616. Congress originally passed CAPTA in 1974, seeking a uniform approach to child abuse. The Act delegated responsibility to the Department of Health, Education, and Welfare (now Health and Human Services) to draft regulations on religious exemption policies. From 1974 to 1983, when the regulations were changed, the Department required states to adopt religious exemptions before they could receive federal funding for child-protection programs. Religious exemptions are no longer federally required but, as discussed above, remain standard state practice.

1607. *See* Baruch Gitlin, Annotation, *Parents' Criminal Liability for Failure to Provide Medical Attention to Their Children*, 118 A.L.R.5th 253 (2004); George L. Blum, Annotation, *Criminal Liability of Nonparent for Failure to Obtain Medical Treatment for Minor Based on Duty of One Acting in Loco Parentis*, 97 A.L.R.6th 539 (2014).

1608. Child Abuse Prevention and Treatment Act (CAPTA), Pub. L. No. 93-247, 88 Stat. 4 (1974), *amended by* Pub. L. No. 104-235, § 115, 110 Stat. 3063, 3078–3079 (1996) (current version at 42 U.S.C. § 5106i (2018)) (providing a carve-out for states to pursue legal remedies to compel medical interventions in cases of "life threatening conditions" and to "prevent or remedy serious harm to the child").

1609. Children's Bureau, Child Welfare Info. Gateway, Dep't of Heath & Hum. Servs., *Definitions of Child Abuse and Neglect* 6 (May 2022), https://www.childwelfare.gov/topics/systemwide/laws-policies/statutes/define (link to PDF).

1610. *See, e.g.*, Ala. Code § 26-14-7.2(a) (2022); Fla. Stat. § 39.01(50) (2022).

1611. *Compare, e.g.*, *In re Willmann*, 493 N.E.2d 1380, 1389–1390 (Ohio Ct. App. 1986) (affirming finding that state should assume guardianship of seven-year-old child with an aggressive, life-threatening form of cancer "because the faith of the parents, as firm and clear as it is, does not permit them, under the law of this state and the nation, to expose [their child] to progressive ill health and death" by refusing treatment), *with People in Interest of D.L.E.*, 614 P.2d 873 (Colo. 1980) (vacating a lower court order that had declared a child a dependent of the state when his mother refused medical treatment, reasoning that the child's life was not "in imminent danger through lack of medical care" and the proposed treatment was potentially dangerous, with serious side effects).

617. Even given the general right to object to medical treatment, state and local vaccine mandates have historically been upheld by US courts, weighing public health interests over personal liberty interests.[1612] However, state and local laws generally allow for exemptions, for medical, religious, or other reasons.[1613] For example, while all fifty states have specific immunization requirements for school children, forty-four states allow for exemptions based on religious and/or philosophical beliefs.[1614] Many states also have vaccination requirements for healthcare workers; only two of those states do not allow for religious or philosophical exemptions.[1615] Although laws have long allowed for such exemptions, to date the Supreme Court has not held that the Constitution requires religious exemptions to vaccine mandates.[1616] Prior to the twenty-first century, those who sought religious exemptions from vaccine mandates were largely members of minority sects who eschewed medical interventions.[1617] By 2021, when COVID-19 vaccines became widely available, several factors led Americans—particularly conservative Christians—to request religious exemptions to vaccine mandates in unprecedented numbers. These factors included the novelty of the vaccine, growing distrust of vaccines and government generally, and the fact that some vaccines available in the United States were developed using fetal cell lines.[1618]

1612. *See, e.g.*, *Jacobson v. Massachusetts*, 197 U.S. 11, 29 (1905) ("[I]n every well-ordered society charged with the duty of conserving the safety of its members the rights of the individual in respect of his liberty may at times, under the pressure of great dangers, be subjected to such restraint, to be enforced by reasonable regulations, as the safety of the general public may demand."); *Zucht v. King*, 260 U.S. 174, 176–177 (2022) (relying on *Jacobson* in holding that a city could make vaccinations compulsory for school children, under government's "broad discretion required for the protection of public health").

1613. *See, e.g.*, *Jacobson*, 197 U.S. at 39 (indicating that exemptions to vaccine mandates are appropriate for medically "unfit" subjects).

1614. California, Connecticut, Maine, Mississippi, New York, and West Virginia do not. *See States with Religious and Philosophical Exemptions from School Immunization Requirements*, NCSL, https://www.ncsl.org/research/health/school-immunization-exemption-state-laws.aspx (last updated Aug. 3, 2023).

1615. Maine and Rhode Island. *See* 10-144-264 Me. Code R. § 3 (LexisNexis 2022); Me. Stat. tit. 22 § 802.4.B (West 2022); 216 R.I. Code R. § 20-15-7.6.1A (LexisNexis 2022). In May 2023, New York announced it would repeal COVID-19 vaccine requirements for healthcare workers, which had not included religious exemptions and had been challenged in the courts.

1616. *See, e.g.*, *Does 1–3 v. Mills*, 142 S. Ct. 17 (2021) (mem.) (denying application for injunction of Maine's immunization mandate for healthcare workers, which does not include a religious exemption). *But see ibid.*, at 19, 21 (Gorsuch, J., with Thomas and Alito, JJ., dissenting) (asserting that injunctive relief should be granted, that Maine's vaccine mandate with no religious exemption should be subject to strict scrutiny, and that the state failed to use the least restrictive means available to achieve its compelling interest of slowing the spread of COVID-19).

1617. However, the founder of the most prominent of such sects, the Christian Science movement, counseled members, "Rather than quarrel over being vaccinated, I recommend that, if the law demand an individual to submit to this process, he obey the law; and then appeal to the gospel to save him from any bad results." *Vaccination: What Did Eddy Say?* (Dec. 20, 2020), Mary Baker Eddy Libr., https://www.marybakereddylibrary.org/research/what-did-eddy-say-about-vaccination.

1618. *See Religious Identities and the Race Against the Virus: American Attitudes on Vaccination Mandates and Religious Exemptions (Wave 3)*, PRRI (Dec. 9, 2021), https://www.prri.org/research/

618. Vaccine mandates in the United States have been imposed in the private sector and in the public sector at local, state, and federal levels. In the private sector, larger employers who impose vaccine mandates for employees must abide by Title VII of the Civil Rights Act, which prohibits religious discrimination.[1619] Title VII requires that employers of more than fifteen employees make reasonable accommodation for religious objections unless doing so would pose an undue hardship on business operations.[1620] In the public sector, a state or local vaccine mandate generally must have a rational basis, requiring that the mandate be reasonably related to a legitimate state interest.[1621] Some Supreme Court justices have asserted in minority opinions that strict scrutiny should apply to state vaccine mandates that allow for exemptions but not religious exemptions.[1622] To date, however, the Court has not issued a majority opinion concluding the same. In early 2022, the Supreme Court considered whether challenged federal COVID-19 vaccine mandates,[1623] which allowed for religious exemptions, should remain in effect while litigation

---

religious-identities-and-the-race-against-the-virus-american-attitudes-on-vaccination-mandates-and-religious-exemptions; Ruth Graham, *Vaccine Resisters Seek Religious Exemptions. But What Counts as Religious?*, N.Y. Times (Sep. 15, 2021), https://www.nytimes.com/2021/09/11/us/covid-vaccine-religion-exemption.html.

1619. 42 U.S.C. § 2000e-2 (2018).

1620. *Ibid.*, § 2000e(j). Suggested "reasonable accommodation" in the context of the COVID-19 pandemic included telework options, for example. *See What You Should Know about COVID-19, the ADA, the Rehabilitation Act, and Other EEO Laws*, § K.12 (*Title VII and COVID-19 Vaccinations*), § L (*Vaccinations—Title VII and Religious Objections to COVID-19 Mandates*), U.S. Equal Emp. Opportunity Comm'n, https://www.eeoc.gov/wysk/what-you-should-know-about-covid-19-and-ada-rehabilitation-act-and-other-eeo-laws#L (last updated May 15, 2023).

1621. *See, e.g.*, *Jacobson v. Massachusetts*, 197 U.S. 11, 25–29 (1905); *Roman Cath. Diocese of Brooklyn v. Cuomo*, 141 S. Ct. 63, 69, 70 (2020) (Gorsuch, J., concurring) (noting that the Court "essentially applied rational basis review" to the state vaccine mandate challenge in *Jacobson*); *Klassen v. Trs. of Ind. Univ.*, 7 F.4th 592, 593 (7th Cir. 2021) (citing *Jacobson* in applying rational basis review to state university students' vaccine mandate challenge); *Norris v. Stanley*, 567 F. Supp. 3d 818, 821–822 (W.D. Mich. 2021) (doing the same in state university employees' vaccine mandate challenge).

1622. *See Does 1–3 v. Mills*, 142 S. Ct. 17, 19, 21 (2021) (mem.) (Gorsuch, J., with Thomas and Alito, JJ., dissenting) (asserting that a Maine law mandating COVID-19 vaccines for healthcare workers, with allowance for individualized exemptions but not religious exemptions, should be subject to strict scrutiny); *Dr. A v. Hochul*, 142 S. Ct. 552, 552, 555 (2021) (mem.) (Gorsuch, J., with Alito, J., dissenting) (asserting the same, relative to a similar New York law). These dissenting opinions cite to Supreme Court majority and minority opinions, including *Fulton v. City of Philadelphia*, 141 S. Ct. 1868, 1881 (2021) (holding that a city contractual provision allowing for exceptions was not generally applicable and thus triggered strict scrutiny); *Tandon v. Newsom*, 141 S. Ct. 1294 (2021) (per curiam) (holding state restrictions on public gatherings were not neutral and generally applicable and thus triggered strict scrutiny, when the regulations allowed exceptions for secular activities but not for comparable religious activities); and *Roman Cath. Diocese of Brooklyn*, 141 S. Ct. at 69, 70–72 (Gorsuch, J., concurring) (asserting that strict scrutiny should apply to government COVID-19-related restrictions where the government fails to "treat religious exercises at least as well as comparable secular activities").

1623. Press Release, White House Briefing Room, Fact Sheet: Biden Administration Announces Details of Two Major Vaccination Policies (Nov. 4, 2021), https://www.whitehouse.gov/briefing-room/statements-releases/2021/11/04/fact-sheet-biden-administration-announces-details-of-two-major-vaccination-policies (announcing COVID-19 vaccine requirement for healthcare workers and employees of large private companies); Exec. Order No. 14043, 86 Fed. Reg. 50989 (Sep. 9, 2021) (requiring COVID-19 vaccines for federal employees); Exec. Order No. 14042, 86 Fed. Reg. 50985 (Sep. 9, 2021) (requiring COVID-19 vaccines for federal contractors).

continued. The Court put a hold on a federal vaccine-or-test mandate for employees of private companies with more than 100 employees, but it allowed a federal vaccine mandate for healthcare workers to be enforced.[1624]

619. When considering whether an individual qualifies for a religious exemption to a vaccine mandate, employers and schools generally have less discretion than the courts to scrutinize the exemption-seeker's beliefs.[1625] Courts must determine if the belief is religious, rather than political or ideological, and if it is sincerely held.[1626] Some courts making this determination have relied solely on the professed personal beliefs of the individual seeking the religious exemption, while others have looked to the relevant religious organization's official position on vaccinations as well as professed belief.[1627] In the post-COVID pandemic era, the law surrounding vaccine mandates and religious exemptions remains controversial and unsettled.

§6. Physician-Assisted Death

620. Physician-assisted death is legal in nine states and the District of Columbia.[1628] Each state statute requires that the patient be at least 18 years of age, capable of making healthcare decisions, and diagnosed with a terminal disease that will lead

1624. *Nat'l Fed'n of Indep. Bus. v. Dep't of Lab.*, 142 S. Ct. 661 (2022); *Biden v. Missouri*, 595 U.S. 87 (2022).

1625. *See, e.g., What You Should Know about COVID-19, supra* n. 1620, § L.2 ("Generally, under Title VII, an employer should assume that a request for religious accommodation is based on sincerely held religious beliefs. However, if an employer has an objective basis for questioning either the religious nature or the sincerity of a particular belief, the employer would be justified in making a limited factual inquiry … ."); Ariz. Rev. Stat. Ann. §§ 15-872, -873 (2021) (requiring, for student exemptions from public-school vaccination mandates, simply a signed statement from parents indicating in part that "due to personal beliefs" they do not consent to having their student vaccinated). *But c.f. B.W.C. v. Williams*, 990 F.3d 614, 622 (8th Cir. 2021) (holding that state requirement for parents to complete a form requesting religious exemption from public-school vaccine mandates did not violate the parents' free speech or free exercise rights).

1626. *See, e.g., Fallon v. Mercy Cath. Med. Ctr.*, 877 F.3d 487, 491–493 (3d Cir. 2017) (outlining factors relevant to determining if hospital employee's beliefs opposing vaccination were sincerely held religious beliefs).

1627. *Compare Kane v. De Blasio*, 19 F.4th 152, 168 (2d Cir. 2021) ("Denying an individual a religious accommodation based on someone else's publicly expressed religious views—even the leader of her faith—runs afoul of the Supreme Court's teaching that '[i]t is not within the judicial ken to question the centrality of particular beliefs or practices to a faith, *or the validity of particular litigants' interpretations of those creeds.*'" (quoting *Hernandez v. Comm'r*, 490 U.S. 680, 699 (1989))), *with Harris v. Univ. of Mass.*, 557 F. Supp. 3d 304, 314 (D. Mass. 2021) (affirming that Catholic student failed to qualify for religious exemption when Catholic Church leaders had encouraged vaccination and the student failed to provide evidence of personal religious beliefs).

1628. *See* (all codes current through 2022) Cal. Health & Safety Code div. 1, pt. 1.85; Colo. Rev. Stat. §§ 25-48-101 to 25-48-123; Haw. Rev. Stat. §§ 327L-1 to -25; Me. Stat. tit. 22, § 2140; N.J. Stat. Ann. §§ 26:16-1 to 26:16-20; N.M. Stat. Ann. §§ 24-7c-1 to 24-7c-8; Or. Rev. Stat. tit. 13, ch. 127; Vt. Stat. Ann. tit. 18, §§ 5281–5293; Wash. Rev. Code §§ 70.245.010 to 70.245.903; D.C. Code §§ 7-661.01 to 7-661.16.

to death within six months.[1629] Oregon and Vermont are the only states to have eliminated residency requirements, thereby allowing non-residents to travel to those states to receive lethal medication.[1630]

621. Montana is the first and only state to legalize assisted death by court decision. The Montana Supreme Court found no indication in Montana law that physician-assisted death to terminally ill, mentally competent adult patients was against public policy.[1631]

1629. *State Statute Navigator*, Death with Dignity, https://deathwithdignity.org/state-statute-navigator (last visited Sep. 30, 2023).
1630. H.B. 2279, 82d Leg. Assemb., 2023 Reg. Sess. (Or. 2023) (amending Or. Rev. Stat. §§ 127.800, .805, .815, and repealing § 127.860); H.B. 190, Gen. Assemb., 2023 Reg. Sess. (Vt. 2023) (amending Vt. Stat. Ann. tit. 18, §§ 5281, 5283).
1631. *Baxter v. State*, 224 P.3d 1211, 1215 (Mont. 2009).

Chapter 7. Non-discrimination

§1. Constitutional Non-discrimination Protections

I. General Provisions

622. Constitutional protections against discrimination can be grounded in either the Establishment Clause or the Free Exercise Clause of the First Amendment among other constitutional provisions, such as the Due Process and Equal Protection Clauses. Indeed, the Free Exercise Clause continues to bar state discrimination on the basis of religion, even after the Supreme Court limited strict scrutiny review to laws burdening free exercise that are not neutral or generally applicable, in *Employment Division v. Smith.*[1632] For additional discussion of *Smith* and its aftermath, *see* Part II (Religious Freedom in General), Chapter 1 (Individual Religious Freedom).

623. In *Fulton v. City of Philadelphia*, for example, the Court reiterated that government may not discriminate against religion when government acts in a "managerial role".[1633] In that case, the Court applied strict scrutiny to a city's contract with foster care agencies because a non-discrimination provision in the contract allowed for discretionary exceptions and, thus, was not "generally applicable". The Court held that the non-discrimination provision, which required agencies to consider placements with same-sex couples, unconstitutionally burdened a Catholic agency's free exercise.[1634]

624. The bar on state discrimination against religion can apply even to laws that appear facially neutral and generally applicable. In *Church of the Lukumi Babalu Aye, Inc. v. City of Hialeah*, the Supreme Court reiterated that "the protections of the Free Exercise Clause pertain if the law at issue discriminates against some or all religious beliefs or regulates or prohibits conduct *because* it is undertaken for religious reasons".[1635] The Court explained that "[f]acial neutrality is not determinative" if the underlying cause of a law is to target a religious group or practice.[1636] In that case, the Court struck down a city ordinance that was facially neutral but was specifically motivated by and targeted at the animal sacrifice practices of a local Santeria congregation.[1637] The Court explained that both the Establishment Clause

1632. *Emp. Div., Dep't of Hum. Res. of Or. v. Smith*, 494 U.S. 872 (1990); *see also Fulton v. City of Philadelphia*, 141 S. Ct. 1868, 1882–1931 (2021) (concurring opinions discussing whether *Smith* should be overruled).

1633. *Fulton v. City of Philadelphia*, 141 S. Ct. 1868, 1878 (2021).

1634. *Ibid.*, at 1878, 1882.

1635. *Church of the Lukumi Babalu Aye, Inc. v. City of Hialeah*, 508 U.S. 520, 532 (1993) (emphasis added). *But see Trump v. Hawaii*, 138 S. Ct. 2392 (2018) (citing the President's broad authority under the Immigration and Nationality Act in upholding an executive order prohibiting individuals from certain countries from entering the US, despite arguments that the travel ban arose from anti-Muslim animus).

1636. *Church of the Lukumi Babalu Aye, Inc.*, 508 U.S. at 532.

1637. *Ibid.*, at 534. Animal sacrifice is an integral component of Santeria beliefs.

and the Free Exercise Clause protect religious groups and practices when examination reveals a motivating animus behind such facially neutral laws.[1638]

625. In addition to striking down religious discrimination in government prohibitions, the Supreme Court has struck down religious discrimination in the granting of government benefits as well. The Court in *Trinity Lutheran Church v. Comer* reiterated that "denying a generally available benefit solely on account of religious identity imposes a penalty on the free exercise of religion that can be justified only by a state interest 'of the highest order'".[1639] In that case, the Court held that a Missouri state playground-resurfacing program could not exclude religious schools from consideration simply because they were religious.

626. Non-discrimination is also strongly implicated by the Establishment Clause, though Supreme Court interpretations of the Establishment Clause are tangled and reflect several different approaches. *See* Part I (Legal Framework and Sources), Chapter 3 (Typology of the System). Some cases focus on separation of religion and the state, and the bar against state support for religion, while others highlight the Establishment Clause ban on discrimination among religions or between religion and non-religion. The latter, like *Trinity Lutheran* (which implicated both free exercise and establishment concerns), typically permit some state support of religious groups, if given without discrimination based on beliefs. *See* discussion in Part VIII (Financing of Religious Communities), Chapter 2 (Indirect Financing).

II. Separation Tests

627. In its first Establishment Clause case, the Supreme Court held that:

> The "establishment of religion" clause of the First Amendment means at least this: Neither a state nor the Federal Government can set up a church. Neither can pass laws which aid one religion, aid all religions, or prefer one religion over another. Neither can force nor influence a person to go to or to remain away from church against his will or force him to profess a belief or disbelief in any religion. No person can be punished for entertaining or professing religious beliefs or disbeliefs, for church attendance or non-attendance. No tax in any amount, large or small, can be levied to support any religious activities or institutions, whatever they may be called or whatever form they may adopt to teach or practice religion. Neither a state nor the Federal Government can, openly or secretly, participate in the affairs of any religious organizations or groups and vice versa.[1640]

1638. *See ibid.*, at 532–542.
1639. *Trinity Lutheran Church of Columbia, Inc. v. Comer*, 582 U.S. 449, 458 (2017) (quoting *McDaniel v. Paty*, 435 U.S. 618, 628 (1978) (plurality opinion)).
1640. *Everson v. Bd. of Educ.*, 330 U.S. 1, 15–16 (1947).

628. Beginning in 1971, the *Lemon* test became a key judicial test for determining whether the Establishment Clause had been violated. First articulated by the Supreme Court in *Lemon v. Kurtzman*, the test did not focus on discrimination per se. Rather, it examined whether government action (1) had a secular primary purpose, (2) had a primary effect that neither advanced nor inhibited religion, and (3) did not foster excessive government entanglement with religion.[1641] From its inception, justices disagreed widely over the value of the *Lemon* test, modified its elements and applicability,[1642] and did not always employ it in Establishment Clause questions.[1643] At least one justice, however, considered it to be "the only coherent test a majority of the Court has ever adopted".[1644]

629. Even so, a majority opinion in 2022 abrogated the *Lemon* test, concluding that the Court had "long ago abandoned" it.[1645] Citing more recent cases, the majority in *Kennedy v. Bremerton School District* explained that "the Establishment Clause must be interpreted by reference to historical practices and understandings … of the Founding Fathers".[1646] Some justices, judges, and scholars have criticized this "history-and-tradition" standard as vague and amorphous,[1647] and it remains to be seen how it will be applied going forward. While the Court has abrogated the *Lemon* test, an understanding of the test remains important to understanding US Supreme Court jurisprudence in the late twentieth and early twenty-first centuries. For discussions of the *Lemon* test's application, *see* Part VIII (Financing of Religious Communities), Chapter 2 (Indirect Financing); and Part IX (Education), Chapter 2 (Religious Schools).

1641. *Lemon v. Kurtzman*, 403 U.S. 602, 612 (1971), *abrogated by Kennedy v. Bremerton Sch. Dist.*, 142 S. Ct. 2407, 2427–2428 (2022).
1642. 1 Durham et al., *supra* n. 157, § 4:6 (*The Three Prongs of the* Lemon *Test*); *see, e.g., Agostini v. Felton,* 521 U.S. 203, 232–233 (1997) (concluding that the entanglement prong could be folded into the effects prong of the *Lemon* test).
1643. 1 Durham et al., *supra* n. 157, § 4:6 (*The Three Prongs of the* Lemon *Test*).
1644. *Wallace v. Jaffree*, 472 U.S. 38, 63 (1985) (Powell, J., concurring).
1645. *Kennedy*, 142 S. Ct. at 2427–2428; *see also Groff v. DeJoy*, 600 U.S. 447, 460 & n.7 (2023) (acknowledging *Kennedy*'s abrogation of the *Lemon* test).
1646. *Kennedy*, 142 S. Ct. at 2428 (internal quotation marks omitted) (quoting *Town of Greece v. Galloway*, 572 U.S. 565, 576–577 (2014), and citing *Am. Legion v. Am. Humanist Ass'n*, 139 S. Ct. 2067, 2087 (2019) (plurality s. II.D)).
1647. *See, e.g., Kennedy*, 142 S. Ct. at 2434, 2450 (Sotomayor, J., with Breyer and Kagan, JJ., dissenting) ("The [majority] reserves any meaningful explanation of its history-and-tradition test for another day, content for now to disguise it as established law and move on."); *Firewalker-Fields v. Lee*, 58 F.4th 104, 122 & n.8 (4th Cir. 2023) ("Open questions abound [regarding the history-and-tradition test]. What kinds of evidence are relevant? What kinds of evidence are the most useful? Which periods of history are relevant—the era of the Bill of Rights, 1791, or the era of the incorporation of the Bill of Rights, 1868—and which period is most important? This last question might matter a great deal in the Establishment Clause context given the evidence that the understanding of that principle changed significantly between 1791 and 1868. We could go on." (citations omitted)).

III. Non-discrimination Tests

630. In contrast to *Lemon*, more recent cases have focused on non-discrimination as a leading principle of the Establishment Clause. In *Trinity Lutheran Church v. Comer*, the Supreme Court held that a state may not discriminate against religious beneficiaries in distributing otherwise generally available state benefits—a guiding principle the Court has applied in other cases as well.[1648] In particular, the Supreme Court has upheld state subsidies for religious education or education at private religious schools when those subsidies come through a generally available subsidy program.[1649]

631. In *Witters v. Washington Department of Services for Blind*, a blind student at a Christian college studying to be a pastor was denied state financial assistance because the state believed subsidizing religious education would violate the Establishment Clause. Applying the *Lemon* test, the Supreme Court held that the subsidy did not violate the Establishment Clause.[1650] The Court reasoned that the financial aid did not "provide greater or broader benefits for recipients who apply their aid to religious education, nor [were] the full benefits of the program limited … to students at sectarian institutions".[1651] The Court concluded that the decision to support religious education was made by the individual receiving the aid, rather than by the state.[1652]

632. In 2020, in *Espinoza v. Montana Department of Revenue*, the Supreme Court upheld a program created by Montana's legislature that offered tax credits for donors to nonprofits providing scholarships for private tuition.[1653] A state agency promulgated a rule that barred the scholarships from being used at religious schools, citing the state constitution's "no-aid" provision prohibiting state funding of religious organizations. The Supreme Court struck down the "no-aid" provision as applied to the program, holding it unconstitutionally discriminated based on religious status.[1654] As in *Witters*, the Court explained that allowing the program's scholarship funds to make their way to religious schools did not violate the Establishment Clause where students independently chose to attend such schools.[1655] Two years later, in *Carson v. Makin*, the Court considered a Maine program that provided tuition reimbursements for secondary school students in rural areas to attend a public or private school, when their small local school districts did not operate a secondary school.[1656] To avoid offending the Establishment Clause, the state did not permit funds to reimburse tuition at private religious schools. The Supreme Court again held that the state's efforts to avoid Establishment Clause issues swung too

1648. *Trinity Lutheran Church of Columbia, Inc. v. Comer*, 582 U.S. 449, 466 (2017).
1649. *See, e.g., Witters v. Wash. Dep't of Servs. for the Blind*, 474 U.S. 481 (1986).
1650. *Ibid.*, at 484–489.
1651. *Ibid.*, at 488.
1652. *Ibid.*
1653. *Espinoza v. Mont. Dep't of Revenue*, 140 S. Ct. 2246 (2020).
1654. *Ibid.*, at 2257–2263.
1655. *Ibid.*, at 2254.
1656. *Carson v. Makin*, 142 S. Ct. 1987 (2022).

widely, in violation of the Free Exercise Clause, stating, "A State's antiestablishment interest does not justify enactments that exclude some members of the community from an otherwise generally available public benefit because of their religious exercise."[1657] And the Court reiterated, once again, that the flow of state funds to religious schools through independent student choice "did not offend the Establishment Clause".[1658] For additional discussion of these cases in the context of the Establishment Clause and non-discrimination in education, *see* Part IX (Education), Chapter 2 (Religious Schools).

§2. Non-discrimination in Speech and Symbolism

I. General Approach

633. Supreme Court opinions on the question of public displays and civil religion reflect inconsistencies found in Establishment Clause decisions generally. In this context, the Supreme Court shifted away from and eventually abrogated the *Lemon* test,[1659] articulating instead a variety of tests related to non-discrimination, coercion, pluralism, and history and tradition.[1660]

II. Speech in School Contexts

634. Students have the right not to be compelled to endorse beliefs or symbols in schools that violate their beliefs.[1661] In rejecting a compulsory flag salute, the Supreme Court stated, "If there is any fixed star in our constitutional constellation, it is that no official, high or petty, can prescribe what shall be orthodox in politics, nationalism, religion, or other matters of opinion, or force citizens to confess by word or act their faith therein. If there are any circumstances which permit an exception, they do not now occur to us."[1662] From 1971, courts used the *Lemon* test[1663] only nominally to determine whether school policies and practices related to religious speech violated the Establishment Clause. Courts more often looked for evidence of state coercion or advancement of religion but have not necessarily been consistent in determining which policies and practices constitute impermissible coercion or advancement.

1657. *Ibid.*, at 1998.
1658. *Ibid.*, at 1997.
1659. *Kennedy v. Bremerton Sch. Dist.*, 142 S. Ct. 2407, 2427–2428 (2022); *see also Groff v. Dejoy*, 600 U.S. 447, 460 & n.7 (2023) (acknowledging *Kennedy*'s abrogation of the *Lemon* test).
1660. *See, e.g.*, *Am. Legion v. Am. Humanist Ass'n*, 139 S. Ct. 2067, 2087–2089 (2019) (plurality section II.D) ("While the *Lemon* Court ambitiously attempted to find a grand unified theory of the Establishment Clause, in later cases, we have taken a more modest approach that focuses on the particular issue at hand and looks to history for guidance.").
1661. *W. Va. State Bd. of Educ. v. Barnette,* 319 U.S. 624 (1943).
1662. *Ibid.*, at 642.
1663. *Lemon v. Kurtzman*, 403 U.S. 602, 612 (1971), *abrogated by Kennedy*, 142 S. Ct. at 2427–2428.

635. In *Lee v. Weisman*, the Supreme Court held that a principal's invitation to a local rabbi to offer a non-sectarian prayer before a public-school graduation ceremony violated the Establishment Clause because the principal's decision to include prayer was "attributable to the State, and from a constitutional perspective it [was] as if a state statute decreed that the prayers must occur".[1664] The principal's choice of a rabbi was similarly "attributable to the State".[1665] The Court explained that "there are heightened concerns with protecting freedom of conscience from subtle coercive pressure in the elementary and secondary public schools"—concerns raised by both perceived and actual school endorsement of a religious message.[1666]

636. In 2000, the Court held that a school district's policy allowing student-initiated, student-led prayer to be broadcast over a high school's public address system before football games was unconstitutionally coercive.[1667] In 2022, however, in *Kennedy v. Bremerton School District*, the Court upheld a high-school football coach's right to kneel and pray quietly at midfield after games, finding the prayers constituted private speech, rather than speech attributable to the school district.[1668] Although some student players knelt with the coach, the Court noted "the absence of evidence of coercion … to persuade or force students to participate".[1669] The Court acknowledged that some might be offended by the practice but reiterated that "[o]ffense … does not equate to coercion".[1670] It also stated that the "Court has long recognized … that secondary school students are mature enough … to understand that a school does not endorse, let alone coerce them to participate in, speech that it merely permits on a nondiscriminatory basis".[1671] In *Kennedy*, the Court abrogated the *Lemon* test, relying instead on the historical tolerance of private religious speech to hold that "[t]he Constitution neither mandates nor tolerates … discrimination" against such speech.[1672]

III. Government Speech in Public Fora

637. Government speech in public fora, such as permanent monuments in public spaces, is not subject to scrutiny under the Free Speech Clause.[1673] The state may select the views it wants to express and is not required to be viewpoint neutral or to accept and publicize similar forms of speech expressing varying views. For example, in *Pleasant Grove City v. Summum*, the Supreme Court did not require a

1664. *Lee v. Weisman*, 505 U.S. 577, 587 (1992).
1665. *Ibid.*
1666. *Ibid.*, at 592; *Santa Fe Indep. Sch. Dist. v. Doe*, 530 U.S. 290, 291 (2000).
1667. *Santa Fe Indep. Sch. Dist.*, 530 U.S. at 312.
1668. *Kennedy*, 142 S. Ct. at 2424–2425.
1669. *Ibid.*, at 2431.
1670. *Ibid.*, at 2430 (internal quotation marks omitted) (quoting *Town of Greece v. Galloway*, 572 U.S. 565, 589 (2014)).
1671. *Ibid.* (internal quotation marks omitted) (quoting *Bd. of Educ. v. Mergens*, 496 U.S. 226, 250 (1990) (plurality opinion)).
1672. *Ibid.*, at 2427–2428, 2433; *see also Groff v. Dejoy*, 600 U.S. 447, 460 & n.7 (2023) (acknowledging *Kennedy*'s abrogation of the *Lemon* test).
1673. *Pleasant Grove City v. Summum*, 555 U.S. 460, 467–468 (2009).

city to erect a small religious group's monument displaying the group's "Seven Aphorisms" in a public park simply because the city had permitted a monument displaying the Ten Commandments.[1674] The Court recognized in *Pleasant Grove* that, while "government speech is not restricted by the Free Speech Clause," it must still "comport with the Establishment Clause" in public fora.[1675] In that case, however, Establishment Clause issues were not raised by the parties or analyzed by the Court.[1676]

IV. Private Speech in Public Fora

638. Most religious speech in public fora involves private religious "speakers" such as religious holiday displays or prayers before legislative meetings. Private religious speech in a public forum is permissible so long as the government does not discriminate based on viewpoint.[1677] The Establishment Clause "prohibits government from appearing to take a position on questions of religious belief or from 'making adherence to a religion relevant in any way to a person's standing in the political community'".[1678]

A. Religious Displays

639. Government may not exclude private religious displays in public spaces that are open to private displays. In such cases, the Supreme Court has noted "a crucial difference between *government* speech endorsing religion, which the Establishment Clause forbids, and *private* speech endorsing religion, which the Free Speech and Free Exercise Clauses protect".[1679] In *Capitol Square Review and Advisory Board v. Pinette*, the Supreme Court held that the state of Ohio could not deny the Ku Klux Klan permission to erect a Latin cross on a public plaza near the Ohio statehouse after the state had permitted a state-sponsored Christmas tree, a privately sponsored menorah, and other exhibits and booths on the plaza.[1680] The state

1674. *Ibid.*, at 472–478, 481.

1675. *Ibid.*, at 468–469.

1676. A concurring opinion suggested, however, that the disputed display would be found constitutional under the Establishment Clause given the Court's approval of similar displays, based on their historical significance and traditional acceptance in their communities. *Ibid.*, at 482, 482–483 (Scalia, J., with Thomas, J., concurring). *But see ibid.*, at 485, 485–487 (Souter, J., concurring) (suggesting other methods for analyzing potential Establishment Clause issues in government speech cases). The current Supreme Court, which has approved the history-and-tradition test for Establishment Clause questions, would likely reach a similar conclusion. *See Kennedy v. Bremerton Sch. Dist.*, 142 S. Ct. 2407, 2427–2428 (2022); *see also supra* para. 377 and accompanying footnotes.

1677. *See Shurtleff v. City of Boston*, 596 U.S. 243, 247–248 (2022); *Capitol Square Rev. & Advisory Bd. v. Pinette*, 515 U.S. 753, 763–764 (1995).

1678. *County of Allegheny v. ACLU*, 492 U.S. 573, 594 (1989), *abrogation acknowledged by Kennedy*, 142 S. Ct. at 2427 (quoting *Lynch v. Donnelly*, 465 U.S. 668, 687 (1984)).

1679. *Bd. of Educ. v. Mergens*, 496 U.S. 226, 250 (1990) (plurality opinion).

1680. *Capitol Square*, 515 U.S. at 770.

claimed that it was barred by the Establishment Clause from permitting the display of a cross, to avoid official endorsement of Christianity. But the Court held that the government did not "promote" or "favor" religion by allowing a religious symbol to be displayed in a public forum where the government had permitted other symbols—including privately sponsored symbols—to be displayed. The Court noted it had "consistently held" that government did not violate the Establishment Clause in enacting "neutral policies that happen to benefit religion".[1681] In *Shurtleff v. City of Boston*, a unanimous Supreme Court found that Boston's flag-raising program, which raised private flags on city property, did not constitute government speech, and therefore, the city could not refuse flags based on viewpoint.[1682] Accordingly, the Court held that the city's refusal to allow a group to raise a "Christian" flag, based on Establishment Clause concerns, constituted viewpoint discrimination in violation of the Free Speech Amendment.[1683]

640. Displays on government property marking traditionally religious holidays must be equally open to non-religious content. In *County of Allegheny v. ACLU*, the Supreme Court held that the Christmas seasonal display of a crèche with a sign reading "Glory to God in the Highest", which was sponsored by a Roman Catholic organization and located on the county courthouse grand staircase, violated the Establishment Clause.[1684] The Court held that the display of a menorah with a Christmas tree outside of the city-county building, however, was an acceptable government recognition of different traditions for celebrating the winter holiday season.[1685] For additional discussion of public displays of religious art and symbols, *see* Part XI (Religion and Culture), Chapter 1 (Religion and Art).

B. Legislative Prayer

641. The Supreme Court has upheld the practice of legislative prayer and prayer before local council or board meetings.[1686] The government body, however, may not

---

1681. *Ibid.*, at 763–764.
1682. *Shurtleff*, 596 U.S. at 258–259.
1683. *Ibid.*
1684. *County of Allegheny v. ACLU*, 492 U.S. 573, 600 (1989), *abrogation acknowledged by Kennedy v. Bremerton*, 142 S. Ct. 2407, 2427 (2022).
1685. *Ibid.*, at 617–618.
1686. *See Town of Greece v. Galloway*, 572 U.S. 565, 578–582 (2014) (holding that prayers opening town board meetings need not be non-sectarian to comply with Establishment Clause); *Marsh v. Chambers*, 463 U.S. 783, 792–793 (1983) (holding that practice of opening state legislature with prayers in Judeo-Christian tradition did not violate Establishment Clause); *see also Fields v. Speaker of the Pa. House of Representatives*, 936 F.3d 142, 153 (3d Cir. 2019) (holding that legislature's policy giving preference to theistic prayers did not violate Establishment Clause); *Barker v. Conroy*, 921 F.3d 1118, 1131 (D.C. Cir. 2019) ("[T]he House's decision to limit the opening prayer to religious prayer fit[s] 'within the tradition long followed in Congress and the state legislatures[.]'") (quoting *Town of Greece*, 572 U.S. at 577 (2014))); *Bormuth v. County of Jackson*, 870 F.3d 494, 497–498 (6th Cir. 2017) (en banc) (finding county board's tradition of opening public meetings with prayer was "consonant with … historical practice" and constitutional, applying *Marsh* and *Town of Greece*).

require that the content of the prayers be non-sectarian or follow a particular pattern, nor may it purposely favor a particular faith tradition.[1687] Even so, the Court has emphasized that non-discrimination does not necessitate extensive solicitation of diversity in the types of prayers offered: "So long as the [government] maintains a policy of nondiscrimination, the Constitution does not require it to search beyond [the community's] borders … in an effort to achieve religious balancing."[1688] For additional discussion, *see* Part V (Religion and Politics), Chapter 3 (Interaction Between Religion and State).

V. Private Speech in Limited Public Fora

642. When government provides a limited public forum for expressive activities, it is not free to discriminate based on particular viewpoints a group may have, such as religious viewpoints. But in contrast to traditional public fora, government is able to define the forum, can set limits on its purposes, and may choose to close it down completely. Limited public fora include spaces open to the public, such as auditoriums and classrooms, as well as public funding for private speech.

643. The Supreme Court held in *Widmar v. Vincent* that permitting religious groups access to public fora does not violate the Establishment Clause.[1689] The Court struck down a state university policy that, out of establishment concerns, prohibited a religious student group from holding meetings in university buildings, which comprised a limited public forum. The Court concluded that "an open forum in a public university does not confer any imprimatur of state approval on religious sects or practices" and that a content-neutral, open-forum policy would provide adequate Establishment Clause protections.[1690] For further discussion of *Widmar* and limited public fora generally, *see* this part, Chapter 3 (Freedom of Expression), above.

644. The Supreme Court has held that state "[d]iscrimination against speech because of its message is presumed to be unconstitutional".[1691] The presumption against viewpoint-based discrimination can be overcome but only under exceptional circumstances. Otherwise, any allocation of state funds or other assistance

1687. *See, e.g.*, *Williamson v. Brevard County*, 928 F.3d 1296, 1299, 1310 (11th Cir. 2019) (holding that process for selecting prayer-givers for board of county commissioners' meetings violated Establishment Clause when it favored monotheistic religions and categorically excluded others); *Freedom from Religion Found., Inc. v. Chino Valley Unified Sch. Dist. Bd. of Educ.*, 896 F.3d 1132, 1150 (9th Cir. 2017) (holding that policy of beginning public portion of school board meetings with prayer violated Establishment Clause where the "policy reinforce[d] the dominance of particular religious traditions"), *reh'g en banc denied*, 910 F.3d 1297 (9th Cir. 2018); *Lund v. Rowan County*, 863 F.3d 268, 272 (4th Cir. 2017) (en banc) (holding that county board of commissioners' exclusive, Christianity-elevating prayer practice violated Establishment Clause).

1688. *Town of Greece*, 572 U.S. at 585–586.

1689. *Widmar v. Vincent*, 454 U.S. 263, 274–277 (1981).

1690. *Ibid.*

1691. *Rosenberger v. Rector & Visitors of U. of Va.*, 515 U.S. 819, 828 (1995).

must be neutral toward religious speech.[1692] In *Rosenberger v. Rector and Visitors of the University of Virginia*, the Court found the presumption of unconstitutionality applied when the university refused to issue payments from a student activities fund to a student-run Christian newspaper.[1693] The Court reasoned that the student activities fund was a type of public forum and thus subject to public forum principles, including neutrality toward religious viewpoints.[1694] The Court found a viewpoint-neutral policy would not unconstitutionally advance or aid a religious cause and would provide sufficient Establishment Clause protections.[1695] Conversely, a policy denying funds to the student newspaper solely based on its viewpoint ran the risk of "fostering a pervasive bias or hostility to religion, which could undermine the very neutrality the Establishment Clause requires".[1696] The Court concluded, "There is no Establishment Clause violation in the University's honoring its duties under the Free Speech Clause."[1697] For another discussion of *Rosenberger*, *see* this part, Chapter 3 (Freedom of Expression), above.

645. In *Good News Club v. Milford Central School*, a city that had opened its public schools to residents for after-school use was not permitted to bar religious groups from using its schools, in particular a children's Christian club. The Supreme Court held that government entities may "be justified in reserving [a limited public forum] for certain groups or for the discussion of certain topics" but may not discriminate based on a particular viewpoint; additionally, any restriction must be "reasonable in light of the purpose served by the forum".[1698] For additional discussions of *Good News Club*, *see* this part, Chapter 3 (Freedom of Expression), above; and Part IX (Education), Chapter 1 (Religious Education in Public and Private Schools).

646. The ability of a state entity like a public university to regulate its limited-purpose public forums via content-neutral regulations can adversely affect religious groups. In *Christian Legal Society v. Martinez*, the Supreme Court held that public universities may condition official recognition and support of a student organization on the group's compliance with viewpoint-neutral policies, which may conflict with the group's religious tenets.[1699] Hastings College of Law in California allowed recognized student organizations to use university resources, provided they adhere to an "all-comers" policy that required groups to accept student members regardless of belief.[1700] The Christian Legal Society required its members "to sign a 'Statement of Faith' and to conduct their lives in accord with prescribed principles. …

1692. *Ibid.*, at 840.
1693. *Ibid.*, at 830–831.
1694. *Ibid.*, at 830.
1695. *See ibid.*, at 840.
1696. *Ibid.*, at 845–846.
1697. *Ibid.*, at 846.
1698. *Good News Club v. Milford Cent. Sch.*, 533 U.S. 98, 106–107 (2001) (internal quotation marks omitted) (quoting *Rosenberger*, 515 U.S. at 829; *Cornelius v. NAACP Legal Def. & Educ. Fund, Inc.*, 473 US. 788, 806 (1985)); *see also Matal v. Tam*, 137 S. Ct. 1744, 1763 (2017). Lower courts have split regarding the application of *Good News Club* to religious or anti-religious advertising on public transportation. *See* cases cited *supra* n. 1439.
1699. *Christian Legal Soc'y Chapter of the Univ. of Cal. v. Martinez*, 561 U.S. 661, 697 (2010).
1700. *Ibid.*, at 671.

[including] the belief that sexual activity should not occur outside of marriage between a man and a woman".[1701] The Supreme Court upheld the all-comers policy and exclusion of the Christian Legal Society from university resources as a reasonable, viewpoint-neutral regulation of a limited-purpose public forum that applied equally to all student groups.[1702]

§3. Significant Statutory Non-discrimination Protections

647. Discrimination based on religion in hiring, employment, and termination from employment is prohibited by the Civil Rights Act of 1964.[1703] To demonstrate that an employer has unlawfully discriminated, an employee must show that an employment action such as hiring, firing, or promoting was motivated by an employer's position toward religion or another protected characteristic.[1704] The Act exempts religious organizations from the prohibition on religious discrimination in hiring practices but does not permit them to discriminate based on other protected characteristics.[1705] For further discussion of religion and employment, *see* Part VI (Labor Law Within Religious Communities), Chapter 1 (Scope of Application of Labor Law) and Chapter 3 (Other Church Employees and Labor Law).

648. The federal Equal Access Act prohibits public schools from discriminating in granting status to student groups as school-affiliated extracurricular clubs.[1706] The Equal Access Act allows students to form extracurricular clubs before or after school so long as those clubs do not disrupt the orderly conduct of the school.[1707] Such clubs must be student led and studentinstigated; school instructors or employees may be present only to supervise and may not participate.[1708] The Act codifies the principle that when a public school allows for school-affiliated student clubs, it creates a limited public forum where viewpoint discrimination—including discrimination based on religious viewpoint—is unconstitutional. In 1990, in a nonbinding opinion, a plurality of the Supreme Court concluded that the Equal Access Act does

1701. *Ibid.*, at 672.
1702. *Ibid.*, at 674, 697–698. *But see Fellowship of Christian Athletes v. San Jose Unified Sch. Dist. Bd. of Educ.*, 82 F.4th 664, 694–696 (9th Cir. 2023) (distinguishing *Martinez* in finding that a district's all-comers policy, which prohibited discriminatory criteria for members and leaders of official student clubs, was "replete with exemptions that treat[ed] comparable secular groups more favourably" than a Christian club, failed strict scrutiny, and likely would not withstand Christian club's free exercise claim).
1703. 42 U.S.C. § 2000e-2(a) (2018).
1704. *See ibid.*, § 2000e-2; *see, e.g.*, *McDonnell Douglas Corp. v. Green*, 411 U.S. 792, 802 (1973) (explaining four-prong method for establishing a prima facie case of racial discrimination, which may shift the burden of proof to the employer to show non-discrimination); *Ortiz v. Werner Enterprises, Inc.*, 834 F.3d 760, 766 (7th Cir. 2016) (distinguishing *McDonnell*'s burden-shifting method of proving discrimination from a holistic method where "all evidence [of discrimination] belongs in a single pile and must be evaluated as a whole").
1705. *See* 42 U.S.C. § 2000e-1(a).
1706. 20 U.S.C. § 4071(a) (2018).
1707. *Ibid.*, § 4071(c).
1708. *Ibid.*

not violate the Establishment Clause.[1709] For further discussion of the Equal Access Act, *see* Part IX (Education), Chapter 1 (Religious Education in Public and Private Schools).

§4. State Statutory and State Constitutional Non-discrimination Provisions

649. Most states have enacted statutes prohibiting discrimination in housing, employment, and "public accommodation" on the basis of race, sex/gender, nationality, and religion.[1710] Some state statutes also prohibit discrimination based on age, gender identity, sexual orientation, marital status, veteran status, military status, and/or pregnancy/childbirth.[1711] In 2023, the California State legislature passed a bill also banning discrimination based on caste—the first state legislature to do so.[1712] Affirmative-action policies in India's universities had led to greater numbers of "lower-caste" individuals gaining education and skills useful in California's tech industry.[1713] While the bill's legislative history contained evidence of caste-based discrimination in California employment and housing, critics argued that the law unfairly targeted Hindus, who were most likely to be accused of such discrimination.[1714] California's governor eventually vetoed the bill, asserting that caste discrimination was already proscribed by existing laws.[1715] For additional discussion of state non-discrimination statutes in employment and how they interplay with federal law, *see* Part VI (Labor Law Within Religious Communities), Chapter 3 (Other Church Employees and Labor Law).

650. Thirty-six state constitutions contain prohibitions on state assistance to religious schools and organizations, often called "Blaine Amendments".[1716] *See* more detailed discussion in Part I (Legal Framework and Sources), Chapter 2 (Other Legislation with Regard to Religion); and Part IX (Education), Chapter 2 (Religious Schools). Such state constitutional prohibitions, however, must not exclude religious groups or institutions "*because of their faith, or lack of it*, from receiving the

1709. *Bd. of Educ. v. Mergens*, 496 U.S. 226, 247 (1990) (plurality opinion).
1710. *See generally State Public Accommodation Laws*, NCSL, *supra* n. 358. *See also supra* paras. 147 & 267 and accompanying footnotes.
1711. *See generally State Public Accommodation Laws*, NCSL, *supra* n. 358. *See also supra* paras. 147 & 267 and accompanying footnotes; *Equality Maps: Nondiscrimination Laws*, MAP, *supra* n. 706.
1712. *See* SB-403, 2023–2024 Reg. Sess. (Cal. 2023).
1713. Kanishka Singh, *California Moves Closer to Historic Caste Discrimination Ban*, Reuters (Aug. 29, 2023), https://www.reuters.com/world/us/california-moves-closer-historic-caste-discrimination-ban-2023-08-29.
1714. Nitish Pahwa, *A Historic Anti-Discrimination Bill in California Sparked Backlash. But the Controversy Isn't What It Seems.*, Slate (Sep. 21, 2023), https://slate.com/news-and-politics/2023/09/california-anti-caste-discrimination-bill-hindu-nationalism-hindutva.html; Amy Qin, *California Could Become the First State to Ban Caste Bias as Prejudices Linger*, N.Y. Times (Sep. 8, 2023), https://www.nytimes.com/2023/09/08/us/california-caste-discrimination.html.
1715. Amy Qin, *Newsom Vetoes Bill Banning Caste Discrimination*, N.Y. Times, (Oct. 7, 2023), https://www.nytimes.com/2023/10/07/us/california-caste-discrimination.html.
1716. 3 Durham et al., *supra* n. 174, §25:14 (*Blaine Amendments in State Constitutions*)

benefits of public welfare legislation".[1717] In *Trinity Lutheran Church v, Comer*, the Supreme Court held that a Missouri state program violated the Free Exercise Clause when it automatically disqualified religious schools from grants offered to schools and day-care centers to purchase recycled-rubber playground surfaces.[1718] Missouri's policy of disqualifying religious entities was based on a Blaine Amendment-like provision in the state constitution.[1719] However, the Supreme Court explained that the state's application of the provision to the grant program led to "greater separation of church and State than is already ensured" under the US Constitution's Establishment Clause, resulting in violation of the Free Exercise Clause.[1720] The Court distinguished its earlier ruling in *Locke v. Davey*, which upheld a restriction on state scholarship benefits for students being trained as ministers.[1721] The Court reiterated that, in *Locke*, the state's anti-establishment interest was at its maximum in not using taxpayer funds for an "essentially religious endeavor", like the training of clergy.[1722] The Court asserted that "nothing of the sort [could] be said about a program to use recycled tires to resurface playgrounds".[1723] The Court also noted that, in *Locke*, scholarship recipients could exercise religious choice in other ways that were accommodated by the scholarship program; whereas Trinity Lutheran, which operated a preschool and day-care center, was required to choose "between being a church and receiving a government benefit".[1724]

1717. *Trinity Lutheran Church of Columbia, Inc. v. Comer*, 582 U.S. 449, 459 (2017) (emphasis in original).
1718. *Ibid.*, at 466.
1719. *Ibid.*, at 471, 473 (Sotomayor, J., with Ginsburg, J., dissenting).
1720. *Ibid.*, at 466 (internal quotation marks omitted) (quoting *Widmar v. Vincent*, 454 U.S. 263, 276 (1981)).
1721. *Ibid.*, at 464–465; *Locke v. Davey*, 540 U.S. 712, 719, 725 (2004).
1722. *Trinity Lutheran*, 582 U.S. at 465.
1723. *Ibid.*
1724. *Ibid.*

Chapter 8. Penal Law and Religion

§1. General Background

651. Most penal laws in the United States are made and enforced at the state level. The Constitution mostly refrains from defining federal crimes, mentioning only treason against the nation,[1725] piracy,[1726] and counterfeiting money.[1727] Instead, it delegates to Congress the responsibility of enacting "necessary and proper" laws and focuses on securing the procedural rights of individuals accused of a crime.[1728] These include protections against unreasonable searches and seizures,[1729] the right to a speedy and public trial by jury,[1730] the right to a defense attorney,[1731] the right to due process and equal protection of the law,[1732] and protections against self-incrimination and double jeopardy.[1733]

652. In the absence of constitutionally established crimes, Congress has used its authority under the Commerce Clause[1734] and Necessary and Proper Clause[1735] to create a comprehensive federal penal code. Federal offenses range from tax evasion to animal trafficking, mail fraud to unlawful acts committed on federal property, unlawful immigration to theft of public money, and violent crimes to international travel undertaken to further unlawful activities. The US Supreme Court has held that Congress's authority to regulate under the Commerce Clause is limited to economic activity that substantially affects interstate commerce; for example, the Court struck down the federal Gun-Free School Zones Act (which was subsequently amended) and a provision of the Violence Against Women Act for having too attenuated a relationship with commerce and thus exceeding congressional authority.[1736]

1725. U.S. Const. art. III, § 3.
1726. *Ibid.*, art. I, § 8.
1727. *Ibid.*
1728. *Ibid.*; *see also, e.g.*, *ibid.*, amend. V.
1729. U.S. Const. amend. IV.
1730. *Ibid.*, amend. VI.
1731. *Ibid.*
1732. U.S. Const. amend. V, XIV.
1733. *Ibid.*, amend V.
1734. *Ibid.*, art. I, § 8, cl. 3 ("The Congress shall have Power … [t]o regulate Commerce with foreign Nations, and among the several States, and with the Indian Tribes … .").
1735. *Ibid.*, art. I, § 8, cl. 18 ("The Congress shall have Power … [t]o make all Laws which shall be necessary and proper for carrying into Execution the foregoing Powers, and all other Powers vested by this Constitution in the Government of the United States, or in any Department or Officer thereof.").
1736. *United States v. Lopez*, 514 U.S. 549, 559, 567–568 (1995) (holding that the Gun-Free School Zones Act exceeded Congress's authority to regulate under the Commerce Clause because the crime prohibited—knowingly possessing a gun in a school zone—was not "economic activity that substantially affected state commerce"); *United States v. Morrison*, 529 U.S. 598, 610, 617–619 (2000) (invalidating the civil remedy provision of the Violence Against Women Act for the same reason). The Gun-Free School Zones Act was later amended to prohibit in school zones only those guns linked to interstate or foreign commerce. *See* 18 U.S.C. § 922(q) (2018).

I. Penal Laws Criminalizing Manifestations of Religion

653. The United States does not permit punishment of manifestations of religious belief qua manifestations of religious belief. Even after the Free Exercise Clause was limited by *Smith*,[1737] the US Supreme Court in a case involving the Church of the Lukumi Babalu Aye held that the clause protects against discrimination on the basis of religious beliefs: "At a minimum, the protections of the Free Exercise Clause pertain if the law at issue discriminates against some or all religious beliefs or regulates or prohibits conduct *because it is undertaken for religious reasons*."[1738] In that case, the Supreme Court struck down a local ordinance that effectively banned religious animal sacrifice, which the Court found was aimed at Santeria beliefs and was "designed to persecute or oppress a religion or its practices".[1739]

654. The federal Religious Freedom Restoration Act (RFRA), as well as state constitutions and statutes with similar standards, offers some protection against the enforcement of generally applicable criminal laws that restrict religious manifestations.[1740] In *Gonzales v. O Centro Espirita Beneficente Uniao do Vegetal*, for example, the US Supreme Court applied RFRA to invalidate a customs seizure of hallucinogenic *hoasca* tea.[1741] The tea was used sacramentally by a religious group, and the Court held that the government failed to show a compelling interest in forbidding such use.

II. Other Penal Laws Related to Religion

655. The Supreme Court has struck down blasphemy statutes as unconstitutional. In 1952, in *Joseph Burstyn, Inc. v. Wilson*, the Supreme Court held that a New York law that allowed government censors to deny screening licenses to films deemed "sacrilegious" violated First Amendment free speech protections.[1742] A few states and local jurisdictions still have not repealed their blasphemy laws, but they no longer have force under current common law.[1743] For further discussion of *Joseph Burstyn*, *see* Part XI (Religion and Culture), Chapter 1 (Religion and Art).

656. Approximately twenty states have statutes that explicitly ban the disruption of religious services or that have been interpreted as applying to religious meetings

1737. *Emp. Div., Dep't of Hum. Res. of Or. v. Smith*, 494 U.S. 872 (1990).
1738. *Church of the Lukumi Babalu Aye, Inc. v. City of Hialeah*, 508 U.S. 520, 532 (1993) (emphasis added).
1739. *Ibid.*, at 547.
1740. *See* 42 U.S.C. § 2000bb (2018).
1741. *Gonzales v. O Centro Espirita Beneficente Uniao do Vegetal*, 546 U.S. 418, 439 (2006).
1742. *Joseph Burstyn, Inc. v. Wilson*, 343 U.S. 495 (1952).
1743. *See* Mass. Gen. Laws ch. 272, § 36 (2022); Mich. Comp. Laws § 750.102 (2022); Okla. Stat. tit. 21, §§ 901–903 (2022); S.C. Code Ann. § 16-17-520 (2022); Wyo. Stat. Ann. § 1-29-106 (2022).

by the state's highest court.[1744] A New York statute categorizes disturbance or interruption of a religious or burial service as a class A misdemeanor, with a penalty of up to one year in prison or USD 1,000.[1745] In 1989, more than 4,000 AIDS activists protested outside St. Patrick's Cathedral in New York City, and several dozen entered the cathedral, severely disrupting a Mass.[1746] The statute was not applied, however, and those charged received only community service sentences. Indeed, even if a state has passed such a statute, incidents involving disruption of religious services are more often addressed through trespass ordinances or (if the incidents are anticipated and/or chronic) injunctive relief, such as a restraining order.[1747]

657. Religious hate crimes—acts of criminal violence motivated by prejudice against the victim's religion—are penalized both by the federal government and by most states. Of the 11,288 single-bias hate crime incidents reported in the United States in 2022, 17.3% were motivated by religious bias, and 3.6% took place in a church, temple, mosque, or synagogue.[1748] Under federal law, hate crimes may be punishable by a fine and by a term of imprisonment up to life.[1749] Religion-motivated hate crimes are codified in all but a few states[1750] and are often a combination of original offense and sentence enhancement. California law, for example, makes it a misdemeanor to damage another's property because of that person's religion and raises other misdemeanors to felonies if motivated by religious bias.[1751] Other states penalize hate crimes solely as original offenses. For example, Michigan law makes "ethnic intimidation" (which includes intimidation or harassment because of religion) a felony punishable by up to two years in prison and/or USD 5,000 in fines.[1752]

1744. *See Stratton v. State*, 13 Ark. 688 (1853); Cal. Penal Code § 302 (West 2023); Fla. Stat. § 871.01 (2023); *Folds v. State*, 51 S.E. 305 (Ga. 1905); *Kidder v. State*, 58 Ind. 68 (1877); *State v. Stroud*, 68 N.W. 450 (Iowa 1896); Mich. Comp. Laws § 750-169 (2022); Mo. Rev. Stat. § 574.035 (2022); Nev. Rev. Stat. § 201.270 (2022); N.C. Gen. Stat. § 14-288.4(a)(7) (2022); Okla. Stat. tit. 21, § 915 (2022); *Commonwealth v. Siwert*, 4 Pa. D. & C.3d 589 (1977); S.C. Code Ann. § 16-17-520 (2022); *Layne v. State*, 72 Tenn. 199 (1879); *Corp. of the President of The Church of Jesus Christ of Latter-day Saints v. Wallace*, 573 P.2d 1285 (Utah 1978); *Commonwealth v. Jennings*, 44 Va. 624 (1846).
1745. N.Y. Penal Law § 240.21 (McKinney 2022).
1746. Jason Deparle, *111 Held in St. Patrick's AIDS Protest*, N.Y. Times, Dec. 11, 1989, at B3.
1747. *See, e.g., Church of Christ in Hollywood v. Superior Court*, 121 Cal. Rptr. 2d 810 (Cal. Ct. App. 2002).
1748. *2022 Hate Crime Statistics*, Dep't of Just., https://www.justice.gov/hatecrimes/hate-crime-statistics (last visited Sep. 30, 2023). Compared to 64.5% motivated by race, ethnicity, or ancestry, 15.9% by sexual orientation, 3.2% by gender identity, 1.4% by disability, and 1.0% by gender. *Ibid.*; *see also 2021 Hate Crime Statistics*, Dep't of Just., https://www.justice.gov/hatecrimes/2021-hate-crime-statistics (last visited Sep. 30, 2023) (reporting 14.1% of single-bias incidents in 2021 were religiously motivated).
1749. *See* 18 U.S.C. §§ 241, 245, 247, 249; 42 U.S.C. § 3631 (2018).
1750. Arkansas, Indiana, South Carolina, and Wyoming have no hate crime statutes. *See ADL Hate Crime Map*, Anti-Defamation League, https://www.adl.org/resources/tools-to-track-hate/hate-crime-map (last visited Sep. 30, 2023).
1751. Cal. Penal Code §§ 422.6(b), 422.7, 422.55 (West 2022).
1752. Mich. Comp. Laws § 750.147b (2022).

§2. Religious Freedom of Incarcerated Persons

I. Basic Framework: RLUIPA

658. Historically, federal and state prisoners in the United States were considered to forfeit personal rights, including the right to freely exercise their religion.[1753] Even so, US prisons have a long history of incorporating mainstream Christian "reformation" principles and allowing inmates to engage in mainstream Christian practices.[1754] The civil rights movement of the late twentieth and early twenty-first centuries had two major effects on the US penal system, however: it placed increased emphasis on rehabilitation and on accommodations for the religious practices of prisoners from minority religious traditions. As a result, courts have increasingly recognized that prisoners—particularly those of minority faiths—maintain religious exercise rights, while still recognizing that incarceration necessarily limits many rights and freedoms.[1755]

659. Questions of religion in the lives of incarcerated persons are now largely governed by the Religious Land Use and Institutionalized Persons Act (RLUIPA),[1756] which, in contrast to RFRA, has been upheld as a valid exercise of federal power vis-à-vis the states.[1757] For more on RFRA (Religious Freedom Restoration Act), *see* Part I (Legal Framework and Sources), Chapter 2 (Other Legislation with Regard to Religion). Like RFRA, RLUIPA imposes a form of "strict scrutiny": RLUIPA prohibits government from substantially burdening the religious exercise of persons institutionalized or incarcerated by the state, even through policies of general applicability, unless the government demonstrates it has a compelling interest in doing so that cannot be achieved by less-restrictive means.[1758] Petitioners bear

1753. *See Pervear v. Massachusetts*, 72 U.S. (5 Wall.) 475, 479–480 (1866) (stating that prisoners charged with offenses under state law have no federal constitutional rights); *see also Price v. Johnston*, 334 U.S. 266, 285 (1948) ("Lawful incarceration brings about the necessary withdrawal or limitation of many privileges and rights … ."); *Ruffin v. Commonwealth*, 62 Va. (21 Gratt.) 790, 796 (1871) ("A convicted felon … not only forfeited his liberty, but all his personal rights except those which the law in its humanity accords to him.").

1754. *See* Elyse Slabaugh, Note, *Dignity, Deference, and Discrimination: An Analysis of Religious Freedom in America's Prisons*, 49 BYU L. Rev. 269, 273–275 (2023).

1755. *See Jones v. Cunningham*, 371 U.S. 236 (1963) (marking a deviation from *Pervear* by holding that a paroled state inmate had a constitutional right to file a writ of habeas corpus in federal court); *see also Wolff v. McDonnell*, 418 U.S. 539, 555 (1974) ("[T]hough his rights may be diminished by the needs and exigencies of the institutional environment, a prisoner is not wholly stripped of constitutional protections … .").

1756. Religious Land Use and Institutionalized Persons Act of 2000, Pub. L. No. 106-274, 114 Stat. 803 (codified at 42 U.S.C. §§2000cc to 2000cc-5 (2018)). *But cf.* Slabaugh, *Dignity, Deference, and Discrimination*, *supra* n. 1754, at 290–305 (discussing other free-exercise-related claims commonly made by prisoners, including First Amendment retaliation claims, under s. 1983, title 42, of the US Code, and equal treatment claims, under the Equal Protection Clause).

1757. *Cutter v. Wilkinson*, 544 U.S. 709 (2005).

1758. 42 U.S.C. 2000cc-1(a) (2018). *But cf.* Slabaugh, *Dignity, Deference, and Discrimination*, *supra* n. 1754, at 290–305 (discussing questions that remain, after the Supreme Court's decisions in *Cutter* and *Holt*, regarding the level of scrutiny and deference courts should employ in analyzing prisoners' First Amendment retaliation claims and equal treatment claims, apart from any free exercise claims made under RLUIPA).

the initial burden of proving that their religious exercise is based on sincere religious belief and that government action substantially burdens their religious exercise.[1759] If that burden of proof is satisfied, the burden shifts to the government to show that the imposed restriction is the least restrictive means to achieve a compelling government interest.[1760] States enjoy sovereign immunity to monetary claims under RLUIPA; plaintiffs can seek equitable relief only.[1761]

660. A handful of claims made by prisoners under RLUIPA have reached the Supreme Court.[1762] The 2015 *Holt v. Hobbs* opinion set important standards for interpreting terms such as "substantial burden" and "compelling interest", as discussed below.[1763] In *Holt*, a Muslim prisoner in an Arkansas detention facility believed that wearing a short beard was an essential religious practice; however, the state prison grooming policy restricted prisoners' growth of facial hair and imposed serious disciplinary action for policy violations. The Supreme Court held that the restriction was impermissible under RLUIPA; the policy placed a substantial burden on the claimant's religious exercise, but the government failed to prove that it had a compelling interest in imposing the regulation and that the regulation was the least restrictive means of furthering that interest.[1764]

A. *"Substantial Burden" under RLUIPA*

661. The Supreme Court in *Holt* noted that Congress intended RLUIPA's expansive provisions to be construed broadly in favor of protecting religious freedom, even to the extent of requiring a prison to incur more expenses in its operations to avoid burdening religious exercise.[1765] Noting the breadth of RLUIPA protections, the Court held that the "substantial burden" test asks whether a prison regulation substantially burdens any religious exercise, not whether the regulation allows the inmate alternative means of worship.[1766] The fact that the petitioner had been allowed a prayer rug and participation in Muslim holidays did not negate the possibility of a substantial burden being imposed by the no-beard policy. A "substantial

1759. *Holt v. Hobbs*, 574 U.S. 352, 360–361 (2015).
1760. *Ibid.*, at 362 (citing 42 U.S.C. § 2000cc-1(a)).
1761. *Sossamon v. Texas*, 563 U.S. 277, 285–287, 293 (2011).
1762. *Cutter*, 544 U.S. at 719–720 (responding to state government officials' facial challenge to RLUIPA's constitutionality in holding RLUIPA provisions related to institutionalized persons "alleviate[] exceptional government-created burdens on private religious exercise" and do not violate the Establishment Clause); *Sossamon*, 563 U.S. at 285–287, 293 (holding that states, by accepting federal funds, do not waive sovereign immunity to private suits for money damages under RLUIPA); *Holt*, 574 U.S. at 361–370 (delineating standards for RLUIPA's "substantial burden" and "compelling interest" provisions in holding that state's prison grooming policy violated RLUIPA); *Ramirez v. Collier*, 142 S. Ct. 1264 (2022) (holding that prison officials failed to show an execution-chamber ban on audible prayer and religious touch by death-row inmate's pastor was the least restrictive means of furthering the state's compelling interests).
1763. *Holt*, 574 U.S. at 361–370.
1764. *Ibid.*
1765. *Ibid.*, at 358 (quoting 42 U.S.C. § 2000cc-3(c), (g)).
1766. *Ibid.*, at 361–362.

burden" has also been defined as a policy that (1) influences adherents to act in a way that violates their religious beliefs or (2) forces them to choose between either adhering to their beliefs or receiving a non-trivial benefit that other inmates receive.[1767]

662. A substantial burden on religious exercise also results when a correctional facility requires verification of an inmate's religion from outside entities before granting religious accommodations.[1768] Prisoners need only provide reasonable evidence of their religious beliefs, although it is appropriate for officials to question whether an inmate's request for religious accommodations is motivated by sincere belief or some other purpose.[1769]

B. "Compelling Interest" under RLUIPA

663. Under RLUIPA, policies that place substantial burdens on religious exercise are valid only pursuant to a compelling government interest. *Holt v. Hobbs* narrows the compelling interest standard to regulations that can be shown to further a specific compelling interest.[1770] Before *Holt*, many lower courts had held that a general interest in prison security was a sufficient reason to restrict particular religious activities such as wearing beards. In *Holt*, the government argued that the specific reason for prohibiting beards was to prevent inmates from hiding contraband in their facial hair and to make it harder for inmates to disguise themselves. The Court agreed that the government articulated specific compelling security interests but held that the beard-length rule was not the least restrictive means to achieve those interests.[1771]

C. "Least Restrictive Means" under RLUIPA

664. RLUIPA requires the government to maintain security and promote other compelling interests using the least restrictive means available. Where various ways of furthering a compelling interest exist, the government must adopt the method that least burdens religious exercise. In *Holt*, the Court invalidated the beard-length rule because the government failed to show it could not adopt less-restrictive means of furthering its security interests, such as searching inmates' beards for contraband, similar to routine searches of inmates' shoes and clothing, and photographing inmates in both clean-shaven and bearded states to facilitate identification.[1772]

1767. *Adkins v. Kaspar*, 393 F.3d 559, 570 (5th Cir. 2004).

1768. *Roberts v. Klein*, 770 F. Supp. 2d 1102, 1112 (D. Nev. 2011).

1769. *See DeMarco v. Davis*, 914 F.3d 383, 388 & n.8 (5th Cir. 2019); *Lovelace v. Lee*, 472 F.3d 174, 187 n.2 (4th Cir. 2006); *Roberts*, 770 F. Supp. 2d at 1111 (citing *Malik v. Brown*, 16 F.3d 330, 333 (9th Cir. 1994)).

1770. *Holt*, 574 U.S. at 362–363.

1771. *Ibid.*, at 362–366, 369–370.

1772. *Ibid.*, at 364–367.

II. Religious Diets

665. Since the 1970s, US courts have maintained that prisoners have the right to a diet that comports with the requirements of their religion, if the expense of providing it is not prohibitive and prison officials can offer no rational reason for denying it.[1773] Prisoners who bring a claim under RLUIPA have the burden to prove that the diet they receive violates their sincere religious beliefs and that the range of available foods substantially burdens their free exercise.[1774] If that burden is met, the government must demonstrate a compelling state interest in not providing the requested diet and narrowly tailored means to achieve that interest.[1775] Inmates have the right to receive a diet that complies with their sincere religious beliefs, even if such a diet is not mandated by their religion.[1776] Cost-effective food production and efficient food distribution have been found to be sufficient government interests, and courts generally defer to a correctional facility's food regulations unless they place a substantial burden on an inmate's religious practices.[1777]

666. Prison authorities have been required to accommodate special fasting requirements and participation in major religious holiday meals or feasts—including providing specific ceremonial foods for those meals—to the extent that the administrative and security costs of making the accommodation are not prohibitive.[1778]

667. Courts have also ruled, however, that a prison is not required to provide specific foods tailored toward a particular religion when it already provides an alternative menu that meets the required dietary restrictions.[1779] But the available alternative must comply with the minimum nutritional standards set forth by the state's

---

1773. *See, e.g.*, *Love v. Reed*, 216 F.3d 682, 691 (8th Cir. 2000); *cf. Cruz v. Beto*, 405 U.S. 319, 322 (1972) (finding "palpable discrimination by the State" where an inmate is "denied a reasonable opportunity of pursuing his faith comparable to the opportunity afforded fellow prisoners").

1774. *See Ackerman v. Washington*, 16 F.4th 170, 180–181 (6th Cir. 2021) (explaining RLUIPA's sincerity prong is "not a difficult hurdle" and is essentially a "credibility assessment" to determine if the plaintiff's religious belief is honest); *Abdulhaseeb v. Calbone*, 600 F.3d 1301, 1314 & n.6 (10th Cir. 2010).

1775. *Ackerman*, 16 F.4th at 179; *Abdulhaseeb*, 600 F.3d at 1312.

1776. *See Koger v. Bryan*, 523 F.3d 789, 797–798 (7th Cir. 2008); *Abdulhaseeb*, 600 F.3d at 1314–1315.

1777. *See Cutter v. Wilkinson*, 544 U.S. 709, 723 (2005); *Cotton v. Cate*, 578 F. App'x 712, 714–715 (9th Cir. 2014); *Patel v. U.S. Bureau of Prisons*, 515 F.3d 807, 813–815 (8th Cir. 2008); *DeHart v. Horn*, 390 F.3d 262, 269–272 (3d Cir. 2004).

1778. *See Ackerman*, 16 F.4th at 170 (striking down under RLUIPA a state policy that did not accommodate Jewish prisoners' need to eat religiously required foods with meals on holidays); *Shakur v. Selsky*, 391 F.3d 106, 120 (2d Cir. 2004).

1779. *See, e.g.*, *Riley v. DeCarlo*, 532 F. App'x 23, 28–29 (3d Cir. 2013) (holding the government was not required to provide Halal meat for all Muslim inmates, which would "significantly impact prison resources", when inmates could choose from available "alternative protein" or "no animal products" diets to meet religious requirements); *Ciempa v. Jones*, 745 F. Supp. 2d 1171, 1197–1198 (N.D. Okla. 2010) (holding state did not violate RLUIPA by not providing Halal diet where plaintiff stated that the kosher food provided met his religious requirements). *But see Hudson v. Dennehy*, 538 F. Supp. 2d 400, 411 (D. Mass. 2008) (holding state's refusal to provide Halal foods to Muslim inmates violated RLUIPA where inmates felt pressured to eat meals that did not conform to their religious beliefs).

department of corrections.[1780] The state imposes a substantial burden on religious practice when it "forces a prisoner to choose between adequate nutrition and religious practice".[1781]

III. Right to Worship

668. Free exercise of religion for incarcerated persons encompasses the possession of religious texts and objects of worship and the right to worship with others of the same faith. Prisons may not pressure inmates into participating in religious activities but are required to allow participation in worship services and possession of religious items as far as security and administrative interests allow.[1782]

669. Concerning objects used for worship, prisoners have only the right to possess personal items that are fundamental to the practice of their religion.[1783] This right may be superseded when the items sought by an inmate potentially compromise security, although prison officials are required to make an effort to provide non-dangerous substitutes.[1784] A prisoner's right to own religious literature is similarly subordinate to a state's compelling interest in safety and discipline, especially when the literature may be used to compromise prison security, promulgate extremist ideas, or recruit members for extremist groups that constitute security threats.[1785] Nevertheless, the state must show that limiting access to literature is the least restrictive means to achieve any such compelling interest.[1786]

670. In many correctional facilities, a single chapel or meeting place serves the congregational needs of all religious groups. Because of limited resources and a multiplicity of faiths, prisons may provide generic services for major religious groups. Prison officials may appropriately allot more time to groups that have more representation in the prison population but should allow reasonably frequent

1780. *See Jones v. Carter*, 915 F.3d 1147 (7th Cir. 2019); *Kretchmar v. Beard*, 241 F. App'x 863, 865 (3d Cir. 2007); *Watkins v. Shabazz*, 180 F. App'x 773, 775 (9th Cir. 2006).

1781. *Carter*, 915 F.3d at 1150 (citing *Thompson v. Holm*, 809 F.3d 376, 380 (7th Cir. 2016) (collecting cases)).

1782. *Cutter v. Wilkinson*, 544 U.S. 709, 720–721 (2005) (noting the exercise of religion involves "physical acts" such as gathering for worship or participating in a sacrament); *DeMarco v. Davis*, 914 F.3d 383, 389–390 (5th Cir. 2019) (finding the seizure of religious books burdened an inmate's religious practice); *Smith v. Allen*, 502 F.3d 1255, 1277–1281 (11th Cir. 2007), *overruled on other grounds by Hoever v. Marks*, 993 F.3d 1353 (11th Cir. 2021) (holding inmate failed to show that state's denying him access to a small crystal, a designated area of worship, and a fire pit substantially burdened his practice of Odinism).

1783. *Allen*, 502 F.3d at 1278.

1784. *Ibid.*, at 1279–1281; *Burke v. N.D. Dep't of Corr. & Rehab.*, 620 F. Supp. 2d 1035, 1050–1051 (D.N.D. 2009).

1785. *See Hayes v. Tennessee*, 424 F. App'x 546, 552–553 (6th Cir. 2011); *Murphy v. Lockhart*, 826 F. Supp. 2d 1016, 1034 (E.D. Mich. 2011) (as amended); *Muntaqim v. Payne*, 628 S.W.3d 629, 639–641 (Ark. 2021).

1786. 42 U.S.C. § 2000cc-1 (2018); *see, e.g., Jesus Christ Prison Ministry v. Cal. Dep't of Corr.*, 456 F. Supp. 2d 1188, 1203–1205 (E.D. Cal. 2006), *withdrawn pursuant to settlement* (Apr. 16, 2007).

meeting-place access to all groups that wish to congregate.[1787] Correctional facilities are required to accommodate group services where inmates show denial of such services would substantially burden the practice of their religion.[1788] But again, rules that restrict group worship are valid if they support a legitimate penological interest and are the least restrictive means of achieving that interest.[1789] For example, a federal district court held that the state had a compelling security interest in not allowing prisoners housed in a special confinement unit to participate in in-person group religious services; however, the court also held that denying those inmates permission to participate via closed-circuit television was not the least restrictive means of achieving the state's compelling security interests.[1790]

IV. Attire and Grooming

671. The wearing of religious apparel must be allowed where it presents no real threat to valid penological interests. Deference is given to prison administrators' determinations that certain restrictions on clothing are necessary to achieve security or other compelling interests, but the interests must be legitimate, and the restrictions must be narrowly tailored.[1791]

672. Permission to wear long hair and facial hair for religious reasons is also subject to penological security, safety, and hygiene interests. Hair-length regulations are valid if they constitute the least restrictive means of meeting a compelling need, such as preventing prisoners from hiding lice, infections, weapons, or contraband in "unsearchable" long hair or dreadlocks.[1792] As discussed above, the Supreme Court held in *Holt v. Hobbs* that the state failed to demonstrate its policy prohibiting beards longer than one-half inch (1.27 cm) was the least restrictive

1787. *Rouser v. White*, 630 F. Supp. 2d 1165, 1182 (E.D. Cal. 2009); *Odneal v. Dretke*, 435 F. Supp. 2d 608, 621–622 (S.D. Tex. 2006), *aff'd in relevant part by* 324 F. App'x 297, 302 (5th Cir. 2009).
1788. *See, e.g.*, *Cavin v. Mich. Dep't of Corr.*, 927 F.3d 455, 458–459 (6th Cir. 2019).
1789. *See, e.g.*, *Hudson v. Dennehy*, 538 F. Supp. 2d 400, 412–413 (D. Mass. 2008); *Thunderhorse v. Pierce*, 418 F. Supp. 2d 875, 895 (E.D. Tex. 2006), *aff'd in relevant part by* 364 F. App'x 141 (5th Cir. 2010).
1790. *Hudson*, 538 F. Supp. 2d at 412–413.
1791. *See, e.g.*, *Muhammad v. Sapp*, 388 F. App'x 892, 895–897 (11th Cir. 2010) (finding restrictions on Sunni Muslim inmate's clothing were narrowly tailored to state's security interests); *Benning v. Georgia*, 864 F. Supp. 2d 1358, 1365, 1369 (M.D. Ga. 2012) (noting courts must apply RLUIPA with "due deference" to experienced prison administrators but finding state grooming policy prohibiting Jewish prisoners from maintaining earlocks was not the least restrictive means to achieve state's compelling interests in safe, secure, and orderly prison operations); *Jihad v. Fabian*, 680 F. Supp. 2d 1021, 1027–1028 (D. Minn. 2010) (finding policy prohibiting Muslim inmate from wearing a Kufi and religious medallion outside of his cell was narrowly tailored to state's compelling security interests).
1792. *See, e.g.*, *Smith v. Owens*, 13 F.4th 1319, 1328–1330 (11th Cir. 2021); *Koger v. Mohr*, 964 F.3d 532, 539–540 (6th Cir. 2020); *Knight v. Thompson*, 797 F.3d 934, 944–947 (11th Cir. 2015); *Williams v. Snyder*, 367 F. App'x 679, 682–683 (7th Cir. 2010). *But see Williams v. Champagne*, 13 F. Supp. 3d 624, 631–632 (E.D. La. 2014) (denying state's motion for summary judgment where state could point to no incidents of lice or contraband hidden in hair and where state offered no evidence that its hair-length policies were the least restrictive means to achieve safety and security interests).

means of preventing prisoners from hiding contraband or disguising their identities.[1793] In a later case, a federal court of appeals affirmed that a state did present sufficient evidence to show (1) that permitting untrimmed beards presented safety and security risks, such as inmates hiding contraband, avoiding identification, and pulling beards in altercations; and (2) that banning untrimmed beards was the least restrictive means to achieve compelling safety and security interests.[1794]

V. Chaplains

673. A prison may provide chaplains and other religious leaders at public expense.[1795] Chaplains minister to inmates' spiritual needs and perform administrative functions, such as managing community volunteers, processing requests for dietary or other religious accommodations, and organizing both secular and religious counselling or educational programs.[1796] Prisoners have the right to access clergy of their own religious persuasion but not a "specific religious advisor of their choice".[1797] When chaplains represent only major religious groups, however, inmates of other religions should be allowed access to clergy of their own faith if denying such access substantially burdens their religious exercise.[1798]

674. Whether RLUIPA requires the presence of a requested chaplain and the performance of requested religious rites at a condemned inmate's execution has been an unsettled issue.[1799] In 2022, the Supreme Court held that a death-row inmate would likely prevail in his claim that the state of Texas had violated RLUIPA by categorically banning chaplains from audibly praying and "laying hands" on inmates during execution by lethal injection.[1800] The Court held that the state failed to show the bans were the least restrictive means of meeting its compelling interests

1793. *Holt v. Hobbs*, 574 U.S. 352, 360–370 (2015).

1794. *Owens*, 13 F.4th at 1326–1334.

1795. *See* 28 C.F.R. § 548.12 (2022); *Sch. Dist. of Abington Twp. v. Schempp*, 374 U.S. 203, 230, 297–298 (1963) (Brennan, J., concurring) ("Since government has deprived [members of the Armed Forces and prisoners] of the opportunity to practice their faith at places of their choice, the argument runs, government may, in order to avoid infringing the free exercise guarantees, provide substitutes where it requires such persons to be."); *Katcoff v. Marsh*, 755 F.2d 223 (2d Cir. 1985) (holding armed services chaplaincy program did not violate the Establishment Clause). The Supreme Court has not issued a decision regarding the constitutionality of prison or military chaplains.

1796. Pew Rsch. Ctr., *Religion in Prisons: A 50-State Survey of Prison Chaplains* 8 (Mar. 22, 2012), https://www.pewforum.org/2012/03/22/prison-chaplains-what-they-do (link to PDF).

1797. *Jihad v. Fabian*, 680 F. Supp. 2d 1021, 1027 (D. Minn. 2010).

1798. *Rouser v. White*, 630 Supp. 2d 1165, 1181–1182 (E.D. Cal. 2009).

1799. *See, e.g., Dunn v. Smith*, 141 S. Ct. 725, 725 (2021) (mem.) (Kagan, J., with Breyer, Sotomayor, and Barrett, JJ., concurring) (concurring in Court's decision to leave circuit court injunction in place, enjoining state policy that excluded pastors from the execution chamber, because the state failed to show policy was necessary to ensure prison security); *Murphy v. Collier*, 139 S. Ct. 1475 (2019) (mem.) (granting stay of execution unless state permitted the presence of a Buddhist spiritual advisor); *Dunn v. Ray*, 139 S. Ct. 661 (2019) (mem.) (allowing execution of Muslim prisoner to proceed where state policy denied the presence of an imam at execution but permitted the presence of a Christian chaplain).

1800. *Ramirez v. Collier*, 142 S. Ct. 1264, 1284 (2022).

in maintaining "security in the execution chamber, preventing unnecessary suffering of the prisoner, and avoiding further emotional trauma to the victim's family members".[1801] The Court noted that those compelling interests could be met by other, less-restrictive means: for example, by allowing a spiritual advisor to stand a few feet away from the prisoner, with a security guard close by; restricting the spiritual advisor's touch to the prisoner's lower leg or foot, far from any IV line; limiting "the volume of any prayer so that medical officials [could] monitor an inmate's condition"; and requiring "silence during critical points in the execution process".[1802]

1801. *Ibid.*, at 1280.
1802. *Ibid.*, at 1280–1281.

Part VIII. Financing of Religious Communities

Chapter 1. Direct Financing

§1. Historical Background

I. Early Disestablishment Efforts

675. Most American colonies and US states were formed with established churches that were financially supported by colonial or state governments.[1803] One of the earliest and most significant efforts to disestablish a state church was the Virginia Statute for Religious Freedom, authored by Thomas Jefferson and enacted by the Virginia General Assembly in 1786.[1804]

676. The Virginia Statute for Religious Freedom presented several reasons for disestablishment: that God created man's mind free and that it should remain free from civil government's attempts to coerce belief, that requiring civil office-holders to hold certain religious opinions fosters only outward conformity with religion and corrupts religion, that attempts by the government to coerce belief are sinful and infringe on free choice, and that the civil government need not control "the field of opinion" or promote or "restrain the profession or propagation of principles", since "truth is great and will prevail" and has "nothing to fear from conflict" with error.[1805]

677. The substantive sections of the Virginia Statute provided several protections: (1) citizens would not be required to attend or support any religious denomination, nor could they be discriminated against for their religious beliefs; (2) individuals were free to express and promote their religious beliefs; and (3) citizens' religious activities would not affect their civic privileges.[1806]

1803. Philip Hamburger, *Separation of Church and State* 9–10, 89–92 (2004).
1804. Va. Code Ann. § 57-1 (2022).
1805. *Ibid.*; Daniel L. Dreisbach, *A New Perspective on Jefferson's Views on Church-State Relations: The Virginia Statute for Establishing Religious Freedom in Its Legislative Context*, 35 Am. J. Legal Hist. 172, 185–186 (1991).
1806. Va. Code Ann. § 57-1; Dreisbach, *A New Perspective*, *supra* n. 1805, at 186.

678. The Virginia Statute and James Madison's *Memorial and Remonstrance*, penned in support of the Virginia Statute, continue to be regarded, including by the Supreme Court, as significant expressions of the Founders' beliefs on church-state separation that led them to write the Establishment Clause.[1807] Others suggest that the record is more complicated and that the First Amendment, although drafted by Madison, was part of a broader discussion that involved compromises between federalists and anti-federalists.[1808] In any case, *Memorial and Remonstrance* has been a key document in the modern interpretation and understanding of the Establishment Clause.

679. In *Memorial and Remonstrance*, Madison argued both against formal establishment and assessment, an alternative idea debated in the Virginia Legislature, which involved levying a tax that would support a number of Christian denominations in Virginia.[1809] Madison argued that assessment would be an establishment of religion that would violate the principle of equality and equal rights, including the right to freedom of religion.[1810] Further, in his view, Christianity did not need assessment because it grew and thrived even when governments were hostile toward it, such as in the early days of Christianity. Assessment, argued Madison, would not only harm the growth of the Christian religion and undermine harmony between the various Christian sects but also create problems for the government. In Madison's view, establishing a church would harm the reputation of the government as an asylum for those who are repressed. Madison saw freedom of religion as a natural right that should not be alienated or abridged by government; since religion is exempt from authority of society, it should be exempt from government, which derives its authority from society. He further argued that if the government could infringe on this right, then it could infringe on other natural rights as well.[1811]

680. Disestablishment proceeded gradually in US states until 1833, when all states had formally disestablished state religions.[1812] For additional details, *see* Part I (Legal Framework and Sources), Chapter 1 (Constitutional Position of Religion).

1807. Daniel L. Dreisbach, *Thomas Jefferson and Bills Number 82–86 of the Revision of the Laws of Virginia, 1776–1786: New Light on the Jeffersonian Model of Church-State Relations*, 69 N.C. L. Rev. 159, 173–174 & nn. 76–79 (1990).

1808. *See, e.g.*, Hamburger, *Separation of Church and State*, *supra* n. 1803, at 104–110; Robert G. Natelson, *The Original Meaning of the Establishment Clause*, 14 Wm. & Mary Bill Rts. J. 73, 76–79 (2005). *See also generally* Noah Feldman, *The Intellectual Origins of the Establishment Clause*, 77 N.Y.U. L. Rev. 346 (2002).

1809. James Madison, *Memorial and Remonstrance Against Religious Assessments, [CA. 20 June] 1785*, Founders Online, Nat'l Archives, https://founders.archives.gov/documents/Madison/01-08-02-0163 (last visited Sep. 30, 2023); Dreisbach, *Thomas Jefferson and Bills Number 82–86*, *supra* n. 1807, at 163–170.

1810. Madison, *Memorial and Remonstrance*, *supra* n. 1809; *see also* Gerald Bauer, *The Quest for Religious Freedom in Virginia*, 41 Hist. Mag. Protestant Episcopal Church 85, 88–89 (1972).

1811. *See* sources cited *supra* n. 1810.

1812. Rhode Island never had an established church, though it did codify Christianity in its early laws. *See* Dye Neumann & Finkelman, *Disestablishment of State Churches*, *supra* n. 167, at 136.

II. Early Constitutional Approaches to State Aid

681. As the Establishment Clause was not applied to the states until incorporation of the First Amendment into the Fourteenth Amendment in the 1940s, few early court cases involved the Establishment Clause. In its earliest case addressing direct aid to religious organizations—*Bradfield v. Roberts*, decided in 1899—the Supreme Court took a permissive attitude.[1813] The Court held that using federal money to build a hospital owned by a religious order did not violate the Establishment Clause.[1814] *Bradfield* implicated the Establishment Clause because the hospital was located in Washington, DC, which brought the case under federal jurisdiction. A group of Roman Catholic nuns used federal funds to finance a hospital that provided medical help to people of all faiths, not just Catholics.[1815] The city of Washington, DC, and the hospital agreed that two-thirds of the building's capacity would be used for indigent patients and that the government would pay for the care of those patients. A taxpayer brought suit, alleging that federal funding of a hospital with "sectarian character" violated the Establishment Clause.

682. The Supreme Court reasoned that the act providing for incorporation of the hospital did not mention religion, or the religious faith of the incorporators, and that the hospital was established for a non-sectarian purpose. Therefore, the Court found that the hospital was a "secular" private corporation providing secular services; the fact that the individuals who ran the hospital held religious beliefs in common did not render the hospital religious or sectarian.[1816] The Court conceded that while "the influence of any particular church may be powerful over the members of a non-sectarian and secular corporation, incorporated for a certain defined purpose and with clearly stated powers", such influence was not enough to convert an otherwise secular organization into a religious one.[1817]

683. The Court's focus on "purpose" was to become a key concept in later Establishment Clause jurisprudence. *Bradfield v. Roberts* was an early precursor of the secular purpose test and exemplifies an early accommodationist approach to state funding of religiously affiliated charitable institutions.

§2. Direct Aid: Separation of Church and State

684. Everson v. Board of Education was the first modern Establishment Clause case decided by the Supreme Court. It concerned a state law that authorized local school boards to reimburse parents for the cost of busing students on public transportation, including students attending religious schools. The Court cited the concept of a "high and impregnable" wall of separation between church and state,

1813. *Bradfield v. Roberts*, 175 U.S. 291, 297–300 (1899).
1814. *Ibid.*, at 297–300.
1815. *Ibid.*, at 292–294.
1816. *Ibid.*, at 297–300.
1817. *Ibid.*, at 298.

drawn from an 1802 letter from Thomas Jefferson to a group of Baptists in Danbury, Connecticut—often referred to as the "Danbury Letter".[1818]

685. In *Everson*, the Supreme Court interpreted the Establishment Clause as requiring strict separation of church and state:

> Neither a state nor the Federal Government can set up a church. Neither can pass laws which aid one religion, aid all religions, or prefer one religion over another. … No tax in any amount, large or small, can be levied to support any religious activities or institutions, whatever they may be called, or whatever form they may adopt to teach or practice religion.[1819]

Nevertheless, the Court allowed the reimbursement program, saying that while the wall of separation must remain "high and impregnable", and that the Court would "not approve the slightest breach", the program did not constitute a breach.[1820] For more on the Court's reasoning in *Everson*, *see* section 3 of this chapter, below.

686. More recently, during the COVID-19 pandemic, the issue of direct government aid to religious organizations arose in relation to Paycheck Protection Program (PPP) loans. The PPP loan program was established temporarily through the Coronavirus Aid, Relief, and Economic Security (CARES) Act[1821] to help certain types of "small businesses"—including faith-based nonprofit organizations with fewer than 500 employees[1822]—meet payroll obligations during the pandemic. While the federal government made clear that receiving a loan would not affect a religious organization's autonomy or rights under the First Amendment, RFRA, or section 702 of Title VII,[1823] many such organizations did not apply for PPP loans, declined loans after receiving approval, or paid them back rather than request available loan forgiveness.[1824] Nevertheless, 122,665 faith-based organizations received PPP loans, averaging nearly USD 75,500 per loan.[1825] Given that these loans constituted direct state aid to religious organizations, the lack of "serious political or

---

1818. *Everson v. Bd. of Educ.*, 330 U.S. 1, 16, 18 (1947) (quoting *Reynolds v. United States*, 98 U.S. 145, 164 (1878)); *see also* Letter from Thomas Jefferson to Danbury, Connecticut, Baptist Association, *supra* n. 526.
1819. *Everson*, 330 U.S. at 15–16.
1820. *Ibid.*, at 18.
1821. Coronavirus Aid, Relief, and Economic Security (CARES) Act, Pub. L. No. 116-136, 134 Stat. 281 (2020) (codified at 15 U.S.C.A. § 9001–9012, 9021–9034, 9041–9063, 9071–9080, and in scattered sections of 2, 17, 21, 26, and 33 U.S.C.A. (West 2023)).
1822. *See* U.S. Small Bus. Admin., *FAQ Regarding Participation of Faith-Based Organizations in PPP and EIDL* 3 (Apr. 3, 2020), https://www.sba.gov/document/support-faq-regarding-participation-faith-based-organizations-ppp-eidl (link to PDF).
1823. *Ibid.*, at 2.
1824. *See* Bob Smietana, *For Some Churches, Paying Back PPP Loans Is Better than Forgiveness*, Religion News Serv., https://religionnews.com/2021/11/02/for-some-churches-paying-back-ppp-loans-is-better-than-forgiveness (Nov. 2, 2021).
1825. *SBA Paycheck Protection Program—Religious Organizations—FederalPay*, FederalPay.org, https://www.federalpay.org/paycheck-protection-program/industries/religious-organizations (last visited Sep. 30, 2023).

public opposition" was perhaps surprising.[1826] While the public objected to large, well-endowed "megachurches" receiving loans, these objections echoed opposition to large for-profit corporations receiving PPP loans and did not appear to reflect Establishment Clause concerns.[1827] Generally speaking, political leaders and the public seemed to consider the pandemic an exigent circumstance that allowed for a temporary breach in the "wall of separation".[1828]

§3. Direct State Aid to Religiously Affiliated Schools

687. Constitutional questions of direct aid to religious organizations usually arise in the context of funding religious schools. The Supreme Court has used various approaches to determine when state aid to religiously affiliated schools constitutes impermissible direct aid. Under the current court doctrine, it appears that aid to private religious schools does not violate the Establishment Clause so long as the aid has a secular purpose, is allocated neutrally, and does not involve an inappropriate continuing relationship between the government and the religious authority. Nevertheless, it remains to be seen how the Supreme Court's abrogation of the *Lemon* test in 2022 will affect the adjudication of questions involving state aid to religiously affiliated schools.[1829] Subsections I through III below address how the Supreme Court's theories of interpretation have developed. Subsection IV addresses the impact of the Free Exercise Clause on direct state aid. For additional discussion of the financing of private religious schools, *see* Part IX (Education), Chapter 2 (Religious Schools).

I. "Child-Benefit" Theory

688. The *Everson* majority opinion allowed the public funding of transportation of students to religious schools. The decision turned on whether the aid in question provided a general and purely secular benefit directed to children of all schools, which was constitutional, or a benefit to "aid one religion, aid all religions, or prefer one religion over another",[1830] which would unconstitutionally breach the wall between church and state. Justice Hugo Black's approach in *Everson*, known as the

---

1826. *See* Ashley Schwartz-Lavares, Faith Abubey & Haley Yamada, *The Inequities of PPP: Megachurches, Large Corporations Receive Money Ahead of Small Businesses*, ABC News (Jan. 18, 2021), https://abcnews.go.com/US/inequities-ppp-megachurches-large-corporations-receive-money-ahead/story?id=75331197 (quoting Professor Micah Schwartzman, University of Virginia).

1827. *See ibid.*

1828. *See ibid.*

1829. *See supra* para. 372 and accompanying footnotes.

1830. *Everson v. Bd. of Educ.*, 330 U.S. 1, 15 (1947); *see also Zobrest v. Catalina Foothills Sch. Dist.*, 509 U.S. 1, 10 (1993) (internal quotation marks omitted) (quoting *Witters v. Wash. Dep't of Servs. for the Blind*, 474 U.S. 481, 488 (1986)).

"child-benefit theory", has been the basis for some, but not all, Supreme Court education-related Establishment Clause cases that followed.[1831]

689. This line of decisions focuses largely on neutrality and private choice as factors determining the constitutionality of state support for private religious schools. The Court has permitted aid where the funds go to religious schools on a neutral basis and the students or their parents can be characterized as the primary beneficiaries (who may then exercise choice in a way that makes religious schools secondary beneficiaries). For example, the Court has held that a state could not deny assistance to a blind student who chose to use generally available state rehabilitation program funds to study for the ministry at a Christian college.[1832]

690. In 2020, the Court held that the state of Montana could not prohibit student recipients from using generally available scholarships at religious schools when those scholarships were indirectly funded through donations that qualified for state tax credits.[1833] The Court noted that state support made "its way to religious schools only as a result of Montanans independently choosing to spend their scholarships at such schools".[1834] Two years later, the Court used similar reasoning to hold that Maine could not prohibit students in rural areas, where the state did not maintain secondary schools, from using state tuition assistance funds at private sectarian schools.[1835] In other cases, the Supreme Court has held that the state may loan secular textbooks to students at sectarian as well as non-sectarian schools,[1836] pay for an interpreter for a deaf student at a private religious school,[1837] and give money to parents in the form of a tax credit allowing them to deduct private school (including religious school) expenses.[1838] For a more detailed discussion of these cases in the context of the Establishment Clause, as well as non-discrimination principles, *see* Part VII (Religious Communities and Protections of the Individual), Chapter 7 (Non-discrimination); and Part IX (Education), Chapter 2 (Religious Schools).

II. "Religious Use" Approach

691. Another line of cases rejects any state funding of private religious schools that can be connected to a "religious use" of the money. This approach traces back to the 1971 Supreme Court decision in *Lemon v. Kurzman*. In that case, the Court held as unconstitutional state salary supplements for teachers of secular subjects in

1831. *Everson*, 330 U.S. at 18 ("The State contributes no money to the [parochial] schools. It does not support them. Its legislation, as applied, does no more than provide a general program to help parents get their children, regardless of their religion, safely and expeditiously to and from accredited schools.").
1832. *Witters v. Wash. Dep't of Servs. for the Blind*, 474 U.S. 481, 482 (1986).
1833. *Espinoza v. Mont. Dep't of Revenue*, 140 S. Ct. 2246, 2254 (2020).
1834. *Ibid.* (noting the parties did "not dispute that the scholarship program [was] permissible under the Establishment Clause" but still finding any such argument would be "unavailing").
1835. *Carson v. Makin*, 142 S. Ct. 1987 (2022).
1836. *Bd. of Educ. v. Allen*, 392 U.S. 236, 238 (1968).
1837. *Zobrest v. Catalina Foothills Sch. Dist.*, 509 U.S. 1, 10–14 (1993).
1838. *Mueller v. Allen*, 463 U.S. 388, 394–404 (1983).

private sectarian schools as well as direct state funding for secular subjects in religious schools. The Court set out a test for Establishment Clause challenges: the state aid must (1) have a secular legislative purpose, (2) have a principal effect that neither advances nor inhibits religion, and (3) not foster an "excessive governmental entanglement with religion".[1839]

692. In *Lemon*, the Court found that the aid had the "secular purpose" of improving the quality of education in religious schools. The Court also found that the aid, as it was restricted to secular subjects, did not have the principal effect of advancing religion. The aid failed the third prong of the *Lemon* test, however. The Court reasoned that the state would have to carry out "comprehensive, discriminating, and continuing" monitoring of classrooms to ensure the aid was not used for religious purposes, since the schools were pervasively religious and teachers played a central role in establishing the religious atmosphere.[1840] The Court held that such monitoring would "involve excessive and enduring entanglement between state and church".[1841] In discussing *Lemon*'s entanglement prong, the Court also noted that the programs in question had the potential of fostering "political division along religious lines" as denominations vied for state aid; this division, the Court reasoned, "was one of the principal evils against which the First Amendment was intended to protect".[1842] The Supreme Court eventually abandoned this "political division" approach, which sought in essence to privatize religion, as a reason for striking down aid.[1843]

693. The Supreme Court used the *Lemon* test and prohibition-on-religious-use line of reasoning to strike down a statutory provision that would have allowed religiously affiliated universities and colleges to use federally financed buildings for religious instruction or worship after a twenty-year waiting period.[1844] In 1985, the Court also relied on *Lemon* in two companion cases that were subsequently overruled, both barring state-paid public-school teachers from providing remedial education in secular subjects to students in private religious schools.[1845] Significantly, in one of the cases, *Grand Rapids School District v. Ball*, the Supreme Court struck down the program in part because the state did not restrict public-school teachers from teaching religion in private school classes.[1846] In the second, *Aguilar v. Felton*, the state imposed such restrictions, but the Court held that the restrictions

1839. *Lemon v. Kurtzman*, 403 U.S. 602, 612–613 (1971), *abrogated by Kennedy v. Bremerton Sch. Dist.*, 142 S. Ct. 2407, 2427–2428 (2022).

1840. *Ibid.*, at 619.

1841. *Ibid.*

1842. *Ibid.*, at 622–624.

1843. *Agostini v. Felton*, 521 U.S. 203, 233–234 (1997).

1844. *Tilton v. Richardson*, 403 U.S. 672, 683–684 (1971).

1845. *Sch. Dist. of Grand Rapids v. Ball*, 473 U.S. 373 (1985), *overruled by Agostini*, 403 U.S. at 672; *Aguilar v. Felton*, 473 U.S. 402 (1985), *overruled by Agostini*, 403 U.S. at 672.

1846. *Ball*, 473 U.S. at 397–398.

required "pervasive monitoring", which constituted impermissible state entanglement with religion.[1847] Thus, the *Lemon* test created what has been called a "Catch-22"[1848] problem.[1849] In paradoxically prohibiting excessive entanglement but requiring monitoring to avoid the advancement of religion (which risks excessive entanglement), the *Lemon* test significantly limited the viability of state funding of private religious schools.

694. The Supreme Court also used the *Lemon* line of reasoning to hold that states may not provide tuition reimbursement for parents sending their children to private religious schools.[1850] The Supreme Court later upheld a variation on tuition reimbursement involving tax credits, however, because no continued state surveillance of the schools was required, which would constitute excessive entanglement.[1851] Significantly, the Court applied a child-benefit approach in the tax credit case, holding that the tax credit did not primarily advance religion but instead reflected a "secular and understandable" decision by the state "to defray the cost of educational expenses incurred by parents".[1852] In the early twenty-first century, the Supreme Court moved away from the *Lemon* test, abrogating it officially in 2022.[1853]

III. Neutral Principles Approach: *Agostini v. Felton*

695. One problem with the *Everson* and *Lemon* lines of cases is that the theories are largely interchangeable. Virtually all aid to private religious schools can be characterized as permissible neutral aid helping children and parents pay for education. Or, conversely, such aid can be characterized as impermissible aid that schools will either use for religious purposes or that will entangle the state in its attempts to ensure aid is not used for such purposes.

696. The Supreme Court attempted to reconcile its own case law in 1997, when it overruled *Aguilar v. Felton.* As discussed above, *Aguilar* involved state payment of public-school teachers for teaching remedial classes in inner-city schools, including religious schools. New York City, which lost the case in 1985, petitioned to reopen the case, citing that it had been required to pay more than USD 100 million

1847. *Aguilar*, 473 U.S. at 412–414.
1848. *Bowen v. Kendrick*, 487 U.S. 589, 615 (1988).
1849. The phrase "Catch-22", which originated with the Joseph Heller novel of the same name, has come to mean a paradoxical situation that is unresolvable because it is grounded in self-contradictory, circular logic. *See* Joseph Heller, *Catch-22* (1961).
1850. *Comm. for Pub. Educ. & Religious Liberty v. Nyquist*, 413 U.S. 756 (1973).
1851. *Mueller v. Allen*, 463 U.S. 388, 402 (1983).
1852. *Ibid.*, at 395.
1853. *Kennedy v. Bremerton Sch. Dist.*, 142 S. Ct. 2407, 2427–2428 (2022); *see also Groff v. DeJoy*, 600 U.S. 447, 460 & n.7 (2023) (acknowledging *Kennedy*'s abrogation of the *Lemon* test).

to comply and arguing that the prior decision could not stand in the face of intervening precedent.[1854] The Court agreed and reversed its prior decision, holding that intervening cases "undermined the assumptions upon which *Ball* and *Aguilar* relied".[1855]

697. In *Agostini v. Felton*, the Supreme Court again applied *Lemon*'s three-pronged test. However, the Court changed the criteria for determining the "primary effects" of the aid, or second prong of the test, moving toward a "neutral principles" approach. The Court held that the primary effect of aid does not advance religion when aid is allocated on the basis of neutral, secular criteria that neither favor nor disfavor religion and when aid is made available to both religious and secular beneficiaries on a non-discriminatory basis. Under such circumstances, aid is less likely to have the effect of advancing religion.[1856] In addition, the Court rejected a basis that it had previously used to find a "primary effect" of advancing religion: the fact that the aid involved some kind of "symbolic union" of church and state. It rejected the presumption that the presence of public-school teachers in parochial classrooms, or of public employees on parochial school grounds, "inevitably results in the impermissible effect of state-sponsored indoctrination or constitutes a symbolic union between government and religion".[1857]

698. The Supreme Court also collapsed the analysis of the second and third prongs of the *Lemon* test, related to "primary effects" and "excessive entanglement":

> Regardless of how we have characterized the issue, … the factors we use to assess whether an entanglement is "excessive" are similar to the factors we use to examine "effect." That is, to assess entanglement, we have looked to "the character and purposes of the institutions that are benefited, the nature of the aid that the State provides, and the resulting relationship between the government and religious authority." Similarly, we have assessed a law's "effect" by examining the character of the institutions benefited (*e.g.*, whether the religious institutions were "predominantly religious"), and the nature of the aid that the State provided (*e.g.*, whether it was neutral and nonideological).[1858]

Thus, under *Agostini*'s neutral principles approach, aid to private religious schools appears permissible so long as the aid has a secular purpose, is allocated neutrally, and does not involve a continuing or excessively involved relationship between the government and the religious authority.

1854. *Agostini v. Felton*, 521 U.S. 203, 213–214 (1997).
1855. *Ibid.*, at 222.
1856. *Ibid.*, at 230–232.
1857. *Ibid.*, at 223–224.
1858. *Ibid.*, at 232–233 (citations omitted).

699. Again, with the Supreme Court's abandonment of the *Lemon* test, it remains to be seen if or how the Court will employ the "child benefit" and "neutral principles" approaches in Establishment Clause cases involving direct state aid to religiously affiliated schools.

IV. Free Exercise Limits on Denying Direct State Aid

700. The previous cases discussing state aid to religious schools examined Establishment Clause limitations on permissible state aid. The Free Exercise Clause, however, also addresses the question of direct state aid to schools. In 2017, the Supreme Court, in *Trinity Lutheran Church v. Comer*, relied on the Free Exercise Clause to hold that a state may not discriminate against religious beneficiaries in the distribution of generally available state benefits simply because of their religious identity. The benefit at issue was scrap rubber for school playground surfaces, available to educational institutions through a Missouri state grant program. The state disqualified Trinity Lutheran Church because of its religious identity, even though the Church objectively qualified as an operator of a day-care center and preschool.[1859] In striking down the program's discriminatory policy, the Court focused on the difference between action and identity. It distinguished *Locke v. Davey*, where the Court had upheld state action barring a student from using state scholarship funds to pay for clerical training. The Court explained that the student in *Locke* was not prevented from using state scholarship funds because of who he was; he was prevented from using state money for one specific act (that is, pursuing a devotional theology degree). Moreover, the state program in *Locke* accommodated religious study in other ways. In contrast, the state program in *Trinity Lutheran* denied the Church state funds because of its religious identity, unconstitutionally burdening the Church's free exercise by forcing it to choose "between being a church and receiving a government benefit".[1860]

701. The impact of *Trinity Lutheran* on direct school aid cases generally is still unclear. Although *Trinity Lutheran* cites language from *Everson v. Board of Education* that religious believers or non-believers cannot be excluded "*because of their faith, or lack of it*, from receiving the benefits of public welfare legislation",[1861] it is premature to state that *Trinity Lutheran* affects *Everson*'s holding more broadly, as the conceptual analyses of the Free Exercise and Establishment Clauses work independently. The Supreme Court has recognized that "there is 'play in the joints' between what the Establishment Clause permits and the Free Exercise Clause compels".[1862] But that "play" has narrowed as free exercise claims have been more

---

1859. *Trinity Lutheran Church of Columbia, Inc. v. Comer*, 582 U.S. 449, 454 (2017).

1860. *Ibid.*, at 466 ("The State has pursued its preferred policy to the point of expressly denying a qualified religious entity a public benefit solely because of its religious character. Under our precedents, that goes too far. The ... policy violates the Free Exercise Clause.")

1861. *Ibid.*, at 459 (quoting *Everson v. Bd. of Educ.*, 330 U.S. 1, 16 (1947)).

1862. *Ibid.*, at 458 (quoting *Locke v. Davey*, 540 U.S. 712, 718 (2004)); *see also Espinoza v. Mont. Dep't of Revenue*, 140 S. Ct. 2246, 2254 (2020); *Carson v. Makin*, 142 S. Ct. 1987, 2002, 2004, 2006 (2022) (Breyer, J., with Kagan and Sotomayor, JJ., dissenting) ("[The play-in-the-joints] doctrine

strictly scrutinized.[1863] In contrast to *Locke*, the Court in *Trinity Lutheran* (involving direct aid to religious schools) and *Espinoza v. Montana Department of Revenue* and *Carson v. Makin* (involving "child-benefit" aid to religious schools) subjected the contested policies to "the strictest scrutiny"—because the policies denied generally available benefits solely based on schools' religious identities—and found the policies violated the Free Exercise Clause.[1864]

---

reflects the fact that it may be difficult to determine in any particular case whether the Free Exercise clause *requires* a State to fund the activities of a religious institution, or whether the Establishment Clause *prohibits* the State from doing so. … [W]e have made clear that States enjoy a degree of freedom to navigate the Clauses' competing prohibitions. This includes choosing not to fund certain religious activity where States have strong, establishment-related reasons for not doing so. And, States have freedom to make this choice even when the Establishment Clause does not itself prohibit the State from funding that activity. … The concept of 'play in the joints' means that courts need not, and should not, answer with 'must' … questions that can more appropriately be answered with 'may'." (citations omitted)).

1863. *See generally Carson*, 142 S. Ct. 1987, 2002, 2002–2012 (Breyer, J., with Kagan and Sotomayor, JJ., dissenting).

1864. *Trinity Lutheran*, 582 U.S. at 462–466; *Espinoza*, 140 S. Ct. at 2260–2263; *Carson*, 142 S. Ct. at 1997, 2002.

Chapter 2. Indirect Financing

702. While religious organizations are not permitted to receive direct state aid for religious activities, numerous forms of indirect financing have long been permitted. There has been some debate as to whether indirect financial benefits to religious organizations should be characterized as subsidies, as exemptions needed to preserve religious autonomy and avoid excessive state entanglement in religion, or as non-discriminatory public funding open to all nonprofit organizations.[1865] For discussion of general principles underlying these approaches, *see* Part I (Legal Framework and Sources), Chapter III (Typology of the System).

§1. Indirect Financing Through Federal and State Tax Codes

I. Federal Tax-Exempt Status

A. Requirements for Tax-Exempt Status Generally

703. The Internal Revenue Code establishes federal tax-exempt status for charitable and religious organizations in section 501(c)(3). Tax-exempt organizations are not subject to federal corporate taxes (the United States has no federal property taxes, sales taxes, or value-added tax), and charitable contributions to them are deductible from the tax base of contributors.

704. To be a federally tax-exempt organization, a religious or charitable organization must meet three primary requirements.[1866] First, it must be "organized and operated exclusively" for exempt purposes, which includes religious purposes. Second, no earnings may inure to the benefit of a private shareholder or individual. And third, the organization must not be an "action organization", meaning a substantial part of its activities cannot involve attempting to influence legislation, nor can it participate in any campaign activity for or against political candidates.[1867] The Internal Revenue Service (IRS) uses two tests to determine whether a religious organization, in reality, meets the first requirement.[1868] The *organizational test* examines whether the group's organization and structure are calculated to achieve one of the tax-exempt purposes listed in I.R.C. section 501(c)(3).[1869] For example, the group's founding documents must "[l]imit the purposes of such organization to one or more

1865. *See generally* Michael W. McConnell & Richard A. Posner, *An Economic Approach to Issues of Religious Freedom*, 56 U. Chi. L. Rev. 1 (1989); Boris I. Bittker, *Churches, Taxes and the Constitution*, 78 Yale L.J. 1285 (1969).
1866. I.R.C. § 501(c)(3) (2018).
1867. *Ibid.*
1868. 26 C.F.R. § 1.501(c)(3)-1 (2022).
1869. *Ibid.*, § 1.501(c)(3)-1(b).

exempt purposes; and … not expressly empower the organization to engage [substantially] … in activities … not in furtherance of one or more exempt purposes".[1870] The *operational test* examines whether a group so organized actually and substantially acts in furtherance of the exempt purposes.[1871] For more on tax-exemption requirements, *see* Part III (Legal Status of Religious Communities), Chapter 1 (Formal Status of Religious Communities); Part V (Religion and Politics), Chapter 1 (Religious Influence in Politics); and Part XI (Religion and Culture), Chapter 4 (Religion and Public Debate).

705. The Internal Revenue Code also provides for a federal parsonage exemption, which permits ministers to deduct any "housing allowance" provided by the minister's religious organization from annual gross income.[1872] For more on the parsonage exemption, *see* Part VI (Labor Law Within Religious Communities), Chapter 2 (Religious Ministers and Labor Law).

B. Requirements for Status as a Tax-Exempt "Church"

706. Religious organizations may choose to claim "church" status under a broad definition in the Internal Revenue Code. The IRS examines whether the organization has a number of qualifying characteristics, including legal existence, ecclesiastical government, creed, literature, history, organization of ordained ministers, place of worship, membership, congregation, worship services, and more.[1873] For a complete list, *see* Part III (Legal Status of Religious Communities), Chapter 1 (Formal Status of Religious Communities). "The IRS generally uses a combination of these characteristics, together with other facts and circumstances, to determine whether an organization is considered a church for federal tax purposes."[1874]

707. Churches that meet the requirements for tax-exempt status are considered automatically exempt and need not apply for and obtain recognition of tax-exempt status by the IRS. They may choose to apply for official IRS recognition, however, to assure leaders, members, and donors of the organization's tax-exempt status.[1875]

1870. *Ibid.*, § 1.501(c)(3)-1(b)(1).
1871. *Ibid.*, § 1.501(c)(3)-1(c).
1872. Internal Revenue Serv., *Ministers Audit Techniques Guide* (Apr. 23, 2009), https://www.irs.gov/businesses/small-businesses-self-employed/audit-techniques-guides-atgs (link to PDF). Section 107 of the I.R.C. states that the following is not to be included in gross annual income for federal tax purposes: "the rental value of a home furnished to [a minister] as part of his compensation[,] or … the rental allowance paid to him as part of his compensation, to the extent used by him to rent or provide a home and to the extent such allowance does not exceed the fair rental value of the home, including furnishings and appurtenances such as a garage, plus the cost of utilities." I.R.C. § 107 (2018). A federal court of appeals upheld the parsonage exemption against a constitutional challenge in *Gaylor v. Mnuchin*, 919 F.3d 420 (7th Cir. 2019).
1873. *See Tax Guide for Churches & Religious Organizations*, *supra* n. 460, at 33.
1874. *Ibid.*; *see also* Edward McGlynn Gaffney, Jr., *Exemption of Religious Organizations from Federal Taxation, in Religious Organizations in the United States: A Study of Identity, Liberty, and the Law* 409, 446 (James A. Serritella et al. eds., 2006).
1875. *See Tax Guide for Churches & Religious Organizations*, *supra* n. 460, at 2.

"Churches" under the Internal Revenue Code also benefit from special rules that reduce annual filing requirements and limit IRS audit authority.[1876] The IRS, of course, retains the right to investigate potentially fraudulent claims. Religious organizations that do not qualify as "churches" generally must apply for tax-exempt status if they wish to be tax-exempt.[1877]

708. The exact number of religious organizations recognized as tax-exempt by the IRS is unknown but has been estimated at 240,000.[1878] In a national survey, 85% of all religious organizations stated that they meet the requirements of Internal Revenue Code section 501(c)(3); an additional 11% were uncertain whether they did.[1879]

C. Additional Benefits from Tax-Exempt Status

709. In addition to the obvious benefits of exemption from corporate taxes and availability of tax-deductible donations, federal tax-exempt status also serves as a gateway to many other indirect government benefits for religious organizations. Religious organizations that wish to accredit military chaplains, for example, must be federally tax-exempt churches.[1880] Applications for state funding of social services also usually require federal tax-exempt status. In large part, this status becomes a marker for being a religious organization able to receive state benefits, parallel in part to meeting upper-tier registration requirements of other countries. What is striking, however, is that not only are there no major additional requirements to qualify, such as a large number of members, long years of existence, or a historical role, but religious organizations need not apply at all, since "churches" under the Internal Revenue Code are automatically considered to have tax-exempt status.

1876. *See ibid.*, at 27–28, 31.

1877. *See ibid.*, at 3. Religious organizations whose gross receipts are normally less than USD 5,000 need not apply formally for tax-exempt status. *Ibid.*, at 3.

1878. *See The Nonprofit Sector in Brief 2019*, *supra* n. 21, at n.2 (citing the National Center for Charitable Statistic's analysis of the February 2016 IRS Business Master File). A 2023 IRS list of tax-exempt organizations contains more than 74,300 occurrences of the term "church", more than 6,400 of "temple", nearly 4,300 of "congregation", nearly 330 of "synagogue/synagogue", and nearly 100 of "mosque". *See Tax Exempt Organization Search Bulk Data Downloads*, Internal Revenue Serv., https://www.irs.gov/charities-non-profits/tax-exempt-organization-search-bulk-data-downloads (link to ZIP file of Organizations Eligible to Receive Tax-Deductible Charitable Contributions (last updated Jul. 23, 2023)).

1879. Rhys H. Williams & John P.N. Massad, *Religious Diversity, Civil Law, and Institutional Isomorphism, in Religious Organizations in the United States: A Study of Identity, Liberty, and the Law* 111, 121 (James A. Serritella et al. eds., 2006).

1880. *See* Dep't of Def., The Appointment and Service of Chaplains, *supra* n. 1542.

D. Public Policy Restrictions on Tax-Exempt Status

710. In a landmark case, the IRS chose to base tax-exempt status on questions of significant public policy. In a 1971 revenue ruling, the IRS announced it would no longer grant tax-exempt status to private schools that practice racial discrimination.[1881] Pursuant to this interpretation of I.R.C. section 501(c)(3), the IRS revoked the tax-exempt status of two religious schools whose policies were racially discriminatory. The US Supreme Court upheld the IRS's interpretation and actions against the schools in 1983, in *Bob Jones University v. United States*. Notably, the Supreme Court held that the IRS could revoke the schools' tax-exempt status for violating public policy—even when the offending school policies were based on sincerely held religious beliefs—without violating the First Amendment's Free Exercise Clause.[1882] For more on *Bob Jones University*, *see* Part V (Religion and Politics), Chapter 2 (Political Influence in Religion); and Part VII (Religious Communities and Protections of the Individual), Chapter 2 (Freedom to Marry).

711. The US Tax Court (an independent judicial authority that adjudicates disputes over federal income tax) has held that requiring "uniform, mandatory participation" in the federal income tax is the least restrictive means to meet compelling government interests in funding social programs; therefore, neither the First Amendment nor RFRA exempts those with religious objections from paying taxes.[1883]

II. Federal Tax Deductibility of Contributions

712. Section 170 of the Internal Revenue Code allows taxpayers to deduct a certain amount of contributions to tax-exempt organizations from their annual gross income on federal personal or corporate income tax returns.[1884] Such contributions are called "charitable contributions". The Internal Revenue Code provides, "There shall be allowed as a deduction any charitable contribution … payment of which

---

1881. Rev. Rul. 71-447, 1971-2 C.B. 230. "A revenue ruling is an official interpretation by the IRS of the Internal Revenue Code, related statutes, tax treaties and regulations. It is the conclusion of the IRS on how the law is applied to a specific set of facts." *Understanding IRS Guidance—A Brief Primer*, IRS, https://www.irs.gov/newsroom/understanding-irs-guidance-a-brief-primer (last updated May 1, 2023).

1882. The two schools the IRS targeted were Bob Jones University (in Greenville, South Carolina) and Goldsboro Christian Schools (in Goldsboro, North Carolina). *See Bob Jones Univ. v. United States*, 461 U.S. 574, 602–604 (1983) ("The governmental interest … in eradicating racial discrimination in education … substantially outweighs whatever burden denial of tax benefits places on petitioners' exercise of their religious beliefs.").

1883. *Adams v. Comm'r*, 110 T.C. 137 (1998).

1884. The Internal Revenue Code limits the maximum possible tax deduction for charitable contributions to 50% of the "taxpayer's contribution base for the taxable year". I.R.C. §§ 170(a), 170(b)(1)(A) (2018). For individuals, these deductions are subject to the limitations in I.R.C. s. 170(b)(1). For corporations, these deductions are subject to the limitations in I.R.C. s. 170(b)(2).

is made within the taxable year."[1885] Charitable contributions may include monetary gifts, in-kind gifts, and future estate gifts.[1886]

713. Since early US history, religious organizations have been funded primarily through private donations. Tax benefits for contributors are considered a crucial incentive that allows these organizations to raise money.[1887] Religious organizations received approximately USD 144 billion in donations in 2022.[1888] Though not all contributions to religious organizations are deducted from income taxes, actual deductions can result in substantial tax savings to individual donors.[1889]

III. State Tax Laws

714. Most states in the United States exempt religious organizations from property, income, and sales taxes.[1890] In some cases, these exemptions are based on state constitutions; in others, the exemptions are statutory.[1891] All states that have a corporate income tax offer exemptions for religious organizations.[1892] Some states directly adopt the federal tax exemptions found in section 501(c)(3) of the Internal Revenue Code, while other states have enacted their own lists of organizations exempted from state taxes.[1893]

1885. I.R.C. § 170(a)(1).
1886. *See* I.R.C. §§ 170(a)(3), 642(c); 4 Durham et al., *supra* n. 178, § 31:12 (*Tithing*), § 31:15 (*Religious and Charitable Gifts and Bequests*).
1887. 4 Durham et al., *supra* n. 178, § 31:1 (*Introduction to Church Financing*), § 31:2 (*Rationale for Tax Exemptions*).
1888. *See Giving USA: Total U.S. Charitable Giving Declined in 2022 to $499.33 Billion Following Two Years of Record Generosity*, IUPUI (Jun. 20, 2023), https://philanthropy.iupui.edu/news-events/news-item/giving-usa:-total-u.s.-charitable-giving-declined-in-2022-to-$499.33-billion-following-two-years-of-record-generosity.html?id=422.
1889. *See* 4 Durham et al., *supra* n. 178, § 31:2 (*Rationale for Tax Exemptions*), § 31:3 (*Donations*).
1890. *See ibid.*, § 32:49 (*State Income Tax Benefits*), § 33:7 (*Legal Sources of Religious Property Tax Exemptions*), § 33:30 (*Sales and Use Taxes and Religious Organizations*).
1891. For example, Alabama's state constitution provides that "[t]he legislature shall not tax … lots one mile or more distant from … cities or towns to the extent of five acres, with the buildings thereon, when same are used exclusively for religious worship … ." Ala. Const. art. IV, § 91. Arkansas statutory law exempts from state income taxes "[c]orporations, trusts, and any community chest, fund, or foundation, organized and operated exclusively for religious … purposes" that meet requirements similar to federal 501(c)(3) requirements. Ark. Code Ann. § 26-51-303(a)(9) (2022).
1892. 4 Durham et al., *supra* n. 178, § 32:49 (*State Income Tax Benefits*).
1893. *Ibid.*, § 32:49 (*State Income Tax Benefits*), § 32:50 (*Chart: State Income Tax Benefits. Compare* Or. Rev. Stat. § 317.080 (2022) (adopting exemptions described in I.R.C. s. 501(c)); Utah Code § 59-7-102(1)(a) (2022) (adopting the same), *with* Del. Code Ann. tit. 30, § 1902 (codifying list of organizations exempt from state income tax); Cal. Rev. & Tax Code §§ 23701, 23701d (West 2023) (codifying the same).

715. States also permit individuals to deduct charitable contributions or receive a tax credit for contributions on their state income tax forms.[1894] Most states with a sales tax allow some sort of sales tax exemption to religious organizations,[1895] although states differ widely as to the details and breadth of a sales tax exemption.[1896] Many states also have a "parsonage exemption" to property taxes similar to the federal income exemption for residences provided to ministers by the church.[1897]

§2. Funding of Religiously Affiliated Social Services

I. Scope of Government-Funded Religiously Affiliated Social Services

716. Religious ideas and organizations have long played a substantial and important role in social service work in the United States.[1898] Historically, many orphanages, food banks, shelters, work-education programs, and other social service programs have been operated by churches.[1899] For example, in 1952, religiously affiliated organizations provided USD 375 million of the USD 675 million

---

1894. *See, e.g.*, Cal. Rev. & Tax Code §§ 24357–24359 (West 2023); La. Stat. Ann. § 47:57(2) (2022); N.C. Gen. Stat. § 105-153.5(a)(2) (2022); Or. Rev. Stat. § 316.747(1) (2022); Utah Code § 59-7-109(1) (2022).

1895. Jennifer C. Root & Norman H. Wright, *Classifying State Sales Tax Exemptions for Religious Organizations*, 11 J. of Tax'n of Exempt Orgs. 279, 281 (2000); 4 Durham et al., *supra* n. 178, § 33:30 (*Sales and Use Taxes and Religious Organizations*).

1896. "While most states follow the federal lead in exempting religious organizations from income taxation, the same is not true in the context of sales and use tax. After two thousand years, the tax collectors are still working the temples. … [The states] have not done so uniformly, but their approaches do fall into discernible categories." Root & Wright, *Classifying State Sales Tax Exemptions*, *supra* n. 1895, at 279.

1897. *See, e.g.*, (all statutes current through 2022) Ala. Code § 40-18-14(3)(g); Ark. Code Ann. § 26-3-303; Cal. Rev. & Tax Code § 17131.6; Idaho Code § 63-602B(1); 35 Ill. Comp. Stat. 200/15-40; Ind. Code § 6-1.1-10-21(b); Me. Stat. tit. 36, § 652(1)(G); Md. Code Ann., Tax—Prop. § 7-204; Mich. Comp. Laws § 211.7s; *State v. Church of Incarnation*, 196 N.W. 802 (Minn. 1924) (holding that Minnesota's state constitution, article 9, section 1, provided for a parsonage exemption); N.J. Stat. Ann. § 54:4-3.6; S.C. Const. art. X, § 3(c); S.D. Codified Laws § 10-4-9; Tenn. Code Ann. § 67-5-212; Tex. Tax Code Ann. § 11.20(a)(3); Wash. Rev. Code § 84.36.020(2)(a).

1898. *See* Ram A. Cnaan, *The Newer Deal: Social Work and Religion in Partnership* 112 (1999); Lew Daly, *God's Economy: Faith-Based Initiatives & the Caring State* 30–37 (2009); Peter Dobkin Hall, *Historical Perspectives on Religion, Government, and Social Welfare in America, in Can Charitable Choice Work?: Covering Religion's Impact on Urban Affairs and Social Services* 78, 78–120 (Andrew Walsh ed., 2001); Sheila Suess Kennedy & Wolfgang Bielefeld, *Charitable Choice at Work: Evaluating Faith-Based Job Programs in the States* 20–21 (2006); Stephen V. Monsma, *When Sacred and Secular Mix: Religious Nonprofit Organizations & Public Money* 5–9 (1996); Lewis D. Solomon, *In God We Trust?: Faith-Based Organizations and the Quest to Solve America's Social Ills* 51 (2003); Bob Wineburg, *A Limited Partnership: The Politics of Religion, Welfare, and Social Science* 29–34 (2001).

1899. *See* Julie Adkins, Laurie Occhipinti & Tara Hefferan, *Social Services, Social Justice, and Faith-Based Organizations in the United States: An Introduction, in Not by Faith Alone: Social Services, Social Justice, and Faith-Based Organizations in the United States* 1, 2–4 (Julie Adkins, Laurie Occhipinti & Tara Hefferan eds., 2010). *See generally* 3 Durham et al., *supra* n. 174, ch. 26 (*Religiously Sponsored Social Services*).

total dollars spent on charitable healthcare by nonprofit organizations—more than 50%.[1900] That same year, religious organizations provided USD 235 million of the USD 1.610 billion total nonprofit dollars—almost 15%—spent on social welfare.[1901]

717. Historically, religiously affiliated social services have received enormous sums of money from the federal and state governments to assist with their work. For example, in the early 1990s "a surprising 75[%] of the annual budget of the New York Roman Catholic archdiocese—some [USD]1.75 billion—[came] from government sources", to fund healthcare and mental healthcare, foster and child care, and similar services.[1902] In 1991, "Catholic Relief Services received [USD]187 million, ... Protestant Church World Services received [USD]6.5 million, and ... Protestant World Vision Relief and Development received [USD]19.3 million" in government funding.[1903] Government funding comes not only through direct grants and payments for particular services but also through low-interest loans or loan guarantees, in-kind donations, free use of government property or facilities, and educational grants and vouchers.[1904]

II. Statutory Restrictions on Religious Organizations Receiving State Aid for Social Services

A. *Historical Restrictions*

718. Until the late 1990s, religious organizations had typically been required to submit to certain requirements to receive public funds for their charitable work. For example, funds available from most state and federal benefits barred their use for religious education or training.[1905] Any employment position funded by public money was protected by anti-discrimination laws (including against religious discrimination), from which religious organizations would otherwise be exempt.[1906] In

1900. Cnaan, *The Newer Deal*, *supra* n. 1898, at 157.
1901. *Ibid.*
1902. Monsma, *When Sacred and Secular Mix*, *supra* n. 1898, at 9–10.
1903. *Ibid.*, at 10.
1904. *See* Esbeck, *Regulation of Religious Organizations via Governmental Financial Assistance*, *supra* n. 1134, at 355–356; Esbeck, *Government Regulation of Religiously Based Social Services: The First Amendment Considerations*, *supra* n. 1143, at 346–347.
1905. *See* Esbeck, *Regulation of Religious Organizations via Governmental Financial Assistance*, *supra* n. 1134, at 361–362.
1906. Kennedy & Bielefeld, *Charitable Choice at Work*, *supra* n. 1898, at 24 ("Prior to passage of [the Charitable Choice provisions of the Personal Responsibility and Work Opportunity Reconciliation Act], ... when religious organizations contracted with government, they usually had to agree that any positions funded with tax dollars would be filled in accordance with applicable state and federal civil rights laws.").

some cases, religious organizations were required to organize separate legal entities to manage charitable work in order to ensure proper separation of charitable and religious activities.[1907]

B. Charitable Choice Initiatives

719. Legislation passed by Congress in 1996, known commonly as "Charitable Choice", altered these religious activity restrictions for federally funded charitable organizations. Federal funding of social services organizations that actively engage in religious activity is permitted under section 104 of the Personal Responsibility and Work Opportunity Reconciliation Act (PRWORA) of 1996.[1908]

720. PRWORA guarantees that government agencies will not discriminate against religious organizations because of their religious nature and guarantees that federal funding will not affect the autonomy and religious freedom of organizations receiving such funding for charitable purposes.[1909] In addition, PRWORA protects the religious rights of welfare recipients by guaranteeing access to alternative welfare providers if the recipient objects to receiving benefits from a religiously affiliated provider; it also prohibits religiously affiliated social services from discriminating against recipients for religious reasons.[1910] PRWORA allows religious organizations to utilize religious qualifications in hiring, however, even for positions funded by public monies.[1911] Religious organizations remain barred from using government funds for "sectarian worship, instruction, or proselytization" under PRWORA.[1912]

1907. Section 104 of the Personal Responsibility and Work Opportunity Reconciliation Act (PRWORA) eventually provided that "religious organizations can retain their organizational form without government interference. This provision was designed to forestall the need for houses of worship to set up separate, nominally secular, corporations as a prerequisite to receiving government grants", which historically had been the practice. Marc D. Stern, *Charitable Choice: The Law as It Is and May Be, in Can Charitable Choice Work?: Covering Religion's Impact on Urban Affairs and Social Services* 157, 158 (Andrew Walsh ed., 2001); *see also* Hall, *Historical Perspectives on Religion, Government, and Social Welfare in America, supra* n. 1898, at 78, 106–107.

1908. 42 U.S.C. § 604a (2018). Section 604a(b) states that the purpose of the provision is to "allow States to contract with religious organizations, or to allow religious organizations to accept … disbursement … on the same basis as any other nongovernmental provider *without impairing the religious character of such organizations, and without diminishing the religious freedom of beneficiaries of assistance funded under such program*". *Ibid.*, § 604a(b) (emphasis added).

1909. Title 42, subss. 604a(c) and (d) of the US Code provide that a religious organization receiving funds "shall retain its independence from Federal, State, and local governments, including such organization's control over the definition, development, practice, and expression of its religious beliefs" and that "[n]either the Federal Government nor a State shall require a religious organization to (A) alter its form of internal governance; or (B) remove religious art, icons, scripture, or other symbols; in order to be eligible to contract to provide assistance, or to accept certificates, vouchers, or other forms of disbursement, funded under a [previously described] program … ." 42 U.S.C. § 604a(c), (d).

1910. *Ibid.*, § 604a(e), (g).

1911. *See* Kennedy & Bielefeld, *Charitable Choice at Work, supra* n. 1898, at 24.

1912. 42 U.S.C. § 604a(j).

721. Individual states have adopted their own versions of PRWORA. State statutes provide express guidelines for the use of government funds, which may be disclosed in the initial announcement of the availability of grant funds. Virginia's statute, for example, establishes that "funds provided for expenditure pursuant to contracts with public bodies shall not be spent for religious worship, instruction, or proselytizing; however, this prohibition shall not apply to expenditures pursuant to contracts, if any, for the services of chaplains".[1913] Arizona, Texas, and Wisconsin adopted federal Charitable Choice language to amend their laws on social services contracting.[1914] For more on PRWORA and Charitable Choice, *see* Part VI (Labor Law Within Religious Communities), Chapter 3 (Other Church Employees and Labor Law).

§3. Constitutional Restrictions on Indirect Financing of Religious Communities

722. Constitutional challenges have been raised concerning state property tax exemptions for religious organizations,[1915] the federal parsonage exemption,[1916] state parsonage exemptions,[1917] state tax deductions to parents whose children attend parochial schools,[1918] and tax exemptions for religious periodicals.[1919] Outside of the school context, indirect benefits for religious communities have largely been upheld.

723. As discussed in Part VI (Labor Law Within Religious Communities), Chapter 1 (Scope of Application of Labor Law), determining what constitutes *permissible indirect aid* and *impermissible direct aid* under the Establishment Clause, most often seen in the school funding context, is complex and often opaque. The Supreme Court's Establishment Clause jurisprudence is not always consistent, and the analytical frameworks often vary depending on the context and precise question involved; therefore, this section examines Establishment Clause cases on indirect funding contextually, by the form of funding challenged.

1913. Va. Code Ann. § 2.2-4343.1 (2022).

1914. Ram A. Cnaan & Stephanie C. Boddie, *Charitable Choice and Faith-Based Welfare: A Call for Social Work*, 47 Soc. Work 224, 227 (2002).

1915. *See Walz v. Tax Comm'n of N.Y.*, 397 U.S. 664 (1970); *Bexar Cnty. Appraisal Review Bd. v. First Baptist Church*, 846 S.W.2d 554 (Tex. App. 1993), *cert. denied*, 510 U.S. 1178 (1994).

1916. *See Gaylor v. Mnuchin*, 919 F.3d 420 (7th Cir. 2019) (holding federal parsonage exemption does not violate the Establishment Clause).

1917. *Freedom from Religion Found., Inc. v. Geithner*, 715 F. Supp. 2d 1051, 1068 (E.D. Cal. 2010) (allowing challenge to two contested state and federal parsonage exemption provisions to go forward). *But see* Order on Stipulation of Dismissal, 715 F. Supp. 2d 1051 (E.D. Cal. 2010) (No. 2:09-CV-02894-WBS-DAD) (stipulating dismissal of future proceedings and settling case jointly).

1918. *See Mueller v. Allen*, 463 U.S. 388 (1983).

1919. *Tex. Monthly, Inc. v. Bullock*, 489 U.S. 1 (1989) (plurality opinion).

I. Constitutionality of Tax Exemptions

724. The seminal US Supreme Court decision on religious tax exemptions is *Walz v. Tax Commission of the City of New York.*[1920] In *Walz*, a New York City resident brought a lawsuit against the municipal government, claiming the tax exemption for religious organizations forced him, as a taxpayer, to provide an indirect subsidy to all religions and, therefore, violated the First Amendment's Establishment Clause. The Court held that New York's property tax exemption for religious organizations did not offend the Constitution. The Court dismissed the indirect sponsorship argument by explaining, "The grant of a tax exemption is not sponsorship since the government does not transfer part of its revenue to churches *but simply abstains from demanding that the church support the state.*"[1921] The Court also observed that tax exemptions had been statutorily extended to churches since the earliest days of the United States, comprising strong evidence that the practice does not violate the Constitution.[1922]

725. However, the Supreme Court framed tax exemptions differently in *Texas Monthly, Inc. v. Bullock*, stating that "[e]very tax exemption constitutes a subsidy that affects nonqualifying taxpayers, forcing them to become indirect and vicarious 'donors.'"[1923] In *Texas Monthly*, the publisher of a secular periodical sued the state of Texas, alleging that a tax exemption for religious periodicals and books violated the First Amendment's Establishment Clause.[1924] The Supreme Court held, in a plurality opinion,[1925] that the state's tax exemption violated the Establishment Clause because it offered the benefit to religious organizations and religious speech without offering similar benefits to other charitable and beneficial organizations, such as charities, hospitals, and nonprofit groups.[1926]

726. In contrast, a federal court of appeals has upheld the federal parsonage exemption as constitutional.[1927] For federal tax purposes, the exemption excludes

---

1920. *Walz v. Tax Comm'n of N.Y.*, 397 U.S. 664 (1970).

1921. *Ibid.*, at 675 (emphasis added).

1922. *Ibid.*, at 676–680 ("It appears that at least up to 1885 this Court, reflecting more than a century of our history and uninterrupted practice, accepted without discussion the proposition that federal or state grants of tax exemption to churches were not a violation of the Religion Clauses of the First Amendment.").

1923. *Tex. Monthly, Inc.*, 489 U.S. at 14 (internal quotation marks omitted).

1924. *Ibid.*, at 5 (quoting Tex. Tax Code Ann. § 151.312 (1982)).

1925. For an explanation of a plurality opinion, *see supra* n. 970; *see also* Kimura, *Legitimacy Model for the Interpretation of Plurality Decisions*, *supra* n. 1459, at 1595–1596.

1926. *Tex. Monthly, Inc.*, 489 at 10–17 ("In all [previous] cases, … we emphasized that the benefits derived by religious organizations flowed to a large number of nonreligious groups as well. Indeed, were those benefits confined to religious organizations, they could not have appeared other than as state sponsorship of religion; if that were so, we would not have hesitated to strike them down for lacking a secular purpose and effect." (citing *Sch. Dist. of Grand Rapids v. Ball*, 473 U.S. 373 (1985), *overruled in part by Agostini v. Felton*, 521 U.S. 203, 236 (1997); *Est. of Thornton v. Caldor, Inc.*, 472 U.S. 703 (1985))).

1927. *Gaylor v. Mnuchin*, 919 F.3d 420 (7th Cir. 2019).

from a minister's gross income "(1) the rental value of a home furnished to him as part of his compensation; or (2) the rental allowance paid to him as part of his compensation".[1928]

II. Constitutionality of Aid to Social Service Providers

727. In 1988, the Supreme Court held in *Bowen v. Kendrick* that a statute giving limited public funding to religious organizations for sexual and family life education did not violate the Establishment Clause.[1929] The Court noted, "this Court has never held that religious institutions are disabled by the First Amendment from participating in publicly sponsored social welfare programs".[1930]

728. In analyzing the statute at issue in *Bowen*, the Supreme Court used the now-abrogated *Lemon* test. *See* this part, Chapter 1 (Direct Financing), above. It held that a statute providing aid for social services, even though it did so through religious providers, had a secular legislative purpose and did not primarily advance religion. In dicta, the Court did suggest that direct government aid might have the primary effect of advancing religion "if the aid flows to institutions that are 'pervasively sectarian'".[1931] "The reason for this", asserted the Court, "is that there is a risk that direct government funding, even if it is designated for specific secular purposes, may nonetheless advance the pervasively sectarian institution's 'religious mission.'"[1932] But the Court held that the statute in *Bowen* survived facial challenge because there was not a substantial risk of "pervasively sectarian" organizations receiving aid, and if such an organization actually received funds under the statute, the issue could be addressed with an "as applied" challenge.[1933]

729. The mere fact that educational services were provided by religiously affiliated organizations in *Bowen* was not enough to invalidate the statute. The Court noted it had previously "refused to presume" that aid flowing "to religiously affiliated institutions that were not pervasively sectarian … would be used in a way that would have the primary effect of advancing religion".[1934] The Court also emphasized that statutes need not contain "an express provision preventing the use of federal funds for religious purposes", so long as there is no intimation in the statute that religious uses are permitted.[1935]

730. In a variety of lower court cases, critics of religiously affiliated social services have challenged the constitutionality of providing public funding to such organizations, and religiously affiliated organizations have challenged state and local

1928. I.R.C. § 107 (2018).
1929. *Bowen v. Kendrick*, 487 U.S. 589, 616–617 (1988).
1930. *Ibid.*, at 609.
1931. *Ibid.*, at 609–610.
1932. *Ibid.*, at 610.
1933. *Ibid.*, at 615–618.
1934. *Ibid.*, at 612.
1935. *Ibid.*, at 614–615.

government decisions to withhold funding.[1936] In *Fulton v. City of Philadelphia*, for example, the city entered into annual contracts with private agencies, including Catholic Social Services (CSS), to place children with foster parents.[1937] Based on religious beliefs, CSS refused to certify same-sex couples as foster parents. The city in turn refused to renew its contract with CSS, citing the contract's non-discrimination provision. Under the terms of the contract, the city had authority to grant exceptions to the non-discrimination provision but refused to grant CSS an exception. Applying strict scrutiny, the Court held that the non-discrimination provision, as applied, violated the Free Exercise Clause. The Court found that the city failed to demonstrate interests compelling enough to justify denying the religiously affiliated organization an exception while making exceptions available to other agencies.[1938]

III. Constitutionality of Funding of Religiously Affiliated Private Schools

731. US Supreme Court jurisprudence in the area of religiously affiliated private schools is somewhat conflicted. Until abrogating *Lemon* in 2022, the Court generally applied *Lemon*'s tripartite test. In a significant 1997 case, *Agostini v. Felton*, the Court held that the primary effect of aid is less likely to advance religion when "aid is allocated on the basis of neutral, secular criteria that neither favor nor disfavor religion, and is made available to both religious and secular beneficiaries on a non-discriminatory basis".[1939] For a more detailed discussion of analytical frameworks applied to the funding of religiously affiliated schools, *see* this part, Chapter 1 (Direct Financing), above.

732. The Supreme Court has held that states may reimburse transportation costs to parents who send children to school (including religious schools) on public transit buses,[1940] loan educational equipment and materials to parochial schools,[1941] provide interpreters for deaf students,[1942] and provide resources to blind students

---

1936. *See, e.g.*, *New Hope Family Servs., Inc. v. Poole*, 966 F.3d 145, 180 (2d Cir. 2020) (holding that a religious adoption agency properly alleged First Amendment claims in its suit challenging threatened closure under a state anti-discrimination statute); *Teen Ranch, Inc. v. Udow*, 479 F.3d 403, 409–410 (6th Cir. 2007), *cert. denied*, 552 U.S. 1039 (2007) (concluding state's moratorium on funding of faith-based residential treatment program for troubled youth was constitutional where the program incorporated religious teachings in activities and treatment); *Freedom from Religion Found., Inc. v. McCallum*, 179 F. Supp. 2d 950, 971, 975–976 (W.D. Wis. 2002) (successfully challenging the state's funding of a religiously based drug rehabilitation program on Establishment Clause grounds); *see also Freedom from Religion Found., Inc. v. McCallum*, 214 F. Supp. 2d 905 (W.D. Wis. 2005) (reaffirming court's previous holding that funding through one state agency of religiously based drug rehabilitation program violated Establishment Clause but holding that funding through another state agency was constitutional where participation was voluntary).

1937. *Fulton v. City of Philadelphia*, 141 S. Ct. 1868, 1874–1875 (2021).

1938. *Ibid.*, at 1882.

1939. *Agostini v. Felton*, 521 U.S. 203, 231 (1997).

1940. *Everson v. Bd. of Educ.*, 330 U.S. 1, 17–18 (1947).

1941. *Mitchell v. Helms*, 530 U.S. 793, 801 (2000) (plurality opinion).

1942. *Zobrest v. Catalina Foothills Sch. Dist.*, 509 U.S. 1, 10 (1993).

attending religious schools, even if a student is attending a religious school to become a minister.[1943] States may also provide tuition vouchers or other tuition assistance to students attending private religious schools[1944] or provide income tax relief to parents of such students, in the form of deductions for some school-related expenses.[1945] A state may permit students at private religious schools to receive scholarship funds funnelled through a state program that offers tax deductions to scholarship fund donors.[1946] Additionally, states may reimburse religious schools for expenses related to mandatory standardized testing,[1947] provide funding for construction (of facilities not used for religious activity) at religious colleges as part of a program available to all universities,[1948] and send public-school teachers to religious schools "to provide remedial education to disadvantaged children".[1949]

733. On the other hand, the US Supreme Court has held that states may not provide salary supplements for teachers of secular subjects in religious schools[1950] and may not create special school districts for religious schools.[1951] States may not provide direct grants to religious schools for "maintenance and repair".[1952] And states may not reimburse parents for education expenses as part of a program that targets mainly religious schools.[1953] For additional discussion of cases involving private religious school funding, *see* Part IX (Education), Chapter 2 (Religious Schools).

734. Many state constitutions limit funding to religiously affiliated private schools more than the federal constitution. In *Espinoza v. Montana Department of Revenue*, the Supreme Court held that a "no-aid" provision in Montana's state constitution—which prohibits any state aid to religiously affiliated schools—was unconstitutional as applied to a state scholarship program.[1954] The state program offered tax credits for donors to nonprofit organizations that provided scholarships to private schools. A state agency, attempting to comply with the no-aid provision, promulgated a rule prohibiting the use of those scholarships at religious schools. The Supreme Court held that the Free Exercise Clause precluded the state from applying the state constitution to ban students from using the scholarships at religious schools. In *Trinity Lutheran Church v. Comer*, the Supreme held that a similar provision in Missouri's state constitution similarly violated the Free Exercise

1943. *Witters v. Wash. Dep't of Servs. for the Blind*, 474 U.S. 481, 489 (1986).
1944. *Carson v. Makin*, 142 S. Ct. 1987, 2002 (2022); *Zelman v. Simmons-Harris*, 536 U.S. 639, 662–663 (2002).
1945. *Mueller v. Allen*, 463 U.S. 388, 403 (1983).
1946. *Espinoza v. Mont. Dep't of Revenue*, 140 S. Ct. 2246, 2260–2263 (2020).
1947. *Comm. for Pub. Educ. & Religious Liberty v. Regan*, 444 U.S. 646, 648 (1980).
1948. *Hunt v. McNair*, 413 U.S. 734 (1973).
1949. *Agostini v. Felton*, 521 U.S. 203, 208–209 (1997).
1950. *Lemon v. Kurtzman*, 403 U.S. 602, 612–613 (1971), *abrogated by Kennedy v. Bremerton Sch. Dist.*, 142 S. Ct. 2407, 2427–2428 (2022).
1951. *Bd. of Educ. v. Grumet*, 512 U.S. 687, 705 (1994).
1952. *Comm. for Pub. Educ. & Religious Liberty v. Nyquist*, 413 U.S. 756, 779–780 (1973).
1953. *Sloan v. Lemon*, 413 U.S. 825, 832–833, 835 (1973).
1954. *Espinoza v. Mont. Dep't of Revenue*, 140 S. Ct. 2246, 2260–2263 (2020); Mont. Const. art. X, § 6.

Clause, as applied.[1955] In that case, the state applied the no-aid provision to exclude religiously affiliated schools from participating in a state grant program for playground resurfacing. For more on state no-aid constitutional provisions, *see* Part IX (Education), Chapter 1 (Religious Education in Public and Private Schools) and Chapter 2 (Religious Schools).

1955. *Trinity Lutheran Church of Columbia, Inc. v. Comer*, 582 U.S. 449, 465–467 (2017).

Part IX. Education

Chapter 1. Religious Education in Public and Private Schools

§1. Development of Public Education

735. Most education in the United States was originally closely tied with or organized by religious organizations.[1956] Beginning in the late 1830s, public schools were established, but universal compulsory public education did not extend throughout the United States until the twentieth century.[1957] Public schools in general had strong Protestant leanings, which prompted a reaction in the form of the development of an extensive Catholic parochial school system.

736. Protestants opposed any public funding for Catholic schools, most notably with the Blaine Amendment, proposed in 1875, which would have revised the First Amendment to prohibit the provision of public funds to sectarian schools.[1958] This measure passed the House but missed passing the Senate by a slim margin.[1959] While the measure failed on a federal level, several states effectively amended their state constitutions to impose strict financial separation requirements in education at the state level.[1960] In some cases, the US Supreme Court has held that the states' application of these amendments to educational funding has violated the First Amendment of the federal constitution.[1961] *See* Part I (Legal Framework and Sources), Chapter 1 (Constitutional Position of Religion) and Chapter 2 (Other Legislation with Regard to Religion), for more about the Blaine Amendment and its state progeny.

737. Even given such sentiments and restrictions, however, some local schools relied on Catholic clergy to staff public schools or used church buildings as public

1956. 3 Durham et al., *supra* n. 174, § 25:2 (*Historical Overview of Private Religious Education*).
1957. Edwin S. Gaustad, *Church and State in America* 87 (2d ed. 2003).
1958. Richard Aynes, *Blaine Amendment, in Religion and American Law: An Encyclopedia* 39, 39–40 (Paul Finkelman ed., 2000).
1959. *Ibid.*, at 40.
1960. W. Cole Durham, Jr., *Treatment of Religious Minorities in the United States, in* Eur. Consortium for Church-State Rsch., *The Legal Status of Religious Minorities in the Countries of the European Union* 323, 333 (1994).
1961. *See, e.g., Espinoza v. Mont. Dep't of Revenue*, 140 S. Ct. 2246, 2261–2263 (2020); *Trinity Lutheran Church of Columbia, Inc. v. Comer*, 582 U.S. 449, 466 (2017).

elementary or secondary schools, particularly in smaller communities.[1962] Most of the US Supreme Court cases that currently define the relationship between religion and education have arisen since the mid-twentieth century as a result of challenges to Protestant practices in public schools or state support for and cooperation with Catholic schools.

738. Educational systems are managed at the state and sub-state (district) levels. Schools are generally structured as follows: elementary school (1st through 5th or 6th grade), middle school/junior high school (6th through 8th, or 7th through 9th grade), and high school (9th or 10th through 12th grade). All states require students to attend school through at least age 16 (approximately 10th grade); in most states, attendance is compulsory through ages 17 or 18, if students have not graduated from high school before reaching that age.[1963]

739. Compulsory education has been challenged by Amish communities, who follow a traditional form of Christianity and share Swiss Anabaptist origins with Mennonites. Most Amish live largely self-sufficient, pre-industrial lifestyles, and some have challenged compulsory education for high school.[1964] In 1972, in *Wisconsin v. Yoder*, the Supreme Court ruled in favor of Amish families who declined to send their children to school after the eighth grade, in violation of Wisconsin's compulsory education law.[1965] The Court held that the state failed to show a compelling state interest narrowly tailored to justify the burdens of compulsory education on the Amish families' religious practice.[1966] The Court found that, while the state had a compelling interest in an educated citizenry, Amish children who left school after eighth grade received adequate continuing, informal education to prepare them for productive, self-sufficient adult lives in their communities. Therefore, the Court concluded that the state requirement of an additional one or two years of compulsory education imposed an unjustified and unconstitutional burden on Amish parents' religious exercise.[1967]

§2. Religious and Denominational Education in Public Schools

I. Denominational Education/Released Time

740. The United States does not permit any form of denominational religious education as part of the compulsory public-school curriculum. The Supreme Court has permitted "released time" education, however, in which students may be dismissed from school early, or for a period during the school day, to attend denominational religious classes at a private location separate from the public school.[1968]

1962. Sarah Barringer Gordon, *The Spirit of the Law: Religious Voices and the Constitution in Modern America* 57 (2010).
1963. *See 50-State Comparison: Free and Compulsory School Age Requirements*, *supra* n. 646.
1964. E.g., *Wisconsin v. Yoder*, 406 U.S. 205, 207–213 (1972).
1965. *Ibid.*, at 234.
1966. *Ibid.*, at 219–234.
1967. *Ibid.*, at 221–227.
1968. *Zorach v. Clauson*, 343 U.S. 306, 315 (1952).

Courts relying on the *Lemon* test, have held that public schools and released time programs may not "entangle" themselves, administratively or otherwise, under the Establishment Clause.[1969] Public schools may cooperate, however, to the extent of receiving released time class attendance records and reporting to parents those students who are repeatedly absent without excuse; doing so helps inform the "legitimate interest[s]" of publics schools and parents "in knowing where their students are during school hours".[1970] The denomination controls entirely the class curricula and the selection and payment of teachers. In contrast, the US Supreme Court has not permitted teaching by religious organizations on public-school grounds, even when the courses were optional and the teachers were paid by the denominations.[1971]

741. In 1980, the Supreme Court held that a Kentucky state law requiring that the Ten Commandments be posted in every public-school classroom violated the Establishment Clause. The Court found that the statute's "pre-eminent purpose" was "plainly religious in nature", despite the state avowing a secular purpose and application for the displays.[1972]

II. Courses about Religion

742. In 1963, in *School District of Abington Township v. Schempp*, the US Supreme Court Study distinguished the teaching *of* religion and teaching *about* religion.[1973] The Court held that a public-school requirement to start the school day with students selecting and reading Bible verses and reciting the Lord's Prayer violated the Establishment Clause.[1974] The Court explained, however, that teaching about religion, such as courses on comparative world religions or the Bible as literature, could be "effected consistently with the First Amendment".[1975] Even so, the

---

1969. *See, e.g., Lanner v. Wimmer*, 662 F.2d 1349, 1353 (10th Cir. 1981).
1970. *See ibid.*, at 1357–1359.
1971. *Illinois ex rel. McCollum v. Bd. of Educ.*, 333 U.S. 203, 209–212 (1948).
1972. *Stone v. Graham*, 449 U.S. 39, 41 (1980) (rejecting the avowed secular legislative application of the displays—based on adoption of the Ten Commandments "as the fundamental legal code of Western Civilization and the Common Law of the United States"—as "not sufficient to avoid conflict with the first Amendment" (internal quotation marks omitted) (quoting Ky. Rev. Stat. § 158.178 (1980))).
1973. *Sch. Dist. of Abington Twp. v. Schempp*, 374 U.S. 203, 224–227 (1963); *ibid.*, at 305, 306–308 (1963) (Golderg, J., with Harlan, J., concurring) (discussing the distinction between constitutionally permissible teaching about religion and impermissible teaching of religion).
1974. *Ibid.*, at 224–227.
1975. *Ibid.*, at 225 (indicating that the study of comparative religion, the "history of religion and its relationship to the advancement of civilization", or the Bible "for its literary and historic qualities" might be "effected consistently with the First Amendment"); *see also Wood v. Arnold*, 915 F.3d 308, 319 (4th Cir. 2019) (upholding a public high school's dedication of a portion of world history coursework to learning about Islam); *Cal. Parents for Equalization of Educ. Materials v. Torlakson*, 370 F. Supp. 3d 1057, 1078–1083 (N.D. Cal. 2019) (holding that state curriculum addressing the role of major world religions in history did not violate the Establishment Clause in teaching Hinduism from a secular perspective and that the curriculum's primary effect was not to disparage Hinduism).

practice of offering public school classes about religion is not widespread; a 2010 survey showed that only 36% of Americans know that comparative religion classes may be taught in public schools.[1976] Several private foundations publish textbooks for teaching about the Bible or religion as history, literature, or culture. Such efforts are viewed by some as attempts to slip religious education through the back door of public schools.[1977] Generally speaking, courses about religion are more likely to be included in the curriculum in the South and rural areas where conservative Protestant majorities are politically powerful.[1978]

III. Challenges to Secular Teachings

743. States may not restrict instructional content when the motivating purpose behind the restriction is religious.[1979] For example, the Supreme Court struck down a state statute that criminalized the teaching of human evolution and Darwinism in *Epperson v. Arkansas*.[1980] The Court held that, since the purpose of the anti-evolution statute was to protect "a particular interpretation of the book of Genesis by a particular religious group", the statute violated the Establishment Clause.[1981] For additional discussion, *see* General Introduction, section 3 (Historical Background).

744. The Supreme Court has also prohibited a state from requiring that scientific creationism be taught in any course that teaches evolution, holding that the religious purpose of the statute violated the *Lemon* test.[1982] The Court's 2022 abrogation of the *Lemon* test and approval of the "history-and-tradition" test[1983] leaves in question how the Court would decide such cases in the future. For additional discussion of *Lemon v. Kurtzman*, *see* Part VII (Religious Communities and

---

1976. Pew Rsch. Ctr., *U.S. Religious Knowledge Survey* (Sept. 2010), https://www.pewforum.org/2010/09/28/u-s-religious-knowledge-survey (link to PDF). This 2010 survey also measured religious knowledge among Americans. It found that the average score was 16 out of 32 questions (50%), even though the questions were fairly basic, such as requiring respondents to identify Moses as the leader of the Exodus in the Bible, or Friday as the day on which the Jewish Sabbath begins. In a 2019 version of the survey, the average score dropped to 14 out of 32 (44%). Pew Rsch. Ctr., *What Americans Know about Religion* (Jul. 23, 2019), https://www.pewforum.org/2019/07/23/what-americans-know-about-religion (link to PDF).
1977. *See, e.g.*, Starita Smith, *Keep Religion out of Public Schools*, Progressive Mag. (Aug. 17, 2005), http://www.progressive.org/media_mpsa1705.
1978. *See, e.g.*, Julie Zauzmer Weil, *A Conservative Christian Group is Pushing Bible Classes in Public Schools Nationwide—and It's Working*, Wash. Post (May 8, 2019), https://www.washingtonpost.com/local/social-issues/a-conservative-christian-group-is-pushing-bible-classes-in-public-schools-nationwide--and-its-working/2019/05/08/f3bb490e-39e8-11e9-a06c-3ec8ed509d15_story.html.
1979. *Epperson v. Arkansas*, 393 U.S. 97, 103, 106–107 (1968).
1980. *Ibid.*, at 106, 109.
1981. *Ibid.*, at 103.
1982. *Edwards v. Aguillard*, 482 U.S. 578, 585–594 (1987).
1983. *Kennedy v. Bremerton Sch. Dist.*, 142 S. Ct. 2407, 2427–2428 (2022); *see also Groff v. DeJoy*, 600 U.S. 447, 460 & n.7 (2023) (acknowledging *Kennedy*'s abrogation of the *Lemon* test).

Protections of the Individual), Chapter 7 (Non-discrimination); and Part VIII (Financing of Religious Communities), Chapter 1 (Direct Financing).

745. Some have tried to challenge a perceived anti-religious bias or lack of respect for religion in the schools, alleging that a secular curriculum establishes a "secular humanist" religion and is barred by the Establishment Clause or that presenting secular material, without allowing students to opt out and have alternative instruction, violates the Free Exercise Clause. Such challenges have failed in federal courts of appeals.[1984]

§3. Prayer, Worship, and Quasi-religious Patriotic Observances in Public Schools

I. Prayer and School-Endorsed Worship

746. Acts of worship that are led or endorsed by teachers, or are otherwise supported by the school, are not permitted in public schools. The US Supreme Court has barred in public schools the use of a voluntary, nondenominational prayer composed by the New York State Board of Regents,[1985] as well as a voluntary devotional Bible reading and recitation of the Lord's Prayer.[1986] These actions were held to involve direct state advancement of religious viewpoints that is impermissible under the Establishment Clause.[1987] For further discussion of Establishment Clause limits on direct state advancement of religion, *see* Part VIII (Financing of Religious Communities), Chapter 1 (Direct Financing).

747. The Supreme Court has also struck down state legislation requiring a moment of silence set aside for meditation or prayer in public schools.[1988] In *Wallace v. Jaffree*, the Supreme Court found that Alabama laws creating a moment of silence had a "wholly religious character" and no secular purpose and thus failed the first prong of the then-valid *Lemon* test.[1989] *See* Part VII (Religious Communities and Protections of the Individual), Chapter 7 (Non-discrimination); and Part

1984. *See Mozert v. Hawkins Cnty. Bd. of Educ.*, 827 F.2d 1058, 1069–1070 (6th Cir. 1987) (holding public-school board's requirement, with no opt-out provision, that students read book series deemed by some parents as promoting secular humanism did not unconstitutionally burden free exercise); *Smith v. Bd. of Comm'rs of Mobile Cnty. Sch.*, 827 F.2d 684, 689 (11th Cir. 1987) (reversing lower court decision that forty-four challenged textbooks "both advanced [secular humanism] and inhibited theistic faiths in violation of the establishment clause"); *see also COPE v. Kan. State Bd. of Educ.*, 821 F.3d 1215, 1219 (10th Cir. 2016) (holding religious organization that challenged state science standards lacked standing).

1985. *Engel v. Vitale*, 370 U.S. 421, 424 (1962).

1986. *Sch. Dist. of Abington Twp. v. Schempp*, 374 U.S. 203, 205 (1963).

1987. *Ibid.*, at 205; *Engel*, 370 U.S. at 424.

1988. *Wallace v. Jaffree*, 472 U.S. 38, 60–61 (1985); *see also May v. Cooperman*, 780 F.2d 240, 253 (3d Cir. 1985) (relying on *Wallace* in finding unconstitutional a state's moment-of-silence law that lacked a secular purpose).

1989. *Wallace*, 472 U.S. at 56–60.

VIII (Financing of Religious Communities), Chapter 1 (Direct Financing) for further discussion of the *Lemon* test. Justice Sandra Day O'Connor, in a concurrence, suggested that not all moment-of-silence laws would violate the Establishment Clause.[1990] Indeed, moment-of-silence laws in Georgia and Virginia have survived appellate review.[1991] Moment-of-silence laws have been much more likely to be upheld when accompanied by a legislative history putting forth a secular reason for the law.[1992]

748. The Supreme Court has barred schools from inviting members of the clergy to offer prayers at a high-school graduation, holding that even a brief, nondenominational prayer violates the Establishment Clause as "a state-sponsored and state-directed religious exercise in a public school".[1993] The Court was also concerned about the subtle coercive pressures on young students to participate and the implicit endorsement of a religious message that the prayer communicated.[1994]

749. In 2000, in *Santa Fe Independent School District v. Doe*, the Supreme Court held that a school district policy allowing student-led prayer to be broadcast over a loudspeaker at a high-school football game constituted inappropriate state endorsement of religion.[1995] The Supreme Court rejected arguments that any prayers offered were student-led, private speech and thus permissible; instead it held that the prayers were culturally important and the circumstances in which they were offered gave the appearance of state endorsement.[1996] In that case, where the district limited pre-football game activities and determined the level of student involvement in the prayer, the Court found that the school district exercised too much control for the prayers to be considered private speech.[1997] Twenty-two years later, in *Kennedy v. Bremerton*, the Court held that the First Amendment protected a public high-school football coach's right to kneel and pray quietly at midfield after games.[1998] The Court contrasted the facts in *Kennedy* with those in *Santa Fe*, noting that the

---

1990. *Ibid.*, at 67, 67, 70–76 (O'Connor, J., concurring).
1991. *Brown v. Gilmore*, 258 F.3d 265, 282 (4th Cir. 2001), *cert. denied*, 534 U.S. 996 (2001); *Bown v. Gwinnett Cnty. Sch. Bd.*, 112 F.3d 1464, 1474 (11th Cir. 1997); *see also* Lee Ann Rabe, *A Rose by Any Other Name: School Prayer Redefined as a Moment of Silence Is Still Unconstitutional*, 82 Denv. U. L. Rev. 57, 63 (2004).
1992. *See Sherman v. Koch*, 623 F.3d 501, 509–510 (7th Cir. 2010) (upholding moment-of-silence law); *Croft v. Governor of Tex.*, 56 F.3d 735, 748–749 (5th Cir. 2009) (upholding the same); *Holloman ex rel. Holloman v. Harland*, 370 F.3d 1252, 1285–1286 (11th Cir. 2004) (holding teacher's practice of daily collecting student prayer requests and bookending daily moment of silence with the phrases "let us pray" and "amen" lacked secular purpose and violated the Establishment Clause); *Brown*, 258 F.3d at 277, 281; *Bown*, 112 F.3d at 1466–1467, 1471–1472.
1993. *Lee v. Weisman*, 505 U.S. 577, 587 (1992).
1994. *Ibid.*, at 592; *see also Freedom from Religion Found., Inc. v. Chino Valley Unified Sch. Dist. Bd. of Educ.*, 896 F.3d 1132, 1146–1147 (9th Cir. 2018) (noting "involuntary" student attendance at board meetings implicated "graver Establishment Clause considerations" than did cases where adult-only school board meetings began with prayer), *reh'g en banc denied*, 910 F.3d 1297 (9th Cir. 2018).
1995. *Santa Fe Indep. Sch. Dist. v. Doe*, 530 U.S. 290, 316–317 (2000).
1996. *Ibid.*, at 309–310.
1997. *Ibid.*, at 302–310.
1998. *Kennedy v. Bremerton Sch. Dist.*, 142 S. Ct. 2407, 2415–2416 (2022).

coach's prayers "were not publicly broadcast or recited to a captive audience" and that, although some students participated on occasion, students were not expected or required to participate in the post-game prayers.[1999] Notably, in *Kennedy* a now-more-conservative Court abrogated the *Lemon* test, on which the Court had relied to reach its holding in *Santa Fe*. Citing precedent, the Court instructed that the Establishment Clause should be interpreted "by reference to historical practices and understandings" instead of the "ahistorical, atextual" *Lemon* test.[2000] The majority reasoned that the coach's actions aligned with private religious worship historically protected by the First Amendment's Free Exercise and Free Speech Clauses and were not coercive in a way to offend the Amendment's Establishment Clause.[2001]

II. Quasi-religious Patriotic Observances in Public Schools

750. In 1943, the US Supreme Court prohibited public schools from requiring student participation in flag salutes or a pledge of allegiance, overruling a prior decision that permitted schools to require such observances.[2002] *See* Part II (Religious Freedom in General), Chapter 1 (Individual Religious Freedom).

751. In 1954, the US Congress amended the Pledge of Allegiance to contain the phrase "under God".[2003] Supporters of the insertion argue that it should be understood as a direct reference to the religious influences that have shaped US history. At the presidential signing of the law adding "under God" to the pledge, for example, President Dwight D. Eisenhower referenced the history of religious influence in the United States and expressed his hope that this influence would continue into the future.[2004]

752. A contested issue in more recent decades is whether encouraging schoolchildren to recite the phrase "one Nation under God" in the Pledge of Allegiance violates the Establishment Clause, the rights of non-believer students (even those who opt out of the observance), or the rights of parents to inculcate in their children their chosen beliefs. A case involving these issues reached the Supreme Court but

---

1999. *Ibid.*, at 2431–2432. *But see ibid.*, at 2434, 2434–2452 (Sotomayor, J., with Breyer and Kagan, JJ., dissenting) (asserting that the majority opinion ignored the similarities between the facts in *Kennedy* and *Santa Fe* and "elevate[d] the religious rights of a school official … over those of his students, who are required to attend school and who this Court has long recognized are particularly vulnerable and deserving of protection").
2000. *Ibid.*, at 2427–2428 (internal quotation marks omitted) (quoting *Town of Greece v. Galloway*, 572 U.S. 565, 576 (2014)).
2001. *Ibid.*, at 2429–2430, 2433.
2002. *W. Va. State Bd. of Educ. v. Barnette*, 319 U.S. 624 (1943), *overruling Minersville Sch. Dist. v. Gobitis*, 310 U.S. 586 (1940).
2003. *See* 4 U.S.C. § 4 (2018). The Pledge of Allegiance states, "I pledge allegiance to the Flag of the United States of America, and to the Republic for which it stands, one Nation under God, indivisible, with liberty and justice for all."
2004. Dwight D. Eisenhower, *Statement by the President upon Signing Bill To Include the Words "under God" in the Pledge to the Flag*, Am. Presidency Project (Jun. 14, 1954), https://www.presidency.ucsb.edu/documents/statement-the-president-upon-signing-bill-include-the-words-under-god-the-pledge-the-flag (last visited Sep. 30, 2023).

was decided on other grounds.[2005] In dicta, the Court suggested that the Pledge should be viewed as primarily a patriotic exercise rather than a religious exercise.[2006] The two federal courts of appeals that have addressed this specific issue have followed this suggestion, upholding the pledge.[2007] For further discussion of individual religious freedom, *see* Part II (Religious Freedom in General), Chapter 1 (Individual Religious Freedom).

III. Non-official Worship and Clubs in Public Schools

753. Individual or group student devotion in public schools is permitted provided there is no state coercion or appearance of state endorsement. For example, students are permitted to wear headscarves or religious symbols in class, and student religious clubs may form and worship together.[2008]

754. Schools may not discriminate against private religious expression by students "but must instead give students the same rights to engage in religious activity and discussion as they have to engage in other comparable activity"; however, schools "may not endorse religious activity or doctrine, nor may they coerce participation in religious activity".[2009]

755. Equal access of religious student clubs in public secondary schools is mandated by the Equal Access Act.[2010] It requires schools to provide access for all student-initiated groups to meet without interference from school instructors, unless the groups "materially and substantially interfere with the orderly conduct of educational activities within the school".[2011] Schools may opt out by prohibiting all non-curriculum-based clubs. But if schools create a "limited open forum" for some such clubs, they may not discriminate based on a club's subject matter.[2012] In *Board*

2005. *Elk Grove Unified Sch. Dist. v. Newdow*, 542 U.S. 1, 5 (2004) (holding that a non-custodial father, who brought suit on behalf of his student daughter, lacked standing).
2006. *Ibid.*, at 6–7; *see also ibid.*, at 18, 25–33 (Rehnquist, C.J., with O'Connor, J., concurring, and with Thomas, J., concurring in part).
2007. *Freedom from Religion Found. v. Hanover Sch. Dist.*, 626 F.3d 1, 10 (1st Cir. 2010); *Newdow v. Rio Linda Union Sch. Dist.*, 597 F.3d 1007, 1014 (9th Cir. 2010).
2008. *See, e.g., A.A. ex rel. Betenbaugh v. Needville Indep. Sch. Dist.*, 611 F.3d 248 (5th Cir. 2010) (holding that school district policy requiring Native American student to hide his long hair violated state's Religious Freedom Restoration Act); *Bd. of Educ. v. Mergens,* 496 U.S. 226 (1990) (holding school that allowed non-curriculum-related student groups to participate in its "limited open forum" triggered statutory obligation to provide equal access to student religious groups).
2009. U.S. Dep't of Educ., Religious Expression in Public Schools: A Statement of Principles 3 (June 1998), https://files.eric.ed.gov/fulltext/ED416591.pdf; *see also Guidance on Constitutionally Protected Prayer and Religious Expression in Public Elementary and Secondary Schools*, U.S. Dep't Educ. (May 15, 2023), https://www2.ed.gov/policy/gen/guid/religionandschools/prayer_guidance.html?exp=1.
2010. Equal Access Act, Pub. L. No. 98-377, 98 Stat. 1302 (1984) (codified at 20 U.S.C. §§ 4071–4074 (2018)).
2011. 20 U.S.C. § 4071(c) (2018).
2012. *Ibid.*, § 4071(a)–(b).

of Education v. Mergens, a plurality of Supreme Court justices concluded that the Equal Access Act does not violate the Establishment Clause.[2013]

756. In *Lamb's Chapel v. Center Moriches School District*, the Court further clarified that government exclusion of a group from any forum—whether public or limited in some way—because of the group's religious viewpoint constitutes impermissible viewpoint discrimination. The Court reiterated that:

> [a]though a speaker may be excluded from a non-public forum [meaning a forum on which the government places limits] if he wishes to address a *topic* not encompassed within the purpose of the forum … or if he is not a member of the class of speakers for whose especial benefit the forum was created …, the government violates the First Amendment when it denies access to a speaker solely to suppress the *point of view he espouses on an otherwise includible subject.*[2014]

In Lamb's Chapel, a school district permitted after-hours use of school facilities for various "social, civic, and recreational uses". But the district denied a religious group's request to use school facilities to show "a religious oriented film series on family values and child rearing".[2015] The Court noted that the district rules allowed "school property to be used for the presentation of all views about family issues and child rearing except those dealing with the subject matter from a religious standpoint".[2016] The Court held that the school district violated the Free Speech Clause by denying forum access based solely on the religious group's viewpoint regarding "an otherwise includible subject".[2017]

757. In *Good News Club v. Milford*, the Supreme Court upheld the rights of a religious student club to use public-school facilities for after-school activities that included prayer, scripture memorization, and Bible lessons.[2018] The Supreme Court rejected lower-court conclusions that the Establishment Clause prohibited the club's use of school facilities because its activities constituted religious instruction and worship. Instead, the Court characterized the club's activities as teaching "morals and character development" from a particular (in this case, Christian) viewpoint, which school policy allowed.[2019] Thus, the Court reasoned, denying the club access

---

2013. *Bd. of Educ. v. Mergens*, 496 U.S. 226, 253 (1990) (plurality opinion). For an explanation of a plurality opinion, *see supra* n. 970; *see also* Kimura, *Legitimacy Model for the Interpretation of Plurality Decisions*, *supra* n. 1459, at 1595–1596.
2014. *Lamb's Chapel v. Ctr. Moriches Union Free Sch. Dist.*, 508 U.S. 384, 394 (1993) (emphasis added) (quoting *Cornelius v. NAACP Legal Def. & Educ. Fund, Inc.*, 473 U.S. 788, 806 (1985)).
2015. *Ibid.*, at 384.
2016. *Ibid.*, at 393.
2017. *Ibid.*, at 394 (quoting *Cornelius*, 473 U.S.at 806). *See also Ne. Pa. Freethought Soc'y v. Lackawanna Transit System*, 938 F.3d 424, 434, 442 (3d Cir. 2019) (holding government ban of religious and atheistic messages on public transportation constituted unreasonable viewpoint discrimination where content-based restriction did not restrict speech based on subject but instead distinguished between religious and secular views "on the same subjects").
2018. *Good News Club v. Milford Cent. Sch.*, 533 U.S. 98 (2001).
2019. *Ibid.*, at 108–112.

to school facilities constituted viewpoint discrimination in violation of the Free Speech Clause.[2020] The Court also distinguished *Good News Club* from cases upholding prayer bans under the Establishment Clause, explaining that the potential for "coercive pressure" with school prayer is absent where after-school club participation is conditioned on parental permission.[2021] For additional discussion of Supreme Court jurisprudence on non-discrimination, *see* Part VII (Religious Communities and Protections of the Individual), Chapter 3 (Freedom of Expression) and Chapter 7 (Non-discrimination).

§4. Creation of Religious School Districts

758. The US Supreme Court has placed limits on institutional accommodation of groups of religious believers, holding that the creation of a school district along religious lines to accommodate a Satmar Hasidic (Orthodox Jewish) village violated the Establishment Clause because it allocated political power based on a religious criterion.[2022] *See* Part III (Legal Status of Religious Communities), Chapter 3 (Fundamental Rights and Religious Communities).

2020. *Ibid.*
2021. *Ibid.*, at 115.
2022. *Bd. of Educ. v. Grumet*, 512 U.S. 687, 690 (1994).

Chapter 2. Religious Schools

§1. RIGHT TO PRIVATE EDUCATION

759. The US Supreme Court upheld the right to form private schools, including private religious schools, in 1925.[2023] States retain power to require attendance at a school that has been accredited, approved, registered, or licensed by or with the state. Each state has its own requirements for private schools, which generally relate to curriculum, length of school year, and health and safety standards.[2024]

760. Private schools in the United States were primarily established by religious—particularly Catholic—organizations, beginning as early as the sixteenth century.[2025] Today the majority of private schools in the United States still have religious affiliations. A US Department of Education 2019–2020 survey showed that 20,241 (66%) of the existing 30,492 private schools were run by religious organizations.[2026] Catholic schools remain the most common, accounting for almost one-third of private schools that had religious affiliations in 2019.[2027] Nondenominational Christian schools were the second most common, constituting 22% of religious private schools.[2028] Jewish and Muslim private schools accounted for 5% and 1% respectively.[2029] While the number of religious private schools stayed fairly level for decades, the percentage of Catholic schools slowly decreased in the late twentieth century and into the twenty-first century.[2030] However, 2019 marked the beginning of an enrolment "boom" in private, conservative Christian schools—an increase attributed to COVID-19 pandemic-related frustrations and "rising parental anxieties" concerning the approach of public schools to issues such as race and transgender student rights.[2031]

761. Increased access to the internet and the growth of online educational resources have allowed both private and public schools to offer technology-based

2023. *See Pierce v. Soc'y of Sisters of the Holy Names of Jesus & Mary*, 268 U.S. 510, 534–535 (1925) (striking down state statute that required parents to send their children to public schools).
2024. *See generally* U.S. Dep't of Educ., State Regulation of Private Schools (July 2009), https://www2.ed.gov/admins/comm/choice/regprivschl/index.html (link to PDF).
2025. Timothy Walch, *Parish School: American Catholic Parochial Education from Colonial Times to the Present* 3 (1996).
2026. *Table 2. Number and Percentage Distribution of Private Schools, Students, and Full-Time Equivalent (FTE) Teachers, by Religious or Nonsectarian Orientation of School: United States, 2019–20*, Nat'l Ctr. for Educ. Stat., https://nces.ed.gov/surveys/pss/tables/TABLE02fl1920.asp (last visited Sep. 30, 2023).
2027. *Ibid.*
2028. *Ibid.*
2029. *Ibid.*
2030. The percentage of Catholic-operated schools decreased from 41% of all private schools in 1989 to 1990 to 35% in 2005 to 2006. *Number of Private Schools, by Religious Orientation and Community Type:1989–90 through 2005–06*, Nat'l Ctr. for Educ. Stat., https://nces.ed.gov/surveys/pss/tables/table_whs_01.asp (last visited Sep. 30, 2023).
2031. *See* Ruth Graham, *Christian Schools Boom in a Revolt Against Curriculum and Pandemic Rules*, N.Y. Times (Oct. 19, 2021), https://www.nytimes.com/2021/10/19/us/christian-schools-growth.html.

education to students, with regulations varying by state. Studies show the number of students engaged in full- and part-time virtual schooling has grown steadily since 2000 and predictably surged during the pandemic.[2032]

762. The COVID-19 pandemic was also a catalyst for an increasing number of US families to choose to homeschool their children rather than continue with remote or in-person public or private schooling. The percentage of homeschooled students nearly doubled from 1.7% to 3.3% of all students from 1999 to 2016,[2033] but by 2021, the percentage had doubled again to approximately 7%.[2034] Although that percentage was expected to decrease as the need for COVID-related contingencies decreased, it has remained well above pre-pandemic figures, at approximately 6%.[2035] A periodic national survey asks parents to identify all reasons important to them for homeschooling their children.[2036] In the 2020–2021 survey, 75% of parents said providing moral instruction was important. Providing religious instruction was important to 59% of parents, with 13% indicating it was the most important reason. The reason cited by the most parents as important (80%) and most important (25%) was concern about the school environment—including concern about "safety, drugs, or negative peer pressure".[2037]

763. Legal requirements and standards for homeschooling vary by state, ranging from states with no regulations to states with requirements such as home visits

2032. In 2020, during the COVID-19 pandemic, "nearly 93% of households with school-age children reported their children engaged in some sort of 'distance learning'", though this percentage was lower for lower-income households. Kevin McElrath, *Nearly 93% of Households with School-Age Children Report Some Form of Distance Learning During COVID-19*, U.S. Census Bureau (Aug. 26, 2020), https://www.census.gov/library/stories/2020/08/schooling-during-the-covid-19-pandemic.html; *see also* Nat'l Educ. Policy Ctr., *Virtual Schools in the U.S. 2019*, at 17 fig.1 (Alex Molnar ed., May 2019), https://nepc.colorado.edu/sites/default/files/publications/Virtual%20Schools%202019.pdf (charting the dramatic increase in number of students enrolled in full-time virtual schools, from 2000 to 2018); *Table 218.20. Percentage of Public School Districts with Students Enrolled in Technology-Based Distance Education Courses and Number of Enrolments in Such Courses, by Instructional Level and District Characteristics: 2002–03, 2004–05, and 2009–10*, Nat'l Ctr. for Educ. Stat., https://nces.ed.gov/programs/digest/d18/tables/dt18_218.20.asp (last visited Sep. 30, 2023) (charting increase in the percentage of public-school districts that enrolled students in some type of technology-based distance learning, from 36% in 2003 to 55% in 2010).

2033. *Table 206.10. Number and Percentage of Homeschooled Students Ages 5 Through 17 with a Grade Equivalent of Kindergarten Through 12th Grade, by Selected Child, Parent, and Household Characteristics: Selected Years, 1999 Through 2019*, Nat'l Ctr. for Educ. Stat., https://nces.ed.gov/programs/digest/d21/tables/dt21_206.10.asp (last visited Sep. 30, 2023).

2034. Brian D. Ray, *How Many Homeschool Students Are There in the United States? Pre-Covid-19 and Post-Covid-19: New Data*, Nat'l Home Educ. Rsch. Inst. (Sep. 9, 2021), https://www.nheri.org/how-many-homeschool-students-are-there-in-the-united-states-pre-covid-19-and-post-covid-19 (estimating that 3.721 million of the 53.771 million school-aged children were homeschooled during the 2020–2021 school year).

2035. Ray, *How Many Homeschool Students Are There in the United States During the 2021–2022 School Year?*, *supra* n. 657.

2036. *See, e.g.*, Nat'l Ctr. for Educ. Stat., *Homeschooled Children and Reasons for Homeschooling*, *supra* n. 658.

2037. Nat'l Ctr. for Educ. Stat., *Homeschooled Children and Reasons for Homeschooling*, *supra* n. 658, at 4.

and curriculum approval by the state.[2038] Homeschooling is typically defined as instruction provided by a parent or legal guardian, but some state definitions also encompass home instruction by private tutor or through programs (often online) provided through a variety of sources including, in some states, the public school system. Consequently, homeschooling regulations vary by type of homeschooling as well as by state; for example, if the student is not taught by a parent or legal guardian, states typically require teacher certification.[2039]

§2. Religious Autonomy

764. Religious groups retain exclusive autonomy over their religious curriculum and the selection of teachers of religious doctrine.[2040] *See* Part III (Legal Status of Religious Communities), Chapter 2 (Autonomy of Religious Communities); and Part VI (Labor Law Within Religious Communities), Chapter 2 (Religious Ministers and Labor Law).

765. Under the Civil Rights Act, Title VII, section 702, a religious educational institution may discriminate on the basis of religion in the hiring of individuals "to perform work connected with the carrying on … of its activities".[2041] This discrimination on the basis of religion is permitted in the hiring of all employees, not just religious teachers and leaders. This right has been upheld against an Establishment Clause challenge in *Corporation of the Presiding Bishop of The Church of Jesus Christ of Latter-day Saints v. Amos.*[2042] For additional discussion of *Amos*, *see* Part III (Legal Status of Religious Communities), Chapter 2 (Autonomy of Religious Communities); and Part VI (Labor Law Within Religious Communities), Chapter 3 (Other Employees and Labor Law).

§3. Financing of Private Schools

766. Private religious schools may be privately funded and seek additional funds and other material support from the state.

767. Riding a wave of anti-Catholic feeling in 1875, the US Congress very nearly passed a "Blaine Amendment" to the US Constitution, which would have barred public funding to religiously affiliated schools.[2043] Although the amendment

2038. *See generally Homeschool Laws by State*, *supra* n. 659.
2039. *See ibid.*
2040. *Hosanna-Tabor Evangelical Lutheran Church & Sch. v. EEOC*, 565 U.S. 171 (2012).
2041. 42 U.S.C. § 2000e-1(a) (2018).
2042. *Corp. of the Presiding Bishop of The Church of Jesus Christ of Latter-day Saints v. Amos*, 483 U.S. 327 (1987).
2043. The text of the proposed Blaine Amendment read:

> No State shall make any law respecting an establishment of religion or prohibiting the free exercise thereof; and no money raised by taxation in any State for the support of public schools, or

was not adopted into the federal constitution, several states adopted into their constitutions similar amendments barring funding of religiously affiliated private schools. Today, thirty-seven states have amendments restricting public funding of religious schools.[2044] In 2017 and 2020, the Supreme Court found state Blaine Amendments unconstitutional as applied by two different states in two different cases; the Court held that the states violated the Free Exercise Clause when they relied on the amendments to prohibit religious educational institutions from receiving state funds offered through generally available programs.[2045] For more about the Blaine Amendment, its state counterparts, and these cases, *see* Part I (Legal Framework and Sources), Chapter 1 (Constitutional Position of Religion) and Chapter 2 (Other Legislation with Regard to Religion); and Part VII (Religious Communities and Protections of the Individual), Chapter 7 (Non-discrimination).

I. Establishment Clause Limits on Financing of Private Schools

768. US Supreme Court case law on whether and when the state may financially or materially assist in private religious education is far from clear and reflects a larger set of conflicting approaches to interpreting the Establishment Clause. For more details, *see* Part I (Legal Framework and Sources), Chapter 3 (Typology of the System). Because the development of case law on this point has been complex, fact specific, and not always consistent, this section (section 3, Financing of Private Schools) focuses on Supreme Court decisions on the financing of private religious schools in some depth, in roughly chronological order, explaining some of the key facts and reasoning of each. For a more doctrinal-based summary, *see* Part VIII (Financing of Religious Communities), Chapter 1 (Direct Financing).

A. *No Direct Aid:* Everson

769. The US Supreme Court's first case involving state material support for religious schools, *Everson v. Board of Education*, established the principle that the state may not provide direct aid for religiously affiliated schools.[2046] While the Court used strong separationist language about the "high and impregnable" wall of separation between church and state, it held that the wall was not breached in that

derived from any public fund therefor, nor any public lands devoted thereto, shall ever be under the control of any religious sect, nor shall any money so raised or lands so devoted be divided between religious sects or denominations.

4 Cong. Rec. 205 (1875).

2044. *Blaine Amendments in State Constitutions*, Ballotpedia, https://ballotpedia.org/Blaine_amendments_in_state_constitutions (last visited Sep. 30, 2023).

2045. *Espinoza v. Mont. Dep't of Revenue*, 140 S. Ct. 2246, 2262–2263 (2020); *Trinity Lutheran Church of Columbia, Inc. v. Comer*, 582 U.S. 449, 466–467 (2012).

2046. *Everson v. Bd. of Educ.*, 330 U.S. 1 (1947).

case.[2047] The board of education in *Everson* had created a transportation reimbursement program for students who used the public bus system to get to school, including students attending parochial schools. A majority of the Supreme Court found that the reimbursement program did not violate the Establishment Clause because it did not contribute money directly to the schools but rather provided "a general program to help parents get their children, regardless of their religion, safely and expeditiously to and from accredited schools".[2048] According to the Court, the First Amendment simply "requires the state to be a neutral in its relations with groups of religious believers and non-believers; it does not require the state to be their adversary".[2049]

770. In *Everson*, the Court focused on the fact that the benefit accrued to the children, not to the religious school. While this is a difficult and somewhat shifting line to draw (since benefits to parents or children may also reduce costs to schools), the Supreme Court has returned to this approach in later cases. *See* Subsection C below and Part VIII (Financing of Religious Communities), Chapter 1 (Direct Financing).

771. Subsequently, in *Board of Education v. Allen*, the Supreme Court used *Everson* as precedent to uphold a state program that loaned textbooks to students attending private schools, both sectarian and non-sectarian.[2050] This decision relied heavily on *Everson*, articulating a test that examines the relevant statute's purpose and primary effect: to be constitutional, the purpose must be secular and the effect may neither advance nor inhibit religion.[2051] Since the purpose of the statute in *Allen* was to increase educational opportunities for children in the state, and the students requested and received the books directly, the Court found that the case was comparable to *Everson* and that the program did not violate the Establishment Clause.[2052]

B. Heightened Limits on State Aid: The Lemon *Test*

772. Until the *Lemon* test was abrogated in 2022,[2053] it served as a key analytical framework for determining the permissibility of aid to private religious schools. First articulated in 1971 in *Lemon v. Kurtzman*, the test adopted the reasoning of *Everson* and *Allen*, formulating the purpose-and-effect analysis into a three-pronged

---

2047. *Ibid.*, at 18 (quoting Letter from Thomas Jefferson to Danbury, Connecticut, Baptist Association, *supra* n. 526).
2048. *Ibid.*
2049. *Ibid.*
2050. *Bd. of Educ. v. Allen*, 392 U.S. 236 (1968).
2051. *Ibid.*, at 242–243 (quoting *Everson*, 374 U.S. at 222).
2052. *Ibid.*, at 243–244, 248.
2053. *Kennedy v. Bremerton Sch. Dist.*, 142 S. Ct. 2407, 2427–2428 (2022); *see also Groff v. DeJoy*, 600 U.S. 447, 460 & n.7 (2023) (acknowledging *Kennedy*'s abrogation of the *Lemon* test).

test: state aid must: (1) have a secular legislative purpose, (2) have a principle effect that neither advances nor inhibits religion, and (3) not foster "an excessive governmental entanglement with religion".[2054]

773. In *Lemon*, the Supreme Court used this test to address challenges to Pennsylvania and Rhode Island state statutes that provided government aid to religiously affiliated schools. The Pennsylvania statute provided financial reimbursement for teachers' salaries and materials for secular subjects in religiously affiliated schools. The Rhode Island statute allowed the state to help attract and retain non-public elementary school teachers by providing a 15% supplement to their annual salaries. In both cases, the funds were limited to non-religious subjects and to teachers teaching non-religious subjects. Both statutes were held to be unconstitutional because monitoring compliance with those limitations fostered excessive entanglement between the church and the government, thus failing the *Lemon* test's third prong.[2055]

774. *Tilton v. Richardson*, handed down the same day as *Lemon*, employed the same test to analyze a statute that provided state grants for the construction of facilities at both public and private colleges and universities, including religiously affiliated institutions.[2056] The challenged statute prohibited religious use of these facilities—but only for a twenty-year period. The Court concluded that the limitation was inadequate and, in the case of private religious universities, would have the effect of state advancement of religion, in violation of the Establishment Clause.[2057] The Court allowed the statute to stand but struck down the twenty-year-prohibition provision and ordered the lower court to enter a judgment requiring the prohibition to remain in place as long as the buildings retained commercial value.[2058] The Court did not find excessive entanglement.[2059] For additional discussion of *Tilton*, *see* Part XI (Religion and Culture), Chapter 1 (Religion and Art).

775. *Committee for Public Education and Religious Liberty v. Nyquist*, decided in 1973, similarly focused on impermissible benefits to religion.[2060] In that case, the Supreme Court barred payment of funds to non-public schools for building maintenance, repair, and tax credits for student tuition. Using the *Lemon* test, the Court determined that those forms of aid were unconstitutional because they directly benefited religion. The Court focused on the fact that the state had no provisions in place for how the funding would actually be spent. Because the statute advanced religion, the Court did not engage in a detailed analysis of whether it also caused excessive entanglement between the state and religion.

2054. *Lemon v. Kurtzman*, 403 U.S. 602, 612–613 (1971).
2055. *Ibid.*, at 615–625.
2056. *Tilton v. Richardson*, 403 U.S. 672 (1971).
2057. *Ibid.*, at 683.
2058. *Ibid.*, at 683–684, 689.
2059. *Ibid.*, at 685–688.
2060. *Comm. for Pub. Educ. & Religious Liberty v. Nyquist*, 413 U.S. 756 (1973).

776. As a practical matter, the standard in *Lemon* created a "Catch-22" problem and, in doing so, proved more separationist than the purpose-and-effect test of *Everson* or *Allen*.[2061] In *Lemon,* for example, the state's attempt to avoid Establishment Clause problems *created* an Establishment Clause problem: the Court held that the state's need to monitor compliance with its own limitations—to prevent teachers and schools that received state funds from teaching religious matters—created excessive entanglement with religion.[2062]

777. Even before the *Lemon* test was abrogated, it was strongly criticized by those both within and outside the Supreme Court.[2063] Most criticism called for a more workable standard—one that lent itself to a more consistent and clear application by the Court. Justice Antonin Scalia, after comparing the test to "some ghoul in a late-night horror movie", provided insight into why the Court retained the *Lemon* test, despite criticism: "The secret of the *Lemon* test's survival, I think, is that it is so easy to kill. It is there to scare us (and our audience) when we wish it to do so, but we can command it to return to the tomb at will."[2064] As Justice Scalia suggested, the flexibility of the test's applicability was both a major target of criticism and a reason the Court retained it in its judicial toolkit for fifty years. In 2022, in *Kennedy v. Bremerton*, the Supreme Court announced the *Lemon* test's abrogation and its replacement: Establishment Clause analysis based on "reference to historical practices and understandings".[2065] It remains to be seen how courts will apply this historical analysis to cases involving the public financing of private schools.

C. *"Child-Benefit" Theory*

778. In several cases after *Nyquist*, and somewhat in tension with *Lemon* and *Nyquist*, the Supreme Court concluded that tax deductions and other indirect aid to religious organizations were permitted under the *Lemon* test. These cases were arguably distinguishable from *Lemon* and *Nyquist* because the program or aid could be said to directly benefit the child or parent rather than the religious school per se.

2061. *See supra* para. 693.

2062. *Lemon v. Kurtzman*, 403 U.S. 602, 615–620 (1971).

2063. *See, e.g.*, Carl H. Esbeck, *The* Lemon *Test: Should It Be Retained, Reformulated or Rejected?*, 4 Notre Dame J.L. Ethics & Pub. Pol'y 513, 543–548 (1990). For more recent discussions of the *Lemon* test among Supreme Court justices, *see* the majority, plurality, concurring, and dissenting opinions in *Am. Legion v. Am. Humanist Ass'n*, 139 S. Ct. 2067 (2019). *See also, e.g.*, *Brown v. Collier*, 929 F.3d 218, 247 (5th Cir. 2019) (collecting USSC cases indicating *Lemon* was not a go-to test); *Doe v. United States*, 901 F.3d 1015, 1019 (8th Cir. 2019) (stating that the USSC had not committed to *Lemon* or any one test).

2064. *Lamb's Chapel v. Cent. Moriches Union Free Sch. Dist.*, 508 U.S. 384, 397, 398–399 (1993) (Scalia, J., with Thomas, J., concurring).

2065. *Kennedy v. Bremerton Sch. Dist.*, 142 S. Ct. 2407, 2427–2428 (2022) (internal quotation marks omitted) (quoting *Town of Greece v. Galloway*, 572 U.S. 565, 576 (2014)); *see also Groff v. DeJoy*, 600 U.S. 447, 460 & n.7 (2023) (acknowledging *Kennedy*'s abrogation of the *Lemon* test).

779. For example, despite overturning the tax credit in *Nyquist*, the Court in *Mueller v. Allen* upheld a statute that provided a personal income tax deduction for educational expenses, including tuition, for parents of students in non-religious or religious schools alike.[2066] Using the *Lemon* test, the Court held that the statute did not primarily advance religion because benefits accrued to religion only through the "numerous, private choices" of individuals. Moreover, it did not create excessive entanglement because the government's only interaction with religion was reviewing textbooks eligible for deduction—an acceptable activity pursuant to *Board of Education v. Allen.*[2067] The private choice or "child-benefit" rationale in *Mueller* invoked the logic used in *Allen* and *Everson v. Board of Education* to approve scenarios where religious schools were benefited only by virtue of the decisions of private citizens.[2068]

780. In *Witters v. Washington Department of Services for the Blind*, the Court again relied on the private choice of an individual as sufficient to overcome Establishment Clause challenges.[2069] In *Witters*, Washington state had established a scholarship program for the blind that focused on recipients, without distinguishing between those who would use the assistance at public or non-public schools. The individuals qualified for the scholarship and then exercised personal discretion as to where to study. The Supreme Court held that the program did not violate the Establishment Clause when some scholarship money went to a religious school because it benefited the school only indirectly through the "independent and private choices of aid recipients".[2070]

781. This principle arose again in *Zobrest v. Catalina Foothills School District*, where the Supreme Court held that the Establishment Clause does not prevent school districts from providing certain public employees to aid students with disabilities enrolled in sectarian schools.[2071] *Zobrest* involved a deaf student who was provided with an American Sign Language interpreter while in public school, under the Individuals with Disabilities Act (IDEA), but was denied an interpreter once he enrolled in a Catholic high school. The school district argued that sending public employees to transmit religious messages would violate the Establishment Clause. The Court determined that IDEA provided benefits "not to schools but to individual handicapped children"; therefore, the benefits only reached religious schools in an attenuated way through the private choices of students and parents.[2072]

782. Since 2000, the US Supreme Court has continued to use "child-benefit" or "private choice" reasoning, upholding state voucher and scholarship programs. In *Zelman v. Simmons-Harris*, a voucher program allocated a set amount of state funding to private citizens, who could choose where to use the voucher to help fund their

2066. *Mueller v. Allen*, 463 U.S. 388 (1983).
2067. *Ibid.*, at 403 (citing *Bd. of Educ. v. Allen,* 392 U.S. 236 (1968)).
2068. *See ibid.*, at 398.
2069. *Witters v. Wash. Dep't of Servs. for the Blind*, 474 U.S. 481 (1986).
2070. *Ibid.*, at 488–489.
2071. *Zobrest v. Catalina Foothills Sch. Dist.*, 509 U.S. 1, 13–14 (1993).
2072. *Ibid.*, at 6, 13.

children's education, including at religious schools.[2073] The Supreme Court held that the program was constitutional because "government aid reache[d] religious schools only as a result of the genuine and independent choice of private individuals".[2074] In *Espinoza v. Montana Department of Revenue*, the Court considered a Montana state program that offered tax credits for donors to nonprofit organizations that provided scholarships to private schools.[2075] A state agency promulgated a rule prohibiting the scholarships from being used at religious schools, citing the state constitution's "no-aid" provision prohibiting public aid to religious organizations. Noting that government funds reached "religious schools only as a result of Montanans independently choosing to spend their scholarships at such schools", the Court held that the scholarship program was permissible under the Establishment Clause and that the no-aid provision, as applied to the program, violated the Free Exercise Clause.[2076] In *Carson v. Makin*, some small rural districts in the state of Maine lacked secondary schools. To help offset education costs for students in those areas, the state transmitted payments to secondary schools chosen by parents but limited payments to non-sectarian schools.[2077] Again, the Supreme Court explained that any benefits flowing to sectarian schools through parent choice would not offend the Establishment Clause; further, the Court held that prohibiting state assistance to parent-chosen sectarian schools was discriminatory, in violation of the Free Exercise Clause.[2078] For additional discussion of these cases in the context of non-discrimination principles and the Establishment Clause, *see* Part VII (Religious Communities and Protections of the Individual), Chapter 7 (Non-discrimination); and Part VIII (Financing of Religious Communities), Chapter 1 (Direct Financing).

783. In 2023, an Oklahoma state board approved a Catholic online charter school[2079] aimed at students in rural areas. The approval provided that the school would be fully funded by taxpayers but include Catholic instruction, raising establishment and free exercise concerns. Opponents of the board's decision, including the Oklahoma State Attorney General, are expected to challenge it in the courts.[2080]

2073. *Zelman v. Simmons-Harris*, 536 U.S. 639 (2002).

2074. *Ibid.*, at 649, 662–663.

2075. *Espinoza v. Mont. Dep't of Revenue*, 140 S. Ct. 2246 (2020).

2076. *Ibid.*, at 2254, 2261–2262.

2077. *Carson v. Makin*, 142 S. Ct. 1987 (2022).

2078. *Ibid.*, at 1997–2002.

2079. The National Charter School School Resource Center, which is funded by the US Department of Education, defines a charter school as:

> a public school that operates as a school of choice. Charter schools commit to obtaining specific educational objectives in return for a charter to operate a school. Charter schools are exempt from significant state or local regulations related to operation and management but otherwise adhere to regulations of public schools—for example, charter schools *cannot* charge tuition or *be affiliated with a religious institution.*

What Is a Charter School, Nat'l Charter Sch. Res. Ctr., https://charterschoolcenter.ed.gov/what-charter-school (last visited Sep. 30, 2023) (emphasis added).

2080. *See* Press Release, Off. Okla. Att'y Gen., Drummond Files Lawsuit Against State Virtual Charter Board Members for Violating Religious Liberty of Oklahoma Taxpayers (Oct. 20, 2023),

D. More Permissive Standard for Indirect State Aid: Agostini

784. In 1997, the Supreme Court liberalized the standard for indirect state aid to religious schools in *Agostini v. Felton*, which decided the reopened 1985 case *Aguilar v. Felton.*[2081] In *Aguilar*, the Supreme Court had barred government funding of teachers at religious schools because supervision to ensure adherence to secular standards required excessive entanglement between the government and religious schools.[2082] In *Agostini*, the Court overruled *Aguilar* because the Court's interpretation of "excessive entanglement" and the Establishment Clause had changed significantly since *Aguilar* was decided.[2083]

785. In *Agostini*, the Court largely collapsed the *Lemon* test into the first step, or the "principal effect" prong. The Court identified three ways that the government could have a principal effect of advancing or inhibiting religion and thus violate the Establishment Clause: (1) by directly participating in indoctrination, (2) by choosing recipients according to religion, or (3) by fostering excessive entanglement between the state and religion.[2084] The Court explained that it no longer presumed any of the three types of violations would occur in a parochial school setting. On re-examining the program that provided federal funds for remedial instruction for disadvantaged children on parochial school premises, the Court concluded that the program had adequate safeguards to avoid any of the three Establishment Clause violations.[2085]

786. Like *Everson*, which laid the groundwork for cases decided under the child-benefit theory, *Agostini* laid the groundwork for a series of cases that would emphasize government neutrality instead of strict separation, which was the focus under *Lemon*. For example, *Agostini* was applied in a 2000 plurality decision in *Mitchell v. Helms* to permit a state to loan educational materials to public and private schools.[2086] While there was no clear majority rationale, a majority of the Court held that this program did not violate the Establishment Clause because it was neutrally applied.

---

https://www.oag.ok.gov/articles/drummond-files-lawsuit-against-state-virtual-charter-board-members-violating-religious; Sarah Mervosh, *A Religious Charter School Faces Pushback from the Charter School Movement Itself*, N.Y. Times (Jun. 8, 2023), https://www.nytimes.com/2023/06/08/us/oklahoma-religious-charter-school.html.

2081. *Aguilar v. Felton*, 473 U.S. 402 (1985), *overruled by Agostini v. Felton,* 521 U.S. 203 (1997).
2082. *Aguilar*, 473 U.S. at 414.
2083. *Agostini*, 521 U.S. at 233–236.
2084. *Ibid.*, at 234.
2085. *Ibid.*, at 234–235.
2086. *Mitchell v. Helms*, 530 U.S. 793 (2000) (plurality opinion). For an explanation of a plurality opinion, *see supra* n. 970; *see also* Kimura, *Legitimacy Model for the Interpretation of Plurality Decisions*, *supra* n. 1459, at 1595–1596.

II. Interaction of the Establishment Clause and Free Exercise Clause in State Aid to Religious Schools

787. The Supreme Court has found that there is "play in the joints", or some flexibility, in state funding questions between impermissible state action that violates the Establishment Clause and actions (or inactions) that violate the Free Exercise Clause.[2087] In *Trinity Lutheran Church v. Comer*, the Supreme Court reiterated, however, that anti-establishment interests are only considered after determining if there is a Free Exercise violation.[2088] In *Trinity Lutheran*, the Court struck down a Missouri playground-resurfacing program under the Free Exercise Clause because it excluded religious schools from participating in the program.[2089] The Court explained that the exclusion unconstitutionally burdened religious exercise by forcing Trinity Lutheran to choose "between being a church and receiving a government benefit".[2090] The Court distinguished *Locke v. Davey*, in which it upheld a state scholarship program available to students at religious and non-religious schools but excluded use for divinity studies.[2091] The *Trinity Lutheran* Court explained that *Locke*'s finding that the state could limit funding under the Establishment Clause was appropriate because the student in that case "sought funding for an essentially religious endeavor."[2092] The Court explained, however, that the Establishment Clause issue was only considered after the Court held that the program did not "require students to choose between their religious beliefs and receiving a government benefit", in which case it would have run afoul of the Free Exercise Clause.[2093]

2087. *See, e.g.*, *Trinity Lutheran Church of Columbia, Inc. v. Comer*, 582 U.S. 449, 458 (2017); *Locke v. Davey*, 540 U.S. 712, 728 (2003); *Walz v. Tax Comm'n of N.Y.*, 397 U.S. 664, 669 (1970); *see also supra* paras. 89, 90, and 701 and accompanying footnotes.

2088. *Trinity Lutheran*, 582 U.S. at 465.

2089. *Ibid.*, at 453–456.

2090. *Ibid.*, at 465.

2091. *Locke*, 540 U.S. at 715.

2092. *Trinity Lutheran*, 582 U.S. at 465 (internal quotation marks omitted) (quoting *Locke*, 540 U.S. at 720–721).

2093. *Ibid.*

Part X. Matrimonial and Family Law

Chapter 1. Legal Position of Religious Marriage

§1. Introduction

788. In the United States, marriage and family law are regulated by civil rather than religious law. Civil legal rights relating to marriage, divorce, and family do not vary by religious community, nor does the religious status of marriage. Marriage and divorce are regulated primarily by state law, however, variance exists from state to state.

789. Many countries do not recognize religious marriage as having civil effect, but in the United States, a religious marriage is civilly binding. Marriage licenses, and the qualifications to receive a license, are regulated by the states. Three-quarters of all states do not require religious officials to be licensed or registered with the state in order to perform civilly binding marriages; the other twelve states have made the licensing/registration process relatively simple.[2094] Thus, once a couple has received a marriage license, a religious figure (who meets state requirements, if any) can perform the marriage, and the marriage becomes binding when the license is signed by the officiant. From a state's point of view, a marriage performed by a state official and a marriage performed by an authorized religious representative (who meets state requirements, if any) have identical civil effect and are regulated under the same civil law standards. For additional discussion, *see* Part VII (Religious Communities and Protections of the Individual), Chapter 2 (Freedom to Marry).

790. Marital status for the purpose of religious standing in a particular religious community is determined by the religious community itself. However, these religious standards do not have civil effect on the legal status of a marriage. Likewise, religious divorces or annulments do not have civil effect because these areas are regulated by civil law.

2094. *See supra* para. 487 and accompany footnotes.

§2. State Law

791. Marriage is primarily regulated in the United States through state law. Typical state requirements for eligibility for marriage include minimum age requirements, legal capacity, prohibitions on relationships involving parties closer than first cousins, and prohibitions on bigamy/polygamy. States are banned from prohibiting interracial marriages, or refusing to recognize legal interracial marriages, by both the US Constitution and federal statute.[2095]

§3. Same-Sex Marriage

792. States cannot exclude same-sex couples from marrying, nor can a state refuse to recognize the validity of a same-sex marriage legally performed in another state.[2096] In 2015, in *Obergefell v. Hodges*, the US Supreme Court held that marriage is a fundamental right for same-sex as well as opposite-sex couples.[2097] In addition, the Court held that same-sex couples could exercise the fundamental right to marry in all states, thus invalidating state laws that prohibited same-sex marriage.[2098]

793. The legalization of same-sex marriage raised a variety of questions, such as whether government and religious officials could be required to perform same-sex weddings and whether private business owners could be required to provide wedding-related services for same-sex couples. In 2022, the US Congress passed the Respect for Marriage Act, which codified the right to same-sex marriage while guaranteeing that nonprofit religious organizations and their employees cannot be required "to provide services, accommodations, advantages, facilities, goods, or privileges for the solemnization or celebration of a [same-sex] marriage" in violation of their beliefs.[2099] The right of wedding-related private business owners to refuse to provide services and goods for same-sex marriages, based on their religious beliefs, has been litigated with mixed results. For a more detailed explanation of *Obergefell* and its implications for religious exercise in this developing area of law, *see* Part VII (Religious Communities and Protections of the Individual), Chapter 2 (Freedom to Marry).

§4. Status of Religious Marriage and Eligibility of Clergy

794. States delegate to religious officials the power to marry, but each religious organization decides for itself who is eligible to perform weddings that will have

2095. *Loving v. Virginia*, 388 U.S. 1 (1967); *Obergefell v. Hodges*, 576 U.S. 644 (2015); Respect for Marriage Act, Pub. L. No. 117-228, 136 Stat. 2305 (2022).
2096. *Obergefell*, 576 U.S. at 675–676 (2015).
2097. *Ibid.*
2098. *Ibid.*, at 681.
2099. Pub. L. No. 117-228, § 6, 136 Stat. 2305, 2306.

religious effect.[2100] They also set forth the requirements for ordination and the ordination process. Certain religions have relevant bodies of law, such as Jewish law or Catholic Canon law, to govern these decisions as well as many other aspects of the religion.[2101] As discussed above, in section 1 (Introduction), thirteen states require religious leaders to be licensed or registered with the state directly to perform civilly binding marriages, but all other states do not.[2102]

§5. Mail-Order and Internet Clergy / Virtual Licensing and Marriages

795. One marriage-related controversy in the United States has involved "mail-in clergy", also known as internet ministers, who are sponsored by organizations such as the Universal Life Church.[2103] These religious officials apply for ordination either online or by mail. From the state's point of view, the question is whether such people are duly ordained ministers. Some states have not recognized marriages performed by ULC ministers, but most states have come to recognize marriages solemnized by "mail-order clergy" as valid unions.[2104] The COVID-19 pandemic precipitated developments relating to virtual ordinations, virtual wedding licensing, and even virtual wedding ceremonies in some states.[2105]

§6. Illegal Marriages

796. Parties to a legally valid marriage must meet three requirements: (1) have the legal capacity to enter a marriage contract; (2) enter the marriage voluntarily; and (3) comply substantially with state statutory requirements.[2106] As mentioned above, state statutory requirements generally relate to age and mental capacity, prohibitions on bigamy/polygamy and incest, and requirements for marriage officiants.[2107] Religious officiants can only marry those who are eligible for marriage

2100. 3 Durham et al., *supra* n. 174, § 23:5 (*Performing Marriages*).
2101. *See, e.g.*, *Code of Canon Law*, Holy See, at bk. IV (*Function of the Church*), tit. VII (*Marriage*), https://www.vatican.va/archive/cod-iuris-canonici/eng/documents/cic_lib4-cann998-1165_en.html #CHAPTER_V (last visited Sep. 30, 2023); Solomon B. Freehof, *American Reform Responsa (ARR) 398-401, 130. Rabbi's Prerogative to Officiate at Weddings*, Cent. Conf. Am. Rabbis, https://www.ccarnet.org/ccar-responsa/arr-398-401 (last visited Sep. 30, 2023) (opining, based on insights from the Talmud and other Jewish authorities, that a Jewish marriage ceremony must be performed by an ordained rabbi).
2102. *See supra* para. 487 and accompany footnotes.
2103. *Universal Life Church—Free Online Ordination*, *supra* n. 1271.
2104. *See supra* para. 488 and accompanying footnotes.
2105. *See supra* para. 488 and accompanying footnotes.
2106. 3 Durham et al., *supra* n. 174, § 23:5 (*Performing Marriages*).
2107. *Ibid.*

under civil law. So, for example, polygamous marriages performed by clergy would not be recognized as civilly valid, since polygamy is illegal in all fifty states.[2108] For more on polygamy, *see* Part V (Religion and Politics), Chapter 2 (Political Influence in Religion).

2108. *See Reynolds v. United States*, 98 U.S. 145 (1878) (holding that federal prohibition on polygamy did not violate the Free Exercise Clause); *Davis v. Beason*, 133 U.S. 333 (1890) (upholding state law that disenfranchised individuals who would not disavow polygamy), *abrogated by Romer v. Evans*, 517 U.S. 620, 634 (1996); *Late Corp. of The Church of Jesus Christ of Latter-day Saints v. United States*, 136 U.S. 1 (1890) (upholding Edmunds-Tucker Act, which dissolved the Church's corporation and seized its assets due to the Church's sanctioning of polygamy); *Cleveland v. United States*, 329 U.S. 14 (1946) (interpreting Mann Act to prohibit transporting women and girls over state lines for purposes of entering polygamous marriages).

Chapter 2. Legal Position of Religious Family Law

§1. Introduction

797. Marriage and family law is largely governed by state law in the United States.[2109] This chapter discusses the intersection of religion and the laws that regulate the creation and dissolution of a civilly binding marriage. For discussions of other topics related to family law, *see* Part VII (Religious Communities and Protections of the Individual), Chapter 2 (Freedom to Marry), discussing same-sex marriage; Chapter 6 (Medical Deontology), discussing reproductive rights; and Chapter 5 (Professional Secrecy), discussing child abuse in the context of mandatory reporting statutes.

798. Civilly binding marriage may be performed by civil officials such as "court clerks, judges, and, in some states, notary publics", by virtue of their offices.[2110] Additionally, unlike many of their counterparts throughout the world, religious officials in the United States may perform civilly binding marriages. In most states, the only requirement for a religious official to perform a civilly binding marriage is that the official be validly ordained or designated as such by a religious denomination. One-quarter of all states require that a religious official be licensed or registered with the state.[2111] States have increasingly recognized ministers ordained through mail-order or internet certification programs as qualified to perform valid civil marriages.[2112] California is unique in allowing local governments to "deputize" friends and family to perform one specific marriage on a specific day, for a small fee, provided the deputized officiant does not use religious wording or references.[2113]

799. Religious officials may, but are not required to, perform marriages for those who do not claim membership in their congregations. While a marriage solemnized in a religious ceremony does not require any validation from the government other than a marriage license, it must conform to government requirements for a valid marriage to be civilly binding.[2114] Religious officials may also require marriage applicants to meet marriage requirements particular to their religious denomination. For additional discussion, *see* this part, Chapter 1 (Legal Position of Religious Marriages), above.

2109. 3 Durham et al., *supra* n. 174, § 23:2 (*Understanding of Marriage in the United States*).
2110. *Ibid.*, § 23:5 (*Performing Marriages*).
2111. *See supra* para. 487 and accompany footnotes.
2112. *See supra* paras. 488 and 795 and accompanying footnotes.
2113. *See* Cal. Fam. Code § 401(b) (West 2022).
2114. *See supra* para. 796 and accompanying footnotes; 3 Durham et al., *supra* n. 174, § 23:5 (*Performing Marriages*).

§2. Prenuptial Agreements and Marriage Contracts with Religious Norms

800. Prenuptial agreements made in anticipation of religious marriage often contain provisions requiring deference to religious law and norms. The Establishment Clause precludes secular courts from inquiring into religious matters; for example, secular courts may not examine, determine, or rule on whether the religious requirements of a religious marriage or divorce have been met.[2115] Thus, many prenuptial agreements between religious couples require either mediation or arbitration through a religious body. While secular courts must steer clear of delving into religious matters or doctrine, they may enforce "neutral principles" of contract law that don't entangle courts in religious controversy.[2116] For example, in *Avitzur v. Avitzur*, the prenuptial agreement between a Jewish couple required any divorce disputes to be arbitrated in front of the Beth Din, a rabbinical court.[2117] Although the couple had obtained a civil divorce, the husband refused to appear before the Beth Din and consent to a religious divorce (*get*). The wife sued in civil court, pointing to the arbitration clause in the prenuptial agreement, which the New York state court of appeals held to be enforceable.[2118] The court reasoned that

> the relief sought by [the wife was] … simply to compel [the husband] to perform a secular obligation to which he contractually bound himself. In this regard, no doctrinal issue need[ed] to be [reviewed], no implementation of a religious duty [was] contemplated, and no interference with religious authority [would] result.[2119]

That court, like others, analogized the prenuptial agreement to other enforceable agreements that require submitting disputes to non-judicial forums.[2120]

801. Courts will not uphold prenuptial agreements that violate constitutional rights or contravene public policy, however, even if they accord with religious norms.[2121] For example, in *In re Marriage of Noghrey*, the court reiterated that prenuptial agreements that promote and encourage divorce offend public policy and are

2115. *Cf. Watson v. Jones*, 80 U.S. (13 Wall.) 679, 727–729 (1871) (articulating what came to be known as the "ecclesiastical abstention doctrine").

2116. *See Jones v. Wolf*, 443 U.S. 595, 602–604 (1979) (approving a "neutral principles" approach to resolving contract and other disputes involving religious organizations and individuals).

2117. *Avitzur v. Avitzur*, 446 N.E.2d 136, 137 (N.Y. 1983).

2118. *Ibid.*

2119. *Ibid.*, at 115.

2120. *Ibid.*, at 113–114; *see also In re Marriage of Goldman*, 554 N.E.2d 1016, 1020, 1025 (Ill. App. Ct. 1990) (explaining that "[m]arriage and divorce are secular, contractual undertakings" and affirming order requiring husband to comply with the marriage contract (*ketubah*) and give his wife an Orthodox divorce (*get*)).

2121. *See, e.g., Tilsen v. Benson*, 347 Conn. 758, 785–786 (2023) (distinguishing *Avitzur* in holding that enforcing a *ketubah*'s provisions would violate the Establishment Clause where it would require the court "to"discern and enforce what Jewish law requires with respect to property division and financial support upon dissolution'); *Aflalo v. Aflalo*, 685 A.2d 523, 540–543 (N.J. Super. Ct. Ch. Div. 1996) (declining to follow *Avitzur* where a wife failed to appear before or seek relief through

unenforceable.[2122] The state court held that an agreement promising the wife in the event of a divorce USD 500,000 or one-half of the assets of the husband, whichever was greater, was against public policy because it encouraged the wife to seek divorce "with all deliberate speed".[2123] Courts have also determined that prenuptial agreements governing the religious upbringing of children are unconstitutional: they (1) "excessively entangle the courts in religious matters" in violation of the Establishment Clause and (2) restrict parents' freedom to question and change their beliefs and instruct their children according to those beliefs in violation of the Free Exercise Clause.[2124] In *Zummo v. Zummo*, a couple agreed by an oral prenuptial to raise their future children in the Jewish faith.[2125] After having three children, the father filed for divorce and wanted to take the children to "occasional Roman Catholic Services", to instill a "bi-cultural upbringing".[2126] The mother protested on the basis of the prenuptial agreement, but the state court concluded that an agreement regarding religious upbringing was not enforceable, especially in the absence of evidence that exposure to Roman Catholic services would present "a substantial threat of present or future physical or emotional harm to the children".[2127] In general, prenuptial agreements do not have to be fair to be upheld, but they cannot be so one-sided as to deprive a spouse or children of all property or support.[2128]

802. US courts may be asked to interpret and enforce prenuptial agreements or marriage contracts created outside the United States, some of which contain religious provisions. Generally, US courts acknowledge non-US choice-of-law provisions where parties have a connection to the chosen foreign forum; however, courts will not uphold these provisions "if the requirements would make the … agreement unconscionable under [US] law".[2129]

---

the Beth Din but sought a court order to compel her husband's appearance before the Beth Din, holding such an order would violate the husband's free exercise rights).

2122. *In re Marriage of Noghrey*, 215 Cal. Rptr. 153, 155 (Cal. Ct. App. 1985).

2123. *Ibid.*, at 156–157.

2124. *Zummo v. Zummo*, 574 A.2d 1130, 1144, 1148 (Pa. Super. Ct. 1990); *see also* Jonathan E. Fields, *Forbidden Provisions in Prenuptial Agreements: Legal and Practical Considerations for the Matrimonial Lawyer*, 21 J. Am. Acad. Matrim. Laws. 413, 433 (2008); Michelle Greenberg-Kobrin, *Civil Enforceability of Religious Prenuptial Agreements*, 32 Colum. J.L. & Soc. Probs. 359, 378–389 (1999).

2125. *Zummo*, 574 A.2d at 1145.

2126. *Ibid.*, at 1141.

2127. *Ibid.*, at 1157.

2128. *See, e.g.*, *Rider v. Rider*, 669 N.E.2d 160, 163–165 (Ind. 1996); *Potts v. Potts*, 303 S.W.3d 177, 187–190 (Mo. Ct. App. 2010); *Unander v. Unander*, 506 P.2d 719, 721–722 (Or. 1973); *Cary v. Cary*, 937 S.W.2d 777, 782 (Tenn. 1996).

2129. John Sill, *The Enforcement of Premarital Agreements at the International Level*, 27 J. Am. Acad. Matrimonial Laws. 245, 255–256 (2015); *see, e.g.*, *Chaudrey v. Chaudrey*, 388 A.2d 1000, 1006 (N.J. Super. Ct. App. Div.1978) (interpreting prenuptial agreement according to the law of Pakistan, which was where the agreement "was freely negotiated and the marriage took place"); *Cohen v. Cohen*, 93 A.D.3d 506 (N.Y. App. Div. 2012) (upholding prenuptial agreement executed in France where it was written in wife's native language and evidence did not support wife's assertion that she agreed to it under duress and without the requisite mental capacity).

803. Bigamy and polygamy are illegal in the United States, even if legally recognized abroad and/or based on religious belief. *See* discussion in General Introduction, section 3 (Historical Background); and Part V (Religion and Politics), Chapter 1 (Religious Influence in Politics). For example, US immigration law prohibits individuals in polygamist or bigamist relationships from becoming naturalized US citizens, even if such relationships are religiously motivated and legally recognized in their home country.[2130] US law has recognized bigamous or polygamous marriages entered legally abroad only in very narrow contexts, such as the distribution of property upon the death of a spouse.[2131]

804. At times, civil courts are called on to enforce provisions in religious marriage contracts such as *mahr* in Islamic marriage contracts—a husband's obligation to give his wife an economic asset. Courts will interpret these agreements if they can rely on neutral contract principles, and courts retain discretion to determine whether enforcement would violate fundamental public policy.[2132]

§3. Religion-Based Alternative Dispute Resolution

805. Alternative Dispute Resolution (ADR) is common throughout the United States, whether religiously motivated or not, and is largely governed by the Federal Arbitration Act and state enactments of the Uniform Arbitration Act.[2133] Many disputes arising out of a religious context, including those concerning religious marriage, are resolved through religiously associated mediation or arbitration bodies.[2134] These bodies attempt to resolve disputes of both secular and religious law with reference to guiding religious principles; the Institute for Christian Conciliation, for example, relies on biblical principles in facilitating ADR.[2135]

806. Despite debates and challenges about the enforceability of awards produced by religious arbitration, civil courts have generally upheld the decisions of

2130. 8 U.S.C. §§ 1427(a), 1101(f)(3), 1182(a)(10)(A) (2018); 8 C.F.R. § 316.10(b)(2)(ix), (b)(3)(i) (2022); *see Al-Hasani v. Sec'y U.S. Dep't of Homeland Sec.*, 81 F.4th 291, 295 (3d Cir. 2023).

2131. *See* Eugene Volokh, *Polygamous Foreign Marriages under U.S. Law* (Nov. 5, 2014), Wash. Post, https://www.washingtonpost.com/news/volokh-conspiracy/wp/2014/11/05/polygamous-foreign-marriages-under-u-s-law (citing *In re Bir's Est.*, 83 Cal. App. 2d 256 (1948)).

2132. *See, e.g.*, *Nouri v. Dadgar*, 226 A.3d 797, 810–811, 817–820 (Md. 2020) (holding that *mahrs* "are not void as against public policy" but that the state court could enforce a *mahr* only if "(1) it can be interpreted under neutral principles of [contract] law, without court involvement in any theological or doctrinal matter; and (2) scrutinize[d] … in purely secular terms, it constitutes an enforceable agreement" (citations and internal quotation marks omitted)).

2133. Federal Arbitration Act, Pub. L. 68-401, 43 Stat. 883 (1925) (codified as amended at 9 U.S.C. §§ 1–16 (2018)); Unif. Arbitration Act (Nat'l Conference of Comm'rs of Unif. State Laws 2010); *see* Walter, *Religious Arbitration in the United States and Canada*, *supra* n. 719, at 517.

2134. Walter, *Religious Arbitration in the United States and Canada*, *supra* n. 719, at 519–521.

2135. *Ibid.*, at 519–520; *see Frequently Asked Questions & Introduction to Christian Conciliation*, Inst. for Christian Conciliation, https://www.aorhope.org/icc-faq (last visited Sep. 30, 2023).

religious arbitrators.[2136] Of course, a civil court may overturn an award for procedural defects, "evident mistake", violation of public policy, deprivation of a constitutional right, or "manifest disregard for the law".[2137] For example, courts have decided that, as a matter of policy, disputes of child custody and visitation cannot be the subject of religious arbitration because secular judicial scrutiny will more likely result in a decision in the child's best interest.[2138]

807. Religious arbitration agreements are particularly common among Jewish couples who, as part of the marriage ceremony, sign an arbitration clause in the *ketubah* (marriage contract) to resolve marital issues before a Beth Din, a rabbinical court. Civil courts will generally uphold religious arbitration clauses if they can do so by applying "neutral contract principles" and without delving into religious doctrine or controversies. And again, to be upheld, such clauses may not violate fundamental public policy standards[2139] or the US Constitution.[2140] For more on religion and arbitration, *see* Part III (Legal Status of Religious Communities), Chapter 4 (Contractual Religious Freedom).

§4. Covenant Marriage

808. Three states—Arizona, Arkansas, and Louisiana—have passed laws allowing marrying couples to choose to enter a "covenant marriage".[2141] Agreeing to a covenant marriage obligates couples to participate in pre-marital counselling and counselling during marriage should the marriage become troubled.[2142] Couples may only divorce where there is a "total breach" of the marriage commitment.[2143] While more robust marriage requirements may appeal to those who place religious value on marriage, only 1% of marriages in Arizona, Arkansas, and Louisiana are covenant marriages.[2144]

2136. Walter, *Religious Arbitration in the United States and Canada*, *supra* n. 719, at 521.
2137. *Ibid.*, at 518.
2138. *See* 3 Durham et al., *supra* n. 174, § 23:7 (*Divorce*).
2139. *See, e.g.*, *In re Marriage of Bellio*, 129 Cal. Rptr. 2d 556, 558 (Cal. Ct. App. 2003) (explaining that prenuptial agreements offend public policy when their terms "promote and encourage dissolution, and thereby threaten to induce the destruction of a marriage that might otherwise endure").
2140. *See, e.g.*, *Aflalo v. Aflalo*, 685 A.2d 523, 525 (N.J. Super. Ct. Ch. Div. 1996) (holding wife was not entitled to court order compelling her husband to abide by arbitration clause in marriage contract (*ketubah*) in violation of his free exercise).
2141. Ariz. Rev. Stat. Ann. § 25-901 (2022); Ark. Code Ann. § 9-11-803 (2022); La. Stat. Ann. § 9:272 (2022).
2142. 3 Durham et al., *supra* n. 174, at § 23:10 (*Overview of Covenant Marriage*).
2143. La. Stat. Ann. § 9:272.
2144. 3 Durham et al., *supra* n. 166, at § 23:10 (*Overview of Covenant Marriage*).

§5. Divorce

809. Unlike solemnization of religious marriages, which may be performed by religious officials, legally binding divorce falls entirely within state power.[2145] Historically, divorce was only available to those who could show fault or a specific, enumerated breach of the marital commitment. Because divorce was so difficult to obtain, beginning in 1969, states enacted "no-fault" divorce laws, which did not require an enumerated breach of the marital commitment. In 2010, New York became the last state to enact a no-fault divorce law. Even though no-fault divorce is an option in all states, individuals may still file for divorce on specific grounds in some states. While no-fault divorce solved some problems, it is not a perfect solution and has been linked with the rise of divorce rates; higher poverty rates for divorced women; and physical, social, and emotional problems for children of divorced parents.[2146]

810. Generally speaking, religious differences are not a major cause of divorce in the United States and cannot be raised as grounds for divorce in states that still allow fault-based filings.[2147] However, as one state court noted, "Although a difference in the religious faith of a spouse does not constitute a ground for divorce, a religious conviction may induce a spouse to do things that would constitute … ground[s]" for divorce, such as disrupting and damaging family life to the point of constituting "extreme cruelty".[2148]

811. Some religious groups have their own laws or practices that govern religious divorce. While these laws and practices by themselves have no legal effect, when integrated with a prenuptial, nuptial, or postnuptial agreement, civil courts may have the task of evaluating the performance of religious divorce requirements that align with basic contract law.[2149] For example, in *Avitzur v. Avitzur*, discussed above, the husband who refused to appear before the Beth Din argued that the obligations of the *ketubah* (marriage contract) arose "solely from Jewish religious law" and that the court's enforcement of its terms would constitute "excessive entanglement between church and State" in violation of the Establishment Clause.[2150] The

2145. *Ibid.*, at § 23:7 (*Divorce*).

2146. *Ibid.*

2147. Mitchell A. Tyner, *Religious Freedom Issues in Domestic Relations Law*, 8 BYU J. Pub. L. 457, 457–458 (1994); 3 Durham et al., *supra* n. 174, § 23:7 (*Divorce*).

2148. *Pater v. Pater*, No. C-890553, 1990 WL 162021, at *2 (Ohio Ct. App. Oct. 24, 1990) (affirming trial court's grant of divorce and custody award to Catholic husband who objected to wife's new religious practices when she became a Jehovah's Witness), *rev'd* 588 N.E.2d 794 (Ohio 1992) (reversing lower court's decisions related to custody and visitation for being "improperly based" on wife's religious beliefs).

2149. 3 Durham et al., *supra* n. 174, § 23:7 (*Divorce*).

2150. *Avitzur v. Avitzur*, 446 N.E.2d 136, 138 (1983).

court disagreed, finding that the *ketubah*'s religious character did not "preclude enforcement of its secular terms" through "the application of neutral principles of contract law".[2151]

812. In many divorce proceedings between parents of differing religions or views, child custody disputes ensue. Child custody necessarily entails the right of a custodian to make decisions regarding the child's religion.[2152] In custody determinations, courts attempt to discern the arrangement that is in the best interests of the child. Courts take into account various factors of custodial fitness, and surprisingly, some courts have weighed the religion, religious knowledge, or religious practices of the potential custodians.[2153] This practice has been criticized as permitting judges to infuse their personal opinions about religion into custody decisions and even as violating the free exercise rights of potential custodians.[2154] In some cases, the justification for considering the religion of potential custodians is that some religious practices may interfere with the ability to properly care for a child.[2155] The willingness of courts to weigh religion as a custodial factor can vary from state to state.[2156]

2151. *Ibid.*, at 138–139; *see also* Lawrence M. Warmflash, *The New York Approach to Enforcing Religious Marriage Contracts: From* Avitzur *to the* Get *Statute*, 50 Brook. L. Rev. 229, 234–235 (1984).

2152. George L. Blum, Annotation, *Religion as Factor in Child Custody Cases*, 124 A.L.R.5th 203 (2004).

2153. *Ibid.*, §§ 7–10.

2154. *See Pater v. Pater*, 588 N.E.2d 794, 798–800 (Ohio 1992) (explaining that the First Amendment forbids denial of parental custody based on "religious practices unless there is probative evidence that those practices will adversely affect the mental or physical health of the child").

2155. *See* Blum, *Religion as Factor in Child Custody Cases*, *supra* n. 2152, § 8[b].

2156. *See generally ibid.*

Part XI. Religion and Culture

Chapter 1. Religion and Art

§1. Introduction

813. Freedom of expression is sometimes considered synonymous with freedom of oral speech, but it includes more than just speech, encompassing art and artistic expression, for example.[2157] The production of both religious art and art that offends religion is broadly protected by the First Amendment.[2158] Although the United States does not have a tradition of publicly funding religious art, art in public places that reflects religious themes is not uncommon, as discussed below. For further discussion of freedom of expression, *see* Part VII (Religious Communities and Protections of the Individual), Chapter 3 (Freedom of Expression).

814. Long before the arrival of the Puritans, Native American tribes incorporated a variety of art, including religious art, into their lives and worship.[2159] Congress has passed laws to protect and preserve sacred ancient Native American art and artifacts, as well as protect and promote the sale of authentic, contemporary religious Native art. For example, the Native American Graves Protection and Repatriation Act of 1990[2160] recognizes the "rights of Indian tribes and their lineal descendants to obtain repatriation of certain human remains, funerary objects, sacred objects, and objects of cultural patrimony from federal agencies and museums."[2161] The Indian Arts and Crafts Act of 1990[2162] was passed "to protect tribal

2157. *See 303 Creative LLC v. Elenis*, 600 U.S. 570, 587 (2023) ("All manner of speech—from 'pictures, films, paintings, drawings, and engravings," to "oral utterance and the printed word'—qualify for the First Amendment's protections; no less can hold true when it comes to speech … conveyed over the Internet." (quoting *Kaplan v. California*, 413 U.S. 115, 119–120 (1973))); *see also* G.A. Res. 217 (III) A, Universal Declaration of Human Rights, arts. 19, 27 (Dec. 10, 1948).

2158. *See infra* this part, s. 6 (Art that Offends Religion), subs. II (Public Funding of Blasphemous Art).

2159. *See* Nat'l Museum of the Am. Indian, *Creation's Journey: Native American Identity and Belief* (Tom Hill & Richard W. Hill, Sr., eds. 1994).

2160. Native American Graves Protection and Repatriation Act (NAGPRA), Pub. L. 101-601, 104 Stat. 3048 (1990) (codified as amended at 18 U.S.C. § 1170; 25 U.S.C. §§ 3001–3013 (2018)).

2161. *Cultural Protection & NAGPRA*, Nat'l Cong. Am. Indians, https://www.ncai.org/policy-issues/community-and-culture/cultural-protection-and-nagpra (last visited Sep. 30, 2023).

2162. Indian Arts and Crafts Act (IACA), Pub. L. 101-644, 104 Stat. 4662 (1990) (codified as amended at 25 U.S.C. §§ 305d, 305e (2018)).

cultural resources by preventing the sale of [arts and crafts] that are falsely represented to have been made by Indians".[2163] The lack of efficacy and enforcement of these laws has been criticized, however.[2164]

815. Religious communities in the United States have varied artistic traditions and modes of expression. While the Puritans' focus on sacred texts helped shape the "American" literary tradition, including both prose and poetry, "visual arts … were neglected and suppressed under the Puritans".[2165] However, the promise of religious freedom eventually attracted immigrant settlers from various faith traditions who brought with them rich artistic traditions. All manner of religious sects, including Catholics, Protestants of many denominations, Jews, Hindus, Buddhists, and Muslims, have brought with them or have developed forms and styles of religious art, which are often integrated into their worship.[2166]

§2. Public Displays of Religious Art and Religious Symbols

816. The First Amendment's prohibition on state establishment of religion and the Establishment Clause doctrine of "separation of church and state" place limits on the public display of religious art and religious symbols. But public display of such art and symbols is more common than the fundamental principles of non-establishment and separation might suggest.

817. Unsurprisingly, given the significant role of religion in US history and society, religious art is often found in public museums and art galleries. Religious art as art[2167] in public places, even government-owned museums, has not been found to violate the Establishment Clause.[2168] For example, a city in California installed a statue of an Aztec deity in one of the city parks.[2169] Although evidence indicated some still believed the statue represented a god, the court held that the installation did not violate the Establishment Clause.[2170] The federal court of appeals reasoned that any New Age concepts of the deity were not based on a formal "shared or comprehensive" doctrine to constitute a "discernible religion for purposes of Establishment Clause analysis".[2171] And while members of a more formal religious

2163. *See Cultural Protection & NAGPRA*, *supra* n. 2161.

2164. *See, e.g.*, *ibid.*; William J. Hapiuk, Jr., Note, *Of Kitsch and Kachinas: A Critical Analysis of the Indian Arts and Crafts Act of 1990*, 53 Stan. L. Rev. 1009, 1009–1075 (2001) (recommending that the "flawed" IACA be supplemented by a robust certification trademark system).

2165. *See* Camille Paglia, *Religion and the Arts in America*, Arion, Spring/Summer 2007, at 1, 3–4.

2166. *See generally ibid.*, at 1–20.

2167. Distinguished from religious symbols, such as the Ten Commandments or a nativity scene.

2168. William M. Howard, Annotation, *First Amendment Challenges to Display of Religious Symbols on Public Property*, 107 A.L.R.5th 1 (2003).

2169. *Alvarado v. City of San Jose*, 94 F.3d 1223, 1225–1226 (9th Cir. 1996).

2170. *Ibid.*, at 1232.

2171. *Ibid.*, at 1230, 1232.

organization believed the Aztec deity symbolized Jesus Christ, they did not consider the symbol to be an object of worship; therefore, the statue did not invoke or implicate religious beliefs in a way that offended the Establishment Clause.[2172]

818. Explicitly religious artwork and imagery are also common in government buildings, including the US Capitol, the Library of Congress, and the US Supreme Court. But the representations of religious figures in these buildings generally are not set in a religious context. In the Supreme Court Building, for example, significant religious figures associated with the law in various ways, such as Moses, Confucius, Muhammad, and Solomon, appear in marble friezes along with other historical law-related figures, including Menes, Charlemagne, and Sir William Blackstone.[2173]

819. Expressly religious displays on public grounds, such as crucifixes, nativity scenes, and monuments displaying the Ten Commandments, have been held to violate the Establishment Clause in some contexts but not in others. In contrast, religious expression and art on private property are broadly protected. For further discussion of religious displays on public property, *see* this section as well as Part VII (Religious Communities and the Protections of the Individual), Chapter 7 (Nondiscrimination).

820. One area of ongoing controversy has been crosses and crucifixes on public land. In San Diego, California, a cross erected in 1913 on city-owned land on Mount Soledad was replaced in the 1920s and replaced again after being blown down by wind in 1952. The cross was dedicated in a 1954 ceremony "as a reminder of God's promise to man of everlasting life and of those persons who gave their lives for our freedom".[2174] In the 1980s, in response to litigation, a plaque was added marking the site and the cross as a war memorial. However, this did not resolve the controversy, as many war veterans felt the cross did not memorialize their efforts in the war. One war veteran explained, "I am not a Christian and the memorial sends a very clear message to me that the government is honoring Christian war veterans and not non Christians."[2175] Courts generally concurred with this view of the cross, found that it violated the Establishment Clause, and ordered it removed, even after the land was transferred to the federal government.[2176] Two appeals to the US Supreme Court failed,[2177] and the land was eventually transferred to a private

2172. *Ibid.*, at 1230–1232.
2173. *Architectural Information*, Sup. Ct. U.S., https://www.supremecourt.gov/about/archdetails.aspx (link to PDF, *Courtroom Friezes: South and North Walls*).
2174. *Trunk v. City of San Diego*, 629 F.3d 1099, 1101 (9th Cir. 2011).
2175. *Ibid.*, at 1125.
2176. *See ibid.*, at 1101–1105, 1125.
2177. *Mount Soledad Mem'l Ass'n v. Trunk*, 573 U.S. 954 (2014) (mem.) (denying certiorari); *Mount Soledad Mem'l Ass'n v. Trunk*, 567 U.S. 944 (2012) (mem.) (denying the same).

memorial association as recommended in the National Defense Authorization Act of 2015,[2178] which has allowed the cross to remain in place.

821. A federal court of appeals held that twelve-foot-tall white crosses erected on public land to honor fallen state highway patrol troopers were unconstitutional.[2179] The American Atheist Society, along with two individual citizens, claimed that the memorial crosses violated the Establishment Clause. The court found insufficient evidence that the cross in that context conveyed "a secular meaning that [could] be divorced from its religious significance".[2180] Thus, the court held that the "memorials ha[d] the impermissible effect of conveying to the reasonable observer the message that the State prefer[ed] or otherwise endorse[d]" Christianity.[2181] In response, the state removed the state highway patrol logo from the crosses and added signage to each cross, indicating that each is a private memorial, approved by surviving family members, and is "not a state endorsement of any religion".[2182]

822. In contrast, in 2019 the US Supreme Court found that a Latin cross erected on public land as a memorial to fallen World War I soldiers did not violate the Establishment Clause.[2183] The Court acknowledged that the cross was "undoubtedly a Christian symbol" but found that, during its 100 years of existence in the community, the cross had acquired "additional layers" of secular and historical meaning.[2184] The Court reasoned that, for those who now viewed the cross as part of the community, "destroying or defacing the Cross … would not be neutral and would not further the ideas of respect and tolerance embodied in the First Amendment".[2185] Four justices signalled the future direction of the Court, supporting a plurality section of the opinion that criticized the *Lemon* test (since abrogated) and looked to historical practices instead.[2186] They referenced the First Congress's practice of having chaplains and chaplain-led prayer in Congress as a constitutional example "of respect and tolerance for differing views, an honest endeavor to achieve

2178. National Defense Authorization Act for Fiscal Year 2015, Pub. L. 113-291, § 2852, 128 Stat. 3292, 3713; *see also* Greg Moran, *Soledad Cross Case Concludes, Leaving Memorial in Place*, San Diego Union-Trib. (Sep. 8, 2016), https://www.sandiegouniontribune.com/sdut-soledad-final-2016sep08-story.html.

2179. *Am. Atheists, Inc. v. Duncan*, 637 F.3d 1095, 1111 (10th Cir. 2010) (amending original decision, 616 F.3d 1145 (10th Cir. 2010), and denying rehearing en banc).

2180. *Ibid.*, at 1122.

2181. *Ibid.*, at 1111.

2182. *The 14 White Roadside Cross Memorials Commemorating Fallen Highway Patrol Officers Beside Roadways Throughout the State of Utah Do Not Constitute an Endorsement of Any Religion by the State*, Utah Highway Patrol Assoc., https://utahtrooper.com/roadside-memorials (last visited Sep. 30, 2023).

2183. *Am. Legion v. Am. Humanist Assoc.*, 139 S. Ct. 2067, 2089 (2019).

2184. *Ibid.*, at 2089–2090.

2185. *Ibid.*, at 2090.

2186. *Ibid.*, at 2087–2089 (plurality section II.D) (foreshadowing the Court's eventual abrogation of the *Lemon* test and approval of analysis referencing historical practices, in *Kennedy v. Bremerton Sch. Dist.*, 142 S. Ct. 2407, 2427–2428 (2022)).

inclusivity and nondiscrimination, and a recognition of the important role that religion plays in the lives of many Americans".[2187] The justices concluded that "[w]here categories of monuments, symbols, and practices with a longstanding history follow in that tradition, they are likewise constitutional."[2188]

823. Public displays of nativity scenes depicting events surrounding the birth of Jesus Christ have also been controversial. In *Lynch v. Donnelly*, a city in Rhode Island annually erected in a private park a Christmas display that typically included a Christmas tree, Santa Claus house, and crèche (nativity scene).[2189] Referring (if somewhat grudgingly[2190]) to the *Lemon* test, the Court held that inclusion of the crèche did not constitute excessive entanglement of church and state, did not impermissibly advance religion, and had a secular purpose, which was to "depict[] the historical origins of [a] traditional event long recognized as a National Holiday".[2191] In a concurrence regularly cited by the Court in subsequent cases, Justice Sandra Day O'Connor reasoned that the crèche passed the "endorsement" test—that evidence failed to show "the particular crèche display at issue … was intended to endorse or had the effect of endorsing Christianity".[2192]

824. The Supreme Court relied largely on the concept of endorsement in *County of Allegheny v. ACLU*, which involved two holiday displays in the Pittsburgh area.[2193] The first challenged display was a large crèche in the Allegheny County courthouse, occupying a space near the building's main staircase. A sign stating "*Gloria in Excelsis Deo*!" (Glory to God in the Highest) stood above the crèche; another sign indicated the crèche had been donated by a Roman Catholic group. The county also displayed a small Christmas tree and poinsettia flowers in the space, which was the site of an annual Christmas-carol program. The second challenge focused on the city of Pittsburgh's display of an eighteen-foot menorah near the city-county building—part of a holiday-season "salute to liberty" display that included a forty-five-foot Christmas tree. A federal court of appeals ruled that each display endorsed religious views in violation of the Establishment Clause. The US

2187. *Ibid.*, at 2089.

2188. *Ibid.*; *see also Kondrat'yev v. City of Pensacola*, 949 F.3d 1319 (11th Cir. 2020) (applying *American Legion* in finding cross maintained on city property did not violate Establishment Clause); *Salazar v. Buono*, 559 U.S. 700, 718–719 (2010) (plurality opinion) (stating, in another cross-monument-on-public-lands case, "The goal of avoiding governmental endorsement does not require eradication of all religious symbols in the public realm. … The Constitution does not oblige government to avoid any public acknowledgment of religion's role in society. … Rather, it leaves room to accommodate divergent values within a constitutionally permissible framework." (citations omitted)).

2189. *Lynch v. Donnelly*, 465 U.S. 668, 672 (1984).

2190. *Ibid.*, at 679 (noting the cases in which the Court chose not to apply the *Lemon* test or found it not useful).

2191. *Ibid.*, at 680–681, 685; *see also see also Woodring v. Jackson County*, 986 F.3d 979, 996–997 (7th Cir. 2021) (applying *American Legion* in finding county's nativity display constitutional, where it was "part of a larger Christmas display that contain[ed] various other symbols of Christmas", including secular symbols).

2192. *Lynch*, 465 U.S. at 687, 694 (O'Connor, J., concurring).

2193. *County of Allegheny v. ACLU*, 492 U.S. 573 (1989), *abrogation acknowledged by Kennedy v. Bremerton*, 142 S. Ct. 2407, 2427–2428 (2022).

Supreme Court affirmed the lower court's judgment regarding the Allegheny County crèche display but reversed the lower court regarding Pittsburgh's menorah display, finding it constitutional. The Court distinguished Allegheny County's crèche display from the display in *Lynch*, noting that the *Lynch* display was on private property and included traditional secular symbols of the holiday season, whereas the Allegheny County display was in a prominent part of a public building and included purely Christian symbols and messages, conveying government endorsement of Christianity.[2194] In contrast, the Supreme Court concluded that the "reasonable observer" would understand Pittsburgh's menorah and Christmas tree display to be a "secular recognition of different traditions for celebrating the winter-holiday season" rather than an "endorsement of Christian and Jewish faiths".[2195]

825. Similar controversies have arisen with respect to public displays of the Ten Commandments. In 2005, the US Supreme Court issued two decisions on the same day in two separate Ten Commandments cases. At issue in *Van Orden v. Perry* was a monolith of the Ten Commandments displayed at the Texas State Capitol; it had been donated by a civic organization and stood among numerous monuments and historical markers.[2196] An individual who frequently passed by the monument sued state officials claiming it violated the Establishment Clause. In a plurality opinion, the Supreme Court disagreed, with several justices concluding that the monument was permitted under the Constitution because it had historical—beyond merely religious—meaning and purpose.[2197] In *McCreary County v. ACLU*, displays of the Ten Commandments were placed in county courthouses after a series of approvals by county officials—approvals that expressed religious motives and purposes behind the displays. After the displays were challenged, the counties revised the displays and their purported purpose, emphasizing the Ten Commandments' position alongside more secular foundational documents of US law. Even so, the Court considered the displays to be motivated by "a predominantly religious purpose" in violation of the Establishment Clause.[2198]

826. In the United States, a number of geographic names and government symbols, such as seals, emblems, and flags, have religious meanings or incorporate religious symbols. Place names with religious origins or connotations include Bethlehem, Los Angeles, Newark, Providence, Sacramento, Salem, San Diego, San Francisco, San Jose, Santa Fe, Zion National Park, and more. The flags of Florida, Georgia, and Mississippi include the words "In God We Trust".[2199] Three state flags incorporate religious imagery: New Mexico's flag represents the spiritual history of the Zia Pueblo through imagery of a red sun with rays extending outward, while the

2194. *Ibid.*, at 598–602.
2195. *Ibid.*, at 617–621.
2196. *Van Orden v. Perry*, 545 U.S. 677, 631–683 (2005) (plurality opinion).
2197. *Ibid.*, at 690–692 (2005). For an explanation of a plurality opinion, *see supra* n. 970; *see also* Kimura, *Legitimacy Model for the Interpretation of Plurality Decisions*, *supra* n. 1459, at 1595–1596.
2198. *McCreary County v. ACLU*, 545 U.S. 844 (2005).
2199. "In God we trust" is also the national motto of the United States. 36 U.S.C. § 302 (2018).

flags of Alabama and Florida display adaptions of St. Andrew's Cross.[2200] In *Briggs v. Mississippi*, the Supreme Court held that Mississippi's flag, which at the time included a version of St. Andrew's Cross, did not violate the Establishment Clause. The Court relied on the *Lemon* test, concluding that the cross's inclusion in the flag had at least one secular purpose and that "any endorsement of or benefit to religion from [the flag's] display [was] at most indirect, remote and incidental".[2201] Legal challenges aimed at changing or removing religious imagery from town symbols have also generally been unsuccessful.[2202] For example, a federal court of appeals held that the city symbol of Las Cruces, New Mexico—which features three Christian crosses—did not violate the Establishment Clause.[2203] The court concluded that the symbol was not a religious statement or endorsement of Christianity, where the city's name means "The Crosses" and derives from the city's historic founding near a cemetery.

827. Religious symbols are common in war memorials and at military cemeteries. Ninety-eight "emblems of belief"—including denomination-specific and more general symbols of belief—are authorized for placement on government headstones for veterans.[2204] One or more emblems may be chosen to represent a "sincerely held belief" of the deceased veteran "that constituted a religion or the functional equivalent of religion and was believed and/or accepted as true by that individual during his or her life".[2205] In 2013, the Department of Veterans Affairs approved a request for the Sandhill Crane to appear as an emblem of belief on the headstone of a military veteran's same-sex spouse—the first same-sex spouse permitted to be buried in a national cemetery.[2206] Although the Sandhill Crane was not a religious emblem or identified with any group, the surviving veteran chose it as a personal symbol of the couple's relationship, and it was added to the emblems of belief register.

§3. Religious Buildings and Architecture

828. Religious buildings in the United States are nearly all privately owned, from churches to temples to mosques to synagogues. Almost all religious buildings

---

2200. Angelina Theodorou, *64 Countries Have Religious Symbols on Their National Flags*, Pew Rsch. Ctr. (Nov. 25, 2014), https://www.pewresearch.org/short-reads/2014/11/25/64-countries-have-religious-symbols-on-their-national-flags.

2201. *Briggs v. Mississippi*, 331 F.3d 499, 505–507 (5th Cir. 2003).

2202. *See, e.g.*, *Salazar v. Buono*, 559 U.S. 700, 718 (2010) (plurality opinion) ("The goal of avoiding governmental endorsement does not require eradication of all religious symbols in the public realm."); *King v. Richmond County*, 331 F.3d 1271, 1286 (11th Cir. 2003) (holding that a superior court clerk's seal, which included an outline of stone tablets representing the Ten Commandments, did not violate the Establishment Clause); *Murray v. City of Austin*, 947 F.2d 147, 158 (5th Cir. 1991) (holding that a Christian cross included in municipal seal was constitutional).

2203. *Weinbaum v. City of Las Cruces*, 541 F.3d 1017, 1033–1035 (10th Cir. 2008).

2204. *Emblems of Belief*, Nat'l Cemetery Admin., U.S. Dep't of Veterans Affs., http://www.cem.va.gov/hmm/emblems.asp (last visited Sep. 25, 2023).

2205. *Ibid.*

2206. Mike Francis, *Coming to VA Cemetery Headstones: The Sandhill Crane*, Oregonian (Jul. 1, 2013), http://www.oregonlive.com/pacific-northwest-news/index.ssf/2013/07/coming_to_va_cemetery_headston.html.

in the United States are built with private funds, as generally neither the federal nor state governments directly fund their construction or maintenance.

829. State and local governments do provide *indirect* aid to religious buildings, however, most importantly through property tax exemptions, the federal and state tax-exempt status of religious organizations, and the tax-deductibility of contributions made to religious and charitable organizations.[2207] The Supreme Court has held that such indirect forms of state support of religion do not violate the Establishment Clause. In 1970, in *Walz v. Tax Commission of the City of New York*, the Supreme Court upheld a New York statute permitting religious organizations to receive property tax exemptions "for properties used solely for worship".[2208] The Court reasoned that the "exemption is not sponsorship since the government does not transfer part of its revenue to churches but simply abstains from demanding that the church support the state".[2209] For more on tax exemptions, *see* Part III (Legal Status of Religious Communities), Chapter 1 (Formal Status of Religious Communities); and Part VIII (Financing of Religious Communities), Chapter 2 (Indirect Financing).

830. In 1971, in *Tilton v. Richardson*, the Supreme Court upheld federal construction grants for academic buildings on religious college and university campuses.[2210] The Court reasoned that the grants were restricted to buildings used for a secular purpose. (The Court struck down a provision, however, that would have allowed the buildings to be used for other purposes, including religious purposes, after a twenty-year period.[2211]). The Court also reasoned that the grants were acceptable because religious colleges generally have a high degree of academic freedom, and college and university students are less prone to indoctrination than elementary- and high-school students.[2212] In a separate case, the Supreme Court upheld state funding through revenue bonds of buildings used for non-sectarian purposes on religious university campuses.[2213] For more on *Tilton v. Richardson*, *see* Part VIII (Financing of Religious Communities), Chapter 1 (Direct Financing); and Part IX (Education), Chapter 2 (Religious Schools).

2207. *See* 1 Durham et al., *supra* n. 157, § 4:43 (*Tax Exemptions*); 3 Durham et al., *supra* n. 174, § 29:1 (*Introduction to Land Use and Property*).

2208. *Walz v. Tax Comm'n of N.Y.*, 397 U.S. 664, 666 (1970).

2209. *Ibid.*, at 675–676.

2210. *Tilton v. Richardson*, 403 U.S. 672 (1971).

2211. *Ibid.*, at 682–684 ("The restrictive obligations of a recipient institution under [the 20-year use-restriction provision] cannot, compatible with the Religion Clauses, expire while the building has substantial value. This circumstance does not require us to invalidate the entire [Higher Education Facilities] Act, however.")

2212. *Ibid.*, at 686–688.

2213. *Hunt v. McNair*, 413 U.S. 734 (1973). *But see Colo. Christian Univ. v. Weaver*, 534 F.3d 1245, 1251 (10th Cir. 2008) (noting that "under the doctrine applicable at the time[*Hunt* was decided], "pervasively sectarian" institutions had to be excluded from direct funding programs in order to fund private education at all. Since that time, the Supreme Court has substantially modified its interpretation of the Establishment Clause" (citing *Zelman v. Simmons-Harris*, 536 U.S. 639, 652 (2002); *Agostini v. Felton*, 521 U.S. 203, 232–234 (1997))).

§4. The National Cathedral

831. The National Cathedral, located in Washington, DC, is a rare exception to the general rule prohibiting state support for religious edifices. Even so, "state support" for the cathedral has been conceptual and symbolic rather than monetary. The National Cathedral was conceived in 1791 by Major Pierre L'Enfant, who was hired by George Washington to create plans for the nation's capital. L'Enfant proposed "a great church for national purposes."[2214] However, the US Congress did not issue a charter for the cathedral until 1893, which finally gave a private foundation the legal status necessary to purchase land.[2215] And construction did not begin until 1907, when President Theodore Roosevelt laid the first cornerstone. The edifice took longer to complete than any other building in the Washington, DC, area, and was not officially completed until 1990.[2216] The cathedral's official name is the Cathedral Church of Saint Peter and Saint Paul; it serves as the home of the Episcopal Diocese of Washington and the wider Episcopal Church in the United States. However, it was also conceived as "a House of Prayer for All People" and is used by various religious groups and for various religious and government functions, including national prayer services and funerals of former US presidents and their spouses.[2217] Contrary to popular belief, the National Cathedral is a private building constructed and maintained solely through private donations; it receives no funding from the federal government or the national Episcopal Church.[2218]

§5. National Historic Landmark Designation

832. A National Historic Landmark (NHL) is a site, structure, object, building, or district officially recognized by the federal government for its historic significance. To be designated an NHL, a landmark must "possess a high degree of integrity of location, design, setting, materials, workmanship, feeling, and association" and meet at least one of six criteria related to historical, artistic, architectural, scientific, and/or cultural significance.[2219] "[P]roperties owned by religious institutions or used for religious purposes" generally are eligible for NHL status only if they derive "primary national significance from architectural or artistic distinction or historical importance."[2220] Nominations for NHL status can come from state, federal,

2214. *Mission & Vision: History*, Wash. Nat'l Cathedral, https://cathedral.org/about/mission-vision (last visited Sep. 30, 2023).

2215. Richard G. Hewlett, *The Creation of the Dioceses of Washington and Washington National Cathedral*, 71 Anglican & Episcopal Hist. 350, 369, 378 (2002) ("At a time when separation of church and state was not a sensitive issue in public discourse, the leaders of the cathedral project in Washington had no compunctions about seeking a congressional charter or promoting the cathedral as a national institution. … To some [Episcopalians,] the vocation was to become the Church of America.")

2216. *Mission & Vision: History*, Wash. Nat'l Cathedral, *supra* n. 2214.

2217. *Learn & Discover: History*, Wash. Nat'l Cathedral, https://cathedral.org/discover/history (last visited Sep. 30, 2023).

2218. *See Mission & Vision: History*, Wash. Nat'l Cathedral, *supra* n. 2214.

2219. 36 C.F.R. § 65.4 (2022).

2220. *Ibid.*

or tribal preservation officers, or from local governments, Indian tribes, or private individuals or organizations.[2221] A National Park System Advisory Board reviews nominations and makes recommendations to the Secretary of the Interior, who makes final designations.[2222] Between 1960, when designations commenced, and 2020, some 2,600 NHLs were designated and approved.[2223] Most NHLs are privately owned, and NHL designation carries both responsibilities and benefits for owners. For example, owners may be eligible for grants or loans for historic preservation of their property, but their property is subject to periodic review by federal authorities and may be subject to limits on alterations or development.[2224] Most state and local governments have their own preservation laws and historic landmark programs and sometimes partner with the federal government in preservation efforts.[2225]

833. On the federal level, tax incentives are available for rehabilitation of historic properties to encourage private-sector investment.[2226] The Federal Historic Preservation Tax Incentives program has been highly successful, creating jobs and leveraging more than USD 116 billion "in private investment to preserve more than 47,000 historic properties since 1976."[2227] Thirty-seven states offer state historic tax credits to motivate private investment in the preservation of historic buildings and communities, although programs vary by state.[2228] In some cases, historic churches and other buildings once owned by religious organizations and exempt from taxes, have been remodelled into taxable properties, with the help of state tax incentives.[2229]

834. Designation as a historic landmark can have significant implications for a religious structure. One historic preservation case, however, had repercussions far beyond the church and municipality involved. In *City of Boerne v. Flores*, zoning authorities rejected a building permit application to enlarge a church because the

2221. *FAQs*, Nat'l Reg. of Hist. Places, Nat'l Park Serv., https://www.nps.gov/subjects/nationalregister/faqs.htm (last visited Sep. 30, 2023).

2222. *Nomination Process*, Nat'l Hist. Landmarks, Nat'l Park Serv., https://www.nps.gov/subjects/nationalhistoriclandmarks/nomination-process.htm (last visited Sep. 30, 2023).

2223. *See List of NHLs by State*, Nat' Hist. Landmarks, Nat'l Park Serv., https://www.nps.gov/subjects/nationalhistoriclandmarks/list-of-nhls-by-state.htm (last visited Sep. 30, 2023).

2224. *See* 36 C.F.R. §§ 65.2, 65.7 (2022).

2225. *Overview of Preservation Programs*, Nat'l Hist. Landmarks, Nat'l Park Serv., https://www.nps.gov/subjects/nationalhistoriclandmarks/preservation-programs.htm (last visited Sep. 30, 2023).

2226. *See* 26 U.S.C. § 47 (2018); 26 C.F.R. § 1.48-12 (2022); *Tax Incentives for Preserving Historic Properties*, Nat'l Park Serv., https://www.nps.gov/subjects/taxincentives/index.htm (Sep. 30, 2023).

2227. *Tax Incentives for Preserving Historic Properties*, Nat'l Park Serv., *supra* n. 2226.

2228. Nat'l Trust for Hist. Preservation, *State Historic Tax Credit Resource Guide* 8–11 (Jan. 2023), https://savingplaces.org/state-historic-tax-credits (link to PDF).

2229. *See, e.g.*, Elaine S. Povich, *State Tax Credits Help Turn Old Churches into Taxable Property*, Stateline (Feb. 2, 2016), https://stateline.org/2016/02/02/state-tax-credits-help-turn-old-churches-into-taxable-property.

church, though not particularly historic, was located in a historic preservation district.[2230] The Catholic Archbishop of San Antonio challenged the decision under the 1993 Religious Freedom Restoration Act (RFRA). However, the US Supreme Court took the opportunity to hold RFRA unconstitutional, as applied to the states. The Court acknowledged Congress's authority under the Fourteenth Amendment to enforce the Amendment's provisions against the states but held that, in enacting RFRA, Congress had exceeded its enforcement authority.[2231] The Court explained that, in legislating "what constitutes a constitutional violation," Congress intruded unconstitutionally into states' general authority to regulate.[2232] For additional discussion of *City of Boerne*, *see* Part II (Religious Freedom in General), Chapter 1 (Individual Religious Freedom).

835. In *St. Bartholomew's Church v. City of New York*, the church building itself and an auxiliary building on the Church's property had been designated a city landmark.[2233] The Church applied to the city's preservation commission to replace the auxiliary building with a forty-seven-story office building, to house and help fund (through lease income) its community outreach and service programs. The commission rejected the application, finding the proposal an "inappropriate alteration" to the landmark under the city's Landmarks Law.[2234] In addition to making a "takings" claim[2235] under the Fifth and Fourteenth Amendments, the Church claimed that the law violated the First Amendment's Free Exercise Clause. Relying on *Employment Division v. Smith*,[2236] the federal court of appeals held that the Landmarks Law was a "valid, neutral regulation of general applicability" that did not violate the Free Exercise Clause, given the lack of evidence showing discriminatory motive, coercion, or the Church's inability to continue its religious practices in the existing facilities.[2237] The court also rejected the Church's takings claim.

836. Some nationally significant historic religious properties and collections have received federal support through Save America's Treasures Grants.[2238] The grant program began in 1999, was paused from 2011 to 2016 due to lack of congressional funding, but resumed in 2017. Through 2017, the program had awarded

2230. *See City of Boerne v. Flores*, 521 U.S. 507, 511–512 (1997).
2231. *Ibid.*, at 511.
2232. *Ibid.*, at 519–520, 534.
2233. *Rector, Wardens, & Members of the Vestry of St. Bartholomew's Church v. City of New York*, 914 F.2d 348 (2d Cir. 1990).
2234. *Ibid.*, at 351.
2235. The "takings clause" of the Fifth Amendment prohibits the government from taking private property "for public use, without just compensation." Const. amend. V. The Fourteenth Amendment applies Fifth Amendment protections to the states, through a constitutional doctrine known as "incorporation." *See St. Bartholomew's Church*, 914 F.2d at 356 n.5.
2236. *Emp. Div., Dep't of Hum. Res. of Or. v. Smith*, 494 U.S. 872, 878–879 (1990) (explaining that free exercise rights do not excuse individuals from complying with an otherwise valid, generally applicable law that prohibits conduct the "State is free to regulate").
2237. *St. Bartholomew's Church*, 914 F.2d at 353–356.
2238. *See* 54 U.S.C. §§ 308901–308905 (2018).

in excess of USD 300 million through more than 1,300 grants.[2239] The federal grants are available to educational, government, tribal, and 501(c)(3) tax-exempt entities, including religious organizations. They are administered through a partnership of federal agencies: the National Park Service, Institute of Museum and Library Services, National Endowment for the Humanities, and National Endowment for the Arts. In the past, religious organizations have received grants for projects as varied as restoration of stained glass windows, remediation of "rising damp", general building restoration, and historic artwork preservation.[2240]

837. After the Supreme Court limited the scope of RFRA's protections in *City of Boerne*, Congress passed the Religious Land Use and Institutionalized Persons Act (RLUIPA), in part to provide protection for churches and religious organizations against discriminatory and excessively burdensome land-use regulations.[2241] Broadly, RLUIPA requires plaintiffs to show that their free exercise has been substantially burdened by government regulation; if plaintiffs meet their burden of proof, the government must show that the regulation constitutes the least restrictive means of furthering a compelling government interest.[2242] This "strict scrutiny" or "substantial burden" standard applies to programs or regulatory schemes under which government entities make individualized assessments of proposed property use.[2243]

838. RLUIPA also contains a specific land-use provision that (1) prohibits governments from imposing land-use regulations "in a manner that treats a religious assembly or institution on *less than equal terms* with nonreligious assembly or institution," (2) "*discriminates* against any assembly or institution on the basis of religion or religious denomination," (3) "*totally excludes* religious assemblies from a jurisdiction," or (4) "*unreasonably limits* religious assemblies, institutions, or structures within a jurisdiction.".[2244] Most RLUIPA land-use claims relate to the "equal terms" provision, which federal courts have interpreted differently, to require different burdens of proof.[2245] In such cases, religious-organization plaintiffs often prevail, with courts finding an equal terms violation when city zoning regulations

2239. *Save America's Treasures Grants*, Hist. Preservation Fund, Nat'l Park Serv., https://www.nps.gov/subjects/historicpreservationfund/save-americas-treasures-grants.htm (last visited Sep. 25, 2023).

2240. *See Save America's Treasures Funded Projects*, Hist. Preservation Fund, Nat'l Park Serv., https://www.nps.gov/subjects/historicpreservationfund/save-america-s-treasures-funded-projects.htm (last visited Sep. 30, 2023).

2241. Religious Land Use and Institutionalized Persons Act (RLUIPA), Pub. L. No. 106-274, 114 Stat. 803 (2000) (codified at 42 U.S.C. §§ 2000cc to 2000cc-5 (2018)).

2242. 42 U.S.C. § 2000cc-2(b) (2018).

2243. *Ibid.*, § 2000cc(a)(2).

2244. *Ibid.*, §2000cc(b) (emphasis added).

2245. *See New Harvest Christian Fellowship v. City of Salinas*, 29 F.4th 596, 606 n.10 (9th Cir. 2022) (discussing the widening circuit split in approaches "to facial challenges under RLUIPA's equal terms provision"); *see, e.g.*, *Tree of Life Christian Sch. v. City of Upper Arlington*, 905 F.3d 357, 373 (6th Cir. 2018) (requiring plaintiffs to present evidence of similarly situated nonreligious assemblies to make a prima facie case of unequal treatment); *New Harvest Christian Fellowship*, 29 F.4th at 605–606 & n.10 (requiring plaintiffs to present evidence that regulation "makes an express distinction between religious and nonreligious assemblies, regardless of whether those assemblies are similarly situated"); *Midrash Sephardi, Inc. v. Town of Surfside*, 366 F.3d 1214,

prohibit places of religious assembly from operating in areas where commercial development is permitted.[2246] As of 2023, the US Supreme Court has not decided a RLUIPA case related to land use, although the Court has issued a handful of opinions relevant to RLUIPA's "institutionalized persons" provisions.[2247] For more information on RLUIPA, *see* Part VII (Religious Communities and Protections of the Individual), Chapter 8 (Penal Law and Religion).

§6. Art That Offends Religion

I. Blasphemous Art and Hate Speech

839. While the First Amendment protects the free exercise of religion, it does not protect religious feelings or sensitivities. Art that is offensive to religion or that is blasphemous is protected by the First Amendment. For example, in a 1952 case, *Joseph Burstyn v. Wilson*, a state statute prohibited the exhibition, sale, lease, or loan of a motion picture that was deemed "sacrilegious."[2248] The Court found the term "sacrilegious" was vague and, as a result, the law vested state censors with unlimited control. The Court cautioned that under such an undefined standard, "the most careful and tolerant censor would find it virtually impossible to avoid favoring one religion over another …, [which] might raise substantial questions under the First Amendment's guaranty of separate church and state with freedom of worship for all."[2249] The Court concluded that the statute's provision allowing the state to ban a film based on a censor's interpretation of "sacrilegious" was an unconstitutional abridgement of free speech and free press. In doing so, it noted "that the state has no legitimate interest in protecting any or all religions from views distasteful to them."[2250]

840. Literature is also protected by the First Amendment, despite offensive content, unless it was "maliciously written for the apparent purpose of promoting and fomenting a bigoted and intolerant hatred against a particular racial or religious

---

1231–1232 (11th Cir. 2004) (requiring government to carry its burden by showing that regulation is narrowly tailored to achieve a compelling government interest, unlike other circuits who do not apply RLUIPA's § 2000cc(a) strict scrutiny standard to § 2000cc(b) "equal terms" challenges); *see also* U.S. Dep't of Justice, C.R. Div., Report on the Twentieth Anniversary of the Religious Land Use and Institutionalized Persons Act 8–11 (Sep. 22, 2020), https://www.justice.gov/crt/case-document/file/1319186/download (discussing RLUIPA land-use cases in US federal courts, 2000–2020).

2246. *See* cases cited *supra* n. 2245.

2247. *See Tree of Life Christian Sch.*, 905 F.3d at 376, 378, 387 (Thapar, C.J., dissenting) ("[T]he courts … have added requirements into RLUIPA that prevent many religious groups from seeking the shelter that Congress sought to provide. … There comes a time with every law when the Supreme Court must revisit what the [federal courts of appeals] are doing. That time has come."). The US Supreme Court has upheld RLUIPA's institutionalized person provisions as applied to the states but has yet to rule on the application of its land-use provisions to the states. *See Cutter v. Wilkinson*, 544 U.S. 709, 715–716, 719–720 (2005); *Holt v. Hobbs*, 574 U.S. 352, 357 (2015).

2248. *Joseph Burstyn, Inc. v. Wilson*, 343 U.S. 495, 497 (1952).

2249. *Ibid.*, at 505.

2250. *Ibid.*

group."[2251] Even in that instance, the author's intent and motive must be considered before such literature is suppressed.[2252] In a New York state court case, *Rosenberg v. Board of Education*, Jewish parents wanted to remove *Oliver Twist* and *The Merchant of Venice* from New York City schools because the works "tend to engender hatred of the Jew as a person and as a race", but the state court found that this was not the authors' intent and not a reason to prohibit students from reading either work.[2253] Furthermore, the court opined that "[p]ublic education and instruction in the home will remove religious and racial intolerance more effectively than censorship and suppression of literary works which have been accepted as works of art and which are not per se propaganda against or for any race, religion or group."[2254]

841. Federal and state laws outline narrow limits to freedom of expression, including obscenity and incitement to violence,[2255] but these limits are interpreted quite narrowly.[2256] The First Amendment's Free Speech Clause does not protect obscene material, and government can restrict such material, subject to specific safeguards. In 1973, in *Miller v. California*, the US Supreme Court articulated a three-pronged test for determining what is "obscene": (1) whether the average person, applying contemporary community standards, would find that the work, taken as a whole, appeals to prurient interests; (2) whether the average person, applying contemporary adult community standards, finds that the work depicts or describes, in a patently offensive way, sexual conduct specifically defined by the applicable state law; and (3) whether a reasonable person finds that the work, taken as a whole, lacks serious literary, artistic, political, or scientific value.[2257] Material that satisfies all three prongs may be found to be "obscene."

842. Content- and viewpoint-based speech restrictions by the state must be "narrowly tailored" to serve "compelling state interest."[2258] Under that standard, hate speech, including speech with religious motivations or targets, is generally protected so long as it does not incite listeners to violence or qualify as other prohibited speech, such as defamation, fraud, "fighting words," "true threats," or

2251. *Rosenberg v. Bd. of Educ.*, 92 N.Y.S.2d 344, 346 (N.Y. Spec. Term 1949).
2252. *Ibid.*
2253. *Ibid.*, at 345–346.
2254. *Ibid.*, at 346.
2255. *See, e.g.*, 18 U.S.C. §§ 1460–1470 (2018) (outlining federal obscenity laws, including prohibitions on visual representations of child sexual abuse); *ibid.*, §§ 2252B, 2252C (outlining federal laws prohibiting misleading domain names, words, or digital images on the internet); *ibid.*, § 2383 (prohibiting incitement of "rebellion or insurrection against" US authority or law).
2256. *See, e.g.*, *Brandenburg v. Ohio*, 395 U.S. 444, 447 (1969) ("[T]he constitutional guarantees of free speech and free press do not permit a State to forbid or proscribe advocacy of the use of force or of law violation except where such advocacy is directed to inciting or producing imminent lawless action and is likely to incite or produce such action.").
2257. *Miller v. California*, 413 U.S. 15, 24–25 (1973); *see also Smith v. United States*, 431 U.S. 291, 300–302, 309 (1977) (clarifying "contemporary adult community standards" standard in prongs one and two); *Pope v. Illinois*, 481 U.S. 497, 500–501 (1987) (clarifying "reasonable person" standard in prong three).
2258. *R.A.V. v. City of St. Paul*, 505 U.S. 377, 395 (1992).

obscenity.[2259] In *R.A.V. v. City of St. Paul*, a city ordinance made it illegal to place, on private or public property, a Nazi swastika, burning cross, or other symbol that "one knows or has reasonable grounds to know arouses anger, alarm or resentment in others on the basis of race, color, creed, religion, or gender."[2260] The Supreme Court found the law unconstitutional when a group of young men burned a cross on the lawn of the only African American family in town. One of the young men charged under the law claimed the law violated his freedom of speech, and the Court agreed, holding that it unconstitutionally discriminated based on content and viewpoint.[2261] The Court acknowledged the city's compelling interests in ensuring the basic human rights of members of groups historically subject to discrimination.[2262] However, it found that the content-specific aspects of the law were not reasonably necessary to achieve that interest, since content-neutral alternatives existed—for example, an ordinance might prohibit the use of "fighting words" without prohibiting a specific viewpoint expressed in those words.[2263] It should be noted that, although the Court upheld the young man's freedom of speech, his actions may have qualified as crimes under laws prohibiting trespass, terroristic threats, arson, and/or criminal damage to property. For additional discussion of *R.A.V. v. City of St. Paul*, *see* Part VII (Religious Communities and Protections of the Individual), Chapter 3 (Freedom of Expression).

843. More recently, in *Matal v. Tam*, the Supreme Court reiterated the principle that "[s]peech may not be banned on the ground that it expresses ideas that offend."[2264] In that case, the lead singer of a rock band was denied a trademark for his band's name, "The Slants," which is widely considered a racial slur. He challenged a provision prohibiting the registration of trademarks that might "disparage … or bring … into contemp[t] or disrepute any persons, living or dead", including members of a racial or ethnic group.[2265] The Supreme Court concluded that the provision was not "narrowly drawn"—that it potentially protected "every person living or dead as well as every institution"—and thus violated the Free Speech

2259. *See* 18 U.S.C. § 1001 (2018) (outlining prohibition on making false, fictitious, or fraudulent statements or representations in federal jurisdictions); *Virginia v. Black*, 538 U.S. 343, 359 (2003) (discussing prohibition on "true threats"); *Texas v. Johnson*, 491 U.S. 397, 398 (1989) (discussing prohibition on "fighting words"); *Miller*, 413 U.S. at 24–25 (discussing prohibition on obscenity); *Brandenburg*, 395 U.S. at 447 (discussing prohibition on incitement); *N.Y. Times Co. v. Sullivan*, 376 U.S. 254, 279–280 (1964) (discussing prohibition on defamation).

2260. *R.A.V.*, 505 U.S. at 380 (1992) (quoting Minn. Leg. Code § 292.02 (1990)).

2261. *Ibid.*, at 391 ("[T]he ordinance applies only to 'fighting words' that insult, or provoke violence, 'on the basis of race, color, creed, religion or gender.' Displays containing abusive invective, no matter how vicious or severe, are permissible unless they are addressed to one of the specified disfavored topics. Those who wish to use 'fighting words' in connection with other ideas—to express hostility, for example, on the basis of political affiliation, union membership, or homosexuality—are not covered. The First Amendment does not permit St. Paul to impose special prohibitions on those speakers who express views on disfavored subjects.")

2262. *Ibid.*, at 395.

2263. *See ibid.*, at 395–396.

2264. *Matal v. Tam*, 582 U.S. 218, 223 (2017).

2265. *Ibid.* (internal quotation marks omitted) (quoting 15 U.S.C. § 1052(a)).

Clause.[2266] For additional discussion of blasphemy and offensive speech, *see* Part VII (Religious Communities and Protections of the Individual), Chapter 3 (Freedom of Expression).

II. Public Funding of Blasphemous Art

844. Public controversies have arisen over public funding of art that is considered blasphemous or otherwise offensive. One such controversy involved a photograph by Andres Serrano titled "Piss Christ," which won an award in a competition sponsored by the National Endowment for the Arts (NEA), a federal agency. Serrano's "Piss Christ" is a photograph of a plastic crucifix submerged in Serrano's urine. Many considered the photograph offensive and questioned the propriety of public funding and government support for such art. In response to the public outcry, Congress amended the National Foundation on the Arts and the Humanities Act, requiring the NEA chairperson to ensure that "artistic excellence and artistic merit are the criteria by which [grant] applications are judged, taking into consideration general standards of decency and respect for the diverse beliefs and values of the American public."[2267] The National Council on the Arts, which advises the NEA Chairperson, then adopted a resolution to implement the amendment by ensuring that advisory panel members represent geographic, ethnic, and aesthetic diversity.[2268] The amendment was challenged in *National Endowment for the Arts v. Finley*, a case brought by four artists who were denied funding before the amendment was enacted. The US Supreme Court rejected the artists' arguments that the new guidelines were unconstitutionally vague and were invalid under the First and Fifth Amendments.[2269] The Court reasoned that "when the Government is acting as a patron rather than as sovereign, the consequences of imprecision are not constitutionally severe."[2270]

2266. *Ibid.*, at 246.
2267. *See* 20 U.S.C. § 954(d)(1) (2018); *Nat'l Endowment for the Arts v. Finley*, 524 U.S. 569, 572 (1998).
2268. *Nat'l Endowment for the Arts*, 524 U.S. at 577.
2269. *Ibid.*
2270. *Ibid.*, at 589.

Chapter 2. Religion and Media

§1. Introduction

845. Church-owned media exists in the same statutory environment as other media, leaving religious groups largely free to own and operate both print and broadcast media on the same terms as other owners and operators.

846. As with non-religious media and speech, government interference in a religious publication or broadcast generally must be narrowly tailored to achieve a compelling state interest, if that interference is based on content or viewpoint.[2271] Content-neutral regulations, however, can be enacted pursuant to less rigorous constitutional standards.[2272] As discussed in the previous chapter, historically some state and local governments criminalized speech deemed "offensive, profane, or blasphemous."[2273] With few exceptions, however, such statutes today are unconstitutional under the First Amendment's application to the states through the Fourteenth Amendment.[2274] For additional discussion of free speech issues, *see* Part VII (Religious Communities and Protections of the Individual), Chapter 3 (Freedom of Expression); and this Part, Chapter 1 (Religion and Art).

§2. Print Media

847. In the United States, religious organizations have long been involved in the production of newspapers, magazines, and other print media. Some religious organizations own national or regional newspapers that focus on reporting general news. Nationally, for example, *The Christian Science Monitor* was founded in 1908 by Mary Baker Eddy, who also founded The First Church of Christ, Scientist. While the Church owns the *Monitor*, the newspaper exercises editorial independence and is a well-respected, much-awarded publication.[2275] Following the fate of numerous other US newspapers in the digital era, *The Christian Science Monitor* is now published largely online but distributes a weekly print edition. *The Deseret News*, the

2271. *See Ward v. Rock Against Racism*, 491 U.S. 781, 791 (1989).

2272. Content-neutral restrictions limit speech regardless of its content or message—for example, bans on leafletting at a shopping mall or placing flyers on car windshields. In evaluating a content-neutral restriction, the Supreme Court uses either deferential, intermediate, or strict standards of review. Under a deferential standard, the Court upholds laws that are rational and further a legitimate government interest. Under an intermediate standard, the Court weighs the substantiality of the government interest against the availability of less-restrictive alternatives. Under strict review, the Court requires that the government have a compelling interest and that the restriction on speech be necessary to advance that government interest. *See* Geoffrey R. Stone, *Content-Neutral Restrictions*, 54 U. Chi. L. Rev. 46, 47–54 (1987).

2273. 2 Antieau on Local Government Law, *Speech Limitations* § 29A.03 (2d ed. 2023) LexisNexis.

2274. *See Cohen v. California*, 403 U.S. 15, 26 (1971); *see also, e.g.*, *Joseph Burstyn, Inc. v. Wilson*, 343 U.S. 495, 497 (1952), as discussed *supra* para. 839.

2275. *About*, Christian Sci. Monitor, https://www.csmonitor.com/About (last visited Sep. 30, 2023).

oldest continuing news publication in the western United States, is owned by The Church of Jesus Christ of Latter-day Saints.[2276]

848. Hundreds of periodicals with an exclusively religious focus are published online and in print in the United States, some of which reflect a generally religious viewpoint (for example, generally Christian or Jewish content).[2277] Others are owned by and reflect the doctrine of particular religious organizations.[2278] And some focus on news relevant to a certain sub-region, sub-community, or sub-population within a larger religious organization or faith community.[2279] Most religious publications are Christian-focused, reflecting the large US Christian population; in the United States, Catholic entities produce more than 150 publications alone.[2280] However, smaller religious communities also publish periodicals, including Jewish, Muslim, Buddhist, Hindu, Humanist, Scientologist, and other groups. Some religious periodicals continue print distribution, but many have transitioned from print to publishing online, while others began exclusively online, avoiding the costs of printing and hard-copy distribution entirely.

849. Religious periodicals are protected by the First Amendment's Free Speech and Free Exercise Clauses; as a result, their content is subject to virtually no state regulation. In 1931, the US Supreme Court decided the landmark case *Near v. Minnesota*, holding a state law unconstitutional where it allowed government officials to "restrain" or censor, prior to production, those publications deemed by public officials to be a "public nuisance."[2281] The Court explained that "the liberty of the press and of speech is within the liberty safeguarded … from invasion by state action" by the First Amendment (as incorporated,[2282] and made applicable to the

2276. *About Us*, Deseret News, https://www.deseret.com/pages/about-us (last visited Sep. 30, 2023).

2277. *See, e.g.*, *Our Ministry*, Christianity Today, https://www.christianitytoday.org/who-we-are/our-ministry (explaining its Christian evangelical-focused "vision" as "[a] church more faithful to Christ and a world more drawn to him") (last visited Sep. 30, 2023); *About*, Jewish Press, https://www.jewishpress.com/about (describing itself as "the largest independent weekly Jewish newspaper in the United States" and as a champion of "Torah values and ideals from a centrist or Modern Orthodox perspective") (last visited Sep. 30, 2023).

2278. *See, e.g.*, *More Than a Century of Signs*, Signs of the Times, https://www.signstimes.com/?p=about (last visited Sep. 30, 2023) (describing the magazine's history as a Seventh-day Adventist publication).

2279. *See, e.g.*, *About*, Catholic Sun, https://www.catholicsun.org (last visited Sep. 30, 2023) (describing itself as "the official source of news for the [Roman Catholic] Diocese of Phoenix", Arizona); *About*, EEW, https://www.eewmagazineonline.com/about-eew-magazine (last visited Sep. 30, 2023) (describing purpose of *Empowering Everyday Women* online magazine as representing "the intersectionality of Blackness, Christianity, and womanhood"); *About Us*, New Voices, https://newvoices.org/about-us (last visited Sep. 30, 2023) (describing itself as "the only Jewish and justice-focused magazine by and for Jews ages 18–24"); *Muslim Media*, Pluralism Project: Harvard U., https://pluralism.org/muslim-media (discussing diverse US Muslim media outlets) (last visited Sep. 30, 2023).

2280. *List of Catholic Newspapers and Magazines in the United States*, Wikipedia, https://en.wikipedia.org/wiki/List_of_Catholic_newspapers_and_magazines_in_the_United_States (last visited Sep. 30, 2023).

2281. *Near v. Minnesota*, 283 U.S. 697 (1931).

2282. For information on the concept of "incorporation", *see supra* para. 124 and accompanying footnotes.

states, through the Fourteenth Amendment).[2283] While conceding that prohibiting "prior restraint" could lead to abuses in the press, the Court reasoned "a more serious evil would result if officials could determine which stories can be published."[2284] The Court carved out some exceptions, explaining that the state may be justified in exercising prior restraint but only in specific scenarios: to maintain national security during times of war, to enforce obscenity standards, and to protect "against incitements or acts of violence and the overthrow by force of orderly government."[2285] *Near* and subsequent press-related cases have severely limited government's ability to restrain or censor the press, including religious publications and media.[2286]

850. While government generally cannot regulate the content of religious publications, civil defamation suits may provide a check. Because content in religious publications can create liability, just as content in more traditional news publications can, fear of damages from a defamation suit may lead religious organizations to limit publication content. In a California state court case, a woman sued her former church and individual church leaders after the leaders made statements critical of her, orally and in a church publication. The court held that the Free Exercise Clause did not bar the defamation action, finding that "protection of a person's good name is a sufficiently important state interest" to allow limitations on the actions and speech of the church and its leaders.[2287] For further discussion of this case and defamation generally, *see* Part VII (Religious Communities and Protections of the Individual), Chapter 3 (Freedom of Expression).

851. Laws at both the federal and state levels allow government tangentially to exercise control over religious publications or, conversely, to facilitate their distribution and social benefits. For example, state and local governments can regulate street use or require a license for "soliciting" (engaging in door-to-door sales), which can affect the ability of religious organizations to propagate their literature.[2288] States can also collect sales taxes from the sale of publications, including religious publications.[2289] In *Texas Monthly, Inc. v. Bullock*, in a plurality decision, the Supreme Court held that an exemption from state sales taxes limited only to religious publications amounts to a government subsidy that "runs afoul of the Establishment Clause."[2290] *See* section 3, below. The US Postal Service, however, does

2283. *Near*, 283 U.S. at 707.
2284. *Ibid.*, at 722.
2285. *Ibid.*, at 716.
2286. *See, e.g.*, *N.Y. Times Co. v. Sullivan*, 376 U.S. 254 (1964) (holding First Amendment free speech protections limit defamation claims by US public officials); *Hustler Mag. v. Falwell*, 485 U.S. 46 (1988) (holding parodies are protected speech under the First and Fourteenth Amendments).
2287. *McNair v. Worldwide Church of God*, 242 Cal. Rptr. 823, 830 (Cal. Ct. App. 1987).
2288. *See, e.g.*, Fate, Tex. Code Ordinances § 8-315 (2022). *But see Busey v. Dist. of Columbia*, 138 F.2d. 592, 596 (D.C. Cir. 1943) (overturning conviction of Jehovah's Witness who sold religious magazines on streets without paying required license fee and finding Washington, DC, license law unconstitutionally interfered with "freedoms of speech, press, and religion" where licensing fees "exceed[ed] the cost of policing sales of religious propaganda").
2289. *Tex. Monthly, Inc. v. Bullock*, 489 U.S. 1, 5 (1989) (plurality opinion).
2290. *Ibid.*

provide special rates for the bulk mailing of nonprofit organizations, including religious organizations.[2291] Federal law details what types of organizations qualify as nonprofit organizations, sometimes called "501(c)(3) organizations."[2292] *See* Part VIII (Financing of Religious Communities), Chapter 2 (Indirect Financing). These organizations do not automatically qualify for the special rates and must submit an application to the Postal Service to receive the benefits.[2293] Among other states, Oklahoma enacted a law allowing nonprofit religious organizations, through their publications, to match people with medical needs with a person of the same faith willing to pay for medical treatments.[2294] These state laws not only legalize the service but also usually provide for exemptions from regulations, such as otherwise applicable insurance requirements.[2295]

§3. Taxation on Sale of Religious Publications

852. The US Supreme Court has permitted states to tax the sale of religious publications, as long as the tax is part of a general program of taxation and does not single out religious materials for either favorable or unfavorable treatment. Such taxes are considered "indirect burdens" on free exercise and constitutionally permissible under the First Amendment, provided they apply in an evenhanded manner to both religious and non-religious publications.[2296] In 1989, in *Texas Monthly, Inc. v. Bullock*, the Supreme Court addressed a challenge to a Texas state law exempting religious publications from state taxes applicable to other, similar publications.[2297] In a plurality opinion, the Court held that the exemption was not required by the Free Exercise Clause and, because it was restricted to religious periodicals only, constituted impermissible state sponsorship of religion in violation of the Establishment Clause.[2298] The plurality implied that a broader exemption encompassing nonsectarian and religious publications alike, to achieve a legitimate government purpose, would have been permissible under the Establishment Clause.[2299] Indeed, religious organizations in many states enjoy a tax exemption from sales taxes through laws broader than the one at issue in *Texas Monthly*—laws that allow exemptions for non-sectarian organizations as well.[2300]

853. The following year, in *Jimmy Swaggart Ministries, Inc. v. Board of Equalization of California*, the Supreme Court concluded that imposing sales taxes on the

2291. *Who Qualifies for Nonprofit Prices?*, Postal Explorer, USPS.com, https://pe.usps.com/businessmail101?ViewName=NonprofitQualifications (last visited Sep. 30, 2023).
2292. I.R.C. § 501(c)(3) (2018).
2293. *How to Apply for Authorization to Mail at Nonprofit Prices*, Postal Explorer, USPS.com, https://pe.usps.com/businessmail101?ViewName=NonprofitApplication (last visited Sep. 30, 2023).
2294. Okla. Stat. tit. 36, § 110 (2022).
2295. *Ibid.*
2296. *See Tex. Monthly, Inc. v. Bullock*, 489 U.S. 1 (1989) (plurality opinion).
2297. *Ibid.*
2298. *Ibid.*, at 24–25.
2299. *Ibid.*, at 14–15.
2300. *See* Root & Wright, *Classifying State Sales Tax Exemptions*, *supra* n. 1895, at 279–281.

sale of religious items (such as recordings of sermons, religious books and pamphlets, and Bible study manuals), along with non-religious items, did not burden the organization's religious practices in violation of the Free Exercise Clause.[2301] While religious organizations are exempt from paying income taxes, they retain tax liability for other taxes in some jurisdictions.[2302] For example, religious organizations are not uniformly exempt from paying or charging sales taxes in all states: states may exempt religious organizations from paying sales tax only on items they purchase, allow them to forgo charging sales tax on items they sell, exempt only certain items from sales tax, or blend these approaches into a "hybrid" system.[2303] This lack of uniformity means that a religious magazine may be exempt from sales tax in one state but not in another state, creating challenges for churches with a wide geographic area of membership.[2304]

§4. Broadcast Media

854. Religious organizations are permitted to own and operate radio and television stations in the United States. Between one-third and one-half of educational channels on major multichannel video programming distributors are managed by religious television stations.[2305] Among non-commercial radio stations, "[a]pproximately 42 percent … have a religious format"; moreover, "[e]ighty percent of the 2,400 Christian radio stations and 100 full-power Christian TV stations are non-profits."[2306] As those numbers imply, Christian radio stations are particularly plentiful, with multiple stations in every state.[2307] Although less numerous, radio and television stations owned and operated by minority religious groups operate across the United States as well.[2308] Podcasts, including religious podcasts, have become increasingly popular since the early 2000s, when high-speed internet access and personal electronic devices became more accessible.

855. Entities that operate radio and television stations using public airwaves are required to obtain a license from the Federal Communications Commission (FCC).[2309] In licensing and other regulatory decisions, the FCC is prohibited by the Communications Act from discriminating based on religion or other protected

2301. *See Jimmy Swaggart Ministries v. Bd. of Equalization of Cal.*, 493 U.S. 378, 392 (1990).
2302. *See* Root & Wright, *Classifying State Sales Tax Exemptions*, *supra* n. 1895, at 279.
2303. *See ibid.*, at 281–286.
2304. *See ibid.*, at 285–287.
2305. Fed. Commc'n Comm., *Religious Broadcasting* (publication date unknown), https://transition.fcc.gov/osp/inc-report/INoC-11-Religious-Broadcasting.pdf (last accessed Sep. 30, 2023).
2306. *Ibid.*
2307. *See generally* Christian Radio, https://www.christianradio.com/stations (last visited Sep. 30, 2023).
2308. *See, e.g.*, America's Islamic Radio, https://americasislamicradio.com/?fbclid=IwAR0_lgtEJJ0dhFoNnKvTu9nMRclYWeKpxaBvdr4XWJMeUwuf6QjRXRaN0Rk (last visited Sep. 30, 2023); N.Y. Jewish Radio, http://www.newyorkjewishradio.com (last visited Sep. 30, 2023).
2309. *See generally The Public and Broadcasting*, Fed. Commc'ns Comm'n, https://www.fcc.gov/media/radio/public-and-broadcasting (link to PDF) (last updated Sept. 2021).

grounds.[2310] Because podcasters do not distribute their content via radio or television airwaves, they are not required to obtain an FCC license, nor are they subject to FCC regulations. However, podcasters are subject to generally applicable laws, including Federal Trade Commission regulations—prohibiting false advertising and requiring disclosure of endorsement agreements, for example.[2311]

856. Generally speaking, religious groups who become broadcast licensees are subject to the same "enforceable public obligations" that apply to non-religious licensees.[2312] The Civil Rights Act, Title VII, section 702, however, allows religious organizations to give employment preference to their members,[2313] whether a job involves strictly religious activities or nonprofit secular activities.[2314] Even so, in 1974 a federal court of appeals interpreted FCC regulations to prohibit religious organizations from conducting preferential hiring for positions that weren't substantially related to on-air communication of a religious message.[2315] But the FCC later expanded its regulations to "permit religious broadcasters to establish religious belief or affiliation as a job qualification for *all* station employees."[2316] For more details, *see* Part VII (Religious Communities and Protections of the Individual), Chapter 3 (Freedom of Expression).

857. Early radio regulators censored speech they deemed socially harmful—sometimes by restricting licensing; the decisions of those regulators often demonstrated a bias toward "more orthodox political, economic and religious views."[2317] Modern regulators and regulations, in contrast, allow for a much freer exchange of ideas.[2318] For some fifty years, the FCC has denied rumors that it will

2310. 47 U.S.C. § 151 (2018).

2311. *See, e.g.*, 16 C.F.R. pt. 255 (2022) ("Guidelines Concerning Use of Endorsements and Testimonials in Advertising"); 15 U.S.C. § 45 (2018) (prohibiting "unfair or deceptive acts or practices in or affecting commerce").

2312. *King's Garden, Inc. v. FCC*, 492 F.2d 51, 60 (D.C. Cir. 1974).

2313. 42 U.S.C. § 2000e-1 (2018).

2314. *See ibid.*; *Corp. of the Presiding Bishop of The Church of Jesus Christ of Latter-Day Saints v. Amos*, 483 U.S. 327, 335–336 (1987).

2315. *See King's Garden, Inc.*, 492 F.2d at 60–61.

2316. *In re Streamlining Broad. EEO Rule & Policies, Vacating the EEO Forfeiture Pol'y Statement & Amending Section 1.80 of the Comm'n's Rules to Include EEO Forfeiture Guidelines*, 13 FCC Rcd. 6322 at 2–3 (1998) (emphasis added); 47 C.F.R. § 73.2080(a) (2022).

2317. *See Radio Censorship and the Federal Communications Commission*, Note, 39 Colum. L. Rev. 447, 447–449 (1939).

2318. *See The FCC and Speech*, Fed. Commc'n Comm., https://www.fcc.gov/consumers/guides/fcc-and-speech (last updated Aug. 31, 2022) ("[T]he FCC has long held that "the public interest is best served by permitting free expression of views." Rather than suppress speech, communications law and policy seeks to encourage responsible "counter-speech" from others. Following this principle ensures that the most diverse and opposing opinions will be expressed, even though some views or expressions may be highly offensive.").

cease issuing licenses to religious broadcasters.[2319] The agency has also continuously affirmed its neutrality toward religious broadcasters, explaining that "no special provisions or restrictions are applied to religious stations or licenses, nor are any changes to that policy contemplated."[2320]

858. While religious broadcasters must abide by generally applicable regulations, some religious broadcasters also regulate themselves to a degree. In the early days of broadcasting, feuding between mainline Protestant broadcasters and increasingly popular Evangelical Christian broadcasters led to Evangelical broadcasters being excluded from national radio networks and relegated to independent stations with much smaller audiences. A series of meetings held by Evangelical church leaders and broadcasters led to the creation of the National Religious Broadcasters (NRB), a private self-regulating association.[2321] NRB is made up of more than 1,100 organizations that use radio, television, or other electronic media to disseminate content reflecting Christian views.[2322] Although it does not have government authority, NRB maintains self-regulatory influence over a large segment of Christian broadcasting in the United States and attempts to influence US media law and policy through lobbying efforts.[2323]

859. Other checks on religious media include legal actions by state authorities. State Attorneys General, for example, have authority to bring cases against nonprofit organizations for fraudulent activities, including fraudulent solicitation.[2324] Individuals who practice fraud, including affinity fraud,[2325] via religious broadcasting can also face criminal charges. In 2020, several municipal and state agencies conducted a joint investigation of a Texas radio host who promoted his financial investment business as a Christian business, via Christian radio. He eventually pled guilty to fraud and money laundering charges, received a twenty-five-year prison sentence, and was ordered to pay more than USD 10 million in restitution.[2326]

860. The Federal Communications Commission (FCC), Federal Trade Commission (FTC), and the Internal Revenue Service (IRS) are the main federal agencies

2319. *Untrue: Religious Broadcaster Ban Rumor*, Fed. Comm's Comm., https://www.fcc.gov/media/radio/religious-broadcast-ban-rumor (last accessed Sep. 30, 2023).
2320. *Ibid.*
2321. *Who We Are*, NRB, https://nrb.org/who-we-are (last visited Sep. 30, 2023).
2322. *Ibid.*
2323. *Ibid.*
2324. *Worldwide Church of God, Inc. v. California*, 623 F.2d 613 (9th Cir. 1980).
2325. Affinity fraud is fraud "targeted towards members of an identifiable group of individuals such as those with a common religion, ethnic heritage, background, or interests. The perpetrators of affinity fraud may pretend or may be members of the targeted group. They exploit the groups' inherent common trust to recruit victims for fraud." *Investor Protection Guide: Affinity Fraud*, LLI: Cornell L. Sch., https://www.law.cornell.edu/wex/investor_protection_guide_affinity_fraud (last visited Sep. 30, 2023).
2326. *William Neil "Doc" Gallagher: Sentenced to 25 Years, $10.3 Million Restitution*, Tex. St. Secs. Bd. (Mar. 27, 2020), https://www.ssb.texas.gov/news-publications/william-neil-doc-gallagher-sentenced-25-years-103-million-restitution.

that can "police" the solicitation of donations by religious organizations and individuals via broadcasting.[2327] In cases of fraud or other violations of relevant statutes and regulations, the FCC has authority to revoke broadcasting licenses, while the IRS has authority to revoke tax-exempt status, sue for unpaid taxes, or file tax fraud charges. In one case, the FCC sanctioned the Faith Center, a nonprofit church corporation that operated a television station, through which it aggressively solicited donations.[2328] The FCC revoked the Center's broadcasting license after reviewing allegations of misuse of church funds. While the allegations were never proven, the FCC based its decision on the Faith Center's failure to cooperate in the federal investigation.[2329] The FCC rarely acts against televangelists or other forms of religious solicitation, however, and its sanctions can be fairly toothless.[2330] After the FCC revoked the Faith Center's license, for example, the Center was able to continue its programming by purchasing airtime on different religious stations.[2331]

§5. Use of Public Media

861. The ability of religious organizations to disseminate content via publicly funded media has evolved, generally toward more restricted access. The Public Broadcasting Service (PBS) is the most prominent publicly funded, noncommercial, nonprofit organization and provider of educational TV content in the United States. PBS is owned by some 350 PBS "member stations," which are themselves owned by other nonprofit groups, educational institutions, or other state-owned or state-related entities.[2332] PBS produces national programming content and distributes it to member stations. Member stations also produce their own local programming and typically broadcast a mix of national and local programs. In the past, member stations regularly broadcast sectarian programming as a public service. For example, a public television station in Washington, DC, broadcast the Catholic program "Mass for Shut-Ins" for almost sixty years.[2333] In 1985, however, PBS enacted

2327. Jonathan Turley, *Laying Hands on Religious Racketeers: Applying Civil RICO to Fraudulent Religious Solicitation*, 29 Wm. & Mary L. Rev. 441, 469–471 (1988).
2328. *Scott v. Younger*, 739 F.2d 1464 (9th Cir. 1984).
2329. *Ibid.*, at 1465.
2330. Turley, *Laying Hands on Religious Racketeers*, *supra* n. 2327, at 470.
2331. *Ibid.*, at 469.
2332. The Corporation for Public Broadcasting (CPB) is a private, nonprofit corporation funded fully by the federal government. Authorized by the Public Broadcasting Act of 1967, CPB provides grant support to PBS for national program production and distributes federal funds to local PBS member stations for local operational and programming support. CPB supports National Public Radio (NPR) and its local "member stations" in a similar way. For more information, *see CPB FAQ*, Corp. for Pub. Broadcasting, https://www.cpb.org/faq#1-2 (last visited Sep. 30, 2023).
2333. Paul Farhi, *PBS Stations Weigh Loss of Affiliation over Religious Content*, Wash. Post (May 16, 2009), http://www.washingtonpost.com/wp-dyn/content/article/2009/05/15/AR2009051503430.html.

bylaws requiring that member station programming be "noncommercial, nonpartisan, and nonsectarian."[2334] In 2009, PBS announced that it was considering cancelling all sectarian programming.[2335] Ultimately, PBS decided to allow current religious programming to continue but to prohibit new religious programming.[2336]

§6. Portrayal of Religion in the Media

862. The prominence and portrayal of religion in US news and entertainment media has fluctuated with social trends and tides. In the nineteenth and early twentieth centuries, religious newspapers—as well as religious essays and news articles in "mainstream" news outlets—were relatively commonplace. By the latter half of the twentieth century, however, news coverage of religion tended to focus more narrowly on religion's intersection with politics or criminal or other wrongdoing, rather than on religious life and theology.[2337] A 2011 US study showed that "religion does not typically receive a lot of attention from the mainstream news media, and … [w]hen religion did make news, it was often because of accusations about extremism or intolerance."[2338]

863. A similar trend is evident in US entertainment media. In the early twentieth century, positive portrayals of religious belief, religious themes, and even scriptural stories were more common in entertainment, as exemplified by popular movies like *The Jazz Singer* (1927), *Boys Town* (1938), *The Ten Commandments* (1956), and *The Sound of Music* (1965). The "counterculture" movement of the 1960s and 1970s, however, led to both (1) fewer overtly religious characters and themes in television and movies and (2) more negative or "irreverent" portrayals of religion when featured in television and movies.[2339] With some notable exceptions,[2340] US entertainment media in the last fifty years has trended toward negative portrayals of organized religion, focusing on hypocrisy, intolerance, or self-serving actions of religious individuals and institutions.[2341] Mirroring the post-World War II trend

2334. PBS, *PBS Editorial Standards and Policies* 3–4 (later version, adopted Jun. 24, 2011), https://publicmediaintegrity.org/wp-content/uploads/PBSEditorialStandardsandPolicies.pdf.
2335. Michael Getler, *The Mailbag: May 22, 2009*, PBS Ombudsman (May 22, 2009), http://www.pbs.org/ombudsman/2009/05/the_mailbag_7.html.
2336. Paul Farhi, *PBS Bans New Religious Programming, Allows Existing Shows to Continue Airing*, Wash. Post (Jun. 17, 2009), http://www.washingtonpost.com/wp-dyn/content/article/2009/06/16/AR2009061603201.html.
2337. S. Robert Lichter, Linda S. Lichter, & Daniel R. Amundson, Ctr. For Media & Pub. Affs., *Media Coverage of Religion in America 1969–1998* at 80–85 (Apr. 2000), https://cmpa.gmu.edu/wp-content/uploads/2013/10/Media_Coverage_Religion_2000.pdf.
2338. Pew Rsch. Ctr., *Religion in the News* 1 (Feb. 23, 2012), https://www.pewresearch.org/journalism/2012/02/23/religion-news-0/ (link to PDF).
2339. *See, e.g.*, *The Omen* (1976); *Carrie* (1976); *Footloose* (1984); *The Last Temptation of Christ* (1988); *South Park* (series, 1997–); *Dogma* (1999); *Lucifer* (series, 2016–2021).
2340. *See, e.g.*, *The Chosen* (series, 2017–); *The Marvelous Mrs. Maisel* (series, 2017–2023); *Seventh Heaven* (series, 1996–2007).
2341. David W. Scott, *Religiosity in* South Park*: Struggles over Institutional and Personal Piety Among Residents of a "Redneck Town"*, 10 J. Media & Religion 152, 162 (2011).

toward disaffiliation from organized religion, "personal," individual religious experiences tend to be treated more positively in US entertainment media.[2342]

864. Under the First Amendment, critical, satirical, irreverent, and "blasphemous" portrayals of religion and religious figures in media are generally protected forms of expression and speech. In 1983, *Hustler* magazine published a satirical advertisement on its inside cover, mimicking a popular alcoholic advertisement that asked celebrities about their first time drinking a certain alcohol.[2343] The satirical advertisement targeted Reverend Jerry Falwell, a conservative pastor and televangelist. *Hustler* "played on the sexual double entendre" of the phrase "first time," suggesting that Falwell's sexual "first time" had been an incestuous encounter "with his mother in an outhouse."[2344] Falwell sued, alleging several causes of action, and the case eventually reached the Supreme Court. The Court held that the First Amendment protected "outrageous" speech of this nature and that offensiveness is insufficient grounds for government intervention in the marketplace of ideas.[2345] A movie based on the case portrayed *Hustler*'s publisher as the hero and the reverend as the villain,[2346] demonstrating how free speech is highly valued in the United States and how the perceived intolerance of religious figures is commonly mocked. *See* Part VII (Religious Communities and Protections of the Individual), Chapter 3 (Freedom of Expression).

2342. *Ibid.*, at 153–154.
2343. *Hustler Magazine, Inc. v. Falwell*, 485 U.S. 46, 47–48 (1988).
2344. *Ibid.*, at 48.
2345. *Ibid.*, at 49–56.
2346. Janet Maslin, Movie Review, The People v. Larry Flynt, N.Y. Times (Dec. 27, 1996), https://archive.nytimes.com/www.nytimes.com/library/film/flynt.html.

Chapter 3. Religion and Civil Society

§1. Historical Background

I. Founding Era

865. The concept of freedom of religion looms large in the American public imagination. The story of the early colonization and settlement of the United States is understood largely as a flight from religious persecution and a search for religious freedom. The Puritans who settled New England were convinced that their break from the Old World was an act of divine providence.[2347] The "beliefs, symbols, and rituals" of these early colonists were foundational to the sense that they had been set apart by God in this country.[2348] Later waves of immigrants to the United States, even to the present day, have often been motivated by fleeing religious persecution for the opportunity to practice their religion freely.[2349]

866. Each of the original American colonies had distinct religious identities based on the religious beliefs of their early white settlers. In Boston, Massachusetts, the dominant religion was Puritanism, characterized by restrictive, reserved behavior and devotion to God.[2350] Other faiths failed to gain a foothold in the region due to the Puritans' demand for conformity and preference for isolationism.[2351] Religious liberty in the eyes of these Puritans was the liberty for other faiths to "keep away."[2352] In contrast, Pennsylvania comprised a mix of religious immigrants and minority groups. These groups were widely viewed as "other," such as the Religious Society of Friends or "Quakers" who were criticized and shunned because of their unique doctrines. Quakers rejected the necessity of church sacraments and conformity with clergy (which put them at odds with both Puritans and Anglicans in other colonies) in favor of individual, direct experience with the divine.[2353] The atmosphere of tolerance for "other" groups in Pennsylvania was a significant reason it became the dominant colony during this period and the location for the constitutional convention.

2347. Jerald C. Brauer, *Puritanism, Revivalism, and the Revolution, in Religion and the American Revolution* 1, 6 (Jerald C. Brauer ed.,1976).

2348. Bellah, *Civil Religion in America*, *supra* n. 925, at 4.

2349. *See, e.g.*, *2022 Report on International Religious Freedom: Afghanistan*, U.S. Dep't State (2022), https://www.state.gov/reports/2022-report-on-international-religious-freedom/afghanistan (discussing US State Department's assistance in relocating "Afghan members of religious minorities through immigration, refugee resettlement, and parole processes"); Katayoun Kishi, *Most Refugees Who Enter the U.S. as Religious Minorities Are Christians*, Pew Rsch. Ctr. (Feb. 7, 2017), https://www.pewresearch.org/short-reads/2017/02/07/most-refugees-who-enter-the-u-s-as-religious-minorities-are-christians; Khalid Duran & Daniel Pipes, *Muslim Immigrants in the United States*, Ctr. for Immigration Stud. (Aug. 1, 2002), http://cis.org/USMuslimImmigrants (discussing religious persecution as one motivating factor in Muslim immigration to the United States, since 1965).

2350. Brauer, *Puritanism, Revivalism, and the Revolution*, *supra* n. 2347, at 7–8.

2351. *See* Jon Meacham, *American Gospel: God, the Founding Fathers, and the Making of a Nation* 48–49 (2007).

2352. *Ibid.*, at 48.

2353. *Ibid.*, at 52.

867. Although religious freedom was a motivating force in the founding of several colonies, most original colonies enacted laws that provided state support for religion.[2354] The charters of eight colonies (Connecticut, Maryland, Massachusetts, New Hampshire, New York, North Carolina, South Carolina, and Virginia) established a state church.[2355] Most other colonies either established a state church legislatively or simply adopted some elements of establishment.[2356] Early government and church authorities used their influence to create civil and criminal laws that reflected the tenets of the state church or majority religion. In response, religious dissenters, minorities, and critics called for the disestablishment of state-endorsed churches. One prominent New England dissenter, Baptist minister Isaac Backus, openly disagreed with many of the requirements imposed by dominant religious sects and proposed amendments to the Massachusetts state charter to secure religious freedom. According to Backus, covenants with God were a personal matter that "each rational soul has an equal right to judge for itself."[2357] Though his views were not immediately adopted in Massachusetts, the idea of disestablishment of state religions was accepted and augmented by many of the Founders.

868. Thomas Jefferson, for example, was well known as a Deist and secularist but also wrote in the Declaration of Independence that "all men are created equal, … endowed by their Creator with certain unalienable Rights."[2358] His ideas, along with those of James Madison and other religious dissenters, successfully led to a statute that disestablished the Anglican Church as the state church of Virginia.[2359] Even members of majority faiths, Madison argued in his *Memorial and Remonstrance*, should reject establishment because it risked government involvement, corrupting the purity of religion, and compromised Christianity's missionary efforts. He further argued that the notion of churches needing state support to function was an insult to religion—that a true religion should be able to succeed on its own merits without government intervention.[2360]

869. A common theme in the founding generation was that civic virtue must exist for the republican experiment to succeed. Thomas Jefferson defined virtue as "a love of others, a sense of duty to them, [and] a moral instinct in short, which

---

2354. "Only Delaware, New Jersey, Pennsylvania and Rhode Island did not compel any taxpayer support for religion." Pew F. on Religion & Pub. Life, *Shifting Boundaries: The Establishment Clause and Government Funding of Religious Schools and Other Faith-Based Organizations* 2 (May 2009), https://www.pewresearch.org/religion/2009/05/14/shifting-boundaries2 (link to PDF); *see also Amdt1.2.2.1 Introduction to the Historical Background on the Religion Clauses*, Const. Annotated, https://constitution.congress.gov/browse/essay/amdt1-2-2-1/ALDE_00013268 (last visited Sep. 30, 2023).

2355. *Religion in the Original 13 Colonies*, Britannica ProCon.org, https://undergod.procon.org/religion-in-the-original-13-colonies (last updated Jan. 6, 2009).

2356. *See Amdt1.2.2.3 State-Established Religion in the Colonies*, Const. Annotated, https://constitution.congress.gov/browse/essay/amdt1-2-2-3/ALDE_00013270 (last visited Sept. 30, 2023).

2357. Miller, *The Religious Roots of the First Amendment*, *supra* n. 71, at 107–109.

2358. *The Declaration of Independence* pmbl. (U.S. 1776).

2359. Miller, *The Religious Roots of the First Amendment*, *supra* n. 71, at 108.

2360. Madison, *Memorial and Remonstrance*, *supra* n. 1809.

prompts us irresistibly to feel and to succour their distresses."[2361] Under such a definition, a commitment to civic virtue enables Americans to believe in and worship their God while also recognizing a duty to respect others' agency to believe and worship differently, or not at all. Somewhat paradoxically, the principle that no one is required to believe in God secures the rights of belief for those who do believe.[2362]

II. Contemporary Understandings of the Founding Era

870. Unlike the French Revolution, which even today is widely understood as a revolution against a dominant state religious establishment, American popular consciousness does not consider the American Revolution to be a fight against a religion or established church.[2363] On the contrary, the American Revolution is perceived as a "moment when precious things" such as religious freedom were preserved for future generations.[2364]

871. The continued salience of the constitutional interpretive doctrine of originalism has led to heated debates about the extent to which the Founders were religious, or motivated by religion, and about their attitudes toward religion in public life. Consolidating religion and public life is often divisive, with secularists claiming the Founders intended to separate church and state, and conservative Christians claiming the Founders were mainly motivated and divinely guided by their Christian faith.[2365] In actuality, the Founding Fathers held divergent religious beliefs—though virtually all agreed that religion was important—and they demonstrated ambivalence, both individually and as a group, about the proper role of religion in civil society.[2366]

III. The Process of State Disestablishment

872. In the early history of the United States, most of the original thirteen states had laws establishing a state church or otherwise authorizing state funding and other support of religion.[2367] Such provisions mirrored the European model that placed "the coercive power of the state, its purse, and its other considerable resources …

2361. *Thomas Jefferson to Thomas Law, 13 June 1814*, Nat'l Archives: Founders Online, https://founders.archives.gov/documents/Jefferson/03-07-02-0307 (last visited Sep. 30, 2023).

2362. *See generally* Va. Code Ann. § 57-1 (2022) (Virginia Statute for Religious Freedom).

2363. *See* Kim R. Holmes, *The Great Divide: The Ideological Legacies of the American and French Revolutions*, Heritage Found. (Aug. 12, 2014), http://www.heritage.org/research/lecture/2014/08/the-great-divide-the-ideological-legacies-of-the-american-and-french-revolutions.

2364. *See* Meacham, *American Gospel*, *supra* n. 2351, at 62–63.

2365. *See ibid.*, at 18–19.

2366. *See ibid. See generally* Martin H. Levinson, *Indexing the Religious Beliefs of America's Founders*, 69 ETC Rev. Gen. Semantics 384 (2012).

2367. *See generally Disestablishment and Religious Dissent: Church-State Relations in the New American States, 1776–1883* (Carl H. Esbeck & Jonathan J. Den Hartog eds., 2019).

behind one church or one religion."[2368] The purpose of this model was in large part to ensure that religion fostered virtue in the state's citizens; however, the Founding Fathers realized that such a system would compromise religious freedom if instituted nationally. As a result, they included the Establishment Clause in the First Amendment to the US Constitution, which dictates that "Congress shall make no law respecting an establishment of religion."[2369]

873. The gradual process of state disestablishment across the United States coincided with a diminishing view that government support "for religion and religious institutions was necessary to ensure religion's salutary effect on public morality and civic virtue."[2370] Many believed America had created a unique democratic system in which the people were personally responsible as citizens for the virtue of the nation, thereby eliminating the need for enforcement of religious ideals by the state.[2371] However, this belief took longer to gain purchase in some states than in others. Massachusetts was the last state to disestablish—in 1833, forty-five years after the US Constitution was ratified—and some states long retained vestiges of state support. For example, Maryland's Constitution still contains requirements for religious oaths and belief "in the existence of God,"[2372] even though the religious oaths requirement was struck down by the US Supreme Court,[2373] and the belief requirement would similarly be struck down if challenged.[2374] For additional discussion of state disestablishment, *see* Part I (Legal Framework and Resources), Chapter 1 (Constitutional Position of Religion).

IV. Religious Involvement in Important Social Movements

874. As one historian has noted, the American Revolution, abolition, fights against tyranny and terror, expansion of women's rights, and the civil rights movement were defining moments in US history in which the religious concepts of justice, liberty, and charity played a significant role.[2375] While these transformative social and political movements did not directly result from conflicts over religion, they were deeply affected by religious actors, beliefs, and movements.

2368. Esbeck, *Dissent and Disestablishment*, *supra* n. 161, at 1395.

2369. U.S. Const. amend. I.

2370. Esbeck, *Dissent and Disestablishment*, *supra* n. 161, at 1395.

2371. *Cf. ibid. But cf.* Olds, *Privatizing the Church*, *supra* n. 89, at 278–282 (discussing various other, less philosophical forces that led to disestablishment in Connecticut and Massachusetts, including political forces and intrareligious divisions).

2372. Md. Const. Declaration of Rights of arts. XXXVI, XXXVII.

2373. *Torcaso v. Watkins*, 367 U.S. 488 (1961).

2374. *See* Michael D. Breidenbach, *Church and State in Maryland: Religious Liberty, Religious Tests, and Church Disestablishment*, *in Disestablishment and Religious Dissent*, *supra* n. 2367, at 309, 322.

2375. Meacham, *American Gospel*, *supra* n. 2351, at 15–16.

875. Both sides of the American Civil War relied on religious arguments to justify their actions.[2376] President Abraham Lincoln acknowledged that both North and South "read the same Bible, and pray to the same God; and each invokes His aid against the other."[2377] But he reasoned that "one [side] *must* be wrong. God can not be *for*, and *against* the same thing at the same time."[2378] When Lincoln issued the Emancipation Proclamation, he explained to his cabinet members that he did so in fulfilment of a promise that he had made to God, attesting that it is not God's will that man should enslave his brother.[2379] Though the Civil War was driven by and involved many issues, at its core it was fought over differing views of religious doctrine on the nature and freedom of man. For additional discussion, *see* General Introduction, section 3 (Historical Background).

876. In the temperance movement of the nineteenth century, religion was the central driving force behind legislation that limited personal rights to sell and consume alcohol.[2380] The movement traced its roots to the Second Great Awakening and was largely successful due to the emphasis that religious leaders placed on societal and personal separation from alcohol-related sins.[2381] Women were heavily involved in the movement, in large part through the Women's Christian Temperance Union, which became the largest American womens' organization in the nineteenth century.[2382] In addition to other social causes, the Union also endorsed women's suffrage and provided important grassroots support for it.[2383]

877. Following the Civil War, discriminatory "Jim Crow" laws and extreme persecution of African Americans persisted in the southern states for a century. In the 1960s, under the leadership of Reverend Martin Luther King Jr., protestors led peaceful "freedom marches" but were often met with vitriol, shows of force, and violence. Many of those involved in the civil rights movement were motivated by religious conviction. In the words of John Lewis, a protégé of King's and long-time US congressman, "Without religion—without the example of Christ ... as the foundation of the movement, it would have been impossible for us to endure the setbacks, and to hope, and to go on."[2384]

2376. *Ibid.*, at 118–129; James M. McPherson, *For Cause & Comrades: Why Men Fought in the Civil War* 62–76 (1997).
2377. Abraham Lincoln, Second Inaugural Address (Mar. 4, 1865), https://www.nps.gov/linc/learn/historyculture/lincoln-second-inaugural.htm.
2378. 5 Abraham Lincoln, *Collected Works of Abraham Lincoln* 403–404 (Roy P. Basler ed., 1953).
2379. *See* Meacham, *American Gospel*, *supra* n. 2351, at 116–117.
2380. *See* Leah Rae Berk, *Temperance and Prohibition Era Propaganda: A Study in Rhetoric*, Brown U. Libr. for Digital Scholarship: Alcohol, Temperance & Prohibition, https://library.brown.edu/cds/temperance/essay.html (last visited Sep. 30, 2023).
2381. *See ibid.*; Underwood, *"Awash in a Sea of Faith"*, *supra* n. 90, at 104–105.
2382. *Women's Christian Temperance Movement*, Case W. Rsrv. U.: Encyclopedia Cleveland Hist., https://case.edu/ech/articles/w/womens-christian-temperance-movement (last visited Sep. 30, 2023).
2383. *Ibid.*
2384. Meacham, *American Gospel*, *supra* n. 2351, at 192.

878. Disputes about abortion and same-sex marriage often involve the potential legal ramifications for religious freedom and how much influence religious beliefs ought to have in the public sphere.[2385] The 1973 Supreme Court decision *Roe v. Wade*, which recognized a constitutional right to access abortion in the first trimester of pregnancy,[2386] had ramifications for the role of religion in public life. Many who had once advocated that religion should stay out of the political process became fearful that government had and would continue to abandon long-held morals.[2387] The debate over religion's role in lawmaking flipped in the wake of the Supreme Court's 2022 decision in *Dobbs v. Jackson Women's Health Organization*. That decision overturned *Roe* and effectively returned authority to regulate abortion to the states, leading to particularly restrictive laws in states with large conservative Christian populations.[2388] Thus, national, state, and local debates have intensified about whether the religious beliefs of many, regarding the sanctity of life, should trump the bodily autonomy and choices of women, or whether women's bodily autonomy and agency should take precedence.

879. While the abortion debate remains heated, and liberty and religious interests remain seemingly at odds in that debate, almost the opposite has occurred with the issue of same-sex marriage. For many—particularly older conservative Americans—the concern about the diminished role of traditional religious values in society was heightened by the 2015 Supreme Court decision *Obergefell v. Hodges*, which requires states to license and recognize same-sex marriage.[2389] Since *Obergefell*, however, support for the *right* to same-sex marriage (if not for the practice of same-sex marriage) has grown considerably, even among traditionally conservative religious individuals and groups.[2390] For more discussion, *see* Part V (Religion and Politics), Chapter 1 (Religious Influence in Politics).

§2. Religious Involvement in Nonprofit and Charitable Activities

I. Charitable Activities of Religious Groups

880. The United States has a large nonprofit sector. Because religious organizations are not required to register with the government or to apply for official IRS recognition for tax-exemption purposes, the exact number of religious congregations is unknown.[2391] But one 2022 study found that at least 18% of the largest nonprofit organizations in the United States "have a religious identity."[2392]

2385. *Ibid.*, at 32.
2386. *Roe v. Wade*, 410 U.S. 113, 162–166 (1973).
2387. Meacham, *American Gospel*, *supra* n. 2351, at 210.
2388. *See After* Roe *Fell: Abortion Laws by State*, *supra* n. 1183.
2389. *Obergefell v. Hodges*, 576 U.S. 644, 680–681 (2015).
2390. *See, e.g.*, *Attitudes on Same-Sex Marriage*, Pew Rsch. Ctr. (May 14, 2019), https://www.pewresearch.org/religion/fact-sheet/changing-attitudes-on-gay-marriage.
2391. *The Nonprofit Sector in Brief 2019*, *supra* n. 21.
2392. Jennifer Altamuro, James Bierstaker, Lucy Huajing Chen & Erica Harris, *Does It Pay to Pray? Religious Nonprofits and Funding*, 41 J. Acct. & Pub. Pol'y 1, 8 (2022) (explaining that study

881. Religious groups are involved in a wide array of charitable activities in the United States and, as a result, receive a significant level of state financial support. In 1899, in *Bradfield v. Roberts*, the Supreme Court found that congressional appropriation of funds to a Catholic hospital, under government contract to treat the poor and afflicted, was not a violation of the First Amendment.[2393] The Court found that, although the hospital was staffed by religious individuals, it was a "secular corporation" with a secular purpose: to provide secular services. Therefore, the Establishment Clause did not bar government funding.[2394]

882. Establishment Clause concerns have waxed and waned throughout US history. In more recent years, due to accommodating interpretations of the Establishment Clause, more legislation allowing state funding of religious social service programs has been enacted. Particularly significant is the Personal Responsibility and Work Opportunity Reconciliation Act of 1996, which authorized the government to partner with religious charities by providing grants and resources to charities that comply with the Act's provisions.[2395] For additional discussion, *see* Part V (Religion and Politics), Chapter 2 (Political Influence in Religion); and Part VIII (Financing of Religious Communities), Chapter 2 (Indirect Financing).

II. Culture of Volunteerism

883. The United States has a strong culture and history of volunteerism, which are largely a reflection of religious culture in the United States. Volunteerism dipped slightly during the COVID-19 pandemic, but even so, between 2020 and 2021, approximately 23% of Americans volunteered formally with charitable and civic service organizations, while 51% informally helped their neighbors.[2396] In the formal sector, from 2021 to 2022, 60.7 million Americans volunteered an "estimated 4.1 billion hours with an economic value of $122.9 billion,"[2397] which calculates to

"code[d] nonprofits as religious if their mission statements contained … religious keywords" but did "not study churches, synagogues, or other houses of worship directly because these organizations are not required to file IRS information tax Form 990 filings" from which the study drew its data); *see also supra* para. 708 and accompanying footnotes.

2393. *Bradfield v. Roberts*, 175 U.S. 291, 297–300 (1899).

2394. *Ibid.*

2395. Personal Responsibility and Work Opportunity Reconciliation Act of 1996 (PRWORA or Welfare Reform Act), Pub. L. No. 104-193, § 104, 110 Stat. 2105, 2161–2163 (codified at 42 U.S.C. § 604a (2018)).

2396. AmeriCorps, *Volunteering and Civic Life in America Research Summary* 2, https://americorps.gov/sites/default/files/document/volunteering-civic-life-america-research-summary.pdf (last accessed Sep. 30, 2023).

2397. *Ibid.*

more than 65 volunteer hours per person. The influence of religious culture is evidenced by the fact that approximately one-third of volunteers offer their time in conjunction with religious groups.[2398] Religious individuals are more likely than non-religious individuals to volunteer their time to both religious and non-religious charitable and civic activities.[2399]

884. Religious-motivated volunteering encompasses a wide variety of activities, such as fundraising, preparing and distributing food, tutoring and teaching, constructing or repairing low-income housing, distributing emergency supplies or otherwise aiding with emergency response efforts, mentoring youth, coaching or refereeing sports teams, making or distributing clothing and bedding, providing general labor, and more.[2400] The type of activity individual volunteers choose to participate in is often determined by demographics; for example, those with children are more likely to coach a youth sports team while those with a college degree are more likely to do administrative or consulting volunteer work.[2401]

III. Monetary Contributions to Charity and Religion

885. Contributions to public charities have consistently increased in the United States, even when adjusted for inflation.[2402] In 1975, the amount donated to charity was around USD 25 billion. By 1990, that number had quadrupled to USD 100 billion. While charitable giving dipped slightly in 2022, due at least in part to the COVID-19 pandemic, it still totalled more than USD 499 billion.[2403] Religious organizations and congregations receive about one-third of total charitable contributions.[2404] These charitable contributions, made by individuals, foundations, bequests, and corporations,[2405] are generally allocated toward operational costs,

2398. *Volunteering in U.S. Hits Record High; Worth $167 Billion*, AmeriCorps (Nov. 13, 2018), https://americorps.gov/newsroom/press-releases/2018/volunteering-us-hits-record-high-worth-167-billion.

2399. Robert D. Putnam & David Campbell, *American Grace: How Religion Divides & Unites Us* 445 (2010); *see also* Pew Rsch. Ctr, *Religion's Relationship to Happiness, Civic Engagement and Health Around the World* 8–9 (Jan. 31, 2019), https://www.pewresearch.org/religion/2019/01/31/religions-relationship-to-happiness-civic-engagement-and-health-around-the-world (link to PDF).

2400. *See, e.g.*, JustServe, https://www.justserve.org (last visited Sep. 30, 2023) (serving as a clearing-house to match individual and group volunteers—religious or otherwise—with needs in their communities or needs that can be met virtually).

2401. Stephanie Boraas, *Volunteerism in the United States*, Monthly Lab. Rev. 3, 5–6 (August 2003).

2402. *See Giving USA*, *supra* n. 1888.

2403. *Ibid.*

2404. *The Nonprofit Sector in Brief 2019*, *supra* n. 21.

2405. *See* Jane G. Gravelle, Donald J. Marples & Molly F. Sherlock, Cong. Rsch. Serv., R45922, Tax Issues Relating to Charitable Contributions and Organizations 15–16 (Sep. 19, 2019), https://crsreports.congress.gov/product/pdf/R/R45922/3 (listing four main sources of charitable contributions).

social programs, missionary programs, and humanitarian projects. Tax benefits accrue to just over half of individuals who contribute to charitable organizations.[2406]

§3. Civil Religion

I. Distinctive American Conception of Civil Religion

886. American civil religion is an "abstract faith" based on a unique combination of ideals originating from both Puritanism and the American Enlightenment.[2407] It encompasses both religious and more secular symbols, ideals, interpretations, and traditions, many of which are reflected and based in America's founding documents.[2408] Influential US scholar Robert N. Bellah distinguished two forms of American civil religion (while conceding they were not necessarily distinguished in the citizenry's consciousness): a "general" or "natural" civil religion and a "special" civil religion.[2409]

887. Natural/general civil religion is comprised of commonly held values and principles—what Bellah calls the "lowest common denominator of church religions" and what Roger Williams believed to be "written in the hearts of all mankind, yea, even in pagans."[2410] George Washington's farewell address described morality and religion as "indispensable supports" to political prosperity, reflecting the natural civil religion principle that adherence to general moral and religious principles was essential to fostering the requisite civic virtue to build a nation.[2411] "Special" civil religion builds on the idea of common morality and civic virtue but extends them to a concern for the common good.[2412] It is embodied in the Declaration of Independence, which states that "all men are created equal, that they are endowed by their Creator with certain unalienable Rights, that among these are Life, Liberty and the pursuit of Happiness.—That to secure these rights, Governments are instituted among Men, deriving their just powers from the consent of the governed ... ."[2413] Special civil religion is also reflected in President

2406. *Ibid.*

2407. Robert N. Bellah, *The Revolution and the Civil Religion, in Religion and the American Revolution* 55, 55–57 (Jerald C. Brauer ed., 1976); Derek H. Davis, *Introduction: Religious Pluralism as the Essential Foundation of America's Quest for Unity and Order, in The Oxford Handbook of Church and State in the United States* 3, 12 (Derek H. Davis ed., 2010) ("On the one hand, American civil religion consists of ideas derived from Puritanism such as the covenanted, millennial, and chosen nation. ... On the other hand, ideas contributed from the American Enlightenment, such as the Declaration's affirmation that 'all men are created equal,' and are entitled to rights of 'life, liberty, and the pursuit of happiness' are clearly more secular, and implicitly universalistic and persuasive in character.")

2408. Bellah, *The Revolution and the Civil Religion, supra* n. 2407, at 55–58.

2409. *Ibid.*, at 55–58.

2410. *Ibid.*, at 57–58.

2411. *Ibid.*, at 58.

2412. *Ibid.*, at 62.

2413. *Ibid.*, at 55, 60; *The Declaration of Independence* pmbl. (U.S. 1776).

Abraham Lincoln's Gettysburg Address, delivered halfway through the Civil War. In that address, Lincoln charged Americans divided over slavery with "the great task" of carrying out the Founding Father's vision of "a new nation, conceived in liberty, and dedicated to the proposition that all men are created equal."[2414] In these terms, Americans fulfil the mission of their "special" civil religion as they strive—individually, collectively, and through the government—to preserve natural, "unalienable" rights for others as well as themselves.[2415]

II. Civil Religion Practices

888. American civil religion is reflected in nondenominational references to God common throughout the government. The US Supreme Court begins its sessions with the phrase "God save the United States and this Honorable Court."[2416] Almost every public address by a US President ends with "God bless the United States of America" or a similar sentiment.[2417] Such invocations of deity and its relation to the nation are a common feature of American politics and civil society. George Washington attended a prayer service after his swearing in as the first US President in 1789; a regular tradition of invocations and benedictions at presidential inaugurations was renewed in the 1930s and continues today. Many school children begin their day saluting the American flag and reciting the Pledge of Allegiance, which includes the phrase "one Nation under God."[2418] And the national motto is "In God we trust."[2419] For additional discussion, *see* Part V (Religion and Politics), Chapter 3 (Interaction Between Religion and State).

III. Controversies Surrounding Civil Religion

889. Since the 1960s, civil religion in government institutions has been increasingly challenged, with mixed results. In 1962, the Supreme Court found it unconstitutional for state officials to compose an official school prayer and encourage recitation of the prayer in public schools.[2420] Twenty years later, in *Marsh v. Chambers*, the Supreme Court determined that government funding for chaplains who

2414. Bellah, *The Revolution and the Civil Religion*, *supra* n. 2407, at 55–56; Abraham Lincoln, *Gettysburg Address Delivered at Gettysburg Pa. Nov. 19th, 1863 [n. p. n. d.]*, Libr. of Cong., https://www.loc.gov/resource/rbpe.24404500/?st=text (last visited Sep. 30, 2023).

2415. *See* Bellah, *The Revolution and the Civil Religion*, *supra* n. 2407, at 62–65.

2416. *The Court and Its Procedures*, *supra* n. 986; *see also* Ashley M. Bell, Comment, "*God Save this Honorable Court": How Current Establishment Clause Jurisprudence Can Be Reconciled with the Secularization of Historical Religious Expressions*, 50 Am. U. L. Rev. 1273, 1274 (2001).

2417. *See supra* n. 985 and accompanying text.

2418. The Pledge of Allegiance states, in full: "I pledge allegiance to the Flag of the United States of America, and to the Republic for which it stands, *one Nation under God*, indivisible, with liberty and justice for all." 4 U.S.C. § 4 (2018) (emphasis added).

2419. 36 U.S.C. § 302 (2018) ("'In God we trust' is the national motto.").

2420. *Engel v. Vitale*, 370 U.S. 421, 424 (1962).

open legislatures with prayer each morning is constitutional.[2421] In the early 2000s, an atheist father sued his daughter's elementary school for conducting daily recitations of the Pledge of Allegiance, which includes the words "one Nation under God." The case went before the Supreme Court, which dismissed the case because the father, as the noncustodial parent, lacked standing to sue on behalf of his daughter.[2422] However, the Court characterized the Pledge as a primarily "patriotic exercise" rather than a religious one,[2423] and that characterization has been employed by other courts to dismiss further Establishment Clause challenges to the Pledge.[2424] For a more detailed discussion of these and related cases, *see* Part V (Religion and Politics), Chapter 3 (Interaction Between Religion and State); Part VII (Religious Communities and Protections of the Individual), Chapter 3 (Freedom of Expression) and Chapter 7 (Non-discrimination); and Part IX (Education), Chapter 1 (Religious Education in Public and Private Schools).

IV. Naked Public Square

890. Some individuals and groups argue for a strict interpretation of the First Amendment that would marginalize or exclude religious viewpoints from public debate in the United States.[2425] This approach has been described as resulting in a "naked public square."[2426] The term comes from the concept that the public arena should be "naked" of any religious references, religiously sourced ideals, or religiously backed agendas, thereby leaving politics to secular dialogue, understanding, and morals.[2427] Though this viewpoint has not been widely held historically, evidence of religious groups losing their influence in policymaking is apparent over the last half-century as some policies justified on religious grounds have been deemed unconstitutional.[2428] *See* discussion in this part, Chapter 4 (Religion and Public Debate), below.

2421. *Marsh v. Chambers*, 463 U.S. 783 (1983); *see also supra* paras. 371–374, 641, and accompanying footnotes.

2422. *Elk Grove Unified Sch. Dist. v. Newdow*, 542 U.S. 1, 11–18 (2004).

2423. *Ibid.*, at 6.

2424. *See, e.g.*, *Newdow v. Rio Linda Union Sch. Dist.*, 597 F.3d 1007, 1014 (9th Cir. 2010).

2425. *See, e.g.*, *About*, Freedom from Religion Foundation, https://ffrf.org/about (last visited Sep. 30, 2023); *About AU*, Ams. United for Separation of Church & State, https://www.au.org/about-au (last visited Sep. 30, 2023).

2426. Richard John Neuhaus, *The Naked Public Square: Religion and Democracy in America*, at vii (1984).

2427. *Ibid.*, at 21.

2428. *See, e.g.*, *Obergefell v. Hodges*, 576 U.S. 644, 679–681 (2015) (affirming that the religiously supported traditional marriage definition in the Defense of Marriage Act was unconstitutional, while also affirming the First Amendment right for "religions, and those who adhere to religious doctrines [to] continue to advocate with utmost, sincere conviction that, by divine precepts, same-sex marriage should not be condoned").

§4. GOVERNMENT RELATIONS WITH RELIGION

I. Minimal and Decentralized Regulation of Religion

891. Compared to many other Western nations, in the United States there is very little government regulation of, or interaction with, religious groups. For example, the federal government does not have a Department of Religious Affairs or national bureaucracy assigned to register, oversee, or regulate religious groups.

892. Federal regulation of religion is decentralized and largely *ad hoc*. It takes place mainly through the federal tax code. The Internal Revenue Service (IRS) is charged with monitoring and enforcing the standards nonprofit tax-exempt organizations must maintain to maintain their tax-exempt status under section 501(c)(3) of the Internal Revenue Code.[2429] Revocation of tax-exempt status, however, is rare. *See* Part III (Legal Status of Religious Communities), Chapter 1 (Formal Status of Religious Communities). Registration of religious groups as legal entities (which is not required but gives groups legal status to facilitate their work) is a matter of state law and typically involves simply filling out basic paperwork to establish a nonprofit corporation. State attorneys general have jurisdiction over nonprofits, including churches, though federal agencies can also exercise jurisdiction in cases involving violations of federal law. Investigations of church activities and legal actions against churches or church leaders are relatively uncommon but have occurred at both state and federal levels.[2430] Wrongdoing by churches and their leaders are addressed principally through ordinary civil law, including land-use regulations and contract law, and ordinary criminal law, including prohibitions on fraud or child sexual abuse. Word of mouth, the media, and social media, together with religious groups' reliance on voluntary donations, provide a disciplining effect on religious groups. *See* this part, Chapter 3 (Religion and Civil Society), below.

II. White House Office

893. In 2001, President George W. Bush formed the White House Office of Faith-Based and Community Initiatives.[2431] While its name and mission have varied somewhat, the Office has essentially been re-established by all subsequent administrations, both Republican and Democratic. Under President Barack Obama's and President Joe Biden's administrations, it has been called the White House Office

2429. *Tax Guide for Churches & Religious Organizations*, *supra* n. 460, at 2, 31–32.

2430. *See, e.g.*, Liam Stack, *Catholic Diocese of Buffalo Will Submit to Government Oversight*, N.Y. Times (Oct. 25, 2022), https://www.nytimes.com/2022/10/25/nyregion/catholic-diocese-buffalo-attorney-general.html (discussing Catholic Diocese settlement with state attorney general in lawsuit regarding cover-up of child sexual abuse); Press Release, U.S. Att'y's Off., Dist. of Utah, Indictment Unsealed Charging FLDS Church Leaders with Conspiracy to Divert SNAP Benefits (Feb. 28, 2016), https://www.justice.gov/usao-ut/pr/indictment-unsealed-charging-flds-church-leaders-conspiracy-divert-snap-benefits (outlining federal indictment against fundamentalist church leaders on fraud and money laundering charges).

2431. White House Press Release (Jun. 26, 2008), *supra* n. 950.

of Faith-Based and Neighborhood Partnerships. Its purpose is to facilitate collaborative partnerships between federal agencies and civil society, including religious organizations, to address social challenges. Under the Biden administration, priorities included addressing COVID-19 and post-pandemic economic recovery, combatting systemic racism, and increasing opportunity for disadvantaged communities domestically, as well as advancing US humanitarian, diplomatic, and development work internationally.[2432] Administrations have assured that the Office respects "church-state separation and freedom for people of all faiths and none" and does not "prefer one faith over another or favor religious over secular organizations."[2433] Nevertheless, since 2001, the establishment, name, and mission of the Office have been somewhat controversial. Some critics believe the Office to be inconsistent with the Establishment Clause and the political and legal ideal of separation of church and state. For additional information, *see* Part V (Religion and Politics), Chapter 2 (Political Influence in Religion) and Chapter 3 (Interaction Between Religion and State).

894. The National Prayer Breakfast takes place annually in Washington, DC, on the first Thursday in February.[2434] The event is attended by approximately 3,500 guests, including members of the US Congress, executive Cabinet members, members of the diplomatic corps, religious leaders, and international invitees. Members of Congress host and help plan the event. The President of the United States is traditionally the keynote speaker. Each year, a different prominent individual is also invited to speak, generally about faith and current issues facing religious individuals and organizations. Religious-related side events involving breakfast attendees and others usually take place before and after the breakfast.[2435] The event has generated some controversies and criticisms, including criticism of its Christian-centric focus.[2436]

III. State Department and International Religious Freedom

895. The International Religious Freedom Act of 1998 requires the US State Department to compile annual reports describing the status of religious freedom in every country of the world except the United States.[2437] Because the annual survey does not include the United States, it has been criticized for ignoring problems with religious freedom in the United States' own "back yard." Nonetheless, the State Department reports have emerged as valuable research tools for social scientists and

---

2432. White House Press Release (Feb. 14, 2021), *supra* n. 952.

2433. *Ibid.*

2434. *See Vision*, Nat'l Prayer Breakfast Found., https://npbfoundation.com/vision (last accessed Sep. 30, 2023).

2435. *See, e.g.*, *About*, IRF Summit, https://irfsummit.org/about (last visited Sep. 30, 2023).

2436. *See* Domenico Montanaro, *Congress Takes Reins of Prayer Breakfast from Secretive Christian Evangelical Group*, NPR (Feb. 2, 2023), https://www.npr.org/2023/02/02/1153705297/congress-takes-reins-of-prayer-breakfast-from-secretive-christian-evangelical-gr.

2437. 22 U.S.C. § 6412 (2018); *see also International Religious Freedom Reports*, *supra* n. 1036 (providing link to latest report, which in turn contains links to individual country reports).

others interested in the state of religious freedom in specific countries and globally. The reports can also serve as authoritative evidence for asylum claims and other immigration-related applications for relief from removal based on religious persecution.[2438] For additional information, *see* Part IV (International, Transnational, and Regional Effects on Religious Communities), Chapter 2 (Transnational Law Effects on Religious Communities); and Part V (Religion and Politics), Chapter 3 (Interaction Between Religion and State).

2438. *See* 8 U.S.C. § 1158(b)(1) (2018).

Chapter 4. Religion and Public Debate

§1. Legal Framework

896. The First Amendment provides a high degree of protection of political speech, including religious-related political speech.[2439] Although political speech may be restricted, strict scrutiny is applied to regulations that burden such speech based on its content.[2440] Challenges to political speech have emerged in the context of political campaigns. For example, in *Republican Party of Minnesota v. White*, a canon of judicial conduct called the "announce clause," prohibited judicial candidates[2441] from announcing their views on disputed legal or political issues.[2442] One candidate filed suit, asserting the announce clause violated the First Amendment by restricting his protected right to political speech.[2443] The US Supreme Court concluded that the clause was not narrowly tailored to a compelling interest in preserving judges' impartiality toward parties to a suit, since it restricted speech about issues rather than speech about parties.[2444] The Court further reasoned that preserving the appearance of judicial impartiality on legal issues did not constitute a compelling state interest, "since avoiding judicial preconceptions on legal issues is neither possible nor desirable."[2445] In holding that the clause violated the First Amendment, the Court reiterated that the role "elected officials play in our society makes it all the more imperative that they be allowed freely to express themselves on matters of current public importance."[2446]

897. Political speech, including allegedly religiously motivated political speech, has been protected even when it is hateful in nature. In *Brandenburg v. Ohio*, film footage broadcast on local and national television showed a Ku Klux Klan leader giving a speech at a Klan rally in which he announced future plans for the group to march on Congress and to take vengeance on the government "if our President, our Congress, our Supreme Court, continues to suppress the white, Caucasian race."[2447]

2439. "Congress shall make no law respecting an establishment of religion, or prohibiting the free exercise thereof; *or abridging the freedom of speech, or of the press*; or the right of the people peaceably to assemble, and to petition the Government for a redress of grievances." U.S. Const. amend. I (emphasis added); *see also Watchtower Bible & Tract Society v. Village of Stratton*, 536 U.S. 150, 153, 160–164 (2002).

2440. *Republican Party of Minn. v.* White, 536 U.S. 765, 774–775 (2002); *McIntyre v. Ohio Elections Comm.*, 514 U.S. 334, 347 (1995) ("When a law burdens core political speech, we apply "exacting scrutiny," and we uphold the restriction only if it is narrowly tailored to serve an overriding state interest.").

2441. Minnesota selects its judges through contested popular elections instead of through an appointment system. *Republican Party of Minn.*, 536 U.S. at 768.

2442. *Ibid.*

2443. *Ibid.*, at 768–770.

2444. *Ibid.*, at 776–777.

2445. *Ibid.*, at 777–778.

2446. *Ibid.*, at 781–732. *But see Wersal v. Sexton*, 674 F.3d 1010, 1024–1028 (8th Cir. 2012) (upholding a restriction on judicial candidates' political speech in Minnesota because the restriction, which prohibited endorsements of other political candidates, was narrowly tailored to serve a compelling government interest).

2447. *Brandenburg v. Ohio*, 395 U.S. 444, 445–447 (1969).

The rally footage also contained images of weapons, a Bible, and a burning cross, as well as audio of other racist speech. The leader was convicted under a state criminal statute for (1) advocating "the duty, necessity, or propriety of crime, sabotage, violence, or unlawful methods of terrorism as a means of accomplishing industrial or political reform" and (2) voluntarily assembling with a group "formed to teach or advocate the doctrines of criminal syndicalism."[2448] The Klan leader challenged his conviction on the grounds that his speech was protected under the First and Fourteenth Amendments. The US Supreme Court held that the statute of conviction unconstitutionally restricted the leader's speech rights, in violation of both amendments.[2449] In so ruling, the Court distinguished advocacy (which cannot be prohibited under the First Amendment, even if offensive) from advocacy that incites imminent lawless action (which can constitutionally be prohibited).[2450] The Court found that the leader's speech fit in the former, rather than the latter, category. *Brandenburg* thus established that, religiously motivated political speech, even when hateful in nature, is constitutional unless it incites imminent lawless action. For a more detailed discussion of religion and free speech, *see* Part VII (Religious Communities and Protections of the Individual), Chapter 3 (Freedom of Expression).

898. The primary limitations on religion in politics are imposed through the tax code. To qualify for tax-exempt status under section 501(c)(3) of the International Revenue Code, religious groups must be "organized and operated exclusively for religious … purposes."[2451] While this language appears to prohibit any political advocacy, IRS regulations interpret "exclusively" to mean "primarily."[2452] To qualify for and retain tax-exempt status, religious organizations must pass two tests: the organizational and operational tests. The organizational test requires that an organization's articles of organization not expressly empower it to engage in non-exempt activities—including political advocacy—other than as an "insubstantial part" of its overall activities.[2453] Under the operational tests, an organization loses its exempt status if (1) more than an insubstantial part of its activities are non-exempt, (2) its earnings benefit private individuals or shareholders, or (3) it is classified as an action organization.[2454] An organization qualifies as an "action organization" if it (a) dedicates a substantial part of its activities to attempting to influence legislation, (b) directly or indirectly participates in political campaigning for or against a candidate, or (c) advocates or campaigns for or against legislation when the organization's institutional purpose can only be completed by passing or defeating the legislation.[2455] Thus, religious organizations that wish to maintain 501(c)(3) nonprofit status must engage in any political advocacy within the bounds of these requirements. For additional discussion of tax-exemption requirements, *see*

2448. *Ibid.*, at 444–445.
2449. *Ibid.*, at 448–449.
2450. *Ibid.*, at 448.
2451. I.R.C. § 501(c)(3) (2018).
2452. Treas. Reg. § 1.501(c)(3)-1(c) (2022).
2453. *See ibid.*, § 1.501(c)(3)-1(b).
2454. *Ibid.*, § 1.501(c)(3)-1(c).
2455. *Ibid.*, § 1.501(c)(3)-1(c)(3).

Part III (Legal Status of Religious Communities), Chapter 1 (Formal Status of Religious Communities); Part V (Religion and Politics), Chapter 1 (Religious Influence in Politics); and Part VIII (Financing of Religious Communities), Chapter 2 (Indirect Financing).

899. For further discussion on the relationship between religion and politics, *see* Part V (Religion and Politics), Chapter 1 (Religious Influence in Politics), Chapter 2 (Political Influence in Religion), and Chapter 3 (Interaction Between Religion and State).

§2. Historical Background

900. As US legal scholar George W. Dent, Jr., has explained:

> Until a few decades ago religion pervaded American debate; it was central to controversies over all our major political events, from the Declaration of Independence and Revolution, through abolition and the Civil War, to the Civil Rights Movement. Not until the 1960's was legal commentary dominated by the idea that a religious basis for law-making is improper and may even render a resulting law invalid. Ironically, at the same time that this idea was gaining ascendancy, the Civil Rights Movement was achieving its greatest triumphs due largely to appeals to religious beliefs. The battle over religion in public discourse has now sunk into a stalemate. While many public speakers still invoke religion, critics decry this practice and sometimes persuade courts to overturn laws deemed religiously motivated.[2456]

§3. Contemporary Debates about Religion and Politics

901. As Dent indicates, religion continues to play a significant role in US political discourse, but that role is debated. Even given the decline of religious devotion and church attendance in the United States over the last several decades, and the sharp increase of religious "nones,"[2457] "religion remains a pervasive influence on American culture, politics and public policy".[2458] Religiosity can vary by region and demographic, but in general, US citizens are still highly religious in comparison with most Western countries.[2459] "Indeed, the citizenry of the United States is one of the most religious—perhaps even the most religious—of the citizenries of the

2456. George W. Dent, Jr., *Religion, Morality and Democracy: New Learning, New Challenges*, 2 Geo. J.L. & Pub. Pol'y 401, 401 (2004).

2457. Pew Rsch. Ctr., *Modeling the Future of Religion in America*, *supra* n. 13, at 19.

2458. *Separation of Church and State*, The Boisi Center Papers on Religion in the United States 1 (2007), https://www.bc.edu/bc-web/centers/boisi-center/publications/papers.html.

2459. Dalia Fahmy, *Americans Are Far More Religious than Adults in Other Wealthy Nations*, Pew Rsch. Ctr. (Jul. 31, 2018), https://www.pewresearch.org/short-reads/2018/07/31/americans-are-far-more-religious-than-adults-in-other-wealthy-nations.

world's advanced industrial democracies."[2460] As a result, religion, religious freedom, free exercise rights, and church-state separation continue to be important in many ongoing political and social debates.

902. A somewhat unique characteristic of the United States is its degree of religious pluralism. Though "Judeo-Christian values" tend to dominate, the diversity among those with religious convictions means that no single sect or denomination necessarily controls the public or political arena. Unsurprisingly, with numerous different religious perspectives and opinions come social friction and divide. "Because the United States is *both* such a religious country *and* such a religiously pluralistic country (now more than ever), the issue of the proper role of religion in politics is anything but marginal to American politics"; in fact it is "a central, recurring issue."[2461]

903. The United States' unique population, history, and government structure lead to frequent tensions over the inclusion of religiously motivated opinions and discourse in political debate: Some believe it appropriate and even essential to enforce strict limits on religion in political debate. Others believe religion has been increasingly marginalized or silenced since the 1960s and should have a permanent place at the public and political "table."[2462] For example, George W. Dent, Jr., quoted above, has asserted, that—given religion's past contributions to American political discourse and its potential for present and future contributions—religion must not be forced to retreat from public debate about "public norms" crises.[2463] Rather, "religious and secular doctrines must compete and cooperate as equally valid participants in democratic colloquy[,] … as a simple matter of justice."[2464] Still others acknowledge religion's deliberative role in political discourse but assert that "discipline is required" in expressing religiously motivated beliefs and opinions—that "a citizen has a duty to reconstruct his or her idiosyncratic convictions into a civic discourse, including the everyday language of business, politics, education and a generalized conception of commonsense."[2465]

904. In the minds of many Americans, "there is an association of religion with superstition, fanaticism, intolerance, reaction, and, in short, illiberalism."[2466] Such perceptions have seemingly grown over the last decades as conflicts involving free exercise and non-discrimination interests, such as LGBTQ+ rights, have arisen in some corners of the public square. This growth further fuels desires and efforts to

2460. Michael J. Perry, *Religious Arguments in Public Political Debate*, 29 Loy. L.A. L. Rev. 1421, 1421 (1996).
2461. *Ibid.*, at 1422.
2462. *See* Tim Shah & Tom Farr, Opinion, *Defending Religion in the Public Square*, N.Y. Times (Dec. 27, 2011), http://www.nytimes.com/roomfordebate/2011/12/22/is-americans-religious-freedom-under-threat/defending-religion-in-the-public-square.
2463. Dent, *Religion, Morality and Democracy*, *supra* n. 2456, at 446–447.
2464. *Ibid.*
2465. Robert Justin Lipkin, *Reconstructing the Public Square*, 24 Cardozo L. Rev. 2025, 2028, 2030 (2003).
2466. *See* Maimon Schwarzschild, *Religion and Public Debate in Liberal Society: Always Oil and Water or Sometimes More Like Rum and Coca-Cola?*, 30 San Diego L. Rev. 903, 903 (1993).

marginalize religion or banish it completely from the political arena. Nevertheless, while the Constitution has been interpreted to require a high degree of separation of *church* and *state*, separation of *religion* and *politics* is not constitutionally required, and they undeniably influence each other. It is because of this reciprocal influence that religion continues to play a significant role in political and public debate, despite the desires of many to lessen or eliminate that role.

§4. Public Reason

905. The idea of public reason, popularized by Harvard philosopher John Rawls, captured the national zeitgeist in the 1970s and 1980s, just as the "culture wars" over women's rights and abortion were dominating social policy. Public reason maintains that religious and other "thick"[2467] ideological commitments are not appropriate in the public square. The basic idea of public reason is both intuitive and appealing: in public discourse, citizens should limit themselves to reasons they can expect all reasonable people to understand and find persuasive. Citizens may have thick normative foundations for their views (such as religious convictions), but they should translate those ideas into a secular vernacular, an idiom that is less partisan, less sectarian, and less religious.

906. Rawls, who became the foremost proponent of public reason in the United States, defined public reason in a democratic society as "the reason of equal citizens who, as a collective body, exercise final political and coercive power over one another in enacting laws and in amending their constitution."[2468] In other words, political power is by its nature "coercive" and "final," and when citizens exercise that power over each other, they have an obligation—a moral obligation, an obligation of civility—to only exercise it pursuant to reasons that their fellow citizens can reasonably be expected to accept or endorse.[2469] For the exercise of political power to be legitimate in a liberal democracy, argues Rawls, it must be exercised pursuant to the limitations imposed by public reason.[2470] Thus, public reason maintains that citizens have strategic, pragmatic, or neighborly reasons for speaking in

---

2467. In philosophy, evaluative concepts and terms are often classified as "thin" or "thick": thin concepts are solely evaluative (for example, *good* or *bad*) whereas thick terms contain evaluative and descriptive elements (for example, *generous* or *selfish*). *See* Pekka Väyrynen, *Thick Ethical Concepts*, Stanford Encyclopedia Phil. (updated Feb. 9, 2021), https://plato.stanford.edu/entries/thick-ethical-concepts. These classifications have been borrowed by social and political scientists to distinguish approaches to social order. In that context, thin approaches are more individualistic and abstractly ideological, whereas thick approaches are sociocentric, normative, and prescriptive, with clear concepts and claims about the way society should be. *See, e.g.*, Seth D. Kaplan, *Human Rights in Thick and Thin Societies: Universality Without Uniformity* 15 (2018).

2468. John Rawls, *Political Liberalism* 214 (Columbia Classics in Philosophy 2005).

2469. *Ibid.*, at 218. "As reasonable and rational, and knowing that they affirm a diversity of reasonable religious and philosophical doctrines, they should be ready to explain the basis of their actions to one another in terms each could reasonably expect that others might endorse as consistent with their freedom and equality. … Understanding how to conduct oneself as a democratic citizen includes understanding an ideal of public reason." *Ibid.*

2470. *Ibid.*, at 217. "And since the exercise of political power itself must be legitimate, the ideal of citizenship imposes a moral, not a legal, duty—the duty of civility—to be able to explain to one

the tongue of public reason, and moral reasons as well. At its core, public reason makes a moral claim—that it is morally wrong to base political arguments, or even positions, on views that are grounded on contestable moral theories or commitments. Accordingly, only public reason is welcome in the public square. Public reason will only make appeals to "plain truths" that are "now widely accepted, or available, to citizens generally."[2471] It will not appeal to "comprehensive religious and philosophical doctrines," matters about which reasonable people may disagree.[2472]

907. The idea of public reason has been highly influential in the United States. As many acknowledge, having a common language is key to successful communication. Further, it can be argued that public reason exhibits a kind of respect for others, in expecting them to be bound only by reasons they can be reasonably obliged to accept as legitimate. It represents one way of achieving what Rawls helpfully describes as an "overlapping consensus" on divisive political and legal issues.[2473]

908. A number of criticisms have been directed at public reason, however. One is its insistence on claiming the status of a moral principle rather than a pragmatic rule of thumb. This claims a normative status for public reason that is controversial and viewed by many as problematic.[2474]

909. A second criticism is that public reason overburdens reason and rationality and overestimates the prospect that reasonable people will reach agreement.[2475] Such criticisms note ample evidence that reasonable and rational people can disagree in fundamental ways about what is good and true and right. Public reason, therefore, may be more optimistic about the promise of reason than society has reason to be.

910. A third objection is that public reason misallocates the burdens of translation, placing the burden of translation into "secularese" on those who are not secular (in other words, on non-native speakers).[2476] Usually, the burden is on native speakers to try to understand those for whom the language is not their primary mode of communication. This begs the conclusion that it is the secular majority who

another on those fundamental questions how the principles and policies they advocate and vote for can be supported by the political values of public reason." *Ibid.*

2471. *Ibid.*, at 225.

2472. *Ibid.*, at 224–225, 241. "[W]e are to appeal only to presently accepted general beliefs and forms of reasoning found in common sense, and the methods and conclusions of science when these are not controversial. … This means that in discussing constitutional essentials and matters of basic justice we are not to appeal to comprehensive religious and philosophical doctrines—to what we as individuals or members of associations see as the whole truth—nor to elaborate economic theories of general equilibrium, say, if these are in dispute." *Ibid.*, at 224–225.

2473. *See ibid.*, at 133–172.

2474. *See* Jonathan Quong, *Public Reason*, Stanford Encyclopedia Phil. (updated Apr. 20, 2022), https://plato.stanford.edu/entries/public-reason.

2475. *See ibid.*

2476. *See* George Tyler, *The Reciprocal Translation Proviso: An Alternative Approach to Public Reason*, 11 Pol. & Religion 717, 721 (2018).

should try to translate religious arguments into a secular voice, rather than placing the burden on religious people, who may be in a minority, to translate their convictions into a secular voice.

911. A fourth objection focuses on the translation metaphor. This critique argues that it is a mistake to think of public reason as imposing simply a requirement of "translation." Rather, what it calls for is an abandonment or disavowal of American foundations, history, culture, and particularity. Under this argument, moral reasoning is often "foundational," and requiring only "public reason" may unfairly hamper foundational systems of thinking.

912. A fifth criticism of public reason is that it rather reflexively echoes liberal conventional wisdom in a noncritical way.[2477] This criticism notes the ease with which secular individuals imagine their preferences to reflect "public reason" while the preferences of other people (especially religious people) reflect irrational biases or inadmissible, irrational—or at least arational—viewpoints. It may be the first part of the phrase (*public*, or popular) that is most characteristic of the practice, rather than the second part of the phrase (*reason*). Public reason may not reflect so much what is "*reason*able" (much less rational) but rather what is popular (or publicly acceptable).

913. A sixth criticism of public reason is that it is blind to claims of conscience. In all its variations, public reason begins with the same analytical approach: it differentiates public reason from private reason.[2478] The premise is that only public reasons are legitimate in public life; private reasons are illegitimate. But this approach can be problematic: claims of conscience are paradigmatic private reasons. Conscience, for example, is often described in metaphors, such as a still small voice, an inner light, or something that pricks the heart or causes inward pain. Within a public reason framework, some argue, the problem is not that claims of conscience are outweighed; it is that they may be given little to no weight at all (at least in the public square).

§5. Ecumenical Politics

914. Public reason is by no means the only powerful model of public discourse. Another influential model is ecumenical dialogue or ecumenical politics. In ecumenical dialogue, representatives of different religious traditions come together to try to discuss issues of common interest. Like public reason, it is (in part) an effort to generate agreement or common ground—not by limiting citizens to translations

2477. *Cf.* Quong, *Public Reason*, *supra* n. 2474.

2478. *See* Rawls, *Political Liberalism*, *supra* n. 2468, at 220; Immanuel Kant, *Answer the Question: What Is Enlightenment?* 4–5 (Daniel Fidel Ferrer trans., 2013); Gerald Gaus, *Hobbes's Challenge to Public Reason Liberalism: Public Reason and Religious Convictions in* Leviathan, *in Hobbes Today: Insights for the 21st Century* 155, 165 (S. A. Lloyd ed., 2013). *But see* Kent Greenawalt, *Private Consciences and Public Reasons* 39–50 (1995).

of their beliefs into "public reason" but by inviting them to provide thick, rich, comprehensive accounts of their moral beliefs, each in turn, and then look for areas of overlap or commonality.

915. Methodologically, an ecumenical approach may be viewed as almost the opposite of public reason. It requires participants in dialogue, with all their particularity, to listen carefully to each other and then look for areas of agreement or overlap. Ideally in such discourse, participants do not restrict themselves to expected areas of overlap but, by each expressing the richness of their viewpoints, can find areas of "overlap." This type of approach represents a markedly different strategy for achieving "overlapping consensus."

916. But ecumenical dialogue has objectives that go beyond achieving consensus. Proponents assert there are reasons to engage in dialogue beyond achieving agreement: Participants may come to understand each other better (that is, understand the grounds or character of their disagreements).[2479] They may come to understand themselves better (that is, understand the character of their own commitments by articulating the grounds for their beliefs).[2480] And participants, in professing their own ideals, are held morally responsible to live (or at least try to live) consistently with those professed ideals.

917. A representative proponent of this type of ecumenical dialogue is law professor Michael J. Perry. Perry argues that such a mode of political discourse would rest upon two practices: "first, a certain kind of dialogue; second, a certain kind of tolerance."[2481] As Perry puts it:

> Ecumenical politics is, above all, both dialogic and communitarian: It is … a politics in which, notwithstanding our religious/moral pluralism, we continually cultivate the bonds of political community—and in which we sometimes succeed in strengthening those bonds, even, occasionally, in forging new bonds—through dialogue of a certain kind. Ecumenical politics institutionalizes a particular conception of the place of religion in American life and of how we should contend with each other's deepest differences in the public sphere.[2482]

2479. Michael J. Perry, *Toward an Ecumenical Politics*, 60 Geo. Wash. L. Rev. 599, 610 (1992).

2480. Michael J. Perry, *Love & Power: The Role of Religion and Morality in American Politics*, 49–50 (1991).

2481. Perry, *Toward an Ecumenical Politics*, *supra* n. 2479, at 599.

2482. Perry, *Love & Power*, *supra* n. 2480, at 45 (1991) (internal quotation marks omitted). Perry continues, "The aim of ecumenical politics is, in words borrowed from *The Williamsburg Charter*, 'neither a naked public square where all religion is excluded, nor a sacred public square with any religion established or semi-established'. The aim, rather, 'is a civil public square in which citizens of all religious faiths, or none, engage one another in continuing democratic discourse'." Perry, *Toward an Ecumenical Politics*, *supra* n. 2479, at 600.

Perry emphasizes there are reasons for dialogue that reach beyond agreement—namely, taking responsibility for one's own moral professions.[2483] He explains, "We must be willing to lend credibility to our convictions by being faithful to them in our lives and not merely in our polemics and our posturing."[2484] He also argues that to engage in genuine ecumenical dialogue, participants must move beyond infallibilism, or in other words, engage with the (genuine) mindset that they might be mistaken. As Perry asserts:

> We must be willing to let our convictions be tested in ecumenical dialogue with others who do not share them. We must let ourselves be tested, in ecumenical dialogue, by convictions we do not share. We must, in short, resist the temptations of infallibilism. … If necessary we must revise our convictions until they are credible to ourselves, if not always or even often to our interlocutors.[2485]

918. Like public reason, ecumenical dialogue also has limits and is subject to powerful criticisms.

919. First, critics contend it can become formulaic, insincere, and thus ineffectual. They point to the common development of a "professional class" of ecumenical dialogue specialists.[2486] And critics note that the concept does not appear to actually influence the way religious life is carried out within religious communities on a daily basis.[2487]

920. Second, ecumenical dialogue is criticized for fostering soft relativism. Those who engage in ecumenical dialogue are sometimes criticized by those within their own community for being sell-outs or denying the distinctive truth claims of their own religious group.[2488] Ecumenical dialogue can result in overgeneralized (and often platitudinous) oversimplifications: *we all believe more or less the same thing*; *why cannot we all get along*; *you have your way, and I have mine*; *there are many roads to the top of the mountain.*[2489]

2483. Perry, *Toward an Ecumenical Politics*, *supra* n. 2479, at 610.
2484. Michael J. Perry, *Morality, Politics, and Law* 183 (1988).
2485. *Ibid.*
2486. *See* Marie Nuar, *Addressing the Difficult Questions*, 7 J. World Christianity 47, 49–51 (2017).
2487. *See* Perry, *Toward an Ecumenical Politics*, *supra* n. 2479, at 612–613.
2488. *See* Nuar, *Addressing the Difficult Questions*, *supra* n. 2486, at 47–48. *Compare* Joseph Pearce, Opinion, *How the Modernists Made "Ecumenical" a Dirty Word*, Crisis Mag. (Nov. 26, 2019), https://crisismagazine.com/opinion/how-the-modernists-made-ecumenical-a-dirty-word ("[T]he modern understanding of *ecumenism* … appears to be the willingness to dilute or delete doctrine in pursuit of a perceived unity among disparate groups of believers, irrespective of what they actually believe."), *with* Jason West, Opinion, *In Defense of Ecumenism*, Crisis Mag. (Dec. 10, 2019), https://crisismagazine.com/opinion/in-defense-of-ecumenism ("[T]he term ecumenism is sometimes bandied about to justify reducing doctrine to the lowest common denominator. … But this would be a false ecumenism, a misunderstanding of the concept, and an abuse.").
2489. *See* Nuar, *Addressing the Difficult Questions*, *supra* n. 2486, at 56.

921. A third criticism of ecumenical dialogue is that it might engage in a feel-good denial or papering-over of differences.[2490] It might also exhibit a reluctance or fear of criticizing those who need criticism, including violent religious extremists.[2491]

922. Although religion in public debate is controversial and contested, in actual practice, the invocation of religion, including criticisms of religion, is often careful and thoughtful. When shared in such a way, religious perspectives have the potential to add depth and richness to public discourse and make it truly reflective of the United States' uniquely pluralistic population.

2490. *See ibid.*, at 51–52.
2491. *See ibid.*, at 56.

Selected Bibliography

Books

Adkins, Julie, Laurie Occhipinti & Tara Hefferan, *Social Services, Social Justice, and Faith-Based Organizations in the United States: An Introduction, in Not by Faith Alone: Social Services, Social Justice, and Faith-Based Organizations in the United States* 1 (Julie Adkins, Laurie Occhipinti & Tara Hefferan eds., 2010)

Ahlstrom, Sydney E., *A Religious History of the American People* (1972)

Backman Jr., Milton V., *Religion at War in Support of the American Revolution, in Lectures on Religion and the Founding of the American Republic* 77 (John W. Welch & Stephen J. Fleming eds., 2003)

Bellah, Robert N., *The Revolution and the Civil Religion, in Religion and the American Revolution* 55 (Jerald C. Brauer ed., 1976)

Breidenbach, Michael D., *Church and State in Maryland: Religious Liberty, Religious Tests, and Church Disestablishment, in Disestablishment and Religious Dissent: Church-State Relations in the New American States, 1776–1883* at 309 (Carl H. Esbeck & Jonathan J. Den Hartog eds., 2019)

Bowers, Amy & Kristen Carpenter, *Challenging the Narrative of Conquest: The Story of* Lyng v. Northwest Indian Cemetery Protective Association, *in Indian Law Stories* 489 (Carole Goldberg, Kevin K. Washburn & Philip P. Frickey eds., 2011)

Bradley, Curtis A., *International Law in the U.S. Legal System* (3d ed. 2020)

Brauer, Jerald C., *Puritanism, Revivalism, and the Revolution, in Religion and the American Revolution* 1 (Jerald C. Brauer ed.,1976)

Bushman, Richard Lyman, *Joseph Smith: Rough Stone Rolling* (2007)

Cannon, George Q., *A Review of the Decision of the Supreme Court of the United States, in the Case of* Geo. Reynolds vs. The People of the United States (1879)

Christian Science, in Christian Science: A Sourcebook of Contemporary Materials 5 (1990)

Clancy, William, *Religion as a Source of Tension, in Religion and the Free Society* (1958)

Cnaan, Ram A., *The Newer Deal: Social Work and Religion in Partnership* (1999)

Controversial Christian Movements: History, Growth, and Outlook, in New Religious Movements and Religious Liberty in America 1 (Derek H. Davis & Barry Hankins eds., 2d ed. 2003)

Daly, Lew, *God's Economy: Faith-Based Initiatives & the Caring State* (2009)

Selected Bibliography

Davis, Derek H., *Introduction: Religious Pluralism as the Essential Foundation of America's Quest for Unity and Order*, *in The Oxford Handbook of Church and State in the United States* 3 (Derek H. Davis ed., 2010)

DellaPergola, Sergio, *World Jewish Population, 2021*, *in American Jewish Year Book* 313 (2021)

Dinnerstein, Leonard, Roger L. Nichols & David M. Reimers, *Natives and Strangers: A History of Ethnic Americans* (6th ed. 2014)

Diouf, Sylviane A., *Servants of Allah: African Muslims Enslaved in the Americas* (15th anniversary ed. 2013)

Disestablishment and Religious Dissent: Church-State Relations in the New American States, 1776–1883 (Carl H. Esbeck & Jonathan J. Den Hartog eds., 2019)

Durham, Jr., W. Cole, *Treatment of Religious Minorities in the United States*, *in* Eur. Consortium for Church-State Rsch., *The Legal Status of Religious Minorities in the Countries of the European Union* 323 (1994)

Durham, Jr., W. Cole & Elizabeth A. Clark (Sewell), *Definition of Religion*, *in Religious Organizations in the United States: A Study of Identity, Liberty, and the Law* 3 (James A. Serritella et al. eds., 2006)

Durham, Jr., W. Cole & Brett G. Scharffs, *Law and Religion: National, International, and Comparative Perspectives* (2d ed. 2019)

Esbeck, Carl H., *Regulation of Religious Organizations via Governmental Financial Assistance*, *in Religious Organizations in the United States: A Study of Identity, Liberty, and the Law* 349 (James A. Seritella ed. 2006)

Ferling, John E., *Adams vs. Jefferson: The Tumultuous Election of 1800* (2004)

Firmage, Edwin Brown & R. Collin Mangrum, *Zion in the Courts: A Legal History of The Church of Jesus Christ of Latter-day Saints, 1830–1900* (1988)

Flake, Kathleen, *The Politics of American Religious Identity: The Seating of Senator Reed Smoot, Mormon Apostle* (2004)

Gaffney, Jr., Edward McGlynn, *Exemption of Religious Organizations from Federal Taxation*, *in Religious Organizations in the United States: A Study of Identity, Liberty, and the Law* 409 (James A. Serritella et al. eds., 2006)

Gage, Matilda Joslyn, *Woman, Church, and State* (Google Books 1893)

4 Garrison, Wendell Phillips & Francis Jackson Garrison, *William Lloyd Garrison, 1805–1879: The Story of His Life Told by His Children* (1894)

Gaus, Gerald, *Hobbes's Challenge to Public Reason Liberalism: Public Reason and Religious Convictions in* Leviathan, *in Hobbes Today: Insights for the 21st Century* 155 (S. A. Lloyd ed., 2013)

Gerstenblith, Patty, *Associational Structures of Religious Organizations*, *in Religious Organizations in the United States: A Study of Identity, Liberty, and the Law* (James A. Serritella et al. eds., 2006)

Gaustad, Edwin S., *Church and State in America* (2d ed. 2003)

Gillman, Howard & Erwin Chemerinsky, *The Religion Clauses: The Case for Separating Church and State* (2020)

Gingerich, Melvin, *Service for Peace: A History of Mennonite Civilian Public Service* (1949)

Goen, C.C., *Broken Churches, Broken Nation: Denominational Schisms and the Coming of the American Civil War* (1985)

Gordon, Sarah Barringer, *The Spirit of the Law: Religious Voices and the Constitution in Modern America* (2010)

Greenawalt, Kent, *Private Consciences and Public Reasons* (1995)

Hall, Peter Dobkin, *Historical Perspectives on Religion, Government, and Social Welfare in America, in Can Charitable Choice Work?: Covering Religion's Impact on Urban Affairs and Social Services* 78 (Andrew Walsh ed., 2001)

Hamburger, Philip, *Separation of Church and State* (2004)

Hammar, Richard R., *Essential Guide to Liabilities and Duties for Church Boards*, https://store.churchlawandtax.com/essential-guide-to-liabilities-and-duties-for-church-boards

Handy, Robert T., *A Christian America: Protestant Hopes and Historical Realities* (1971)

Haupt, Claudia E., *Religion-State Relations in the United States and Germany: The Quest for Neutrality* (2011)

Heller, Joseph, *Catch-22* (1961)

Kaczorowska-Ireland, Alina, Public International Law (5th ed. 2015), 274

Kant, Immanuel, *Answer the Question: What Is Enlightenment?* (Daniel Fidel Ferrer trans., 2013)

Kaplan, Seth D., *Human Rights in Thick and Thin Societies: Universality Without Uniformity* (2018)

Katz, Sanford N., *Marriage, in Family Law in America* 43 (3d ed. 2021)

Kennedy, Sheila Suess & Wolfgang Bielefeld, *Charitable Choice at Work: Evaluating Faith-Based Job Programs in the States* (2006)

Kundnani, Arun, *The Muslims Are Coming!: Islamophobia, Extremism, and the Domestic War on Terror* (2014)

Lambert, Frank, *Religion and the American Revolution, in* 1 *The Cambridge History of Religions in America* 570 (Stephen J. Stein ed., 2012)

Land, Gary, *Historical Dictionary of the Seventh-day Adventists* (2d ed. 2014)

Levy, Leonard W., *The Establishment Clause: Religion and the First Amendment* (2d ed. 1994)

5 Lincoln, Abraham, *Collected Works of Abraham Lincoln* (Roy P. Basler ed., 1953)

Macedo, Stephen, *Just Married: Same-Sex Couples, Monogamy, & the Future of Marriage* (2015)

Manza, Jeff & Clem Brooks, *Religion, in Social Cleavages and Political Change: Voter Alignments and US Party Coalitions* 85 (1999)

Marty, Martin E., *Pilgrims in Their Own Land: 500 Years of Religion in America* (1984)

McBride, Spencer W., *Joseph Smith for President: The Prophet, the Assassins, and the Fight for American Religious Freedom* (2021)

McDonald, Robert M. S., *Was There a Religious Revolution of 1800?, in The Revolution of 1800: Democracy, Race, and the New Republic* 173 (James Horn, Jan Ellen Lewis & Peter S. Onuf eds., 2002)

McPherson, James M., *For Cause & Comrades: Why Men Fought in the Civil War* (1997)

Meacham, Jon, *American Gospel: God, the Founding Fathers, and the Making of a Nation* (2007)

Meyerson, Michael I., *Endowed by Our Creator: The Birth of Religious Freedom in America* (2012)
Miller, Nicholas P., *The Religious Roots of the First Amendment: Dissenting Protestants and the Separation of Church and State* (2012)
Monsma, Stephen V., *When Sacred and Secular Mix: Religious Nonprofit Organizations & Public Money* (1996)
Nat'l Museum of the Am. Indian, *Creation's Journey: Native American Identity and Belief* (Tom Hill & Richard W. Hill, Sr., eds. 1994)
Nelson, William E., *Dispute and Conflict Resolution in Plymouth County, Massachusetts, 1725–1825* (1981)
Neuhaus, Richard John, *The Naked Public Square: Religion and Democracy in America* (1984)
Pascoe, Peggy, *What Comes Naturally: Miscegenation Law and the Making of Race in America* (2009)
Perry, Michael J., *Love & Power: The Role of Religion and Morality in American Politics* (1991)
Perry, Michael J., *Morality, Politics, and Law* (1988)
Pfeffer, Leo, *Religious Freedom* (1979)
Pierceson, Jason, *Same-Sex Marriage in the United States: The Road to the Supreme Court* (2013)
Putnam, Robert D. & David Campbell, *American Grace: How Religion Divides & Unites Us* (2010)
Rawls, John, *Political Liberalism* (Columbia Classics in Philosophy 2005)
Regan, Richard J., *The American Constitution and Religion* (2013)
Religious Freedom, LGBT Rights, and the Prospects for Common Ground (William N. Eskridge, Jr. & Robin Fretwell Wilson eds., 2018)
Selby, Gary S., *Martin Luther King and the Rhetoric of Freedom: The Exodus Narrative in America's Struggle for Civil Rights* (2008)
Sherman, Natalie & David Gergen, *Religion & Politics: Seeking a Reconciliation, in Religion & Public Policy* 307 (Sumner B. Twiss, Marian Gh. Simion & Rodney L. Petersen eds., 2015)
Solomon, Lewis D., *In God We Trust?: Faith-Based Organizations and the Quest to Solve America's Social Ills* (2003)
Steinhardt, Ralph G., Paul L. Hoffman & Christopher N. Camponovo, *International Human Rights Lawyering: Cases and Materials* (1st ed. 2008)
Stern, Marc D., *Charitable Choice: The Law as It Is and May Be, in Can Charitable Choice Work?: Covering Religion's Impact on Urban Affairs and Social Services* 157 (Andrew Walsh ed., 2001)
Stout, Harry S. & Christopher Grasso, *Civil War, Religion, and Communications: The Case of Richmond, in Religion and the American Civil War* 313 (Randall M. Miller, Harry S. Stout & Charles Reagan Wilson eds., 1998)
Thiemann, Ronald F., *Religion in American Public Life: A Dilemma for Democracy* (1996)
Tribe, Laurence, *American Constitutional Law* (1st ed. 1978)
Underwood, Grant, *"Awash in a Sea of Faith": America and the Second Great Awakening, in Lectures on Religion and the Founding of the American Republic* 97 (John W. Welch & Stephen J. Fleming eds., 2003)

Walch, Timothy, *Parish School: American Catholic Parochial Education from Colonial Times to the Present* (1996)

Wardle, Lynn Dennis, William C. Duncan & Laurence C. Nolan, *Family and Succession Law in the USA* (4th ed. 2019)

Wasserman, Rhonda, *Procedural Due Process: A Reference Guide to the United States Constitution* (2004)

Williams, Rhys H. & John P.N. Massad, *Religious Diversity, Civil Law, and Institutional Isomorphism, in Religious Organizations in the United States: A Study of Identity, Liberty, and the Law* 111 (James A. Serritella et al. eds., 2006)

Wineburg, Bob, *A Limited Partnership: The Politics of Religion, Welfare, and Social Science* (2001)

Witte, Jr., John & Joel A. Nichols, *Religion and the American Constitutional Experiment* (4th ed. 2016)

Wood, Gordon S., *The Radicalism of the American Revolution* (1992)

Articles

Achey, Thomas S. & Ashley T. Robertson, *Conscientious Objection: A Review of State Pharmacy Laws and Regulations*, 57 Hosp. Pharmacy 268 (2022)

Adamczyk, Amy, Chunrye Kim & Leevia Dillon, *Examining Public Opinion about Abortion: A Mixed-Methods Systematic Review of Research over the Last 15 Years*, 90 Socio. Inquiry 920 (2020)

Adams, Arlin M. & William R. Hanlon, Jones v. Wolf*: Church Autonomy and the Religion Clauses of the First Amendment*, 128 U. Pa. L. Rev. 1291 (1980)

Albert, Richard, *Religion in the New Republic*, 67 La. L. Rev. 1 (2006)

Altamuro, Jennifer, James Bierstaker, Lucy Huajing Chen & Erica Harris, *Does It Pay to Pray? Religious Nonprofits and Funding*, 41 J. Acct. & Pub. Pol'y 1 (2022)

Archibold, Randal C., *Archdiocese Loses Case to Keep Former Priests' Records Secret*, N.Y. Times (April 18, 2006), http://www.nytimes.com/2006/04/18/washington/18church.html

Assisted Reproductive Technologies, 20 Geo. J. Gender & L. 313 (Jenna Casolo et al. eds., 2019)

Bailey, Sarah Pulliam, *Major Evangelical Nonprofits Are Trying a New Strategy with the IRS That Allows Them to Hide Their Salaries*, Wash. Post (January 17, 2020), https://www.washingtonpost.com/religion/2020/01/17/major-evangelical-nonprofits-are-trying-new-strategy-with-irs-that-allows-them-hide-their-salaries

Barclay, Stephanie Hall & Michalyn Steele, *Rethinking Protections for Indigenous Sacred Sites*, 134 Harv. L.R. 1294 (2020)

Barnes, Morey Elizabeth, Comment, *Falling Short of the Mark: The United States Response to the European Union's Data Privacy Directive*, 27 Nw. J. Int'l L. & Bus. 171 (2006)

Bassett, William, *Church Records and the Courts: Recent Court Rulings Undermine the Churchs* [sic] *Promise of Confidentiality*, Am.: Jesuit Rev. (October 29, 2007), http://americamagazine.org/issue/631/article/church-records-and-courts

Bauer, Gerald, *The Quest for Religious Freedom in Virginia*, 41 Hist. Mag. Protestant Episcopal Church 85 (1972)

Selected Bibliography

Bell, Ashley M., Comment, "*God Save this Honorable Court": How Current Establishment Clause Jurisprudence Can Be Reconciled with the Secularization of Historical Religious Expressions*, 50 Am. U. L. Rev. 1273 (2001)

Bellah, Robert N., *Civil Religion in America*, 96 Dædalus 1 (1967)

Bennett-Smith, Meredith, *Pastors to Challenge IRS Ban on Political Speech with "Pulpit Freedom Sunday"*, Huffington Post (September 20, 2012), https://www.huffpost.com/entry/pastors-conservative-groups-challenge-irs-pulpit-free-sunday_n_1901080

Berg, Thomas C., *Anti-Catholicism and Modern Church-State Relations*, 33 Loy. U. Chi. L.J. 121 (2002)

Berg, Thomas C., *What Same-Sex Marriage and Religious-Liberty Claimants Have in Common*, 5 Nw. J.L. & Soc. Pol'y 206 (2010)

Biblarz, Timothy J. & Greg Gottainer, *Family Structure and Children's Success: A Comparison of Widowed and Divorced Single-Mother Families*, 62 J. Marriage & Fam. 533 (2000)

Bittker, Boris I., *Churches, Taxes and the Constitution*, 78 Yale L.J. 1285 (1969)

Blair, Keith S., *Praying for a Tax Break: Churches, Political Speech, and the Loss of Section 501(c)(3) Tax Exempt Status*, 86 Denv. U. L. Rev. 405 (2009)

Blocher, Joseph, *Institutions in the Marketplace of Ideas*, 57 Duke L.J. 821 (2008)

Boraas, Stephanie, *Volunteerism in the United States*, Monthly Lab. Rev. 3 (August 2003)

Boulter, Brandon S., Note, *Expensive Speech:* Citizens United v. FEC *and the Free Speech Rights of Tax-Exempt Religious Organizations*, 2010 BYU L. Rev. 2243

Bowman, Jr., Robert M., *Argument for the Silent: A Biblical Case Against Abortion*, Reasons to Believe (April 1, 2001), http://www.reasons.org/articles/argument-for-the-silent-a-biblical-case-against-abortion

Bradley, Curtis A., *The* Charming Betsy *Canon and Separation of Powers: Rethinking the Interpretive Role of International Law*, 86 Geo. L.J. 479 (1998)

Bradley, Gerard V., *Dogmatomachy: A "Privatization" Theory of Religion Clause Cases*, 30 St. Louis U. L.J. 275 (1986)

Brady, Kathleen A., *Religious Organizations and Free Exercise: The Surprising Lessons of* Smith, 2004 BYU L. Rev. 1633

Brunson, Samuel, *Dear I.R.S., It Is Time to Enforce the Campaigning Prohibition. Even Against Churches*, 87 U. Colo. L. Rev. 143 (2016)

Campbell, David E., John C. Green & Geoffrey C. Layman, *The Party Faithful: Partisan Images, Candidate Religion, and the Electoral Impact of Party Identification*, 55 Am. J. Pol. Sci. 42 (2011)

Cary, Nathaniel, *Bob Jones University Regains Nonprofit Status 17 Years after It Dropped Discriminatory Policy*, Greenville News (February 16, 2017), https://www.greenvilleonline.com/story/news/education/2017/02/16/bju-regains-nonprofit-status-17-years-after-dropped-discriminatory-policy/98009170

Cate, Fred H., *The Changing Face of Privacy Protection in the European Union and the United States*, 33 Ind. L. Rev. 173 (1999)

Charo, R. Alta, *Vigilante Injustice – Deputizing and Weaponizing the Public to Stop Abortions*, N. Eng. J. Med. (October 14, 2021), https://www.nejm.org/doi/full/10.1056/NEJMp2114886

Chemerinsky, Erwin, *Rethinking State Action*, 80 Nw. U. L. Rev 503 (1985)

Cherlin, Andrew J., *Rising Nonmarital First Childbearing Among College-Educated Women: Evidence from Three National Studies*, Proc. Nat'l Acad. Scis., June 25, 2021, at 2, https://www.pnas.org/doi/full/10.1073/pnas.2109016118

Citron, Danielle Keats & Daniel J. Solove, *Privacy Harms*, 102 B.U. L. Rev. 793 (2022)

Clark, Bradford R., *Domesticating Sole Executive Agreements,* 93 Va. L. Rev. 1573 (2007)

Cnaan, Ram A. & Stephanie C. Boddie, *Charitable Choice and Faith-Based Welfare: A Call for Social Work*, 47 Soc. Work 224 (2002)

Collins, Allison L., *"I Will Not Pronounce You Husband and Husband": Justice and the Justice of the Peace*, 61 Ala. L. Rev. 847 (2010)

Collins, Lois M., *Israel Must Recognize Marriages Performed Online Through Utah County Portal*, Deseret News (March 17, 2023), https://www.deseret.com/u-s-world/2023/3/17/23644985/israel-must-recognize-marriages-performed-online-by-utah-county

Cook, Tony et al., *Indiana Governor Signs Amended "Religious Freedom" Law*, USA Today (April 2, 2015), http://www.usatoday.com/story/news/nation/2015/04/02/indiana-religious-freedom-law-deal-gay-discrimination/70819106

Cross, Christina, Opinion, *The Myth of the Two-Parent Home*, N.Y. Times (December 9, 2019), https://www.nytimes.com/2019/12/09/opinion/two-parent-family.html

Dallas, Kelsey, *How Should Black Churches Respond to the Fight for LGBTQ Rights?*, Deseret News (April 30, 2022), https://www.deseret.com/faith/2022/4/30/23045434/how-should-the-black-church-respond-to-the-fight-for-lgbtq-rights-gay-transgender

Dallas, Kelsey, *Is the "DEFCON 3 Culture War" over Religious Freedom Bills Coming to an End?*, DeseretNews (May 15, 2021), https://www.deseret.com/2021/5/15/22421195/is-the-culture-war-over-state-level-religious-freedom-bills-coming-to-an-end-rfra-first-amendment

Dane, Perry, *"Omalous" Autonomy*, 2004 BYU L. Rev. 1715

Daniels, John D., *The Indian Population of North America in 1492*, 49 Wm. & Mary Q. 298 (1992)

DeForrest, Mark Edward, *An Overview and Evaluation of State Blaine Amendments: Origins, Scope, and First Amendment Concerns*, 26 Harv. J.L. & Pub. Pol'y 551 (2003)

Dent, Jr., George W., *Religion, Morality and Democracy: New Learning, New Challenges*, 2 Geo. J.L. & Pub. Pol'y 401 (2004)

Deparle, Jason, *111 Held in St. Patrick's AIDS Protest*, N.Y. Times, December 11, 1989, at B3

Dreisbach, Daniel L., *A New Perspective on Jefferson's Views on Church-State Relations: The Virginia Statute for Establishing Religious Freedom in Its Legislative Context*, 35 Am. J. Legal Hist. 172 (1991)

Dreisbach, Daniel L., *Thomas Jefferson and Bills Number 82–86 of the Revision of the Laws of Virginia, 1776–1786: New Light on the Jeffersonian Model of Church-State Relations*, 69 N.C. L. Rev. 159 (1990)

Epstein, Carl H., *An Extended Essay on Church Autonomy*, 22 Federalist Soc'y Rev. 244 (2021)

Epstein, Richard A., Citizens United v. FEC: *The Constitutional Right That Big Corporations Should Have but Do Not Want*, 34 Harv. J.L. & Pub. Pol'y 639 (2011)

Esbeck, Carl H., *Dissent and Disestablishment: The Church-State Settlement in the Early American Republic*, 2004 BYU L. Rev. 1385

Esbeck, Carl H., *Government Regulation of Religiously Based Social Services: The First Amendment Considerations*, 19 Hastings Const. L.Q. 343 (1992)

Esbeck, Carl H., *The Establishment Clause as a Structural Restraint on Government Power*, 84 Iowa L. Rev. 1 (1998)

Esbeck, Carl H., *The Establishment Clause as a Structural Restraint: Validations and Ramifications*, 18 J.L. & Pol'y 445 (2002)

Esbeck, Carl H., *The* Lemon *Test: Should It Be Retained, Reformulated or Rejected?*, 4 Notre Dame J.L. Ethics & Pub. Pol'y 513 (1990)

Eskridge, Jr., William N., *A Jurisprudence of "Coming Out": Religion, Homosexuality, and Collisions of Liberty and Equality in America*, 106 Yale L.J. 2411 (1997)

Estlund, Cynthia L., *Free Speech and Due Process in the Workplace,* 71 Ind. L.J. 101 (1995)

Farhi, Paul, *PBS Bans New Religious Programming, Allows Existing Shows to Continue Airing*, Wash. Post (June 17, 2009), http://www.washingtonpost.com/wp-dyn/content/article/2009/06/16/AR2009061603201.html

Farhi, Paul, *PBS Stations Weigh Loss of Affiliation over Religious Content,* Wash. Post (May 16, 2009), http://www.washingtonpost.com/wp-dyn/content/article/2009/05/15/AR2009051503430.html

Feldman, Noah, *The Intellectual Origins of the Establishment Clause*, 77 N.Y.U. L. Rev. 346 (2002)

Feldman, Stephen M., *Divided We Fall: Religion, Politics, and the* Lemon *Entanglements Prong*, 7 First Amend. L. Rev. 253 (2009)

Fields, Jonathan E., *Forbidden Provisions in Prenuptial Agreements: Legal and Practical Considerations for the Matrimonial Lawyer*, 21 J. Am. Acad. Matrim. Laws. 413 (2008)

Fishman, James J., *The Development of Nonprofit Corporation Law and an Agenda for Reform*, 34 Emory L.J. 617 (1985)

Francis, Mike, *Coming to VA Cemetery Headstones: The Sandhill Crane*, Oregonian (July 1, 2013), http://www.oregonlive.com/pacific-northwest-news/index.ssf/2013/07/coming_to_va_cemetery_headston.html

Freedman, Samuel G., *A Man's Existentialism, Construed as Blasphemy*, N.Y. Times (March 20, 2009), https://www.nytimes.com/2009/03/21/us/21religion.html

Garnett, Richard W., *A Quiet Faith? Taxes, Politics, and the Privatization of Religion*, 42 B.C. L. Rev. 771 (2001)

Gedicks, Frederick Mark, *An Unfirm Foundation: The Regrettable Indefensibility of Religious Exemptions*, 20 U. Ark. Little Rock L.J. 555 (1998)

Goodstein, Laurie & Neela Banerjee, *Obama's Talk Fuels Easter Sermons*, N.Y. Times, March 23, 2008, at A1

Graham, Ruth, *Christian Schools Boom in a Revolt Against Curriculum and Pandemic Rules*, N.Y. Times (October 19, 2021), https://www.nytimes.com/2021/10/19/us/christian-schools-growth.html

Graham, Ruth, *Vaccine Resisters Seek Religious Exemptions. But What Counts as Religious?*, N.Y. Times (September 15, 2021), https://www.nytimes.com/2021/09/11/us/covid-vaccine-religion-exemption.html

Green, Steven K., *Justice David Josiah Brewer and the "Christian Nation" Maxim*, 63 Alb. L. Rev. 427 (1999)

Greenberg-Kobrin, Michelle, *Civil Enforceability of Religious Prenuptial Agreements*, 32 Colum. J.L. & Soc. Probs. 359 (1999)

Gross, Jenny & Maria Cramer, *The Latest Issue in Divorces: Who Gets the Embryos?*, N.Y. Times (April 3, 2021), https://www.nytimes.com/2021/04/03/health/IVF-frozen-embryo-disputes.html

Hamilton, Marci A., *The Endorsement Factor*, 43 Ariz. St. L.J. 349 (2011)

Hapiuk, Jr., William J., Note, *Of Kitsch and Kachinas: A Critical Analysis of the Indian Arts and Crafts Act of 1990*, 53 Stan. L. Rev. 1009 (2001)

Hardy, B. Carmon, *That "Same Old Question of Polygamy and Polygamous Living," Some Recent Findings Regarding Nineteenth and Early Twentieth-Century Mormon Polygamy*, 73 Utah Hist. Q. 212 (2005)

Harris, Anne-Marie G., *A Survey of Federal and State Public Accommodations Statutes: Evaluating Their Effectiveness in Cases of Retail Discrimination*, 13 Va. J. Soc. Pol'y & L. 331 (2006)

Harris, Séan Alonzo, *The Last Shakers*, Deseret News (March 24, 2022), https://www.deseret.com/faith/2022/3/24/22989812/the-last-shakers-sabbathday-lake-maine-shaker-village

Hastings, Sarah J., *Cinderella's New Dress: A Better Organizational Option for Churches and Other Small Nonprofits*, 55 Drake L. Rev. 813 (2007)

Heinsz, Timothy J., *The Revised Uniform Arbitration Act: Modernizing, Revising, and Clarifying Arbitration Law*, 2001 J. Disp. Resol. 1

Hewlett, Richard G., *The Creation of the Dioceses of Washington and Washington National Cathedral*, 71 Anglican & Episcopal Hist. 350 (2002)

Ho, Jeremiah A., *Once We're Done Honeymooning:* Obergefell v. Hodges, *Incrementalism, and Advances for Sexual Orientation and Anti-Discrimination*, 104 Ky. L.J. 207 (2016)

Huhn, Wilson R., *The State Action Doctrine and the Principle of Democratic Choice*, 34 Hofstra L. Rev. 1379 (2006)

Johnson, Stephen D., Joseph B. Tamney & Ronald Burton, *Pat Robertson: Who Supported His Candidacy for President?*, 28 J. Sci. Study Religion 387 (1989)

Jonassen, Frederick B., *"So Help Me?": Religious Expression and Artifacts in the Oath of Office and the Courtroom Oath*, 12 Cardozo Pub. L. Pol'y & Ethics J. 303 (2014)

Kaysen, Ronda, *Condo Tower to Rise Where Muslim Community Center Was Proposed*, N.Y. Times (May 12, 2017), https://www.nytimes.com/2017/05/12/realestate/muslim-museum-world-trade-center.html

Kazin, Michael, *The American People and the New Deal*, 1 Fed. Hist. J. 1 (2009)

Kesavan, Vasan, *The Three Tiers of Federal Law*, 100 Nw. U. L. Rev. 1479 (2006)

Kimura, Ken, Note, *Legitimacy Model for the Interpretation of Plurality Decisions*, 77 Cornell L. Rev. 1593 (1992)

Klosowski, Thorin, *The State of Consumer Data Privacy Laws in the US (and Why It Matters)*, N.Y. Times: Wirecutter (September 6, 2021), https://www.nytimes.com/wirecutter/blog/state-of-privacy-laws-in-us

Knaplund, Kristine S., *Assisted Reproductive Technology: The Legal Issues*, Prob. & Prop., March/April 2014, 48

Koch, Alexander, Chris Brierley, Mark M. Maslin & Simon L. Lewis, *Earth System Impacts of the European Arrival and Great Dying in the Americas after 1492*, 208 Quarternary Sci. Rev. 13 (2019)

Kohn, Sally, *When Minorities Demand Equal Respect*, Atlantic (November 13, 2015), https://www.theatlantic.com/politics/archive/2015/11/the-revealing-roots-of-political-correctness/415812

Kroll, Daniel, *Faith-Based Arbitration: First Amendment Freedom or Major Concern?*, Colum. Undergraduate L. Rev. (January 8, 2023), https://www.culawreview.org/journal/faith-based-arbitration-first-amendment-freedom-or-major-concern

Kuhlmann, Fred L., *Communications to Clergymen—When Are They Privileged?*, 2 Val. U. L. Rev. 265 (1968)

Laycock, Douglas, *Continuity and Change in the Threat to Religious Liberty: The Reformation Era and the Late Twentieth Century*, 80 Minn. L. Rev. 1047 (1996)

Laycock, Douglas, *The Wedding-Vendor Cases*, 41 Harv. J.L. & Pub. Pol'y 49 (2018)

Laycock, Douglas, *Towards a General Theory of the Religion Clauses: The Case of Church Labor Relations and the Right to Church Autonomy*, 81 Colum. L. Rev. 1373 (1981)

Levinson, Martin H., *Indexing the Religious Beliefs of America's Founders*, 69 ETC Rev. Gen. Semantics 384 (2012)

Lipkin, Robert Justin, *Reconstructing the Public Square*, 24 Cardozo L. Rev. 2025 (2003)

Lockerbie, Brad, *Race and Religion: Voting Behavior and Political Attitudes*, 94 Soc. Sci. Q. 1145 (2013)

Lund, Christopher C., *Religious Liberty after* Gonzales: *A Look at State RFRAs*, 55 S.D. L. Rev. 466 (2010)

Lupu, Ira C., Hobby Lobby *and the Dubious Enterprise of Religious Exemptions*, 38 Harv. J.L. & Gender 35 (2015)

Lusty, Kathryn, Note, *Proselytizers, Pamphleteers, Pests, and Other First Amendment Champions:* Watchtower Bible and Tract Society of New York, Inc. v. Village of Stratton, 18 BYU J. Pub. L. 229 (2003)

Marshall, William P., *The Case Against the Constitutionally Compelled Free Exercise Exemption*, 40 Case W. Res. L. Rev. 357 (1989)

Maslin, Janet, Movie Review, The People v. Larry Flynt, N.Y. Times (December 27, 1996), https://archive.nytimes.com/www.nytimes.com/library/film/flynt.html

McClellan, Melissa, Note, *Faith and Federalism: Do Charitable Choice Provisions Preempt State Nondiscrimination Employment Law?*, 61 Wash. & Lee L. Rev. 1437 (2004)

McConnell, Michael W., Essay, *Is There Still a "Catholic Question" in America? Reflections on John F. Kennedy's Speech to the Houston Ministerial Association*, 86 Notre Dame L. Rev. 1635 (2011)

McConnell, Michael W. & Richard A. Posner, *An Economic Approach to Issues of Religious Freedom*, 56 U. Chi. L. Rev. 1 (1989)

Medford, Roberta, Opinion, *In Theory: The IRS Gave Nonprofit Status to a Satanic Church. Will All Hell Break Loose?*, L.A. Times (July 2, 2019), https://www.latimes.com/socal/burbank-leader/opinion/tn-blr-me-intheory-20190702-story.html

Mellen, Ruby, *The History of Meetings Between U.S. Presidents and Pontiffs*, Wash. Post (October 29, 2021), https://www.washingtonpost.com/world/interactive/2021/biden-francis-popes-presidents

Mervosh, Sarah, *A Religious Charter School Faces Pushback from the Charter School Movement Itself*, N.Y. Times (June 8, 2023), https://www.nytimes.com/2023/06/08/us/oklahoma-religious-charter-school.html

Middlebrook, David O., *Pastoral Confidentiality: An Ethical and Legal Responsibility*, Assemblies God (February 2, 2010), https://news.ag.org/en/Features/Pastoral-Confidentiality-An-Ethical-and-Legal-Responsibility

Moorman, Sara M. & Megumi Inoue, *Persistent Problems in End-of-Life Planning among Young- and Middle-Aged American Couples*, 68 J. Gerontology Series B Psych. Scis. & Soc. Scis. 97 (2013)

Moran, Greg, *Soledad Cross Case Concludes, Leaving Memorial in Place*, San Diego Union-Trib. (September 8, 2016), https://www.sandiegouniontribune.com/sdut-soledad-final-2016sep08-story.html

Morrissey, Daniel J., *The Separation of Church and State: An American-Catholic Perspective*, 47 Cath. U. L. Rev. 1 (1997)

Nadler, Ben, *Controversial Georgia "Religious Liberties" Bill Stalls*, AP (March 4, 2019), https://apnews.com/article/b588b00d0728401d95e42bcb39749cdd

Natelson, Robert G., *The Original Meaning of the Establishment Clause*, 14 Wm. & Mary Bill Rts. J. 73 (2005)

Newport, Frank, *Personal Religiosity and Attitudes Toward Abortion*, Gallup (May 13, 2022), https://news.gallup.com/opinion/polling-matters/392648/personal-religiosity-attitudes-toward-abortion.aspx

Newport, Frank, *The Religion of the Supreme Court Justices*, Gallup (April 8, 2022), https://news.gallup.com/opinion/polling-matters/391649/religion-supreme-court-justices.aspx

Newport, Frank & Lydia Saad, *Religion, Politics Inform Americans' Views on Abortion*, Gallup (April 3, 2006), http://www.gallup.com/poll/22222/religion-politics-inform-americans-views-abortion.aspx

Nuar, Marie, *Addressing the Difficult Questions*, 7 J. World Christianity 47 (2017)

O'Hara, James B., *The Modern Corporation Sole*, 93 Dick. L. Rev. 23 (1988)

Olds, Kelly, *Privatizing the Church: Disestablishment in Connecticut and Massachusetts*, 102 J. Pol. Econ. 277 (1994)

Oman, Nathan B., *Natural Law and the Rhetoric of Empire:* Reynolds v. United States, *Polygamy, and Empire*, 88 Wash. U. L. Rev. 671 (2011)

Opinion Letters, *College Campuses: Are They Too P.C.?*, N.Y. Times (August 14, 2019), https://www.nytimes.com/2019/08/14/opinion/letters/college-diversity.html

Paglia, Camille, *Religion and the Arts in America*, Arion, Spring/Summer 2007, at 1

Pahwa, Nitish, *A Historic Anti-Discrimination Bill in California Sparked Backlash. But the Controversy Isn't What It Seems.*, Slate (September 21, 2023), https://slate.com/news-and-politics/2023/09/california-anti-caste-discrimination-bill-hindu-nationalism-hindutva.html

Pascoe, Peggy, *Race, Gender, and Intercultural Relations: The Case of Interracial Marriage*, 12 Frontiers J. Women Stud. 5 (1991)

Paulsen, Michael Stokes, *The Irrepressible Myth of* Marbury, 101 Mich. L. Rev. 2706 (2003)

Pawelski, James G. et al., *The Effects of Marriage, Civil Union, and Domestic Partnership Laws on the Health and Well-Being of Children*, 118(1) Pediatrics 349 (2006)

Pelley, Virginia, *What Is the Divorce Rate in America?*, Fatherly (last updated July 4, 2022), https://www.fatherly.com/life/what-is-divorce-rate-america

Perry, Michael J., *Religious Arguments in Public Political Debate*, 29 Loy. L.A. L. Rev. 1421 (1996)

Perry, Michael J., *Toward an Ecumenical Politics*, 60 Geo. Wash. L. Rev. 599 (1992)

Peterson, Larry R. & Armand L. Mauss, *Religion and the "Right to Life": Correlates of Opposition to Abortion*, 37 Socio. Analysis 243 (1976)

Pearce, Joseph, Opinion, *How the Modernists Made "Ecumenical" a Dirty Word*, Crisis Mag. (November 26, 2019), https://crisismagazine.com/opinion/how-the-modernists-made-ecumenical-a-dirty-word

Pierard, Richard V., *Billy Graham and the U.S. Presidency*, 22 J. Church & St. 107 (1980)

Pitofsky, Robert, *Father Robert F. Drinan*, 95 Geo. L.J. 1721 (2007)

Povich, Elaine S., *State Tax Credits Help Turn Old Churches into Taxable Property*, Stateline (February 2, 2016), https://stateline.org/2016/02/02/state-tax-credits-help-turn-old-churches-into-taxable-property

Prosser, William L., *Privacy*, 48 Cal. L. Rev. 383 (1960)

Qin, Amy, *California Could Become the First State to Ban Caste Bias as Prejudices Linger*, N.Y. Times (September 8, 2023), https://www.nytimes.com/2023/09/08/us/california-caste-discrimination.html

Qin, Amy, *Newsom Vetoes Bill Banning Caste Discrimination*, N.Y. Times, (October 7, 2023), https://www.nytimes.com/2023/10/07/us/california-caste-discrimination.html

Rabe, Lee Ann, *A Rose by Any Other Name: School Prayer Redefined as a Moment of Silence Is Still Unconstitutional*, 82 Denv. U. L. Rev. 57 (2004)

Radio Censorship and the Federal Communications Commission, Note, 39 Colum. L. Rev. 447 (1939)

Raines, Howell, *A Provocative Candidate*, N.Y. Times, November 4, 1983, at A1

Rauch, Jonathan, *Meeting in the Middle on Religious and LGBTQ Rights*, Deseret News (May 4, 2021), https://www.deseret.com/2021/5/4/22417652/meeting-in-the-middle-religious-freedom-lgbtq-rights-fairness-for-all-equality-act

Rauch, Jonathan & Peter Wehner, Opinion, *We Can Find Common Ground on Gay Rights and Religious Liberty: It Does Not Have to Be All or Nothing*, N.Y. Times (June 22, 2020), https://www.nytimes.com/2020/06/22/opinion/gay-rights-religious-liberty.html

Root, Jennifer C. & Norman H. Wright, *Classifying State Sales Tax Exemptions for Religious Organizations*, 11 J. of Tax'n of Exempt Orgs. 279 (2000)

Rubenfeld, Jed, *Antidisestablishmentarianism: Why RFRA Really Was Unconstitutional*, 95 Mich. L. Rev. 2347 (1997)

Ryan, Meghan J., *Can the IRS Silence Religious Organizations?*, 40 Ind. L. Rev. 73 (2007)

Sagers, Christian, Opinion, *Are Latter-day Saint Voters Turning Blue?*, Deseret News (May 12, 2021), https://www.deseret.com/opinion/2021/5/12/22432312/latter-day-saint-voters-turning-blue-mormon-trump-republican-democrat

Sarabyn, Kelly, *Free Speech at Private Universities*, 39 J.L. & Educ. 145 (2010)

Sataline, Suzanne, *Obama Pastors' Sermons May Violate Tax Laws*, Wall St. J. (March 10, 2008), http://www.wsj.com/articles/SB120511457633523621

Scharffs, Brett G., *The Autonomy of Church and State*, 2004 BYU L. Rev. 1217

Schwartz, Jeremy & Jessica Priest, *Churches Are Breaking the Law and Endorsing Elections, Experts Say. The IRS Looks the Other Way*, Tex. Trib. (October 30, 2022), https://www.texastribune.org/2022/10/30/johnson-amendment-elections-irs

Schwarzschild, Maimon, *Religion and Public Debate in Liberal Society: Always Oil and Water or Sometimes More Like Rum and Coca-Cola?*, 30 San Diego L. Rev. 903 (1993), 854

Scott, David W., *Religiosity in* South Park*: Struggles over Institutional and Personal Piety Among Residents of a "Redneck Town"*, 10 J. Media & Religion 152 (2011), 815.1

Seavey, Warren A., Comment, *Dismissal of Students: "Due Process"*, 70 Harv. L. Rev. 1406 (1957)

Shah, Tim & Tom Farr, Opinion, *Defending Religion in the Public Square*, N.Y. Times (December 27, 2011), http://www.nytimes.com/roomfordebate/2011/12/22/is-americans-religious-freedom-under-threat/defending-religion-in-the-public-square

Shannon, Peter, *Deference or Neutral Principles: The Dual Approach by Civil Courts to Ecclesiastical Disputes*, 49 Canon L. Soc'y Am. Proc. 105 (1987)

Shapiro, Edward, *World War II and American Jewish Identity*, 10 Mod. Judaism 65 (1990)

Shipler, David, *The Faustian Bargain Between Church and State*, Atlantic (May 7, 2015), http://www.theatlantic.com/politics/archive/2015/05/the-faustian-bargain-between-church-and-state/392630

Shippee, R. Seth, *"Blessed Are the Peacemakers": Faith-Based Approaches to Dispute Resolution*, 9 ILSA J. Int'l & Compar. L. 237 (2002)

Sill, John, *The Enforcement of Premarital Agreements at the International Level*, 27 J. Am. Acad. Matrimonial Laws. 245 (2015)

Singh, Kanishka, *California Moves Closer to Historic Caste Discrimination Ban*, Reuters (August 29, 2023), https://www.reuters.com/world/us/california-moves-closer-historic-caste-discrimination-ban-2023-08-29

Slabaugh, Elyse, Note, *Dignity, Deference, and Discrimination: An Analysis of Religious Freedom in America's Prisons*, 49 BYU L. Rev. 269 (2023)

Smietana, Bob, *For Some Churches, Paying Back PPP Loans Is Better than Forgiveness*, Religion News Serv., https://religionnews.com/2021/11/02/for-some-churches-paying-back-ppp-loans-is-better-than-forgiveness (November 2, 2021)

Smith, Starita, *Keep Religion out of Public Schools*, Progressive Mag. (August 17, 2005), http://www.progressive.org/media_mpsa1705

Stack, Liam, *Catholic Diocese of Buffalo Will Submit to Government Oversight*, N.Y. Times (October 25, 2022), https://www.nytimes.com/2022/10/25/nyregion/catholic-diocese-buffalo-attorney-general.html

Stanley, Erik W., *LBJ, the IRS, and Churches: The Unconstitutionality of the Johnson Amendment in Light of Recent Supreme Court Precedent*, 24 Regent U. L. Rev. 237 (2012)

Stark, Rodney, *The Rise and Fall of Christian Science*, 13 J. Contemp. Religion 189 (1998)

Stephens, Bret, Opinion, *Diversity, Inclusion and Anti-Excellence*, N.Y. Times (August 2, 2019), https://www.nytimes.com/2019/08/02/opinion/university-campus-diveristy-inclusion-free-speech.html

Stone, Geoffrey R., *Content-Neutral Restrictions*, 54 U. Chi. L. Rev. 46 (1987)

Strom, Stephanie, *The Political Pulpit*, N.Y. Times, September 30, 2011, at B1

Taylor, Barry W., *Diversion of Church Funds to Personal Use: State, Federal and Private Sanctions*, 73 J. Crim. L. & Criminology 1204 (1982)

Taylor, Jessica, *True Believer? Why Donald Trump Is the Choice of the Religious Right*, NPR (September 13, 2015), https://www.npr.org/sections/itsallpolitics/2015/09/13/439833719/true-believer-why-donald-trump-is-the-choice-of-the-religious-right

Teachout, Zephyr, *The Historical Roots of* Citizens United v. FEC: *How Anarchists and Academics Accidentally Created Corporate Speech Rights*, 5 Harv. L. & Pol'y Rev. 163 (2011)

Turley, Jonathan, *Laying Hands on Religious Racketeers: Applying Civil RICO to Fraudulent Religious Solicitation*, 29 Wm. & Mary L. Rev. 441 (1988)

Tyler, George, *The Reciprocal Translation Proviso: An Alternative Approach to Public Reason*, 11 Pol. & Religion 717 (2018)

Tyner, Mitchell A., *Religious Freedom Issues in Domestic Relations Law*, 8 BYU J. Pub. L. 457 (1994)

Volf, William, *Mormon Polygamy in the Nineteenth Century: The Practice of "The Principle" in Reality*, 15 Neb. Anthropologist 39 (1999)

Volokh, Eugene, *Polygamous Foreign Marriages under U.S. Law* (November 5, 2014), Wash. Post, https://www.washingtonpost.com/news/volokh-conspiracy/wp/2014/11/05/polygamous-foreign-marriages-under-u-s-law

Wadlington, Walter, *The* Loving *Case: Virginia's Anti-miscegenation Statute in Historical Perspective*, 52 Va. L. Rev. 1189 (1966)

Walsh, James, *Tax Treatment of the Church of Scientology in the United States and the United Kingdom*, 19 Suffolk Transnat'l L. Rev. 331 (1995)

Walter, Nicholas, *Religious Arbitration in the United States and Canada*, 52 Santa Clara L. Rev. 501 (2012)

Warmflash, Lawrence M., *The New York Approach to Enforcing Religious Marriage Contracts: From* Avitzur *to the* Get *Statute*, 50 Brook. L. Rev. 229 (1984)

Warren, Samuel D. & Louis D. Brandeis, *The Right to Privacy*, 4 Harv. L. Rev. 193 (1890)

Weil, Julie Zauzmer, *A Conservative Christian Group is Pushing Bible Classes in Public Schools Nationwide – and It's Working*, Wash. Post (May 8, 2019), https://www.washingtonpost.com/local/social-issues/a-conservative-christian-group-is-pushing-bible-classes-in-public-schools-nationwide--and-its-working/2019/05/08/f3bb490e-39e8-11e9-a06c-3ec8ed509d15_story.html

Weinberger, Lael, *The Limits of Church Autonomy*, 98 Notre Dame L. Rev. 1254 (2023)

West, Jason, Opinion, *In Defense of Ecumenism*, Crisis Mag. (December 10, 2019), https://crisismagazine.com/opinion/in-defense-of-ecumenism

Wheeler, David R., *Gay Marriage and the Future of Evangelical Colleges*, Atlantic (July 14, 2015), http://www.theatlantic.com/education/archive/2015/07/evangelical-colleges-struggle-gay-marriage-ruling/398306

Whitfield, Stephen J., The Preacher and the Presidents: Billy Graham in the White House *by Nancy Gibbs and Michael Duffy*, 123 Pol. Sci. Q. 523 (2008) (book review)

Wilcox, W. Bradford, *The Evolution of Divorce*, 1 Nat'l Aff. 81 (2009)

Wilson, Robin Fretwell, *Summary of the Utah Compromise* (March 24, 2015), https://papers.ssrn.com/sol3/papers.cfm?abstract_id=2584543

Wilson, Robin Fretwell, *The Calculus of Accommodation: Contraception, Abortion, Same-Sex Marriage, and Other Clashes Between Religion and the State*, 53 B.C. L. Rev. 1417 (2012)

Wilson, Robin Fretwell, *When Governments Insulate Dissenters from Social Change: What* Hobby Lobby *and Abortion Conscience Clauses Teach about Specific Exemptions*, 48 UC Davis L. Rev. 703 (2014)

Electronic Sources

16 Striking Findings from 2016, Pew Rsch. Ctr. (December 21, 2016), https://www.pewresearch.org/fact-tank/2016/12/21/16-striking-findings-from-2016

2020 Christian Coalition Voter Guide: Presidential Election, Christian Coal. of Am., https://cc.org/wp-content/uploads/2020/10/2020-Voter-Guide-President-1-sided_N.pdf

2021 Hate Crime Statistics, Dep't of Just., https://www.justice.gov/hatecrimes/2021-hate-crime-statistics (last visited September 30, 2023)

2022 Hate Crime Statistics, Dep't of Just., https://www.justice.gov/hatecrimes/hate-crime-statistics (last visited September 30, 2023)

2022 Report on International Religious Freedom: Afghanistan, U.S. Dep't State (2022), https://www.state.gov/reports/2022-report-on-international-religious-freedom/afghanistan

2022 Service Year Report of Jehovah's Witnesses Worldwide, Jehovah's Witnesses, https://www.jw.org/en/library/books/2022-Service-Year-Report-of-Jehovahs-Witnesses-Worldwide/2022-Grand-Totals (last visited September 30, 2023)

50-State Comparison: Free and Compulsory School Age Requirements, Educ. Comm'n States (August 2020), https://reports.ecs.org/comparisons/free-and-compulsory-school-age-requirements-all

Selected Bibliography

Abortion, Gallup, https://news.gallup.com/poll/1576/Abortion.aspx (last visited September 30, 2023)

About AU, Ams. United for Separation Church & State, https://www.au.org/about-au (last visited September 30, 2023)

About, Catholic Sun, https://www.catholicsun.org (last visited September 30, 2023)

About, Christian Sci. Monitor, https://www.csmonitor.com/About (last visited September 30, 2023)

About Congressional Apportionment, U.S. Census Bureau, https://www.census.gov/topics/public-sector/congressional-apportionment/about.html (last visited September 30, 2023)

About, EEW, https://www.eewmagazineonline.com/about-eew-magazine (last visited September 30, 2023)

About, Freedom from Religion Foundation, https://ffrf.org/about (last visited September 30, 2023)

About, IRF Summit, https://irfsummit.org/about (last visited September 30, 2023)

About, Jewish Press, https://www.jewishpress.com/about

About NLRB: 1947 Taft-Hartley Substantive Provisions, Nat'l Lab. Rels. Bd., https://www.nlrb.gov/about-nlrb/who-we-are/our-history/1947-taft-hartley-substantive-provisions (last visited September 30, 2023)

About NLRB: Collective Bargaining (Section 8(d) & 8(b)(3)), Natl'l Lab. Rels. Bd., https://www.nlrb.gov/about-nlrb/rights-we-protect/the-law/collective-bargaining-section-8d-8b3 (last visited September 2023)

About NLRB: Employer/Union Rights and Obligations, Nat'l Lab. Rels. Bd., https://www.nlrb.gov/about-nlrb/rights-we-protect/your-rights/employer-union-rights-and-obligations (last visited September 30, 2023)

About NLRB: Jurisdictional Standards, Nat'l Lab. Rels. Bd., https://www.nlrb.gov/about-nlrb/rights-we-protect/the-law/jurisdictional-standards (last visited September 30, 2023)

About REAL ID, U.S. Dep't Homeland Sec., https://www.dhs.gov/real-id/about-real-id (last updated November 16, 2022)

About Treaties, U.S. Senate, https://www.senate.gov/about/powers-procedures/treaties.htm (last visited September 30, 2023)

About Us, Deseret News, https://www.deseret.com/pages/about-us (last visited September 30, 2023)

About Us, New Voices, https://newvoices.org/about-us (last visited September 30, 2023)

About Us, Off. Int'l Religious Freedom, U.S. Dep't State, https://www.state.gov/about-us-office-of-international-religious-freedom (last visited September 30, 2023)

Adams, J. Stuart & Robin Fretwell Wilson, *Protecting Religious Liberty Requires Protections for All*, Religious Freedom Inst. (July 12, 2016), https://religiousfreedominstitute.org/2016-7-12-protecting-religious-liberty-requires-protections-for-all

ADL Hate Crime Map, Anti-Defamation League, https://www.adl.org/resources/tools-to-track-hate/hate-crime-map (last visited September 30, 2023)

After Roe *Fell: Abortion Laws by State*, Ctr. for Reproductive Rts., https://reproductiverights.org/maps/abortion-laws-by-state (last visited September 30, 2023)

Al Sharpton, Britannica, https://www.britannica.com/biography/Al-Sharpton (last updated September 29, 2023)

Am. Bar Ass'n, Res. 113A, *Court's Use of International Law or Doctrine of Particular Religion* (August 9, 2011), https://www.americanbar.org/content/dam/aba/administrative/crsj/religious-freedom.pdf

Amdt1.2.2.1 Introduction to the Historical Background on the Religion Clauses, Const. Annotated, https://constitution.congress.gov/browse/essay/amdt1-2-2-1/ALDE_00013268 (last visited September 30, 2023)

Amdt1.2.2.3 State-Established Religion in the Colonies, Const. Annotated, https://constitution.congress.gov/browse/essay/amdt1-2-2-3/ALDE_00013270 (last visited September 30, 2023)

America's Islamic Radio, https://americasislamicradio.com/?fbclid=IwAR0_lgtEJJ0dhFoNnKvTu9nMRclYWeKpxaBvdr4XWJMeUwuf6QjRXRaN0Rk (last visited September 30, 2023)

America's Treasures Grants, Hist. Preservation Fund, Nat'l Park Serv., https://www.nps.gov/subjects/historicpreservationfund/save-americas-treasures-grants.htm (last visited September 25, 2023)

AmeriCorps, *Volunteering and Civic Life in America Research Summary*, https://americorps.gov/sites/default/files/document/volunteering-civic-life-america-research-summary.pdf (last accessed September 30, 2023)

Am. Soc'y for Reprod. Med., *Oversight of Assisted Reproductive Technology* (2021), https://www.asrm.org/about-us/media-and-public-affairs/public-affairs/oversight-of-assisted-reproductive-technology (link to PDF)

Amnesty Int'l USA, *Economic, Social and Cultural Rights: Questions and Answers* (June 26, 2008), https://web.archive.org/web/20080626051117/http://www.amnestyusa.org/escr/files/escr_qa.pdf

Anti-Muslim Legislation Map, Othering & Belonging Inst. UC Berkeley, https://belonging.berkeley.edu/islamophobia/anti-muslim-legislation-map (last visited September 30, 2023)

Architectural Information, Sup. Ct. U.S., https://www.supremecourt.gov/about/archdetails.aspx (link to PDF, *Courtroom Friezes: South and North Walls*)

Armstrong, Christopher & Grant Wacker, *The Scopes Trial*, Nat'l Humans. Ctr.: TeacherServe, Divining Am., http://nationalhumanitiescenter.org/tserve/twenty/tkeyinfo/tscopes.htm (last modified October 2000)

Attitudes on Same-Sex Marriage, Pew Rsch. Ctr. (May 14, 2019), https://www.pewresearch.org/religion/fact-sheet/changing-attitudes-on-gay-marriage

Beckman, Joanne, *Religion in Post-World War II America*, Nat'l Humans. Ctr.: TeacherServe, Divining Am., http://nationalhumanitiescenter.org/tserve/twenty/tkeyinfo/trelww2.htm (last modified October 2000)

Berk, Leah Rae, *Temperance and Prohibition Era Propaganda: A Study in Rhetoric*, Brown U. Libr. for Digital Scholarship: Alcohol, Temperance & Prohibition, https://library.brown.edu/cds/temperance/essay.html (last visited September 30, 2023)

Selected Bibliography

Billy Graham: Pastor to the Presidents, Billy Graham Evangelistic Ass'n (February 17, 2023), https://billygraham.org/gallery/billy-graham-pastor-to-the-presidents

Black Churches and Gay Marriage, PBS: Religion & Ethics News Weekly (July 16, 2004), https://www.pbs.org/wnet/religionandethics/2004/07/16/july-16-2004-black-churches-and-gay-marriage/13200

Blaine Amendments in State Constitutions, Ballotpedia, https://ballotpedia.org/Blaine_amendments_in_state_constitutions (last visited September 30, 2023)

Botero, Catalina (OAS/IACHR Special Rapporteur on Freedom of Expression) et al., *Joint Declaration on Defamation of Religions, and Anti-Terrorism and Anti-Extremism Legislation* (December 9, 2008), https://www.osce.org/files/f/documents/4/b/35639.pdf

Burke, Daniel, *What Is Neil Gorsuch's Religion? It's Complicated*, CNN (March 22, 2017), https://www.cnn.com/2017/03/18/politics/neil-gorsuch-religion

Bush, President George W., *Rallying the Armies of Compassion* (January 2001), http://archives.hud.gov/reports/rally.pdf

Business Filings & Trademarks Fee Schedule, Tex. Sec'y State, https://direct.sos.state.tx.us/help/help-corp.asp?pg=fee (last visited September 30, 2023)

Byrne, Julie, *Roman Catholics and Immigration in Nineteenth Century America*, Nat'l Humans. Ctr.: TeacherServe, Divining Am., http://nationalhumanitiescenter.org/tserve/nineteen/nkeyinfo/nromcath.htm (last modified November 2000)

Cerna, Christina M., *Reflections on the Normative Status of the American Declaration of the Rights and Duties of Man*, Inter-Am. Ct. H.R. (February 2, 2009), https://www.corteidh.or.cr/tablas/r31598.pdf

Chapter 2.206 Homeschooling and School Choice, Digest of Educ. Stat., Nat'l Ctr. for Educ. Stat., https://nces.ed.gov/programs/digest/2021menu_tables.asp (last visited September 30, 2023)

Charitable Solicitation – State Requirements, IRS, https://www.irs.gov/charities-non-profits/charitable-organizations/charitable-solicitation-state-requirements (last visited September 30, 2023)

Child Welfare Info. Gateway, Children's Bureau, U.S. Dep't of Health & Hum. Servs., *Clergy as Mandatory Reporters of Child Abuse and Neglect* (April 2019), https://www.childwelfare.gov/topics/systemwide/laws-policies/statutes/clergymandated (link to PDF)

Children's Bureau, Child Welfare Info. Gateway, Dep't of Heath & Hum. Servs., *Definitions of Child Abuse and Neglect* (May 2022), https://www.childwelfare.gov/topics/systemwide/laws-policies/statutes/define (link to PDF)

Chilton Furniture Me., *The Sabbathday Lake Shakers*, YouTube (February 15, 2015), https://www.youtube.com/watch?v=8ZZbT8NVlZ8

Christian Radio, https://www.christianradio.com/stations (last visited September 30, 2023)

Christian Sci. Monitor, https://www.csmonitor.com (last visited September 30, 2023)

Churches, Integrated Auxiliaries, and Conventions or Associations of Churches, IRS, https://www.irs.gov/charities-non-profits/churches-integrated-auxiliaries-and-conventions-or-associations-of-churches (last updated April 26, 2023)

Code of Canon Law, Holy See, https://www.vatican.va/archive/cod-iuris-canonici/eng/documents/cic_lib4-cann998-1165_en.html#CHAPTER_V (last visited September 30, 2023)

Commissioners, U.S. Comm'n on Int'l Religious Freedom, https://www.uscirf.gov/commissioners (last visited September 30, 2023)

Countries of Particular Concern, Special Watch List Countries, Entities of Particular Concern, U.S. Dep't State, https://www.state.gov/countries-of-particular-concern-special-watch-list-countries-entities-of-particular-concern (last visited September 30, 2023)

CPB FAQ, Corp. for Pub. Broadcasting, https://www.cpb.org/faq#1-2 (last visited September 30, 2023)

Cultural Protection & NAGPRA, Nat'l Cong. Am. Indians, https://www.ncai.org/policy-issues/community-and-culture/cultural-protection-and-nagpra (last visited September 30, 2023), 770

Dep't of Def., DoD Instruction 1300.17, Religious Liberty in the Military Services (September 1, 2020), https://www.esd.whs.mil/Portals/54/Documents/DD/issuances/dodi/130017p.pdf

Dep't of Def., DoD Instruction 1304.28, The Appointment and Service of Chaplains (May 12, 2021), https://www.esd.whs.mil/Portals/54/Documents/DD/issuances/dodi/130428p.pdf

Diamant, Jeff, *Faith on the Hill*, Pew Rsch. Ctr. (January 3, 2023), https://www.pewresearch.org/religion/2023/01/03/faith-on-the-hill-2023

Dinan, John, *Constitutional Amendment Processes in the 50 States*, State Ct. Rep. (July 24, 2023), https://statecourtreport.org/our-work/analysis-opinion/constitutional-amendment-processes-50-states

Discrimination and Harassment in the Workplace, NCSL, https://www.ncsl.org/labor-and-employment/discrimination-and-harassment-in-the-workplace (last updated August 12, 2021)

Dolak, Kevin, *"Pulpit Freedom Sunday" to Defy IRS*, ABC News (September 25, 2010), http://abcnews.go.com/US/defiant-pastors-irs-pulpit-freedom-sunday/story?id=11726610

Download 2020 Voter Guides, Christian Coal. of Am., https://cc.org/download-2020-voter-guides (last visited March 31, 2023)

Duran, Khalid & Daniel Pipes, *Muslim Immigrants in the United States*, Ctr. for Immigration Stud. (August 1, 2002), http://cis.org/USMuslimImmigrants

Durham, Jr., W. Cole, et al., *Response to the UN's Call for Input to a Thematic Report: Freedom of Religion or Belief (FoRB) and Sexual Orientation and Gender Identity*, Talk About: L. & Religion (February 16, 2023), https://talkabout.iclrs.org/2023/02/16/response-to-the-uns-call-for-input

Ebel, Jonathan H., *Religion (USA)*, 1914–1918 Online: Int'l Encyclopedia First World War, https://encyclopedia.1914-1918-online.net/article/religion_usa (last visited September 30, 2023)

EEOC Comp. Man. § 2.B.I (*Threshold Issues: Partial Exemptions/Exemptions for Discrimination Based on Religion*) (May 12, 2000), https://www.eeoc.gov/laws/guidance/section-2-threshold-issues

Selected Bibliography

EEOC Comp. Man. § 12.C.1 (*Religious Discrimination: Exceptions/Religious Organizations*) (January 15, 2021), https://www.eeoc.gov/laws/guidance/section-12-religious-discrimination

Eggleston, Casey & Jason Fields, *Census Bureau's Household Pulse Survey Shows Significant Increase in Homeschooling Rates in Fall 2020*, U.S. Census Bureau (March 22, 2021), https://www.census.gov/library/stories/2021/03/homeschooling-on-the-rise-during-covid-19-pandemic.html

Eisenhower, Dwight D., *Statement by the President upon Signing Bill to Include the Words "under God" in the Pledge to the Flag*, Am. Presidency Project (June 14, 1954), https://www.presidency.ucsb.edu/documents/statement-the-president-upon-signing-bill-include-the-words-under-god-the-pledge-the-flag (last visited September 30, 2023)

Emblems of Belief, Nat'l Cemetery Admin., U.S. Dep't of Veterans Affs., http://www.cem.va.gov/hmm/emblems.asp (last visited September 25, 2023)

Employer and Employee Relationships, Seventh-day Adventist Church, https://www.adventist.org/guidelines/employer-and-employee-relationships (last visited September 30, 2023)

Equality Maps: Nondiscrimination Laws, MAP: Movement Advancement Project, https://www.lgbtmap.org/equality-maps/non_discrimination_laws

Employment: Private Employment, Unlawful Discrimination, 50 State Statutory Surveys, Westlaw 0060 Surveys 25 (database updated November 2022)

Facts and Statistics: Worldwide Church, Church Jesus Christ Latter-day Saints, https://newsroom.churchofjesuschrist.org/facts-and-statistics (last visited September 30, 2023)

Fahmy, Dalia, *Americans Are Far More Religious than Adults in Other Wealthy Nations*, Pew Rsch. Ctr. (July 31, 2018), https://www.pewresearch.org/short-reads/2018/07/31/americans-are-far-more-religious-than-adults-in-other-wealthy-nations

Fair Employment Practices Agencies (FEPAs) and Dual Filing, U.S. Equal Emp. Opportunity Comm'n, https://www.eeoc.gov/fair-employment-practices-agencies-fepas-and-dual-filing (last visited September 30, 2023)

Faith-Based and Other Neighborhood Organizations, U.S. Dep't Housing & Urb. Dev., https://www.hud.gov/program_offices/faith_based/execorders (last visited September 30, 2023)

FAQs, Nat'l Reg. of Hist. Places, Nat'l Park Serv., https://www.nps.gov/subjects/nationalregister/faqs.htm (last visited September 30, 2023)

FAQ – What's a Right to Work Law?, Nat'l Right to Work Comm. (October 1, 2019), https://nrtwc.org/faqs-right-to-work-laws

Fed. Commc'n Comm., *Religious Broadcasting* (publication date unknown), https://transition.fcc.gov/osp/inc-report/INoC-11-Religious-Broadcasting.pdf (last accessed September 30, 2023)

Filing & Other General FAQs, Tex. Sec'y State, http://www.sos.state.tx.us/corp/filingandothergeneralfaqs.shtml (last visited September 30, 2023)

Franklin Roosevelt Administration: Report on Meeting of Jewish Leaders with Roosevelt (December 8, 1942), Jewish Virtual Libr., https://www.jewishvirtuallibrary.org/report-on-meeting-of-jewish-leaders-with-roosevelt-december-1942 (last visited September 30, 2023)

Freehof, Solomon B., *American Reform Responsa (ARR) 398-401, 130. Rabbi's Prerogative to Officiate at Weddings*, Cent. Conf. Am. Rabbis, https://www.ccarnet.org/ccar-responsa/arr-398-401 (last visited September 30, 2023)

Frequently Asked Questions, IRS, https://www.irs.gov/faqs/small-business-self-employed-other-business/entities/entities-5 (last updated June 15, 2023)

Frequently Asked Questions, U.S. Dep't Interior: Indian Affs., https://www.bia.gov/frequently-asked-questions (last visited September 30, 2023)

Frequently Asked Questions & Introduction to Christian Conciliation, Inst. for Christian Conciliation, https://www.aorhope.org/icc-faq (last visited September 30, 2023)

Frequently Asked Questions: IRF Report and Countries of Particular Concern, U.S. Dep't State, https://www.state.gov/frequently-asked-questions-irf-report-and-countries-of-particular-concern (last visited September 30, 2023)

Getler, Michael, *The Mailbag: May 22, 2009*, PBS Ombudsman (May 22, 2009), http://www.pbs.org/ombudsman/2009/05/the_mailbag_7.html

Giving USA: Total U.S. Charitable Giving Declined in 2022 to $499.33 Billion Following Two Years of Record Generosity, IUPUI (June 20, 2023), https://philanthropy.iupui.edu/news-events/news-item/giving-usa:-total-u.s.-charitable-giving-declined-in-2022-to-$499.33-billion-following-two-years-of-record-generosity.html?id=422

Glossary —U.S. v. Avarez, U.S. Cts., https://www.uscourts.gov/educational-resources/educational-activities/glossary-us-v-alvarez (last visited August 30, 2023)

Guidance on Constitutionally Protected Prayer and Religious Expression in Public Elementary and Secondary Schools, U.S. Dep't Educ. (May 15, 2023), https://www2.ed.gov/policy/gen/guid/religionandschools/prayer_guidance.html?exp=1

Holmes, Kim R., *The Great Divide: The Ideological Legacies of the American and French Revolutions*, Heritage Found. (August 12, 2014), http://www.heritage.org/research/lecture/2014/08/the-great-divide-the-ideological-legacies-of-the-american-and-french-revolutions

Homeschool Laws by State, Home Sch. Legal Def. Ass'n (HSLDA), https://hslda.org/legal (last visited September 30, 2023)

How Did Scientology Start, Scientology Newsroom, https://www.scientologynews.org/faq/how-did-scientology-start.html (last visited September 30, 2023)

How to Apply for Authorization to Mail at Nonprofit Prices, Postal Explorer, USPS.com, https://pe.usps.com/businessmail101?ViewName=NonprofitApplication (last visited September 30, 2023)

Insurance Coverage by State, Resolve: Nat'l Infertility Ass'n, https://resolve.org/learn/financial-resources-for-family-building/insurance-coverage/insurance-coverage-by-state (last visited September 30, 2023)

Internal Revenue Serv., *Ministers Audit Techniques Guide* (April 23, 2009), https://www.irs.gov/businesses/small-businesses-self-employed/audit-techniques-guides-atgs (link to PDF)

Internal Revenue Serv., Pub. No. 1828, *Tax Guide for Churches & Religious Organizations*, https://www.irs.gov/pub/irs-pdf/p1828.pdf (last visited September 30, 2023)

Internal Revenue Serv., Pub. No. 4220, *Applying for 501(c)(3) Tax-Exempt Status*, https://www.irs.gov/pub/irs-pdf/p4220.pdf (last accessed September 30, 2023)

Selected Bibliography

Internal Revenue Serv., Publication 15-A, *Employer's Supplemental Tax Guide* (December 19, 2022), https://www.irs.gov/pub/irs-pdf/p15a.pdf

International Religious Freedom Reports, U.S. Dep't State, https://www.state.gov/international-religious-freedom-reports (last visited September 30, 2023)

Investor Protection Guide: Affinity Fraud, LLI: Cornell L. Sch., https://www.law.cornell.edu/wex/investor_protection_guide_affinity_fraud (last visited September 30, 2023)

Irons, Charles F., *Religion in the Civil War*, Encyclopedia Va., http://www.encyclopediavirginia.org/religion_during_the_civil_war (last modified December 7, 2020)

Jesse Jackson, Britannica, https://www.britannica.com/biography/Jesse-Jackson (last updated October 4, 2023)

John F. Kennedy, Address to the Greater Houston Ministerial Association (September 12, 1960), https://www.jfklibrary.org/learn/about-jfk/historic-speeches/address-to-the-greater-houston-ministerial-association (link to transcript) (last visited September 30, 2023)

JustServe, https://www.justserve.org (last visited September 30, 2023)

King, Jr., Martin Luther, *"I Have a Dream ... ", Speech by the Rev. Martin Luther King at the "March on Washington"* (1963), https://teachtnhistory.org/file/I%20Have%20A%20Dream%20Speech.pdf (last visited September 30, 2023)

Kishi, Katayoun, *Most Refugees Who Enter the U.S. as Religious Minorities Are Christians*, Pew Rsch. Ctr. (February 7, 2017), https://www.pewresearch.org/short-reads/2017/02/07/most-refugees-who-enter-the-u-s-as-religious-minorities-are-christians

Learn & Discover: History, Wash. Nat'l Cathedral, https://cathedral.org/discover/history (last visited September 30, 2023)

Lichter, S. Robert, Linda S. Lichter, & Daniel R. Amundson, Ctr. For Media & Pub. Affs., *Media Coverage of Religion in America 1969–1998* (April 2000), https://cmpa.gmu.edu/wp-content/uploads/2013/10/Media_Coverage_Religion_2000.pdf

Lincoln, Abraham, *Gettysburg Address Delivered at Gettysburg Pa. Nov. 19th, 1863 [n. p. n. d.]*, Libr. of Cong., https://www.loc.gov/resource/rbpe.24404500/?st=text (last visited September 30, 2023)

Lincoln, Abraham, Second Inaugural Address (March 4, 1865), https://www.nps.gov/linc/learn/historyculture/lincoln-second-inaugural.htm

Lipka, Michael, *Republicans and Democrats Agree Religion's Influence Is Waning, but Differ in Their Reactions*, Pew Rsch. Ctr. (November 15, 2019), https://www.pewresearch.org/fact-tank/2019/11/15/republicans-and-democrats-agree-religions-influence-is-waning-but-differ-in-their-reactions

Lipka, Michael, *The Most and Least Racially Diverse U.S. Religious Groups*, Pew Rsch. Ctr. (July 27, 2015), https://www.pewresearch.org/short-reads/2015/07/27/the-most-and-least-racially-diverse-u-s-religious-groups

List of Catholic Newspapers and Magazines in the United States, Wikipedia, https://en.wikipedia.org/wiki/List_of_Catholic_newspapers_and_magazines_in_the_United_States (last visited September 30, 2023)

List of NHLs by State, Nat' Hist. Landmarks, Nat'l Park Serv., https://www.nps.gov/subjects/nationalhistoriclandmarks/list-of-nhls-by-state.htm (last visited September 30, 2023)

Livingston, Gretchen, Pew Research Ctr., *The Changing Profile of Unmarried Parents* (April 25, 2018), https://www.pewresearch.org/social-trends/wp-content/uploads/sites/3/2018/04/Unmarried-Parents-Full-Report-PDF.pdf

Madison, James, *Memorial and Remonstrance Against Religious Assessments, [CA. 20 June] 1785*, Founders Online, Nat'l Archives, https://founders.archives.gov/documents/Madison/01-08-02-0163 (last visited September 30, 2023)

Marriage and Divorce, Ctrs. for Disease Control & Prevention, https://www.cdc.gov/nchs/fastats/marriage-divorce.htm (last updated April 24, 2023)

Marriage Officiant Registration, Off. City Clerk, City N.Y., https://www.cityclerk.nyc.gov/content/marriage-officiant-registration (last visited September 30, 2023)

Masci, David, *American Religious Groups Vary Widely in Their Views of Abortion*, Pew Rsch. Ctr. (January 22, 2018), https://www.pewresearch.org/short-reads/2018/01/22/american-religious-groups-vary-widely-in-their-views-of-abortion

Masci, David, *Where Major Religious Groups Stand on Abortion*, Pew Rsch. Ctr. (June 21, 2016), https://www.pewresearch.org/fact-tank/2016/06/21/where-major-religious-groups-stand-on-abortion

McElrath, Kevin, *Nearly 93% of Households with School-Age Children Report Some Form of Distance Learning During COVID-19*, U.S. Census Bureau (August 26, 2020), https://www.census.gov/library/stories/2020/08/schooling-during-the-covid-19-pandemic.html

Md. Off. of the Att'y Gen., *The State of Marriage Equality in America* (April 2015), https://www.marylandattorneygeneral.gov/Reports/The%20State%20of%20Marriage%20Equality%20in%20America%202015.pdf

Mintz, Steven, *Historical Context: The Constitution and Slavery*, Gilder Lehrman Inst. Am. Hist., https://www.gilderlehrman.org/history-resources/teaching-resource/historical-context-constitution-and-slavery (last visited September 30, 2023)

Mission & Vision: History, Wash. Nat'l Cathedral, https://cathedral.org/about/mission-vision (last visited September 30, 2023)

Montanaro, Domenico, *Congress Takes Reins of Prayer Breakfast from Secretive Christian Evangelical Group*, NPR (February 2, 2023), https://www.npr.org/2023/02/02/1153705297/congress-takes-reins-of-prayer-breakfast-from-secretive-christian-evangelical-gr

Moorhead, James Howell, *Religion in the Civil War: The Northern Perspective*, Nat'l Humans. Ctr.: TeacherServe, Divining Am., http://nationalhumanitiescenter.org/tserve/nineteen/nkeyinfo/cwnorth.htm (last modified October 2000)

More Than a Century of Signs, Signs of the Times, https://www.signstimes.com/?p=about (last visited September 30, 2023)

Movement Advancement Project & Nat'l Ctr. for Transgender Equality, *Religious Refusals in Health Care: A Prescription for Disaster* (March 2018), https://www.lgbtmap.org/file/Healthcare-Religious-Exemptions.pdf

Muhammad, Mother Tynnetta, *Nation of Islam in America: A Nation of Beauty & Peace*, Nation Islam (March 28, 1996), http://www.noi.org/noi-history

Muslim Media, Pluralism Project: Harvard U., https://pluralism.org/muslim-media (last visited September 30, 2023)

Selected Bibliography

Nat'l Ctr. for Educ. Stat., *Homeschooled Children and Reasons for Homeschooling* (May 2022), https://nces.ed.gov/programs/coe/indicator/tgk/homeschooled-children#suggested-citation (link to PDF)

Nat'l Educ. Policy Ctr., *Virtual Schools in the U.S. 2019* (Alex Molnar ed., May 2019), https://nepc.colorado.edu/sites/default/files/publications/Virtual%20Schools%202019.pdf

Nat'l Trust for Hist. Preservation, *State Historic Tax Credit Resource Guide* (January 2023), https://savingplaces.org/state-historic-tax-credits (link to PDF)

News Release, The Church of Jesus Christ of Latter-day Saints, President Uchtdorf, Other Faith Leaders Meet with President Obama on Immigration (April 15, 2014), https://newsroom.churchofjesuschrist.org/article/church-apostle-joins-other-faith-leaders-in-meeting-with-president-obama-on-immigration

N.Y. Jewish Radio, http://www.newyorkjewishradio.com (last visited September 30, 2023)

Nomination Process, Nat'l Hist. Landmarks, Nat'l Park Serv., https://www.nps.gov/subjects/nationalhistoriclandmarks/nomination-process.htm (last visited September 30, 2023)

"Nones" on the Rise, Pew Rsch. Ctr. (October 9, 2012), https://www.pewforum.org/2012/10/09/nones-on-the-rise

Nortey, Justin, *Most White Americans Who Regularly Attend Worship Services Voted for Trump in 2020*, Pew Rsch. Ctr. (August 30, 2021), https://www.pewresearch.org/fact-tank/2021/08/30/most-white-americans-who-regularly-attend-worship-services-voted-for-trump-in-2020

NSA Spying, Electronic Frontier Found., https://www.eff.org/nsa-spying (last visited September 30, 2023)

Number of Private Schools, by Religious Orientation and Community Type: 1989–90 through 2005–06, Nat'l Ctr. for Educ. Stat., https://nces.ed.gov/surveys/pss/tables/table_whs_01.asp (last visited September 30, 2023)

Off. of the Dir., Nat'l Insts. of Pub. Health, Notice No. NOT-OD-21-111, Update on Changes to NIH Requirements Regarding Proposed Human Fetal Tissue Research (April 16, 2021), https://grants.nih.gov/grants/guide/notice-files/NOT-OD-21-111.html

Office of International Religious Freedom, U.S. Dep't State, https://www.state.gov/bureaus-offices/under-secretary-for-civilian-security-democracy-and-human-rights/office-of-international-religious-freedom (last visited September 30, 2023)

Overview of Preservation Programs, Nat'l Hist. Landmarks, Nat'l Park Serv., https://www.nps.gov/subjects/nationalhistoriclandmarks/preservation-programs.htm (last visited September 30, 2023)

Privacy, State Cal. Dep't Just., https://oag.ca.gov/privacy (last visited September 30, 2023)

Online Social Security Handbook, Soc. Security Admin., https://www.ssa.gov/OP_Home/handbook/handbook.11/handbook-1130.html (last visited September 30, 2023)

Org. of Am. States & Inter-Am. Comm'n on Hum. Rts., *Informational Booklet: Petition and Case System* (2022), https://www.oas.org/en/IACHR/jsForm/?File=/en/iachr/mandate/petitions.asp (link to PDF)

Osterman, Michelle J.K., Brady E. Hamilton, Joyce A. Martin, Anne K. Driscoll & Claudia P. Valenzuela, Ctrs. for Disease Control & Prevention, *Births: Final Data for 2021*, Nat'l Vital Stat. Rep., January 31, 2023, https://www.cdc.gov/nchs/data/nvsr/nvsr72/nvsr72-01-tables.pdf

Our Ministry, Christianity Today, https://www.christianitytoday.org/who-we-are/our-ministry

Parentage Act, Unif. L. Comm'n, https://www.uniformlaws.org/committees/community-home?CommunityKey=c4f37d2d-4d20-4be0-8256-22dd73af068f (last visited September 30, 2023)

Parliamentary Taxation of Colonies, International Trade, and the American Revolution, 1763–1775, U.S. Dep't State, Off. Historian, https://history.state.gov/milestones/1750-1775/parliamentary-taxation (page retired and archived) (last visited September 30, 2023)

PBS, *PBS Editorial Standards and Policies* (later version, adopted June 24, 2011), https://publicmediaintegrity.org/wp-content/uploads/PBSEditorialStandardsandPolicies.pdf

Pew F. on Religion & Pub. Life, *Shifting Boundaries: The Establishment Clause and Government Funding of Religious Schools and Other Faith-Based Organizations* (May 2009), https://www.pewresearch.org/religion/2009/05/14/shifting-boundaries2 (link to PDF)

Pew Rsch. Ctr., *About Three-in-Ten U.S. Adults Are Now Religiously Unaffiliated* (December 14, 2021), https://www.pewresearch.org/religion/2021/12/14/about-three-in-ten-u-s-adults-are-now-religiously-unaffiliated (link to PDF)

Pew Rsch. Ctr., *America's Changing Religious Landscape* (May 12, 2015), https://www.pewforum.org/2015/05/12/americas-changing-religious-landscape (link to PDF)

Pew Rsch. Ctr., *Faith and the 2016 Campaign* (January 27, 2016), https://www.pewforum.org/2016/01/27/faith-and-the-2016-campaign (link to PDF)

Pew Rsch. Ctr., *Measuring Religion in Pew Research Center's American Trends Panel* (January 14, 2021), https://www.pewresearch.org/religion/2021/01/14/measuring-religion-in-pew-research-centers-american-trends-panel (link to PDF)

Pew Rsch. Ctr., *Modeling the Future of Religion in America* (September 13, 2022), https://www.pewresearch.org/religion/2022/09/13/modeling-the-future-of-religion-in-america (link to PDF)

Pew Rsch. Ctr., *Religion in Prisons: A 50-State Survey of Prison Chaplains* (March 22, 2012), https://www.pewforum.org/2012/03/22/prison-chaplains-what-they-do (link to PDF)

Pew Rsch. Ctr., *Religion in the News* (February 23, 2012), https://www.pewresearch.org/journalism/2012/02/23/religion-news-0/ (link to PDF)

Pew Rsch. Ctr, *Religion's Relationship to Happiness, Civic Engagement and Health Around the World* (January 31, 2019), https://www.pewresearch.org/religion/2019/01/31/religions-relationship-to-happiness-civic-engagement-and-health-around-the-world (link to PDF)

Pew Rsch. Ctr., *The Future of World Religions: Population Growth Projections, 2010–2050* (April 2, 2015), https://www.pewresearch.org/religion/2015/04/02/religious-projections-2010-2050 (link to PDF)

Pew Rsch. Ctr., *U.S. Religious Knowledge Survey* (September 2010), https://www.pewforum.org/2010/09/28/u-s-religious-knowledge-survey (link to PDF)

Pew Rsch. Ctr., *What Americans Know about Religion* (July 23, 2019), https://www.pewforum.org/2019/07/23/what-americans-know-about-religion (link to PDF)

Pew Rsch. Ctr., *Wide Gender Gap, Growing Educational Divide in Voters' Party Identification* (March 20, 2018), https://www.pewresearch.org/politics/2018/03/20/wide-gender-gap-growing-educational-divide-in-voters-party-identification (link to PDF)

Pierce, Sarah & Jessica Bolter, Migration Pol'y Inst., *Dismantling and Reconstructing the U.S. Immigration System: A Catalog of Changes under the Trump Presidency* (July 2020), https://www.migrationpolicy.org/sites/default/files/publications/MPI_US-Immigration-Trump-Presidency-Final.pdf

Plan B One-Step (1.5 Levonorgestrel) Information, U.S. Food & Drug Admin. (December 23, 2022), https://www.fda.gov/drugs/postmarket-drug-safety-information-patients-and-providers/plan-b-one-step-15-mg-levonorgestrel-information

Pre-employment Inquiries and Religious Affiliation or Beliefs, U.S. Equal Emp. Opportunity Comm'n, https://www.eeoc.gov/pre-employment-inquiries-and-religious-affiliation-or-beliefs (last visited September 30, 2023)

Press Release, FBI, Liying Lin Found Guilty of Immigration Fraud Offenses Following One-Week Jury Trail in Manhattan Federal Court (February 26, 2014), https://archives.fbi.gov/archives/newyork/press-releases/2014/liying-lin-found-guilty-of-immigration-fraud-offenses-following-one-week-jury-trial-in-manhattan-federal-court

Press Release, IACHR, IACHR and Its Special Rapporteurship for Freedom of Expression Urge the State of Nicaragua to End Persecution of the Church and to Enable a Plurality of Voices (May 27, 2022), https://www.oas.org/en/iachr/jsForm/?File=/en/iachr/media_center/preleases/2022/119.asp

Press Release, Off. Okla. Att'y Gen., Drummond Files Lawsuit Against State Virtual Charter Board Members for Violating Religious Liberty of Oklahoma Taxpayers (October 20, 2023), https://www.oag.ok.gov/articles/drummond-files-lawsuit-against-state-virtual-charter-board-members-violating-religious

Press Release, U.S. Att'y's Off., Dist. of Utah, Indictment Unsealed Charging FLDS Church Leaders with Conspiracy to Divert SNAP Benefits (February 28, 2016), https://www.justice.gov/usao-ut/pr/indictment-unsealed-charging-flds-church-leaders-conspiracy-divert-snap-benefits

Press Release, White House Briefing Room, Fact Sheet: Biden Administration Announces Details of Two Major Vaccination Policies (November 4, 2021), https://www.whitehouse.gov/briefing-room/statements-releases/2021/11/04/fact-sheet-biden-administration-announces-details-of-two-major-vaccination-policies

Press Release, White House Briefing Room, Fact Sheet: President Biden Reestablishes the White House Office of Faith-Based and Neighborhood Partnerships (February 14, 2021), https://www.whitehouse.gov/briefing-room/statements-releases/2021/02/14/fact-sheet-president-biden-reestablishes-the-white-house-office-of-faith-based-and-neighborhood-partnerships

Press Release, White House Off. of the Press Sec'y, Fact Sheet: Embryonic Stem Cell Research (August 9, 2001), https://georgewbush-whitehouse.archives.gov/news/releases/2001/08/20010809-1.html

Press Release, White House Off. of the Press Sec'y, President Bush Attends Office of Faith-Based and Community Initiatives' National Conference (June 26, 2008), http://georgewbush-whitehouse.archives.gov/news/releases/2008/06/20080626-20.html

"Pro-Choice" or "Pro-Life" Demographic Table, Gallup, https://news.gallup.com/poll/244709/pro-choice-pro-life-2018-demographic-tables.aspx (last visited September 30, 2023)

Public Sees Religion's Influence Waning, Pew Rsch. Ctr. (September 22, 2014), http://www.pewforum.org/2014/09/22/public-sees-religions-influence-waning-2

Publication 517, Social Security and Other Information for Members of the Clergy and Religious Workers, IRS, https://www.irs.gov/publications/p517 (last updated December 29, 2022)

Quaker Opposition to the Constitution's Provisions Concerning Slavery, Univ. Wis.–Madison: Ctr. for Study Am. Const., http://csac.history.wisc.edu/quaker_opposition.htm (last visited September 30, 2023)

Quick Facts: United States, U.S. Census Bureau, https://www.census.gov/quickfacts/fact/table/US/PST045219 (last visited September 30, 2023)

Quong, Jonathan, *Public Reason*, Stanford Encyclopedia Phil. (updated April 20, 2022), https://plato.stanford.edu/entries/public-reason

Race and Ethnicity in the United States: 2010 Census and 2020 Census, U.S. Census Bureau (August 12, 2021), https://www.census.gov/library/visualizations/interactive/race-and-ethnicity-in-the-united-state-2010-and-2020-census.html

Ray, Brian D., *How Many Homeschool Students Are There in the United States During the 2021–2022 School Year?*, Nat'l Home Educ. Rsch. Inst. (September 9, 2021), https://www.nheri.org/how-many-homeschool-students-are-there-in-the-united-states-during-the-2021-2022-school-year

Ray, Brian D., *How Many Homeschool Students Are There in the United States? Pre-Covid-19 and Post-Covid-19: New Data*, Nat'l Home Educ. Rsch. Inst. (September 9, 2021), https://www.nheri.org/how-many-homeschool-students-are-there-in-the-united-states-pre-covid-19-and-post-covid-19

Ray, Brian D., *Research Facts on Homeschooling: General Facts, Statistics, and Trends*, Nat'l Home Educ. Rsch. Inst. (revised July 20, 2023), https://www.nheri.org/research-facts-on-homeschooling

Religion in the Original 13 Colonies, Britannica ProCon.org, https://undergod.procon.org/religion-in-the-original-13-colonies (last updated January 6, 2009)

Religious Exemption Laws: Marriage Solemnization, Movement Advancement Project, https://www.lgbtmap.org/equality-maps/religious_exemption_laws/religious_exemption_solemnization (updated October 27, 2023)

Religious Identities and the Race Against the Virus: American Attitudes on Vaccination Mandates and Religious Exemptions (Wave 3), PRRI (December 9, 2021), https://www.prri.org/research/religious-identities-and-the-race-against-the-virus-american-attitudes-on-vaccination-mandates-and-religious-exemptions

Selected Bibliography

Religious Landscape Study: Views about Abortion, Pew Rsch. Ctr., https://www.pewresearch.org/religion/religious-landscape-study/views-about-abortion (last visited September 30, 2023)

Right to Work States Timeline, Nat'l Right to Work Comm., https://nrtwc.org/facts/state-right-to-work-timeline-2016 (last September 30, 2023)

Save America's Treasures Funded Projects, Hist. Preservation Fund, Nat'l Park Serv., https://www.nps.gov/subjects/historicpreservationfund/save-america-s-treasures-funded-projects.htm (last visited September 30, 2023)

SBA Paycheck Protection Program – Religious Organizations – FederalPay, FederalPay.org, https://www.federalpay.org/paycheck-protection-program/industries/religious-organizations (last visited September 30, 2023)

Schwartz-Lavares, Ashley, Faith Abubey & Haley Yamada, *The Inequities of PPP: Megachurches, Large Corporations Receive Money Ahead of Small Businesses*, ABC News (January 18, 2021), https://abcnews.go.com/US/inequities-ppp-megachurches-large-corporations-receive-money-ahead/story?id=75331197

Scientology Religion, Scientology Newsroom, https://www.scientologynews.org/quick-facts/scientology.html; *Church of Scientology International*, Scientology Newsroom, https://www.scientologynews.org/quick-facts/church-of-scientology-international.html (last visited September 30, 2023)

Separation of Church and State, The Boisi Center Papers on Religion in the United States (2007), https://www.bc.edu/bc-web/centers/boisi-center/publications/papers.html

Seventh-day Adventist World Church Statistics 2021, Seventh-day Adventist Church, https://www.adventist.org/statistics (last visited September 30, 2023)

Shaker Historical Background: An Ongoing Story, Shaker Village: Sabbathday Lake, Me., https://www.maineshakers.com/shaker-historical-background (last visited January 31, 2023)

Special Rules Limiting IRS Authority to Audit a Church, IRS, https://www.irs.gov/charities-non-profits/churches-religious-organizations/special-rules-limiting-irs-authority-to-audit-a-church (last updated April 25, 2023)

State and Territory Infertility Insurance Laws, Am. Soc'y for Reproductive Med.: ReproductiveFacts.org, https://www.reproductivefacts.org/patient-advocacy/state-and-territory-infertility-insurance-laws (last visited September 30, 2023)

State Laws and Policies: Medication Abortion, Guttmacher Inst., https://www.guttmacher.org/state-policy/explore/medication-abortion (last updated August 31, 2023)

State Laws and Policies: Refusing to Provide Health Services, Guttmacher Inst., https://www.guttmacher.org/state-policy/explore/refusing-provide-health-services (last updated August 31, 2023)

State of the Law: Speech Codes, Found. for Individual Rts. in Educ., https://www.thefire.org/in-court/state-of-the-law-speech-codes (last visited September 30, 2023)

State Public Accommodation Laws, NCSL, http://www.ncsl.org/research/civil-and-criminal-justice/state-public-accommodation-laws.aspx (last updated June 25, 2021)

State Statute Navigator, Death with Dignity, https://deathwithdignity.org/state-statute-navigator (last visited September 30, 2023)

Statement about Race at BJU, Bob Jones Univ. (November 20, 2008), https://www.bju.edu/about/what-we-believe/race-statement.php

States with Religious and Philosophical Exemptions from School Immunization Requirements, NCSL, https://www.ncsl.org/research/health/school-immunization-exemption-state-laws.aspx (last updated August 3, 2023)

Style Guide – The Name of the Church, Church Jesus Christ Latter-day Saints, https://newsroom.churchofjesuschrist.org/style-guide (last visited September 30, 2023)

Surrogacy Laws by State, Legal Pro. Grp.: Am. Soc'y Reproductive Med., https://connect.asrm.org/lpg/resources/surrogacy-by-state?ssopc=1 (last visited September 30, 2023)

Table 2. Number and Percentage Distribution of Private Schools, Students, and Full-Time Equivalent (FTE) Teachers, by Religious or Nonsectarian Orientation of School: United States, 2019–20, Nat'l Ctr. for Educ. Stat., https://nces.ed.gov/surveys/pss/tables/TABLE02fl1920.asp (last visited September 30, 2023)

Table 206.10. Number and Percentage of Homeschooled Students Ages 5 Through 17 with a Grade Equivalent of Kindergarten Through 12th Grade, by Selected Child, Parent, and Household Characteristics: Selected Years, 1999 Through 2019, Nat'l Ctr. for Educ. Stat., https://nces.ed.gov/programs/digest/d21/tables/dt21_206.10.asp (last visited September 30, 2023)

Table 218.20. Percentage of Public School Districts with Students Enrolled in Technology-Based Distance Education Courses and Number of Enrolments in Such Courses, by Instructional Level and District Characteristics: 2002–03, 2004–05, and 2009–10, Nat'l Ctr. for Educ. Stat., https://nces.ed.gov/programs/digest/d18/tables/dt18_218.20.asp (last visited September 30, 2023)

Tax Exempt Organization Search Bulk Data Downloads, Internal Revenue Serv., https://www.irs.gov/charities-non-profits/tax-exempt-organization-search-bulk-data-downloads

Tax Incentives for Preserving Historic Properties, Nat'l Park Serv., https://www.nps.gov/subjects/taxincentives/index.htm (September 30, 2023)

Texas Abortion Ban Emergency Exceptions Case: Zuraski v. State of Texas, Ctr. for Reproductive Rts. (March 6, 2023), https://reproductiverights.org/case/zurawski-v-texas-abortion-emergency-exceptions/zurawski-v-texas

Texas CBAR, *Forming a Nonprofit Tax-Exempt Corporation in Texas* (2018), https://www.sos.state.tx.us/corp/nonprofit_org.shtml (link to PDF) (last visited September 30, 2023)

The 14 White Roadside Cross Memorials Commemorating Fallen Highway Patrol Officers Beside Roadways Throughout the State of Utah Do Not Constitute an Endorsement of Any Religion by the State, Utah Highway Patrol Assoc., https://utahtrooper.com/roadside-memorials (last visited September 30, 2023)

The Biblical Basis for Being Pro-Choice, Beliefnet, http://www.beliefnet.com/News/2003/01/The-Biblical-Basis-Forbeing-Pro-Choice.aspx?p=3 (last visited September 30, 2023)

The Constitution, White House, https://www.whitehouse.gov/about-the-white-house/our-government/the-constitution (last visited September 30, 2023)

The Court and Its Procedures, Sup. Ct. U.S., http://www.supremecourt.gov/about/procedures.aspx (last visited September 30, 2023)

Selected Bibliography

The FCC and Speech, Fed. Commc'n Comm., https://www.fcc.gov/consumers/guides/fcc-and-speech (last updated August 31, 2022)

The Legislative Branch, White House, https://www.whitehouse.gov/about-the-white-house/our-government/the-legislative-branch (last visited September 30, 2023)

The Nonprofit Sector in Brief 2019, Urban Inst.: Nat'l Ctr. for Charitable Stat. (June 4, 2020), https://nccs.urban.org/publication/nonprofit-sector-brief-2019#the-nonprofit-sector-in-brief-2019

The Public and Broadcasting, Fed. Commc'ns Comm'n, https://www.fcc.gov/media/radio/public-and-broadcasting (link to PDF) (last updated September 2021)

Theodorou, Angelina, *64 Countries Have Religious Symbols on Their National Flags*, Pew Rsch. Ctr. (November 25, 2014), https://www.pewresearch.org/short-reads/2014/11/25/64-countries-have-religious-symbols-on-their-national-flags

Thomas Jefferson to Thomas Law, 13 June 1814, Nat'l Archives: Founders Online, https://founders.archives.gov/documents/Jefferson/03-07-02-0307 (last visited September 30, 2023)

Timeline of a Crisis, Nat'l Cath. Rep. (July 6, 2015), https://www.ncronline.org/blogs/ncr-today/timeline-crisis; *Roman Catholic Church Sex Abuse Cases*, N.Y. Times, https://www.nytimes.com/topic/organization/roman-catholic-church-sex-abuse-cases

Topic No. 417, Earnings for Clergy, IRS (last updated August 24, 2023), https://www.irs.gov/taxtopics/tc417

Tracking Anti-Muslim Legislation Across the U.S., S. Poverty L. Ctr., https://www.splcenter.org/data-projects/tracking-anti-muslim-legislation-across-us (last visited September 30, 2023)

Transcript: JFK's Speech on His Religion, NPR, http://www.npr.org/templates/story/story.php?storyId=16920600 (last visited September 30, 2023)

Two Acts of Toleration: 1649 and 1826, Md. State Archives, http://msa.maryland.gov/msa/speccol/sc2200/sc2221/000025/html/intro.html (last visited September 30, 2023)

Understanding IRS Guidance – A Brief Primer, IRS, https://www.irs.gov/newsroom/understanding-irs-guidance-a-brief-primer (last updated May 1, 2023)

Universal Life Church – Free Online Ordination, Universal Life Church Monastery, http://www.themonastery.org/ordination (last visited September 30, 2023)

Untrue: Religious Broadcaster Ban Rumor, Fed. Comm's Comm., https://www.fcc.gov/media/radio/religious-broadcast-ban-rumor (last accessed September 30, 2023)

U.S. Comm'n on C.R., *School Choice: The Blaine Amendments & Anti-Catholicism* (2007), https://www.usccr.gov/files/pubs/docs/BlaineReport.pdf

U.S. Dep't of Com., Bureau of the Census, *Bicentennial Edition: Historical Statistics of the United States, Colonial Times to 1970* (*Unemployment: 1890 to 1970*) (September 1975), https://www.census.gov/library/publications/1975/compendia/hist_stats_colonial-1970.html

U.S. Dep't of Educ., Religious Expression in Public Schools: A Statement of Principles (June 1998), https://files.eric.ed.gov/fulltext/ED416591.pdf

U.S. Dep't of Educ., State Regulation of Private Schools (July 2009), https://www2.ed.gov/admins/comm/choice/regprivschl/index.html (link to PDF)

U.S. Dep't of Justice, C.R. Div., Report on the Twentieth Anniversary of the Religious Land Use and Institutionalized Persons Act (September 22, 2020), https://www.justice.gov/crt/case-document/file/1319186/download

U.S. Dep't of State, *Treaties in Force: A List of Treaties and Other International Agreements of the United States in Force on January 1, 2020*, https://www.state.gov/treaties-in-force (link to PDF) (last visited September 30, 2023)

U.S. Small Bus. Admin., *FAQ Regarding Participation of Faith-Based Organizations in PPP and EIDL* (April 3, 2020), https://www.sba.gov/document/support-faq-regarding-participation-faith-based-organizations-ppp-eidl (link to PDF)

Vaccination: What Did Eddy Say? (December 20, 2020), Mary Baker Eddy Libr., https://www.marybakereddylibrary.org/research/what-did-eddy-say-about-vaccination

Väyrynen, Pekka, *Thick Ethical Concepts*, Stanford Encyclopedia Phil. (updated February 9, 2021), https://plato.stanford.edu/entries/thick-ethical-concepts

Ventura, Stephanie J. & Christine A. Bachrach, Ctrs. for Disease Control & Prevention, *Nonmarital Childbearing in the United States, 1940–99*, Nat'l Vital Stat. Rep., October 18, 2000, https://pubmed.ncbi.nlm.nih.gov/11060989 (link to PDF)

Vision, Nat'l Prayer Breakfast Found., https://npbfoundation.com/vision (last accessed September 30, 2023)

Volunteering in U.S. Hits Record High; Worth $167 Billion, AmeriCorps (November 13, 2018), https://americorps.gov/newsroom/press-releases/2018/volunteering-us-hits-record-high-worth-167-billion

Wacker, Grant, *Religious Liberalism and the Modern Crisis of Faith*, Nat'l Humans. Ctr.: TeacherServe, Divining Am., http://nationalhumanitiescenter.org/tserve/twenty/tkeyinfo/liberal.htm (last modified October 2000)

Welcome, Quakers & Slavery Conf., https://web.tricolib.brynmawr.edu/speccoll/quakersandslavery (last visited September 30, 2023)

What Is a Charter School, Nat'l Charter Sch. Res. Ctr., https://charterschoolcenter.ed.gov/what-charter-school (last visited September 30, 2023)

What Is Christian Science?, Christian Sci., http://christianscience.com/what-is-christian-science#history-of-cs (last visited September 30, 2023)

What the Muslims Want, Nation Islam, http://www.noi.org/muslim-program (last visited September 30, 2023)

What You Should Know about COVID-19, the ADA, the Rehabilitation Act, and Other EEO Laws, U.S. Equal Emp. Opportunity Comm'n, https://www.eeoc.gov/wysk/what-you-should-know-about-covid-19-and-ada-rehabilitation-act-and-other-eeo-laws#L (last updated May 15, 2023)

Who Are Seventh-Day Adventists?, Seventh-day Adventist Church N. Am. Div., https://www.nadadventist.org/about-our-church/who-are-adventists (last visited September 30, 2023)

Who Qualifies for Nonprofit Prices?, Postal Explorer, USPS.com, https://pe.usps.com/businessmail101?ViewName=NonprofitQualifications (last visited September 30, 2023)

Who We Are, NRB, https://nrb.org/who-we-are (last visited September 30, 2023)

Wilcox, W. Bradford, Wendy Wang & Ian Rowe, *Less Poverty, Less Prison, More College: What Two Parents Mean for Black and White Children*, Inst. for Fam.

Stud. (June 17, 2021), https://ifstudies.org/blog/less-poverty-less-prison-more-college-what-two-parents-mean-for-black-and-white-children

William Neil "Doc" Gallagher: Sentenced to 25 Years, $10.3 Million Restitution, Tex. St. Secs. Bd. (March 27, 2020), https://www.ssb.texas.gov/news-publications/william-neil-doc-gallagher-sentenced-25-years-103-million-restitution

Women's Christian Temperance Movement, Case W. Rsrv. U.: Encyclopedia Cleveland Hist., https://case.edu/ech/articles/w/womens-christian-temperance-movement (last visited September 30, 2023)

Other Sources

Congressional Materials

4 Cong. Rec. 205 (1875)

138 Cong. Rec. 8071 (1992)

139 Cong. Rec. S384–385 (daily ed. January 20, 1993)

140 Cong. Rec. 14,326 (1994)

147 Cong. Rec. S422–423 (daily ed. January 22, 2001)

155 Cong. Rec. S668–669 (daily ed. January 20, 2009)

163 Cong. Rec. S364–365 (daily ed. January 20, 2017)

167 Cong. Rec. S77–78 (daily ed. January 21, 2021)

H.R. Journal, 1st Cong., 1st Sess., 121 (1789)

H.R. 619, 84th Cong., Pub. L. 84-140, 69 Stat. 290 (1955) (codified at 31 U.S.C. §§ 5112(d)(1), 5114(b) (2018))

H.R.J. Res. 1, 44th Cong., 1st Sess., 4 Cong. Rec. 205 (1875)

H.R.J. 396, 84th Cong., Pub. L. No. 84-851, 70 Stat. 732 (1956) (codified at 36 U.S.C. § 302 (2018))

J. Res. 11, 53d Cong., 1st Sess., 28 Stat. 980 (1893)

S. Journal, 1st Cong., 1st Sess., 88 (1789)

Brougher, Cynthia, Cong. Rsch. Serv., R40515, Legal Analysis of Religious Exemptions for Photo Identification Requirements (September 5, 2012), https://www.everycrsreport.com/reports/R40515.html (link to PDF)

Brougher, Cynthia, Cong. Rsch. Serv., R41099, Faith-Based Funding: Legal Issues Associated with Religious Organizations That Receive Federal Public Funds (February 9, 2011), https://www.everycrsreport.com/reports/R41099.html (link to PDF)

Cong. Rsch. Serv., R40484, The United Nations Convention on the Rights of the Child (updated July 27, 2015), https://crsreports.congress.gov/product/pdf/R/R40484/25

Cong. Rsch. Serv., RL34447, Churches and Campaign Activity: Analysis under Tax and Campaign Finance Laws (October 9, 2012), https://www.everycrsreport.com/files/20121009_RL34447_22d86a9c9b98adab4e9846c34dccff3dc741b652.pdf

Cong. Rsch. Serv., S. Prt. 106-71, Treaties and Other International Agreements: The Role of the United States Senate (January 2001), https://www.congress.gov/106/cprt/SPRT66922/CPRT-106SPRT66922.pdf

Forsberg, Vanessa C., Cong. Rsch. Serv., R44065, Overview of Health Insurance Exchanges (March 17, 2023), https://sgp.fas.org/crs/misc/R44065.pdf

Garcia, Michael J., Cong. Rsch. Serv., RL32528, International Law and Agreements: Their Effect upon U.S. Law (September 24, 2015), https://www.everycrsreport.com/files/20150924_RL32528_2ce3cbc59891da783bdb9fa34756754810d4d301.pdf

Gravelle, Jane G., Donald J. Marples & Molly F. Sherlock, Cong. Rsch. Serv., R45922, Tax Issues Relating to Charitable Contributions and Organizations (September 19, 2019), https://crsreports.congress.gov/product/pdf/R/R45922/3

Liu, Edward C. & Wen W. Shen, Cong. Rsch. Serv., IF 12167, The Hyde Amendment: An Overview (July 20, 2022), https://crsreports.congress.gov/product/pdf/IF/IF12167

Mulligan, Stephen P., Cong. Rsch. Serv., RL32528, International Law and Agreements: Their Effect upon U.S. Law (update July 13, 2023), https://crsreports.congress.gov/product/pdf/RL/RL32528

Staff of the J. Comm. on Tax'n, JCX-29-05, Historical Development and Present Law of the Federal Tax Exemption for Charities and Other Tax-Exempt Organizations (April 19, 2005), https://www.jct.gov/CMSPages/GetFile.aspx?guid=91d1c71d-866b-4423-84a7-0f1ec352edf8

Constitutions

State Constitutions

US Constitution

Selected Bibliography

Executive Orders

State Executive Orders

N.Y. Exec. Order No. 202.20 (April 18, 2020), **473**

Federal Executive Orders

Exec. Order No. 11246, 30 Fed. Reg. 12319, 12935 (September 29, 1965), **423**
Exec. Order No. 11478, 34 Fed. Reg. 12985 (August 13, 1969), **423**
Exec. Order No. 13279, 67 Fed. Reg. 77139 (December 12, 2002), **424, 425**
Exec. Order No. 13435, 72 Fed. Reg. 34591 (June 20, 2007), **585**
Exec. Order No. 13505, 74 Fed. Reg. 10667 (March 9, 2009), **586**
Exec. Order No. 13559, 75 Fed. Reg. 71317 (November 17, 2010), **424, 425**
Exec. Order No. 13672, 79 Fed. Reg. 42971 (July 21, 2014), **423**
Exec. Order No. 13798, 82 Fed. Reg. 21675 (May 9, 2017), **316**
Exec. Order No. 13831, 83 Fed. Reg. 20715 (May 3, 2018), **359**
Exec. Order No. 14015, 86 Fed. Reg. 10007 (February 18, 2021), **359, 372**
Exec. Order No. 14042, 86 Fed. Reg. 50985 (September 9, 2021), **591.1**
Exec. Order No. 14043, 86 Fed. Reg. 50989 (September 9, 2021), **591.1**

Federal Government Reports

U.S. Gov't Accountability Off., GAO-22-106096, Consumer Data: Increasing Use Poses Risks to Privacy (September 2022), https://www.gao.gov/products/gao-22-106096 (link to PDF), **447**

Fed. Trade Comm'n, FTC Report to Congress on Privacy and Security (September 13, 2021), https://www.ftc.gov/reports/ftc-report-congress-privacy-security (link to PDF), **447**

Historical Documents

The Declaration of Independence (U.S. 1776), **2, 3, 14, 54, 65, 323, 342, 436, 820, 838, 851**

Magna Carta (1215), https://www.bl.uk/magna-carta/articles/magna-carta-english-translation (last visited September 30, 2023), **526**

International Agreements, Conventions, Declarations, Treaties

Charter of the Org. of Am. States, 2 U.S.T. 2394, 119 U.N.T.S. 3 (April 30, 1948), **308, 309**

Convention on the Rights of the Child, *adopted* November 20, 1989, 1577 U.N.T.S. 3, **288**

Convention Relating to the Status of Refugees, *approved* July 28, 1951, 19 U.S.T. 6259, 189 U.N.T.S. 150, **284, 304**

G.A. Res. 36/55, Declaration on the Elimination of All Forms of Intolerance and of Discrimination Based on Religion or Belief (November 25, 1981), **281**

G.A. Res. 40/144, Declaration on the Human Rights of Individuals Who Are Not Nationals of the Country in Which They Live (December 13, 1985), **282**

G.A. Res. 47/135, Declaration on the Rights of Persons Belonging to National or Ethnic, Religious and Linguistic Minorities (December 18, 1992), **283**

G.A. Res. 217 A (III), Universal Declaration of Human Rights (December 10, 1948), **279, 769**

G.A. Res. 2200A (XXI), International Covenant on Civil and Political Rights (December 16, 1966), **279**

International Covenant on Civil and Political Rights, *adopted* December 19, 1966, 999 U.N.T.S. 171, **286**

International Covenant on Economic, Social and Cultural Rights, *adopted* December 16, 1966, 993 U.N.T.S. 3, **287**

International Convention on the Elimination of All Forms of Racial Discrimination, *opened for signature* December 21, 1965, 660 U.N.T.S. 195, **285**

OAS Res. XXX, American Declaration of the Rights and Duties of Man, May 2, 1948, 1 *Annals of the O.A.S.* 130 (1949), **280**

Org. of Am. States, American Convention on Human Rights, *adopted* November 22, 1969, S. Treaty Doc. No. 95-21, 1144 U.N.T.S. 123, O.A.S.T.S. No. 36, **289, 308, 311**

Vienna Convention on the Law of Treaties, May 23, 1969, 1155 U.N.T.S. 331, **268**

Regulations, Proposed Rules, Rules

State Rules, Regulations; Municipal Ordinances

Ala. Admin. Code § 670-X-4-.01 (2022), **383**
24 Del. Admin. Code § 2500-3.0 (3.1.2.4) (2022), **573**
Ga. Comp. R. & Regs. §§ 186-1-.02 to -.03 (2022), **383**
Ga. Comp. R. & Regs § 480-5-.03(n) (2022), **151**
10-144-264 Me. Code R. § 3 (LexisNexis 2022), **591**
Minn. Leg. Code § 292.02 (1990), **797**
Mont. Admin. R. 37.85.207 (2022), **582**
Ohio Admin. Code § 5160-2-03, **582**
216 R.I. Admin. Code § 40-15-1.16 (West 2022), **573**
216 R.I. Code R. § 20-15-7.6.1A (LexisNexis 2022), **591**
Fate, Tex. Code Ordinances § 8-315 (2022), **805**

Federal Regulations, Proposed Rules, Rules

8 C.F.R. § 316.10(b)(2)(ix), (b)(3)(i) (2022), **761.1**
16 C.F.R. pt. 255 (2022), **808.1**
16 C.F.R. pt. 312 (2022), **442**
26 C.F.R. § 1.48-12 (2022), **789**
26 C.F.R. § 1.1402(e)-2A (2022), **409**
26 C.F.R. § 1.501(c)(3)-1 (2022), **199, 316, 317, 319, 666**
26 C.F.R. § 54.9815-2713(a)(1)(iv) (2022), **565**
28 C.F.R. § 548.12 (2022), **639**
29 C.F.R. § 1605.2(d)(2) (2022), **261**
29 C.F.R. § 2590.715-2713(a)(1)(iv) (2022), **565**
36 C.F.R. § 65.4 (2022), **788**
36 C.F.R. §§ 65.2, 65.7 (2022), **788**
45 C.F.R. § 88.3(c) (2022), **559**
45 C.F.R. pt. 147 (2022), **106, 569**

45 C.F.R. §§ 147.130, .131, .132 (2022), **565, 566, 567**
45 C.F.R. pt. 160 & 164 (2022), **442, 445**
47 C.F.R. § 73.2080 (2022), **517, 809**
Treas. Reg. § 1.501(c)(3)-1 (2022), **97, 191, 199, 849**
Fed. R. Civ. P. 26, **450**
Coverage of Certain Preventive Services under the Affordable Care Act, 78 Fed. Reg. 39870 (July 2, 2013), **105**
Coverage of Certain Preventive Services under the Affordable Care Act, 80 Fed. Reg. 41318 (July 14, 2015), **567**
Coverage of Certain Preventive Services under the Affordable Care Act, 88 Fed. Reg. 7236 (proposed February 2, 2023) (to be codified at 26 C.F.R. pt. 54; 29 C.F.R. pt. 2590; 45 C.F.R. pt. 147, 156), **106, 569**
Establishment of Safeguards and Program Integrity Requirements for Health and Human Services–Funded Extramural Research Involving Human Fetal Tissue, 86 Fed. Reg. 2615 (proposed January 13, 2021), **586**
Federal Agency Final Regulations Implementing Executive Order 13,559: Fundamental Principles and Policymaking Criteria for Partnerships with Faith-Based and Other Neighborhood Organizations, 81 Fed. Reg. 19353 (April 4, 2016), **424**
Religious Exemptions and Accommodations for Coverage of Certain Preventive Services under the Affordable Care Act, 82 Fed. Reg. 47792 (October 13, 2017) (codified at 45 C.F.R. pt. 147 (2022)), **106, 569**

Model Statutes, Uniform Acts, Restatements

Model Act Governing Assisted Reproductive Tech. (Am. Bar Ass'n 2019), **577**
Restatement (Second) of Torts (Am. L. Inst. 1977), **509**
Restatement (Third) of the Foreign Rels. L. of the U.S. (Am. L. Inst. 1987), Westlaw REST 3d FOREL (database updated 2023), **277**
Model Nonprofit Corp. Act (Am. Bar Ass'n 4th ed. 2022), **188, 225**
Unif. Arbitration Act (Nat'l Conference of Comm'rs of Unif. State Laws 2010), **262, 763**
Unif. Marriage & Divorce Act (Unif. Law Comm'n 1973), **470, 472**
Unif. Parentage Act (Nat'l Conf. of Comm'rs on Unif. State L. 2017), **577, 579**
Unif. Partnership Act (Unif. Law Comm'n 1914), (Unif. Law Comm'n 1997), (Unif. Law Comm'n 2013), **183**

Non-US Regulations, Cases

Regulation (EU) 2016/679 of the European Parliament and of the Council of 27 April 2016 on the Protection of Natural Persons with Regard to the Processing of Personal Data and on the Free Movement of Such Data, and Repealing Directive 95/46/EC (General Data Protection Regulation), 2016 OJ (L 119/1), **301, 302**
Case C-311/18, *Data Prot. Comm'r v. Facebook Ireland Ltd. (Schrems II)*, ECLI: EU:C:2020:559, **303**
Case C-362/14, *Schrems v. Data Prot. Comm'r (Schrems I)*, ECLI:EU:C:2015:650, **303**
Schüth v. Germany, App. No. 1620/03 (Eur. Ct. H.R. 2010), **433**

Treatises, Law Reports

12 Am. Jur. 2d *Blasphemy and Profanity* § 5 (*Validity of Blasphemy Laws*), Westlaw AMJUR BLASPHEMY § 5 (database updated October 2023), **508**

16 Am. Jur. 2d *Constitutional Law* § 542 (*Limited Public Forums for Purposes of Free Speech and Press Protections*) n.2, Westlaw AMJUR CONSTLAW § 542 (database updated May 2023), **519**

52 Am. Jur. 2d *Marriage* § 17 (*Minimum Age for Capacity to Marry*), § 21 (*Criteria for Determination of Mental Capacity to Marry*), Westlaw Amjur MARRIAGE §§ 17, 21 (database updated May 2023), **465**

2 Antieau on Local Government Law, *Speech Limitations* § 29A.03 (2d ed. 2023) LexisNexis, **800**

1 Bassett, William W., W. Cole Durham Jr., Mark A. Goldfeder & Robert T. Smith, *Religious Organizations and the Law*, Westlaw RELORGS (database updated December 2022), **83, 89, 110, 139, 156, 182, 183, 187, 188, 190, 211, 215, 216, 217, 218, 219, 220, 225, 226, 233, 325, 328, 331, 396, 516, 518, 597, 785**

2 Bassett, William W., W. Cole Durham Jr., Mark A. Goldfeder & Robert T. Smith, *Religious Organizations and the Law*, Westlaw RELORGS (database updated December 2022), **207, 221, 222, 223, 227, 228, 332, 418, 450, 451, 452, 534, 535, 536, 537, 538, 539, 541, 547, 548, 549**

3 Bassett, William W., W. Cole Durham Jr., Mark A. Goldfeder & Robert T. Smith, *Religious Organizations and the Law*, Westlaw RELORGS (database updated December 2022), **87, 111, 150, 332, 472, 509, 514, 531, 616.1, 678, 697, 752.1, 755, 756, 758, 763.1, 764, 765, 766, 767, 785**

4 Bassett, William W., W. Cole Durham Jr., Mark A. Goldfeder & Robert T. Smith, *Religious Organizations and the Law*, Westlaw RELORGS (database updated December 2022), **88, 200, 224, 317, 319, 406, 408, 409, 674, 675, 676, 677**

Blum, George L., Annotation, *Criminal Liability of Nonparent for Failure to Obtain Medical Treatment for Minor Based on Duty of One Acting in Loco Parentis*, 97 A.L.R.6th 539 (2014), **588**

Blum, George L., Annotation, *Religion as Factor in Child Custody Cases*, 124 A.L.R.5th 203 (2004), **768**

Brazener, Robert A., Annotation, *Validity of Blasphemy Statutes or Ordinances*, 41 A.L.R.3d 519 (1972), **508**

Campbell, Andrew M., Annotation, *What Constitutes Employer's Reasonable Accommodation of Employee's Religious Preferences under Title VII of Civil Rights Act of 1964*, 134 A.L.R. Fed. 1 (1996), **73**

Cross, M.L., Annotation, *What Constitutes Duress Sufficient to Warrant Divorce or Annulment of Marriage*, 16 A.L.R.2d 1430 (1951), **467**

Gitlin, Baruch, Annotation, *Parents' Criminal Liability for Failure to Provide Medical Attention to Their Children*, 118 A.L.R.5th 253 (2004), **588**

2 Greenwald, David M., Michele L. Slachetka & Caroline L. Meneau, Testimonial Privileges § 6:5 (3d ed.), Westlaw PRIVILEGES (database updated February 2023), **542**

Hammar, Richard R., *Pastor, Church & Law* (5th ed. 2019), **432, 450, 451**

Howard, William M., Annotation, *First Amendment Challenges to Display of Religious Symbols on Public Property*, 107 A.L.R.5th 1 (2003), **773**

Keatinge, Robert R. & Ann E. Conaway, *Keatinge and Conaway on Choice of Business Entity: Selecting Form and Structure for a Closely Held Business* § 2:5 (*Organic Statutes–Partnership Statutes*), Westlaw CHOICEBE (databased updated October 2023), **183**

Kramer, Donald T., Annotation, *Supreme Court Cases Involving Establishment and Freedom of Religion Clauses of Federal Constitution*, 37 L. Ed. 2d 1147 (LexisNexis 2012), **117**

3 Larson, Lex K., *Labor and Employment Law*, at ch. 76, § 76.10[3] (*Reasonable Accommodation–General*), Lexis/Matthew Bender (database updated May 2023), **247**

Schopler, E.H., Annotation, *Right of Student to Hearing on Charges Before Suspension or Expulsion from Educational Institution,* 58 A.L.R.2d 903 (1958), **533**

9 Witkin, B.E. et al., Witkin Summary of California Law, at ch. XIII.X.D, § 404 (*Examination by Attorney General*), Westlaw WITSUM (database updated May 2023), **190**

Reference Materials: Dictionaries, Encyclopedias, Law Reports

Aynes, Richard, *Blaine Amendment, in Religion and American Law: An Encyclopedia* 39 (Paul Finkelman ed., 2000), **698**

Benson, Reed A. & Sheri Dew, *Benson, Ezra Taft, in Encyclopedia of Mormonism* 100 (Daniel H. Ludlow ed., 1992), **313**

Churchill, Robert Paul, *Conscientious Objection, in An Encyclopedia of War and Ethics* 99 (Donald A. Wells ed., 1996), **145**

Defamation, Black's Law Dictionary (11th ed. 2019), Westlaw, **509**

Finkelman, Paul, *Maryland Toleration Act (1649), in* 1 *Encyclopedia of American Civil Liberties* 975 (Paul Finkelman ed., 2013), **51**

McHenry, James, *Fourteenth Amendment, in* 2 *The Encyclopedia of Civil Liberties in America* 394 (David Schultz & John R. Vile eds., 2015), **122**

Meigs-Jaques, Donna L. & R. Kevin Jaques, *Islam, in Encyclopedia of Religion in the South* 394 (Samuel S. Hill, Charles H. Lippy & Charles Reagan Wilson eds., 2d ed. 2005), **39**

2 Merriman, Scott A., *Religion and Nineteenth-Century Reform, in Religion and the Law in America: An Encyclopedia of Personal Belief and Public Policy* 416 (2007), **330**

2 Merriman, Scott A., *Religion and the Defense of Slavery, in Religion and the Law in America: An Encyclopedia of Personal Belief and Public Policy* 413 (2007), **325, 326**

1 Merriman, Scott A., *Religion in Times of War, in Religion and the Law in America: An Encyclopedia of Personal Belief and Public Policy* 72 (2007), **323**

2 Merriman, Scott A., *Religious Elements of the Civil Rights Movement, in Religion and the Law in America: An Encyclopedia of Personal Belief and Public Policy* 428 (2007), **331**

2 Merriman, Scott A., Roe v. Wade, *in Religion and the Law in America: An Encyclopedia of Personal Belief and Public Policy* 439 (2007), **332**

Neumann, Michelle J. Dye & Paul Finkelman, *Disestablishment of State Churches, in Religion and American Law: An Encyclopedia* 136 (Paul Finkelman ed., 2000), **86, 645**

Religious Texts

Ephesians 6:5 (King James), **59**
Leviticus 25:44–46 (King James), **59**
1 Peter 2:18 (King James), **59**
Joseph Smith—History 1:18–19, 33, *in Pearl of Great Price* (The Church of Jesus Christ of Latter-day Saints 2013), **33**
Joseph Smith, *The Articles of Faith of The Church of Jesus Christ of Latter-day Saints*, at art. 12, Church of Jesus Christ of Latter-day Saints, https://www.churchofjesuschrist.org/comeuntochrist/article/articles-of-faith (last visited September 30, 2023), **350**
Wilford Woodruff, *Official Declaration – 1, in Doctrine and Covenants* 291 (The Church of Jesus Christ of Latter-day Saints 2013), **350**

Media

Boys Town (1938), **815.1**
Carrie (1976), **815.1**
Dogma (1999), **815.1**
Footloose (1984), **815.1**
Lucifer (series, 2016–2021), **815.1**
Seventh Heaven (series, 1996–2007), **815.1**
South Park (series, 1997–), **815.1**
The Chosen (series, 2017–), **815.1**
The Jazz Singer (1927), **815.1**
The Last Temptation of Christ (1988), **815.1**
The Marvelous Mrs. Maisel (series, 2017–2023), **815.1**
The Omen (1976), **815.1**
The Sound of Music (1965), **815.1**
The Ten Commandments (1956), **815.1**

Other

Brief Amicus Curiae of United States Conference of Catholic Bishops in Support of Respondents and Supporting Affirmance, *Obergefell v. Hodges*, 574 U.S. 1118 (2015) (mem.) (Nos. 14-556, 14-562, 14-574), **374, 497**
Brief of National Ass'n of Evangelicals as Amicus Curiae Supporting Hobby Lobby and Conestoga, et al., *Burwell v. Hobby Lobby Stores, Inc.*, 573 U.S. 682 (2015) (Nos. 13-354, 13-356), **374**
Brief of The Church of Jesus Christ of Latter-day Saints as Amicus Curiae in Support of Respondents, *City of Boerne v. Flores*, 521 U.S. 507 (1997) (No. 95-2074), **356**
Center for Church/State Studies, DePaul University College of Law, 1994 Report on the Survey of Religious Organizations at the National Level, Q4 (unpublished survey on file with the Center for Church/State Studies, DePaul University College of Law), **184**
Letter from Gerald Reynolds, Assistant Sec'y, Off. for C.R., Dep't of Educ., to "Colleague" (July 28, 2003), https://www2.ed.gov/about/offices/list/ocr/firstamend.html, **513**

Letter from Stephen Wise, President, Am. Jewish Cong., to President Franklin D. Roosevelt (December 2, 1942) (on file with National Archives), https://www.docsteach.org/documents/document/american-jewish-congress-fdr, **374**

Letter from Thomas Jefferson to Danbury, Connecticut, Baptist Association (January 1, 1802) (The Thomas Jefferson Papers at the Library of Congress: Series 1, General Correspondence, 1651 to 1827, Manuscript Division), https://www.loc.gov/item/mtjbib010955 (last visited September 30, 2023), **204, 360, 649, 730**

Memorandum from Reed Rubinstein, Principal Deputy Gen. Couns., U.S. Dep't of Educ., Off. of Gen. Couns., to Kimberly M. Richey, Acting Assistant Sec'y of Off. for C.R. (January 8, 2021), https://www2.ed.gov/about/offices/list/ocr/correspondence/other/ogc-memorandum-01082021.pdf, **96**

Memorandum from Margo Schlanger, Officer for C.R. & Civ. Liberties, to U.S. Dep't Homeland Sec. Component Heads, Guidance for Accommodating Religious Beliefs in DHS Policies Requiring Fingerprinting or Photographic Identification (December 30, 2011), https://www.dhs.gov/publication/guidance-accommodating-religious-beliefs-dhs-policies-requiring-fingerprinting-or (link to PDF), **108**

Petition for Writ of Certiorari at 16–23, *City of Salinas v. New Harvest Christian Fellowship*, 143 S. Ct. 567 (2023) (No. 22-309), 2022 WL 4781694, **127**

Petition for Writ of Certiorari at 31, *Fulton v. City of Philadelphia*, 141 S. Ct. 1868 (2021) (No. 19-123), 2019 WL 3380520, **135.1**

Table of Cases

Table of Cases

Table of Statutes

State Statutes

Federal Statutes

Index

The numbers here refer to paragraph numbers.

Index

Index

Index

www.ingramcontent.com/pod-product-compliance
Lightning Source LLC
Chambersburg PA
CBHW080437300625
28844CB00063B/454
* 9 7 8 9 4 0 3 5 3 9 1 8 8 *